LITTLE MANILA IS IN THE HEART

LITTLE MANILA
IS IN THE HEART

*The Making of the
Filipina/o American Community
in Stockton, California*

DAWN BOHULANO MABALON

DUKE UNIVERSITY PRESS

DURHAM AND LONDON   2013

© 2013 Duke University Press

All rights reserved

Printed in the United States of America on
acid-free paper ∞

Designed by Heather Hensley

Typeset in Arno Pro by Tseng Information Systems, Inc.

Photo credit (frontispiece): A group of friends gather
on Lafayette Street in the 1930s. From left to right,
unknown man, Coleta Delgado Luisen, Angelina
Bantillo Magdael, and Domingo Tuason. Courtesy of
the Angelina Bantillo Magdael Family Collection.

Photo credit (p. vi): The northern end of Little Manila,
El Dorado and Washington Streets, in the late 1920s.
Photo by Frank Mancao, courtesy of the Filipino
American National Historical Society.

Photo credit (p. viii): A gathering of friends in the
campo in Stockton in the late 1920s. Photo by Frank
Mancao, courtesy of the Filipino American National
Historical Society.

Library of Congress Cataloging-in-Publication Data
Mabalon, Dawn Bohulano.
Little Manila is in the heart : the making of the
Filipina/o American community in Stockton,
California / Dawn Bohulano Mabalon.
p cm
Includes bibliographical references and index.
ISBN 978-0-8223-5325-6 (cloth : alk. paper)
ISBN 978-0-8223-5339-3 (pbk. : alk. paper)
1. Filipinos — California — Stockton — History — 20th
century. 2. Immigrants — California — Stockton —
History — 20th century. 3. Filipino Americans —
California — Stockton — History — 20th century.
4. Stockton (Calif.) — History — 20th century. I. Title.
F870.F4M33   2013
305.899′21073079455 — dc23
2013005280

This book is for

my mother, Christine Bohulano Bloch, my first teacher,

and my father, Ernesto Tirona Mabalon, who taught me how to become a historian;

my grandparents, whose sacrifices made our lives possible, Isabel Tirona Mabalon and Pablo Magdaluyo Mabalon and Concepcion Moreno Bohulano and Delfin Paderes Bohulano;

my family, whose love and support sustained the writing of this book;

all the *manangs* and *manongs* of Little Manila,

all Filipinas/os who call Stockton their home,

and all the future generations of Filipina/o Stocktonians

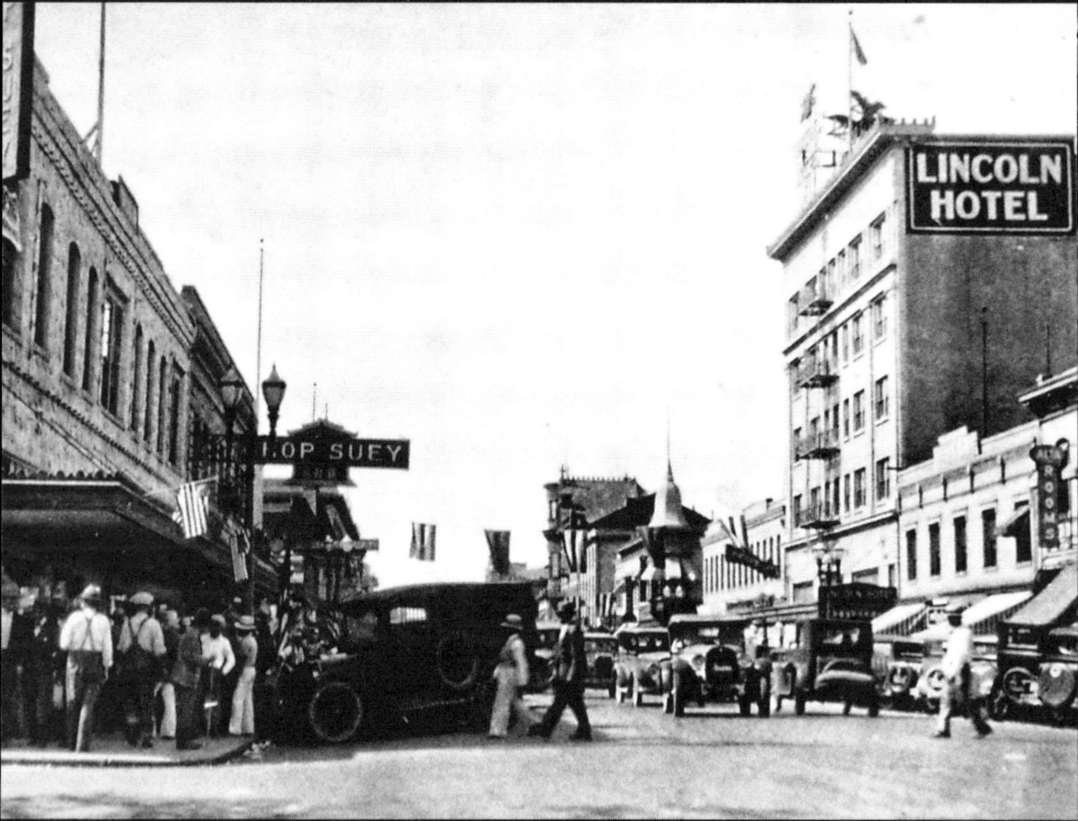
LINCOLN
HOTEL
ROOMS

CONTENTS

ix   ILLUSTRATIONS

xi   ACKNOWLEDGMENTS

1   INTRODUCTION Remembering Little Manila

23   **PART I. PUTTING DOWN ROOTS: 1898–1940s**

    1. From the Provinces to the Delta: Life on the Eve
      of Emigration to the United States 25

    2. Toiling in the "Valley of Opportunity" 61

    3. Making a Filipina/o American World in Stockton 101

149   **PART II. GROWING A COMMUNITY: 1930s–1960s**

    4. Women, Families, and the Second Generation 151

    5. Searching for Spiritual Sustenance 192

    6. The Watershed of World War II 217

267   **PART III. DESTRUCTION AND DISPLACEMENT: 1950s–2010**

    7. Losing El Dorado Street 269

    8. Building a Filipina/o American Movement in Stockton 299

335   EPILOGUE Coming Home to Little Manila

351   NOTES

403   BIBLIOGRAPHY

423   INDEX

ILLUSTRATIONS

MAPS

1. The Philippines 43
2. Stockton and the San Joaquin Delta 64
3. Little Manila in the 1920s 116
4. Little Manila in the 1930s 120
5. Little Manila in the 1940s 236
6. Little Manila in the 1950s and 1960s 280
7. Little Manila in the 1970s to 2012 338

PHOTOGRAPHS

1. Primo Villaruz 37
2. Fortunata Montayre Naranda and Remedios Fortunata 53
3. Monton family and friends 56
4. Pablo Mabalon 58
5. The Filipino Employment Agency 62
6. Filipina/o Students at Stockton High School 67
7. Mary Arca 70
8. Asparagus crew 74
9. Asparagus workers 77
10. The Cano family 81
11. Playing cards in the campo 83
12. White women in the campo 87
13. Little Manila 102
14. Bombed headquarters of the Filipino Federation of America 105
15. Daguhoy Lodge 108
16. "Positively No Filipinos Allowed" 114
17. Lafayette Lunch Counter 118
18. Los Filipinos Tailoring 122
19. Claro Candelario Restaurant 123

20. Pinoys on El Dorado Street, 1920s 125
21. Filipino Federation of America Parade Contingent 126
22. Rizal Social Club 136
23. Ernie Hernandez's Jazz Band 137
24. Carido wedding 152
25. Jose and Francisca Navalta 156
26. Asuncion Guevarra Nicolas 158
27. Angelina Bantillo Magdael in a black dress 175
28. Helen Nava 178
29. Filipina Club of Stockton 184
30. Lighthouse Mission 197
31. Filipino Agricultural Laborer's Association meeting 223
32. Bulosan and Candelario 228
33. Members of Legionarios del Trabajo marching 234
34. Mabalons reunited 247
35. Members of the Manuel Roxas Post 251
36. Rudy Delvo 255
37. Strikers march in 1948 256
38. Claro Candelario 257
39. Larry Itliong 258
40. Carmen Saldevar 270
41. Lafayette and El Dorado streets 271
42. Bohulano family gathering 274
43. Manongs in Little Manila 287
44. Path of the Crosstown Freeway 297
45. Association of Filipino American Professionals 302
46. Leo Giron and Dan Inosanto 312
47. Filipino Center groundbreaking 326
48. Filipino Center 332
49. Lafayette Lunch Counter historic banner 340
50. Freeway entrance 341

ACKNOWLEDGMENTS

This book has been guided and supported by a community of mentors, scholars, activists, librarians, and archivists, as well as my friends and family, to all of whom I give my most heartfelt gratitude. Most importantly, I want to thank my community in Stockton for embracing me and this book project when I came back home in 1997. I thank the members of the Stockton Chapter of the Filipino American National Historical Society, especially Maria "Terri" Torres, Violet Dutra, Anita Bautista, Virgie Melear, Mel and Gail LaGasca, Buster Villa, Leatrice Perez, Rosalio "Sleepy" Caballero, Emily Rosal, Juliana Homan, and Marilyn Guida. Deepest thanks to the Little Manila Foundation board members and volunteers: Dillon Delvo, Rebecca Abellana-Delvo, Tony Somera, Elena Mangahas, Addie Suguitan, Florence Quilantang, Rico Reyes, Sylvia Oclaray, Lailani Chan, Lorenzo Romano, Reggie Romano, Debbie Panganiban Louie, Fay Olympia, Jennifer Mashburn, Flora May Teague, Sandi Olega-Miyai, Alma Riego, Brian Batugo, Stacey Arquines, Sarah May Olarte, Arianne Suguitan, and all our interns. I also thank the teachers and students of our Little Manila Afterschool Program. Thanks also to the many people around the nation who offered their help and materials.

I am deeply grateful to the many community members and organizations who so generously shared their stories, photographs, and other materials with me. I thank them all, especially Alma Alcala, Moreno Balantac, Anita Navalta Bautista, Christine Bohulano Bloch, Fred and Dorothy Cordova, Dillon Delvo, Violet Juanitas Dutra, Jimmy and Phyllis Ente, Lillian Galedo, Luna Jamero, Eudosia Bravo Juanitas, Laurena Cabañero Knoll, Eulogio "Ted"

Lapuz, Rene Latosa, Flora Arca Mata, Nelson Nagai, Angelina Candelario Novelozo, Jaime Patena, Leatrice Bantillo Perez, Rizaline Monrayo Raymundo, Sharon Monton Robinson, Emily Behic Rosal, Antonio Somera, Jr., Terri Torres, Buster Villa, Art Villaruz, and the Perez and Bantillo/Magdael family. I also thank the entire Filipina/o American community of Stockton and vicinity, especially the Old Pinoys, Trinity Presbyterian Church, Legionarios del Trabajo in America, the Daguhoy Lodge, Filipino Federation of America, the Numancia Aid Association, and the Association of Filipino American Educators for their support of this project.

I am grateful to those community members who shared memories and materials with me but passed away before this book was completed: Jerry Paular; Lorenzo Romano Sr.; Frank Perez; Camila Carido; Angelina Bantillo Magdael; Paula Dizon Daclan; Deanna Daclan Balantac; Eleanor Olamit; Asuncion Guevarra Nicolas; Segunda Reyes; Juan "Johnny" Malumay Macahilas; Manuel Antaran; Frank Acoba; Toribio "Terry" Rosal; Carmen Saldevar; Helen Lagrimas Liwanag; Frank Acoba; Susanna Mangrobang; Concepcion Lagura; Claro Candelario; my aunt, Florencia Mabalon Pastrana; my grandmother, Concepcion Moreno Bohulano; and my father, Ernesto Tirona Mabalon. I offer my deepest gratitude to them all.

This book began as a dissertation, and the members of my committee at Stanford — Gordon H. Chang, Albert Camarillo, and Anthony Antonio — offered invaluable suggestions and critical comments. I am forever indebted to my adviser, Gordon Chang, for his guidance, integrity, advice, and example. For helping me to shape my ideas, I also thank Estelle Freedman, Richard White, Rudy Busto, Karen Sawislak, Michael Thompson, and the late George Frederickson. I also thank my Stanford sisters for their warm friendship, assistance, and support: Marisela Chávez, Kim Warren, Monica Perales, Shana Bernstein, Gina Marie Pitti, Shelley Lee, Cecilia Tsu, and Gabriela Gonzalez.

For their important advice and suggestions, I thank my colleagues in history and Asian American studies at San Francisco State University: Chris Chekuri, Sarah Curtis, Julyana Peard, Steve Leikin, Laura Lisy-Wagner, Eva Sheppard-Wolf, Dan Gonzales, Allyson Tintiangco-Cubales, Bill Issel, the late Jules Tygiel, and the late Paul Longmore. I also thank my department chair, Barbara Loomis, and the past chair, Richard Hoffman, and the administrative staff, Deborah Kearns, Smithy Blackwell, and Sheri Kennedy, for their encouragement and support. Deep thanks to my former dean, Joel Kassiola, for his support in the completion of this project. Fellowships and grants enabled me to complete this book, including a San Francisco State University Summer Stipend, the Affirmative Action Award, and the Presidential

Fellowship. I am very grateful for the sabbatical and networks provided by the Ford Foundation's Postdoctoral Fellowship.

I am grateful to my earliest mentors, particularly my auntie and uncle, Drs. Fred and Dorothy Cordova, who welcomed me with open arms into the field of Filipina/o American history, and into the National Pinoy Archives of the Filipino American National Historical Society (NPA FANHS) in Seattle, Washington. We are all the beneficiaries of their work through FANHS in recovering, preserving, and disseminating our community's history. I thank my cousin/auntie/*ninang* Joan May Timtiman Cordova; her co-editor, Alexis Canillo; and Filipino Oral History for inspiring us with *VOICES* and for allowing me to use their archives. I offer heartfelt gratitude to the professors who instilled in me a passion for Filipina/o American studies, American history, and community work: Nelson Nagai, Delmar McComb, Albert Ortiz, and Richard Bastear, of San Joaquin Delta College, and from the University of California, Los Angeles, the late Royal "Uncle Roy" Morales; and the late Steffi San Buenaventura, Pauline Agbayani-Siewert, Valerie Matsumoto, Don Nakanishi, Enrique de la Cruz, Henry Yu, and Michael Salman. Special thanks to Catherine Ceniza Choy, whose generous mentorship since my undergraduate years and suggestions for the revision of this manuscript have helped me more than I can express.

I thank my colleagues and friends, many of whom took time to offer support, critiques, advice, and materials, and/or asked me to speak about my work or published parts of this book. Many thanks and *maraming salamat* go to Dan Gonzales, Kuya Oscar Peñaranda, Emily Porcincula Lawsin, Scott Kurashige, Estella Habal, Ray San Diego, Maria Luisa Alaniz, Kay Dumlao, Leny Mendoza Strobel, Joaquin Gonzalez, Dorothy Fujita-Rony, Theo Gonzalves, Barbara Posadas, Roland Guyotte, Melinda L. de Jesus, Al Acena, Linda Revilla, James Sobredo, Linda España Maram, Eric Estuar Reyes, Christine Bacareza Balance, Darlene Rodrigues, Robyn Magalit Rodriguez, Jonathan Okamura, Tony Tiongson, Nerissa Balce, Mitchell Yangson, Liza Erpelo, Michelle Magalong, Joanne Rondilla, Rudy Guevarra, and Frank Samson. I am also grateful to the members of the Asian/Pacific American Program at the Smithsonian Institution, especially Gina Inocencio, Franklin Odo, and Konrad Ng; and to the Critical Filipino Studies Collective.

Heartfelt thanks to Ken Wissoker, the editorial director at Duke University Press, for his patience and for believing wholeheartedly in this project. I also thank Dorothy Fujita-Rony for her helpful comments, and the copyeditors for their attention to detail. I thank other presses and editors for allowing me to include previously published material in the book. Portions of chapter 4 are from "Writing Angeles Monrayo into the Pages of Pinay History," in *Tomorrow's Memories: A Diary, 1924–1928*, by Angeles Monrayo and edited by Rizaline R. Raymundo, University of Hawai'i Press. An earlier version of chapter 7 was published as "Losing Little Manila: Race and Redevelopment in Filipina/o Stockton, California," in *Positively No Filipinos Allowed: Building Communities and Discourses*, edited by Tony Tiongson, Temple University Press. The second half of chapter 4 was published as "Beauty Queens, Basketball Players, and Bomber Pilots" in *Pinay Power: Peminist Critical Theory*, edited by Melinda de Jesus from Routledge.

I am indebted to many local historians, archivists, and librarians across the nation: the late Leslie Crow of the Cultural Heritage Board; Alice Van Ommeren of the Cultural Heritage Board; Lynn Damouny and the Filipino Federation of America archives; Marilyn Guida, Susan Benedetti, Kimberly Bowden, and Tod Ruhstaller of the Haggin Museum in Stockton; Katherine Gong Meissner, retired city clerk of Stockton, and her staff members Geoff Aspiras and Raeann Cycenas; Mitchell Yangson, director of the Filipino American Center at the San Francisco Public Library; the reference librarians who went out of their way to help despite diminished staff at the Cesar Chavez Main Branch of the San Joaquin County Library, particularly Rebecca Hill Long and Gretchen Louden; Donald Walker, Janine Turner, and Patricia Richards of the Special Collections of the University of the Pacific Holt Atherton Library; William Maxwell of the Bank of Stockton archives; the librarians at the University of Washington Special Collections; Catherine Powell, director of the Labor Archives and Research Center at San Francisco State University; Christina Moretta of the San Francisco History Center/San Francisco Public Library; Suzanne Harris and Bob Ellis of the National Archives in Washington, D.C.; William Nealand and William Crouse of the National Archives in San Bruno, Calif.; Rita Cacas and Eric Van Slander of the National Archives at College Park, Maryland; the Ricaforte family and Gran Oriente Library; Jeff Liu, associate director at the media arts organization Visual Communications; the staff of the Filipiniana Room and Special Collections of the University of the Philippines at Diliman and Ateneo de Manila University; and the staff at the Museo It Akean in Kalibo, Aklan province. Much appreciation to Ben Pease of Pease Press, who makes maps that help us find our way home. I am grateful to Trinity Presbyterian Church the late Reverend Richard Litherland, whose collection of Filipina/o American materials found its way into my grateful hands. *Maraming salamat po* to Marie Romero of Arkipelago Bookstore in San Francisco. I also thank the San Francisco Giants (especially Tim Lincecum, of the Asis family of Stockton), who, by winning two World Series championships as I completed this book, provided me with more joy and distraction than I could ever imagine.

While this is a book about my hometown, I could not have completed it without the love and support and assistance of the many communities that have also made me feel at home in San Francisco and beyond. It has been a great honor to serve on the FANHS National Board of Trustees, and I thank all my fellow board members for their support of this project. Deepest gratitude to my beloved late mentors, the International Hotel activists Manong Bill Sorro and Manong Al Robles, who first inspired me when I watched *The Fall of the I-Hotel* as an undergraduate at the University of California, Los Angeles, then took me under their wings when I moved to San Francisco. I was honored to serve alongside them on the Manilatown Heritage Foundation Board. I also thank the friendship and support of my fellow members both past and current of the Pin@y Educational Partnerships board, and the warm and welcoming community of the Asian Pacific Islanders in Historic Preservation network, especially Michelle Magalong, Donna Graves, Lisa Hasegawa, Bill Watanabe, and Jill Shiraki. I am also grateful to the staff of the San Francisco office of the National Trust for Historic Preservation, especially Anthony Veerkamp, Anthea Hartig (now at the California Historical Society), and Hugh Rowland, for believing in Little Manila. I also thank the filmmaker Marissa Aroy for her wonderful film *Little Manila: Filipinos in California's Heartland* and for sharing with me her research for her upcoming film *The Delano Manongs*, on Larry Itliong and the early Agricultural Workers Organizing Committee and the United Farm Workers.

Heartfelt thanks to my research assistants and transcribers: Karmela Hererra, Jaylyn Hernandez, Cynthia Manuel, Adrianne Francisco, Jaymee Castrillo, Mike Solis, Mark Ramos, Tes Esparrago, Melissa Fernandez, Kei Fischer, Angelo Mayo, Allan Lumba, Melissa Nievera, Ed Curammeng, Anne Rose Duenas, Alma Riego, Brian Batugo, and Aldrich Sabac. I especially thank Ray San Diego for reading through the manuscript and for his suggestions, critiques, and assistance. I also thank all of the teachers of the Pin@y Educational Partnerships Project at San Francisco State University; and all of my students, who motivate and inspire me. And I thank all of my teaching assistants, whose help made this book possible, especially Alisha Vasquez, Matt Cropp, Gerson Rosales, Joseph Stancer, Nicole Roberts, Aliyah Dunn-Salahuddin, Natalie Novoa, Jesse Davis, Ben Graber, José Barocio, Jeffrey Mitchell, Lindsey Loscutoff, Celerah Hewes, Mark Portuondo, and Catherine Roth, Justin Coburn, and Andres Uribe.

For their friendship and love, I thank Allyson and Val Tintiangco-Cubales, Rico Reyes, Andrew Ardizzoia, Kay Dumlao, Donna Pascua-McAllister and Keith McAllister, Ben de Guzman, Jeanne Batallones, Christine Capacillo, Cindy Evangelista and Lakan de Leon, Olivia Malabuyo-Tablante, Christine

Bacareza Balance, Anna Alves, Oliver Savia, JR and Lorie Saria, Tricia and Ron Ramos, Norm and Kristi Pabros, Terry and Rachana Valen, Trina Villanueva, April Veneracion, Rod and Arlene Daus-Magbual, Kuya Oscar Peñaranda, E. Ivan Fructuoso, Ninong Dan and Ninang Linda Gonzales, and Emily Porcincula Lawsin and Scott Kurashige. The friendship and sisterhood of my colleague, best friend, and *comadre* Allyson Tintiangco-Cubales sustained me as an intellectual, scholar, activist, professor, and Pinay.

My deepest thanks go to my family, especially the Mabalon/Pastrana and Bohulano clans, the Nellie and Willie Ureta family, the Rhonda and Doug Ureta-Villalos family, Ninang Joan May Timtiman Cordova, the Tintiangcos, Suguitans, Sonia Jhao and family, and Lourdes and James Sobredo. I thank all our kin and *kabanua* around the globe for reminding me of the enduring ties of family and love. I owe a deep debt to my late grandmother, Concepcion Moreno Bohulano. Her legacy lives on in this book and in my life's work. I thank all of my extended family for their love and encouragement: Uncle Mel and Auntie Addie Suguitan, Auntie Virginia Bohulano, Uncle Del and Auntie Wendy Bohulano, and the late Florencia Mabalon Pastrana, and all my first cousins and nieces and nephews on both sides of my family, especially those who shared stories and materials with me: Tex Mabalon Jr., Cynthia Mabalon, Lucy Pastrana, and Ruby Ibabao. I also thank my godchildren, my *inaanaks*, for their love and laughter: Tayondee Isabella Concepcion Kelley, Mahalaya Tintiangco-Cubales, and Triston Noel Ureta-Villalos.

Special thanks to my beloved sister, Darleen Mabalon, and her children, my nieces Tayondee and Nonaiya Jean Kelley, and my nephew Cayden Jerrell Kelley for their love. Lastly, I thank my parents, Christine Bohulano Bloch, and the late Ernesto Tirona Mabalon. I could not have undertaken this project without my father's encyclopedic knowledge about our community history, translation skills, and guidance: this is also his book. I am so grateful that my mother, a retired public-school teacher, shared her memories with me and always encouraged me on this long journey. I hope that this book honors the sacrifices that my parents and grandparents made to give us lives that are full of promise and possibilities. Lastly, *maraming salamat sa asawa ko* to my spouse and partner, Jesus Perez Gonzales, for being my patient research assistant and the cameraman on many interviews; and for his love, humor, music, and pots of home-cooked *munggo* and Filipino spaghetti. He gives me a reason to look forward to the future.

REMEMBERING LITTLE MANILA

I was born and raised in Stockton, California, the daughter and granddaughter of Filipina/o immigrants who called Stockton home for much of the twentieth century. In my earliest memory of Stockton's Little Manila neighborhood, it was 1977, and I was a precocious five-year-old. My *tatay*—my father, Ernesto Mabalon—led me across busy El Dorado Street to the corner of Lafayette and El Dorado and nodded greetings to the elderly Filipinos standing there, surrounded by the din and fumes from the Crosstown Freeway. The uncles stuffed dollar bills and quarters into my hands, and they greeted my father effusively in Tagalog, Illonggo, Aklanon, and English. *"Anong balita?"* (What's the news?) was my father's smiling response. Within minutes, I was balanced on a stool at the counter of my grandfather's diner, the Lafayette Lunch Counter, the tips of my toes brushing the footrest. My white-haired, dimpled *lolo*, Pablo "Ambo" Mabalon, set a plate of my favorite steaming hotcakes in front of me. As I ate, I listened to the elders around me, who were making *kuwento*—telling stories—and roaring with laughter. This was not history to me, at least not then. This was just another morning, my father's day off from work in the fields, with my favorite breakfast.

Almost two decades later, I was a student at the University of California, Los Angeles, and was home for the weekend. I had just read a riveting book, *America Is in the Heart*, by a Filipino author, Carlos Bulosan, which was required reading in my Filipino American history course. I asked my father about Bulosan, and the story he told me continues to intrigue and astound me. From the 1930s to the early 1950s, Bulosan used the Lafayette Lunch Counter at 50 East Lafayette Street as his permanent address in Stockton. Whenever he came to town, he picked up his letters at the community mailbox, an old shoebox my grandfather kept for this purpose, and sat at the counter and sifted through his mail. Bulosan usually ate free at the restaurant because my soft-hearted Lolo couldn't bear to see Filipinas/os starve, my Tatay said. In return, Bulosan gave my Lolo a signed copy of *America Is in the Heart*. My father remembered that when his niece Cynthia Mabalon was a toddler, she used the book—cast off by the family as scratch paper—as her scribbling pad. Skeptical of my father's story, I consulted Bulosan's papers at the University of Washington. In one letter there, a girlfriend tells Bulosan that she sent her letters to "Pablo" in Stockton for him. Suddenly, my father's memories became history, corroborated by archival evidence, and framed by my deeper understanding and embrace of my hometown's Filipina/o American history. This discovery was a life-altering one, for with all the kuwentos that my family shared with me, there was still a terrible silence about the history of our community.

My Lolo sold the restaurant in the early 1980s, when he was too old to run it any longer. In 1997 I went to the shuttered Lafayette Lunch Counter and peeked through the dusty windows, imbued with a deep longing to understand what had brought thousands of Filipinas/os to the intersection of El Dorado and Lafayette and the kind of community that they created here. Two years later, the Lafayette Lunch Counter was reduced to rubble, cleared for an urban redevelopment project dubbed the Gateway Project, intended to beautify the freeway exit in downtown Stockton with such structures as a gas station and a McDonalds. The destruction of the restaurant inspired me to explore this community's history while working on a dissertation at Stanford, which was the start of this book.

When I was growing up, my elders rarely spoke about the Little Manila community that had thrived in downtown Stockton or the demolitions that destroyed it in the 1960s and 1970s. Moreover, few of them ever talked of the intense racism and discrimination that they had survived in Stockton. Very few old-timers ever spoke of Bulosan, and those who remembered him regarded the celebrated author as an alcoholic Communist who never worked in the fields, yet wrote as though he did. He died in Seattle in 1956, forgotten by the Stockton community he immortalized in his 1946 ethnobiography. My book is an attempt to understand the silences, recover and find meaning in the memories of Stockton's community members, and interpret and tell their stories. I wrote this book with the deep and unquenchable hope that these stories might inspire community members to continue to challenge and, eventually, defeat capitalism's ruthless and persistent attempts to reduce to dust what is left of this historic community.

Little Manila Is in the Heart is about how Filipinas/os created a distinctive community and identity in the city of Stockton in California's San Joaquin Delta throughout the twentieth century. I argue that the racialized ethnic community they built in Little Manila, the neighborhood itself, and its institutions—labor unions, fraternal lodges, hometown mutual aid associations, and ethnic businesses—offered sites for the construction of a unique Filipina/o American ethnic identity and culture by Ilokana/o, Visayan, and Tagalog immigrants, shaped by their racialization in Stockton as brown "others" and their collective experiences in the fields and in the streets of Little Manila. This book weaves together many threads of Filipina/o American experiences in Stockton over the span of a century.

This journey to uncover my community's long-buried past has been emotional and highly personal. My family's history is inextricably linked with the history of Little Manila and of Filipinas/os in Stockton. My mother, Christine Bohulano, was born in Cebu City and arrived in the United States in 1952. Her father, Delfin Bohulano, met and married her mother, Concepcion, during World War II in Leyte, when he was fighting with the First Filipino Infantry Regiment. My grandfather brought his young family back to the San Joaquin Delta in 1952 and found work as a labor contractor in Tracy, twenty miles south of Stockton. The family spent every weekend in Little Manila, seeing movies, visiting friends, and eating at the Lafayette Lunch Counter. The Veterans Administration loan program allowed my grandparents to purchase a home in South Stockton in 1955. My mother was among the first Filipinas/os in Stockton to have the opportunity to leave the fields. She attended the University of California, Davis, and became a schoolteacher in nearby Lathrop in 1970.

My grandfather Pablo Mabalon, who had emigrated to Stockton in 1929, was able to send for his older son, my father, Ernesto, because immigration laws allowed American citizens to bring over their immediate family members. My father arrived in Stockton in 1963 with a medical degree from the University of Santo Tomas in Manila. My grandfather's work at his restaurant had put my father through college in the Philippines. Unable to get his medical license in the United States because of discriminatory laws, my father became a labor contractor in the Delta fields. It was work that he embraced as honorable and dignified. Community life was my father's passion: he served as president of the Filipino Community of Stockton in the 1980s and was a longtime member and leader of the Legionarios del Trabajo, a fraternal order of workers with lodges in the Philippines and the United States. My grandfathers Delfin and Ambo hailed from the Visayas, the central Philippines, and both came from the town of Numancia, in Aklan province on the island of

Panay, and my parents met at the Mabalon family restaurant in the 1960s. The restaurant was a gathering place for Filipina/o immigrants, especially those from the Visayas. My parents married and settled in south Stockton, with all of their immediate relatives within one mile of them.

My grandparents and parents came to Stockton as part of a massive stream of Filipinas/os to that Delta town, a flow that began in 1898. According to Stockton's old-timers, the first Filipina/o immigrant to arrive and settle in Stockton was a man they remembered simply as Villareal. Villareal jumped ship at the port of San Francisco in 1898, made his way to Stockton, and worked harvesting fruit and on the railroads. Soon he became Stockton's biggest booster among the early Filipina/o arrivals to the West Coast in the 1910s. When he met Filipinas/os arriving at the port of San Francisco, he encouraged them to take advantage of job opportunities in Stockton. Vicente Roldan, a prolific writer who contributed to several Filipino newspapers in California, recalled that these immigrants "were not convinced nor converted," but their interest had been piqued. "But they became Stockton conscious, so that when they went back home, just to brag about their adventures among relatives, friends and acquaintances, they talked about what he told them in their own ways and in a very lurid manner," he wrote. "They talked of the valley of opportunity with Stockton as its axis." According to Roldan, some of the earliest immigrants, *pensionados* (Filipina/o college students sponsored by the United States colonial regime) who were studying at University of California, Berkeley, and University of the Pacific (first in San Jose, now in Stockton), worked in the fields around Stockton as early as 1914.[1]

Roldan came from the same town as my grandfather, Ambo Mabalon. By the late 1920s, several hundred Aklanons—and thousands of Filipinas/os from all over the Philippines, especially the provinces in the Ilocos and other places in the Visayas—had settled in Stockton. The story of Stockton is in many ways, the story of Filipina/o America. By World War II, so many Filipinas/os had flocked to Stockton that the columnist Frank Perez dubbed the Stockton area, and the downtown Filipina/o neighborhood, "Little Manila."[2] Stockton became, in the words of the old-timer Pete Valoria, the hometown of the entire Filipina/o American community, and the intersection of Lafayette and El Dorado streets in Little Manila was a literal crossroads of Filipina/o America. By World War II, the city was home to the largest Filipina/o community outside of the Philippines, a distinction the community held well into the 1960s. Stockton became the capital of Filipina/o America.

When my Lolo Ambo died, in August 1987, the Ilocano journalist Frank Perez called him "Mr. Little Manila" with great affection in an obituary on the front page of the *Philippines Press (USA)*.[3] My humble Lolo would have protested, but Perez was accurate in understanding that his life story was not unlike those of thousands of other lower-middle-class and poor young men and women who left rural villages in the Philippines to settle in Stockton. My grandfather left for the United States because he could not earn enough money in the Philippines to feed his five children and wife, Isabel. His family's poverty was a direct result of the death of his father, Guillermo, in the 1902 cholera epidemic that was a tragic consequence of the Philippine-American War.

Filipina/o American experiences in Stockton are part of a larger history of American imperialism. After brutal wars of conquest — the Spanish-American War in 1898 and the Philippine-American War in 1899–1913 — that wrested control of the Philippines first from Spain and then from Filipina/o nationalists, the islands became an American colony. As colonial wards, or "nationals," Filipina/o students and workers streamed into the United States until the Tydings-McDuffie Act of 1934 promised Philippine independence and restricted immigration to only fifty people per year. By the end of World War II, more than 150,000 Filipinas/os lived in Hawai'i and on the U.S. mainland.

By the 1920s, San Joaquin County growers had become dependent on Filipino labor. The entry of thousands of Filipinas/os in the 1920s and 1930s provided California growers with the cheap, immigrant labor they needed to harvest the "green gold" growing from the fields and orchards of the Central Valley and Delta. Stockton was at the center of a West Coast migratory labor circuit in which Filipinas/os worked in the salmon canneries of Alaska and the vineyards of Southern California. Thousands of other Filipinas/os did not follow the crops and stayed in and near Stockton because the area provided work year-round, with pruning in the wintertime and picking asparagus in the spring and tomatoes and grapes in the summer and fall.[4]

Moreover, Stockton became a destination point for these early Filipina/o immigrants because there simply were not enough domestic service and restaurant jobs for Filipina/o workers in Seattle, San Francisco, and Los Angeles, especially during the Depression, and because the farmers of the fertile San Joaquin Valley and Delta needed cheap, transient farm labor for their expanding industrialized farms. Filipinas/os became specialists in labor-intensive produce like asparagus, a multimillion-dollar crop in the region. In the 1920s and 1930s, approximately five thousand to six thousand Filipinas/os lived in the Stockton area. During the asparagus season, from late February to June, the Filipino population would double.[5]

The pull to Stockton soon became so strong for some Filipina/o immigrants that they came to the city almost immediately after landing in San Francisco, Seattle, or Los Angeles. The activist and writer Carey McWilliams noted that Filipinos were exploited in a "weird California whirligig" from the moment they arrived on American soil. McWilliams noted that "fly-by-night taxi drivers" waited at San Francisco's Embarcadero for newly arrived Filipina/o immigrants. The drivers took the immigrants to Stockton, charging them $65–75 in taxi fare. The immigrants didn't know that the bus or train would cost them only $2.[6]

From the 1920s until the 1970s, Filipina/o families, community organizations, and businesses thrived in an area of downtown Stockton called Little Manila, four to six square blocks near Chinatown and Japantown in Stockton's West End. In that part of Stockton, Chinese, Japanese, and Filipinos shared cramped quarters in a working-class area full of hotels, rooming houses, bars, pool halls, dance halls, saloons, grocery stores, storefront missions and churches, union halls, dry goods stores, and barbershops. By World War II, the number of Filipinas/os in Stockton had mushroomed to around 15,000. According to 2010 Census figures, Filipinas/os are the second-largest Asian American group nationwide, the third-largest minority group in California, and the largest Asian American group in San Joaquin County. Though most Filipinas/os now live in urban areas such as Los Angeles and the San Francisco Bay Area, thousands of Filipina/o Americans can trace their roots to Stockton's Little Manila.

Three themes are central to this book. I am particularly concerned with the politics of historical memory in Stockton and the ways in which we remember, and forget, the history of the community. This book is organized around the historical processes of racialization and cultural transformations that turned provincial immigrants into Filipina/o Americans, and it considers the central roles that race, place, and space played in shaping a unique Filipina/o American identity in the twentieth century. The third theme is the politics of historical memory and the demands and logic of capitalism that led to the urban redevelopment policies that caused the destruction of much of the community in the 1960s and the 1990s.

This book grew from my interest in the politics of historical memory, the power of place to shape ethnic identities and memories, and the ways in which the Filipina/o community tries not to forget its ethnic neighborhood. According to the historian David Blight, the study of historical memory is the "study of cultural struggle, of contested truths, of moments, of events, or even texts in history that thresh out rival versions of the past which are in turn put to the service of the present."[7] The urban redevelopment projects of the 1950s, 1960s, and 1990s scraped the landscape almost completely bare of the Filipina/o ethnic neighborhood that had once flourished there, giving rise to a kind of traumatic forgetting in which the historical memory of the thriving ethnic community was almost lost. If, as Dolores Hayden argues in *The Power of Place*, "identity is intimately tied to memory: both our personal memories (where we have come from and where we have dwelt) and the collective or social memories interconnected with the histories of our families, neighbors, fellow workers and ethnic communities," and "urban landscapes are storehouses for these social memories," then the destruction of most of Little Manila in the 1960s and the 1990s not only destroyed the physical community but also threatened to obliterate the collective memory of this important place.[8]

This book also explores the relationship of Filipinas/os in Stockton to their history and their memories of their community. The historian Michael Frisch writes, "The relationship between history and memory is particularly and perhaps uniquely fractured in contemporary American life."[9] The rupture between Filipinas/os and their history in Stockton was forged by the destruction of Little Manila, streams of new immigration, and the invisibility of Filipina/o Americans in the media, local government, and the racist environment of Stockton. The loss of Little Manila in the 1960s as a result of urban redevelopment left a traumatic wound for old-timers and second-generation Filipinas/os. The pain of the loss of their community prevented older generations from speaking openly about the destruction of that community. There are no monuments to Filipina/o American history in Stockton. Young Filipinas/os in the city's public or private schools do not learn about Filipina/o American culture or history, much less the history or contributions of Filipinas/os in the city. Frisch charges those of us engaged in public history with the repair of this rupture, so that we can enhance our "ability to imagine and create a different future through a reuse of the past."[10] This book is an attempt to answer Frisch's challenge: to recover the memories of the past in order to reimagine a better present and future for the Filipina/o American community of Stockton.

The arguments in this book rest heavily on Michael Omi and Howard Winant's theory of racial formation, in which racial categories are "created, inhabited, transformed and destroyed."[11] The emigrants arriving in Stockton in the first decades of the twentieth century brought with them ideas about race, ethnicity, culture, and difference that were shaped by their ethnic, linguistic, and cultural identities — which in turn were tied to their kin networks and hometowns in the Philippines — and by their racialization as brown colonial wards of the American empire. It was only in their parents' generation that the *indios* began calling themselves Filipinas/os, a term that had been reserved primarily for those Spaniards who were born in the islands. In fact, the totalizing experience of American colonialism would provide even more impetus for the residents of the islands to begin thinking of themselves as Filipina/o, as the racial colonial state imposed a new language (English) on all Filipinas/os and racialized them as one people. As Paul Kramer argues in his important work on race making and empire in the Philippines, the American colonial regime ushered new racial formations. The earliest ideas about race derive from the Philippine-American War, with the racialization of the insurgent enemy as "goo-goos" and as "niggers."[12] Kramer argues that the American colonial administration constructed "a new racial state organized around an aggressively optimistic colonialism of 'capacity'" for self-rule. At the heart of this new racial formation was the split of the population of the Philippines into Christian and non-Christian peoples. Kramer argues that this was an inclusionary racial formation that both "invited and delimited Filipino political agency in colonial state building."[13]

When emigrants arrived in Stockton, they brought with them these ideas about Filipina/o national identity. However, the identities that were most meaningful were those tied primarily to their class and the region, province, and the town from which they hailed. Emigrants saw themselves first as Ilocanas/os, Visayans, or Tagalogs. The Philippines consists of more than seven thousand islands, and its people speak almost a hundred languages and dialects. Partly as a result of this geography and abusive Spanish colonialism, a sense of nationalism had developed primarily among the elite Filipinas/os in Manila and the Tagalog-speaking provinces, and only in the generation of the emigrants' parents and/or grandparents. For almost all of the early emigrants, their first and only visit to Manila, the national capital, or Cebu, the oldest city in the Philippines, was on the eve of their departure, as they prepared to board ships at the ports of those cities. Even more specifically, they organized themselves around their hometowns and villages: Palomponganons (from Palompon, Leyte) or Numanciahanons (from Numancia, Aklan), or Calapeñas/os (from Calape, Bohol), or Tarlekanians (from Tarlac, in Central Luzon). Their segregation in the labor market, which limited them to agricultural work and the domestic and service sector; antimiscegenation laws and the extremely unbalanced sex ratio, which enforced bachelorhood; their status as "nationals" who were unfit to be naturalized; and their identity as colonial wards of the United States all served to racialize these provincial immigrants into despised brown others, into Filipinas/os.

This book explores their experiences as racialized colonials, and how space and place—that is, the fields of the San Joaquin Delta and the streets and buildings of Little Manila—as well as historical events such as World

War II and the residents' work in the fields, labor activism, political activism, and religious activities and involvement in community organizations all helped shape ethnic identities and Filipina/o American culture. Over time, the racialized, gendered, and sexualized space of Little Manila (often called Skid Row by local officials) became a site for the negotiation of a local Filipina/o American identity that was shaped by the work they performed as farm laborers, by the distorted sex ratio that influenced marriage and family formation for decades, and by the racial violence and repression of Stockton.

As immigrants found themselves racialized as despised brown people, they turned to their family networks and to fellow immigrants to survive, constructing a social world and ethnic identity formed both by their provincial identities and the world they now inhabited in Stockton. As George Sanchez argues in his study of Mexican Americans in Los Angeles, "ethnicity . . . was not a fixed set of customs . . . but rather a collective identity that emerged from daily experience in the United States."[14] In exploring the ways in which Visayan, Ilocana/o, and Tagalog emigrants became Filipina/o Americans in Stockton, I take to heart the call for a new kind of Filipina/o American history heralded by the late historian Steffi San Buenaventura, who insisted that early Filipina/o American history "should be as much a narrative of the cultural world they brought with them as it is an account of their life in the new country."[15]

This book traces how historical events and their lived realities created Filipina/o American racial and ethnic identity, culture, and community throughout the twentieth century. What we know of the turbulent early colonial period tells us that the racial and ethnic identities and cultural worlds of Filipina/o immigrants were already in flux by the time they began arriving in the United States in large numbers in the 1920s. At the same time that Filipinas/os were leaving for Hawai'i and the United States, the upheaval of the Philippine-American War and the American colonial regime had already made an indelible impact on the identities and lived realities of immigrants, which is why this book begins with an exploration of life and culture in the provinces of the Philippines in the first two decades of American colonial rule. Immigrants hailed from different provinces and lacked a unifying language besides English to allow them to communicate with one another. In the earliest years of the community, those who did not speak English fluently preferred to associate mainly with other people from their own hometown, province, or region. Class differences between educated and uneducated immigrants and between urban and rural immigrants also created divisions.

The 1920s and 1930s were crucial decades for the forging of a powerful Filipina/o American culture, identity, and community in Stockton. Filipinas/os in Stockton may have seen themselves in the 1920s as students and adventurers whose stay in the metropole would be exciting yet brief. By the mid-1930s this attitude had been transformed. The brutality of industrialized agriculture and the devastating joblessness of the Depression years; pitiful agricultural wages and conditions; anti-Filipina/o violence, exclusion, and deportation; and labor repression marked the first years of the 1930s. After 1934, Filipinos/os were reclassified as aliens. The Filipino Repatriation Act of 1935 was essentially a deportation measure, as it offered Filipinas/os a one-way ticket back to the Philippines if the immigrant promised never to attempt to return.

The fact that Filipinas/os weathered the Depression, exclusion, repatriation, violence, and poverty while refusing to leave showed that the community that they had built in Stockton in the 1920s and early 1930s had given them the resources that allowed them to survive, and even flourish. Just as the Mexican Americans of whom Sanchez writes created new identities and possibilities for themselves in the 1930s and 1940s, by the 1930s so had Filipina/o immigrants developed and assumed "a new ethnic identity, a cultural orientation which accepted the possibilities of a future in their new land."[16]

Immigrants responded to their racialization and new identities in surprising and diverse ways. When my grandfather Delfin Bohulano, a native of Kalibo, Aklan, applied for Social Security in 1936, he scrawled "brown" in between spaces for "white" and "Negro" on the line that asked him to indicate his color. When asked to identify himself on his World War I draft card, Eleno Ninonuevo, an immigrant from Libacao, Aklan, also wrote in "brown." When presented with these documents during lectures on the ways in which the immigration experience racialized immigrants and initiated them into the puzzling logic of ever-changing American racial categories, my students always laugh and say my grandfather must have been confused when he wrote "brown." I gently remind them that the collective experiences of early Filipina/o immigrants led them to believe that they inhabited a despised place below whites and near blacks, a category that reflected their skin color: brown. Moreover, their new lives in America afforded them an opportunity to remake and reshape new ethnic and racial identities.

A third theme in this book is about how the logic of capital, with its prioritizing of urban redevelopment, demolition, and displacement over the preservation and revitalization of ethnic communities, ultimately destroyed the Little Manila neighborhood. The story of Little Manila demonstrates the destructive impact of federal, state, and local urban redevelopment and freeway construction policies that continue to disproportionately affect poor neighborhoods of color—often wiping them off the map, both physically and psychologically. The Little Manila community is a case in point. This book describes how the politics and strong ties of the community and its historical memory have attempted to challenge urban redevelopment's scrape-and-burn policies toward Little Manila.

Little Manila Is in the Heart builds on and challenges the histories of Filipina/o Americans produced by scholars in the last three decades. In its largest context, this book's most ambitious goal is to rewrite the dominant narrative of Asian American history, which has downplayed Filipina/o American community building to favor a male-centered, sojourner narrative; and to examine the important local communities, identities, and institutions built by early immigrants and investigate how they were constructed and changed over time.[17] This book also challenges historians of the Asian American experience to broaden their ideas about the emergence, creation, and maintenance of Asian ethnic communities in the United States.

For example, in his *Strangers from a Different Shore*, Ronald Takaki asserts that Filipinas/os did not develop their own neighborhoods in American cities, nor did they open their own businesses.[18] The story I tell in this book challenges histories that have downplayed or denied the existence of important Filipina/o American enclaves by describing Filipina/o immigrants as roving bands of workers who, some historians assert, rarely settled in West Coast cities. The migratory nature of Filipina/o life in the early to mid-twentieth century pushed Filipinas/os to create flexible notions of family, community, and home, but Stockton remained a mecca for even those Filipinas/os who traveled frequently throughout the West Coast. And although I focus on Stockton, I believe that this book also provides frameworks for understanding the development of other Filipina/o communities on the West Coast — such as those in San Francisco, Salinas, Los Angeles, Watsonville, and San Diego — and other communities throughout the nation.

When Fred Cordova, along with his wife Dorothy, published *Filipinos: Forgotten Asian Americans* in 1983, that pioneering book was one of the few sources on Filipina/o American history. The plethora of books and articles produced in the last decade by academic and community scholars has endeavored to correct the dearth of scholarship on Filipina/o American history so evident in the 1980s and 1990s. Books, dissertations, and articles have explored themes of American empire, Filipina/o community building, ethnic cultural production, gender relations, and interracial relationships and conflict. Notable among these publications are Arleen de Vera's and Eiichiro Azuma's work on Filipina/o-Japanese relations in the Delta region, Dorothy Fujita-Rony's book on Filipina/o Seattle, Linda España-Maram's book on Filipina/o male youth culture, and Catherine Ceniza Choy's book on Filipina nurse migration. Filipina/o American scholars in the social sciences are also studying the impact of place on Filipina/o American histories and identities; examples include Benito Vergara's study of Daly City and Rick Bonus's and Yen Le Espiritu's books on Filipinas/os in San Diego, and Joseph Galura and Emily Lawsin's collection of oral histories of Filipino women in Detroit.[19] Most important, their work has noted how historical Filipina/o American identities have been contingent, varied, and dynamic.[20]

The most groundbreaking recent works on the urban West have focused on interethnic and interracial relations and the interplay between communities and urban space. These works remind us that peoples of color in the West did not live in a vacuum, hermetically sealed off from one another in segregated communities. In fact, the works show how working-class people and people of color struggled to live and get along together, challenged racism and exploitation, created new ethnic cultures and identities, and made the most of their often meager resources in their urban working-class communities. Matt Garcia's book on Mexican labor and community formation in Los Angeles, Scott Kurashige's groundbreaking work on blacks and Japanese in Los Angeles, Mark Wild's book on multiethnic communities in Los Angeles, and Allison Varzally's study on interracial marriage all attempt to understand how different groups interacted with one another in California, and how these interactions forged new identities and communities.[21]

A FRAGMENTED PAST

In *America Is in the Heart*, Bulosan's protagonist, Carlos, sat wearily at the bare table in his kitchen and "began piecing together the mosaic of our lives in America." "Full of loneliness and love," Carlos began to write.[22] A mosaic is an apt metaphor for the fragments of materials and memories I would encounter as I began research for this book. In the mid-1990s, when I began to explore my community's history for an undergraduate paper, I interviewed my father's best friend, Claro Candelario, whom I called Uncle Claro. He revealed to me that he was the restaurateur–turned–radical labor activist, the character "Claro," in *America Is in the Heart*, and a close friend of Bulosan. He explained, the bitterness still fresh, how a relative, in an attempt to clean out his garage, had taken everything to the trash heap—the old letters, newspapers, photographs, records of his time with Bulosan in the Committee for the Protection of Filipino Rights, and more. Uncle Claro's daughter, Angelina Novelozo, was able to save a few of her father's precious photographs and documents, and some of them are published here.

I had known Uncle Claro my entire life. I had to leave Stockton and encounter him in a completely different context—as a character in a book assigned in one of my classes—to begin to appreciate and understand who he was, and the role he had played in our community's history. Old-timers rarely spoke openly of their early experiences, perhaps because the past was painful. And when they did share their stories with us, like Uncle Claro did, they often fell on deaf ears. My peers and I, most of us in our teens when the old-timers were in their twilight years, were unable to connect their memories to the larger history of the United States or to our own identities. When we finally knew the right questions to ask, many of our elders had already passed on, or their memories had grown too dim. In the process of writing this book, I have often been filled with a shameful regret that many of the members of my Filipina/o American generation, who came of age in Stockton in the 1980s and 1990s, did not engage in enough conversations with our elders because we were too naive or too ignorant to understand their memories as history.

These attitudes about our history have roots in colonial mentality and the internalization of hatred of Filipinas/os in Stockton. We have lost much of our community's history because of the assumption that our past is not history, that it is not an American experience worthy of interpretation and analysis. As I was gathering materials for this project in the 1990s, many descendants of pioneering families had already thrown away the newspapers, community programs, photo albums, documents, and other ephemera that historians need to piece together the stories of the past. To some people, these materials were only junk, or at best someone else's memories, rather than history. At several junctures in this project, research involved trying to race families—at one point, my own—to the trash bins. In too many cases, it was too late. Locating sources for this project that lay deep in basements, attics, and garages required patient excavation, and sometimes begging and pleading.

This idea that our community's past as one that is not historically important has been compounded by our invisibility in the curriculum of the K–12 public educational system in Stockton. There is no Filipina/o American history course at San Joaquin Delta College or the University of the Pacific. Most Filipinas/os in Stockton are largely unaware of how central their experiences have become to understanding the history of American colonialism, twentieth-century immigration, ethnic community building, the history of American agriculture and labor, and the building of the urban and agricultural U.S. West. Prominent figures such as Carlos Bulosan and Larry Itliong—widely known in academic, activist, and community circles in Seattle, the San Francisco Bay Area, and Los Angeles—are unknown to most Filipina/o Stocktonians, young or old.

The lack of materials on Filipina/o Americans in local archives compounds this problem. None of the dozens of local organizations or community leaders donated their papers to a local library, university, or historical society, resulting in a deafening silence about Filipina/o community life in local archives. Moreover, no local Filipina/o American ethnic community organization, with the possible exception of the fraternal order Legionarios del Trabajo, has preserved its papers, and that group's papers are not open to researchers. The search for information about the past of the labor leader Larry Itliong is just one example of the unique challenges that Filipina/o American historians face: it was extremely difficult to find memories or materials in Stockton about him. Though within the past two decades there has been a resurgence of interest in Itliong's life and his cofounding of the United Farm Workers, it is impossible to find any local archival materials or anyone who can speak about Itliong's life and work in Stockton, since almost no one who had worked closely with him is still alive.

Though most of the documents of Stockton's Filipina/o American history have been relegated to the trash heap, there has been progress. Because of the dedicated efforts of the Filipino American National Historical Society chapter in Stockton and the National Pinoy Archives in Seattle, photographs, newspapers, documents, and oral histories have been preserved for researchers and community members. In 2005 Antonio Somera, a member of the Daguhoy Lodge and grand master of Bahala Na Escrima, began to clean out the basement of the lodge, at 203 East Hazelton Street in Stockton. The building had been purchased by the lodge in 1937, and over the decades, the lodge members had tossed all manner of boxes and trash into the basement until it was full to bursting. "Take it all out, and do whatever you want with it," they told Somera. Under many layers of trash, he discovered hundreds of photographs, old uniforms of the lodge, band instruments, clothing, pomade jars, citizenship test materials, documents, and several dozen steamer trunks full of the personal belongings of lodge members who had passed away in the 1930s, leaving no next of kin. This discovery, which deserves its own book, could be counted as one of the most significant finds in Filipina/o American history to date. With these materials, he created a museum in the basement. Several photographs that Tony found are featured in this book.

Because of the dearth of archival and printed sources on the history of Filipinas/os in Stockton, oral histories provided the richest source of information on the history of my community. I am indebted to my father, Ernesto T. Mabalon, and my grandmother, Concepcion M. Bohulano—two family members who, until their recent deaths, were just as passionately dedicated to Stockton's history as I am. They opened up their well-worn address books and drew on their web of kin and community to identify people who were willing to share their stories with me. These community members graciously entrusted me with their memories, shared photographs and historical documents, and talked for hours. As Alessandro Portelli writes, oral histories show us that "memory is not a passive depository of facts, but an active process of the creation of meanings."[23] Their stories brought to life the rich and vibrant community that was Little Manila. In our talks, we journeyed back in time to provinces in the Philippines, Hawai'ian sugar plantations, asparagus fields in California, Lafayette and El Dorado streets, cramped and suffocating hotel rooms in Little Manila, Fourth of July parades, boxing matches, and cockfights.

Each interview provided me with a unique and nuanced perspective on the themes of this book. Sometimes my interviewees' memories and opinions contradicted one another. At other times, their total agreement on certain themes was illuminating and deeply moving, as in the case of the shock and grief that the entire community felt about the destruction of Little Manila. I was also blessed to be able to draw on oral histories conducted by scholars who interviewed old-timers in the 1970s and 1980s. These voices, so essential to this project, were recorded and preserved by the Filipino Oral History Project in Stockton, the Filipino American National Historical Society in Seattle, and the collections of the Washington State Oral/Aural History project and the Demonstration Project for Asian Americans.

The many Filipina/o American newspapers of the period, as well as government records, city directories, and Census information, allowed me to reconstruct the Little Manila neighborhood decade by decade by providing concrete locations of Filipina/o, Japanese, and Chinese businesses and organizations in downtown Stockton, and showing the neighborhood's changes over time. To obtain information on the settlement and eventual destruction of Little Manila, I relied heavily on the archival records of the City of Stockton, including the official records regarding the area which encompassed Little Manila, Japantown, Chinatown, and the Mexican community. Some families had saved diaries, photograph albums, letters, and other documents and graciously shared them with me. My family's collection of documents and photographs, organized by my grandmother, Concepcion Bohulano, was invaluable.

Manuscript collections and ethnic newspaper archives at the University of the Pacific and the Haggin Museum, as well as at the University of the Philippines, yielded important historical material, including correspondence about the Little Manila community, church records, and the activities of selected Filipina/o social organizations. Indispensable for the book were the priceless archival collections of the Filipino American National Historical Society, especially the growing collection of the Stockton chapter, and the National Pinoy Archives in Seattle, which housed a significant amount of material on the Filipino American experience in the Stockton area. The Filipina/o American ethnic newspapers collected by the Filipino American Experience Research Project at San Francisco State University were absolutely invaluable. The Bancroft Library at the University of California, Berkeley, houses the papers of James Wood, an economics doctoral student who studied Filipinas/os and left boxes of his notes, interviews, drafts, and articles for future researchers. The new technologies that have made passenger ship lists, naturalization records, Census data, and military records easily accessible allowed me to glean insights about the arrivals and provincial origins of the earliest Filipina/o immigrants to Stockton, where they lived and worked, with whom they lived, and their families.

The lack of a wealth of conventional archival materials led me to use creative ways in which to uncover the history of this community. As the historians Antoinette Burton and Dolores Hayden remind us, physical sites and buildings can become archives and important sites of memory.[24] The walls and interiors of the remaining buildings of Little Manila—the Iloilo Circle, Daguhoy Lodge, Mariposa Hotel, Rizal Social Club, Emerald Restaurant/ Filipino Recreation Center, and the Caballeros de Dimas Alang house— spoke of the history of a community determined to stay and build places to live and thrive in the face of racism. The celebrations and gatherings of our community were sites of memory to which I went in search of its history: church services including masses, novenas, and rosaries; family birthday parties, weddings, christenings, and funerals; the annual Barrio Fiestas; meetings of fraternal orders such as the Legionarios del Trabajo and the Filipino Federation of America; events at the county senior center, neighborhood card rooms, and ethnic restaurants and businesses; family and generational reunions; and the meetings of clubs, provincial associations, and professional organizations such as the Association of Filipino American Educators. In these gatherings, I found documents, community stories, oral history interviewees, and most important, the spirit of community and resilience that has sustained Filipina/o American Stocktonians over many decades. I hope that this book can inspire succeeding generations of Filipina/o Americans in Stockton, particularly the children and grandchildren of immigrants who arrived after 1965, to begin to see that the materials of everyday life—their grandparents' stories, documents, photographs, and other belongings—are history, and therefore, priceless.

I also went to the Philippines several times for archival research, as well as to visit the rural provinces to which many Filipinas/os in Stockton trace their roots. Riding hulking inter-island steamers, jeepneys, buses, and on the motorbike and bicycle-powered "tricycles" that carry whole families which abound throughout the Philippines, and, in some cases, traversing towns on foot, I visited ancient churches and historic sites, cemeteries and town plazas, lush rice and coconut fields, and beaches. I visited the towns of Loboc and Tagbilaran in Bohol, the towns of Palompon and Ormoc in Eastern Leyte; the towns of Numancia, Lezo, Makato, Ibajay, and Kalibo in Aklan province; Cebu City and the towns of Talisay and Carcar; the towns of Binalonan and Dagupan in Pangasinan; tiny villages like Masinloc on the coast of Zambales; the American colonial town of Baguio; the emerald rice terraces of Banaue; and drove through the provinces of Nueva Ecija, Nueva Vizcaya, and the bustling city of Davao in Mindanao.

Visiting the provinces about which the old-timers waxed sentimental allowed me to better understand how colonialism, poverty, and dreams of big-city life and college educations pushed emigrants to the United States. Most important, seeing the provinces, the white sand beaches and impossibly turquoise oceans, the million shades of green in the rice and coconut fields, and meeting families torn apart by immigration—especially my own relatives—taught me about the ache of homesickness that the first generations of Filipinas/os in the United States must have felt. As I flew above the lush archipelago in 1997 on a short island hop between Manila and Cebu, I was choked with emotion as I looked down at the tiny green islands in turquoise water through my plane window. What kinds of poverty and dreams could have pushed my grandparents to leave such a beautiful land, and how might it have felt to build a new home thousands of miles away?

OUTLINE OF THE BOOK

This book describes how Filipina/o American ethnic identities and the Filipina/o American community were constructed and changed over time in Stockton's Little Manila. Part I presents the stories of the members of Little Manila from their lives in the provinces to the initial Filipina/o settlement in downtown Stockton in the 1910s. Chapter 1 examines life in the Philippines on the eve of the emigration of thousands of Filipinas/os to Hawai'i and the mainland. I argue that Filipinas/os came to the United States not only because of the pervasive influence of American colonialism, especially public education, but also because changes in the economy of the Philippines extinguished any hope that peasants and members of the lower middle class would be able to hold onto their family land and obtain gainful employment in their home provinces. Chapter 2 examines the development of industrialized agriculture in the San Joaquin Delta and Valley, and how Filipinas/os became the solution to severe labor shortages in the area after 1924. Their horrific working conditions racialized and radicalized them, and they responded to those conditions by abandoning regionalism and embracing ethnic solidarity and labor militancy.

Part II explores how community members created their own world in Stockton, establishing institutions such as churches, labor unions, and community organizations. Chapter 3 explores how Filipinas/os carved out a social world for themselves through their community institutions and in the development of their corner of Stockton, Little Manila, in the decades before World War II. Filipina/o American ethnic identity in Stockton is shaped from the unique culture that emerges from the lodges, organizations, and streets of Little Manila. I also discuss how the attempts to exclude and deport Filipinas/os failed, as Filipinas/os decided to stay in Stockton permanently.

Chapter 4 explores women's lives in Little Manila from the 1920s to World War II. The extremely imbalanced sex ratio—fourteen Pinoys to one Pinay in the prewar years—prevented large-scale family formation in Little Manila. Interestingly, however, the imbalance and relative youth of the immigrant population provided immigrant and second-generation Filipinas to challenge and transform traditional gender roles. I also discuss how Filipinas/os shaped the contours of a new kind of Filipina/o American family in Stockton. The second part of chapter 4 turns to the experiences of second-generation Filipina/o Americans from the late 1930s to the 1960s, with a focus on young women's ethnic identity and culture.

Chapter 5 examines the religious life of Filipina/o immigrants and their families and explores the conversion and Americanization efforts of evangelical Protestant missionaries. This chapter also explores the role that the church played in sustaining the Filipina/o farm labor movement in the early 1960s. Chapter 6 shows how World War II was a watershed moment for Filipinas/o in Stockton, as changing racial discourses and the war in the Pacific remade Filipinas/os into the good Asians. Before the war, workers organized the most militant and successful farm labor union the West Coast had witnessed. The forced removal of Japanese Americans from Stockton during World War II allowed Filipina/o entrepreneurs to expand the borders of Little Manila. Citizenship, a baby boom, and new immigration caused the community to grow exponentially in this period. Furthermore, the labor movement was represented by the powerful Local 7, the leaders of which, such as Larry Itliong, would go on to lead the Delano Grape Strike and co-found the United Farm Workers Organizing Committee.

Part III describes how by 1968, much of the Little Manila and Chinatown area had been destroyed by urban redevelopment. Moreover, new immigration threatened to tear apart the delicate fabric of the community. The Crosstown Freeway cut through the heart of Little Manila, and by 1972, only two struggling blocks remained. The destruction of Little Manila as a result of the city's postwar scrape-and-burn urban renewal policies and the California State Highway Commission's policy of freeways at all costs is described in chapter 7. The Crosstown Freeway wiped out two blocks of Little Manila in the late 1960s, displacing thousands of Filipina/o residents and destroying dozens of businesses, residential hotels, and community institutions. Chapter 8 describes the five-year struggle of a group of postwar immigrants, second-generation Filipinas/os, and progressive old-timers who proposed the creation of a Filipino Center as a solution to the displacement of thousands of Filipina/o old-timers and several Filipina/o businesses. This last chapter explores how the community forged an elusive unity by coming of age politically, banding together to speak to power, and demanding federal funding for the center.

In the epilogue, I reflect on the legacies and burdens of Stockton's Filipina/o American history, and the politics of history and memory in ethnic community building. The community's heated debates over what to preserve and why, disputes over the memories of the special place that was Little Manila, and the economic and cultural challenges of revitalization and historic preservation remind us that Filipinas/os in Stockton continue to struggle with issues of history, memory, and power.

ON THE TERMS AND THE TITLE

Several terms used in this book are defined and explained here for greater clarity. I chose to use *F* instead of *P* in reference to the Filipina/o American community for several reasons. "Pilipina" and "Pilipino" are as commonly used as "Filipina" and "Filipino" by both pre-1965 and post-1965 immigrants and their descendants for various reasons, including the lack of the *F* sound in Tagalog. Filipina/o American activists in the 1960s and 1970s rejected the *F* and its Spanish and American colonial legacy, preferring to use the *P*.[25] However, in Stockton, "Filipina/o" was used more widely throughout the twentieth century by the community members. Following the lead of the historians Dorothy Fujita-Rony, Teresa Amott, and Julie Mattaei, I have used "Filipina/o" (and "Ilokana/o" and so forth) throughout this book to call attention to the gendered nature of the Filipina/o experience.[26]

When referring to Filipina/o immigrants before World War II, I have occasionally used "manong" for men and "manang" for women, but only when writing from my own point of view or from the viewpoints of younger generations. In Ilocano, Visayan, and Tagalog, these are honorific terms used for one's elders. In the 1960s, younger generations of Filipinas/os began to use the terms to refer to those Filipinas/os who immigrated to the United States before World War II. Because some people use "manong" and "manang" to refer only to close relatives, many prefer the term "old-timer" to denote people who came to the United States before 1965. I sometimes use the terms "old-timers" and "pioneers" for those immigrants who arrived in Hawai'i or the United States before 1965. When referring to any Filipina/o in the United States, I use the words "Pinoy" (Filipino American male) and "Pinay" (Filipina American female). According to first-generation immigrants, these terms were developed specifically by Filipina/o immigrants as a nickname for Filipinas/os living or born in the United States.[27] The earliest documented appearance of the term "Pinay" was in 1926 in the *Filipino Student Bulletin*.[28] "Pinoy" and "Pinay" are now used for any Filipina/o in the Philippines or in the Diaspora. How fitting that the etymological roots of these terms lie in the experiences of the pioneers of the Filipina/o Diaspora: the Pinays and Pinoys of Stockton's Little Manila.

The book's title, *Little Manila Is in the Heart*, was inspired by *America Is in the Heart*, Bulosan's classic 1946 ethnobiography of the Filipina/o American experience in the 1930s. Bulosan split his time among the great centers of Filipina/o American life—Stockton, Seattle, and Los Angeles—and a number of significant events in his book take place in Little Manila or elsewhere in Stockton. Carlos, the wide-eyed idealist who is the protagonist of *America Is in the Heart*, yearned to be part of the America of his colonial education and his most optimistic dreams, an America of racial and social justice and equality, a nation that would reciprocate his loving embrace. In the last chapter of the book, as the tumult of World War II created a new world for Carlos and other Filipina/o Americans, he felt "the American earth was like a huge heart unfolding to receive me." "It was something that grew out of the sacrifices and loneliness of my friends, of my brothers in America, and my family in the Philippines—something that grew out of our desire to know America, and to become part of her great tradition, and to contribute something to her final fulfillment," Bulosan writes. "I knew that no man could destroy my faith in America that had sprung from all our hopes and aspirations, ever."[29]

As Bulosan knew too well, this faith in America, and the hopes and aspirations of the first generations of Filipina/o immigrants, stood in stark contrast to their lived realities. Nonetheless, life in Stockton, before World War II, with the barriers erected to prevent the immigrants' settlement, and the urban redevelopment policies that wreaked destruction on Little Manila from the 1960s to the 1990s, did not in the end deter Filipinas/os from making their homes in Stockton. From the earliest years of the community, as Bulosan writes in *America Is in the Heart*, emigrants cherished the hope that they would one day find a real home in their adopted country. This deep faith in America sustained them through decades of sacrifice and poverty; racial violence; denial of the rights to immigrate, become citizens, and marry whom they wished; and labor repression.

Through these long decades, they married and established families, brought over their relatives from the Philippines, created enduring institutions and a vibrant ethnic community, made their voices heard politically— in short, used their imagination and creativity to become that new entity, Filipina/o Americans. In so doing, they themselves created the America of which they dreamed: the Little Manila of their hearts, a beloved ethnic community and a unique and special world in Stockton. Though the buildings are gone, and the old-timers have passed away, the power and promise of the Little Manila community remains in the hearts of every Filipina/o who remembers and reclaims its legacy.

PART I PUTTING DOWN ROOTS

1898–1940s

The Filipino youth has learned the great achievement of America, its economic prosperity, its gigantic industrial institutions, the high wages paid, its beautiful cities, its big buildings and skyscrapers, and other wonders and opportunities. All of these fires the imagination of the Filipino youth and creates in his mind the love of adventure.

His education increased his wants.

— *Hermenegildo Cruz, Director, Philippine Bureau of Labor, 1931*

The growing and harvesting season of the farm crops orchestrated the rhythm of our lives. Asparagus, starting in February; thinning fruits, sugar beets; picking cherries in spring, potatoes, tomatoes, tokay grapes in summer; and in the fall and winter, pruning grape vines, cutting celery, thinning onions, and planting garlic was our general cadence. . . . Like the weary traveler when he beds down at night, closes his eyes but still sees the rushing pavement, I would see the tomatoes, smell the pungent vines, feel the oppressive unrelenting afternoon heat, and totally, unconditionally accept this way of life.

— *Gussie Gesulga Bowden, writing in 1985*

Stockton
magic city
streets of the happy life
poolhalls, girls and grass . . . Stockton!
. . .
Stockton,
I remember you
gaudy, happy, sinful
Stockton
meeting place and clearing house for 20,000 Pinoys.

— *"Stockton, 1950," Lanosa, in* Liwanag

CHAPTER 1

FROM THE PROVINCES TO THE DELTA

Life on the Eve of Emigration to the United States

My grandfather Pablo Magdaluyo Mabalon had poignant memories of the Philippine-American War. When he was four years old, he watched Tagalog and U.S. troops burn houses in the *barangay* (neighborhood) of Albasan, in Numancia, Capiz province, in 1901. The following year, his father, Guillermo Mabalon, became one of the estimated 200,000 victims of the cholera epidemic that raged across the Philippines in the wake of the war.[1] Guillermo left behind his wife, Victorina, and two children, one of whom was my grandfather. He remembers that without his father, the family spiraled into deep poverty: "As far as my memory could recall, no special family celebration of any kind was ever held due to our poverty." There were other families who were poorer, however, he recalled: "My family was in a position to still have three meals a day and have less worry where to get the next meal."[2]

Like thousands of other poor provincial families in the immediate aftermath of the Philippine-American War and with the advent of American colonial rule, the Mabalons traveled to Manila to find work. Pablo, also called "Ambo," was a fifth grader in a colonial public school when his uncle Sacarias Macavinta hired him to work in his restaurant. At dawn, ten-year-old Pablo delivered heavy bags of hot rolls, called *pan de sal*, throughout Manila and then returned to the restaurant to work.[3] In his twenties, he met Isabel Timtiman Tirona, a young woman from Makato, a town just north of Numancia. Isabel's family had also relocated to Manila to find better opportunities. A Protestant priest married the couple in the Malate neighborhood in 1919, and they moved to Numancia and had five children. Pablo's work as a *matanzero* (butcher) and Isabel's business as a weaver of abaca and *sinamay* (a coarse, open-weave textile derived from abaca) could barely feed their young children, Rodrigo, Florencia, Ernesto, Teqio, and Francisco.[4] Rodrigo and Francisco died in childhood as a result of illness and malnutrition. In 1929 Pablo decided that the only way the family could survive would be if he traveled to the United States. He sold his meager inheritance — his grandmother Clara Macavinta's rice and coconut fields, a sliver of rich land that fronted the province's narrow main road.[5] He traveled to Manila and, for 75 pesos, bought a steerage class ticket for Seattle. On March 2, 1929, Pablo, with a group of relatives and fellow town mates, left for Seattle on the steamship *President Jackson*, a ship operated by the Dollar Steamship line, which dominated prewar Pacific steamship travel.

It must have been with mixed emotions that my grandfather left behind his wife and their three surviving children. Foremost on his mind, however, must have been the dream of seeing his surviving children fed and educated.[6] His daughter, Florencia, nicknamed "Puring," then only seven, thought that he was only going on a short trip to Manila.[7] Ernesto, my father, was then four and has dim memories of his father's departure: "When [he] left in 1929, I was almost five. I don't have a clear picture of how he looks. I had no feeling about where he was going, and I wasn't aware that he was going away for long. A five-year-old can be lured into believing that your father is just going out, and he never comes back."[8] It would be seventeen years before they would see their father again.

My grandfather was one of 150,000 mostly Ilocano and Visayan men with meager landholdings, hungry families, and little cash for their children's education who left their homes for the United States in the first half of the twentieth century. His story tells us that Filipinas/os would have never come to the United States in significant numbers in the early twentieth century if the United States had not first colonized the Philippines in 1898. By 1899 the United States had fought two wars — one with Spain and a much longer war with Filipina/o nationalists — that would forge a new American empire in the Pacific. The violence, death, and dislocation caused by the American conquest of the Philippines would disrupt life across the provinces in ways that would reverberate over the generations and play a central role in the movement of Filipinas/os to the United States. The expansion of the American empire in the Pacific sparked the massive movement of Filipinas/os to the metropole in two important ways: the totalizing influence of the colonial public education system served to convince Filipinas/os of the superiority of American culture and institutions; and the shift to a capitalist, export economy so exacerbated the extreme poverty of rural life that leaving home was, for some, the only option.

This chapter examines the lives of Filipinas/os in the provinces of the Philippines in the first decades of the twentieth century, on the eve of massive emigration to Hawai'i and the United States. To attempt to understand the motivations behind this first massive wave of emigration, I explore life in the hometowns and provinces of these early emigrants, with a particular focus on the Ilocos region in Northern Luzon and the Visayas, the two regions that sent the most emigrants to the United States in the last century. The first half of this chapter explores the ways that American imperialism and capitalism, particularly through the public education system, shaped life in the provinces; racial, cultural, and political identities; economic opportunities; gender roles; and family lives for the generation coming of age in the 1910s and 1920s. The second half of the chapter explores the motivations and experiences of those who left the provinces to work as contract laborers (*sakadas*) on the sugar plantations of Hawai'i in the first two decades of the twentieth century. From these sugar plantations came most of the first Filipina/o immigrants to arrive in the San Joaquin Valley and Delta in the 1910s and 1920s.

Exploring province life and life on the sugar plantations of Hawai'i in the early years of the American regime reminds us that emigrants did not immediately imagine themselves as Filipinas/os; rather, they identified primarily with others from their town, province, and region. Their primary identities were based on their kin networks, villages, towns, and regional languages and/or dialects. They sought the company of others from their towns when they arrived in the United States not only because those people were likely to be members of their extended kin networks, but also because it was easier to communicate with those speaking the same, or at least a similar, dialect or language. Until universal use of English was mandated, there was no national language that tied Filipinas/os together across the thousands of islands. Spanish was a language of the elite. Few Spaniards actually went to the Philippines, and friars, who were the primary representatives of the Spanish Crown there, learned local languages and dialects and did not force indios (the name the earliest Spanish explorers, who had hoped to reach India, gave to the indigenous population of the Philippines) to speak Spanish. Moreover, English fluency ranged dramatically. Emigrants who were high school graduates were able to read and write with great fluency in English, but emigrants who had not gone beyond elementary school were less fluent.

American colonial rule made it possible—and, for some, necessary—for Filipinas/os to emigrate to the United States. As Dorothy Fujita-Rony argues, the advent of American empire in the Philippines and colonialism as practiced by other Western powers "created new opportunities and sites around the globe, dramatically changing the realm of the possible for people around the globe."[9] Because of their status as colonial wards, Filipinas/os were classified as nationals, not aliens as other Asians were. And as nationals, they were not subject to the immigration exclusion laws of the late nineteenth and early twentieth centuries—laws that barred Chinese laborers in 1882, Japanese laborers in 1907, and South Asian immigrants in 1917. This special status would facilitate the massive immigration wave that brought thousands of Filipinas/os to the United States, and then to Stockton. Their lives under the American flag and their collective experiences in Hawai'i and, later, in Stockton transformed and racialized them from *provincianas/os* into Filipinas/os and, eventually, Filipina/o Americans.

THE PHILIPPINE REVOLUTION AND AMERICAN EMPIRE

Those emigrants who arrived in Stockton in the first decades of the twentieth century were following a path carved out by people from the Philippines who came to the New World as early as the sixteenth century. Ferdinand Magellan reached the islands of Cebu and Mactan in 1521, beginning three centuries of Spanish colonial rule. The lucrative trade between China, Manila, and Acapulco that commenced in 1565 and lasted until 1815 brought the first indios to the New World, where they worked as shipbuilders, prostitutes, sailors, and slaves on the Spanish galleons.[10] The earliest recorded arrival of Filipinas/os in what would become California was on October 18, 1587, when a group of "Luzon Indios" landed near what is now Morro Bay.[11] The first permanent New World communities of Filipinos were formed as early as 1763 in the Louisiana bayous by indios who jumped ship at ports in the Gulf of Mexico.[12]

While these communities were establishing themselves across the globe, Spain relegated the governing of its far-flung colony to Mexico and the Roman Catholic Church.[13] By the late nineteenth century, the abuses and oppression of the friars had inflamed the outrage of the educated elite—called *illustrados*, or enlightened ones—who demanded representation in the Spanish *Cortes* and an end to the friars' abuses. Most prominent among the elite was José Rizal, a wealthy doctor educated in Madrid, whose two books, *Noli Me Tangere* (1887) and *El Filibusterismo* (1891), offered scathing criticisms of Spanish corruption and abuse. Rizal insisted that the indios be called Filipinos, a name formerly reserved for Spaniards born in the Philippines. He established the Liga Filipina, an anticolonial political organization, in 1892. One of its earliest members was Andres Bonifacio, a native of Tondo. In 1892, drawing on his experiences as a Philippine freemason (Bonifacio, Rizal, and almost all of the illustrados and many mestizo elites were freemasons, which incensed the Catholic hierarchy), Bonifacio formed the secret society Katipunan ng Kataastaasan ng Kagalanggalangan ng Anak ng Bayan (Highest order of the brotherhood of the children of the nation).

The Katipunan began the Philippine Revolution in August 1896, fighting the Spanish throughout Luzon and in Negros and Panay.[14] Rizal was immediately imprisoned and killed by a firing squad in Luneta Park in December 1896.[15] A power struggle among the Katipunan leadership ensued, and Emilio Aguinaldo and his relative Daniel Tirona, both members of the Cavite elite, asserted that Bonifacio's lack of education disqualified him from leading the organization. When he attempted to reassert control over it, Bonifacio was executed for treason on the order of Aguinaldo, who then became the group's leader. In 1898 Aguinaldo agreed, under the Pact of Biak-na-bato, to retreat to Hong Kong in return for a payment of $400,000 and the promise of Spanish reforms. There he plotted his next move.

By the late nineteenth century, the race for empire among Western countries had whetted the appetite of American politicians, military leaders, and other elite groups for building an American empire in the Pacific. The United States and Spain began the Spanish-American War in May 1898, in the midst of the Cuban and Philippine Revolutions, after the United States blamed the explosion of the USS *Maine* in Havana on Spain (it was actually caused by a malfunction in the ship). Immediately, the United States sent Admiral George Dewey and the Pacific fleet to Manila Bay.[16] To save face, Spanish officials agreed to stage a mock battle in which they would surrender to the Americans instead of to the Philippine nationalists.[17] Confident of U.S. support, Aguinaldo sailed for Manila and declared the independence of the Philippines on June 12, 1898, from the balcony of his family mansion in Kawit, Cavite. In the summer and fall of 1898, Aguinaldo declared himself president of the Philippine Republic and presided over a constitutional convention at the new capital, Malolos, in Bulacan province, north of Manila, which resulted in the nation's first constitution and Malolos Congress. Meanwhile, thousands of U.S. troops, including several all-black regiments, began to arrive in Manila. That fall, Spain and the United States negotiated the Treaty of Paris, which ceded the Philippines, Guam, and Puerto Rico to the United States for $20 million. The treaty was signed on December 10, 1898, and then sent to the U.S. Senate for ratification. President William McKinley then issued the Benevolent Assimilation Proclamation, which promised that the Americans came as friends and not as conquerors.[18] The treaty ignited a fierce debate in Congress and among the American people over whether or not the United States should possess a colony in Asia.[19]

A vocal pro-imperialist majority, led by such figures as McKinley and Senator Alfred J. Beveridge, argued that the United States had a racial and religious duty to spread American democracy and capitalism, Protestant Christianity, and Western civilization to the dark and savage peoples of the Philippines. In the fall of 1899, in a speech to Methodist ministers, McKinley framed the taking of the Philippines as the ultimate Christian sacrifice, telling his audience that "there was nothing to do but to take them all, and to educate the Filipinos, and uplift and civilize and Christianize them, and by God's grace do the very best we could by them, as our fellow-men for whom Christ also died."[20] An 1899 poem by Rudyard Kipling, "The White Man's Burden," exhorted Americans to grow into their masculine, Anglo-Saxon destiny and take a colony of "new-caught, sullen peoples" as the rest of Europe had already done.[21]

Anti-imperialists included African Americans who drew parallels between Jim Crow racism and the conquest of the Philippines; intellectuals, reformers, and civil rights leaders who decried imperialism as unconstitutional, racist, and unjust; labor unionists who feared the influx of cheap labor; eugenicists and other racial scientists who abhorred the idea of extending American citizenship to Filipinos; and American businessmen who feared competition from Philippine exports. The most prominent anti-imperialists were Mark Twain, W. E. B. DuBois, Jane Addams, Bishop Henry Turner, and the steel magnate Andrew Carnegie.[22]

As the debate raged in the United States, troops in Manila traded shots. The Philippine-American War officially began on the evening of February 4, 1899, when Willie Grayson, a veteran of the U.S. Indian wars, shot at a group of Filipino soldiers near San Juan, a neighborhood in Manila. After opening fire on them, he returned to camp, yelling: "Line up, fellows; the niggers are in here all through these lines."[23] General Arthur MacArthur ordered his troops to advance. In a proclamation given the next day from the new capital of Malolos, Aguinaldo assured the new nation that the nationalists would be victorious, although so far "all my efforts have been useless against the measureless pride of the American Government and of its representatives in these islands, who have treated me as a rebel because I defend the sacred interests of my country and do not make myself an instrument of their dastardly intentions."[24] Two days after the hostilities commenced, the U.S. Senate ratified the Treaty of Paris by a single vote.

The Philippine-American War was brutal and protracted. The U.S. government preferred the term "Philippine Insurrection" for the hostilities, casting the Filipinas/os as insurgents against their rightful government.[25] As Paul Kramer argues, the Philippine-American War was as much a race war as it was one of national independence. American troops committed horrifying atrocities and mass killings to subdue the nationalists.[26] By September 1900

Aguinaldo and the members of the Malolos Congress had retreated to Pala-nan, Isabela, but guerrilla warfare continued throughout the islands. When Aguinaldo was captured on March 23, 1901, fighting was still raging in many provinces. As noted in the introduction, U.S. soldiers called Filipinos "nig-gers" and "goo-goos." They also burned villages, killed civilians (sparing most children, but not young adolescents), and employed such methods of torture as the "water cure"—now known as waterboarding.[27] The nationalists' use of guerrilla tactics, including attacks with bolo knives (long, sharp machete-like blades), spurred a response in which Americans destroyed crops, which led to starvation and malnutrition. The policy of concentrating civilians in camps and designated areas in the provinces led to overcrowding and un-sanitary conditions, and water supplies were tainted by the filth and trash that the U.S. army left in its wake. The result was a cholera epidemic of such horrific proportions that between 150,000 to 200,000 people died across the Philippines.[28]

Amid intense fighting, William Howard Taft was sworn in as first governor-general of the Philippines in 1901. President Theodore Roosevelt declared the war over on July 4, 1902, although fighting continued in some areas until 1915. In 1901 some Filipinas/os, particularly those from Pangasi-nan, had joined new military forces such as the Philippine Scouts for mop-up operations with Americans in the provinces where revolutionary activity per-sisted, particularly in the Visayas and in Mindanao. This was why my grand-father Pablo remembered Tagalog (more likely, Macabebe or Pangasinense) troops burning homes in his village in 1902.[29] Historians now estimate that up to one million Filipinos were killed during the fighting from battle, dis-ease, and malnutrition.

MAKING THE FILIPINA/O COLONIAL SUBJECT

The American colonial project in the Philippines transformed the culture, politics, and economy in both countries in ways that historians still struggle to fully understand.[30] Under the Spanish regime, only the Philippine elite could send their children to private Catholic schools, which left much of the population without a formal education. American colonial policymakers set themselves apart from other imperial powers by their policy of "benevo-lent assimilation," in which the majority of the populace could come under colonial control through public education and preparation for eventual self-rule. U.S. military and political officials moved swiftly to co-opt national-ist Filipina/o elites by offering them positions of power and influence and implementing a public education system in English that transformed Fili-pinas/os into loyal colonials.[31] With this policy, American officials could reject anti-imperialist criticism and thus make an argument for American exceptionalism in the race for empire in the late nineteenth and early twentieth centuries.

Perhaps more than any other colonial institution, the American educational system transformed the Philippines from a distant, long-neglected Spanish outpost into a full-fledged American colony. So important was "civilization"—and the pacification that Americans hoped would result from it—of the indigenous population through public education in English that military leaders such as General William Otis established public schools and handpicked textbooks and curricula even as the war continued to rage in 1899. Within a month of the entry of U.S. troops into the city of Manila in August 1899, seven schools were opened under the direction of the chaplain of the California Regiment.[32] In the 1899–1900 school year, the first year of the war, officials counted almost 7,000 students enrolled in American public schools.[33] Taft said that it was the "genius of the American people that even among their soldiers, waging a war to subdue insurrection among the Filipino people, there should be found an earnest desire and effort to better the people by education."[34] Officials were convinced that education would be embraced. "Wherever our flag was raised a public school was soon established, soldiers often serving as teachers, and the moral effect of this upon the Filipinos was very great," wrote former Philippine Secretary of the Interior Dean C. Worcester in his memoirs of the first years of conquest.[35] On January 21, 1900, Worcester, along with his fellow members of the Philippine Commission, the body of American officials tasked with governing the Philippines, passed Act No. 74, which established a free public primary school system and a normal school in Manila for the purpose of training teachers, and mandated that all instruction be conducted in English.[36]

American officials rebuffed criticism that education would be wasted on the "savage" natives in the Philippines, arguing that the United States was undertaking a project in social reform more challenging and exceptional than any European nation had attempted in any colonial venture. "Has any nation unselfishly, earnestly and in good faith tried the experiment of bettering the social, moral and intellectual condition of the people of the tropics?" asked James F. Smith, secretary of public instruction, in an address given in Manila in 1904. "Or is the conclusion drawn from the fact that the nations alleged to be the most successful in dealing with races of another color have declined to undertake the experiment?"[37] For this project, American teachers and administrators were imported en masse. On August 23, 1901, approximately 368 men and 141 female teachers arrived in the Philippines on the U.S. transport ship *Thomas* and were dubbed "Thomasites." These "bearers of benevolence," as the historians Mary Racelis and Judy Celine Ick call them, set to work teaching the more than 200,000 students enrolled in the 1901–2 school year.[38] Hundreds of teachers would follow them during the first two decades of American rule. In 1915, the last year that historians recorded evidence of skirmishes between American troops and Filipina/o nationalists, more than half a million Filipina/o children were attending public schools across the nation.[39]

To create the system of public education in the Philippines, American educators, reformers, and policymakers had only to look at what had been hailed at the end of the nineteenth century as a successful solution to the problem of what to do with the peoples of the Americas: the American Indian boarding-school system, developed in the late nineteenth century. Christian boarding-school education was regarded as a more practical and moral approach to the Indians than the genocide and forced removal from their territory that had been the previous hallmarks of Indian policy. The motto "Kill the Indian in him, and save the Man," voiced by Richard H. Pratt, president of the Carlisle Institute, directed teachers to destroy all vestiges of Indianness (culture, values, language, food, and dress) in order to create good Americans.[40] If the Indian could be remade — that is, if the "savage" inside could be civilized and taught to give up Indian ways — the Indian "problem" would cease, reformers argued. The historian Anne Paulet argues that the educational system in the Philippines and the boarding-school system for Indians allowed Americans to claim that their colonial project was superior to European imperialism because it was used "to transform the cultures of their subjects and prepare them for self-government rather than continued colonial control."[41] It made sense to model the educational system in the Philippines after the American Indian one. As Walter Williams has argued, the status of American Indians set the precedent for the colonial status proffered to Filipinas/os, making them, like the Indians, "wards" of the state, and thus ineligible for citizenship.[42]

By 1905 at least one school had been established in every municipality, with English as the lingua franca. Not surprisingly, reaction to the schools was mixed. Some barrio families refused to allow their children to attend American schools, especially devout Roman Catholics who were suspicious of secular education. Many, however, were anxious to allow their children to become literate. By 1931, 1.2 million students were attending American public schools.[43] American teachers initially, and then the American-trained Filipina/o ones, raised literacy rates. These teachers were also the main transmitters of American colonial culture, and their ideas about public health, cleanliness, and hygiene — as well as the view that American culture and institutions were superior to those of the Philippines—would challenge and disrupt indigenous beliefs and practices and transform the identities and aspirations of the generation coming of age after the end of the war.

Kramer argues that the policy of using English in the public schools and as the lingua franca of the colonial state was both pragmatic and ideological. The American colonial regime had few resources to devote to making its administrators fluent in Filipino languages, of which there were almost a hundred. Furthermore, U.S. policymakers believed that only through a common language could a self-ruling Philippine nation be constructed. And if the U.S. conquest and subsequent rule of the Philippines was proof of Anglo-Saxons' racial and political superiority, then English, with its "transformative, liberating power," was "the necessary vehicle for tutelage," Kramer writes. The widespread teaching of its lingua franca to its colonial wards—in contrast to the typical policies of other Western powers in their colonies—bolstered U.S. claims to exceptionalism.[44] In 1908, when the Philippine Assembly, the lower house of the legislature in the Philippine Islands that consisted of Filipinos, proposed a bill that would replace English with the local or regional dialect as the medium of instruction, the Philippine Commission, which consisted of Americans appointed by the federal government, moved to reject the bill outright, arguing that it would delay the spread of English.[45]

The American school system—which the colonizers touted as essential in preparing the Philippines for self-government—would prove to be the most effective tool for American control of the Filipina/o population. Education, as the historian Renato Constantino argues, was the "handmaiden of colonial policy." "In exchange for a smattering of English, we yielded our souls," wrote Constantino in his 1966 essay "Miseducation of the Filipino," a classic of postwar nationalist historiography. "The stories of George Washington and Abraham Lincoln made us forget our own nationalism," he added. "The American view of our history turned our heroes into brigands in our own eyes, distorted our vision of the future." For Constantino, the educational system was the death knell of the independence movement in the Philippines: "The surrender of the Katipuneros was nothing compared to this final surrender, this leveling down of our last defenses."[46] The historian Nick Joaquin argues that the generation that came of age in the 1920s was "the first of several generations of Filipinos . . . that would identify entirely with the American, lovingly assuming that American and Philippine interests were identical."[47] By 1925 the civil service exam was given entirely in English. Some Filipinas/os considered those who still spoke Spanish to be of an older, obsolete generation.

By then, Filipina/o public school teachers, not Americans, were the most powerful agents of the American colonial regime. These Filipinas/os followed the example of their white predecessors and were just as harsh, if not harsher, in inculcating thousands of Filipinas/os with American colonial identities. Even in the 1920s, when the majority of teachers were Filipinas/os trained by Americans, the policy of using only English in instruction was strictly enforced. My grandmother Concepcion Moreno Bohulano remembers that her Filipina teacher would strike her and her classmates with a ruler or fine them if they were caught speaking Cebuano in her public school in the 1920s and 1930s. Camila Labor Carido remembers that English was the only language allowed on the school grounds in her barrio of Hinundayan, Leyte. "If you're caught talking Bisaya, oh my God, they slap or spank you with a ruler in the *lobot* [bottom]," she recalled. "And they say go over there in the corner. And then, they go *bang, bang, bang* with the ruler."[48]

American public education and the changing colonial economy also transformed Philippine gender roles. The American colonial period ushered in changes for upper-class women in politics, in the community, and in their roles as waged workers. Educational opportunities began to broaden for landowning and elite women as the American colonial government implemented women's and coeducational public education at every level throughout the Philippines, such as the University of the Philippines, established in 1908. Though some elite women were encouraged to complete college degrees, their career choices were still limited to nursing and teaching. Catherine Ceniza Choy argues that nursing programs established in the first decade of the American colonial period provided opportunities that had never previously been available to Filipinas, regardless of their class. However, she notes that these opportunities—mostly in nursing, domestic science, and teaching—"perpetuated America's gendered assumptions about labor, constructing the separate women's sphere that many white American men and women of the period claimed to be one of the foundations for 'civilization.'"[49] Some of these middle-class women—including Segunda Reyes, a teacher, and Eudosia Bravo Juanitas, a nurse—came to Stockton in the 1920s and 1930s.

But not all gender-role transformations were liberating for Filipinas. If the goal of colonial education was to shape loyal servants of the empire, then the domestic science curricula required for young girls in the Philippines—cooking, knitting, sewing, crocheting, and household sanitation—sought to civilize them in the model of middle-class, white Victorian womanhood or, at the very least, her perfectly trained servant. In the late nineteenth century, white middle- and upper-class women promoted domestic science as a way to professionalize the domestic sphere by marrying the scientific and managerial techniques of modern industrialization to the domestic labor of cooking, cleaning, and child raising.[50] Domestic science made a deep impression on Filipinas growing up in the first half of the twentieth century. Camila Carido remembers bitterly that her education in Leyte province consisted not of reading, arithmetic, and the sciences, but of domestic science and domesticity. "We are not educated," she remembered angrily. "We go to school to learn how to write our name. You are [just] prepared to take care of your husband and your children. We are just taught how to be a good wife, darn and sew, cook for your husband. That's our life in the Philippines, to serve your husband even if he kills you for not doing it."[51]

REPRESENTATIVES OF AMERICAN EMPIRE:
THE PENSIONADAS/OS

One of Taft's pet policies was the pensionado program, created in 1903 by the Philippine Commission.[52] The program handpicked sons and daughters of the elite, as well as ambitious and bright students to study at American universities as "disciples of democracy," as the historian H. Brett Melendy writes; these students would be shining examples of the benevolence and exceptionalism of the American colonial project. They were then to return to the Philippines to assume positions in local and regional politics, the colonial government, education, and business.[53] The program served to consolidate further the growing relationship of patron and client between the American colonial government and the Filipina/o elite. The first group of 102 pensionadas/os was sent to the United States in October 1903.[54] Their success, fabled or real, ignited a desire among many young men and women to attend a prestigious U.S. college and to return to take an important political or business role in the Philippines, a phenomenon I will discuss in greater detail later in this chapter.[55]

One of the several hundred pensionadas/os who traveled to Stockton was Primo Villaruz, of Capiz province, Panay (see figure 1). Villaruz graduated from the University of California, Berkeley, with a degree in chemical engineering. He had intended to go back to the Philippines, where he could work to upgrade the water and sanitation system in his home province, but he was offered a position as a chemist at the California Water Service in Stockton, a rare feat for a Filipina/o.[56] In Stockton, he met his wife, Rita, a mestiza whose father had been an American army officer. Villaruz never returned to the Philippines, but many other pensionados did go back, after attaining degrees from elite universities.

A small but not insignificant number of pensionadas/os were women. One of the most prominent was the feminist historian Encarnacion Alzona, the

1. Shown here as a chemistry student at UC Berkeley in the early 1920s, Primo Villaruz was the first Filipino chemist hired by the California Water Service. He was elected the first president of the Filipino Community of Stockton and Vicinity in 1930. Courtesy of Arthur Villaruz.

first Filipina to earn a PhD.[57] The women studying in prestigious U.S. universities through the pensionado program were still limited by gender-role expectations to traditional women's careers. The *Filipino Student Bulletin*, a publication by and for the pensionadas/os in the 1920s and 1930s, reported that although two women had "invaded the sacred and hitherto exclusively men's realm of business and politics, the rest have proved true to form and graced the fields where women are expected to give their finest contributions: nursing, home economics, and social service." The *Bulletin* also called these young Filipinas studying in America by a new name, invented to differentiate them from Filipinas in the Philippines: they were called Pinays, and their male counterparts were called Pinoys.[58]

The vast majority of emigrants to Stockton—even those with only a few years of schooling in the Philippines—credited the pensionadas/os, their teachers, and the American public school system with impressing on them the superiority of American culture and the vast possibilities that awaited them across the ocean. Emigrants recalled that it was their American teachers who inspired them to yearn to travel to the United States, citing "education" and "adventure" as the main reasons for their emigration.[59] Writing in 1931, as Filipina/o emigration to the United States had peaked, the director of the Philippine Bureau of Labor, Hermenegildo Cruz, observed that all Filipino youth believe that "America is the land of promise." The school system taught young people about "the great achievement of America, its economic prosperity, its gigantic industrial institutions, the high wages paid, its beautiful cities, its big buildings and skyscrapers, and other wonders and opportunities," he wrote. "All of these fires the imagination of the Filipino youth and creates in his mind the love of adventure." Unfortunately, there were only limited opportunities in the Philippines, Cruz noted.[60]

Anastasio Pagala, an Ilocano from Laoag who arrived in San Francisco in 1927 and settled in Stockton, remembers that his teachers taught him that the United States was a "country of opportunity," and this instilled in him a "great desire" to emigrate. Returning pensionadas/os impressed him: "Those people that came here and went [to the Philippines] on their vacation always had good jobs."[61] Segunda Reyes, who left Tacloban, Leyte, for Stockton in 1930, said she learned that "America was a great country. You have lots of opportunities."[62] Camila Carido was told by her village teachers that America was the "land of paradise," where immigrants could "pick up the money on the sidewalk." Carido's father had left for the United States in the early 1920s, and on her walks through the village, her thoughts often turned to him and his life in the United States. "I used to stand over there on top of a hill and wonder, 'How far is America?'" she said. "They have lots of money. They have the big phonograph, and they have lots of music in the house. They have big lights, no more coconut lantern."[63] One Pinoy old-timer remembered what brought him to Stockton in the 1920s: "I hear about the prosperity of the best country in the world. That's why I came here. I wanted to see the beautiful United States. I wanted work. I wanted adventure."[64] When Pablo Mabalon was attending public school in Manila, America represented freedom, because the United States "came to the Philippines to take possession of the Islands and also to free us from the tyranny of imperial Spain."[65] Like many Filipinas/os in his generation, his education was limited: he went only as far as the fifth grade. However, the positive impressions of the United States that his teachers gave him endured throughout his life.

Many children in rural areas stopped attending school after the elementary grades because not every barrio and town had a high school, and often their parents needed them to work. Bright students yearned for more education, especially after American teachers and returning pensionadas/os bragged of the opportunities for higher education at universities and colleges in the United States. But only elite families could afford to send their children to the two private, Catholic venerable institutions of higher learning in the Philippines: the University of Santo Tomas, established in 1611, and the Jesuit-run Ateneo de Manila, established in 1859, both in Manila. The establishment of the University of the Philippines allowed middle- and lower-middle-class Filipinas/os to attend college, but even then, few families could afford to send their children to Manila for an extended period. In large families with few resources, perhaps only one very bright child could be sent to college.

Thus, many children of the aspiring middle and lower middle classes became increasingly convinced that it would be less expensive, and more prestigious, to obtain a college education in the United States rather than in the Philippines. So popular was the image of the Filipina/o student who went abroad to America that thousands of self-supporting immigrants like Felipe Napala sold or mortgaged family land in order to pursue such higher education. "To go to high school I have to venture to the other island," recalled Napala, a native of Limasawa, a tiny island near Leyte in the Visayas. "It costs us money. . . . So my mother inspired us to venture, go someplace where maybe you can find a better life out there because you don't have nothing here in the island."[66] Napala went to the United States because he wanted to get an education and a job that paid well, and he eventually made his home and raised a family in Stockton.

Some emigrants decided to leave because of the limited opportunities in the province for those who were bright and educated. Claro Candelario was born to a poor family in San Fernando, La Union, in 1905. He was an extremely bright and articulate young man who yearned for more education than his small barrio school could offer. In high school, he excelled and impressed local school officials with his intelligence and potential. After two years of high school, he began to work as a houseboy for the superintendent of schools, an American. His employer took him to Manila, where Candelario attended the Philippine Normal School. He returned to his home province, where he became assistant principal of the public school. At home in San Fernando, Candelario married his childhood sweetheart, Ines Nufable—a fellow schoolteacher and the daughter of one of the town's richest landowners. Candelario felt the need for more education and better pay. On May 30, 1930, he left his wife and Angelina, their toddler daughter, in San Fernando and boarded the *Empress of Russia*, a Canadian ship bound for Victoria, Canada. That same day, Ines gave birth to a son.[67] Candelario, on whom his friend Carlos Bulosan based the character Claro in *America Is in the Heart*, settled in Stockton.

Benicio Catapusan, a pensionado who earned a PhD in sociology at the University of Southern California, estimated that almost 14,000 Filipina/o immigrants studied at American educational institutions between 1910 and 1938.[68] Most of those students that Catapusan counted were self-supporting. In 1931, Manuel Adeva, a pensionado in New York City, estimated that 95 percent of the almost 1,000 Filipina/o college students in the United States that year were self-supporting, with only a small fraction receiving partial governmental support, and an even smaller handful receiving full support.[69] "I wanted to come to the United States for two purposes," said George Montero, a native of Santa Maria, Pangasinan, who later settled in Stockton. "First, to get an education to continue studying and going to high school. And, of course, to find employment. But really it was my intention to come here first to study if I could support myself."[70] Nemesio Paguyo attempted to go to Manila to attend college but realized there was no money: "My other two sisters, younger than me, they were both in high school at the time I graduated. . . . And if I went to college, then one of them will probably have to stop studying and go to work. So I decided . . . that I should leave." Paguyo boarded the *President Tyler* in Manila in February 1930 and landed in San Francisco on March 9, 1930. He settled in Stockton, where he worked, raised a family, and lived out the rest of his life, never realizing his dream of a college education.[71]

LIFE IN THE PROVINCES

As the American colonial education system transformed the minds of young Filipinas/os attending public schools, their families in the provinces struggled to adjust to the new economic and social order imposed on the Philippines by American colonialism. The economic shifts that were a result of the changing economy created conditions that, along with colonial education, pushed thousands of Filipinas/os to look for better opportunities and wages overseas. American capitalism indelibly changed the economies of the provinces—particularly the northernmost provinces of Luzon and in the Visayas, notably in the Ilocos region and on the islands of Cebu, Bohol, and Panay—as the economy shifted from one of barter and subsistence to one dependent on cash, and as small landholders struggled to adjust to the new focus on exports.

The deteriorating economy of the provinces, the stories told by returning pensionadas/os, and the heavy recruitment of Filipino laborers for the sugar plantations of Hawai'i all were major factors in the emigration of Filipinas/os to Hawai'i and the United States in the first decades of the twentieth century. The Hawai'ian Sugar Planters Association (HSPA), which began heavy recruitment in the Visayas and the Ilocos in the 1910s, eventually brought more than 126,831 Filipinos to Hawai'i between 1909 and 1946. About 16 percent of this population eventually moved to the West Coast, including California.[72] By the 1910s and 1920s, emigration to Hawai'i or the United States became a viable alternative to migration to new lands in the Cagayan Valley (for Ilocanos), migration to the city, or sending the oldest children in a family to be educated in Manila or Cebu. Thousands of families responded

to economic conditions and the promise of an American education by sending family members, mostly sons, to Hawai'i and the United States, with the
hope that they could improve the family fortunes.[73]

Families in the provinces were already struggling during the Philippine
Revolution. The arrival of the Americans did little to disrupt the system of
landownership in place under the Spanish. In fact, the entry of American
monopoly capital worsened landlord-tenant relationships and benefited only
the most elite families and American business interests. Constantino argues
that the Americans had a vested interest in increasing the landholdings of
families who already had large haciendas, because these landholdings produced the raw exports (especially sugar, copra, and hemp) desired by American capitalists. To meet the demand for export crops, *hacenderas/os* strove to
enlarge their holdings. In sum, Constantino writes, the Philippines was exporting most of its raw materials, such as sugar, copra and hemp, while purchasing American manufactured goods in a drastically uneven ratio. In 1900
the total American share of the value of the import and export trade in the
Philippines was a paltry 11 percent. By 1935 it was 72 percent. In 1899, only
9 percent of all imports to the Philippines came from the United States. By
1933, Filipinas/os purchased 64 percent of their total imports from the United
States. American companies and elite landowners reaped the benefits.[74] As a
result of these economic dislocations, thousands of lower-middle-class and
poor families and single men and women migrated from the Ilocos and the
Visayas to Manila and Cebu for work, which strained the urban infrastruc-
tures that had to handle many new unskilled and unemployed arrivals.[75]

In the first decades of American rule, wages were lower than during the
late Spanish period, with workers earning an average of P1 (peso) a day, and
four out of five families lived below the poverty level in Manila. Conditions
were worse in the provinces: even in prosperous sugar-producing areas such
as Pampanga and Negros, annual income averaged P185, half of what was
considered subsistence-level annual income.[76] The American regime also
brought new opportunities for the landholding class in every region. In the
Ilocos region, elite families emphasized education and political participation
in the American regime. To finance an education in Manila, lower-middle-
class families were forced to mortgage or sell off parcels from their already
small landholdings. After the onset of American rule, an increasingly attractive option for elite families and small landholders was to leave for Hawai'i or
the United States for an education and work. Sadly, when migrants returned
from Hawai'i and/or the mainland, flush with cash, they were hampered by
inflation caused by the high demand for land amongst returnees.[77]

Most of the immigrants who arrived in Stockton before World War II were Ilocanas/os and Visayans from lower-middle-class families who were small landowners or tenant farmers who could sell farm animals, mortgage parcels of land, or sell crops; they were not peasant laborers, the starving poor, or the elite. Some immigrants had resources and land and came to the United States for adventure. Some had educations, but they could find no jobs in the small towns and remote provinces of the Philippines — or if they did, the wages were too low to support a family. Tenant farmers, the poorest of the poor, had nothing to mortgage or sell to raise the P180 for a steamship ticket and thus could not leave the Philippines.

Almost all of the emigrants to Stockton came from impoverished provinces in the Ilocos region on the island of Luzon and provinces near Ilocos, such as Pangasinan and Tarlac (see map 1). A smaller number were Visayan immigrants who came from rural provinces on the islands of Cebu, Panay, Leyte, and Bohol in the central Philippines.[78] From 1906 to 1924, Ilocos Norte and Ilocos Sur sent approximately 32,707 immigrants to Hawai'i. Other areas that sent large numbers of immigrants included Pangasinan, Cebu, Bohol, and La Union.[79] In 1929 the provinces of Ilocos Norte, Pangasinan, Ilocos Sur, Tarlac, La Union, and Abra, all on Luzon, sent the most immigrants to the United States. In 1928, Ilocos Norte sent the most immigrants to the United States, approximately 2,833. Pangasinan sent 2,226; Ilocos Sur, 2,045; Tarlac, 519; La Union, 872; and Abra, 271. Almost 90 percent of Filipina/o immigrants to the United States before 1930 were of Ilocana/o origin.[80]

The Ilocos region is a dry stretch of land that emerges from Pangasinan province at the Lingayen Gulf and extends north for 160 miles. The soil is rocky and, for the most part, lacks the fertile richness of the rice- and coconut-growing lands directly to the south. Most farmers in the region, before and immediately after the American colonial period, practiced subsistence-level farming. All of these provinces had an extremely high population density. In the provinces of Ilocos Sur and La Union, as well as on the island of Cebu, there were almost 500 people per square mile. Furthermore, the average landholding in these regions was only about an acre.[81] Because of a lack of land, there were few large haciendas in Ilocos. Even at the end of the Spanish colonial period, few families owned more than sixty hectares each.

Historians have noted that as early as the sixteenth century, Ilocanas/os had responded to the lack of fertile land and increasing population pressure by migrating to new areas. When families had multiple children, as was usually the case among Catholics, landholdings were further divided, and not all children could inherit land, which increased tenancy, landlessness, and poverty. By the beginning of the American colonial period, large numbers of

1. The Philippines. The shaded provinces are those that sent the most immigrants to the United States from the early twentieth century through 1965.
MAP BY BEN PEASE.

Ilocanas/os were emigrating across Luzon.[82] By the early twentieth century, Ilocanas/os began to leave the region altogether and work in Pampanga in the sugar centrals, or in Hawai'i or the United States.[83]

The hardships of farming created an Ilocana/o regional culture that valued thrift, hard work, and frugality, with a high value placed on migration to new land for better opportunities. By the twentieth century, these cultural values earned Ilocanas/os, rather unfairly, a reputation among other Filipinas/os as people who were "naturally" adventurous, as well as "pushy, aggressive, hot-headed, land-hungry, excessively jealous, overly quick to resort to violence, and extremely provincial," according to one anthropologist doing research among Ilocanas/os in the 1960s and 1970s.[84] The sociologist Miriam Sharma argues that the stereotype of Ilocana/o immigrants as lovers of adventure misses the point: Ilocanas/os migrated to survive. The poor soil in the region and the economic pressures placed on farmers by the export-oriented economy forced thousands to sell their land and leave the region.[85]

American colonial officials ensured that the Philippines remained dependent on the United States for most of its imports and exports, Sharma notes, and the U.S. demand for sugar, copra, and hemp created a disastrous situation for peasants and small landowners. Politically powerful elite landlords who owned large haciendas blocked agrarian reforms, and the American colonial government hesitated to change the feudal agricultural system that was hundreds of years old.[86] Sharma writes that the main industry in the Ilocos region soon became "the production, reproduction, and subsequent export of human resources."[87] Moreover, the effect of exporting Ilocano labor on the struggling families left behind was not at all what the emigrants expected. The onset of the American period inflated the price of land. Inflation was made worse when thousands of dollars of remittances from workers in Hawai'i and the mainland began flowing into the region in the 1920s. Sadly, many who left to find work in the United States found that they could not afford to buy land when they returned.[88]

The tribulations of the family of the protagonist in Carlos Bulosan's *America Is in the Heart* illustrate the brutal struggle to survive in the provinces of the Ilocos region in the 1920s and 1930s. The book's first part tells a heartbreaking story of crop failure, usury, land loss, and starvation in Binalonan, Pangasinan, just south of the Ilocos region, where many Ilocanas/os had settled. The family of the main character, Allos, places its hopes on the eldest sons, who are studying to become schoolteachers. In order to pay for their education, the family mortgaged its small farm, and Allos's mother worked as a trader in the village market, as did many women in the rural provinces.[89] Hectare by hectare, the family land is lost to moneylenders, until there is nothing left.[90] When the prospects of completing their expensive educations are dashed, Allos's brothers decide to leave for work in the United States, and Carlos reluctantly follows them. "Only Macario and I were left, and I did not want our family to disperse further," says Allos. "But circumstances stronger than my hands and faster than my feet were inevitably dividing us, and no matter what I did our family was on its way to final dissolution and tragedy."[91] Eventually, Allos leaves Binalonan to join his brothers Macario and Amado in the United States. Although the details of Bulosan's story are largely fictional, the book was based on his own family's experiences, the stories of his friends, and the tragedies he witnessed as a young boy growing up in Pangasinan.

The stories of the Mabalon and Dionisio families show that Visayan immigrants were under similar pressures to those facing Ilocanas/os. Pablo "Ambo" Mabalon's family was among the thousands who left rural provinces for Manila soon after the American occupation began. Juan Dionisio Sr. also left Numancia for Manila to find work. A farmer with a small plot of land, Dionisio left his wife and two children in Tagayon, Kalibo, in Capiz province, to travel to Manila. There he found employment as a coal worker on a steamship that plied the Pacific between Seattle and Manila. But he soon jumped ship in Seattle and began working in the timber industry in Washington State. Left behind with his mother and sister, with little to no contact from his father, Juan Dionisio Jr. itched to go to the United States after excelling at the private high school in his province. The family mortgaged the little land they had left to raise the P180 for passage to the United States, plus P220 for expenses. The usurer who loaned them the money charged 60 percent interest on every 100 pesos borrowed. "And if you do not pay it in one year, the agreement you signed with him says that the land belongs to him," remembered Juan Dionisio Jr., known as Johnny.[92] He bought a steamship ticket and was settled in Stockton by the late 1930s. Felipe Napala's family owned several plots of land on which several tenant families raised rice, corn, bananas, and sweet potatoes. The Napala family survived by asking their tenant families for a small share of their crops and by bartering the rice and corn for some of the daily catch of the village fishermen.[93] "They were in normal conditions," said Nemesio Paguyo, a native of Laoag, Ilocos Norte, of his family. "They were all right. They were not so hard, except they were not as rich as the people who were rich. They have enough food. They were the average family."[94] Pablo Mabalon's parents, Victorina Magdaluyo Mabalon and Guillermo Mabalon, were lower-middle-class landowners who owned rice and coconut fields in the same village. Pablo's inheritance, a small coconut and rice field, was sold to pay for his steamship ticket.[95]

Families' desperation, gender-role expectations, and reliance on the overseas earning potential of their sons, husbands, and fathers had a significant impact on the extreme imbalance of the sex ratio of the early Filipina/o American immigrant community. Another cause was the sojourner mentality of some Filipino immigrants, who believed they would only be gone for a few years. Filipinas did not immigrate in large numbers because of patriarchal cultural values that dictated that women should stay at home, and because sugar plantation labor recruiters shifted their focus from family units in the Visayas to single male laborers from the Ilocos region by the early 1920s. Though educational and employment opportunities and a broader role in community and government changed middle-class Filipinas' lives, little changed in the sexual division of labor in the home or in the general expectation that all women's lives, especially those of poor and working-class women, would revolve around the home. Upper-class women benefited the most from changes, but they could afford household helpers who did the brunt of domestic work. In any case, traditional families regardless of class insisted that marriage and family remain the primary goals for women.

Families were more likely to use their resources to help their sons emigrate. My maternal great-grandparents, Paz Paderes Bohulano and Severo Bohulano, mortgaged their rice fields in Numancia, Capiz province, to send their oldest son, my grandfather Delfin, to America in 1929. He was responsible for sending some of his wages home to support his eight brothers and sisters.[96] Nonetheless, the Bohulano family, like Allos's family, was never reunited, and the family remained mired in poverty. According to the Stocktonians Frank and Leatrice "Letty" Perez, "it was all a family could afford to pay for one to have a chance at a better life in America with the hope that the rest of the family could follow."[97] When Frank Perez left Bantay, in Ilocos Sur, in the late 1920s, his family sold a water buffalo, a cow, and part of their land to pay for his fare.[98] After a brief stint in Los Angeles, Perez settled in Stockton during World War II, where he met and married Letty Bantillo in 1948.

Emigrants from the Ilocos and the Visayas were mostly young, male, and single. The majority of the immigrant population during these years was under thirty, and more than half of all female immigrants were under twenty-two. The early Stockton Filipina/o community—like many other Filipina/o American centers, including those in San Francisco, Seattle, and Los Angeles—was largely devoid of elders.[99] More than half were unmarried, though there were some, like Candelario and Pablo Mabalon, who had left their wives and families behind. More than 31,000 Filipinas/os landed in the ports of San Francisco and Los Angeles from 1920 to 1929, but more than 93 percent of them were male. Of the 100,000 Filipino immigrants in Hawai'i and the United States in 1946, fewer than 20,000 were women.[100] About 40 percent of the Filipinas who went to America before World War II were married and had entered the country with their husbands.[101] Eudosia Bravo Juanitas and Segunda Reyes had gone to college and gotten married before they came to Stockton with their husbands in the 1930s. Eudosia Bravo, a public health nurse, had met her husband, Cirilo Juanitas, when he was on a trip home to her village in the Visayas. She encountered little resistance from her family when she told them she would marry him and accompany him back to Stockton. "You know people who are coming from America," she said. "They are so excited about those people. Everyone approved my marriage to him."[102]

Some of the women who settled in Stockton—such as Camila Carido, Asuncion Nicolas, and Paula Dizon Daclan—came at the behest of family members already in the United States.[103] Since arriving in Hawai'i after World War I, Camila Carido's father had remarried, had two children, and been widowed when he sent for Camila. With few opportunities in her village on the island of Leyte, Camila decided to leave her province for the United States. The boat ride was incredibly lonely for Camila, who had seldom ventured beyond her village. "I cried and cried, and I was saying, 'How come I'm going?' I almost really jumped off the boat," she recalled. "That's the first time I felt lonesome for my mother, my sister, and all my friends."[104] Paula Daclan's aunt and uncle had already moved to the United States and had traveled back to her province of Pangasinan to invite the rest of the family to join them. Paula, then twelve, ecstatically agreed, though leaving her parents and brothers and sisters was painful. "Then I made a promise to myself," she remembered. "I'll go back [one day] and see them."[105] Asuncion Nicolas's mother, Juliana Lazaro, was already a businesswoman in Stockton when she sent for sixteen-year-old Asuncion in 1929. Eudosia Juanitas's mother warned her that in America she would be without her family. "My mother said, 'You'll be the only one there. Nobody will help you,'" Eudosia recalled. "So I made up my mind. I had to fight. So I was not afraid."[106]

Many Filipinas simply refused to leave the Philippines, preferring life there to an uncertain future and probable hardship in America. "We do not have any intention of coming to America," one Filipina wrote on a questionnaire circulated in the Philippines asking women why they were reluctant to emigrate. "We will stay here at home where they left us years ago. We want them to come back."[107] In the provinces of the Ilocos region and in provinces in the Visayas such as Capiz and Antique, from which many people emigrated, 13–19 percent of households were headed by women; the average across the rest of the country was close to 11 percent. The wives and the children left behind in the provinces shouldered incredible burdens of work after the departure of their husbands and fathers.[108]

KASLA GLORYA TI HAWAI'I: HAWAI'I IS GLORIOUS

Most Filipinas/os arriving at the port of San Francisco from 1920 to 1927 had embarked not from Manila, but from Honolulu.[109] One of the thousands of immigrants who left Hawai'i to settle in Stockton was Cirilo Yongque Juanitas, who had been born in 1892 in Barbaza, Antique province, on Panay. Though his parents owned their own farmland, Cirilo was one of eleven children. When families were this large, it was next to impossible for all the children to inherit land. Twenty-one-year-old Cirilo was recruited in 1913 to work on a sugar plantation in Lihue, Kauai. After his contract expired, he took the SS *Lurline* to San Francisco in 1916. By 1917 he had become the first Filipino hired by Stockton's Holt Manufacturing, the company that invented the tractor.[110]

Juanitas and the thousands of other Filipinas/os who arrived in Hawai'i in the early twentieth century came to answer the labor needs of American sugar plantation owners, who had wrested control of Hawai'i from the monarchy in 1898. Unable to force native Hawai'ians to work the sugar and pineapple plantations in the mid- to late nineteenth century, plantation owners relied on imported Chinese, Japanese, and Korean laborers. When Asian exclusion laws in the United States barred their entry, and other attempts to get more labor failed—including the importation of Puerto Ricans—the HSPA turned to the Philippines. In 1906 a recruiter for the HSPA, Albert F. Judd, tried to recruit three hundred Filipina/o families to work in Hawai'i. He was able to entice only fifteen Ilocanos he encountered in Manila, and he put them to work at the Olaa Plantation on the Big Island of Hawai'i.[111] Judd was largely unsuccessful in finding more recruits, partly because he was unfamiliar with the regions and languages of the Philippines. He had a difficult time convincing any women to go to Hawai'i.[112]

In 1909 the HSPA began recruiting Filipina/o workers in earnest. After paying a $6,000 fee to the Philippine colonial government, the organization began to recruit workers in two areas: the Visayas and the Ilocos region.[113] The HSPA actively recruited Filipinas/os until 1926, when they stopped because so many thousands were coming to Hawai'i on their own. The first Filipinas/os who arrived in large numbers in the early 1910s were families from the Visayas. Historians have yet to find evidence as to why the HSPA first concentrated its efforts on the recruitment of families in Bohol, Cebu,

Panay, and Romblon, but it could be that the tradition of entire Visayan families migrating to Negros seasonally to work the sugar plantations made these families seem more skilled and likely to adapt; another reason may be because the Ilocos region was far from the main ports of Manila and Cebu.[114] These workers were called sakadas, the name given to migratory laborers in the Negros sugarcane plantations.[115]

Stories of the abusive recruitment system and harsh conditions filtered back to Philippine officials, and after 1915 the Philippine government forced the HSPA to provide return passage for laborers after the end of a three-year contract.[116] The HSPA set up a main office in Manila, with agents and sub-agents in recruiting offices in Cebu, Iloilo, Capiz (now Aklan province), and Negros Oriental. Per recruit, agents and subagents were paid P7 for Visayans and Ilocanas/os, but only P5 for Tagalogs, because they had been found to be picky about their work conditions and resistant to strict supervision, according to the HSPA. Agents showed films of the good life in Hawai'i and bragged about the high wages workers could receive.[117] "They would show the Filipino a nice silver dollar, and tell him that there were lots of them to be had in Hawai'i," said Felix Tapia, who settled in Stockton. "They also told them that there was plenty to eat, that it was easy to get good clothes, and to have a good time there."[118]

Beginning in the 1920s, HSPA recruiters focused on single Ilocanos, particularly those who were illiterate (and therefore more easily manipulated) and could perform hard manual labor. Ilocanos and Visayans who could read and write but were desperate for work often lied and pretended to be illiterate in order to be chosen to go to Hawai'i. To ensure that their recruits could handle sugar plantation work, recruiters looked for calloused, hard palms.[119] Ceferino Jamero was an educated man in his barrio of Garcia-Hernandez, Bohol, but he purposely chafed his soft palms on rocks to fool the recruiter and pretended to be illiterate, according to his daughter, Luna Jamero. It worked, and Garcia went to work in Hawai'i for a time before traveling to the United States. There he worked in the fields around Stockton, finally settling in Livingston, about fifty miles south of Stockton.[120] Between 1906 and 1935, the HSPA brought more than 120,000 Filipinas/os to work on sugar plantations in Hawai'i.[121]

The recruitment films were enticing, but the best advertisement for work in Hawai'i came from the letters and money sent back from the first sakadas. Villagers were deeply impressed by the fancy, well-dressed *Hawai'ianas/os* who returned to the Philippines after three-year contracts, their *maletas* (suitcases) groaning under the weight of their American-made gifts. The writer Manuel Buaken remembered when a fellow town mate, a sakada named Masong, began to earn the enormous sum of $3 a day, which he sent to his wife, Benita. He returned in glory, confidently dressed in an American business suit, with $3,000 in savings. Buaken writes that Masong was called "the shrewd and lucky adventurer from the rich sugar-cane and pineapple plantations." Buaken remembers that a dozen HSPA agents swarmed through Ilocos Sur, dazzling Ilocanas/os with promises of wages of $2 a day and repeating the "hypnotic" story of Masong's incredible success.[122] In 1917, in Virgilio Felipe's village in Ilocos Norte, the success of the earliest Hawai'ianos convinced the provincianas/os that Hawai'i was a place to pick up money. That year, Felipe's brother-in-law Miguel began sending $40 home every two months, impressing his in-laws and neighbors. When Miguel returned from work at Puunene Plantation on Maui, he brought back mirrors, tools, ready-made clothing, a sewing machine, and a phonograph player. "We were so amazed by the machines," Felipe recalled.[123]

Felipe decided to go to Hawai'i because "when people talked in those days, they said, 'Kasla Glorya ti Hawai'i.' Like heaven is Hawai'i.'" Felipe and his friends and relatives were struck by the rich Hawai'ianas/os returning to the province. "Because those Hawai'ianos, Pilipinos who went to Hawai'i, when they came back they were very showy," Felipe remembered. "They walk around with white high-heeled shoes, even in the dust, and wore these *Amerikana* suits, and Stetson hats, even on hot days in town. They looked so rich, and true they had some money to blow on the outside. And those who came to Hawai'i would soon send back so much money! In no time."[124] The stories of sakada success proved so tantalizing that in 1927, Agapito Formoso and Emilio Balanzat decided to start a regular ship line between the Philippines and Hawai'i. The first voyage began on July 3, 1927, reported the *Manila Bulletin*, and the ship carried 776 Ilocana/o workers. The record is silent on whether or not other such voyages took place—but this voyage, taken against warnings of its foolhardiness by government officials because the workers lacked contracts—illustrates how fervently Ilocana/o laborers desired work in Hawai'i.

Preferring instead to allow myth and rumor to make their experiences seem glamorous, or perhaps because descriptions of the conditions they had lived in might prove too humiliating, returning sakadas rarely shared their true experiences with their families. When they arrived at the plantation, sakadas were forced to live in barracks and subsist on substandard wages. Filipina/o workers were living in "odious" and "desperate" situations, according to Prudencio Remigio, the Filipino labor commissioner appointed to work among Filipina/o nationals in Hawai'i. Workers found the ten-hour-a-day, six-day-a-week schedule of cutting sugar cane almost unbearable. In the province, the ability to control one's own time made farm work less arduous than the never-ending work on the clock demanded by the lunas (supervisors).

The richly detailed diaries of Angeles Monrayo, a Romblon native and later a Stockton resident, tell us a great deal about life in the Visayan community in Honolulu and about the migration of Visayans from Hawai'i to the West Coast in the mid-1920s. Monrayo was a baby when she and her mother, Valeriana; her father, Enarciso; and her brother, Julian, left Romblon, a small island in the Visayas, for Hawai'i. They arrived in 1912. Her mother, Valeriana, took a lover and left Enarciso to raise the children alone. What Valeriana did was not uncommon. The extremely imbalanced sex ratio among Filipinas/os in Hawai'i transformed marital relations and courtship, and the scarcity of women led to violent altercations between male emigrants. Stories abound of instances in which men "stole" wives or women left their husbands for new partners in a practice called *coboy coboy* (meaning "cowboy," probably so called because of the ways cowboys would swoop down and lasso cows; the practice is described in chapter 4). With her mother gone, Angeles had to help support the family.[125]

Another Visayan family recruited to Hawai'i were the Alcoys of Carcar, Cebu. Poor farmers, the Alcoys had been scratching out a living on less than five acres, where they grew *gabi* (taro), string beans, breadfruit, *ube* (purple yam), and munggo (mung beans). In 1904 the family was left destitute when the crops were ruined by disease and drought, and the father passed away in 1908. "And then my dad left the five acres of land to us, but we cannot do the land, you know, plant something, because we are small yet," Alberta Alcoy Asis remembered. Her mother went to Cebu City to find work, and there she met an HSPA recruiter. "They give us ten pesos for our expenses," Alberta remembered. "They give Momma clothes and they give us clothes." Alberta was only ten when she and her mother and siblings arrived in Hawai'i on Christmas Day in 1910. "The boss, the plantation boss, they give us a house and we are forty-seven people, fifty-seven people [including the children]," she recalled.[126] Alberta Alcoy married another sakada, Genaro Asis, a native of Mindanao, and the Alcoy and Asis families worked in the sugarcane fields before leaving for Stockton.

As the last group to arrive in Hawai'i, Filipinos had the lowest status of any ethnic group in the racial hierarchy there. Stereotyped as oversexed and irrational, and nicknamed "poke-knives" by members of other ethnic groups because of their reported propensity for fighting with knives over women and gambling, Filipinas/os struggled to find allies outside of their ethnic group and solidarity within. Their penchant for gambling, arguments, and violence over women, as well as their love for cockfights and playing pool on Sundays, incited the ire of other groups in Hawai'i, Lawrence Fuchs argues.[127] There were deep ethnic, cultural, and linguistic differences among the Filipinas/os, a situation they would also encounter in Stockton. In Hawai'i, Ilocanas/os, Visayans, and Tagalogs "eyed each other with suspicion and dislike," writes Bienvenido Junasa.[128] With English fluency ranging widely among the immigrants, Filipinas/os in Hawai'i found it difficult to communicate with one another, and distrust grew as stereotypes about one another abounded. According to Junasa, Visayans considered themselves sophisticated, educated, and urbane, and they looked down on Ilocanas/os, whom they considered to be cheap, tight-fisted, illiterate rubes. Many Visayans maintained that Ilocanas/os were to blame for the Filipino stereotypes of hypersexuality and explosive temper. In turn, many Ilocanas/os believed that Visayans were lazy, impulsive, unreliable, and extravagant with their money. Ilocanas/os were more frugal than their Visayan counterparts, averaging twice the savings of Visayans and having very little debt by comparison.[129]

Though Ilocanas/os, Tagalogs, and Visayans were often in direct conflict outside of the plantation, all Filipina/o emigrants suffered horrific conditions and low wages. One of the most prominent labor organizers was a self-educated lawyer, Pablo Manlapit, a Tagalog immigrant from Lipa City, Batangas, who was recruited by the HSPA in 1910. Manlapit led two strikes, in 1920 and 1924. The failure of both strikes, particularly the 1924 sugar strike, resulted in Filipina/o evictions from the plantations and the blacklisting of Filipina/o labor union members. Considered dangerous and subversive by officials in Hawai'i, the HSPA, and the American government in the Philippines, Manlapit was deported. He traveled to California in the late 1920s to organize workers and exhorted Filipino asparagus workers from Stockton to strike in 1929.[130] The evictions forced thousands of Visayans and Ilocanas/os to relocate to Honolulu, where they could not find work.[131] Because most Visayans immigrated as families, rather than single men, there was a preponderance of Visayan families in Honolulu, while the majority of the Ilocanas/os were single men. After the strikes, many of the Visayan families left Hawai'i for the West Coast, and they were later followed by single Ilocanos. The Alcoy-Asis, Arca, Lagrimas, and Monrayo families were among the thousands of mostly Visayans and Tagalogs who left Hawai'i for greater opportunities in Stockton (see figure 2).[132]

Enarciso Monrayo had participated in the 1924 strike, and after that he had difficulty finding work in Honolulu. One by one, his relatives and friends began leaving Hawai'i for the West Coast. Enarciso decided that migration to Stockton would be best for the whole family. Angeles's brother, Julian, was the first to go, and he sent fare money back for Angeles and their father.

2. In 1918 Remedios Tenedor and her aunt, Fortunata Montayre Naranda, commemorated their departure from Hawai'i for Stockton with a formal portrait. A native of Cebu, Remedios had a typical story: her family had worked in the sugarcane fields in the 1910s, moved to Honolulu, and then went to Stockton in search of better opportunities. Courtesy of NPA FANHS.

"They are going to America next month to work over there," Angeles wrote of her brother's and father's plans in her diary on February 2, 1927. "They say that there are [sic] plenty of work there."[133] Alberta Alcoy Asis's husband, Genaro, had been an organizer during the 1920 and 1924 sugar strikes on Oahu. His union activity angered his boss, and eventually the couple and their children left Hawai'i and moved to the Stockton area.[134]

The Lagrimas family, Tagalogs from Laguna and Bulacan provinces, were also greatly affected by the 1924 strikes. The family left Hawai'i for Stockton in 1913, where one daughter, Helen Lagrimas Liwanag, was born. Liwanag remembers that her parents returned to Hawai'i with her and her two siblings soon after her birth because the dry air of the San Joaquin Valley aggravated her mother's asthma. Liwanag's father was a *compadre* of Pablo Manlapit and often brought food from the commissary at Pearl Harbor to the strike camps in Honolulu. She recalled: "During that time, Filipinos were having a hard time and there were so many of them and they were in a camp." Her father empathized with the strikers and cooked for them for a significant period of time. When her mother passed away, her father remarried and they all returned to Stockton.[135]

Flora Arca Mata was a young girl when she arrived in Stockton from Honolulu in 1923 with her parents — José Montano Arca, a laborer from the Tagalog province of Cavite, and Victoria Salcedo Arca, an immigrant from the city of Bacolod, in Negros — and several brothers and sisters. Her parents had met in Hawai'i. She recalled: "My father said he heard about Filipinos in Stockton, so he said maybe that's a better place." After their arrival they settled near Little Manila, at 329 East Lafayette Street.[136] Jose Arca found work as a labor contractor in the Delta. Mata remembers that when ships arrived at the port of San Francisco, her father would meet the new immigrants at the dock and bring them to Stockton, where they could find work. Jose Arca died in a tragic automobile accident in 1930, leaving Victoria Arca to raise their five children alone. Census records locate the family in Stockton in 1930, with Victoria listed as head of the household.[137]

STEAMSHIPS AND THE JOURNEY

Although favorable immigration policies, colonial culture, strikes in Hawai'i, and depressed wages and land loss were major factors that contributed to massive Filipina/o emigration in the first decades of the twentieth century, it was the advent of cheap, trans-Pacific travel via steamship in the late nineteenth century that made it physically possible for thousands of Asian immigrants to travel to Hawai'i and the West Coast. After 1927 the majority of Filipina/o immigrants arriving in San Francisco and Los Angeles came directly from the Philippines, bypassing the sugar plantations entirely to find work and educational opportunities on the West Coast. Third-class steerage on the Dollar Steamship presidential liners (which were named after American presidents) transported thousands of Filipinas/os to Hawai'i and/or the United States from the 1910s through the 1960s. With routes between Manila, Yokohama, Honolulu, San Francisco, and Seattle, the Dollar Steamship Company (later renamed the American Presidential Lines in 1938 when it was taken over by the U.S. Maritime Commission) dominated trans-Pacific travel and carried the majority of Asian immigrants to Hawai'i and the mainland from the beginning of the twentieth century up to the 1970s.[138]

The Dollar Steamship Company began to market its steerage tickets to Filipinas/os as a result of U.S. Asian exclusion laws by establishing ticket counters in the larger towns of provinces in the Ilocos and the Visayas, and hiring provincial subagents to entice Filipinas/os onto its ships. Ticket agents and subagents operated throughout the provinces that sent the most immigrants to the United States: Ilocos Norte, Ilocos Sur, La Union, Pangasinan, Cebu, and Iloilo. Agents plied Filipinas/os with exaggerated stories of success and high wages in the United States. "Steamship companies in every province unquestionably are making exaggerated promises," complained a Filipino minister in 1930. "Leaflets of the companies, while they do not misrepresent, advertise cheap fares (at $75) and make it seem a great advantage to take this trip. Their agents verbally state that work here [in the United States] can easily be found at $5 an hour or some fantastic sum. I have heard them say so." A Filipino student told a researcher in 1929 that "boosters [were] sent to all parts of the Islands. Their agents were everywhere, telling and convincing young people of the bright aspects of life here. They told stories of 'streets strewn with gold.'" An agent earned a 2–3 percent commission on every ticket sold.[139] To prospective emigrants, boarding West Coast–bound, towering steamships named after former U.S. presidents must have added to the glamorous experience that was the first part of their passage to America. In careful script, my grandmother Concepcion Moreno Bohulano wrote "Arrived on the President Wilson in 1952" on her souvenir *President Wilson* postcard and saved it as one of her most cherished keepsakes.

PICTURES OF SUCCESS: THE ENTICEMENT
OF LETTERS AND PHOTOGRAPHS

But zealous ticket agents, the influence of American colonial schools, and diminishing expectations for a prosperous future on the farm were not the only factors that encouraged Filipinas/os to leave home in the mid- to late 1920s. The letters, photographs, and money sent home by Hawai'ianas/os — from their time in Hawai'i and then after they left for the mainland — the pensionadas/os, and the first waves of emigrants played a significant role in influencing thousands of later arrivals. Officials of the Dollar Steamship Line, defending the company against claims that its exaggerated stories of success overseas had inflated emigration, stated that by the late 1920s, the letters and money sent home from earlier emigrants created more of the demand for passage to the United States than any propaganda they had spread through the islands.[140] These letters, which were passed around among relatives and friends, contained photographs of emigrants wearing well-cut suits (see figure 3) and included glowing accounts of life in Hawai'i and the United States.

A Philippine sociologist who had studied the letters of more than a thousand Hawai'ianas/os and emigrants to the United States noted that the documents were worn and folded, evidence that they had passed through many hands. Emigrants rarely revealed the hardships they endured in the United

3. Members of the Monton family and friends from Bohol pose for a photograph in 1928. The extremely unbalanced sex ratio among early immigrants is illustrated here. Courtesy of Sharon Monton Robinson/FANHS Stockton.

States when they wrote home, the scholar observed. A Filipino student writing in the late 1920s observed that "they say that if anyone writes home of difficulties encountered here, no one will believe him."[141] Preferring to pepper their letters with exaggerated stories of success rather than tales of failure, the earliest emigrants inadvertently encouraged thousands of others to follow. This correspondence created an enduring impact on those left behind. In his 1933 thesis on Filipino immigration, the pensionado Honorante Mariano argues that letters and flashy photos sent home to impoverished families had a profound impact on younger brothers and cousins who had been left behind.[142] Those receiving the letters and photographs were deeply impressed. "You see, I had a cousin who was here in the U.S.," a Stockton oldtimer recalled. "He'd usually write to my relatives in the Philippines, and he'd tell us about the life in the United States. He always sent us a good picture of himself; in photos he'd be all dressed up, you know, in a suit with a nice Stetson hat and cane and even sporty black and white shoes. That influenced me. I thought if I could go to the U.S., maybe I would have clothing like that."[143] The journalist Frank Perez was enticed by a photograph of his cousin, Joe Palacpac, who immigrated to California in 1927. "His parents were showing us how successful he looked," Perez recalled. "There he stood with his Stetson hat on his well-groomed head, clad in a handsome Macintosh suit, an expensive overcoat draped over one arm, an impressive cane in one hand and leather gloves on his hands. He was a picture of success." When Perez found his cousin in San Francisco, he was shocked to find him sweating in a white apron while working in a restaurant.[144]

In a 1931 editorial, the editors of the Stockton-based Filipina/o American newspaper *Three Stars* admonished their readers for sending exaggerated stories of success back to their families and friends in the Philippines. "Every paisano ought to tell the truth, nothing but the truth, to friends over in the Philippines," wrote D. L. Marcuelo. "Each of us must not write of boastful descriptions, of fictitious properties we have come into. What we should do is unravel the tragic sufferings [that] one might encounter in America."[145] But for struggling Filipina/o immigrants, to tell the truth would be a humiliation too overwhelming to bear.

MAKING THE JOURNEY

Once the decision was made to leave, young men and women gathered their pesos, bought passage in steerage from the local Dollar Steamship Line ticket agent, and bid goodbye to their families. In steerage, these young provincianas/os found themselves in cramped quarters together with hundreds of other emigrants from all over the Philippines, some bound for Hawai'i and some for the United States. For the first time, these emigrants were in close contact with Filipinas/os from different regions, and with people of diverse backgrounds from all over the world. Tagalogs, Visayans, and Ilocanas/os struggled to communicate, with those who spoke even broken English having an advantage. "The passengers were mostly men," said Laoag native Sixto Nicolas, who arrived in San Francisco in 1923 as an ambitious student and later moved to Stockton to work as a barber in Little Manila. "They were from all sections of the Philippines. We were only six students. . . . There were three of us Ilocanos and three Visayans that boarded the ship with these immigrants to the Hawai'ian islands."[146]

On the *President Jackson*, the ship that carried my grandfather Pablo Mabalon (see figure 4) to the United States in the spring of 1929, were hundreds of immigrants, mostly from Ilocano and Visayan provinces in the Philippines. Approximately half of them hailed from the provinces of the Ilocos region: Abra, La Union, Tarlac, Pangasinan, and Ilocos Sur and Ilocos Norte. Most of the other half hailed from Capiz, Pablo's home province. A handful came from other islands in the Visayas: Bohol, Cebu, and Leyte. Pablo was traveling with a tightly knit group that included seven other young men from his hometown of Numancia, some of them his relatives: his sixteen-year-old nephew Braulio Cordova, Benito Mabalon, Ambrosio Macavinta, José Crispino, Santiago Constantino, Cenon Rey, Emil Tolentino. These seven men

4. The author's paternal grandfather, Pablo Mabalon, left his wife and five children behind when he left Numancia, Aklan, for the United States in 1929. From the author's personal collection.

in Pablo's inner circle were among the three dozen immigrants from Capiz province on the ship. All the young men were under thirty, with the exception of my grandfather Pablo, who was a comparatively mature thirty-two.[147]

By arriving in a group, these men, who called themselves the "Original Seven" (Benito fell ill and returned to the Philippines soon after their arrival), became each other's family and community in the United States.[148] When they reached Seattle, the eight kabanua,[149] or fellow town mates, crowded into a room at the Freedom Hotel at King and Jackson streets in Chinatown and looked for work.[150] When asked about his first impression of the United States, Pablo Mabalon recalled being astounded. America "was big and beautiful and [had] lots of work almost everywhere," he recalled. Fortunately for Pablo (but not for his relatives), he was the only one chosen for work in an Alaskan salmon cannery. Before he left, he charged $60 worth of groceries and rice for them so they would not go hungry.[151]

After Seattle, my grandfather and his town mates found work as agricultural laborers and began following the crops of asparagus, lettuce, peaches, grapes, and other fruits and vegetables up and down the West Coast. In the summers, they canned salmon in Alaska, stooped to pick lettuce in Salinas, and bent over sugar beets in the blistering heat of the Imperial Valley. Sometimes Pablo would draw on his restaurant experience and cook for people in the labor camps.[152] In 1931 he and his relatives went to Stockton, where the rapidly growing population of Filipinas/os in the area had by then earned the city, as well as the ethnic neighborhood, the nicknames "Little Manila" and "The Manila of California."[153]

CONCLUSION

Transformed by American colonialism, pushed from their farms by the rapidly changing agricultural economy, and eager to see the fabled "motherland" of the United States, thousands of provincianas/os left their barrios and villages for an uncertain future in the United States in the first decades of the twentieth century. Whether they were more influenced by the American public school curriculum and their teachers or by the poverty in the provinces, no Filipina/o growing up in the years between the Philippine-American War and World War II could escape the pervasive influence of the American colonial state, ideas about the superiority of the American way of life and popular culture, or the notion that there were limitless possibilities awaiting immigrants in the metropole.

If, for its architects, the main goals of a system of free, public education conducted in English were to inculcate love of the United States and inspire a devotion to American culture and institutions, the Philippine colonial education system was successful beyond the wildest dreams. Public schools played the primary role in turning Filipinas/os into loyal, English-speaking colonials. The students in American public schools in the Philippines were regaled with so many exaggerated stories of the superiority of American culture that the generation coming of age in the 1910s and 1920s was convinced that America was the greatest country on earth. The educational system created good colonials — hyper-Americans, even — who yearned to travel to the metropole. Provincianas/os and sakadas confronted and negotiated American colonial culture by resisting, embracing, and adapting to the massive transformations wrought by the arrival of American capitalism and public schools. For those growing up in the 1910s and 1920s, the heroes of the revolution were soon replaced by other role models: the white American official and teacher, the pensionadas/os, and, by the 1910s, the returning Hawai'iano, his pockets fat with money from his work on a sugar plantation and his rattan suitcases heavy with American products like phonograph players and records.

But American rule also triggered massive changes in the economies of the rural provinces and increased poverty, tenancy, and landlessness, so much so that for thousands of emigrants, their departure for America was the only way for their family to survive. Economic hardship in the Philippines played the most significant role in the decision to migrate. The fact that the vast majority of immigrants quickly abandoned their dreams of college and went immediately to work in the only jobs open to them — farm work — in order to send money home illustrates this clearly.

Two events in 1924 would forever transform the movement of Filipinas/os to the West Coast of the United States from a trickle of colonial wards from the periphery to the metropole into a massive movement of workers, students, and families. In 1924 Congress passed the National Origins Act, which barred all aliens ineligible for citizenship from entry. The act placed strict quotas on immigration from Southern and Eastern Europe, established the U.S. Border Patrol, and required Mexicans to pay head taxes to enter the United States. But in the small print of the law was a loophole. Filipinas/os were nationals — wards of the state, owing allegiance to the American flag — not aliens, and their entry to the United States was therefore not restricted.[154] On ship passenger lists they were listed as "United States Citizens." When ships from Asia approached San Francisco, Filipinas/os were taken straight to the port of San Francisco, along with other American citizens. In contrast, other Asian immigrants had to go to Angel Island, the detention station built in 1910 in San Francisco Bay.

Immigration exclusion cut off the United States' main sources of cheap agricultural labor, and the arrival of Filipinas/os could not have come at a more opportune juncture for California farmers. The workers involved in the 1924 sugar plantation strike in Hawai'i were blacklisted and could not return to plantation work; worse yet, opportunities in Honolulu for work were nonexistent. The handful of sakadas who went to the West Coast when their contracts ended began sending back word that farmwork was plentiful in California. What began as a trickle of adventurers, sakadas, pensionadas/os, and self-supporting students at the beginning of the twentieth century became a massive movement that eventually brought 150,000 Filipinas/os to the United States and Hawai'i by the end of World War II.

CHAPTER 2

TOILING IN THE "VALLEY OF OPPORTUNITY"

In 1917 twenty-five-year-old Eleno Ninonuevo, a native of Liba-cao, Capiz province, was working as a janitor for the AT&T company in Los Angeles when he was drafted to fight in World War I. After the war, he and his wife migrated to San Joaquin County to work in the fields. Ninonuevo became a labor contractor and started the Filipino Employment Agency, eventually becoming the wealthiest Filipina/o in Stockton (see figure 5). In 1928 D. L. Marcuelo wrote in his Stockton newspaper, the *Three Stars*, that it was due to Ninonuevo's "unswerving determination, grim endurance, and bulldog tenacity" that he became a success. "Undoubtedly, Ninonuevo did all the stooping and dust eating," Marcuelo wrote. "Let us stoop and eat dust to conquer."[1] Ninonuevo's story was an inspiring one for the thousands of Filipinas/os who had gathered in Stockton and the surrounding San Joaquin Delta and who were, literally, eating the dust and laboring in brutal conditions in the late 1920s.[2]

The influence of American colonial public schools, the lack of opportunities for work and higher education in the provinces, the poor wages and working conditions on the plantations in Hawai'i, the failure of the 1920 and 1924 sugar strikes, and the need for cheap farm labor in the wake of the restrictive 1924 Immigration Act all played key roles in bringing Ninonuevo and thousands of other Filipinas/os to the West Coast. Once in the United States, early migrants were drawn to Stockton by its plentiful, year-round agricultural work, high wages for farm work, and location near San Francisco and between the canneries of Alaska and the fields and orchards of Southern California. Small numbers of Filipinas/os who had left Hawai'i and some pensionadas/os attending colleges

5. Eleno Ninonuevo was a pioneering labor contractor whose Filipino Employment Agency recruited and transported hundreds of Filipina/o laborers to area farms in the 1920s and 1930s. Courtesy of Holt-Atherton Special Collections, University of the Pacific Library.

such as University of California, Berkeley, and the University of the Pacific began working in the fields around Stockton in 1909.[3]

Between 1907 and 1929, approximately 150,000 Filipinas/os left the Philippines for the United States and Hawai'i. From 1923 to 1929, Filipinas/os came to the mainland at a rate of 4,177 per year.[4] The majority (56 percent) came from Hawai'i, with the rest coming directly from the Philippines. By 1930 there were more than 30,000 Filipinas/os in California, and approximately 10,000 of them lived and worked in or near Stockton, with thousands more passing through the city seasonally for work.[5] Soon the migrants added a new vocabulary of islands to the ones they had known from the Philippines: Delta islands called Roberts, Bacon, and Ryer; and a dozen others on which Filipinas/os would toil for much of the twentieth century. The city became an anchor community for the thousands of Filipina/o immigrants arriving on the West Coast in the 1920s and early 1930s. So many thousands of immigrants came through, lived in, and worked in Stockton that the city became the crossroads of early Filipina/o America.

This chapter focuses on the first decades of Filipina/o settlement in Stockton and describes how agricultural labor served to racialize and dehumanize Filipinas/os, while also fostering enduring ties among immigrants in the San Joaquin Delta. From the late 1920s until after World War II, Filipinas/os were the primary laborers in the agricultural economy of San Joaquin County, primarily because racism barred them from any other jobs, especially during the Depression.[6] Much less frequently, Filipinas/os found work in domestic service and in hotels and restaurants. In Stockton, Filipinas/os from a wide range of backgrounds worked together in the fields as exploited laborers — as brown others. Visayans, Ilocanas/os, and Tagalog immigrants soon came to the humiliating realization that the dominant society treated them all alike, regardless of their class background or regional origins. Nor did their supposedly special status as wards of the American flag and having American educations make any difference. Ilocanos who had come as sakadas from the sugar plantations of Hawai'i cut asparagus next to Tagalog pensionados studying for their PhDs, and Illonggo and Ilocana/o schoolteachers sowed celery seed and topped onions next to teenage provincianas/os from Capiz, La Union, Tarlac, and Pangasinan who aspired to be doctors and engineers.

Even the most educated immigrants worked in the California fields or as domestic servants. The racialization, exploitation, and degradation they experienced in the fields brought these Ilocana/o, Visayan, and Tagalog immigrants together, allowing them to transcend and challenge differences of region, class, and language and view their experiences collectively and themselves as part of a larger racial or ethnic community. By 1930 being Filipina/o, then, for the earliest immigrants was as much about a common homeland and cultural heritage as it was about the brutal experience of racialization as Filipinas/os, nonwhite people who were limited to agricultural labor and were barred from citizenship, congregating outside of their ethnic neighborhood, marriage to whites, and owning property.

In 1942 the writer and activist Carey McWilliams lamented that to be a Filipina/o in California was "to belong to a blood brotherhood, a freemasonry of the ostracized."[7] Although farmers and the white elite saw Filipina/o bodies as specially suited to farm work, Filipinas/os began to view their labor in the fields as highly skilled, honorable, and dignified work worthy of higher wages and better working conditions. As early as the mid-1920s, they began to form labor unions that engaged in some of the most militant and radical labor organizing that the San Joaquin Delta, if not the entire West Coast, had ever witnessed, laying the groundwork for the farmworkers' movement of the 1960s.

THE "VALLEY OF OPPORTUNITY"

Located at the northern end of California's Central Valley, and at the eastern edge of the Sacramento–San Joaquin Delta, Stockton lies at the center of one of the most fertile agricultural areas in the world (see map 2). The town's

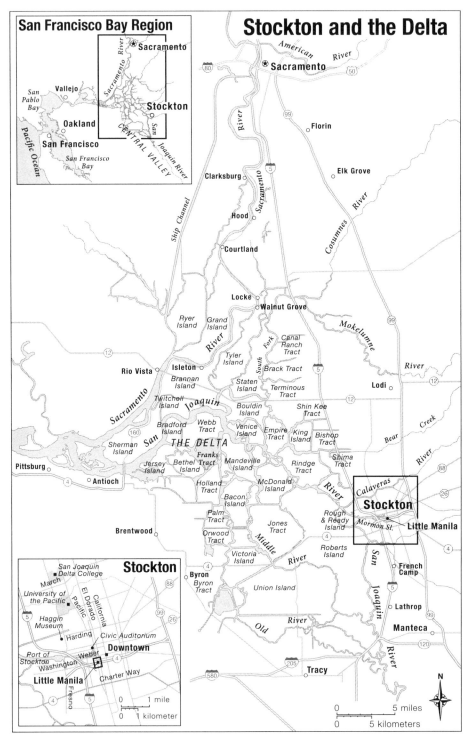

2. Stockton and the San Joaquin Delta. Stockton's location at the foot of the Delta. MAP BY BEN PEASE.

founder, the German immigrant Charles Weber, named it after Commodore Robert F. Stockton, a hero of the Mexican-American War.[8] The California gold rush transformed the settlement into a thriving transportation hub and supply center to the mother lode and the southern gold mines.[9] Thousands of settlers streamed to the Stockton area to find their El Dorado.[10] Fittingly, the city's main north-south thoroughfare was named El Dorado Street. Trains from across the nation stopped at its Southern Pacific Railroad Depot, and ferries and steamers plied the Delta between Stockton and San Francisco daily for the nine-hour trip.

After the gold rush, the manufacture of farm machinery and agriculture became the city's twin economic engines, and boosters were dubbing Stockton the "Chicago of the Far West."[11] The rich, organic peat soil of the Delta was prone to erosion in the region's marshy swamps of the Delta. But that problem was solved when Chinese immigrants were hired to build an intricate system of levees that transformed the marshland into islands of highly fertile farmland. The reclamation of the Delta, however, led to the destruction of one of the state's most important estuaries.[12] The majority of area farmers depended on wheat, barley, hay, and orchard crops, with the lucrative asparagus harvest—the "queen" (or most profitable) crop of the Delta—first planted in 1892 on Bouldin Island, and with Chinese farmers pioneering in truck farming and potatoes.[13] By the 1880s, San Joaquin County was being called the "breadbasket of the world."[14] The railroads and the river to the Bay Area carried the county's crops across the nation.

Local farmers grew even richer when, in the early twentieth century, California agribusiness underwent a transformation from family farms to large-scale agricultural "factories" dependent on cheap migratory labor.[15] Italian, Portuguese, and German immigrant families, along with white migrants from the Midwest, South, and East Coast, built a powerful agricultural economy in the Delta that relied on the labor of Asian and Mexican immigrants.[16] In the late nineteenth century, the majority of farm laborers were Chinese immigrants. Japanese and South Asian immigrants soon followed, attracted by the availability of farm work and entrepreneurial opportunities. In 1912, immigrants from the Punjab region of India established the first American *gurdwara* (Sikh temple) in Stockton.[17] The historian Sucheng Chan argues that the Delta provided the most favorable conditions in the state for the establishment of stable Asian communities.[18]

White and, later, Japanese and Chinese tenant farmers realized incredible profits as a result of the booming economy during World War I. The end of the war signaled the beginning of a kind of industrial feudalism in California agriculture, with farmers dependent on vast tracts of land and on thousands of laborers who would work cheaply. According to McWilliams, in response to their huge profits, farmers "expanded production, rationalized methods, speeded up labor, consolidated their control, imported thousands of alien laborers, built up their labor reserves, disregarded all thought of permanent social planning, and created a situation ripe for collapse and disaster."[19] By 1924, the county ranked second in the state and twelfth in the nation in crop output.[20] After years of dredging projects, the Port of Stockton was officially opened in 1933 and became California's largest inland port, making it possible for ocean-going vessels to bring more of the area's products directly to the Port of San Francisco and, from there, across the globe.[21]

Beginning in the late nineteenth century, in order to prevent unionization and strikes, growers manipulated the area's racial and ethnic groups—poor whites, Chinese, Japanese, Mexicans, and South Asians—by pitting them against one another with segregated housing, the use of different contractors for each group, differential wage scales, and the relegation of the worst jobs to those lowest on the racial hierarchy (usually Filipinos).[22] In the 1920s, a Delta farmer told a reporter that he had used Mexicans and South Asians against one another to prevent labor unrest. "Last year our Hindu workers struck," he said. "So this year we mixed half Mexicans in with them, and we aren't having any more labor trouble."[23]

Asian immigrants and their descendants began demanding higher wages, going into business for themselves, and purchasing and leasing their own farmland by the 1910s, triggering a labor shortage.[24] Japanese and Chinese immigrants were able to become farmers by circumventing the 1913 Alien Land Law that barred aliens from owning land by leasing farmland, establishing farm corporations and leasing farmland through them, and placing land titles in the names of their native-born children.[25] One of the more prominent Asian immigrant farmers in the Delta was George Shima, dubbed the Potato King of Stockton.[26] By 1920 Japanese American farms in California occupied 361,276 acres and were producing crops valued at $67 million annually.[27] On the eve of World War II, 10 percent of the state's agricultural output was owned or controlled by ethnic Japanese.[28] A spokesperson for Zuckerman Farms told a researcher that Filipina/o laborers began coming into the Delta "just when we began to need them."[29] By 1922 several gangs of Filipino workers were working in asparagus, and white, Chinese, and Japanese growers in the Delta had begun to rely heavily on Filipina/o labor.[30]

STUDENTS BECOME WORKERS

Many of the sakadas who came to Stockton from Hawai'i in the 1910s and 1920s went immediately into farm work. Most who came directly from the

6. In 1929, Filipino students at Stockton High School formed a club and are pictured here in the school yearbook, the *Guard and Tackle*. Their officers for the fall semester were Daniel Dancel, president; Hoyolito Sajonia, vice president; Atanasio L. Alcala, secretary-treasurer; and Simplicio Bilinario, sergeant-at-arms. Spring semester officers were Juan Montermeso, president; Simplicio Bilinario, vice president; Mary Arca (third row, second from left, next to her sister, Conching Arca), secretary-treasurer; and Eulalio Aguinaldo, sergeant-at-arms.

Philippines in the mid- to late 1920s arrived hoping to attend college. In 1930, when a university researcher surveyed hundreds of Filipina/o immigrants in the Delta, the vast majority said that they had come to California to further their education.[31] Some self-supporting students tried to prepare for college by attending high school in the United States and working in the fields during school vacations. In 1930 a group of about thirty Filipinos attended the Stockton Part-Time School for about a month at a time. Their conscientiousness impressed their teacher, Edith Reynolds. "The Filipino studies very hard, harder, I believe, than any other race which attends the school," she told a researcher, adding that they were focused on learning English and improving their penmanship.[32] So many Filipinas/os were attending Stockton High School in the late 1920s that they formed a Filipino Club in 1929 (see figure 6).

One student in the Filipino Club at Stockton High School who wanted to go to college was Atanasio Alcala, a native of Laoag, Ilocos Norte, who had had a civil service job in his province. He arrived in San Francisco in 1926 with just $5 in his pocket and spent his first night sleeping outdoors. With other Ilocanos, he went to Stockton to pick pears. "They were all talking in Ilocano, telling stories to each other," his daughter Alma Alcala remembered. "They told him: 'If I knew what you know, if I had your education, I wouldn't be picking pears here.'" Atanasio Alcala decided to try to find work as a houseboy.[33] He knocked on doors, asking for work, and was eventually hired by the Cohn family, owners of the exclusive downtown department store, The Wonder.[34] In the eighteen years that he worked for the Cohns, he graduated from Stockton High School but never attended college.[35] Just as the hiring of a Chinese cook in the late nineteenth century was a mark of elite status for whites in the West, the hiring of a Filipino houseboy elevated the status of wealthy whites in Stockton in the early twentieth century. In 1930 the president of the Stockton Labor Council complained that Filipinos were dominating the domestic service trade. "They have cut us out of a good deal of the work that we used to get—particularly in club work and in the aristocratic homes in North Stockton—catering and the like," said William Burtz. "The society people like to dress a Filipino up in some clever little outfit and they think, then, that he is just as cute as can be."[36]

But Alcala's situation—that he could depend on one relatively stable job for so many years—was rare. Those arrivals who already had a college education found that racism shut them out of all professions, and fieldwork was often the only work available to them. The Depression crushed the hopes of self-supporting college students, who found that once wages plummeted, they could not pay their tuition. Some immigrants worked to support their family in the Philippines and helped relatives in college. "Even though I am 37 years old I am trying to get an education," one immigrant told a researcher in 1930. "I have a wife and 3 children in the Islands. Helping a brother in University of Washington too. Sending him $70 over a semester."[37] George Montero, a native of Santa Maria, Pangasinan, arrived in California in March 1930 hoping to find a good job and continue his college education, but he was disappointed. "Even if you have the education that you could pass tests—like if you want to work in the post office or teaching, Filipinos were not given the chance to get those jobs," he said. "Because there were so many educated Filipinos who could do it but there was just no opening, or they don't hire them. Like teachers."[38]

Fausto Rabaca, a native of Santa Catalina, Ilocos Sur, was a high school graduate with a teaching job—but that job was in Mindanao, far from his hometown, so in May 1930 he decided to go to college in the United States. He landed in Seattle and then went to Stockton, where his uncle had found him a job hoeing asparagus in the Delta. "When we went to work I felt homesick because I never did that kind of work when I was in the Philippines, so I want [sic] to go back if I could," he said. "But . . . there is no way of going back."[39] Nemesio Paguyo—a native of Laoag, Ilocos Norte, who arrived in Stockton in 1930—said that youthful naivete and hopeful dreams had lured Filipinas/os to Stockton. "We were young, coming [to] this country, mostly teenagers," he said. "What do you expect from a 17-year old coming here? [We] come over here to better ourselves. But when we got here, there was no way to better ourselves, because everything around us is against us. There was nothing available to us."[40]

ENDURANCE AND EXPLOITATION

Filipinas/os became part of a massive army of seasonal migratory workers toiling up and down the West Coast and in the Midwest and Southwest. In 1929 state inspectors visiting agricultural camps in San Joaquin County found Filipinas/os working primarily with asparagus, celery, and grapes. By the late 1920s, Filipinas/os had become essential to processing the most important crops in the San Joaquin Delta, particularly asparagus.[41] By 1930 they comprised over 80 percent of the asparagus workers in the Delta region, and almost 14 percent of the total farm labor force in California.[42] These laborers worked with many crops: lettuce, sugar beets, asparagus, tomatoes, peaches, apples, berries, melon, hops, celery, and other fruits and vegetables. Although most of the workers were men, a number of women worked alongside men, doing repair work and working in the shed, a large wooden structure for sorting and packing vegetables and fruits. They dressed in men's clothes and earned the same wages as men (see figure 7). Women also worked as bookkeepers, contractors, and *campo* cooks.[43]

By the 1920s, many of the farms in California were operating as "industrial plantations," relying on mechanization and gangs of cheap, seasonal labor.[44] Filipina/o immigrants from farming families were not accustomed to these "factories in the fields," as McWilliams called them in his book by that title. Those employed in these "factories" had to work on the clock at backbreaking tasks for eight to twelve hours at a time, with only very brief breaks for meals. On his first day of work, thinning lettuce with a short-handled hoe — a tool eventually outlawed in California in the 1970s because its shape caused terrible back pain for workers — George Montero began to question his decision to immigrate to the United States. "I worked about six hours that day and I said to myself, 'Why did I come to this country?' when my back was hurting," he remembered. "I was doing easy in the Philippines. Boy, the next day I could hardly sit down because all my back and body was sore. But then I said to myself, 'I'll get used to it.'" To bolster his spirits, he tried to draw strength from the veteran sakadas' work ethic. "There were some older men and they come from Hawaii, you know, some maybe 50 [years old]," he said. "So if they could do it, I could do it."[45]

Filipinas/os occupied the lowest rung of the racial hierarchy of farm labor, and labor activists took note of the abuse and exploitation reserved particu-

7. Born in Hawai'i, Mary
Arca migrated to Stockton
with her family in 1923 and
worked in the fields to help
support her family. Here, she
takes a break from fieldwork
for a photo sometime in
the 1920s. After World
War II, she became a public
school teacher in Stockton.
Courtesy of FOHP.

larly for Filipinas/os in the California fields. "With the exception of the Mexican, the Filipino has been the most viciously exploited of any of the various races recruited by California agriculturists to make up their vast army of 'cheap labor,'" wrote McWilliams in 1935.[46] The farmers' exploitation of Filipina/o workers could take various forms, from low wages and substandard working and living conditions to unscrupulous hiring and payroll practices. Farmers and contractors sent recruiters to the port in San Francisco to bring new immigrants directly to the camps. "They get bunches of them and run them into some of the camps," said Deputy Labor Commissioner Charles F. Crook in an interview in February 1930. "Here they are kept apart from other Filipinos and are kept green."[47]

The demands for seasonal labor resulted in a West Coast migratory labor circuit in which Filipinas/os traveled as far north as Alaska for salmon cannery work in the early summer and as far south as the Imperial Valley in the early fall, with stops in Stockton, Salinas, and other agricultural centers in between. In her study of Seattle's Filipina/o community and Filipina/o migratory labor patterns, Dorothy Fujita-Rony notes that the position of Filipinas/os at the bottom of the labor market, and in the worst paid and hardest agricultural work, resulted in their need for constant mobility in search of work.[48] With San Joaquin County and the Delta as a home base, Filipinas/os also followed the crops to Dinuba, Suisun, Fairfield, Delano, Santa Maria, Salinas, Watsonville, Lompoc, San Luis Obispo, Sacramento, and the Santa Clara Valley in California, and to the states of Washington, Idaho, and Montana.

Filipina/o laborers in the Delta and San Joaquin Valley could find agricultural work for approximately ten months out of the year. The Delta farming season usually began in late February, with the beginning of the asparagus harvest. Late spring and summer brought peaches, pears, lettuce, and other fruits and vegetables. When the asparagus season ended in late June, thousands of workers would leave for Alaska salmon canneries, while most of their families remained in Stockton. Harvesting grapes, berries, and other fruits would begin in August. After August, the slack season would begin, with stretches of unemployment from October to January, with the exception of the sugar beets and grape pruning in the fall and the celery harvest in November.[49]

Filipinas/os who went north to work in the Alaskan salmon canneries could go either for the long season, which started in April, or the regular season, which began in June. Stockton-based Filipinas/os were more likely to leave for the regular season so they could finish the asparagus season in Stockton. In the early 1920s, Filipinas/os could make up to $250 for four months of work in Alaska.[50] In his first season in Alaska in 1929, my grandfather Pablo Mabalon remembered that the workers' white boss woke them up every morning by knocking on the bunkhouse door with the butt of his gun. "Working to survive was real hard work in the Alaskan cannery," my grandfather recalled. "At that time, there was no machinery and much of the hauling was done by pure manual labor. Ours was the work of a mule. The work schedule was indefinite and the hours were long. You needed will and strength to keep up with the work in those early days."[51] Pablo worked in the canneries every summer until his retirement in the 1960s. For many decades, his children, grandchildren, and other relatives did the same every summer.[52] Filipinos formed a strong cannery labor union, Local 37, in 1934.[53] Many of these labor leaders, including Larry Itliong and Chris Mensalvas, went to Stockton to organize farm laborers.

However, the salmon season lasted only for the summer. The seasons of the San Joaquin Delta and surrounding areas shaped life for the entire Filipina/o American community on the West Coast. "The growing and harvesting season of the farm crops orchestrated the rhythm of our lives," remembered Gussie Gesulga Bowden, a second-generation Pinay. "Asparagus, starting in February, thinning fruits, sugar beets; picking cherries in spring, potatoes, tomatoes, tokay grapes in summer; and in the fall and winter, pruning grape vines, cutting celery, thinning onions, and planting garlic was our general cadence," she wrote. "Like the weary traveler when he beds down at night, closes his eyes but still sees the rushing pavement, I would see the tomatoes, smell the pungent vines, feel the oppressive unrelenting afternoon heat, and totally, unconditionally accept this way of life."[54]

Of all the crops grown in the area, asparagus was the one that was a multimillion-dollar industry. Americans developed a taste for green asparagus around 1925. Area farmers began planting it widely throughout the Delta, and almost all of the canned asparagus eaten in the United States before World War II came from the area. Most asparagus farms were located on the southern end of the Delta—on Shima Tract, Union Island, and Lower Roberts Island. The fertile, light, and loose soil of the Delta, and the area's cold nighttime and wintertime temperatures, proved to be ideal for asparagus.[55] Also ideal for the profitable growing of asparagus is a tractable, cheap labor force to do the backbreaking work of harvesting.

In the early days, farm work paid relatively well. One of the reasons that so many Filipinas/os were drawn to Stockton was that workers there earned substantive wages. In 1937 community leaders estimated that Filipina/o workers had earned more than $36,150,000 between 1917 and 1932. In 1930 Stockton's postmaster estimated that $300 per day was being sent home to the Philippines.[56] But generally, Filipinas/os were paid 20 to 30 cents less an hour than whites and Japanese earned. Even with this disparity, Filipinas/os received approximately 30 to 50 cents per hour, and up to $5 per day between the late 1910s and mid-1920s.[57] These relatively high wages were due to a number of factors, including the enormous profits reaped by area farmers during and immediately after World War I.

But wages plummeted and working conditions worsened by the mid-1920s. Farmers who wanted fatter profits began to hire more workers per acre, at a lower hourly rate. From 1920 to 1923, wages averaged 45 cents per hour, then dropped to 40 cents per hour between 1924 and 1926. In 1927 each Filipina/o could expect to earn 30 cents per hour. In one Delta camp, the daily earnings per worker fell 38 percent between 1925 and 1929, from $6.06 to $3.75. During those years, the number of workers in that corporation's camps grew almost 30 percent.[58] Wages dropped steeply once the Depression began. Farm labor wages dropped almost 50 percent, and Filipina/o workers began to earn only 10 to 12 cents per hour.[59] In 1934 there were more workers than available jobs: 142 workers for every 100 jobs.[60] In 1934 wages rose slightly, to an average of $3.30 per day.[61]

In the first years of Filipina/o settlement in the Delta, naive and desperate immigrants were willing to put up with low pay and deplorable conditions. This contributed to the belief that Filipinas/os were docile, tractable, and easily exploited, especially in comparison to Mexican and Japanese laborers.[62] Growers maintained that that their size, skin color, and other racial qualities made Filipinas/os ideal to perform "stoop labor" and to work on wet soil for hours on end.[63] Warren Atherton of California Delta Farms believed that white labor was "too long in the back" for stoop labor.[64] According to Frank Waterman of the State Employment Agency, it was the Filipinas/os' darker skin that helped them to work in the dirt. "The white man can't stand the itch which results from working in the peat fields of the Delta," Waterman told a researcher in 1930.[65] Another farmer told a researcher with the state of California that Filipinas/os were desirable workers because they were agreeable to working in all kinds of weather, even the rain.[66]

But Filipinas/os proved to be indispensable in the San Joaquin Delta not because of their supposed racial disposition for stoop labor, but because of their speed, skill, efficiency, and willingness to work in large crews. Most important, these crews were particularly productive because their members were bound to one another by kinship and town and regional relationships. In one labor camp near Stockton in the early 1930s, the researcher James Earl Wood found eighty-four Visayans who all hailed from the same town, one Tagalog, and six Ilocanos.[67] In fact, the Iloilo Circle, a Stockton-based hometown organization founded in 1939 by former residents of the area around Iloilo, a major city on the island of Panay, has its origins in a work crew comprised of, and headed by, Illonggos.[68] Some crews traveled and worked together for their entire working lives (see figure 8).

Farm labor contractors in the Delta were independent entrepreneurs who recruited laborers, set wages and work conditions, and then sold the workers' services as a total package to growers. Contractors were also in charge of board, room, and payroll for a crew of workers. Early on, these crews were headed by Japanese contractors, who usually worked for a white or Japanese foreman who had been hired by a grower. Although Japanese contractors sometimes led Filipino work crews, it was rare to see a Filipino contractor heading a Japanese work crew.[69] Delta Japanese workers considered Filipinos racially inferior and treated them accordingly. According to one Filipino labor contractor named Cinco, Japanese contractors exploited Filipinos to curry favor with white growers. "We have had a great deal of trouble with the Japanese contractors," he said. "The Japanese live somewhat cheaper than the Filipinos. . . . They want to show their bosses how economical they are, and when they are asked for advice concerning what wages should be for a particular season, they advise paying less than the current wage." Cinco ac-

8. A Delta asparagus crew made up of a group of relatives and fellow townmates poses for a photograph in the late 1930s. Photograph by Frank Mancao, courtesy of NPA FANHS.

cused Japanese contractors of paying Filipina/o workers up to 10 cents an hour less than other work crews. Because of their reputation, Filipinas/os only worked for Japanese contractors if they could not get work with a Filipino. In 1930 Japanese contractors were paying Filipinos only 25 cents an hour, much less than the standard rate of 30 to 40 cents paid to Mexican or white workers. Japanese contractors also had a reputation for swindling Filipinas/os.[70] "We have case after case of the 'boys' being taken advantage of by white employers and Japanese contractors," said the wife of D. L. Marcuelo, the editor of the local newspaper *Three Stars*.[71] Filipina/o contractors soon took the place of Japanese, however.

Filipina/o contractors tended to be better educated, older, and more experienced than other Filipina/o workers. They raised the productivity and efficiency of crews because most used the *encloso* system, in which workers accepted piece, pound, and per box rates instead of hourly wages. In this system, asparagus cutters could expect to make anywhere from $2 to $3 per day, with wages based on the pounds of asparagus cut.[72] When Juan "Johnny" Latosa—a native of Mambusao, Capiz province—was a young laborer in the 1920s, he received 90 cents per 100 pounds of asparagus.[73] After picking or cutting, sorting, washing, packing, and sealing crates, the total earnings of the harvest were added. Expenses such as groceries and work tools were then deducted from the total earnings, which were then divided equally among the members of the work crew. The cook, who was sometimes an elder or the wife of a laborer or the contractor, would also receive a cut.

Growers paid contractors through commissions and profits from the services provided to workers, such as lodging and board. The encloso system, which made for happier and more efficient Filipina/o labor crews, continued well throughout the twentieth century among Filipina/o work crews and exists to this day on many California farms.[74] The writer Manuel Buaken noted that Filipino students liked to work with asparagus because they were able to earn enough money in the encloso system to return to school in the fall.[75] Jerry Paular remembered that the encloso system, especially during and after World War II, allowed Filipinas/os to receive much higher wages than other workers. "Some others are making $2 a day," he said. "And the Filipino, he is making $8."[76] George Montero, a contractor, preferred the encloso system and made sure his men were well fed. "If we are twenty people I divide it that one or two men will cook one day," he said. "Tomorrow, another cook one day. And then we divide all the expenses among ourselves. When you pay board, you got no choice. You have to eat whatever they fix." Montero remembered the men sharing expenses to feast on roast pig, chicken, and anything else they craved.[77]

In most contracts, the farmers paid the contractor the majority of the money toward the end of the harvest, when the terms of the contract (acreage covered or pounds harvested) were likely to be almost fulfilled. Because the labor contract was between the contractor and the laborers, the farmers were not held liable for the wages owed to the workers. In collusion with farmers, some contractors—including some Filipinas/os—fleeced many Filipinas/os out of their wages, taking further advantage of an already exploited workforce.[78] Labor contractors and farmers sometimes absconded with the wages near or at the end of the season. Buaken's younger brother told him that at the end of one season, a white potato farmer left for the bank and never returned with the workers' money. "He disappeared, and with him all our wages—pay of $120 for each of the Filipino workers," Buaken wrote.[79] In *Three Stars*, Marcuelo suggested that it was absolutely "imperative" that Filipino workers accompany the contractor to the bank and then back to the farm to ensure that they were paid. Marcuelo also warned Filipinos to toughen themselves against exploitation by other Filipinos: "In business, we cast aside sentiment and friendship, and when we talk friendship let us cast business aside." Marcuelo also advised Filipinos to save a percentage of their pay.[80]

Contractors and growers also saved money by feeding workers substandard food, and they gouged workers for room and board. A spokesperson for Zuckerman Farms admitted that he saved money on food by feeding his Filipina/o workers only rice and fish, which cost just 70 cents per worker per day.[81] Workers were often charged 75 cents per day for room and board. Lorenzo Romano, a native of Pangasinan, came to Stockton to work in 1931, so he could send his siblings to school. The meager amounts he was earning frustrated him. "Well, sometimes at the end of the month you only have $20 in your check," he said. "During [the Depression] in 1933, '34, your check in one month is only $20, sometimes $30. Your board is 50 cents a meal. You work ten hours. That's a really hard time. . . . Room, if you sleep in a hotel, 50 cents a night. If you don't pay you don't sleep."[82] Even between seasons, some contractors continued to charge workers 75 cents per day for room and board. The destitute workers would owe the contractor anywhere from $75 to $80 by the time new work appeared. "Sometimes you don't have enough to pay your board," recalled Montero.[83]

The most respected Filipina/o contractors took extra care to ensure fair wages and working conditions for their workers. Because these contractors often recruited workers from their own families, towns, and regions, their workers had a deep sense of responsibility and loyalty to them. According to Paular, ethical, community-minded Filipina/o labor contractors were essential to the survival of many Filipina/o American families, particularly during the Depression. "The contractors enabled our families to survive," he remembered. "Without their willingness to accept the responsibility of our welfare and to bargain on behalf of the people they represented, we would have no one to represent us before the landowner. They were men of substance, being more vocal, brash, and tenacious. They'd go broke before they'd see a family starve."[84]

My father, a medical doctor, became a labor contractor when he immigrated to Stockton in 1963 to join his father, Pablo Mabalon, and his brother, Tex. In Stockton, my father could not find work as a doctor. He worked as a contractor every year from 1963 to 2005, when he passed away at the age of eighty during the asparagus harvest in April. He typed out lists of his workers on his manual typewriter, calculated payroll every week on his ancient adding machine, and called his workers in the beginning of the seasons to be ready for pruning and harvesting grapes, peaches, and asparagus. So dedicated was my father to his crop, his crew, and to the Yamadas, the Japanese American farming family for whom he worked for four decades, that even when he fell suddenly ill at the asparagus packing shed and had to be rushed to the hospital, he agonized about his workers and the crop. When my father died several days later, some of his workers grieved alongside my sister and me as if their own father had died.

9. By the 1920s, Filipina/o workers were in high demand by asparagus farmers, who appreciated their cutting skills and work ethic. The asparagus season, which lasted from February to June, swelled the Filipina/o population in the Delta to more than 10,000. Here, cutters pose in the 1920s. Photograph by John Y. Billones, courtesy of FANHS Stockton.

EATING THE DUST

Low pay, bad food, and disputes over wages and payments were only part of the workers' misery. Working conditions for farm laborers in the San Joaquin Delta and Central Valley were horrific because of the backbreaking work, intense heat, and dust. Peat dust choked laborers, and local doctors routinely had to swab the workers' throats clean. The fine soil itched uncontrollably, so even in broiling heat, most workers covered themselves head to toe with long-sleeved clothing, kerchiefs, hats, and wraps, and they made sure to wrap a piece of cloth or tie a string around their pant legs to prevent the peat dirt from creeping up their legs (see figure 9). Cipriano Insular, a native of Iloilo, remembered being relieved to get a kitchen job in the asparagus camp on Terminus Island because the peat dust was unbearable. "That even goes inside your shoes, even how tight your shoes," he said. "When you take your shoes off you see about [an] inch of dust inside."[85]

Cutting asparagus, both then and today, is grueling work that requires great skill. Each spear must be cut by hand in an exhausting pattern of walking, stooping, and thrusting the wooden-handled, two-foot-long asparagus knife into a precise point at the stalk, being careful not to disturb asparagus growing underground near the stalk. Paguyo remembered the process of the asparagus harvest:

> The asparagus are lined up about six feet apart. But the asparagus are planted close together. Before the asparagus goes out in February, they

are being disked. What I mean [by] disked is the ground is being turned down so that the 'gras will go up. And that shoot of the 'gras will come out. And there we had a knife, a sharp knife. Then under there we see the 'gras coming out and that's where we stick the knife under the root of the 'gras and we pick it up with the left hand and hold it until we got a handful and then drop it into the ridge. Then a sled come around and pick them up, a machine or a horse pulled up sleds and come around and pick up those 'gras and put them in the sled and take them to the shed. Where in the shed, there are boys over there to pick them up and put them against the wall so they will be cut into the size of about seven, eight inches long. And from there they are put into a box and from there they are taken to market. The truck will pick them up and then take them into the market to be sold to different places — San Francisco, Sacramento, and Los Angeles and all that.[86]

The asparagus season began in late February and lasted until June. When temperatures rose into the 90s and 100s in late spring, two harvests a day were sometimes required. Each worker was required to cover at least eight to ten acres per day.[87] The relentless afternoon heat of the Delta and Central Valley in the spring and early summer forced workers to rise as early as 3:00 AM so they could complete their work by the early afternoon, right before the heat became unbearable. Camila Labor Carido remembered the appalling conditions her family members endured. Some, she remembered, had to work all day in the rain, and asparagus work began before the sun rose. "My uncle bought a flashlight and put it on his head so he starts cutting at 3 o'clock in the morning so by 2 or 4 PM they finished cutting the whole field," she said. "They have to cut the field. They don't care if you're crawling! They're mean to the Pilipinos!"[88]

Some Pinoys dropped dead in the fields because of heat and exhaustion. In the 1950s, Demetrio "Jimmy" Ente, a second-generation Pinoy, worked as a sled boy in charge of collecting the asparagus at the ends of the rows and conveying it by truck to the packing shed (in the 1920s and 1930s, such work was done not with a truck but with a horse pulling a sled). "There was an old man, I was sledding, and the one old man — he must've been in his eighties — he died right there, about a couple of lines from me, poor guy," he said. "We took his asparagus knife and put it in the ground, put his hat on it. Some of the guys took his body back to the camps. I'll never forget that."[89] During the asparagus season, cutters worked without weekends or holidays off. I remember asking my father every year if he would be accompanying us to church on Easter Sunday. My father would retort: "Asparagus knows no holiday!" Easter usually fell during the height of the season in late March or early April, when the asparagus harvest was almost nonstop.

Workers who did not go to Alaska in the summertime toiled in the tomato fields, which also required skill and a strong back. Tomatoes had to be planted by seed, thinned once or twice, and weeded once or twice before harvest. Weeding was done by hand and with the despised short hoe. Only twelve inches long; it required workers to stoop over close to the ground. Latina/o farmworkers called the hoe *la herramienta del Diablo* (the devil's instrument). At harvest time, work in the tomato field was twelve hours a day, seven days a week. Bob Cabigas—a second-generation Pinoy, who worked with his father and uncles in the tomato fields near Stockton in the 1950s and 1960s—remembered waking up at 4:30 AM in the campo to the smell of cigars and rubbing liniment and the sounds of roosters crowing. Workers dressed for protection against the sun and peat dust in boots; loose, cotton clothes; long-sleeved cotton shirts; a wide bandanna or cloth to mop up perspiration; and a wide-brimmed Stetson.

After a quick breakfast of hot coffee and toast or donuts, the lead man set the pace. "Bent over keeping close to the ground, chop chop chop, on we went," Cabigas remembered. "Conversation was loud and plentiful about home, family, and money. Mostly about the beautiful blonde they were going to dance with on the next trip into town." As heat rose, the Pinoys—who were, by then, in their fifties and sixties—were getting tired and taking frequent breaks. After a half-hour lunch of rice, meat, fish, and vegetables prepared by the lead man, the crew would return to work, now slower and more fatigued. "You wouldn't raise your head, only to glance to see the end of every row," Cabigas remembered. "It looked like a lake of water, but it was waves of heat rising from the ground." The toilets were far from the field, so men would have to relieve themselves in the fields. Toilet paper was a commodity as precious as dollar bills. Instead, the workers used newspaper or cotton shirts. "No trees or bushes," Cabigas recalled. "If you had to go, pull your pants down and go. It was degrading and embarrassing to me."[90]

The America that their teachers had bragged of in the Philippines, the image of a modern city on a hill, was far from the reality of the campo. Even up to the 1970s, Filipina/o workers in the Delta and Central Valley lived without electricity, running water, or flush toilets in segregated ramshackle wooden bunkhouses, old barns together with animals, or abandoned boxcars in the campo. Bunkhouses ranged in size from those that could house hundreds of workers to deteriorating cabins with dirt floors. A Japanese grower in the Delta made his crop profitable by using Filipina/o labor and substandard housing. "I don't like Fils, but I have to use them," he told a researcher in 1930. "I can get them in large enough gangs. The Mexicans and Spaniards bring their families with them and I have to fix up houses." But, he said, laughing, "I can put a hundred Filipinos in that barn."[91] Workers had to use outhouses in which a hole in the ground was the toilet.[92] On some farms, dozens of workers were forced to bathe in the same bathwater, one right after another, in large corrugated metal tubs heated by a fire below them.

Montero was shocked at the labor camp conditions. "I expect that it was nice you know, that you got good jobs," he said. "But really, I expect that when I came here I'll go to a place to stay that have [sic] electricity . . . you know we have to use this kerosene lamp and then we don't have also what we call inside restrooms or toilets. We have them outside. So I said to myself, 'Well, is this America?'"[93] Sebastian Inosanto left Libacao, Capiz, in May 1925 and found work in Stockton.[94] "During this time, the Filipinos were largely unorganized, and because of this, the abuses were not known," he recalled. "We were housed in dwellings with dirt floors and the windows were made of cardboard. When we slept, we put curtains around our beds to keep the wind out. We called ourselves 'Tao Sa Lupa,' or men of the earth."[95] Ulpiano Morania, also a native of Libacao, Capiz, remembered the campo well. "You could maybe call it unsanitary?" he said, laughing. "You have to take it. You got to go outside for your toilet. The bunkhouse. . . . You got all the dust when the wind comes."[96] Men had to sleep on cots and bring their own bedding. Montero remembered the bunkhouses being choked full of cigarette and cigar smoke.[97] When it rained at night, workers scurried to move their cots, Paguyo recalled: "At night when it rains, you had to find a place where it is not dripping so that the rain does not drip on your bed."[98]

Unsanitary conditions abounded throughout the campo. Paguyo remembered that the main water source for drinking and bathing was the San Joaquin River. "There was nothing sanitary in there, nothing," he said. "We had to boil our drinking water to make it clear."[99] Dozens of workers took turns sipping from a single tin dipper used with a communal can of tepid water, which was wrapped in wet burlap and placed in shade or up in a tree to keep cool.[100] Ramona Acompañado Napala—a war bride from Leyte who arrived in Stockton with her husband, Felipe Napala, in 1947—vividly remembered dozens of Filipinas/os having to share one cup. After they reached Stockton, she and her husband went to work in the grapes. "You know, the cook have [sic] to bring a can of water to the field and then everybody drinks from the same cup," she remembered. "And then they dip it in there for everybody, and they just go around. And I said, I can't drink from that. But there's no way. You have to drink. You're so thirsty, you know, in the heat.

10. Many Filipina/o pioneer families settled in Stockton. Pictured here is the Cano family in 1936, taken in the campo in Terminous Tract near Highway 4. From left to right: George, Faustina Juntilla, Laura, Felicidad "Phyllis" (Ente), Constancia "Connie" (Estante), and Toribio "Terry" (Rosal). Courtesy of Phyllis Ente.

106 [degrees], in the field . . . so I just close my eyes and drink water." Felipe Napala cried when he saw how his wife struggled to adjust.[101]

Migrant families had an especially difficult time in the campo (see figure 10). Segunda Reyes, a native of Tacloban, Leyte, had been a schoolteacher in the Philippines when she and her husband immigrated to California so her husband could study for a master's degree at the University of California, Berkeley. When he lost a nighttime dishwashing job, they began following the crops around Stockton. "But the worst part of it was we did not have no [sic] decent place to live," she remembered. "We can live in a bunkhouse and then some of them didn't even have a floor in the bunkhouse. We have a bed but it will just be on the ground." When the family worked the grapes in Lodi, Reyes had to give birth to their second son, Thomas, in an old cabin in the middle of a rainstorm. "They give us a cabin but the cabin had no double walls," she said. "They have holes in the walls. . . . We did not have no gas in the car to go to town. We didn't have no telephone to call the doctor. So Thomas was born and it was raining so hard. No midwife. . . . He was born and we didn't have no doctor. . . . And then my husband was boiling water outside with cornhusks, no wood. So what we did, Thomas's umbilical cord was cut the next morning because my husband walked to our boss to use the telephone to have the doctor come."[102]

When she was an infant, Rizaline Raymundo lived with her family in a railroad car in the back of the campo. "There wasn't any room in the bunk house or another room available for us, so when Dad saw the railroad car he asked if we could use it as our housing," recalled Raymundo, who was born in Stockton in 1929. Her parents stacked crates for their belongings and used bleached rice sacks as curtains. There was no clean, running water in any of the bunkhouses, Raymundo remembered. For food, the family scavenged for whatever was edible. "Most of the time the food was rice and mushroom, rice and fish—whatever was on the table we ate it," Raymundo recalled. "I learned how to eat fish head, shells from the river, tripe, fried intestines, chicken feet, frog legs—you name it we ate it. Filipinos have a knack for making any kind of food edible and delicious."[103] Anita Bautista, who lived in the campo with her parents and eight brothers and sisters, remembered that families planted gardens; gathered wild mustard greens and mushrooms; fished in the creeks and rivers; shot birds; and ate whatever they could procure. Beef, pork, and chicken were rare luxuries, as Filipinas/os utilized game and vegetables readily available in the Delta. "I remember my father making jackrabbit adobo," she recalled. "And him shooting these illegal swans out in the asparagus field. There was always food."[104]

CAMPO LEISURE TIME: JAZZ, COCKFIGHTS, ESCRIMA, AND WOMEN

Life in the campo was not all drudgery. At the end of the workday, Filipinas/os bathed scrupulously to wash off the dirt and sweat and then turned to leisure activities. Some played games like volleyball. Many brought with them, or developed in America, a love of jazz, and they passed the time in the campo with music. Many of the campo pictures taken during time off from work in the fields feature Pinoys with their beloved guitars, banjos, saxophones, and drums. In addition to playing sports, practicing martial arts (*arnis escrima*), and playing jazz during their leisure time, Pinoys in the campo engaged in vice: visiting prostitutes, gambling, playing cards (see figure 11), and illegal cockfighting (*sabong*).

Significant numbers of workers used their free time in the campo to covertly practice arnis escrima (sometimes called just *escrima* or *kali*), an ancient system of Philippine martial arts that utilized sticks, blades, spears, improvised weapons, and bare hands.[105] Some immigrants brought with them

11. Pinoys gather to play cards in the campo after a long day in the fields, sometime in the 1930s. Courtesy of FOHP.

to the United States deep knowledge of these ancient arts.[106] The coming together of Visayans, Tagalogs and Ilocanas/os in Stockton also brought regional escrima systems together, for the first time in some cases. Victorino Ton—who was born in 1895 in La Paz, Abra province, in the Ilocos region— began learning escrima when he was ten years old and brought the skill with him to Stockton. In 2011 Ton was still practicing escrima.[107] Lacking the traditional *bolos* (long swords), spears, rattan sticks, *balisong* blades, and other traditional weapons in the campo, Filipinas/os improvised, brilliantly adapting asparagus knives and grape knives to their practice of escrima.[108] According to Antonio Somera, grandmaster of Bahala Na Escrima and a historian of Filipina/o American martial arts, one of the favored weapons to use in practicing escrima was the asparagus knife. "After using this tool for hours upon hours, days upon days, weeks upon weeks, these young labor warriors would become experts in the thrusting and cutting style of *Sonkete* (poking) much like the style of European fencing," Somera writes. *Escrimadors* would use the grape knife in a reverse grip, holding it like an icepick. A small, short tool with a blade of two to three inches that curved inward, the grape knife was designed to cut grape stems with precision.

Each camp usually had one expert in escrima. He might specialize in the *cabaroan* or the *cadaanan* systems, which had their origins in the Ilocos region; the methods of the Cebuano system or Bohol and Elustrisimo systems; or such other styles as *serrada, espada y daga, decuerdas,* or *cadena de mano.*[109]

Somera writes that the identity of the expert was kept secret, and after a time, the expert would pick a worthy apprentice: "After each day of work they would go deep into the grape vineyards, pear orchard or behind the barn or bunkhouse of the asparagus camp to play [train] in the deadly arts of Filipino Escrima, Arnis and Kali."[110] Before he arrived in the United States in the 1920s, Leo Giron had trained in escrima when he was a young boy in his barrio of Bayambang, Pangasinan. Near Yuba City, he met an accomplished escrimador named Vergara Flaviano. "We played far away from the camp since Flaviano would not teach in the presence of another person," Giron writes in his memoirs. "He was very careful to see that no one should acquire his rare knowledge and represent it in a way that might discredit him." Giron met Flaviano again during World War II, when they were both soldiers in the First Filipino Infantry and stationed at Fort Ord in Central California. They cut up old broomsticks and played between the bunks.[111]

Daniel Inosanto, the son of Stockton labor contractors Mary and Sebastian Inosanto, remembers watching Pinoys practice arnis escrima with twenty-six-inch-long asparagus knives during lunchtime breaks in the fields. He later learned arnis escrima from Stockton old-timers—including Leo Giron, Angel Cabales, and Juanito Lacaste—and became one of the world's most renowned martial artists.[112] Rene Latosa, also a world-famous escrimador who learned his craft in Stockton from such old-timers as Leo Giron and Angel Cabales, said that his father, Johnny Latosa, had secretly learned escrima in the hills of Capiz province, in the Visayas, and brought the knowledge with him to Stockton.[113] This extreme secrecy was necessary, Dan Inosanto writes, since the art was sacred.[114] Also, in the violent period of the 1920s and 1930s, Filipina/o experts kept their knowledge of the martial arts a secret so that they could defend themselves against surprise attacks.

Most Filipina/o workers did not spend their leisure time practicing escrima, however. Most dabbled in gambling, cockfights, and prostitution during their leisure time. Half of the annual earnings of Filipinas/os in California went to gambling and prostitution; in Stockton alone, $2 million was being spent annually on gambling, cockfights, and prostitutes in the 1930s.[115] But gambling offered Pinoys a way to earn more money, and with wages so low, the possibility of winning big and being able to send more money home—or even just to have more pocket money—was almost irresistible. In her study of gambling among Pinoys in Los Angeles's Chinatown and Little Manila from the 1920s to the 1930s, Linda España-Maram makes a similar argument.[116]

The most popular form of gambling in the campo was cockfighting. The practice of training, and then forcing, roosters to fight to the death as spectators placed bets, is so entrenched in Philippine culture that the Venetian chronicler Pigafetta saw Filipinos betting on cockfights in Palawan in 1521. During his brief presidency, Emilio Aguinaldo banned cockfighting, but to no avail: today, every barrio and big city boasts a cockfighting arena.[117] In the Philippine cockfight, a deadly, three-inch, razor-sharp blade is attached to the cock's leg with a spur. Filipinas/os all over California engaged in cock-fighting on their days off, especially on Sundays. Pete Valoria — who was born in Vigan, Ilocos Sur, and came to Stockton in 1927 — remembered stories of legendary wins of expert *sabongeros* (practitioners of sabong, or cockfight-ing). "Oh my God, sometimes they bet $1,500, oh yeah," he remembered, laughing. "There's one guy in Delano, he bought three houses, just from one chicken. *He bought three houses! One chicken only!* He got a good chicken, boy!" Such stories enticed Filipinas/os to bet large sums on cards or cock-fights. Valoria remembered cockfight bets as high as $5,000 and $10,000 in the years after World War II.[118]

Cockfighting became central to Filipina/o life in the campo. Angelina Ban-tillo Magdael, a second-generation Pinay, remembers seeing Pinoys squat-ting on the ground, caressing fighting roosters and obsessing over their care and diet. Angelina's widely respected mother, Virgilia Bantillo, did not hesi-tate to give advice to sabong-crazed Pinoys. "To this Filipino husband my mother would say, 'If your wife will receive some of that stroking there will not be problems in your marriage,'" Angelina remembered.[119] Men, women, and children all attended the fights on Sundays. "Cockfights in Stockton was number one," remembered Connie Amado Ortega, who settled in Seattle. "Everybody used to love to go to the cockfights. They go out where the as-paragus ranches are and that's where they get all their cockfights."[120] The farm town of Livingston, fifty miles south of Stockton on Highway 99, was also a center of cockfighting. Peter Jamero has fond memories of the Sunday afternoon sabong near his family's campo in Livingston. "Sabong was more than a cockfight; it was like a county fair, Filipino market day, and commu-nity celebration all rolled into one," Jamero wrote in his memoirs.[121] At the cockfights, Pinays sold homemade snacks like *biko*, a sweet rice cake; sweet potato fritters; *binangkal*, a Visayan deep-fried, sesame-seed-covered donut; and *adobo*, the popular dish of pork and/or chicken braised in vinegar, salt, garlic, pepper, and bay leaves.

Through much of the twentieth century, San Joaquin County officials at-tempted to shut down illegal cockfighting in the local camps. In early May 1943, at the height of the asparagus season, the county sheriff and his depu-ties used undercover officers and the entire sheriff's department to raid a massive cockfight north of Stockton near Terminous and arrested 170 Filipinos. The officials were shocked to find a hundred birds, some of them dead; cockfighting equipment, such as slashers and spurs; and a beer stand. Those arrested were given a choice: a $50 fine or twenty-five days in jail. Most chose jail; only fifty-three could afford to pay the fine.[122] But the illegality of cockfighting, with the threat of hefty fines and raids, did not deter avid sabongeros. Valoria had been arrested and fined many times but still loved to go to cockfights every weekend. "That's my favorite," he remembered. "*Three times I was fined!* $180. When I was nine years old I got three chickens in the Philippines. I love that sabong. That's one thing I love very much. I don't know why they're forbidden."[123] Authorities in the San Joaquin Delta and near Livingston in Merced County turned to light planes for surveillance to break up cockfights. In Livingston, Luna Jamero remembered her uncles just moved under trees to avoid detection.[124]

In their time off, if they weren't engaged in sports, music, or gambling, or in Little Manila, many Filipinos spent time with prostitutes. The imbalanced sex ratio and the California antimiscegenation law, which outlawed Filipino-white marriage, exacerbated the loneliness felt by single Filipinos. Most Filipino immigrants were in the prime of their sexual lives, and they turned to the services of prostitutes. Sex with prostitutes was such a central part of the early Filipino male immigrant experience that Carlos, the protagonist of Bulosan's *America Is in the Heart*, has his first sexual experience with a prostitute in the campo almost as soon as he arrives in America. Although Carlos is repelled by the act's brutality and exploitation, his peers view it as his initiation into a new, masculine, American life.[125]

Lonely Filipino men spent much of their earnings on prostitutes, particularly white women, according to Charles F. Crook, Deputy Labor Commissioner of San Joaquin County, who was interviewed by the researcher James Earl Wood in the early 1930s. Pimps, growers, and unscrupulous farm labor contractors in San Joaquin County made thousands of dollars annually by providing prostitutes directly to workers in the camps. According to Crook, one company in Stockton made $500 per month by bringing prostitutes into the Delta island camps (see figure 12). Crook noted that Filipinos desired women who were under twenty-five years of age, white, and under 100 pounds. "One of these women is good for about a week in a camp," Crook said. "They are worked through the islands and down toward the coast to the city. Then, they are worked back again. This bringing them in and taking them out of the valley is a continuous process, and plenty of money is made out of it."[126] In his memoir, *I Have Lived with the American People*, Buaken wrote that the prostitution rings brought "deliberate and wanton destruction" to Filipinos in the United States. While working near Stockton at Terminal

12. The female relatives and friends of workers on this Delta campo accidentally chose an interesting day to visit: a day when pimps brought white prostitutes to the campo. Their dissatisfaction is quite obvious. This photograph was taken in the late 1920s or early 1930s. Photograph by Frank Mancao, courtesy of NPA FANHS.

Landing, Buaken remembered that a man driving a Cadillac brought three blondes to the campo one evening. "The man with the three blondes made fat collections that night," he wrote. "When this man got all the available business, he went to see the head man of the farm and asked him if he could recommend other places where Filipinos worked in that section of Stockton. Within a week he was back again, this time he had different girls."[127]

Stories of the hypersexuality or sexual inadequacy of Filipino men were favorites among some whites in Stockton. One prostitute who served primarily Filipinos bragged that she could "make two or three times as much money in dealing with Filipinos. I can accommodate half a dozen of them in the time that it would take to satisfy just one white man." C. D. Crowell, who operated a garage in downtown Stockton, told a researcher that the "Filipinos are hot little rabbits, and many of these white women like them for this reason."[128] These stories served to dehumanize Filipino workers, racializing them as hypersexual (or, alternately, sexually inadequate) monsters interested only in debasing white women. Furthermore, as Rhacel Salazar Parreñas argues in her study of Filipino-white relations in the taxi dance halls, the willingness of certain working-class white women to engage in sexual relations with these "brown monkeys"—either as prostitutes or in genuine, romantic unions—confirmed middle-class whites' beliefs that the women were immoral and impure "trash."[129] Furthermore, the penchant of Pinoys for white girls incited the rage of the white community in Stockton.

The dominance of Filipinas/os in farm work, white Stockton's anger at the union of white women and Filipinos, and the increasing militancy of Filipina/o laborers dovetailed with increasing violence against the immigrants in the late 1920s. By the early 1930s, Filipina/o labor in the Delta was essential and central to the local economy, but in the words of one farmer, the immigrants were beginning to be seen as troublemakers and Communists, both "contemptuous" and treacherous.[130]

Contrary to the opinion of white organized labor, most Filipinas/os, especially the most respected labor contractors, despised the low wages they were paid. The increasing militancy of disgruntled Filipina/o workers came as a shock to most growers. The first Filipina/o strike in the Stockton area was a wildcat strike by grape workers near Lodi in 1924, which took farmers by surprise.[131] In 1927 Filipina/o workers at the Stockton Box Factory discovered that they had been hired at 35 cents per hour when the usual rate was 40 cents. Enraged, they walked off the job. Unfortunately, they were barred from collective bargaining with the company and abandoned by local labor groups who barred Asians, and their strike failed.[132]

By the mid-1920s, Filipina/o crews in San Joaquin County were engaging in small, intense "gang strikes" in which workers all refused to work at crucial points in the harvest—usually right before or at the peak of the harvest, when a strike would hurt the grower the most. Deputy Labor Commissioner Crook faulted the Filipino labor contractors for encouraging these strikes. "The Filipinos are handled by their leaders, and [they] have perfect control over them," he told a researcher in 1930: "You have a good example of what the leaders can do in the 'gang' strikes. They quit all at one time, usually just at the time when labor is needed most in order to get in a perishable crop." But the gang strikes were not always effective. One Delta farmer said that if he were faced with a gang strike, he would "tell them to go to hell, and then get our [Japanese] foremen to pick up some more men." In 1930 a Stockton farmer warned: "The Filipinos are not dangerous now because they are not organized. But if they do succeed in organizing, as they have been trying to do, it will present a dangerous situation."[133]

Conditions were ripe for labor unrest throughout the California fields in the 1920s and 1930s. According to the historian Cletus Daniel, the combination of communist radicalism and farmworker militancy of the early 1930s created the most turbulent and significant era in agricultural unionism in California.[134] To counter unions, farmers consolidated themselves into powerful grower cooperatives that sought to crush any organizing activity among workers. The Valley Fruit Growers of San Joaquin County, organized in 1921, was the first such organization in the Stockton area. The most highly developed was the Agricultural Labor Bureau of the San Joaquin Valley, organized in 1925. By estimating the number of laborers needed for a specific harvest, establishing a low, uniform wage scale across each crop, and using automobiles to move laborers around to snuff out strikes, these organizations reduced labor costs by as much as 30 percent. One of the largest and most powerful groups opposed to Filipina/o naturalization was the Associated Farmers, a right-wing coalition of growers backed by the Southern Pacific Railroad, the Holly Sugar Company, Spreckels Investment Company, and Pacific Gas and Electric.[135] In 1935 Congress passed the National Labor Relations Act, also called the Wagner Act, which authorized labor unions to bargain collectively with employers. However, because of powerful lobbying from the grower cooperatives, the act did not protect farmworkers. As the labor historian Stuart Jamieson argues, these anti-union grower cooperatives and their strategies disempowered workers to such a degree that, ultimately, they incited more labor rebellion and stronger calls for unionization.[136] The publicist for one of the large shipper-grower organizations called the Filipina/o "the most worthless, unscrupulous, shiftless, diseased semi-barbarian that has ever come to our shore."[137]

Filipinas/os were not ignorant of the power and usefulness of unions; labor unions were organized in Manila as early as 1910.[138] In fact, the powerful Philippine workers' fraternity with several lodges in the Delta, the Legionarios de Trabajo, grew out of the 1912 Manila Electric Company strike.[139] Moreover, many Filipinas/os who came to Stockton had left Hawai'i because they had been blacklisted by the plantations there as a result of their participation in labor unions and the failed 1924 strike. Pablo Manlapit—a brilliant, self-educated lawyer—was forced to leave Hawai'i after the strike. He arrived in Los Angeles on August 19, 1927, and immediately set out to organize Filipinas/os in the United States.[140]

According to the labor historian Howard DeWitt, Manlapit went to Stockton in February 1928 and attempted to convince two hundred asparagus workers to strike, but he was unsuccessful. When he returned to Los Angeles later that month, the Federal Bureau of Investigation suspected him of attempting to organize thousands of Filipino asparagus workers in Stockton, accused him of membership in the Communist Party, and detained him for three hours of questioning. Manlapit was released and continued to speak throughout California. He founded the highly political, pro-labor newspaper

Ang Bantay in Los Angeles and returned to Hawai'i in 1932. The Stockton Filipina/o American newspaper *Three Stars* wrote effusively about Manlapit and his radicalism.[141]

At the time when Manlapit visited Stockton, Filipina/o labor demands were becoming more militant. In 1928 Manuel M. Insigne and D. L. Marcuelo, the editors of the Stockton-based newsmagazine the *Philippine Advertiser*, warned Filipina/o laborers not to be manipulated as cheap labor: "The American laborers, together with the rest of the laboring element in this community are watching with keen eyes the steps the Filipino laborers are going to take in view of the fact that they too are affected by other competitors. The Filipino laborers therefore are between hell and fire. While they do not intend to harm one another, they are unconsciously making themselves the victims of unfair and dastardly treatment of their employers."[142] The editors were correct: white labor was watching the Filipina/o situation in the fields. In 1930 the *Stockton Labor Journal* welcomed Filipina/o workers into Stockton if work was plentiful, but the editors suggested that during economic downturns, they were not welcome. The editors also suggested a minimum wage to discourage racism in hiring.[143]

In the spring of 1928, a group of contractors organized themselves into the Filipino Workers Delegation and issued a powerful proclamation to asparagus growers in the *Philippine Advertiser*. D. Tolio, Tomas Espanola, Francisco T. Albano, Sebastian N. Inosanto, and the journalists D. L. Marcuelo and N. C. Villanueva invited the growers to meet with them to "consult one another in an atmosphere of friendliness and good will," to set wages for the season. The delegation reminded the growers that Filipina/o workers desired to "uphold and EMULATE the STANDARD OF AMERICAN WAGES" (emphasis in the original), so that Filipina/o workers would not be reproached for lowering wages.[144] How farmers responded is unknown, but wages continued to drop through the late 1920s and early 1930s.[145] The plummeting wages of the late 1920s as a consequence of the Depression only served to incite more labor militancy. "When we come here, [first to] Seattle, it's 45 cents an hour," Juan "Johnny" Malumay Macahilas recalled. "But in Depression time, that's when it was nine cents an hour!"[146]

The first formal Filipino American labor organization was the Stockton-based *Anak ng Bukid*, or Children of the Farm, organized in June 1928 by Luis Agudo and Marcuelo.[147] The next month, Marcuelo launched a new Stockton Filipina/o American newspaper, the pro-labor *Three Stars*, headquartered in Little Manila at 306 Center Street. The Anak ng Bukid was intended to obtain labor contracts, broker work for farm laborers, and "promote the moral, social, and economic condition of Filipinos" in the United

States.[148] In August 1928 the organizers of the Anak ng Bukid invited all of the major Filipina/o American fraternal groups to a meeting in Stockton, where the new organization hoped to make alliances.[149] The Anak ng Bukid operated like a labor union and a mutual aid society that worked for the welfare of Filipina/o laborers, especially in banning Chinese gambling halls. By 1929 the group had additional chapters in Salinas, Guadalupe, and San Francisco.

Macahilas joined the Anak ng Bukid soon after its organization. A native of Numancia, Aklan, he arrived in California in June 1928. His brothers had all left Numancia for work in Manila, and then in the United States, by the early 1920s. He explained his reasons for emigrating by saying: "We want to be adventurers."[150] But when the family's *carabaos* (water buffaloes, used as beasts of burden on farms in the Philippines) all died of disease, the family was devastated. "So we came here," he remembered. "No carabao to plow." Macahilas traveled the West Coast work circuit, picking hops in Washington State; working in the Alaskan salmon canneries; pruning grapes; picking peas, spinach, and peaches; harvesting walnuts; and cutting asparagus. Of the many Filipina/o community organizations that were founded in the United States in the 1920s, Macahilas joined only one: the Anak ng Bukid.

In January 1929, the editors of the *Three Stars*, who were also the leaders of the Anak ng Bukid, begged Filipina/o workers to refuse to accept the wage of a dollar per hundred pounds of asparagus in a front-page story in January 1929. "That is almost slavery!" Marcuelo wrote. "Demand for a good, reasonable price, that is your right and privilege. If you do not get it do not work at all." Marcuelo assured the workers that if they would hold out for a higher wage, the farmers would be forced to capitulate. "Be always conscious of your power, not of your backbone but of your head and not let those growers bluff you every year," Marcuelo admonished his countrymen. "Now let's go and get a man's wage and not a horse's wage!"[151]

"THE THIRD ASIATIC INVASION"

In May 1930 the local photographer and longtime local Filipino businessman Juan "John" Y. Billones, who had arrived in Stockton in 1912, visited asparagus camps across the San Joaquin Delta and estimated that Filipinas/os in the fields would make $14 million for area farmers that asparagus season. He told the *Three Stars* that he wanted "to show those destroying the name of the Filipinos that after all they are not a menace to the people of this state."[152] However, the idea that the Filipinas/os were the most recent alien menace persisted through the 1920s and 1930s. As immigration peaked and labor militancy among Filipinas/os grew, white labor groups and xenophobic politicians began to issue urgent calls for Filipina/o exclusion. Beginning in

1927, the California State Federation of Labor and the American Federation of Labor passed resolutions at their annual conventions demanding Filipino exclusion.[153] One of the most ardent early anti-Filipina/o agitators was the German immigrant Paul Scharrenberg, secretary-treasurer of the California State Federation of Labor. In a highly influential essay in *Pacific Affairs* published in the winter of 1929, Scharrenberg called Filipinas/os the "third Asiatic invasion" and argued that they were displacing whites in agriculture and culinary trades, on steamships, and in domestic and service work.[154] The American Federation of Labor remained viciously anti-Filipina/o and rejected the repeated requests of Filipina/o laborers for membership. At its annual convention in 1931, the organization passed a resolution calling for Filipino exclusion and for Philippine independence.[155]

One of the first politicians to jump on the bandwagon of anti-Filipina/o sentiment was a Republican congressman, Richard Welch of San Jose. Beginning in 1928, he proposed a series of exclusion bills that would have changed the status of Filipinas/os from national to alien. As aliens, Welch argued, they would then be subject to exclusion by the 1924 Immigration Act, which prohibited the entry of aliens ineligible for citizenship. Filipinas/os in the United States, including the resident commissioners, appointed officials who represented Filipinos as nonvoting members of the House of Representatives, protested every exclusion attempt in Congress. They argued that exclusion would be a grave injustice, as well as illegal and immoral, if full independence was not also simultaneously given to the Philippines.[156] In 1929 the Commonwealth Club in San Francisco brought together so-called experts and scientists who proffered their judgment: the Filipinas/os, like the Chinese and Japanese before them, must go. They argued that Filipinas/os lowered wages and displaced white workers, as well as having an inferior racial character and a penchant for white women, and being unassimilable.[157]

By 1929 most white labor organizations were calling for complete exclusion. Though white workers never competed with Filipinas/os for the same jobs, the historian Mae Ngai argues that it was the whites' perception that Filipina/o labor would lower wages and displace whites that provided the impetus for white labor to begin to agitate against the immigrants.[158] Ironically, the whites who felt most displaced by Filipinas/os were themselves newcomers. The population of California exploded in the 1920s as 1.8 million migrants from other states entered California, and thousands of Dust Bowl migrants settled in Stockton and the surrounding San Joaquin Valley.[159] Most white migrants to the area came from states like Texas, Oklahoma, and Arkansas, where Jim Crow segregation, lynchings, mob violence, and racial terror were part of the regional culture. "After the Depression, all the people in the South mostly come here to California and they have nothing," Johnny Macahilas explained. "The farmers, they used Filipinos, because they know the Filipinos worked [better] than Americans."[160] Camila Carido said that everyone knew the kind of *puti* (whites) who preyed on Filipinas/os: those from "Oklahoma, [those] Okies."[161]

The first recorded incidence of anti-Filipina/o violence in the United States took place in Stockton on New Year's Eve, 1926. Eight whites and Filipinos were stabbed and beaten when white men entered hotels and pool halls, looking for Filipinos to attack. Instead of placing the blame on the white thugs, the local paper—the anti-Filipina/o *Stockton Daily Evening Record*—reported that "Filipinos ran amuck, attacking whites."[162] Racist terror and violence peaked in the fall and winter of 1929–30 as the economy hit rock bottom, with white mobs using dynamite, bombs, and guns to intimidate Filipinas/os across the state. The atmosphere was so hostile for the immigrants that Bulosan would later write that 1930 was "the year of the great hatred: the lives of Filipinos were cheaper than those of dogs."[163]

In late October 1929, in the Tulare County town of Exeter, a mob of several hundred whites roamed through camps where Filipinas/os worked in the fig harvest, beating immigrants, smashing cars, and burning down bunkhouses.[164] "Work no Fils Or We'll Burn This Town Down," read one note hastily scribbled by a vigilante.[165] On January 10, 1930, in Pajaro, the Northern Monterey Chamber of Commerce passed a series of racist resolutions that incensed Filipinas/os throughout California. A local judge, D. W. Rohrback, condemned the immigrants as cheap laborers who were only "ten years removed from a bolo and a breechclout" and were diseased degenerates who subsisted on rice and fish. Stockton Filipinas/os were outraged, and the staff of the *Three Stars* called Rohrback's proclamations inflammatory lies.[166]

In neighboring Watsonville on January 19, Filipinos leased a dance hall and hired nine white girls. On the 21st, an armed white mob approached the hall and engaged in a shoot-out with Filipinos until the sheriff arrived. Four days of mob terror ensued, in which whites shot at and beat Filipinos indiscriminately. The terror culminated with the shooting death on the 22nd of January of Fermin Tobera, who was sleeping inside a bunkhouse when a bullet pierced his chest.[167] But the violence continued into 1930 as Filipinas/os and whites clashed in labor camps and cities. In San Jose on January 24, 1930, a Filipino stabbed a white man.[168] On January 29, a white mob bombed the Filipino Federation Building at 2049 South San Joaquin Street in Stockton. No one was killed, but the attack sent a sobering message.[169]

On January 31, students at the University of the Philippines in Quezon City demonstrated against the anti-Filipina/o violence in the United States, condemned the bombing in Stockton, and announced plans for a massive meeting that Sunday in Manila.[170] On February 2, more than 10,000 workers, representatives from labor organizations, professors, and students gathered in Manila's Luneta Park to memorialize Fermin Tobera in what was dubbed a "National Day of Humiliation." Jorge Bacobo, the dean of the University of the Philippines Law School and a former pensionado, addressed the crowd: "Would we be worthy of our sacred past and of any glorious future if we did not protest against the humiliating events in America?"[171] Attendees wore black armbands and wept through the speeches.[172] "Americans were welcomed to the Philippines with open arms, but Filipinos are welcomed in California with coffins," said the political leader Jose de Jesus, in a speech that electrified the crowd.[173]

Writing soon after the Stockton bombing, Marcuelo raged against the hostility against Filipinas/os across California. "Let us Filipinos have our independence immediate and complete, and in this way solve the whole problem for all time," he wrote. "But—to drive the Filipinos, insult them because they are brown, which is not a matter of their own choosing, hounding them from pillar to post, and bombing their homes, depriving them of limb and even of life, as well as preventing their pursuit of happiness, all the time withholding their country from them is a travesty beyond human comprehension—and if that is justice then let us serve the devil!"[174]

As noted above, white migrants from the South and Midwest brought Jim Crow with them to California, with its segregation and tactics of racial terror. Filipinas/os were beaten and lynched in terrifying parallels to the violence used to enforce deference to whites in the South. Between 1890 and World War I, at least two or three black Southerners were hanged, burned at the stake, or murdered each week.[175] Anti-Filipino incidents were reported in the San Francisco Bay Area, the San Joaquin Valley, in Dinuba, Delano, Fresno, and Reedley. On June 14, 1930, after it was claimed that he had been seen with white girls, the mutilated body of Robert B. Martin, a local lumber worker and Filipino veteran of World War I, was found hanging in a tree in Susanville, a hundred miles north of Stockton.[176] On July 29, 1930, a bomb was found at the Ferry building in San Francisco with a note attached: "Death to all Filipinos."[177] In the first week of August, Marcuelo went to each of these towns to help rally Filipinas/os against the mob violence.[178] In early August 1930, the *Three Stars* reported that a contractor driving near Lodi, just north of Stockton, saw two Filipinos hanging from a tree, and one burned body propped up against the tree trunk. "The last line has been crossed in our forbearance, and with our back against the walls anything may happen," wrote Marcuelo in the newspaper's August 15 issue.[179]

The Ku Klux Klan was experiencing a national revival in the 1920s; one meeting of the group drew more than a thousand people to the Stockton Civic Auditorium on February 23, 1924.[180] Jerry Paular recalled that the Klan used terror and violence to run Filipinas/os out of towns in the San Joaquin Valley. He remembered one incident in a town near Stockton in the 1920s, in which a two-year-old Filipino boy was burned to death when the Klan set fire to the family's home: "They came back and the house was on fire and the big KKK was there and the kid was swollen up dead." The family and the entire Filipina/o community were devastated. "My mother never wanted to talk about it. Until the day she died, [the mother] never wanted to talk about it," Paular said.[181]

Because armed mobs usually targeted the bunkhouses, Filipinas/os sometimes slept outdoors. Johnny Macahilas missed a bomb attack on his bunkhouse because he slept outside instead of inside the stifling bunkhouse. "I was laying down in the oranges, because in the summertime, I don't go in the house, I stay outside, mostly," he remembered. "So lucky I wasn't in that cot!" he remembered. "Because when the bomb was thrown, I was out already! When I come back over there, all the dirt is in my cotbed!"[182] Camila Carido remembered the white mobs vividly: "There were nights when they couldn't sleep in the houses because people from the South, they would throw bombs in the fields because they were blaming the Pilipinos that they would take the jobs away from them."[183]

When threatened with gun violence, Filipinos were not afraid to shoot back. Johnny Latosa participated in shoot-outs between Filipinos and white vigilante mobs, most of them Dust Bowl migrants, in San Joaquin County in the 1920s and 1930s, said his son, Rene Latosa. Johnny told his son "they would have people from other states that wanted their jobs," Rene remembered. "And he said there would be shoot-outs. And this is when he was younger and they would just shoot back. They would drive by, and boom boom boom, and then they'd keep going. This is how they lived during that Depression. They fought for their jobs. He said that they [would] drive by every night."[184] Rene said his father carried a small pistol with him at all times, a practice that was a holdover from that era.

As terror against Filipinas/os continued, national movements for their exclusion gathered steam. Soon after the Watsonville riots, Congressman Welch blamed the violence on the unassimilability of Filipinas/os and argued that the solution to race riots was exclusion.[185] Resident Commissioner Camilo Osias responded that the only way for the problem to go away would be to grant the Philippines immediate independence.[186]

As white vigilantes attacked Filipinas/os up and down the West Coast, the battle between the farmworkers, who demanded the right to organize, and the growers and their allies was becoming increasingly violent. On one side were the farmworkers. On the other side were "the Associated Farmers, American Legionnaires, deputy sheriffs, highway patrolmen, vigilante prosecutors, intemperate judges, and complaisant grand juries using the language and psychosis of red scare to protect their hegemony and investments," writes the historian Kevin Starr.[187] DeWitt describes the activities of the Associated Farmers and other anti-Filipina/o groups as "farm fascism."[188] The resentment of white labor, the pandering of local politicians to racist and nativist constituencies, and anti-Filipina/o violence served to unify Filipina/o workers and strengthen their resolve to organize into formal labor unions in the Delta. But they initially struggled to find allies. The Industrial Workers of the World, known as the Wobblies, maintained an office at 344 South El Dorado Street, in the heart of Little Manila—next to the Caballeros de Dimas Alang, a Filipino nationalist fraternal group, and the *Three Stars* newspaper.[189] But the Wobblies were largely ineffectual in the Delta.

The only organization willing to defend Filipinas/os and advocate on their behalf was the Communist Party. The *Daily Worker*, the party's newspaper, was the only non-Filipina/o publication to come to the defense of Filipina/o workers in the Salinas-Watsonville area in 1930, and the party began to recruit Filipinas/os and Mexicans throughout California in the early 1930s, through the Cannery and Agricultural Workers Industrial Union (CAWIU).[190] The Communist organizers in the union were fearlessly dedicated to organizing the most despised and exploited laborers in California: Filipina/o, Mexican, and poor white farmworkers. Filipinas/os responded positively to Communist organizers for a number of reasons. The most important was that Communist labor unions were the only white labor institutions that defended Filipinas/os against mob violence. Also, Filipinas/os learned how to organize from the Communists. DeWitt argues that Communist-led unions were highly skilled at organization and strike tactics, including picketing and worker grievance committees.[191]

However, the vast majority of Filipina/o workers did not become Communists, as DeWitt notes. Some workers became deeply influenced by the concepts of leftist organizing and Marxist-Leninist theories, among them such organizers as Ernesto Mangaoang and Crispulo Mensalvas, who became radicals and members of the Legionarios del Trabajo fraternal order, whose secret internal teachings included American labor history. Mensal-

vas and Mangaoang later organized Salinas lettuce workers with Rufo Canete, D. L. Marcuelo, and Luis Agudo in 1934, and helped organize cannery
workers with other labor leaders in Alaska into the Cannery Workers' and
Farm Laborers' Union 18257.[192] Bulosan, a close associate of Mensalvas, became one of the more prominent Communist writers of the late Depression
and postwar period.[193]

By the early 1930s, Filipinas/os in California had gained the reputation of
being the most militant and radical workers in the fields.[194] Certainly, the
militancy and cohesion of the Filipina/o union organizing work that emerged
in the 1930s derived from the highly organized, efficient, and close-knit
bonds that Filipina/o work crews had developed in the gang strikes of the
1920s. Militancy was also a response to the violent vigilante mobs that threatened Filipina/o workers in the fields from the late 1920s to the mid-1930s.[195]
Filipina/o laborers became militant in the early days because, in comparison
to other farmworkers, they were more likely to be young, single laborers. In
addition, they expected to return to the Philippines after making their fortune or earning a college degree. Largely free from worrying about feeding
their families, unlike Mexican and white laborers, Filipinas/os were willing
to go head to head with police, armed guards, and scabs to defend their jobs.

Most important, the militancy of Filipina/o workers became part of their
identities. Immigrants from the Tagalog, Visayas, and the Ilocos regions
shared the same poor wages and working conditions. The white mobs that
began to terrorize Filipinas/os in the late 1920s did not differentiate between
Visayans, Tagalogs, and Ilocanas/os when they bombed bunkhouses and attacked camps with drive-by shootings. Organized white labor and politicians
ignored any differences among Filipinas/os. Ilocanas/os, Tagalogs, and Visayans were coming to the realization that they were all in the same situation:
they were degraded and racialized as inferior, unassimilable, and easily ex-
ploitable, regardless of individuals' regional or class origins or educational
attainment. For example, Filipinas/os did not hesitate to turn on each other if
they discovered that another crew had crossed a picket line. The *Sacramento
Bee* reported that on June 5, 1932, a violent confrontation between two Filipino factions working in the Delta asparagus fields had resulted in three men
being sent to the hospital. When fifteen Filipino lettuce cutters were hired to
replace an asparagus crew that was on strike, a full-blown brawl erupted at
Third and M streets in Sacramento, with both sides wielding knives. Though
the crowd dispersed as soon as the police arrived, three Filipinos were arrested.[196]

The Anak ng Bukid disbanded in the early 1930s, when Marcuelo and
Agudo left Stockton to organize workers in the Salinas lettuce fields. Mar-

cuelo, Agudo, and Canete formed the Filipino Labor Union in 1933 and organized a massive strike of Filipino lettuce cutters that spring. That strike showcased growing Filipina/o unity and courageous militancy. "The Filipino is a real fighter and his strikes have been dangerous," McWilliams wrote, reflecting on the absolute determination of the 3,000 Filipina/o workers in Salinas to win the right to collective bargaining despite the order of the American Federation of Labor to return to work and the violent repression of the strikers.[197] Though the strike was moderately successful, and the Filipino Labor Union had spawned seven locals by 1934, the union was eventually killed by the combined pressure of growers, factionalism, and white labor's racism.[198]

Increasingly, Filipinos turned to formal labor unions to settle labor disputes, especially after 1930. From 1930 to 1934, organized by the CAWIU, Filipinos and Mexicans participated in ten major strikes across California. Filipinas/os walked off their jobs and demanded higher wages and better working conditions across the state, in Santa Maria Valley, Orange County, Imperial Valley, and San Diego. In March 1934, asparagus workers in the Delta struck for higher wages. By the mid-1930s, independent Filipino labor unions began to emerge that were not affiliated with either the Communist Party or the American Federation of Labor. Filipinas/os in Stockton organized several ethnic unions in California through the 1930s, including the Filipino Labor Association, the Filipino Labor Supply Association, and, in 1939, the Filipino Agricultural Laborer's Association. The Filipino Labor Supply Association of Stockton refused membership to non-Filipina/o contractors.[199]

But the contractors and workers were split on whether or not to affiliate with larger unions such as the American Federation of Labor, which began to actively court Filipina/o and Mexican workers by the mid-1930s. Leftist organizers such as Mensalvas advocated a broader organizing strategy and were not opposed to allying with the federation to accomplish this, but advocates of independent, all-Filipino unions opposed the idea. This ideological split would lead to a splintering of Filipino labor unions in the Salinas area. In 1936 Mensalvas formed the Filipino Independent Labor Union and broke with the more conservative Canete. In the 1940s, Mensalvas would become a leader in Alaska's Local 7 of the United Cannery and Packing and Allied Workers' Union, a new affiliate of the Congress of Industrial Organizations that had been born as the original Filipino cannery workers' union in 1933.[200]

In late 1936, Filipino workers in Stockton organized Local 20221 of the Agricultural Workers Union, affiliated with the American Federation of Labor. The union organized celery workers in the San Joaquin and Sacramento Delta and called a strike in November 1936. Among its demands were a 10-cent wage increase, recognition of the union, and the creation of a hiring hall. Growers refused to capitulate to the workers' demands, insisting that the union was just a front to collect money from its members rather than a legitimate union. Police erected barricades to keep workers miles from the fields, and farmers brought in strikebreakers. The strike failed.[201] The next year, on March 12, 1937, Filipino asparagus workers on Union Island under the labor contractor C. Tonie went on strike, demanding a 20-cent increase per 100 pounds, from the 95 cents the growers were offering to $1.15. The Agricultural Workers Union locals of Stockton and Sacramento were demanding $1.25–1.75 per 100 pounds that season.[202] As the 1930s came to a close, Filipinos were still split over whether or not to affiliate with the American Federation of Labor or the more progressive Congress of Industrial Organizations, or to organize along racial lines in independent unions limited to Filipinas/os. The story of the emergence in 1939 of the Stockton-based Filipino American Laborer's Association (later renamed the Filipino Agricultural Laborer's Association), the most powerful Filipino American union ever to emerge in the United States, will be told in chapter 6.

CONCLUSION

When people in the Philippines mortgaged land, borrowed money, and sold farm animals to pay for the one-way journey to the United States, they imagined a bountiful, modern nation, full of opportunity and jobs that would help pay their tuition at a prestigious university. Instead, as soon as they arrived they went to work performing stoop labor in some of the worst jobs they could have ever imagined, in some of the crudest living conditions they would ever experience. Work in the fields, and horrific farm labor conditions, low wages, and industrialized agriculture taught Filipina/o immigrants their place: at the bottom of the racial hierarchy in Stockton. However, they refused to accept their labor conditions passively, nor did they allow regionalism and factionalism to destroy hard-won solidarity with one another. In the campo, Filipina/o workers resisted their dehumanization and formed bonds with one another as they gambled, played escrima, and engaged in cockfights.

Most important, they came together as militant laborers who fought tenaciously for fair wages. Their heartbreaking experience in the United States—the racist violence, segregation, and labor exploitation of the 1920s and 1930s—led to their passionate defense of their right to live and work in the United States, not as debased colonials, but as workers and human beings. Some of the most highly organized Filipina/o American ethnic organizations were the militant farm labor unions that grew out of worker unrest in the 1920s and 1930s in the San Joaquin Delta. Beginning with the intense but tiny gang strikes they used to shock farmers in the 1920s and moving to the enormous strikes of the 1930s that froze entire industries, Filipinas/os soon earned a reputation for being among the most radical and militant workers in the United States.

But just as Filipinas/os were learning how to come together in the late 1920s, racist hatred of them also brought whites together across class and regional origins in a campaign of violent repression. This anti-Filipina/o movement on the West Coast from the late 1920s to the mid-1930s brought together Dust Bowl migrants and other recent white arrivals; wealthy growers and other powerful businessmen; and politicians like Richard Welch, a California congressman who pandered to all of these constituencies. In the face of extreme racial repression on the streets of Little Manila and in the fields of the Delta, Filipinas/os turned to one another and created a complex and vibrant community in Stockton. In the next chapter, I discuss the origins of ethnic organizations and the key roles these groups played in helping Filipinas/os survive the Depression, together with the vibrant street culture of Little Manila.

CHAPTER 3

MAKING A FILIPINA/O AMERICAN WORLD IN STOCKTON

On July 27, 1927, an anxious fourteen-year-old Angeles Monrayo boarded a steamship and left Honolulu for San Francisco with her father, Enarciso. When they arrived in Stockton that fall, they moved into a residential hotel in a neighborhood that was swiftly becoming the center of Filipina/o life in the United States: the four square blocks surrounding the intersection of Lafayette and El Dorado streets, next to Chinatown and Japantown (Nihonmachi). Early immigrants like the Monrayos flooded to Stockton in such numbers during the 1920s that the city, as well as the ethnic neighborhood that was home to many businesses and immigrants, was called Little Manila, the Manila of California, and Manila of the United States. When the Monrayos arrived in Stockton, there were approximately 7,000 Filipinas/os living in and near the city (see figure 13).[1]

In their first months in California, the Monrayos looked to other Visayans—particularly those from Romblon and Panay—for work, shelter, and friendship. Angeles had learned to read and write in English in Hawai'i, but her father, a sakada who left the island of Romblon for Hawai'i in 1912, could not even write his name. In their reliance on people from their hometown and others who spoke their dialect, Hiligaynon, the Monrayo family was typical. The lack of a common language among many Filipina/o immigrants and their strong regional identities posed barriers to the formation of a broader community early in the immigrants' experience. But the Monrayos, like others, soon found that they would be identified in the United States not as Ilocanas/os, Tagalogs, and Visayans, but as Filipinas/os whose presence was met with violent resentment.

13. Photographer Frank Mancao captured the northern end of Little Manila, at El Dorado and Washington streets, in the late 1920s. Courtesy of NPA FANHS.

The preceding chapter described how the fields served as a site in which a militant Filipina/o identity could be articulated by different ethnic and linguistic groups of immigrants from the Philippines. In this chapter, I explore how, in the first three decades of Filipina/o settlement in Stockton, the immigrants responded to their racialization and the rigid segregation in Stockton by creating their own distinct world in the Little Manila neighborhood in downtown Stockton, forging identities as Filipina/o Americans and creating a community that served their needs and consisted of a complex web of social relations, obligations, and identities. In Stockton's Little Manila, Pinoys were engaged in the creation of a homosocial, aggressively masculine culture of fashion, gambling, boxing matches, dance halls, dancing and sex with prostitutes, and music in which Filipino sexuality and purchasing power were on full display, a similar cultural phenomenon to what Linda España-Maram describes regarding Filipinas/os in Los Angeles's Little Manila.[2]

This chapter describes this Pinoy masculine world in Stockton, as well as the larger community these immigrants created before World War II. As the city's whites and other groups carried on a reign of terror that sought to drive Filipinas/os from their streets, and as a larger, national anti-Filipina/o movement among white labor, elites, business interests, and politicians terrorized Filipinas/os up and down the West Coast, the immigrants increasingly reached across ethnic and regional lines. They learned that race, more than class, ethnicity, dialect, or regional origin, shaped one's opportunities and social status in Stockton. To survive the brutal years of the Depression and the violence of anti-Filipino sentiment, immigrants and their families turned first to their relatives and others from their province. They increasingly turned also to dozens of fraternal groups, mutual aid associations, religious groups, hobby clubs, women's organizations, labor unions, and regional and hometown associations. These networks were integral to the survival of the Filipina/o American community in the 1920s and 1930s, and membership in a close-knit group that was not technically kin was central to the construction of Filipina/o American identity in Stockton. Through identification with other Filipinas/os in Stockton, Ilocanas/os, Visayans, and Tagalogs in Little Manila became Filipina/o American, adding this identity to the one based on their hometown and language group.

COMING TOGETHER

The task of forging a unified identity and community in Stockton was complicated by the linguistic and regional differences among immigrants. However, the desire to congregate solely with others from the same town or region may have had less to do with regionalism and interethnic prejudice than with language: many Ilocanas/os, Visayans, and Tagalogs were most comfortable communicating in their own languages and dialects. Almost ninety different languages and dialects have been identified in the Philippines. Only 25 percent of the total Philippine population spoke Tagalog when it was made the national language of the Philippines after World War II, and most immigrants spoke Visayan or Ilocano. Some had only a perfunctory command of English, and very few spoke Spanish.[3] Mary Arca, who moved to Stockton with her family in the early 1920s, learned to speak Illonggo, Cebuano, Tagalog, and Ilocano. "Each group seemed to segregate into the dialect one seemed comfortable to be with," Mary wrote.[4]

There were linguistic differences even among Visayan immigrants. Angeles Monrayo's family and others from northern Panay spoke Hiligaynon, the main language spoken throughout the western Visayas; they may have also spoken or understood Romblomanon, Kinaray-a, Aklanon or Capiceño, other dialects and languages spoken by residents of the provinces of Iloilo, Aklan, Antique and Capiz on Panay, the island adjacent to Romblon. Most emigrants from Cebu, Bohol, and Leyte spoke Cebuano or Waray-Waray. Angeles's diaries give us ample evidence of the ways that linguistic barriers prevented Filipinas/os from creating relationships across regional lines. Antagonism and stereotyping certainly existed among Visayans, Tagalogs, and Ilocanas/os; Angeles writes several times that her father hated Tagalogs, but she doesn't understand why. Some Filipinas/os raised in the United States, like Angeles, learned English in addition to several other dialects and languages. Angeles spoke English, Aklanon, and Cebuano.[5] The most powerful community leaders brought many factions and people from different regions together by speaking several dialects and languages. For example, Sebastian Inosanto and Larry Itliong, both powerful labor contractors and union organizers in Stockton, spoke Tagalog, Ilocano, and several Visayan dialects. Inosanto spoke nine different Philippine languages and dialects.[6]

However, the racial violence aimed at Filipinas/os along the West Coast — there were more than thirty incidents of anti-Filipina/o incidents including bombings, riots, and shootings in the late 1920s and early 1930s — rendered regionalism, factionalism, linguistic differences, and class divisions increasingly unimportant.[7] When Watsonville was wracked by anti-Filipina/o violence in the winter of 1930, the Stockton Filipina/o American community believed it was safe from race riots. Bruno E. Dato of Anak ng Bukid, a labor union and mutual aid society, told the *Stockton Daily Evening Record* that people lived in harmony in Little Manila: "The whites and Filipinos are in perfect harmony and, as far as I know, there has not been any ill feeling here since the rioting started." Cornelio Clenuar, of the Filipino Federation of America in Stockton, told the newspaper that he doubted that the rioting would spread to Stockton. However, the newspaper reported that police were already taking precautionary measures by patrolling Little Manila, which had been quiet, and preventing large crowds of Filipinas/os from gathering.[8] "Although Stockton is the Filipino center of the United States and there are more than 6,000 of the race here, there has been no hostility between Filipinos and whites," the *Record* reported on January 27.[9]

Two days after that story appeared, a group of whites bombed the building at 2049 South San Joaquin Street, several blocks south of Little Manila, just after midnight. The building was the Stockton headquarters of one of the largest Filipina/o American organizations, the Filipino Federation of America. Though more than forty people were inside the Victorian mansion at the time of the bombing, no one was killed, and only one person was slightly injured. The explosion blew off the porch and shattered windows in homes hundreds of feet away (see figure 14). Police accused other Filipinas/os of the bombing and refused to investigate. The bombing shook the Filipina/o community to its core and brought hundreds of immigrants together in Stockton to protest and urge officials to undertake a proper investigation of the bombing.

John Y. Billones, a respected elder and businessman who owned a photography studio on El Dorado Street, called a mass meeting at the Japanese Hall on Washington Street the day after the bombing. Billones told the hundreds of assembled Filipinas/os that the violence was meant to scare them into re-

14. Members of the Filipino Federation of America pose with their building after it was bombed in 1930. Though the original building is no longer there, the organization maintains its headquarters on the same site today. Courtesy of FANHS Stockton.

turning to the Philippines, and he urged them to stay peaceful. A committee of concerned Filipinas/os was appointed and elected as its president Primo Villaruz, an articulate former pensionado who was the chemist for the city's water utility. The *Stockton Daily Evening Record*, probably to the great relief of most whites in the city, reported that the Filipinas/os were not seeking revenge. In a rare show of unity, members of the Filipina/o community decided to remain peaceful because they wanted to be perceived as good neighbors by Stockton's white residents and as colonials worthy of the independence of their homeland.[10] "The 'boys' are brave, and will fight back," Mrs. D. L. Marcuelo told a researcher less than a week after the bombing. "But at a time like this it is better that they not fight back."[11] The Filipino Federation of America refused to move and repaired its headquarters.[12]

On February 7, 1930, just over a week after the bombing, the Filipina/o community held another mass meeting. For three hours, Filipina/o and sympathetic white community leaders again urged the immigrants to refrain from seeking revenge. Villaruz told those assembled to "live a clean and noble life" and to live up to the example of the national hero, José Rizal. D. L. Marcuelo, editor of the *Three Stars*, told immigrants to control their tempers and warned them that their conduct in the United States directly affected the Philippine independence movement. "Your conduct here lets the American people know whether you are good or bad," he told the group. "We must live here in such a manner to reflect the best that there is in the Filipino people. We must give them the right impressions." The white allies included Reverend Long of the Presbyterian Church, and a former mayor of Stockton; they assured the Filipinas/os that they wanted "the right thing to be done."[13] At the meeting, Billones played a piece on his violin that he dedicated to the memory of Fermin Tobera, the Filipino shot to death during the Watsonville riots. But after two and a half hours of speeches, most people in the audience grew restless with the rhetoric and left. The Filipina/o community canceled a huge Philippine Independence demonstration that had been set for Saturday, February 8, for fear of more anti-Filipina/o violence.[14]

Other Filipinas/os nationwide also opposed retaliation, arguing that they must act as though they were fit for independence. In the fall of 1930, after almost a year of racial terror inflicted on Filipinas/os up and down the West Coast, the Filipino attorney Vincent Villamin spoke at the Hotel Stockton on his tour of major cities in the United States, reminding local Filipinas/os to turn the other cheek when under attack and to act like model Americans. "Violence will only aggravate the situation," he told a crowd. "I advise the Filipinos, in their turn, to do their duty, abide by the laws, be friendly even under provocation, and they will eventually be welcomed by the community where they are workers." Villamin was rather naively convinced that American law would protect Filipinas/os.[15] Filipinas/os in Stockton turned instead to community organizations for a collective voice and protection.

CREATING A COMMUNITY

Creating a cohesive Filipina/o American community in Stockton was no simple task. The proliferation of Filipina/o American labor and community and ethnic organizations in the city—by the 1970s, more than forty of these three types of organizations were competing for members—is evidence of how community leaders struggled, especially in the years before World War II, to unite Little Manila in terms of ethnic identity, purpose, and politics.[16] The sheer number of groups is also evidence of the intense internal divisions and internecine fighting within organizations that often split them apart. Divisions were sometimes provoked by dissension about a group's structure, its distribution of power, and ideas about nationalism and citizenship. An inability to share power could break up even a Bible study class, wrote Emory Bogardus in his study of Filipina/o American organizations.[17]

So many organizations were formed in the early years of the community's settlement that a group of Filipinas/os organized the Filipino Community of Stockton and Vicinity in 1927, an umbrella group that struggled to bring together the competing voices, agendas, and interests of the many Filipina/o organizations in Stockton.[18] Its first president, the well-respected

Primo Villaruz, soon learned that creating a community was a frustrating task. Residents of Little Manila balanced larger community concerns — especially those regarding discrimination, labor battles, citizenship struggles, and Philippine independence — with concerns about the care of their families back in the Philippines.

Almost all Filipinas/os in the United States of the generation who came of age before World War II were members of least two ethnic organizations.[19] The organizations that proliferated in Stockton at this time became a surrogate family and support network for the thousands of single men and young families who had left their extensive kin networks behind in the Philippines. Without these organizations, Filipinas/os would never have survived the Depression. As noncitizens, Filipinas/os, were not eligible for New Deal relief programs, and they were too proud to stand in the bread lines. The fraternal, Masonic, and regional or hometown associations that were founded in Stockton before World War II all offered mutual aid insurance benefits such as cash assistance for doctor's bills, hospitalizations, and funerals; wedding and funeral rituals; social events; housing; and a network of friends and family.[20] These organizations carried many single men and families through some of the most joyous and some of the most challenging times of their lives in the United States.

The most formal, largest, and long-lived of these Filipina/o American religious, political, and community organizations were the American branches of Philippine fraternal and Masonic orders. The Masonic order Gran Oriente was founded by the Filipino Merchant Marines in San Francisco in 1925, and the order established the Mayon Lodge in Stockton. The nationalist Caballeros de Dimas Alang (CDA) fraternity was founded in San Francisco in 1920. The Legionarios del Trabajo (Legionnaires of Labor, or LDT) fraternity, founded in Manila in 1916 to honor the brotherhood of workers, was brought to San Francisco in 1924. All three organizations — the Gran Oriente, CDA, and LDT — were closely based on the secret organizational structure, ideologies, and nationalist creed of Andres Bonifacio's secret revolutionary society, the Katipunan, which itself was based on the principles of freemasonry.[21] And these organizations — as well as the Filipino Federation of America, founded in Los Angeles by Hilario Camino Moncado in 1925 — stressed belief in a higher power, Philippine nationalism, morality, and a commitment to Philippine independence and national progress.[22]

The leftist LDT, the largest of the three fraternal orders, boasted more than 80,000 members in the Philippines and the United States in the 1920s and 1930s. The group's founder, Domingo Ponce, was a Marxist organizer in Manila who recruited peasants and working-class Filipinas/os to the or-

15. The Worshipful Daguhoy Lodge of the Legionarios del Trabalo was organized in Stockton in 1926 in the Mariposa Hotel, mainly by immigrants from Bohol. In Bohol, Francisco Daguhoy led the longest revolt against Spanish authorities. Photograph by Frank Mancao, courtesy of NPA FANHS.

ganization.[23] The group's membership base mushroomed when its radical leaders engaged in a militant strike against the Manila Electric Company in 1919. Ponce focused on inspiring nationalism and labor consciousness among the group's members and engaged in vocal political debates about American colonial rule, anti-Filipino sentiment in the United States, agrarian reform, and collective bargaining.[24] The LDT was so inspired by American labor radicalism that it honors Nina Van Zandt, an American labor radical and the spouse of the jailed radical labor activist August Spies (one of the Haymarket defendants) with an annual Nina Van Zandt queen contest that continues to this day.[25]

The Gran Oriente, CDA, and LDT named their lodges after such nationalist heroes as Andres Bonifacio, Artemio Ricarte, and Apolinario Mabini and after notable Philippine landmarks, such as Mount Mayon, a massive, active, cone-shaped volcano in Southern Luzon. Immigrants from Bohol chartered the first LDT lodge in the San Joaquin Valley and Delta, the Worshipful Daguhoy Lodge No. 528, in the Mariposa Hotel at 130 E. Lafayette Street in Little Manila in 1926 (see figure 15). The men named their lodge after Francisco Daguhoy, the leader of a protracted revolt against Spanish rule in Bohol. The Daguhoy Lodge bought a large temple and rooming house at 203 E. Hazelton Street near Little Manila in 1937.[26] By 1940 there were thirty-one

LDT lodges in Hawai'i, Washington, California, and New York.[27] The first LDT women's lodge, the Teodora Alonzo Lodge (named after José Rizal's mother), was formed in Stockton in 1935. The CDA chartered the Regidor Lodge in Stockton in the early 1920s and a women's lodge, the Maria Clara, in Stockton in 1928.

Hilario Camino Moncado, who founded the Filipino Federation of America (FFA) in 1925, was a native of Barrio Pondol, Balanban, Cebu. He went to Hawai'i in 1914 to work as a sakada before coming to the United States.[28] The historian Steffi San Buenaventura argues that the FFA was uniquely Filipina/o American because it chose to orient itself toward the immigrant community in Hawai'i and the United States, operated solely in English, and was founded not in the Philippines, but in the United States.[29] From the beginning, Moncado exhorted his followers to set themselves apart from other Filipinas/os by their Christian morality and "clean living," according to San Buenaventura. They ate a strictly vegetarian diet; shunned drinking, gambling, smoking, cockfighting, and dance halls; and were resolutely anti-union, thereby positioning themselves as the conservative, anti-labor solution to Filipina/o problems in California.[30] Soon after the FFA was founded, it purchased its Victorian house at 2049 South San Joaquin Street.

Because of the strict moral code and diet of its members; the conservative, anti-union stance of Moncado; and the secretive nature of the religious and political organization, the FFA was highly controversial within the Filipina/o American community. Moncado's claims of greatness — he was an attorney who had attended several American universities and a hero of the Philippine Revolution — were heavily criticized outside of the organization. One Filipino contractor, a Mr. Cinco, felt that the FFA's doctrines and practices, including its members' vegetarian diet, reflected badly on Filipinas/os. "It is composed mainly of ignorant people. . . . They are weak on the job, probably because of their no-meat diet, and they give Filipinos a bad name," he said, and he complained that the group's leaders preyed on newcomers and the most uneducated immigrants.[31] Despite these criticisms, the FFA was an important organization for hundreds of immigrants and their families. The organization and its headquarters still thrive to this day in Stockton, albeit on a much smaller scale.

San Buenaventura has argued that organizations like the FFA, LDT, CDA, and Gran Oriente were "formal institutions that sought to project a collective voice of Filipinos and present a unified image of the group to the outside world."[32] For young, single, vulnerable Filipinas/os in the United States, the FFA, CDA, and LDT were powerful political families bound by ties of secrecy, nationalism, and shared struggle. Membership in organizations gave immigrants dignity, prestige, honor, power, and a collective voice in the political landscape of the Philippines and Filipina/o American communities. They also became members of a kind of super family, with an extensive and close-knit brotherhood and sisterhood of thousands of Filipinas/os tied together through shared values and beliefs, class and racial identity, and sworn secrecy. In the absence of immediate family members in the United States, it was meaningful that members of the lodges called each other "Brother" and "Sister." In photographs, the members gaze at the camera with steely pride and dignity, resplendent in their hats, aprons, swords, and other lodge regalia.[33] Lodge leaders were called "Worshipful Master" or "Worshipful Matron." As Vicente Rafael has argued in his analysis of the photographs of the illustrados, Filipinas/os of this time period were self-consciously marking their dignity, humanity, and nationalist pride through their photographed bodies. A similar argument could be made about the photographs of the members of the fraternal orders.[34]

Hometown and mutual aid associations began to multiply in the 1930s, with the aim of providing social support and kin network, and also formalizing the process by which aid could be sent back to hometowns in the Philippines. By assessing dues, hometown associations provided money for medical bills, illnesses, funerals, marriages, and christenings to their members; these associations avoided politics. Some of the first hometown and regional associations grew out of farm labor work crews, as discussed in the previous chapter. The Numancia (Aklan/Capiz) Aid Association was founded by thirteen Numanciahanons in a Tracy asparagus camp in 1935; the Iloilo Circle was founded by Illonggos in a Delta farm labor camp in 1939; and the United Sons of Santa Catalina (Ilocos Sur) was founded in 1939.[35] Other Stockton-based hometown associations founded before World War II include the Sons of Naga, the Siquijor Association, the Clarin-Tubigon-Calape Association (Bohol), the Sibunga (Cebu) Association, the Bohol Circle, the Sons of Batac (Ilocos Norte), and the Talisay (Cebu) Association.[36] At a time when Filipinas/os lacked access to medical, life, and burial insurance or the support of their immediate families and the large extended families of their barrios, the hometown, mutual aid, and fraternal organizations played a critical role in the survival of their members and in ensuring that the major milestones in their lives would be celebrated and recognized—stepping in to help in the same way that family and extended kin would have done in the Philippines.

Fausto Rabaca, one of the founders of the United Sons of Catalina, remembered that his peers felt the need for an organization when their town mates began dying or got sick or hurt in work or car accidents. "We have to go from friends to friends to beg for help for the funeral of [someone]," he said.

For many years, the Sons of Catalina paid generously for their members' weddings, christenings, childbirths, and all medical and burial expenses.[37] Nemesio Paguyo had joined a Filipino Masonic organization in the 1920s, but when its members moved to work in other parts of California, the group splintered. He soon found friendship and comfort in other organizations: "I joined the other organizations because probably we need some friends, and to help one another in case of trouble, to help if we needed help." Often, Paguyo said, members have a meal together in a restaurant after their meetings. "So you are not alone in there," he said. "You have somebody to go to and depend on if you have any trouble."[38] Most hometown associations hosted annual benefit dances, picnics, and other social events that assuaged members' homesickness, loneliness, and boredom.

Jimmy Ente remembered how single Filipinas/os depended on these mutual aid associations to serve the role that large families would have in the provinces, especially at times of death. "A lot of the Filipinos joined these clubs because they found that if someone died, if you got twenty, thirty guys in a club, they are going to help pay for this burial," he said. "So, that was the main purpose of this whole big organization, not only to get together, but to pay for these guys that passed away; and for the family, give them some money 'cause back then you didn't have no welfare."[39] Fred Cordova remembered that his mother, Lucia, helped to gather money to bury destitute Filipinas/os at either of the two funeral parlors in downtown Stockton, Chapel of the Palms and Frisbee-Warren. "Mama was always running around asking for [donations], meaning for every time there was a lot of people who might have died, there was always a collection that was given to pay for the expenses," he said.[40]

Like organizations and lodges, new Filipina/o institutions and annual events built community ties. In August 1929 Dr. Felipe Amistad opened the Filipino Hospital in Little Manila, which could hold thirty patients and employed mostly white workers.[41] However, the hospital had closed by the early 1930s. Dr. Macario Bautista, a Tagalog immigrant from Imus, Cavite, arrived in Stockton at that time and began to provide medical services to the community. Bautista, a former pensionado, had studied at the College of Physicians and Surgeons in San Francisco. His close relationship to his hundreds of Filipina/o patients, and his sympathy for their plight, would push him into labor organizing; in 1939 he became president of the Filipino Agricultural Laborers Association.[42] In 1937 the community hosted a carnival in Stockton that featured entertainments, rides, sports contests, queen contests, and — for the first time in Stockton — Filipina/o American theater. For the carnival, Lucia F. Cordova, a Visayan immigrant, wrote a play called *Walang Kama-*

tayang Pagibig (Love eternal), a Tagalog *zarzuela* (a Spanish form of theater); most of the cast members were young, second-generation Pinays and Pinoys.[43]

Community-based newspapers provided an important means by which community members could come together. A number of immigrants, including D. L. Marcuelo, Manuel Insigne, Juan Dionisio, and Vicente Roldan, had backgrounds in journalism and writing. They published a number of monthly, weekly, and biweekly papers in Stockton beginning in the 1920s, such as the *Philippine Advertiser, Three Stars, Torch, Filipino Pioneer, Philippine Record, Philippine Examiner,* and *Philippine Journal.* These newspapers were among approximately forty Filipina/o American publications that were published in the early twentieth century across the United States, according to the scholar Jean Vengua Gier.[44] These publications provided an important source for news of the Philippines and of Filipina/o American community life in Stockton and other West Coast cities. Many of the newspapers, such as *Three Stars,* published stories in English, Tagalog, Cebuano, and Ilocano. Editors of these papers, especially Marcuelo and Dionisio, were also involved in community organizations and labor organizing.

Bound together by kinship and regional origin and further united through the bonds created by newspapers, fraternal lodges, institutions, and organizations that brought them together as Filipinas/os, Pinays and Pinoys in Stockton found comfort and community with one another during the most violent and terrifying years of the Depression and anti-Filipina/o sentiment. The Little Manila neighborhood served as an important place in which immigrants could create community and define a unique Filipina/o American identity.

EL DORADO STREET: CROSSROADS OF FILIPINA/O AMERICA

When Filipinas/os began arriving in Stockton in the early 1920s, the city had more than 40,000 residents. Most were European immigrants or white transplants from the South and Midwest, with smaller populations of African Americans, Mexicans, Chinese, Asian Indians, and Japanese. The city boasted a bustling downtown with almost a hundred hotels and luxurious department stores that served the city's white middle and upper classes. But Stockton's whites maintained Jim Crow segregation: people of color were barred from living north of Main Street and were forced to live south of downtown, in the West End or Skid Row neighborhood. This area had a statewide reputation as a district of saloons, gambling and card rooms, houses of prostitution, and dance and pool halls, holdovers from the heady gold rush days. But it was also full of residential hotels, inexpensive diners, lunch counters and restaurants, soda fountains, grocery stores, and movie theaters, as well as ethnic neighborhoods.[45] A corner of the West End was dubbed the "Oriental Quarter" and was home to Chinatown and Nihonmachi, or Japantown.

The only place Filipinas/os were allowed to live and congregate in downtown was south of Main Street, in the Oriental Quarter. Most institutions, businesses, and gathering places outside of the campo and the streets of the West End were strictly forbidden to Filipinas/os. Many hotels in downtown Stockton outside of the West End refused to rent rooms to them. Immigrants recalled seeing the signs that warned Filipinas/os not to let the sun set on them in the city. "I personally saw signs on some hotel stairways on El Dorado Street, openly discriminating against Filipinos saying 'Positively No Filipinos Allowed' or 'No Filipinos or Dogs Allowed,'" remembered Anita Bautista, a second-generation Pinay (see figure 16). "When we frequented the upscale department stores in Main Street, we were made to wait or were not served. When Filipino youths cruised Pacific Avenue on the north side [of town], they were told by police to 'go back to your own side of town.' Stockton real estate ads openly stated 'No Filipinos.'"[46]

The Oriental Quarter was first settled by Chinese immigrants in the late nineteenth century. Early Chinatown was bordered by Market Street on the north, Lafayette Street on the south, El Dorado Street on the west, and Hunter Street on the east.[47] Japanese immigrants began moving into rooming houses and apartments on Market Street in 1907 and created a thriving district they called Nihonmachi, or Nihonmachi, centered just west of Chinatown between Market, El Dorado, and Washington streets.[48] When Filipina/o immigrants began moving into the district in the 1920s, they settled near the intersection of El Dorado and Lafayette streets. By this time, the borders of Chinatown, Nihonmachi, and the budding Little Manila district often blurred and overlapped, with Chinatown concentrated near Market and Washington streets, Nihonmachi's center near El Dorado and Market streets, and Little Manila centered at El Dorado and Lafayette streets. The relegation of Filipinas/os to downtown's poorest area mirrored the pattern of Filipina/o segregation in other West Coast cities such as San Diego, as Rudy Guevarra's research has shown.[49]

By the late 1920s, this neighborhood was being called Little Manila or El Dorado by Filipina/o immigrants. In the years before World War II, the Little Manila district became famous nationwide among immigrant and second-generation Filipina/o Americans for its concentration of Filipinas/os and their businesses and institutions. The district encompassed the blocks between Center and Hunter streets and Washington and Hazelton streets. El Dorado Street became the central artery of Little Manila, as it was of Stock-

16. This Stockton hotel, photographed in 1945, was one of many area establishments, including restaurants, public pools, department stores, and other public places, that barred Filipinas/os. Courtesy of NPA FANHS.

ton itself. The city's founders named the street as a reference to Stockton's key role in the gold rush (El Dorado literally means land of gold). But for Filipinas/os crowding into Stockton in the late 1920s, it might have seemed like a bitter irony that they were segregated to the poorest part of the city on a street named for a land of riches. By the late 1920s, Little Manila had been carved up according to language and regional origin; Ilocanas/os gathered on one side of Lafayette Street, Visayans on the other side.[50]

When Carlos Bulosan's character Carlos arrives in Stockton in midsummer, in *America Is in the Heart*, he goes to El Dorado Street to find other Filipinos. "It was like a song, for the words actually mean 'the land of gold,'" Bulosan writes. "I saw many Filipinos in magnificent suits standing in front of poolrooms and gambling houses. There must have been hundreds in the street somewhere, waiting for the night. . . . I walked eagerly among them, looking into every face and hoping to see a familiar one. The asparagus season was over and most of the Filipino farmhands were in town, bent on spending their earnings because they had no other place to go."[51] El Dorado Street had a similar pull for the Monrayos of Honolulu.

In 1928, when Enarciso Monrayo arrived in Stockton with his young daughter, Angeles, and his son, Julian, he went immediately to El Dorado Street, where he ate at Filipino restaurants, played pool in halls owned by Filipinas/os, and looked for others from his province.[52] Anita Bautista, who lived on a campo and visited Little Manila on weekends with her father and uncles, remembered a self-reliant and self-sustaining community: "Filipino Americans developed pride in their own enclave to support the needs of the Filipino community. This Filipino enclave had all of the businesses needed to sustain its people."[53]

My father, Ernesto Tirona Mabalon, who left Manila and arrived in Stockton in 1963, told me that the name Little Manila probably came from the fact that there were so many Filipinas/os standing on the streets in the neighborhood that it literally looked like a street scene in Manila. "It was almost people-to-people carpeting," recalled Fred Cordova. "Especially during asparagus seasons, when the crops were up. The men would come back into town. They had no place else to go but El Dorado."[54] The Pinoy journalist Frank Perez moved from Los Angeles to Stockton toward the end of World War II and was struck by the massive crowds in Little Manila. In one of the often sarcastic and witty columns he wrote in the monthly *Philippine Examiner*, published in Stockton, he noted that he was growing to like his new hometown, dubbing it the "Capital City of the Filipinos in the West Coast." "The endless parade of our sun-bitten brothers on El Dorado Boulevard," he wrote. "The inviting tingling of silver from dens of game-of-chance."[55]

In the neighborhood's earliest years, Chinese and Japanese residents had an almost total monopoly on its businesses. Before World War II, Japanese managed more than fifty-four single resident occupancy–style walk-up hotels in the Oriental Quarter and the larger West End district.[56] Chinese and Japanese businesspeople ran all of the drugstores, hotels, grocery stores, dentists' offices, doctors' offices, midwife businesses, hospitals, restaurants, photography studios, garages, laundries, dry goods stores, beauty shops, florist shops, barbershops, and soda fountains in the Oriental Quarter, leaving Filipinas/os with little room for expansion in the early 1920s.[57] In the fall of 1928, before the Depression caused farm wages to fall precipitously, the editors of *Three Stars* encouraged Filipinas/os to capitalize on the business opportunities presented by the more than 5,000 Filipinas/os who called the area home. "The

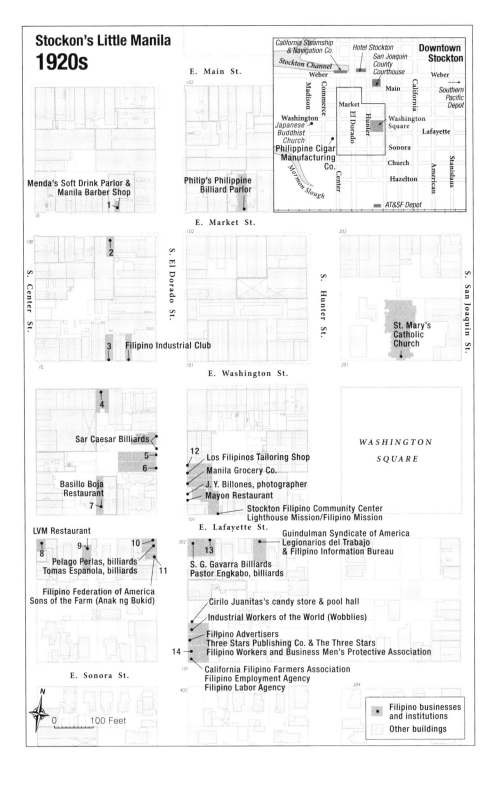

Stockon's Little Manila
1920s

Menda's Soft Drink Parlor &
Manila Barber Shop
1

E. Main St.

Philip's Philippine
Billiard Parlor

E. Market St.

Philippine Cigar
Manufacturing
Co.

Downtown Stockton

California Steamship
& Navigation Co.
Stockton Channel
Weber

Hotel Stockton
San Joaquin
County
Courthouse
Main

Weber

Southern
Pacific
Depot

Madison
Commerce

Market
El Dorado
Hunter

California

Washington
Square

Lafayette

Washington
Japanese
Buddhist
Church

Sonora

Church

American

Stanislaus

Center

Hazelton

Mormon Slough

AT&SF Depot

S. El Dorado St.

2

3 Filipino Industrial Club

S. Center St.

S. Hunter St.

E. Washington St.

S. San Joaquin St.

St. Mary's
Catholic
Church

4

Sar Caesar Billiards

5
6

Basillo Boja
Restaurant
7

WASHINGTON

SQUARE

12 Los Filipinos Tailoring Shop
Manila Grocery Co.
J. Y. Billones, photographer
Mayon Restaurant
Stockton Filipino Community Center
Lighthouse Mission/Filipino Mission

LVM Restaurant

9   10
8

Pelago Perlas, billiards
Tomas Espanola, billiards   11

Filipino Federation of America
Sons of the Farm (Anak ng Bukid)

E. Lafayette St.

13

Guindulman Syndicate of America
Legionarios del Trabajo
& Filipino Information Bureau

S. G. Gavarra Billiards
Pastor Engkabo, billiards

Cirilo Juanitas's candy store & pool hall

Industrial Workers of the World (Wobblies)

Filipino Advertisers
Three Stars Publishing Co. & The Three Stars
14 Filipino Workers and Business Men's Protective Association

California Filipino Farmers Association
Filipino Employment Agency
Filipino Labor Agency

E. Sonora St.

N

0   100 Feet

• Filipino businesses
  and institutions

  Other buildings

3. Little Manila in the 1920s. Filipina/o American businesses began cropping up in the early 1920s near the Chinatown and Japantown neighborhoods around El Dorado and Lafayette streets in downtown Stockton. SOURCE: POLK CITY DIRECTORIES, 1920–29. MAP BY BEN PEASE.

Numbers within parentheses indicate the businesses' chronological order at the sites.

1. (1) V. G. Mapa (barber); (2) Menda's Soft Drink Parlor and Manila Barber Shop; (3) V. J. Mafea (barber) and Respicio Santos (pool hall)
2. (1) E. V. Aception (barber) and Steph Perez (shoe shiner); (2) Philippine Barber Shop; (3) Estrella Trinidad (shoe shiner) and E. D. Medallo (barber)
3. (1) International Photo Studio; (2) P. R. Montano; (3) J. M. Castillo
4. Marcelo Robinal (restaurant)
5. Pedro Caballo (bootblack)
6. (1) Concepcion Angel (pool hall); (2) Bueno Nemecio (pool hall)
7. (1) Basillo Boja Restaurant; (2) International Café
8. (1) Hotel Franklin; (2) Agapeto Restaurant
9. (1) Cotleco Ernado Restaurant; (2) LVM Restaurant
10. (1) C. Desano; (2) Sar Caesar (cleaners)
11. (1) Rizal Barber Shop; (2) Auntentico Romeo (barber); (3) Filipino Federation of America; (4) Sons of the Farm (Anak ng Bukid)
12. Martisano Eugenio (shoe shiner)
13. P. D. Lazaro (tailor)
14. (1) Sambahang Filipino Mission; (2) Filipino Sales Promotion and Service

Filipinos in the San Joaquin Valley had been, in the past, dilly-dallying on the question of what things are most needed for ourselves," wrote D. L. Marcuelo. He insisted that the community needed practical businesses: "If the Filipinos in San Joaquin Valley ever needed something, it is a grocery store, a dry goods store, and a meat and fish market. Today, we have enough pool halls, restaurants, cigar stands and soft drink parlors."[58]

The earliest Little Manila businesses included the candy store and pool hall owned by Cirilo Juanitas at 342 South El Dorado Street, established in 1922 (see map 3). Another of Little Manila's pioneering entrepreneurs was, like Juanitas, from Antique province: Tomas Espanola, a sakada who had worked as a cook on the Ewa plantation before coming to Stockton in the late 1910s with his wife, Patricia, and son, Tony.[59] Espanola had arrived in San Francisco in 1911 but then returned to Hawai'i to work. He and his wife opened another pool hall, at 303 South El Dorado Street, in 1927. In 1930 the couple and their son were living above that pool hall, along with lodgers named Bruno Dato, Pedro Oposa, Bonansio Sollis, and Marcelino Opialdo.[60]

17. From 1931 to 1983, Pablo Mabalon (on left) served heaping plates of hotcakes, diniguan, and adobo at his popular Lafayette Lunch Counter at 50 E. Lafayette Street. Author's personal collection.

Another early settler was Pastor Engkabo, a Cebuano who was working in the Rindge Tract in the San Joaquin Delta in 1918.[61] In 1927 Engkabo and his family opened a pool hall across the street from the Espanola pool hall, at 302 South El Dorado. Other early businesses include the Filipino Employment Agency (352 South El Dorado Street), established in 1928 by Elino Ninonuevo; the Stockton Filipino Community Center (111 E. Lafayette Street), established in 1926; Sar Caesar's pool hall (223 S. El Dorado Street), 1927; and the Mayon Restaurant (242 S. El Dorado Street), 1927.[62] By 1930 thousands of Filipina/o laborers were living in the dozens of residential hotels in the Little Manila area, and many families had made the neighborhood their home, among them the Arca, Bantillo, Villaruz, Engkabo, and Espanola families.[63]

But with the onset of the Depression, it became almost impossible for Filipinas/os to leave farm work and start a business. One of the few entrepreneurs who did so during the Depression was my paternal grandfather, Pablo "Ambo" Mabalon. In 1931, he bought the Lafayette Lunch Counter at 50 E. Lafayette Street from Margarita Balucas, an Ilocana who, after leaving Hawai'i for Stockton, had made a fortune with the restaurant and a pool hall popular among Ilocanas/os (see figure 17). Pablo drew on his childhood experiences of working in his uncle Sacarias's restaurant in Manila to serve freshly cooked, homemade-style food familiar to Visayans and Tagalogs. By adjusting some recipes, like the one for adobo, he was also able to cater to many different regional appetites. He used the leftover fat from cooking to make his own soap, which he also sold to other Filipinas/os; he made his own dried beef, or *tapa*, by hanging it in the restaurant. The pork blood soup called *diniguan* in Tagalog and Visayan and *dinardaraan* in Ilocano was one of his specialties. By using local ingredients and those harvested and brought in by Filipina/o workers — such as salmon and asparagus — he helped to create a distinctive Filipina/o American cuisine in Stockton. Filipino jazz bands on their way to gigs at the Little Manila dance halls or at community events would stop first to eat at the Lafayette Lunch Counter and check their reflections in the mirror behind the counter.[64] "The first spot [we hung around at] was Pablo's Lafayette Lunch, that corner, where they had the pool hall of that old man before, from Antique," Policarpo Porras remembered, referring to Tomas Espanola's pool hall. "That's the first spot we hung around. So that Lafayette Lunch is the oldest Filipino restaurant in Stockton! It's older than me!"[65]

By making his restaurant not just a café but a community center, Pablo Mabalon had one of the most popular and enduring businesses in Little Manila. Pablo also offered credit and a permanent address to which customers could send their mail while they followed the crops. When Pinoys arrived in Stockton after stints in Alaska or Southern California, they would check for their mail in a shoebox that Pablo kept on the counter. The growing number of restaurants, pool halls, barbershops, grocery stores, and other ethnic businesses in Little Manila served similar roles for Filipinas/os in the neighborhood. They were also informal banks, community post offices, social halls, employment centers, and gathering points for Filipinas/os from certain regions. For example, labor contractors often visited pool and gambling halls to find workers.

By the late 1920s, the pool halls and restaurants opened by early Filipina/o entrepreneurs were joined by more Filipina/o businesses, including additional pool halls, barbershops, grocery stores, newspapers, churches, shoeshine stands, and community halls (see maps 3 and 4).[66] Significant businesses on South El Dorado Street included the Billones Photography Studio at number 240, where many immigrants took formal photographs to be sent back to the Philippines; the *Filipino Pioneer* newspaper office; and the Los Filipinos Tailoring Shop at number 232, owned by the Lazaro family, Visayan immigrants from Iloilo (see figure 18). Dr. Macario Bautista practiced at 241 South El Dorado Street from 1930 to 1941.[67] The neighborhood soon had a national reputation for being the center of Filipina/o life in the United States, not only because there were so many Philippine immigrants gathered

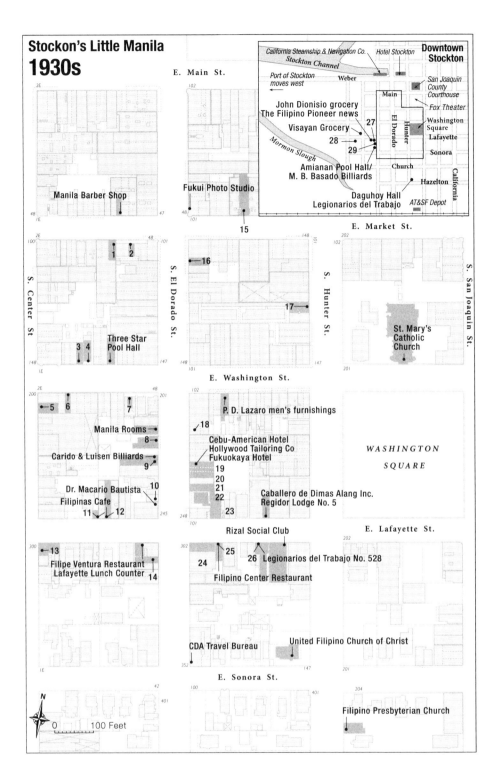

4. Little Manila in the 1930s. Little Manila became a bustling, thriving neighborhood in the 1930s. SOURCE: POLK CITY DIRECTORIES, 1930–39. MAP BY BEN PEASE.

Numbers within parentheses indicate the businesses' chronological order at the sites.

1. (1) Estrella Trinidad (shoe shiner); (2) E. D. Medallo (barber)
2. (1) B. C. Magracia (barber); (2) Victor Ramos (shoe shiner)
3. Melecio Rilorcasa (restaurant)
4. (1) Ray Cruz (barber) and Jos. Francia (pool hall); (2) Pony Recomio (pool hall)
5. M. Robinal (pool hall)
6. (1) Silbia Cristobal (barber); (2) M. M. Balot (barber)
7. Esteban Villanueva Restaurant
8. (1) M. S. Florita; (2) V. Sosona; (3) C. Galea
9. Rado Jos (shoe shiner)
10. (1) Stockton Barber Shop, Sawat Simeon; (2) E. M. Cipano (barber)
11. Isabelo Bautista Restaurant
12. (1) A. T. Licong Restaurant; (2) Francisca Baccus Restaurant; (3) Filipinas Café; (4) Machila Francisco (pool hall)
13. (1) Louis Villanueva Restaurant; (2) L. L. Tactacan Restaurant
14. (1) Sajonia Hispolito Restaurant; (2) S. J. Merida Restaurant; (3) Max Palmos Restaurant
15. Elite Jewelry and Novelty
16. (1) Carrasco Salvador (shoe shiner) and J. S. Mendiola (barber); (2) Bath House Barber Shop
17. A. B. Bantillo (furnished rooms)
18. (1) Marcelina Cordova Restaurant; (2) Charles Toy (fruits); (3) Philippine Barber Shop (Damaso Paminsan)
19. (1) Eugenio Martisano and Philip Gonzalez (shoe shiners); (2) T. C. Lai (Chinese); (3) Policarpo Parino (shoe shiner); (4) Chuzo Takahashi (grocer, Japanese)
20. (1) Catalico Maruico Restaurant; (2) E. Bautista Restaurant; (3) V. J. Cabebe Restaurant
21. (1) Mrs. Anastasia Villamor Restaurant; (2) Casil Norman (restaurant); (3) Delgado Benigno (pool hall)
22. Mrs. Melecia Alcos Fish
23. (1) V. S. Cabaccang Restaurant; (2) Francisca Baccus Restaurant
24. (1) Inez Marmelino (pool hall) and Damaso Paminsan (barber); (2) Bert Magracia (barber)
25. (1) Filipino Center Restaurant; (2) Dumangas Restaurant
26. (1) Legionarios del Trabajo No. 528; (2) Caballeros de Dimas Alang Inc.; (3) Regidor Lodge No. 5; (4) General Ricarte Lodge #36
27. (1) Garcalea Mocordo (pool hall); (2) Tigayon Pool Hall
28. Hotel Dorin
29. G. R. Rabang Restaurant

18. The Lazaro family owned the Los Filipinos Tailoring Shop, shown here in the early 1930s, at 232 South El Dorado Street. Placido Lazaro (on left); his wife, Juliana (third from left); and their daughter, Asuncion Guevarra (Nicolas), in the white dress, hailed from Iloilo, Panay. The Pinoy and Pinay penchant for sharp suits and beautiful Filipina dresses kept the shop bustling. Photo by Frank Mancao. Courtesy of NPA FANHS.

in one place but also because nowhere else in the nation were there so many Filipina/o businesses and institutions.

In the decades before World War II, Chinese, Filipina/o, and Japanese businesses competed fiercely for the Filipina/o dollar in Stockton. In 1930 after a visit to Stockton, the researcher Wood observed that Filipinas/os had a difficult time staying in business in Little Manila because they competed with Japanese and Chinese entrepreneurs, and Filipinas/os in business in Little Manila complained of the disloyalty of Filipinas/os in the district. In ads taken out in Filipino newspapers, businessmen pleaded with their compatriots: "When you come to town, see us and patronize your people."[68] Japanese merchants marketed themselves to Filipinas/os by serving Filipino dishes. In an ad in the *Philippine Advertiser*, a Japanese restaurant at 37 East Lafayette Street boasted in Tagalog that it served both "Sukiyaki at Sinigang." Sukiyaki is a Japanese soup with thinly sliced beef; *sinigang* is a sour soup popular in many regions of the Philippines.[69]

Claro A. Candelario, owner of the Luzon Café at Lafayette and El Dorado streets (see figure 19), complained bitterly of this disloyalty—of the tendency of Filipinas/os to patronize Japanese and Chinese businesses rather than Filipina/o ones, especially restaurants. He often gave credit to jobless Filipinos at his restaurant. But when Filipinas/os came to town on payday, he would see his debtors dining at Chinese-owned chop suey restaurants.[70]

19. Claro Candelario hosted the Consul General Benigno Pidlaon at his Luzon Café at 112 East Lafayette Street in 1951. The restaurant and Candelario are featured in Carlos Bulosan's *America Is in the Heart*. In the book, a character named Claro, a political activist, comforts the character named Carlos with food and political education at the restaurant. Courtesy of Angelina Candelario Novelozo and FANHS.

Nonetheless, quite a few of the entrepreneurs endured. Though many businesses were short-lived, some lasting for less than a year because of the Depression, there were several dozen Filipina/o American businesses and community organizations crowded together at the intersection of Lafayette and El Dorado streets on the eve of World War II.

Despite the West End's reputation as a vice district, Gussie Bowden, a second-generation Pinay, remembered Little Manila as a warm, comforting ethnic neighborhood. "In playing baseball, going to dances or picnics, we were all Filipinos," she wrote. "All my friends, girls and boys, were Filipinos. We bought from Filipino businesses — gas, food, clothing, dry cleaning, haircuts. Surrounded by Filipinos while walking down El Dorado. . . . I felt everyone was the same."[71] Second-generation residents coming of age in the 1930s and during World War II saw El Dorado Street in its heyday. "Filipinos were very close-knit," remembered Flora Arca Mata, a Pinay born in Hawai'i but raised in Stockton. "We all lived on Lafayette Street." The Arcas lived in Little Manila. In 1930 the family consisted of Flora; her mother, Victoria; her sisters Felicidad, Conching, and Mary; and her brothers, Cecil and Albert.[72]

From the 1940s to the 1960s, Peter Jamero often made the fifty-mile drive north from Livingston to Stockton with his father and uncles to attend boxing matches, dances, and parties; to recruit workers for his parents' labor camp; and to go to the Fourth of July celebrations. "El Dorado Street was the closest thing to the Philippines I could imagine," he wrote in his memoir, *Growing Up Brown*. "It was crowded mostly with Filipino farmworkers eager to meet up with longtime kababayans and admire the dalagas, who were invariably chaperoned by their parents. . . . Stockton was an exciting place in the 1930s and 1940s." Jamero's uncles, flush with asparagus earnings, would treat him to Chinese food at Gan Chy Restaurant or a movie at the Star or Lincoln theaters. The newer Main Street theaters were off limits to Filipinas/os, Jamero recalled.[73]

Rizaline Raymundo also has fond memories of El Dorado. "El Dorado in Stockton was, to me, the 'Filipino Highway,'" she remembered. "We'd go down the street and there was nothing but Filipinos in the street, on the corners, along the sidewalk, and we'd go down the street, and call out, 'Hi! Hi!' and my father would honk the horn. It was just like going on a parade. That's what made me feel comfortable with Stockton and I really have a soft spot for it, a sense of family."[74] As a teenager, Jerry Paular, a second-generation Pinoy born in Hawai'i of Tagalog and Visayan parents, pumped gas at the MacArthur Garage, located at El Dorado and Lafayette streets. "I fell in love with the lights of El Dorado Street," he recalled. "If you would have seen El Dorado Street you would have fell [*sic*] in love with it because everything was Filipino. There was so much hustle and muscle and commercial activity. There were thousands in the street. All of the businesses, 95 percent of them, catered only to Filipinos. If you were in business . . . you catered to the biggest dollar that floated around the Valley."[75]

Filipinos took every opportunity to wear their glamorous McIntosh and, later, zoot-style suits on El Dorado Street and took great care to look sharp when they came to town, Fred Cordova remembered.[76] Paular recalled that after work most Pinoys would check into a hotel room, bathe, and then don a well-cut, immaculate suit. "They came into town in a fashion that even Hollywood took a note of it . . . and Filipinos didn't emulate them in the way they dressed. The public imitated the Filipino," Paular recalled (see figure 20).[77] But they even made sure they were stylish when they were working, Fred Cordova remembered. "They had a flair, the men," he said. "They just didn't put on a hat, it had to be tilted the right way, it had to be the right kind of straw hat with the right kind of crown. They couldn't look like bums out in the field because if you were lucky you had women working out in the fields, single women. Now you're not going to look like a bum out there in

20. Pinoys gather in front of the Fukuokaya Hotel at 228 S. El Dorado Street in the heart of Little Manila in the late 1920s. Courtesy of FANHS Stockton.

the middle of an onion field if that's the only way you're going to have some kind of socializing with women."[78]

Holidays, Christmas, and New Year's Eve drew Filipinas/os from all over the West Coast to Little Manila. And they looked forward all year to the Fourth of July, which was tantamount to an annual gathering of the entire West Coast Filipina/o American community on the streets of Little Manila.[79] The timing of the holiday was perfect, because the asparagus season ended in late June, and most of the workers took a break before leaving for the Alaskan salmon canneries. Organizations used the holiday to hold benefit dances, and reunions of people from particular hometowns or regions. Filipinos were "all dressed up like hell," remembered Pete Valoria. "People came from all over—Fresno, Delano, Tracy, San Jose, San Francisco," he remembered. "You should see all the Filipinos! This is the hometown of the Filipino. Stockton!"[80]

The Stanford-trained sociologist and labor organizer Trinidad Rojo studied Little Manila in 1937 and found massive numbers of Filipinas/os in the Little Manila district around the Fourth of July. On one afternoon in late June, on just one side of one block, he counted approximately 263 Filipinos. They were "standing, eating, passing, sitting, playing on the sidewalk, in the cars, in the pool halls, in the restaurants, in the stores on one side of a block of the street."[81] Farmers, foremen, and contractors—like Ceferino Jamero of nearby Livingston—used the holiday to recruit workers. "Fourth of July in Stockton was the busiest day of the year for Filipinos," Ceferino's son, Peter

21. Members of the Filipino Federation of America march in a Fourth of July parade in the late 1930s or early 1940s. Courtesy of FANHS.

Jamero, remembered. Peter felt intimidated by the urban Filipina/o Stocktonians: "They seemed so much more sophisticated in dress and in their knowledge of music and cultural fads."[82]

In the city's Fourth of July parade up and down Main Street, so many Filipina/o American organizations had marching contingents and floats that they soon had their own competitive division, a tradition that lasted well into the 1960s. The local Filipina/o community's embrace of the city's annual performance of American identity and citizenship demonstrates the ways in which Stockton Filipinas/os strove to prove the fitness of the Filipina/o character. They wanted to support Philippine independence and demonstrate the patriotism and loyalty of immigrant Filipinas/os and their children to the United States, and their fitness for U.S. citizenship. The parades also gave Filipinas/os an opportunity to show off the strength and numbers of their many organizations, and to wear with pride their regalia or matching outfits. In 1939 the second-generation group Daughters of the Philippines raised funds to buy matching capes that they proudly wore as they walked down Main Street. The Filipino Federation of America's enormous marching band was singularly impressive (see figure 21). "They went out in their band with purple and gold capes," recalled Fred Cordova. "I mean, that really looked sharp. And then the different fraternal groups came out with their hats and their caps."[83] Jerry Paular said that the federation's contingent, hundreds strong and marching in perfect sync in their matching outfits, probably scared the local Klan out of its plans for anti-Filipina/o violence.[84]

Boxing matches also brought thousands of Filipinas/os together in downtown Stockton. From the 1920s up to the 1960s, the golden age of Filipina/o boxing in the United States, thousands of Filipinas/os flocked to Stockton to watch champion Filipino boxers pummel Mexican and white boxers. The filmmaker Corky Pasquil dubbed the period "the Great Pinoy Boxing Era" in his film.[85] Whenever a Filipino boxer was on the ticket, cheering Filipina/o boxing fans filled local arenas such as the humble Oak Park Arena in Central Stockton and the Civic Auditorium, built in the 1920s and located just north of Little Manila. According to España-Maram, American soldiers brought Western-style boxing to the Philippines.[86] Talented Filipino boxers mixed American-style boxing with Philippine punches and techniques, and promoters began to bring these fighters to the United States. The first to achieve massive fame in the United States was the flyweight Francisco "Pancho Villa" Guilledo, a native of Iloilo, who stood five foot one and weighed 110 pounds.[87]

By the 1920s, these Filipino boxers became beloved brown heroes and inspired immigrants and second-generation Pinoys to begin to train. Fred Pearl, a Stockton boxing promoter, organized amateur nights for aspiring local Filipino boxers. The boxer with the best bout of the evening was paid $10, a princely sum in a 1935, when farmworkers were lucky to make a dollar a day in the fields.[88] Even my maternal grandfather, Delfin Paderes Bohulano, tried his luck as an amateur boxer in Los Angeles and Stockton in the 1930s.[89] For young Filipinos, boxing was a way out, a way up, wrote Peter Bacho. Moreover, it gave Filipinos an opportunity to "be judged as an equal, which every Pinoy craved." Bacho wrote that the ring "suspended society's norms, those rules that embodied a racial and social order favoring color over ability, class over potential."[90] Matches that pitted whites and Filipinos were the biggest draws. "Filipinos versus white fighters are . . . their favorite matches," a Filipino promoter noted.[91] The boxing ring gave Filipinos a place to physically respond to racism without fear of reprisal. In boxing, Bacho notes, "a Filipino could beat a white man with his fists and not get arrested."[92] These matches reflected the larger battles in the outside world. A victory against a Mexican fighter symbolized the crushing of Mexican labor competition; knocking out a white fighter challenged ideologies of white supremacy and allowed Filipinas/os to take some revenge in watching one of their own beat up a white man.

To maximize their profit, promoters timed many matches at the Civic Auditorium to coincide with the end of the asparagus season. The Pacific Coast bantamweight champion Diosdado Posadas, called "Speedy Dado," made two appearances in Stockton in July 1931. Dado knocked out Leonard Rahming at the Civic on the Fourth of July, then returned to knock out De-los "Kid" Williams on the 31st.[93] The next year, the Mexican fighter Chato Laredo defeated Speedy Dado in Los Angeles. At the Civic on New Year's Eve in 1934, thousands of vengeful Filipinas/os cheered as Star Frisco, an up-and-coming Filipino fighter, knocked out Laredo.[94] On Fourth of July in 1939 at the Civic, Ceferino Garcia, a Cebuano fighter, bested Bobby Pacho with his sweeping "bolo" punch, a hybrid of a right hook and uppercut that used the sweeping motion of cutting sugar cane with a bolo knife (a long machete) — which he said he learned while working on sugar plantations.[95]

The boxing matches served to bring Ilocanas/os, Visayans, and Tagalogs together as Filipinas/os, according to Jerry Paular. Boxing "was the first common denominator without question that brought them together more than anything else," he said. "They didn't care if a person was Visayan, Ilocano, Tagalog, Boholano, Cebuano . . . and you can just see the expressions on their faces in the auditoriums, and especially when the Pinoy comes out the winner, and Ilocano was embracing the Visayan and the Tagalog!"[96] By the 1940s and 1950s, homegrown Stockton Pinoy boxing champions such as Jimmy Florita, Sleepy Caballero, and Joey Caballero were drawing crowds and creating excitement.[97] In school, the day after a big victory, we "walked down the hall, chins raised high," Paular said. "Jimmy put the whole school on notice that we've arrived."[98]

The immense racial pride that Filipinas/os drew from boxing victories against whites led the State Boxing Commission to announce an immediate moratorium on boxing matches featuring Filipino pugilists the day after the January 29, 1930, bombing of the Filipino Federation of America building. William H. Hanlon of the Boxing Commission reasoned that bouts of Filipino and white boxers had the potential to cause race riots, especially if the Filipino boxer was victorious.[99] "The little islanders, in the lightweight classes, have a disagreeable habit of winning their fights," according to an editorial in the *Stockton Daily Evening Record*.[100] However, boxing simply made too much money for everyone to be shut down, and Filipinos were soon fighting again at the Civic. Boxing and its intrigues were as important to the local community as the labor struggles and exclusion and independence battles of the 1930s. España-Maram writes that Filipina/o boxing fans in Stockton boycotted the Civic Auditorium briefly in 1937 when they suspected promoters were rigging contests. Those most angered were those who had made bets.[101]

Boxing matches brought the entire community — children and women, as well as men — to the Civic Auditorium. The arrival of world-class Pinoy boxers like Francisco "Pancho Villa" Guilledo, Ceferino Garcia, Dado Marino, Speedy Dado, Small Montana, Lil Dempsey, Bernard Docusen, Young Tommy, or Flash Elorde at the Civic would spur an exodus from the dusty nearby towns and campos to Stockton.[102] Piling into their cars to go Stockton for a boxing match at the Civic, for Peter Jamero, was "always a celebration." The weekend ritual for his family included a stop to eat Chinese food and visit with other Pinoys on El Dorado Street in Little Manila before or after the match.[103] If the Filipino boxer won, Little Manila would explode, with boisterous crowds in the streets. "When uncles would come, we'd be thrilled to death because we knew we'd be able to go the boxing, because they would come and take us," Anita Bautista remembered. "They'd say, 'Oh, let's go Chop Suey.'"[104] The West End's numerous Cantonese chop suey joints were enormously popular. Bautista and her family, like many others, favored Gan Chy Restaurant at 215 South El Dorado Street, which featured favorites like chop suey, sweet and sour pork, and *hum ha yuk* (pork braised in *bagoong*, or shrimp paste). The restaurant had private booths enclosed in curtains.[105]

The beginning of the end for the golden years of Pinoy boxing came as Filipina/o exclusion cut off the annual infusion of new blood into the sport, and World War II cut short the rise of any new boxing stars. Interest in boxing waned as attention shifted from the fighting in the ring to the real, bloody fighting of the war. Wartime jobs in the defense industry, military service, and, after the war, citizenship and the possibilities of better-paying jobs gave Filipina/o Americans other ways to make money besides the boxing ring.[106]

PORNADA! LOSING IT ALL IN THE GAMBLING DENS

Boxing was only one of the draws of downtown Stockton. After work in the campo, Pinoys often went wild gambling in Chinese gambling halls in Little Manila. "After staying [in camp] for awhile I would come to the city and spend all that I had made in just a few days, and so would my friends," one Filipino admitted in 1930. "One week I spent $45. After being in the camp for a long time you go wild the first few days in the city."[107] Pete Valoria arrived in Stockton in 1927, after stints in Los Angeles and San Francisco, and fell in love with Little Manila. When his work as a cook in a local restaurant ended, he would go immediately to the *sikoy sikoy* (gambling halls) to play gin rummy. "I think Stockton is the best—I've been to San Francisco, I've been to Hollywood, but there's no fun there," he remembered. "We have a lot of fun here in Stockton. I love Stockton. If you're not gambling, you play pool. You are tired at nighttime, you go to the dancing halls." Valoria remembered playing pool in Stockton with another Ilocano, Carlos Bulosan, when the two were teenagers.[108] "Oh, the life of the Filipino! Oh God!" Policarpo

Porras remembered. "Every Filipino here before the war, when they are crazy about dancing, gambling, you know—they lost a lot of money. The payday [come], then [he sees] the taxi dancer over there and he just signs the check. The check is gone! But not me!"[109]

The Stockton police department told a researcher that Filipinos were jailed for gambling more often than for all other crimes. "He gives some trouble with regard to sex offenses, and occasionally the Filipinos—as do other foreign people—fight among themselves. There are usually knife fights. But, in gambling, the Filipino is a constant offender," said an officer in 1930.[110] P. C. Morantte, a writer for the *Filipino Pioneer*, visited a gambling hall in Stockton's Chinatown in the spring of 1938, at the height of the asparagus season, when thousands of Filipina/o laborers were in town. Morantte observed one Pinoy, still in his work clothes, who spent all of his money on the "Pai-Q [sic]" betting (also known as Pai-Gow, a Chinese dominoes game). When he spent his last cent, he remarked, "God-demit, hindi pa ito manalo, ay, na pornada ang one week ko sa asparagus!" (Goddamn it, I didn't win this! For nothing, one week of my wages in the asparagus!) Morantte pitied the asparagus workers, who came to town, "working hard and throwing their money away."[111] He estimated that from two o'clock in the afternoon, when most asparagus workers came into town, to midnight, the gambling house owners had made $1,000 from Filipino workers. The next day, workers would return to the gambling halls and attempt to win back their lost wages. It was a tragic cycle.

By the late 1930s, Stockton's Filipina/o American community organizations had begun to voice opposition to the vice industries, such as gambling, taxi-dance halls, and prostitution, in the hope of preventing the exploitation of Filipinas/os in the Little Manila district and quelling anti-Filipina/o sentiment. Stockton's Chinese vice lords were the main culprits, reformers claimed. Much of the Chinese and Filipina/o friction in the Oriental Quarter and Little Manila was tied to the gambling halls. In 1924 a fight in a gambling hall sparked a "wild race riot" between Filipino immigrants and Stockton Chinese. The *Stockton Daily Evening Record* characterized the ensuing violence as a "small war" that involved more than 200 Filipinos and "Chinamen" at 102 East Washington Street, in the heart of Chinatown. The fight erupted when two Filipinos allegedly held up two Chinese gambling hall operators. It took squads of police with billy clubs and shotguns to subdue the violence. Three Filipinos were taken in for questioning and were found guilty.[112]

In *America Is in the Heart*, Carlos becomes embroiled in a violent gambling dispute in a Stockton Chinese gambling den and finds refuge and home in Claro's café, where Claro warns Carlos to avoid being exploited. "Stay away from Stockton, stay away from the Chinese gambling houses, and the dance halls and the whorehouses operated by Americans," Claro says. "Don't come back to this corrupt town until you are ready to fight for your people."[113] Bulosan's Claro was based on a real person—Claro Candelario, the owner of the Luzon Café—but he was also modeled on the many Filipina/o reformers who expressed disgust at the ways the Chinese gambling lords in Stockton fleeced gullible Filipino immigrants out of thousands of dollars every year.

In 1930 the leadership of the Anak ng Bukid appealed to local officials to close the Chinese gambling dens to Filipinas/os, to no avail. "During our fight to close the Chinese gambling dens to Filipinos, I had had many exciting as well as funny experiences with some of the City Officials," Luis Agudo wrote in a letter to the researcher James Earl Wood in September 1930. "I am now convinced that the two peoples, Americans and Filipinos, can not live side by side in harmony. Because racial problems will forever be a sensitive problem between peoples who emerged from different origins."[114] Despite Agudo's efforts, the city remained a wide-open town, in part because local officials were among the most corrupt in the state. In 1942, Carey McWilliams wrote that though gambling was illegal, Stockton police and city officials looked the other way. Corruption was rampant in the police force and city politics, and "various interests" encouraged gambling as a way of keeping the Filipino workforce in Stockton.[115]

The exploitation of Filipinos by Chinese gambling hall operators became a paramount concern in the late 1930s. In 1938 a convention of national Filipina/o American leaders in Sacramento estimated that Filipina/o laborers were spending more than $2 million annually in the gambling, pool, and dance halls and houses of prostitution in the Oriental Quarter.[116] *Three Stars* hinted that a special arrangement had been made between Chinese gambling hall owners and the police: "Carloads of Filipinos, arrested in gambling dens, are daily dumped into the jail in Stockton. Filipinos in these places are being arrested and charged with vagrancy, yet gambling operators and henchmen are 'immune.' Arresting Filipinos in these places develops into a business proposition, it swells the coffers of the city in the form of fines which bring in thousands of dollars."[117] Policarpo Porras also suspected corruption in the Stockton police: "That's a racket by the city and the owner of the gambling, you know. Once a month, you know, they raid. About 15 guys go to jail, go to court, then they put them back again. And the next hour they open again."[118]

In 1938 the local journalists Vicente Roldan and Simon Bellosillo estimated that Filipina/o workers had contributed a total of $42,930,000 to the Stockton economy. They came to that conclusion by estimating the Filipina/o population in San Joaquin County and the average wages earned each year.

The highest wages were paid before 1920, when Filipinas/os could earn $5 per day. Those wages plummeted at the onset of the Depression, when workers made approximately 12 cents per hour. "In view of the velocity of the spending habit of the Filipinos, not even a millionth part of these moneys have reached their native country," Roldan wrote. "It is very evident, therefore, that the local merchants, business men and manufacturers benefited."[119] But the merchants, businessmen, and manufacturers were not the only Stockton businesspeople who benefited from Filipina/o spending. Prostitution and taxi-dance halls in the Oriental Quarter drained thousands of dollars from Filipina/o earnings annually.

LOVE, COMPANIONSHIP, AND SEX IN LITTLE MANILA

Prevented from marrying whites by the state's strict antimiscegenation laws and hindered by the extremely imbalanced ratio of Filipinas to Filipinos in the community, single Filipino men turned to prostitutes and dancers for hire to ease their loneliness and fulfill their desires for romance, sex, and love. In the taxi-dance halls that proliferated throughout downtown Stockton and other working-class urban districts in the early twentieth century, men bought tickets to dance with women for a few minutes at a time. The name taxi dancer derives from the fact that the dancer is paid much in the way a taxi driver is paid for length of service.[120] Most taxi dancers were working-class white women (many were daughters of European immigrants); smaller numbers of them were Mexicans and African Americans. All of the dancers were considered "trash" by middle-class and elite whites.[121] Almost no Filipinas worked in dance halls; strict Catholic culture and elders forbade such work. Moreover, Filipinas did not need dance halls to attract Filipino attention, as I will discuss in the next chapter.

There were several taxi-dance halls in the Oriental Quarter by the mid-1930s, all seeking to capitalize on the Filipino demand for companionship. The Lu-Vi-Min Club, located at 20 East Lafayette near El Dorado Street, was named after the major regions of Luzon, Visayas, and Mindanao, but it had Chinese owners at first (by late 1937, a Filipino named G. E. Lagrimas was running the club). Another club was located at Hunter and Lafayette streets. In most of the clubs, a live band played popular jazz tunes of the day, though some establishments made do with a phonograph. After the day's work was done, and particularly on the weekends, thousands of Pinoys would converge on the Little Manila district, dressed in their best suits, ready to go to the taxi-dance halls. Inside the smoky halls, where Pinoy bachelors could enjoy a moment of intimacy, it was possible to spend several days' earnings on the dance tickets, the source of a saying that was popular among the members of that generation: "dollar a day, dime a dance."

Anita Bautista recalled that one of her uncles, Segundo Bautista, was such a smooth dancer that he was nicknamed "Ballerino." Handsome Uncle Segundo personified the suave Pinoy of the years before World War II. "He was always ready each evening, dressed in his $100 McIntosh suit, expensive Florsheim shoes, cologned with Tabu, his hair pomaded with Three Flowers and his hair carefully parted with a straight piece of wire he used just for this purpose," Anita wrote.[122] Modesto Lagura, from Calape, Bohol, spent many nights at the dance halls. "Well, the Filipinos got no wives," he recalled with laughter. "So we go to the hotel and that's it. Happiness, then go home. As long as you got money to pay." After his job at a cousin's Filipina/o grocery store, he went immediately to the Rizal Social Club, which was open every night. "That's where all my money was spent," he said. "I don't save nothing, because, you know, women. You have to be so nice. And we'll go eat. And the dancing. That's where all my money went. I got broke. I always have nothing saved."[123]

It was this situation—poor Filipinos made penniless by the vice industries—that many Filipinas/os condemned. For the thousands of bachelor Filipinos looking for companionship, prostitutes and taxi-dance halls provided intimacy, however fleeting.[124] España-Maram writes that the dance halls "legitimized the creation of desire and sensuality denied them in their everyday lives."[125] The Filipino desire for sex and dancing with white prostitutes and dancers enraged white communities wherever Filipinos engaged in taxi dancing, from Stockton, Seattle, and San Francisco to Chicago, where Filipinos made up a significant portion of the patrons of taxi-dance halls.[126] Pinoys especially desired blondes, who, they believed, most embodied white womanhood and were therefore forbidden fruit.

As noted in chapter 2, enraged white Stocktonians racialized Filipinos as either hypersexual or impotent monsters. A manager at the Big Three Labor Company in Stockton dismissed stories of Filipino virility by saying that a "number of Filipinos can be satisfied in the time it takes to satisfy one white man."[127] Filipino-white relations at once astounded, bewildered, and angered working-class white men. "Those Filipino boys are good dancers too," said a homeless white man. "They can dance circles around these 'white' boys, and the white boys don't like it—especially when the Filipinos dance with 'white' girls, and that's what most of it is."[128] In March 1930, the *Stockton Daily Evening Record* took a stand against dance halls, writing that the "little brown brothers" who flocked to Stockton were "unassimilable and miscegenation would be unthinkable."[129] But despite these attitudes, Filipinos continued to pursue white women. "You got to sneak!" recalled Policarpo Porras. "You sneak, you hide it because [if] the police see you . . . they will put you in jail!"[130] Porras, who ran a successful barbershop in Little Manila, could afford to go the taxi-dance halls every night. But most Filipinos believed they were fully in their rights to pursue sexual and romantic relations with white women, which was a bold affront to long-established racial boundaries in Stockton.

White taxi dancers and prostitutes soon found that they could easily get Filipinos to spend copious amounts of money on them by making them jealous or playing Pinoys against one another. The savviest dancers called gullible Filipinos "fish."[131] "Filipinos are very emotional," a Pinoy told a researcher in 1930. "Women are his weakness. Indecent women [are] his only chance of association [with women]. He resorts to taxi dance. Women can pick up any Filipino on the streets. Easy prey."[132] Carlos Bulosan's short story "The Romance of Magno Rubio," published after World War II, tells the story of a diminutive, illiterate Ilocano who sends money to a blonde pen pal, only to be heartbroken when she is revealed to be a scam artist.[133] Bulosan's story is an allegory for the betrayal that many Filipinas/os felt about their life in America—from the emotionally empty relations they had with prostitutes and taxi dancers, to the much more shattering realization that life in the United States, as symbolized by the buxom blonde in his story, was nothing like what they had been promised.

Jealousy and bitter fights over girls would sometimes break out among Filipinos, especially between Ilocanos and Visayans, in the dance halls. In July 1937 as more than twenty local Filipinos opposed to the dance halls picketed in front, Juan Rosario and Andres Quimin were arrested and booked for participating in what the local press called "disturbances" in front of the Lu-Vi-Min Club. Both men went to jail and paid hefty fines.[134] In March 1938 the collision of two Pinoys on the dance floor at the Rizal Social Club resulted in a violent altercation in which two other men were hurt; they were sent to the hospital, and the two men who had collided were arrested.[135] Filipinos began to carry knives with them for protection, and Jimmy Ente remembered that there was always a box full of knives confiscated by the front door security men at the Rizal Social Club, which was owned by his father, Demetrio.[136]

Demetrio Ente, a native of Bohol, arrived in Seattle in 1917. There he met and married a Filipina who also hailed from Bohol, and they raised a family. He opened a small restaurant at 605 King Street, in Seattle's Chinatown, and noticed that people loved dancing to the music playing on his jukebox. Ente procured a loan from the local tongs to expand and then renamed his place the Rizal Social Club. After visiting Stockton's Little Manila, Ente decided to relocate there. "At that time, there was Filipinos all over Stockton, you thought you were back in the islands," Jimmy Ente recalled. He remembered arriving by train as a ten-year-old and coming into Little Manila on a hot summer night in 1937. "And it was just — at night time, at summer — and the Filipino people was just all over El Dorado," he said. "You could smell different kind of foods, cigars. The minute you just look out the window, it was something to see 'cause it was alive with people. It was quite a place there." In March 1937, Demetrio Ente leased the Lucca Inn at Weber and Commerce streets and renamed it the Rizal Social Club.[137] He soon ran into opposition from the Little Manila community and from local police.

Most of those opposed to the dance halls and prostitution were Filipinas/os who were devout Catholics and Protestants, and those who worried about the negative publicity the vice industry would bring to Filipinas/os. On March 5, six days before the Rizal Social Club officially opened, the Filipino Community of Stockton, Inc., passed a resolution denouncing the club and sent it to local officials, business groups, women's groups, and local ministers. Undaunted, Ente opened the Rizal, arguing that it was a private social club. He charged $1.00 for a three-month membership. Members could bring guests to the club, and if they wanted to dance, Ente assessed a cover charge of 50 cents. He told the Little Manila newspaper the *Filipino Pioneer* that if a member arrived alone and wanted to dance with any of the girls at the club, it was up to him. Ente hired private security and barred white men to prevent racial violence.[138]

Those who opposed the dance halls were not merely conservatively moralizing; they were deeply concerned for the welfare of the community. Establishments that brought white women together with Filipino men drained the workers of their wages and, even worse, stoked anti-Filipina/o violence. "In all probability, there will be no trouble in the hall itself," Filipino Community president Eddie Wasan told the *Filipino Pioneer*. "However, trouble always arises from the public association of Filipino boys with white girls. There is liable to be plenty of trouble originating in the dance hall and coming to a head far away from the place where it starts."[139] However, there were competing agendas even within the organization. The Filipino Community did not refuse Ente's half-page advertisement in its souvenir program for the First Filipino Carnival in Stockton in 1937. In the ad, Ente extended "a Cordial Invitation to Have a Real Good Time While Visiting Stockton During the Filipino Carnival." Surely, the meaning of "Real Good Time" was not lost on anyone.[140]

Soon after the club opened, a white woman tipped police off that Ente

22. Demetrio Ente moved his Rizal Social Club from Seattle to Stockton in 1937 and built a plush deco moderne club at 138 E. Lafayette Street. The Rizal was a popular taxi-dance hall where patrons bought tickets to dance with women. It became a community hall in the 1950s and a boxing gym in the 1960s. Here, patrons celebrate the Fourth of July in 1938 with a costume contest. Courtesy of FOHP.

had hired her sixteen-year-old daughter to dance, and the police raided the club immediately.[141] Ente was warned that he would be cited if any more minors were caught working at the club. In August 1937 all three dance halls in Stockton were closed because of local tensions over interracial dancing and the "white hostesses" who would be dancing with the Filipino men.[142] The Lu-Vi-Min Club reopened, only to be closed again by another general police crackdown on all of Stockton's dance halls in November 1937, in compliance with the city's newly passed taxi-dance hall ordinance that forbade the solicitation of male persons for dancing in public dance halls. The proprietor, G. E. Lagrimas, and eighteen white girls employed at the club were brought before Judge Cyril B. Kenyon for various infractions, including vagrancy. The *Stockton Daily Evening Record* reported that the girls "paraded smilingly to the bench" and that the smiling judge, after commenting on their beauty, dismissed all charges and ordered them all to leave town. Lagrimas, like Ente, protested that he was running a private social club, not a public dance hall.[143]

Though the police routinely closed dance halls in Little Manila, including his own, Demetrio Ente decided to build a new one, a private club for members only, not a public dance hall, in order to comply with the city ordinance. In the fall of 1937, he formed a corporation with a local contractor, J. C. Nunley, and the next year, opened a sleek new Rizal Social Club at 138 E. Lafayette Street, in the heart of Little Manila.[144] When the sleek deco moderne club opened, it was billed as the first air-conditioned dance club in America (see figure 22).[145] Although it catered specifically to Filipinos, even

23. The jazz pianist Ernie Hernandez had been a pensionado who found his way to Stockton in the 1930s. His jazz band—which also featured Cornelio "Charlie" Bautista on tenor sax, Pedro Corpuz on bass, and Eddie Navarro and Patero Bolong on trumpet—was a fixture at the Rizal Social Club. Courtesy of the Angelina Bantillo Magdael family collection.

Japanese Americans living in nearby Nihonmachi, such as Nelson Nagai's Nisei father, were members and patrons of the club.[146]

The dance halls also provided a place for local Filipina/o musicians to play, as España-Maram points out. The music at the Rizal Social Club was provided by a seven- to nine-piece jazz band led by Ernie Hernandez, a pianist (see figure 23). Nelson Nagai remembers that the band would eat and practice first at the Lafayette Lunch Counter, then walk across El Dorado Street to the Rizal Social Club, where they would begin playing.[147] Several Filipino jazz bands called Stockton home, and the city became a hub for Filipina/o American jazz musicians. The local Tenio family was famed for their talent. A jazz pianist named Rudy Tenio and his sister, the jazz singer Josephine Tenio Canion, performed at many Filipina/o and mainstream jazz concerts.

Ente's new club stayed open because he paid the famously corrupt Stockton police officer Jack O'Keefe large sums of cash to look the other way. "You couldn't get in that dance hall without getting searched by the police," said Jimmy Ente. "Who was at the door was Jack O'Keefe."[148] O'Keefe eventually became chief of police. Police continually raided the Rizal Social Club, but the raids were largely for show. Ente eventually became so rich that he paid $60,000 for the most opulent mansion in Stockton, the Wong Mansion on Clay Street, and diversified his investments into onion fields, two auto garages, and two Little Manila hotels. The demand for businesses that offered

Pinoys gambling, dancing, and women did not abate until well after World War II. In 1948 Ente invested $175,000 into building the cavernous Filipino Recreation Center next door to the Rizal Social Club. The hall hosted taxi dancing, Filipina/o social dances, union meetings, and Filipino movie screenings.[149] The ground floor was a gambling hall. The building also included private upstairs rooms for high rollers. From the 1990s to 2011, the Emerald Restaurant operated in the building. After the Rizal Social Club closed in the 1950s, the building became a boxing gym until it was shuttered in the 1980s.

Dance halls were only one of many venues where Filipinos could find companionship. For sex, they could go to dozens of brothels throughout the West End. It was an open secret that gay men gathered in front of the Fox Theater on Main Street, and some Filipinos could be found there, looking for male companionship.[150] Some taxi-hall dancers worked as prostitutes, so when the dance hall closed, Filipino men invited the women to their hotel rooms in Little Manila. For a night, white women charged $2.50; African American and Mexican women charged 50 cents.[151] Brothels were located throughout Little Manila, and Filipina/o families sometimes lived in awkward proximity to them. In the 1940s Fred Cordova and his parents moved into a former brothel at Market and Washington streets, and his mother's friends visited often. "For first couple of days or so, we had a couple of women visiting Mama," he remembered, laughing. "There was a knock at the door. A Pinoy comes in. Steps in for a few minutes and looks at all the women, [and says,] 'I'll take this one. No, no, no, no. All right, I'll take that one,' and I said, 'Manong, this is not [a brothel] anymore. This is a house we're living in.'"[152] Cordova said that he and his mother later found a suitcase full of condoms in the apartment. His mother, Lucia Cordova, was a devout Roman Catholic, and she turned one of the rooms in their apartment into a chapel full of religious statues, perhaps as a way to cleanse the home of its prior taint.[153]

In 1930, when asked by a researcher if most Filipinos in Stockton would go back to the Philippines, Felixberto Tapia smiled sheepishly. "Most of them would," he said. "But there are many boys, like myself, who wouldn't want to go back and face their parents. We couldn't tell them some of the things that we've done."[154] The first decades of Filipina/o settlement in Stockton were full of tantalizing new experiences for these mostly young and single men. More often than not, however, immigrants experienced crushing disappointment and disillusionment. But as Filipinas/os struggled to build a community across regional and linguistic barriers, white supremacists in Stockton endeavored to crush it by creating an atmosphere of racial terror.

Despite the fun of gambling and dancing in Little Manila, life on the streets of downtown Stockton before World War II could be precarious. "After the bombing of the Filipino club here, some of these men on the street remarked that if they had blown up all the Filipinos over here it would have been a damn good thing for the country," said the manager of a labor company in Stockton in 1930.[155] When Angelina Bantillo Magdael was a young girl living in a rooming house in Little Manila in the late 1920s, her father often came home late at night with chilling news that he would whisper to her mother: someone had been "*bug-bug*," or beaten, by a white man. This happened so often that Angelina came to distrust her father's stories. But when she worked at the Sharpe Army Depot in nearby Lathrop in the 1960s, she overheard a white man in the lunchroom boasting that his favorite pastime was to go down to El Dorado Street with brass knuckles to beat up Filipinos. Enraged and emotional, she was then convinced that her father had told the truth.[156]

A week after the Watsonville riots, a reporter blamed anti-Filipina/o sentiment and racial violence on jealous whites and credited the American colonial regime for inculcating a love for all things American in Filipinas/os. "No Filipino has been condemned by the mass opinion of his Nordic California neighbors for relapsing into Tagalog tribal custom or for starting an Igorrite [sic] head hunting expedition in the wilds of the San Joaquin Valley, or for tryin [sic] to introduce the fashionable residents of Los Angeles to the Moro outdoor sport of running amok," wrote Duncan Aikman. He pointed out that as a result of their American education and tutelage, Filipinas/os embraced the consumer and popular culture that pervaded American life in the 1920s and were really no different from white working-class people in doing so. All young working-class men in the United States yearned to wear the latest fashions, take girls out on romantic dates, and dance with attractive young white women in dance halls. What enraged white men, Aikman pointed out, was the fact that suave Filipinos all did these things better than they did. Filipinas/os were being demonized not because they were "practicing unfamiliar Oriental customs but for practicing American ones, in some cases better than the Americans do themselves."[157]

It should have come as no surprise to most educated Americans that Filipina/o immigrants would eagerly embrace all that America offered them, because the immigrants' teachers had promised them a future of liberty, equality, and the pursuit of happiness. Their American colonial teachers had told them only about the success they would surely experience in the United

States, not about the racism, racial customs, and hierarchies they would encounter in the metropole. Filipinas/os in Stockton spoke English and paraded down El Dorado Street wearing flashy, well-cut suits. They pooled their money to buy new cars and flaunted their romantic and sexual prowess with white women. They established businesses in Little Manila, had children, and intended to stay and make Stockton their home. To make matters worse, they quickly understood the power of labor unions by the late 1920s, built solidarity, and had the audacity to strike for higher wages at opportune moments.[158]

The problem with Filipinos, it seemed to white Stocktonians, was that they did not know their place in the racial hierarchy: they thought themselves equals to whites. "He has helped build this Valley," admitted a local farmer. "But the Filipino is crowding out both the Mexicans and whites. He drives in the best cars and wears the best clothes. He's runnin' things here. A Filipino chambermaid over here showed me [her Filipino employer's] wardrobe of five suits and five hats, and so on, and when he went to bathe he had silk underwear."[159] Furthermore, the ease with which Filipinas/os associated with white women startled white men in Stockton. "They won't stay to themselves," complained a white fruit worker in 1931. "They want to step right in amongst whites. A Filipino asked my sister to dance at a street dance and [I] took a poke at him. They think they're just as good as you are."[160] The *Stockton Daily Evening Record* complained that Filipinas/os expected equality: "The insistence of the Filipinos that they be treated as equals by white girls has been the chief cause of friction between the races here."[161] The thought of mongrel children of what were called white trash and brown monkeys was abhorrent to many whites. Even those sympathetic to Filipina/o problems complained of the immigrants' audacity. Writing in *Sociology and Social Research* in 1931, the sociologist Donald Anthony identified the "Filipino" problem: "He will not 'take his place' as the Oriental races have done."[162]

To put Filipinas/os in their place, Stockton's political elite, white mobs, and police created an atmosphere of extreme racial repression. Theaters, hotels, restaurants, and stores above Main Street were segregated or off limits to Filipinas/os altogether. The elegant Fox Theater on Main Street had segregated seating until well after World War II. "I recall when I went to the upscale Fox, a Main Street theater, Filipinos and other minorities were not allowed to sit in the downstairs center section of the theater," remembered Bautista. "We were relegated only to the side rows against the walls or to the upper parts of the balcony."[163] The city's only bowling alley barred Filipina/o entry. Signs, posters, and handbills appeared in Stockton periodically that appealed to Filipinas/os to return to the Philippines.[164] Anti-Filipina/o sentiment in the city was so durable that even during World War II, when many Americans began regarding Filipinas/os in a more positive light as a result of the Bataan Death March, Stockton maintained its rigid segregation. In 1945 photographers from *Look* snapped a photograph of a hotel that had proudly emblazoned "Positively No Filipinos Allowed" on its entrance.[165]

In the early years of Filipina/o settlement in Stockton, Visayans and Ilocanas/os blamed one another for behavior that provoked anti-Filipina/o repression. "The Ilocano who came here [before], the discrimination is not bad, you know," said Policarpo Porras. "But when the people from Hawaii [came], you know, those sakadas, they are ignorant people. That's what started the discrimination in town." But Porras later realized that all Filipinas/os, regardless of regional origin or class, were lumped together. "Now when you are a Filipino . . . as long as you are a Filipino, you are discriminated [against]," he said.[166] The 1926 New Year's Eve race riot and the bombing of the Filipino Federation of America building were only two of the many instances of racist violence targeted at Filipinas/os in Stockton in the prewar years.

Police waited at Main Street with billy clubs for Filipinos who dared cross that street, the city's Mason-Dixon line, which separated white Stockton from the rest of the city. "They don't respect much [Filipinas/os]," said Eudosia Juanitas about the Stockton police. "Sometimes they kick [us]!"[167] One old-timer remembered: "Filipinos couldn't cross Main Street or else there would be big trouble. . . . The cops then were really mean. Before, when we were standing on the sidewalks — there were so many Filipinos standing on the sidewalk like that — nobody could pass by, so the cops would get mad 'cause they [Filipinos] were blocking the sidewalk and they would pick you up. Police would beat them up. Filipinos who didn't work would get picked up for stealing. Detectives would beat you up if you were with a white woman, 'cause they thought you were doing something bad."[168]

Marauding white mobs went to El Dorado Street to taunt and beat Filipinas/os standing on the street, harassing them with names like "brown monkey." Atanasio Alcala wrote letters to the editor and short stories that described the violence experienced by Pinoys in Little Manila. "All the Americans were just beating up the Pinoys," said Alma Alcala, Atanasio's daughter. "I have some [of his] stories, [and he writes] of the cops just brutalizing the Filipinos there on El Dorado Street because there were so many of them. They didn't have anywhere to go, they didn't have anything to do. And just standing there was a crime."[169] Buster Villa, a second-generation Pinoy, also recalled that police arrested Filipinos at random who were standing on Little Manila streets, packed them in the Black Maria, or paddy wagon, and took them to the county jail.[170]

In the mid-1930s, Nemesio Paguyo and some friends were at a pool hall near the border between white and brown Stockton when a group of white boys burst in and beat them up. Undeterred, Paguyo and his friends went to a pool hall even closer to white Stockton, at Stanislaus and American streets. The mob soon burst in again and tried to beat them up once more. "But then we were prepared," he remembered. "When they come in, you know those pool cues—we used that [sic] to hit them, hit them American boys. We hit them bad, some of them. The policeman had to come around."[171] Surprisingly, the pool hall owner testified that the Filipinos were acting in self-defense, and Paguyo and his friends were not jailed. Filipinas/os were not easily intimidated by white violence but took care to avoid going to town alone. Most Pinoys made sure to bring at least one other person—a friend, relative, or town mate—with them to downtown in case they needed any kind of help.[172]

Instead of coming to their defense, elites in the Philippines instead blamed working-class Filipinas/os for their plight. Only a few months after he blasted American racism as responsible for the Watsonville riots, Jorge Bacobo, dean of the law school at the University of the Philippines, identified gambling and fraternization with white women as the reason why Filipinas/os were treated so miserably in the United States. The gambling in Stockton was the Filipinos' "greatest curse," Bacobo wrote, noting that he had heard of one Stockton Filipino who had lost $12,000 and was in an insane asylum. "While a majority of Filipinos in the United States are honest and hardworking, there is an increasing minority whose misconduct has vividly given the American people a wrong impression of Filipino character, capacity and culture," Bacobo wrote. Moreover, he blamed anti-Filipino sentiment on Filipinas/os' expectations of being treated as equals, Filipinos' associations with white women of "doubtful character," and their fights with whites as the reasons for being "shunned and despised." "It is absolutely useless to go on with the independence campaign unless at the same time we try hard to solve the disgraceful conditions produced by the growing number of Filipinos in America," he concluded.[173]

Even the resident commissioner Joaquin Miguel Elizalde had little sympathy, though he was charged with the supervision and care of Filipinas/os in the United States (beginning in 1937, only one resident commissioner was appointed per year). Francisco Varona, a staff member at the commissioner's office, told a newspaper that the prejudice against Filipinas/os "has been brought about by the past conduct of our countrymen, who, without proper guidance or better example, showed irresponsibility and inability to adapt themselves to conditions and have discredited the Filipinos in general." The blame lay with the Philippine colonial government, Varona argued, which allowed "thousands of discreditable Filipinos to go to the United States." In so doing, they had presented "the worst possible propaganda for our country among the masses of the American people who have come into contact with them."[174]

EXIT THE FILIPINA/O

As discussed in chapter 2, the national movement for Filipina/o exclusion that began in the late 1920s gained steam as the Depression worsened. Most of the politicians and groups in the movement—such as the American Federation of Labor, American Legion, Native Sons of the Golden West, eugenicists, and congressmen such as San Jose's Richard Welch and Sacramento's V. S. McClatchy—were veterans of other anti-Asian campaigns.[175] As historians of American immigration policy have pointed out, the testimonies of eugenicists and so-called scientists of race who claimed that the entry of nonwhites would be devastating to the racial makeup of the nation played a central role in the 1924 Immigration Act and the law that eventually excluded Filipinas/os.[176] During the hearings on the Welch bill, Senator Samuel Shortridge insisted that Filipinas/os were racially unfit for citizenship. "Speaking generally, we belong to the Caucasian branch of the human family," Shortridge said. "They of the Orient belong to another and different branch of the human family; and for reasons for which I need not go into, these two branches of the human family are unassimilable."[177]

In 1929 the Commonwealth Club of San Francisco brought together experts in law, medicine, and science to debate Filipina/o immigration. The most incendiary testimony came from David Barrows of the University of California, formerly superintendent of schools in Manila and director of education in the Philippines, who confirmed anxieties about Filipina/o racial difference and Filipina/o hypersexuality. "Their vices are almost entirely based on sexual passion," he reported. "The defects of the race are not intellectual but moral, and it is on the moral side that Filipinos require inflexible standards and constant support." Despite their reputation as good boxers, he concluded that they were weak and diseased, and he opposed Filipino-white marriage.[178] Eugenicists were alarmed at the prospect that the progeny of white trash and Filipinos would become American citizens. In 1931 the eugenicist C. M. Goethe of Sacramento characterized Filipinas/os as jungle folk who were vain, lazy, and arrogant. "The Filipino tends to interbreed with near-moron white girls," he wrote, and he warned of "the danger to our future generations" if Filipinos were granted citizenship, as "primitive island folk such as the Filipinos do not hesitate to have nine children." Goethe estimated that at this rate, a typical Filipino married to a white would have 729 descendants, while a white couple would only have 27.[179]

Welch hit on a new solution: if the movement for Philippine independence could be married to the campaign for Filipina/o exclusion, exclusion could gain traction. The Depression brought pressure from farm states regarding imports of Philippine products, and Republican lawmakers began to warm to Philippine independence. In April,1934, Senator Millard Tydings of Maryland and Rep. John McDuffie of Alabama authored a successful independence bill. The Tydings-McDuffie Act provided for the independence of the Philippines in ten years, changed the status of Filipinas/os from nationals to aliens, and limited immigration to fifty per year. The bill was then sent to the Philippine Senate for approval.[180]

As Congress awaited the Philippine Senate, there were several hundred Filipinas/os on steamships en route to the West Coast. Among them was seventeen-year-old Primitivo Gonzales of Numancia, Capiz, who left Manila for San Francisco on April 18, 1934, on the USS *President Hoover*. He listed his final destination as Stockton. The Philippine Senate ratified Tydings-McDuffie on April 30. When Gonzales left Manila, he was a national owing allegiance to the American flag. Overnight, he became a deportable alien under the provisions of the 1924 Immigration Act. On May 9, 1934, Gonzales and 143 other Filipinos aboard the *Hoover* were brought to the detention station built on Angel Island in San Francisco Bay in 1910, where they were detained and questioned. Gonzales, who had only $10 in his pocket, told immigration officials that he was to meet his uncle, Saturnino Turipiel. His permanent address in the United States was 50 East Lafayette Street, my grandfather Pablo Mabalon's restaurant. Gonzales and the other Filipinas/os in his situation appealed their detention, and the Immigration and Naturalization Service (INS) paroled them to the custody of the International Institute (a leftist immigrant advocacy organization in San Francisco) and ordered them to return to Angel Island until their appeals could be ruled on. But Gonzales disappeared, and so did almost all of the several hundred Filipinas/os who landed in Los Angeles, Seattle, and San Francisco the week after the Tydings-McDuffie Act was passed.[181] The INS then embarked on an aggressive manhunt for the almost three hundred Filipinas/os who had been let out on parole.[182]

While the INS scrambled to find them, Welch launched his next anti-Filipina/o campaign: deportation. His Repatriation Act, passed in 1935, provided free transport back to the Philippines for any Filipina/o wishing to return. Section 4 of the act stipulated that any Filipina/o who went back could never return. The INS did allow those Filipinas/os who had been in the

United States prior to May 1, 1934, to go to the Philippines for brief visits and return without having to secure one of the fifty visas issued annually under the Tydings-McDuffie Act.[183] Most Filipinos saw it for what it was: a deportation measure.[184]

Until the program was suspended in 1938, the INS sought to convince Filipinas/os that the act was intended to help, not deport, Filipinas/os. Officials pressured community leaders to write positively about repatriation in Filipina/o American newspapers and to translate the act into different Filipino dialects to be posted in pool halls and restaurants.[185] Officials also embarked on a tour of major Filipina/o American communities to encourage Filipinas/os to apply for repatriation. Edward Cahill, the INS commissioner, took to the radio in the summer of 1935 to assure Filipinas/os that the act was borne of paternalism, not racism. "This act . . . is a Big Brotherly act on the part of the United States, and we ask all our Filipino friends to recognize it as such," Cahill said. "One thing I would like to make absolutely clear is that this departure is purely a voluntary act on the part of the Filipinos. It is not deportation in any sense. There is no compulsion."[186] For three days at the end of August 1935, INS officials set up an information desk at the San Joaquin County courthouse in Stockton to encourage Filipinas/os to apply.[187]

For many Filipinas/os, taking the one-way ticket home meant accepting failure. It was already rather shameful to return to the Philippines without a college degree and a fortune; it was quite another kind of humiliation to have been deported.[188] As a result, response to the Repatriation Act ranged from lukewarm to bitter. The first handful to return to the Philippines sent back word that they were being treated like criminals, confirming Filipina/o suspicions. In 1937 *Filipino Pioneer* reported that Filipinas/os experienced poor food and prison-like conditions on Angel Island, which they called Devil's Island. "If the United States really want us to go home as repatriates—this free transportation is in no way called a favor because we have more than paid for it with our labor in this country—we must at least be given a decent treatment from the officials who are concerned," a Stockton Pinoy wrote in the *Pioneer*.[189] To counter these reports, the INS tried to intimidate community leaders they believed were spreading negative propaganda, including the Roque De Las Yslas of the Legionarios del Trabajo and Manuel Insigne, publisher of the *Philippines Mail*, and pressured President Manuel Quezon, president of the Philippine Commonwealth, to issue a welcome message for repatriates.[190] In "Exit the Filipino," McWilliams noted that Filipinas/os regarded the act "as a trick, and not a very clever trick, to get them out of this country."[191]

Records of the INS show that Primitivo Gonzales applied to return to the

Philippines in 1938 under the Repatriation Act, but he didn't appear at an arranged meeting in Watsonville with an official who was to escort him to his ship. By the end of World War II, the INS had finally given up looking for Gonzales and most of the other Filipinas/os who arrived the week after the Tydings-McDuffie Act was passed. Apparently, Gonzales decided to stay, as did almost every Filipina/o in the country. Only approximately 2,165 Filipinas/os took the offer of the free one-way ticket home to the Philippines, out of more than 150,000 in the U.S. mainland and Hawai'i.[192]

By 1935 life for Filipina/o Americans had reached its nadir, and the year represented a significant turning point. They were now aliens excluded from entry into the United States, criminals deported by the INS, workers exploited by growers and unscrupulous contractors, and targets of the police and white mobs. But instead of returning to the Philippines and the comfort of their families, Filipinas/os in Stockton refused to look back and were fiercely determined to make the city their permanent home. The flowering of Filipina/o American organizations and businesses founded in Stockton in the 1930s was testament to this determination.

CONCLUSION

As they soon learned, their regional origins and class background did not shield immigrants from the rampant and violent discrimination against Filipinas/os in Stockton. All of the immigrants found that their skin color and status as wards of the American colonial state — as nationals — mediated any class or regional difference, or privilege, they might have brought with them from the Philippines. All of them were second-class citizens in the land they had been taught to believe was paradise. In the depths of the Depression, when wages were pitiful and work conditions deplorable, George Montero was struck with a deep wave of loneliness. "I miss my old friends and family," he said. "But then I said, 'Well, if I stayed home I cannot improve myself.' Because I said to myself, 'I got nobody here now to tell me what to do. It's up to me to think of my future.'" After a few years in Stockton, he began to enjoy it. "Because after two years, yeah, after two–three years I start going [out], knowing some Filipinos. Then I start to go to my social affairs like dances. And I feel happy, meeting new friends."[193]

By World War II, most Filipinas/os in Stockton belonged to a fraternal organization, a hometown association, and/or a labor union, and most lived in Little Manila or passed through it regularly. For Filipinas/os living in racially hostile Stockton, these organizations and spaces played a pivotal role in their lives as the economy crashed and the Depression deepened, and as anti-Filipina/o sentiment reached its peak. In addition to providing such basic services as food, shelter, funeral services, and monetary assistance, organizations and community institutions played multiple and pivotal roles in the cultural, political, and personal lives of Filipinas/os in Little Manila. The need for social and economic support was particularly acute, because as aliens, most Filipinas/os were ineligible for New Deal relief.

Moreover, community organizations, the boxing matches, the Little Manila neighborhood, and their labor unions (as discussed in chapter 2) became places for Ilocanas/os, Visayans, and Tagalogs to find solidarity and common ground and imagine themselves as Filipina/o Americans whose lives were open to many possibilities. In these spaces, they rejected the identity of the debased, exploited, faceless laborer hunched over endless miles of asparagus, celery, or beets. Dressed in impeccable suits and moving out of their stifling hotel rooms and into the shade of the palm trees in front of Washington Square Park or in front of St. Mary's Church on Washington Street, or gathered with their friends on El Dorado Street or inside a pool hall or restaurant, Filipinas/os asserted their right to flourish on the streets of Stockton. The work crews, labor unions, and organizations they created strengthened and fostered the development of a distinctive Filipina/o American, Stockton-based ethnic identity and facilitated their further participation in American political and cultural life.

However, Jim Crow segregation limited their mobility within the city to the West End. In Little Manila, Filipinas/os were exploited by merchants, gambling hall owners, prostitution rings, and taxi-dance hall owners and dancers. The enclave could not shelter Filipinas/os from racist violence, as mobs harassed them on the streets of downtown Stockton, and police actively sought to brutalize them. Unions and strikes, the anti-Filipina/o exclusion movement, the 1930 bombing of the Filipino Federation of America's building, the rigid segregation of Stockton's downtown, and the exclusion of Filipina/o immigrants in 1934 and the passage of the Repatriation Act in 1935 brought immigrants together as Filipinas/os. In the face of rising anti-Filipina/o sentiment, labor unions and ethnic organizations bolstered Filipina/o unity, fought injustice, and fostered community.

Even if some Filipinas/os felt that life in Stockton was a gamble, and even when the government offered free passage back home, almost everyone stayed. One factor preventing a mass return was the shame and embarrassment of returning to the Philippines empty-handed, without a large bank account or a college degree. But more important, Filipinas/os in San Joaquin County who refused to take the repatriation money had ceased looking back to the Philippines and expected to make Stockton their permanent home. In the next part, I explore how Filipinas/os, despite the precariousness of their lives, endeavored to grow their community by pursuing romantic relationships, marrying, and creating families as well as durable organizations and more powerful labor unions.

PART II GROWING A COMMUNITY

1930s–1960s

Before in 1929, we are diamonds to the Filipinos.
When you come over here, you are the belle of the town!

— *Camila Carido*

This is the hometown of the Filipino. Stockton.

— *Pete Valoria*

CHAPTER 4

WOMEN, FAMILIES, AND THE SECOND GENERATION

When she was growing up in a barrio in Hinundayan, Leyte, Camila Labor Carido's teachers had told her that gold could be picked up in the streets in America. So when Camila's father, Manuel Labor, asked her to join him in Stockton in 1929, where he had settled after a stint of harvesting sugar in Hawai'i, she jumped at the opportunity. When she and an uncle arrived in San Francisco on June 26, they journeyed immediately to Stockton.[1] Camila, a Visayan teenager with a grade-school education, had a background similar to those of the thousands of immigrants from the Philippines also streaming to the area before World War II. However, because she was a woman in a community made up almost entirely of single men, she occupied a unique place. When she arrived, Pinays were so rare and, therefore, so valuable in the community, they were like "gold" and "diamonds," according to Camila. "Before in 1929, we are diamonds to the Filipinos," she said. "When you come over here, you are the belle of the town!"[2] Within two years of her arrival, she married Leon Carido, a native of the town of Clarin, Bohol (see figure 24).[3] Instead of picking up gold on the streets, she was soon picking and harvesting fruits and vegetables and cooking for work crews in the peat fields surrounding Stockton.

Far fewer Filipinas traveled to the United States before World War II because of narrow gender roles based on Catholic colonial culture that confined them to the domestic sphere, expectations that male immigrants would send money home, and limited financial resources for travel expenses for daughters. As Dorothy Cordova argues, those who did immigrate left the Philippines because of a lack of economic opportunities there, a yearning for an Ameri-

24. Camila Labor, a native of Hinundayan, Leyte, married Leon Carido, a native of Bohol, in 1932 in Stockton. Courtesy of FANHS Stockton.

can education, and a belief in the promise of American opportunity.[4] The majority of the first Filipina/o families to settle in Stockton were Visayans who left the sugar plantations of Hawai'i after the failure of the 1924 strikes.[5] A sizable Filipina/o American population, the presence of other women and families, the availability of year-round work, and the Little Manila community in Stockton helped to make the area an attractive place to these early families. The flow of Filipinas/os to Stockton had as much to do with the desire of immigrants to be close to family members and people from their hometowns as it did with the supply of work.

So few Filipinas arrived, however, that the gender imbalance was staggering. The 1930 Census counted 2,500 women out of a total of 42,500 Filipinas/os in California.[6] Approximately 40 percent of the female immigrants were married and came with their spouses.[7] Outnumbered ten to one in Hawai'i, fourteen to one in California, thirty-three to one in Washington State, and forty-seven to one in New York, and constituting only 7 percent of the Filipinas/os on the U.S. mainland, these women were a tiny minority within a minority. Because of this, most historical accounts of Filipina/o American communities before World War II pay little attention to women's roles.[8] However, I maintain that Filipinas and their Filipina/o American families were at the center of the Filipina/o American world in Stockton.

In this chapter, I argue this extreme imbalance in Little Manila offered Filipinas and Filipinos an opportunity to negotiate and transform gender roles and expectations, forge women's networks as well as community institutions, redefine the contours of the Filipina/o American family, and create and preserve Filipina/o American culture. Because of their rarity, the women wielded significant power within their community and families and were held in the highest esteem as representatives of the women left behind in the Philippines.[9] As a result, despite their small numbers, Filipinas played a critical and central role in constructing the rich and dynamic ethnic community and distinctive Filipina/o American culture and identity in Stockton. Changing perceptions of women's roles in the Philippines and the United States, the extreme imbalance in the sex ratio, the lack of elders who would uphold traditional views, the large number of interracial and interethnic families in Stockton, and the entry of Filipinas into the wage labor market created a situation in which Filipinas/os could reshape and transform ideas about gender, femininity, and family in Stockton. Traditional ideas about Filipina womanhood brought from the Philippines clashed with the material realities faced by Filipino immigrants, creating a conflict between idealized and romanticized notions of Filipina womanhood and the stark reality of Filipina life in Stockton.

I explore here the lives of Filipina immigrant women and of Filipina/o American families in Little Manila, and the second half of this chapter builds on the historian Fred Cordova's understandings of the second generation as the "bridge" between the first-generation immigrants and postwar immigrants. I expand his analysis by examining the lives of second-generation Pinoys and Pinays in Little Manila, and the ways that they engaged in constant negotiation with mass culture, forces of Americanization, and their immigrant parents over gender roles, labor, leisure, courtship, and their roles as second-generation Filipina/o Americans in the ethnic community.

THE NEW FILIPINA

In the first decades of the twentieth century, Filipinas were transforming gender roles and perceptions in the Philippines as they responded to larger historical and economic pressures. The literature on gender roles in the Philippines characterizes women as "queens" of the domestic sphere.[10] The queen archetype might have its origins in many Philippine legends and myths, in which women are highly esteemed or have relative equality with men.[11] According to the historian Encarnacion Alzona, in the precolonial Philippines, women enjoyed equal rights with men, and kinship was traced through both parents.[12] However, feminist scholars such as Fe Mangahas and Elizabeth Uy Eviota note that the precolonial division of labor between men and women "already carried the seeds of inequality" because women were responsible for the domestic sphere while men were responsible for hunting, fishing, fighting, and governing.[13] Spanish friars insisted on a model of Filipina womanhood that required them to be demure, modest, and devoutly Catholic, as was Maria Clara, the fair-skinned, prim *mestiza* heroine of José Rizal's nationalist novel *Noli me Tangere*. A book translated into local languages by Spanish priests, *Urbana at Felisa*, told native girls to observe "modesty in dress, speech and manners; virginity before marriage, patience and obedience at all times."[14] Gender ideologies shifted again as the American colonial regime imported Victorian racial, gender, and colonial hierarchies into the Philippines, with a compulsory domestic science curriculum for girls, as discussed in chapter 1.

By the first decades of the twentieth century, the American archetype of the "New Woman"—educated, wage-earning, athletic, and independent—had become a new model of womanhood for Filipinas.[15] The establishment of coeducational institutions such as the University of the Philippines and Philippine Women's University, hospitals, and the civil service in the Philippines increased the demand for educated women professionals. Upper- and middle-class women began entering universities to become nurses, educators, doctors, lawyers, accountants, and other professionals, and a handful of women went overseas to study as pensionadas.[16] Some Filipinas became entrepreneurs and wage laborers in cities and villages, and a significant number of women became labor union organizers. Filipina suffragists won the vote in 1937. In Manila and Cebu, women founded groups devoted to educational advancement and better working conditions for women and children.[17] Men of the elite classes began to complain that women were becoming too American. "Shall this new Filipina, the unconscious victim of Modernity, be allowed to lose her characteristic simplicity?" a Filipino complained. "Women are already walking about alone, a little handbag under the arm, like a true bold little American missus."[18] Even those emigrants from the remotest villages were exposed to some extent to these transformations in gender roles and opportunities.

LOVE, COURTSHIP, AND MARRIAGE

In the Philippines, courtship and marriage rituals were closely and strictly monitored by parents and family members, as marriage meant the union of two families and their resources. In many provinces in the early twentieth century, courtship (*ligaw* in Tagalog) was a complex process that involved the suitor's providing the girl's family with his labor and gifts of food or farm animals, as well as negotiations between the families over land and dowries. A suitor would customarily bring his parents and a respected, articulate elder to serve as a spokesperson to his prospective bride's home, where he could ask the bride's father for permission to marry his daughter.[19] Such deeply traditional rituals were still observed by some families in Stockton. Bienvenido Magdael brought my grandfather, Pablo Mabalon, to serve as his spokesperson when he asked Anastasio Bantillo for the hand of his daughter Angelina, just after World War II.[20]

For the most part, however, complicated courtship rituals from the Philippines were rendered fairly obsolete in Stockton because of a number of factors. Early on, the community was largely devoid of extended family and elders who could enforce strict courtship rituals. The sex ratio imbalance shifted the balance of power toward women in regards to courtship, marriage, love, and sex. The competition for the handful of marriageable women was intense, and because fathers were so protective of their young daughters, most immigrant Pinoys had no chance at marriage until after World War II, when more women emigrated, the young daughters of the pioneering families came of age, anti-miscegenation laws were struck down, and legislation allowed veterans to bring war brides into the country. And in the early days, even if young men could find romance with a young Pinay, strict fathers preferred to marry their daughters to older, established labor contractors, as I will discuss in greater detail in this chapter.

As a result, Filipinos in San Joaquin County often turned to Mexican, Native American, white, and African American women for sex, love, companionship, and marriage. The sociologist Benicio Catapusan found about two hundred mixed marriages in Stockton in 1939.[21] Although most Filipino men who did marry did so with white women, Filipino-Mexican unions occurred because the two groups spent the most time together at work. Moreover, they shared similar cultural experiences under Spanish colonialism, and most members of both groups were Roman Catholics. Some Filipinos met and married Native American women when they went to Alaska to work in the canneries. But Filipino-white marriage was fraught with danger for the man, and involved incredible sacrifice for both partners. Even marriage between Mexican women and Filipino men was potentially dangerous, if the Mexican woman's skin tone was light. Filipino-white couples walking in the streets of Little Manila could trigger a race riot. White and Mexican women who married Filipinos were often disowned by their families.

This was the case for Francisca Leon, a Mexican American who met José Navalta, a native of La Union, in the cotton fields near Phoenix, Arizona, when she was only fifteen. The couple fell in love, despite her parents' disapproval. They eloped, driving through the night to the closest city that would allow interracial marriage: Lordsburg, New Mexico (see figure 25). Francisca

25. Because California's anti-miscegenation laws prohibited their union, José Navalta and Francisca Leon drove overnight from Stockton to Lordsburg, New Mexico, to marry. They were married on November 26, 1931. Courtesy of Anita Navalta Bautista.

and José settled on a farm labor campo near Stockton, where their daughter Anita Bautista and her eight younger brothers and sisters were born.[22] Many other couples of mixed heritage were forced to marry in New Mexico, since California classified Mexicans as white and anti-miscegenation laws barred marriage between whites and blacks, Mongolians, and, after 1933, Malays. Nine states (Arizona, California, Georgia, Idaho, Missouri, Mississippi, South Dakota, Utah, and Wyoming) barred marriages between whites and Mongolians or Malays. Nebraska barred marriage between whites and someone with one-eighth or more black, Japanese, or Chinese blood.[23] These laws forced Filipino men and their white, Mexican, African American, and Native American partners to travel hundreds, if not thousands, of miles to marry.

Some couples of mixed heritage went to Canada to get married. George Montero and his girlfriend, Corinne Fagan, met at a dance in Salinas in May 1941. George and Corinne planned to be married by a liberal Lutheran minister in Vancouver, British Columbia, on December 9, Montero's birthday. The bombing of Pearl Harbor failed to deter them, and they departed under the darkness of air-raid blackouts. Guided only by moonlight, they drove hundreds of miles to Seattle, and then on to Vancouver. No hotel would let them have a room, so they slept in the car and returned to Salinas the next day. "That was our wedding and honeymoon!" he said.[24] Filipinos were more likely to marry whites, Mexican, and African American women than Chinese or Japanese women because racial hierarchies and sexual stereotyping made parents in the latter two groups unwilling to allow their daughters to marry Filipinos. Moreover, Filipina/o relations with Japanese farmers, labor contractors, and merchants were often antagonistic. Claro Candelario recalls that Japanese merchants and farmers treated Filipinos as if "we are below their feet!"[25]

In early February 1930, soon after the Filipino Federation of America building had been bombed, Filipina/o-Japanese relations soured further when Felixberto Tapia, a Filipino immigrant, eloped with a Nisei girl, Alice Saiki, on February 3, 1930. When Saiki tried to go home to retrieve her belongings, her father hid her away in Sacramento. The father owned a pool hall that served primarily Filipinos. When he kidnapped his daughter, the Filipino community organized behind Tapia and called an immediate boycott of Japanese merchants in the Oriental Quarter in early February 1930.[26] After 1948, when antimiscegenation laws were abolished in California, mixed-heritage marriages in San Joaquin County began to rise. Allison Varzally notes that of the 1,803 marriages in the county from the second half of 1948 through 1949, 9 were Mexican-Filipino couples and 20 were white-Filipino couples.[27] The progeny of these mixed-heritage couples — the mestizas and mestizos — along with the smaller numbers of children born to parents who were both of Filipina/o descent, formed the foundation of the community's second generation. Most bachelor Pinoys, however, persisted in their attempts to marry a Filipina.

The jealousy among Filipinos for the attention of Pinays was intense, Camila Carido recalled. When a new Filipina arrived in town in the 1920s and 1930s, Carido remembered that scores of well-scrubbed, pomaded Filipinos would don their sharply pressed McIntosh, zoot, or double-breasted wool suits, in spite of the burning heat of the Central Valley summer, to impress the woman. Dances provided the best opportunities to socialize, but "when you go to a dance and they ask to dance with you, you have to tell them, 'You are number five,'" Carido said.[28] George Montero remembered feeling frustrated when he went to dances sponsored by Filipina/o community groups or in dance halls. "The problem is that maybe there are 20 to 30 men to one [woman] in a dance," he said. "Maybe half Filipinas and maybe half Mexican Americans. You have to go to her and say, 'May I have this dance?' and maybe they count sometimes and say, 'You are number 7.'"[29] Eventually, the large benefit dances put on by prominent organizations, families, contractors, and businesspeople in Little Manila were not a draw for single Pinoys. "I wouldn't want to go there and dance with them," said one Pinoy of the older ladies. "They're married and they're too old and they don't dance very well."[30]

Filipinas in Hawai'i and the United States quickly realized that because there were so few Filipinas and so many bachelors, they could take their time

26. Asuncion Guevarra left Iloilo, Panay, and arrived in the United States in 1929 with her mother and stepfather, Placido and Juliana Lazaro. She married a local barber, Sixto Nicolas, and they settled in Stockton and raised a family. Here, she is pictured in 1930, running for Rizal Day queen. Photos like these were distributed during queen contests to drum up ticket sales. Photograph by John Y. Billones, courtesy of FANHS Stockton.

and did not have to marry someone they did not love. Moreover, divorce, which was banned in the Philippines, was legal in the United States. "You could say I'm gonna get married, or not, you take it or leave it," Asuncion Guevarra Nicolas remembered. Asuncion remembered that even women who "were not educated" and who were not considered attractive married handsome Filipinos. "Because they loved Filipinas to be their wives!" she said. "So many are after me. I am ugly, I know I do not have looks at all!" (see figure 26). Asuncion was a teenager when she met and married her husband, Sixto Nicolas, in San Francisco, where he was studying to be a barber.[31]

Many of the girls that Pinoys courted from the 1920s to the 1940s were young teenagers, the daughters of the Visayan sakadas who had immigrated to Stockton. "Here, in this distant country, when a Pinay is as young as 12 or 13, she makes her debut in Filipino community," wrote Hellen Rillera, a San Francisco teenager, in the *Philippines Mail* in 1934. "She is immediately swarmed with admirers. An innocent, unknown child, who should be out in the streets playing with youngsters of her own age, is shoved into a world of glamour and sophistication."[32] When she wanted to wait until she was nineteen to marry Rosauro Daclan, Paula Dizon's girlfriends teased her that she would be an old maid. "We had about five in our group of girls," she said. "Some of them fourteen and fifteen years old, and they get married already.

They had children."[33] In Hawai'i, where the sex ratio imbalance was also extreme, the courting of very young girls by older Pinoys came to be seen as evidence of the sexual deviance of Filipino men. However, as the scholar Jonathan Okamura writes, older Filipinos' pursuits of young Pinays were "expressions of their keen desire for family life under historical conditions not of their making in which it was extremely difficult for them to marry." Pensionado Ramon Cariaga, who studied Filipina/o families in Hawai'i in the 1920s and 1930s, writes that Filipina/o families with an eligible daughter found themselves plied with "presents of all kinds from hopeful suitors," from money and groceries to automobiles, jewelry, personal gifts, loans, and favors.[34] Filipinos in Stockton went to similar extremes to impress the families of Filipinas.

Another phenomenon caused by the extremely imbalanced sex ratio in Hawai'i was coboy-coboy, an adaptation of the word "cowboy." This was a type of wife abduction, in which a group of Filipino men would kidnap a Filipina on another plantation. In most cases, the kidnapped woman became the wife of one of the coboys; however, sometimes the woman was raped by all of the unattached men on a plantation. Men fearful of coboy-coboy sent their wives back to the Philippines or left them in the Philippines.[35] Alberta Alcoy Asis recalled that her mother, Tomasa, feared living in the Filipino camps. "My mama said, 'If we live in that Filipino camp, too much trouble,'" Alberta recalled. "Because you know that time in 1910 until 1917–18, all those trouble in there, [because] not enough women." All women were susceptible, she remembered: "So they call that cowboy, they pick the women, even [if] they got husband."[36] Although there are many stories of coboy-coboy on Hawai'ian plantations and even in the United States, most women who left their husbands did so of their own accord, according to oral histories and family stories in Stockton. In her diaries, Angeles Monrayo writes that her father delivered a cruel beating to her mother, Valeriana, when she tried to escape and live with her lover in Honolulu.[37] Filipinos whose wives left them for another Pinoy may have exaggerated the tales of coboy-coboy in order to save face.

Desperate Pinoy bachelors in Stockton knew that Pinays had their choice of men and courted married women, though husbands surely saw this threatening behavior as reminiscent of coboy-coboy. "They do anything to win, as long as they are married to one Filipina," recalled Asuncion Nicolas. "I told them you better watch it, or I'll tell my husband and you'll be walking with no head."[38] Eudosia Bravo, a native of Barbaza, Antique, met and married Cirilo Juanitas, a widower, when he went home to Antique to find a new wife and mother for his four children. She arrived in Stockton in 1936.[39] She avoided going to community dances because Pinoys continued to court her although she was married. "Even if you have a husband, they will court you, because they want Filipino women!" she remembered, laughing.[40] Concepcion Bulawit Lagura came to the United States with her husband in 1938 from Calape, Bohol, and had four children, but she was still pestered by bachelors. "Even if you are married, the boys are after you," she remembered. "That's the truth. Even though you are married, some of them will say, 'When is her husband going to die so I could marry her?'"[41]

Reporters from the Filipina/o American newspapers *Three Stars* and the *Philippines Mail* and periodicals like the *Philippine Yearbook* highlighted the minute details of the life of Filipinas in the Central Valley and Pacific Coast communities, writing about their social activities, birthdays, graduations, romances, and weddings. The press placed Filipinas and their daughters on pedestals, and the pressure from Filipino men on these women to uphold traditional gender roles was intense. All eyes were on their behavior, appearance, social skills, grace, femininity, and personality traits. Rillera criticized the community's surveillance of young Pinays: "From the minute she becomes known in the community, her every step is measured and judged — her faults are exaggerated, her good points mocked. No matter how sweet she may be, no matter what good aims and thoughts she entertains in her mind, there is always something wrong, or so it seems to those who always find something to criticize."[42]

Pinoys who were rejected by women were harshly critical of Pinays to save face. Pinays' growing power frustrated Filipinos, as indicated in an essay in *Sociology and Social Research* by the pensionado Trinidad Rojo, in which he complained that Pinays seemed to be more "fickle" than girls in the Philippines, because "a pretty Filipino girl has several times more admirers than if she were in the Islands."[43] Camila Carido recalls Filipino men giving her a hard time because she was not as "friendly" as they expected her to be.[44] Filipina/o teenagers — both immigrant and second-generation young people — turned to advice columnists for help, much like their young Jewish American and Japanese American counterparts.[45] In columns in *Three Stars* and the *Philippines Mail*, lovestruck Filipinos asked for guidance. "In the Valley of the Moonstruck," a column in the *Philippines Mail*, "Aunt Dearie," an older Filipina immigrant, doled out advice to younger Filipinas/os. "All my friends say I am beautiful and charming," wrote Alicia, a sixteen-year-old from Fresno. "I have scores of boyfriends . . . at present, I am in love with three of them. Everyone is just as good and handsome as the other. I am in a state of quandary about making my choice." Aunt Dearie answered that Alicia had "too many irons in the fire," a common problem among Pinays.[46]

Competition for women could sometimes turn violent and deadly, when jealous Pinoys reacted bitterly and angrily to rejection. Rillera wrote that there would be two hundred men and only ten or fifteen young Filipinas with whom to dance at social gatherings, and men would react violently if they were rejected: "What does the poor girl do but choose one of them; and those who are disappointed lose their tempers, and openly insult or try to injure either the girl or the rivals. Weapons have, too often, threatened many a life—sometimes actually done injury."[47] In the summer of 1929, *Three Stars* reported that in Salinas a Filipino had been fatally stabbed by another Filipino who had become obsessed with his wife.[48] That fall in Vallejo a thirty-six-year-old Filipino shot and killed a fourteen-year-old girl and then turned the gun on himself when she refused his advances.[49] Anita Bautista remembered that one of her mestiza girlfriends was stabbed along with a family member when she refused a proposal from a Filipino elder in the 1940s. The rejection had deeply insulted him, because he had been giving gifts to the girl's family and assumed he would marry her.[50]

"JUNGLE JUSTICE"

One of the most harrowing examples of jealousy over Filipina attention played out in the summer of 1933 in Stockton, when the murder of the twenty-eight-year-old Cecelia Navarro over her alleged infidelity by members of the Caballeros de Dimas Alang (CDA) attracted the attention of the entire West Coast. Navarro, a native of Carcar, Cebu, had left Hawai'i with her family and settled in Stockton in 1918. In 1924 she married an Ilocano farmworker, Ignacio Navarro, and they had four children.[51] In 1928 she and a handful of local Filipinas organized a women's lodge of the CDA—the Maria Clara Lodge—in Stockton. In May 1932 Navarro called the police after witnessing a violent altercation among Filipinos at a boardinghouse in Little Manila. The police arrested four members of the CDA and charged them with the assault and kidnapping of Frank Pepita and A. Perales, who had helped the white wife of one of the CDA members escape from her husband. At their trial, Navarro testified that she had seen the four men kidnap Pepita and Perales, and the four men were sent to San Quentin.[52] After the trial, as Navarro prepared to leave town with her husband, the Maria Clara Lodge of the CDA accused her of adultery, and she disappeared on November 19.[53]

Her body was not found until April 1, 1933, when Pablo Bustamente, a member of the Regidor Lodge of the CDA (a men's lodge), led police to her body in a shallow grave near Leon Quintanilla's labor camp on Jersey Island, thirty-one miles west of Stockton, in the Delta in Contra Costa County.[54] Bustamente told police that the CDA had held a five-hour trial on November 20, 1932, at Redmen Hall in Stockton. He said that, with her hands bound and blindfolded, Navarro was beaten by her lodge sisters and accused of being unfaithful to her husband. The "jury" sentenced her to burial alive at midnight, and her body was taken to the camp for burial. Bustamente claimed that by going to the police he had been marked for death by violating the oath of secrecy of the CDA.[55] Autopsy reports later found that Navarro had died of suffocation.

Three men and four women, all members of the CDA, were arrested and indicted for the murder; they plead not guilty. In testimony before a grand jury, a Maria Clara Lodge leader admitted that the group had tried Cecelia Navarro three times for adultery, based on reports from Bustamente. Navarro had plead guilty, the lodge leader said, and was punished by being forced to crawl on her hands and knees on a floor covered with uncooked beans. The lodge members maintained that her adultery had brought shame and disgrace on the Filipina/o people.[56] Two of the indicted women claimed that it was Bustamente who accused Navarro of infidelity and ordered them to bury her alive, facedown.[57] A week after the indictments, Cecelia Navarro's sisters told the district attorney that she had been kidnapped and accused of adultery by the CDA before.[58]

The murder made front-page news throughout Northern California, which only served to fuel ideas about Filipina/o racial otherness and alien culture.[59] In lurid, sensational stories, newspapers blamed the murder on a fanatical cult engaged in bizarre, barbaric tribal rituals. The *Stockton Daily Evening Record* identified the CDA as the "Kalaya-an" cult and reported that, according to that cult's teachings, if a woman is "unfaithful to her husband, or husbands, the entire tribe will suffer through poor crops and bad trading."[60] The burial, the *Record* wrote, was a form of "Jungle Justice."[61] The *San Francisco Chronicle* reported that the murder had taken place during a midnight ritual by women around a voodoo fire. Newspapers called the crime "barbarous" and "one of the most cruel and inhumane murders ever committed in the state."[62]

The CDA leaders in San Francisco responded quickly by hiring high-powered attorneys, and they condemned the murder publicly.[63] The Filipino Community of Stockton called a meeting of more than a thousand Stockton Filipinas/os, blamed the murder on "irresponsible Filipino characters," and assured everyone that the Filipina/o community in the city considered the crime "despicable." The organization's leaders were also quick to remind the larger public that such practices were not part of Philippine culture and exhorted the larger community to blame only the seven individuals indicted for murder, rather than the entire Filipina/o race.[64]

The entire Filipina/o American community on the West Coast was fascinated by the trial that summer, as witnesses for the prosecution refused to testify, invoked the Fifth Amendment, or began to have memory lapses or difficulty with English. Defense witnesses said that Pablo Bustamente had been in love with Cecelia Navarro, an assertion that Navarro's family denied.[65] When she spurned him, defense witnesses reported, he sought to punish her by forcing her lodge sisters to punish her. The accused maintained that it was Bustamente who strangled and killed Navarro, ordered lodge members to bury her, and then swore the rest of his men's lodge to secrecy under threat of death. Defense witnesses said that after Navarro's death, a drunken Bustamente visited a labor camp on Roberts Island, muttering, "My love is gone."[66] On July 29, 1933, the jury voted to acquit all of the accused.[67]

The ghastly murder of Cecelia Navarro—whether the result of a jealous suitor's revenge or a punishment meted out by a group of Filipina/o lodge members in retaliation for Navarro's incriminating testimony against other CDA members—is an extreme example of the struggles Filipinas/os in Stockton experienced as a result of competition for women's attention, women's power, and the need some Filipinas/os felt to control mainstream perceptions of Filipina/o racial and moral characteristics and fitness for independence and citizenship. The jealousies, power relationships, and gender dynamics in the lodges reflect the complex relationships among Filipinas/os in the community, and between men and women. Tragically, the punishment and murder of a lodge member for violating the lodge's ultranationalist code of morals only served to further embarrass and humiliate all Filipinas/os at a time when the community could least afford bad publicity. In November 1933 Pablo Bustamente went back to the Philippines, and the murder faded from the spotlight.[68]

THE QUEEN OF THE HOUSE: THE WORK
OF MARRIAGE AND FAMILY

The sex ratio imbalance strengthened Filipinas' position as queens within the domestic sphere, where they wielded considerable power and influence. As Fred Cordova wrote, "Pinay mothers . . . decided where the children went to school, what to eat, what to wear, where to live, when to go to church, whether the family could afford to buy things, or whether the children should go to college."[69] "He's the one who wears the pants in the family," said Camila Carido, referring to her husband. "But I am queen of the house, so you better respect me, too! The mother is queen of the house." In America, she continued, unlike the Philippines, Filipino men and women were partners, "100 percent," and "whatever we do, we agree together."[70]

But not every Filipina/o American household shared decision-making and household burdens equally. According to the Filipina feminist scholar Elizabeth Uy Eviota, the Philippine archetype of the mother as queen actually represents "men's ability to shed their responsibility for housework and child care." Eviota argues that the decision-making power held by Pinays increased their workload.[71]

Historians have suggested that the family is a "culture of resistance" for women of color. For Filipina/o immigrants in Stockton, home and family were havens, and a strong sense of family and a reliable kinship network helped Filipina/o immigrants cope with harsh conditions. However, feminist historians also argue that the family has also been a site of oppression for the same women.[72] For example, the burdens placed on Pinays in the decades before World War II could be overwhelming. Eudosia Juanitas, stressed out with caring for eight children, decided to take a short vacation from her family just after the war. "He could not do anything, because whatever I say, I do," she said of her husband's reaction. "You know they value Filipino women so much at that time. He might be scared if I leave him, because taking care of eight children is so depressing and so much work on the nerves." Eudosia returned to her family after her short break.[73]

For Filipinas/os in Stockton, "family" meant more than just the nuclear family, and Filipina/o Americans drew on the power of an extended family network to help them survive. Filipinas had a central role as the gatekeepers of the family network by shaping and controlling family boundaries. Pinays in Stockton became magnets for the many bachelors who yearned for family. When a Filipina/o arrived in Stockton, he or she first searched for blood relatives, then people from the same town and province, and then those from the same region. With single, lonely Filipinas/os in America searching for companionship, even unrelated town mates became like blood relatives. Everyone was adopted into a complex kinship network in which women were the centers. Because women are primarily responsible for the work of kinship, as Micaela di Leonardo has asserted in her study of Italian American women in California,[74] it was the handful of Filipinas who performed the work that maintained the networks essential to the psychological well-being and survival of all Filipinas/os.

Once married, Filipinas were caretakers not only of their immediate family members, but also of this extended network. "We have lots of people who come to our house," said Camila Carido, who, with her husband and five children, lived in a tiny apartment in Little Manila through most of the Depression. "They would say, 'Can we sleep with you and we can help pay the grocery?'" she recalled. "How can they afford to go to the hotel at 25 cents a night? So we have to help them. That's why we always housed somebody. They buy the food, and we cook, and eat. They would bring rice, and I was just cooking and washing and ironing."[75] Angelina Bantillo Magdael recalled that though the Depression years were lean and she had seven brothers and sisters, there were always "others dining around our table," since her mother, Virgilia, was known for her hospitality and cooking. But in the leanest times, sometimes all they had to eat was rice with a little cream and sugar, Angelina remembered.[76]

Filipina/o American families in Stockton and on the West Coast also depended heavily on the *compadrazgo* (the bonds created by godparenthood) system of kinship, deeply rooted in both Philippine indigenous kinship networks and Roman Catholic traditions. Mexican American families relied on the same system.[77] These godparents served as sponsors for various Catholic sacraments: for an infant's baptism, a child's First Communion or confirmation, or a young adult's wedding. Women called the godmothers of their children comadre and men called the godfathers of their children compadre. But the compadre, or cofather, and comadre, or comother, played significant roles in the Filipina/o American extended family that went beyond religious commitments; godparents and their godchildren, comadres and compadres, and godbrothers and sisters became like blood kin. Filipina/o children in the Philippines and the United States called their godfathers Ninong and their godmothers Ninang. Godsisters and brothers called each other Igsoo (or igso) in some Visayan dialects. The relationship between comadres and compadres, as well as that among godsisters, godbrothers, and godparents, was a sacred and "irrevocable relationship," Fred Cordova argues, a relationship as binding as blood.[78] In the absence of elders and blood kin in the United States, comadres and compadres played a crucial role among Filipina/o Americans. Godparents often stepped in when parents died, lost their jobs, or became ill. In the lonely and often uncertain years of early Filipina/o American life, such a bond was invaluable.

Comadres often shared the burdens of reproductive labor—all the labor within the home—with one another, by helping with babysitting and cooking. This was critical, since almost all Filipinas, immigrant and/or American born, worked for wages outside of the home in addition to all of the labor they performed for their families. According to the 1930 Census, Pinays worked in canneries; as farmworkers, contractors, cooks, and bookkeepers; and in service-sector jobs in the food industry as waitresses and cooks or in domestic service.[79] It could be argued that—expected to keep the family together, rear children, and take care of the home, and contribute to the survival of the family through wage work—Filipinas and the wives of Filipino men, like other women of color, never stopped working. Despite their exalted place as diamonds in the Filipina/o community, their work experiences were just as harsh as, if not harsher than, those of their male counterparts. Filipinas/os and their spouses and children formed an economic partnership in order to survive. Louise Tilly and Joan Scott call this strategy "the family wage economy."[80] In the family wage economy, all members of the family pool their income to help the entire family stay afloat.

Many Filipina immigrants were more educated than their husbands, but few women were able to find professional work, especially during the Depression.[81] Though she was trained as a nurse, Eudosia Juanitas was unable to practice nursing until after World War II, when citizenship laws finally allowed Filipinas/os to become naturalized citizens. "When you read books about America, everything is nice," she said. "Then when I arrived here, my God! It's hard because of the prejudice. I graduated [from] nursing [school] but was not allowed to apply for nursing [work] because of the Americans. Even if you had had a career, you could not work in a hospital." In addition to caring for her eight children and husband, Juanitas worked in a celery packing shed in Terminous Island in the Delta, as a crew boss with several men under her and as the farm's bookkeeper.[82] As nationals and, after 1934, as aliens, Filipinas found it difficult to find any work with good pay. "You cannot have any jobs in offices unless you were a citizen of the United States before the war," recalled Asuncion Nicolas. "No matter how intelligent you are, no matter what degree you have. Most of our people who were graduates of the university . . . they were picking fruit in the fields."[83]

For second- and third-generation immigrants in Stockton, college was prohibitively expensive. Mary Arca Inosanto had won a full scholarship to Stanford University but went to work in the fields to help support her family, eventually putting her younger sisters and brothers through college. Mary's wages helped to send her sister, Flora Arca, to the University of California, Los Angeles, in the late 1930s. But when Flora became one of the university's first Filipina graduates, she had to go to the Philippines to find a teaching job because no one would hire her in the United States. When she was hired by the Stockton Unified School District after World War II, she became the first Asian American public school teacher in Stockton. Her sister, Mary, eventually attended the local University of the Pacific and also became a Stockton public school teacher.[84] Like Mary Arca, Angelina Magdael prepared to attend college, but her pragmatic father pressured her to take bookkeeping, shorthand, and typing at Stockton High instead. After graduation, Magdael found a job at the Sharpe Army Depot, in nearby French Camp. "Of course I couldn't go to college, because there was no money, my father was a part-time employee, and times were really tough," she said. "So I had to work, so I went to work right away for the government and in the end I worked there for thirty-nine years. It killed my dreams for college."[85]

College dreams were completely dashed for immigrants and most members of the second and third generation as soon as they married and began having children, as work in the home was constant and grueling. Asuncion Nicolas had to drop out of college when she married Sixto Nicolas. "Really, people think that [women] are not supposed to work," Paula Daclan said. "Like there in the house, you're working! You're not sitting down! There are so many things you have to do."[86] For the women who had to work on farms, such as Eudosia Juanitas, Segunda Reyes, and Camila Carido, the day began long before the sun rose. Since most Filipina/o families had multiple children (for example, Eudosia Juanitas had eight, Virgilia Bantillo had seven, Camila Carido and Asuncion Nicolas each had five, and Segunda Reyes had three), women's lives centered around raising their children. Having so many children meant constant cooking, cleaning, ironing, laundry, and sewing. Carido laughed as she recalled raising two younger siblings and then her own five children without the modern conveniences of disposable diapers, dishwashers, bathtubs, refrigerators, washing machines, electric irons, and television to occupy the children. "Imagine, no Pampers!" she said.[87]

In addition to this household labor, most Stockton Pinays, married or single, worked in the fields. They worked under a blistering sun in horrific conditions, and women's wages were substandard: Filipinas generally earned even less than the average pay of Filipinos, which was 10 to about 40 cents an hour during the Depression. On summer vacations and after school, second-generation Pinays worked to feed their families, buy school clothes and other necessities, and, in rare cases, pay college tuition. Filipina Americans—like most working-class women, no matter what their racial or ethnic group—rarely kept their earnings, and most contributed them to the family pool.[88]

Angelina Magdael began sorting potatoes for ten hours a day in the relentless heat of the summer for Zuckerman Farms in the Delta when she was thirteen. "Sorting potatoes in the nearby islands during the summer was a job any young person would want since there were no other jobs," she remembered. Some women, she recalled, would throw something into the machine to break the conveyor belt so the women could rest.[89] In her later teens, she worked as secretary to the Filipino Agricultural Laborer's Association and in the Filipino-owned ice cream and soda shop on El Dorado Street in downtown Stockton. Her younger sister, Leatrice, worked as a waitress in my grandfather's Little Manila diner, the Lafayette Lunch Counter, through World War II.[90] All Angelina's wages, she remembered, went to their mother, who was the family accountant.[91] Mary Arca Inosanto remembers one grueling summer picking tomatoes to earn money for school clothes. "Visions of sweaters, skirts, shoes encouraged me to bend and grab the first ripe tomato," she remembered. "It was so hot that perspiration was pouring down and I had to stop and wipe my face. This was a delay, and a vision of only one sweater was my goal for the day."[92] Eleanor Galvez Olamit picked prunes in the summers during her girlhood and when she was a young mother. "That's the hardest work, picking prunes," she said. "I cried."[93] "We would sit down in the car, so tired," Camila Carido said of the prune harvest. "Then I got to go home, cook for my father, wash, and iron."[94] The workday began at two in the morning for women in the agricultural camps. "I cried when I get up, I'm so sleepy," said Segunda Reyes. "But here we are. We have to work."[95] Families endured ramshackle bunkhouses, polluted water, and outhouses.

Camila Carido recalled long, hot days in the fields cutting and packing asparagus, while her children waited in the car. Both Reyes and Carido remembered bringing bottles and diapers to the fields because there were no babysitters. "I think we never stayed in one place for a long time," said Reyes. "Two weeks, three weeks at the most. And that was the time during the Depression. Already banks were closing."[96] Because they, too, were paid low wages and suffered poor working conditions in the fields, women supported men's strike activity in the 1930s. During the successful 1939 asparagus strike, Filipino women rallied behind the Filipino Agricultural Laborer's Association. Virgilia Bantillo and many other Filipinas cooked for several days to help feed the thousands of Filipina/o strikers. "Our kitchen was full of activity," recalled her daughter, Angelina Bantillo Magdael.[97]

In addition to wage labor and reproductive labor, many Filipinas were also responsible for organizing the family's finances and budget, a role Filipinas have held, some historians have suggested, since before Spanish colonialism.[98] "I handled all the money, and he worked hard, sixteen hours a day," recalled Asuncion Nicolas. "I paid the bills and everything."[99] This responsibility also led Filipinas to seek out ways to find extra money with which to augment the family's meager earnings. In the late 1930s, Eudosia Juanitas cooked for labor crews in the celery fields of the San Joaquin Delta. As a side job, she sewed mosquito netting to supplement the family budget and grew vegetables to sell. She also later managed the Juanitas Grocery, the family's grocery store in Little Manila that she founded.

In her diaries, Virgilia Bantillo kept records of the earnings of her husband, Anastasio, a tailor who also worked odd jobs. She also recorded the wages of her sons and daughters.[100] And she kept detailed financial records of her side business, making and selling *maduya* (banana fritters) and *lumpia*

(spring rolls) in Little Manila throughout the 1920s and the 1930s. Her husband would take the maduya and sell them to Pinoys in the pool halls for
a few cents. In addition to making lumpia, Virgilia would sell her homemade delicate, paper-thin lumpia wrappers to other Pinays. Her youngest
daughter, Leatrice, was her delivery girl. "I had to walk from our home from
downtown to West Charter Way and brought a package of lumpia wrappers,
which my mother sold a dime a piece," remembered Leatrice. "She'd made
a hundred, so she made ten dollars, I think, for that. And that, you know,
that helped the expenses, [it was] a little extra."[101] But even with her side
business, the Depression was difficult for Virgilia, who was responsible for
the family economy, and the rest of the family. "Very unlucky day for us,"
she wrote in her diary on March 19, 1939. "Broke like anything. I feel blue. I
shed tears."[102]

Some Filipinas turned their business talents into successful enterprises.[103]
Margarita Balucas was one of Stockton's most prominent Filipina businesswomen; she owned a pool hall and the Lafayette Lunch Counter, a popular
Filipino American restaurant she sold to my grandfather in 1931. "Mother had
the busiest pool hall in Stockton," remembered Catherine Bilar Autentico,
Margarita's daughter. Her mother's pool hall was so successful, Catherine
recalled, that she was able to buy a new black Cadillac.[104] Juliana Lazaro —
an Illongga who arrived in the United States in the 1920s with her daughter
Asuncion Guevarra (Nicolas) — opened Los Filipinos Tailoring, with her
husband Placido Lazaro. Eudosia Juanitas started the Juanitas Grocery in
the late 1930s, and the Carido family ran the Three Star Pool Hall.

SUSTAINING ETHNICITY, CREATING CULTURE,
AND BUILDING COMMUNITY

Although regarded as special within the community, Filipinas were continually reminded of their status as female immigrants of color when dealing with
teachers, police, real estate agents, and salespeople in Stockton department
stores. When Leon and Camila Carido wanted to buy a house as a gift deed
for their children in the late 1930s (the Alien Land Law in California prohibited aliens from purchasing land, so Filipinas/os and other Asians bought
land in the names of their American-born children), real estate agents told
them that the house they were interested in had already been bought. "At
that time, I did not know how to fight yet," Camila Carido sighed. "I'm not
experienced in that. I was sad, I said, 'That's okay.' I did not have the madness in my heart."[105] The Caridos eventually found a real estate agent who
was willing to work with Filipinas/os. Some Filipinas simply ignored Stockton's segregation and discriminatory housing practices. "If they don't want

you there, why do you have to go there?" said Paula Daclan, referring to the whites-only hotels and department stores. "Stockton is big." She believed racism was of little concern to the Filipina/o community because Filipinas/os had created their own world. "In that time, we group ourselves together," she recalled. "We're happy. We don't have to mix with anybody."[106]

Faced with such blatant exclusion from Stockton's white world, Filipinas/os turned to each other, as described in detail in chapter 3. Through the 1920s and 1930s, Filipinas in Stockton organized a plethora of fraternal, mutual aid, regional, hometown, and women's ethnic organizations that offered Filipinas/os a sense of cohesion, belonging, and unity. The Filipino Women's Club of Stockton had several incarnations; one group, called the Mothers of the Philippines, was organized in 1930 by Virgilia Bantillo, Juliana Lazaro, Natividad Moquite, Juliana Lazaro, and Rita Villaruz; another was organized by Segunda Reyes and Paula Daclan in 1942. Filipinas also formed their own women's lodges in the Legionarios del Trabajo (LDT) and the CDA. As noted above, the Maria Clara Lodge of the CDA was formed in 1928, and Carido and several other wives of members of the LDT organized Teodora Alonzo Lodge in Stockton in 1935. Women also joined the Filipino Federation of America.

From these community organizations, women forged bonds of sisterhood and unity with each other that extended to the larger Filipina/o American community. Scholars such as di Leonardo have noted that the work of kinship, community building, and cultural retention, as well as ethnicity construction, production, and transmittal is just that — work.[107] And Filipinas did the bulk of it. Through these groups, Filipinas created the networks responsible for organizing queen contests, dances, fund-raisers, conventions, parades, carnivals, sports tournaments, cultural performances, and church functions — all events and sites within which Filipina/o American cultural traditions were created. Immigrant Filipinas brought their regional and provincial cultural traditions, particularly foodways, with them, transforming them within an American context and creating new ones. In the process, they helped to forge a distinct Filipina/o American ethnic identity that bridged the differences among Filipinas/os from different regions and language groups. As nationals ineligible for any kind of New Deal social services or welfare, Filipina/o immigrants were forced to depend on one another to survive the Depression. There was "caring and sharing and compassion for one another," wrote the second-generation Pinay Mary Inosanto in her journals.[108] "The bread line, from Lafayette Street, goes for three miles," Camila Carido said. "But you see no Filipino there. The Pinoy has to go to work. We managed. We made an effort to feed ourselves!"[109] Membership in organizations gave support in times of sadness and joy and created social networks important to the psychological well-being of Filipinas.

Working within community organizations helped Filipinas forge identities in addition to those of wife and mother and, in some cases, enabled those who were highly educated and/or were charismatic leaders to utilize their skills in writing and public speaking. In the time that these women spent together, they shared recipes, child-rearing techniques, and tips on home-making; their class and regional differences were muted as they forged bonds of sisterhood with one another. "In those days," Eleanor Olamit said, "it was just enough to live and see that we all got along together. That's the word: unity. If you only knew how hard it was to get along, and there were so few Filipino women in those days."[110]

Pinays who were members of lodges and women's organizations were able to socialize among themselves in the United States in spaces without men and children, where they could gain dignity and a sense of self independent from an identity forged in relation to men or children. In meetings, they taught each other how to read and write, how to raise children and run a household, how to deal with husbands and in-laws, and, most important, how to take advantage of new opportunities in America. As a young woman from the Philippines with just a seventh-grade education, Camila Carido described herself as "uneducated" and credited her lodge sisters with teaching her leadership and organizational skills and expanding her worldview. She eventually rose in the ranks of the LDT to serve as worthy matron (head) of the Teodora Alonzo Lodge and was a highly respected leader in the LDT's national organization.[111] Carido stressed that networks like the lodges were important because there were so few Pinays and their burdens were so great. "You cannot just stay home!" she said. "We gotta go out, too! I'll go crazy if I stay home!"[112] The lodge enabled her to "go alone with other ladies." "We also educated other women who don't want to go out [of the house] and who would just say 'Oh no' [at joining an organization]," Carido recalled. "She would say, 'I don't know how to speak English.' And I would say, 'Speak it in Pilipino and someone would translate!' Then they are inspired, and they go, because it gives them an incentive to be there. If you stay home, you learn nothing. We don't have a TV anyway, and we don't know what is happening outside."[113]

On their meeting nights, women could delegate the care of younger children to husbands or older children. Virgilia Bantillo's diaries noted the Friday evening meetings of the Mothers of the Philippines in her diaries. On one Friday night, the women played bingo and snacked on sandwiches, and Bantillo did not return home until 11:30 PM. At another meeting in the mid-1930s, she drew on her public speaking experience as a teacher in the Philippines and gave a talk titled "Husbands."[114] In addition, women in the lodges and organizations gained leadership experience through administrative work and through community organizing; their status in the community rose because they were members of an organization. At the 1941 Inter-Filipino Community Conference, held in Oakland, four of the five delegates who represented Stockton were Filipinas: Mrs. Francisco Lardizibal, Mrs. Placido (Juliana) Lazaro, Mrs. Sebastian (Mary) Inosanto, and Mrs. Pastor Engkabo.[115]

In the process of sustaining Filipina/o ethnic identity and adapting to American mainstream culture, Filipinas, working with limited financial and cultural resources, created distinctly Filipina/o American traditions. Like the Mexican immigrants George Sanchez has studied, Filipinas/os, with a long history of colonialism and occupation, have long been accustomed to cultural blending, transformation, and rearticulation.[116] Community organizations—many of them led by men but held together by women—held dances, parades, and other gatherings to celebrate American and Filipino holidays such as Rizal Day, Mother's Day, Father's Day, the Fourth of July, and Christmas and created uniquely Filipina/o American traditions. They maintained the vibrant community life that sustained Filipinos in times of hardship and sacrifice, as well as the vital women's networks that helped Pinays cope with their hectic lives. "That was the happiness of our people," said Camila Carido of the dances, plays, sports tournaments, parades, and carnivals of the 1930s and 1940s.[117] Even plays and cultural shows were penned and directed by Filipina immigrants.[118]

Their activities within the home also transformed Filipina/o American ethnicity and culture. More than just sustenance, food is a celebration of ethnicity, group identity, and shared history; as such, it is a powerful vehicle for both cultural maintenance and cultural synthesis.[119] Stockton's Filipinas/os clung to their family's cherished Philippine recipes and the specialties of their hometowns and provinces. Virgilia Bantillo noted in her diaries that family celebrations usually included biko (sweet rice cake), lumpia, *lechon* (roast pig), and maduya, as well as American foods like chicken, Virginia ham, and a sheet cake. For the Bantillo family's Thanksgiving celebration in 1938, American foods took center stage. "Attended Bible class," wrote Virgilia in November 1938, "then went to buy pumpkin pie with Titang at Mother Lee's." The next day numerous relatives and friends came over to feast on the roast turkey for Thanksgiving dinner. As readily as she served Philippine foods to her family, Bantillo introduced American foods to her family's meals. She wrote that she often cooked American-style breakfasts of grapefruit, oranges, cereal, eggs, ham and sausage, and buns with butter.[120]

Bantillo's creative attempts at sustaining ethnicity through foodways despite the limitations of the Depression and American grocery stores were common among Pinays. Those women who came as young girls—such as Eleanor Olamit's mother, Maria Galvez; Asuncion Nicolas; and Paula Daclan—learned how to cook Philippine food in America. "My mother was so young when she came here, she had to learn from other women how to cook," recalled Olamit, whose mother came to the Central Valley when she was ten. "They came so young from the Philippines, and you don't know all of these things. You still had to learn."[121] Asuncion Nicolas said that her mother, Juliana, learned how to cook Philippine food from other Filipinas/os in the United States, not in the Philippines, where their family had had cooks. She taught herself, Nicolas remembered, and became an acclaimed cook.[122]

Filipinas, cooking for work crews and their own families in Hawai'i and the United States, created a new cuisine—Filipina/o American food—by cooking with vegetables, fish, and meats native to Hawai'i and California and using Philippine methods and seasonings. Ilocano, Visayan, Capampangan, and Tagalog regional cooking styles were shared among women. "The woman who cooks *ginataan* [coconut milk soup], she is from Luzon, where Manila is," recalled Camila Carido. "You come to the Visayan islands, and we have different ways of cooking. And the women who came from the southern part, Mindanao—they have different cooking, too, because they are Moros [Muslims] there."[123] Creative adaptations such as sinigang made with salmon heads were common in Filipina/o American households; sinigang is a traditional sour soup in the Philippines, but salmon is native to the West Coast. Deanna Daclan Balantac—whose father, Rosauro Daclan, hailed from Cebu, and whose mother, Paula Dizon Daclan, came from Pampanga province, on Luzon—remembered that her Cebuano-Tagalog family often ate corn instead of rice. Corn, Balantac noted, is even more popular than rice in some areas of Cebu.[124]

Immigrant Pinays developed a special place for themselves within the ethnic community as the centers of kinship networks, wage earners and businesswomen, queens of the domestic sphere, community leaders and organizers, and retainers and producers of Filipina/o American culture. Moreover, these women transformed traditional gender roles in regard to the family, work, and the community, laying a strong foundation for women's leadership and power in Little Manila for their second-generation daughters and the war brides who would arrive after World War II.

THE BEAUTY QUEEN CIRCUIT AND THE SECOND GENERATION
When Anastacio Bantillo asked his teenage daughter Angelina to run for the 1942 queen contest of the CDA, she was adamantly opposed. Anastacio, who

had arrived in San Francisco in 1904 from his native Kalibo, Aklan, was a leader of the Stockton Regidor Lodge, a men's lodge of the CDA based in Stockton. Thus, it was important to him that his daughter would represent the family by running for queen. But Angelina resisted because the Filipina/o American queen contest circuit required that Pinays attend social functions dressed in traditional Philippine dress and sell tickets (which counted as "votes" for them) to community members in the Delta campos. The popular Filipina/o American beauty queen contests that arose in the 1920s brought the community together to promote Philippine nationalism and a positive Filipina/o American identity, and they raised money critical to the survival of community organizations.

Angelina felt the beauty queen circuit was exploitative, but in the patriarchal Bantillo family, "my father's word was an order in our family." To express her resistance, Angelina wore an austere, knee-length black dress to the vote tabulation dance, while other young daughters of prominent Filipino community leaders wore elaborate, floor-length Filipino gowns either imported from the Philippines or painstakingly sewn and embroidered by their mothers. "I felt like I was in mourning and that was my expression of my resistance," she remembered (see figure 27). When a photographer came to the family home to take publicity photos for the campaign, Anastacio ordered his daughter to change into her Philippine dress. "I was an obedient daughter, and I kept my mouth shut and I changed to my Filipina dress and I was all set for the photographer," she recalled. "Just before I was supposed to go and pose for the photographer, I suddenly broke out and just cried and sobbed and I couldn't stop crying."[125] Incensed, Angelina's mother, Virgilia, intervened and allowed her to bow out of the contest.

Angelina's strict upbringing and her yearning to resist the confines of an ethnic culture that prescribed rigid gender roles for women illustrate the kinds of pressures, negotiations, and responses experienced by young Pinays in the Filipina/o American community as the second generation came of age from the 1930s to the 1950s. In 1941, the teenage Angelina was one of fewer than two hundred second-generation Pinays in Little Manila and the nearby area. Like her peers, she was born into a large family and worked two jobs to contribute to the family pot, downtown at a soda shop in Little Manila and, in the summers, in the Delta potato fields.

Angelina and her peers belonged to a large cohort of Filipina/o Americans born to immigrants who arrived in Hawai'i or the United States prior to World War II. Fred Cordova calls this cohort the "Bridge Generation," because these Filipina/o Americans were a bridge between the early immigrants and Filipinos who immigrated after 1965.[126] The members of this

27. In this photograph from the 1943 *Philippine Song Book*, Angelina Bantillo (Magdael) wears a black dress to protest the queen contest circuit. Courtesy of the Angelina Bantillo Magdael family collection.

bridge generation, according to Cordova, himself one of them, "had their own special way of dressing, dancing, speaking, eating and surviving," which differed from the ways of their immigrant parents and from other teen-agers.[127] Scholars have called attention to the ways that the category of teen-ager became a relevant marketing and social category during the 1930s, just as the second generation of Filipina/o boys and girls came of age.[128] Scholarship by several historians describe the ways in which Asian American women, and other young women of color, drew on a variety of sources to create new ethnic and gender identities in the mid-twentieth century.[129] The historian Vicki Ruiz calls attention to the ways in which "immigrants and their children pick, borrow, retain and create distinctive cultural forms" and reminds us of the importance of the ways in which racism and patriarchy "constrain aspirations, expectations and decision making."[130] Valerie Matsumoto's re-search has shown how Nisei women dealt with multiple roles and pressures to create a distinctly Japanese American urban youth culture and identity.[131]

Stockton public schools were not segregated, but Filipina/o youth attending other local schools acutely felt the entrenched racial segregation and racism in San Joaquin County. Toribio "Terry" Rosal, who was born in Hawai'i and moved to Stockton in the 1920s, attended segregated elementary schools for Filipino, Chinese, and Japanese children in the nearby Delta towns of Isleton and Walnut Grove. As an adolescent, he experienced intense racism from children in Lodi, a mostly white farm town just north of Stockton. "I went to Lodi High, and that's a [racist] town; lots of Germans, and Norwegians," said Rosal. "We weren't segregated, but it was a prejudiced school. I went to school for six months and I couldn't stand it anymore. I quit. They [whites] wouldn't play with us, or talk to us."[132] Moreover, even if they attended integrated local schools in Lodi and in Stockton, Filipina/o youth were excluded from the leisure activities of the white teens in Stockton and therefore sought to create their own social world of dances, fund-raising for the community and World War II war bonds, cultural events, and sports tournaments. These young girls and boys listened to jazz and swing, wore knee-length skirts and bobby sox like their classmates, and drank Cokes at the Little Manila soda fountain.

Though daughters were still heavily surveilled by their parents and by the ethnic community, parents were less likely to restrict their daughters if the members of their peer networks were drawn from the Little Manila community. But there were still high expectations for young Pinays. Through the beauty queen contests and social box dances (described below), as well as articles and photos in the ethnic press, journalists and community leaders (mostly men) instructed young women to uphold standards of womanhood brought over from the Philippines, although those ideologies were already being criticized. If their mothers were hardy, unconventional women who bucked tradition to travel to the United States and wielded astonishing power in their marriages and families, Filipina/o American community leaders still pushed second-generation girls to emulate their nostalgic ideal.

The beauty queen contests and social box dances served as the main vehicles by which to order and constrain Filipina American bodies and force them to resemble demure, submissive, ultra-feminine, and traditional Filipinas. From the 1920s to the 1950s, the Filipina/o American community relied heavily on these dances and contests as lucrative events, raising money through the commodification of Pinay bodies and repressive ideas about Filipina womanhood and standards of beauty, with shapely, demure, fair-skinned girls usually winning. For example, in the Miss Philippines contest for the 1929 Pacific Coast Joint Rizal Day celebration, Estelita de la Peña's campaign manager, Celestino Alfafara, wrote in *Three Stars* that an ideal Filipino woman "is religious, obedient, loving, kind, sweet, faithful, modest, and is a good housekeeper." Queen contest winners embodied the best aspirations and virtues of the new nation, and voting for his candidate, Alfafaro insisted, was "honoring our race and the memory of Dr. José Rizal."[133]

In a social box dance, men placed money in boxes held by young women to dance with them. These were large celebrations that were often fund-raising affairs for the community center, offering Pinays opportunities to make money (women would take home half of their box earnings), Pinoys a chance to ease their loneliness, and a space for the community to come together for entertainment. The *dalagas* (young, unmarried women) were brought to the dance by their parents or chaperones. Almost every week-end from the Depression into the 1950s, Filipina/o families from as far away as Watsonville and San Francisco converged on the Stockton Civic Auditorium for queen contest tabulation dances and fund-raising social box dances. Families and single men attended dressed in their best clothes, with most of the dalagas dressed in traditional Filipina dresses called *terno*—made of taf-feta and organza, with stiff butterfly sleeves. The 1941 *Philippine Yearbook's* promotion of an upcoming social box dance for a Filipino community build-ing fund used the promise of romance with the young girls as an incentive for men to attend: "Do you remember that dance when you held them in your arms? How sweet and irresistible were their voices and smiles . . . and you flattered them for their winsome and charming ways . . . you probably did not have a chance to express your love sentiments, that night when they were 'making eyes at you.' Yes, the ladies are here again!"[134]

The clothing that men and women wore to these events is evidence of the fact that Americanization and acculturation were gendered processes. At community events, Filipinos flaunted and performed their Americanness and modernity with their zoot and McIntosh suits (such men were called *Americanos* in the Philippines), like elite Filipinos in the American colonial period who wore Western suits because they desired to be seen as modern, powerful men, argues the historian Mina Roces.[135] From the 1920s to the 1950s, at community events and in formal photographs, most Pinays dressed in modified versions of the Hispanized Philippine terno or mestiza dress with a shawl (*panuelo*) and stiff, butterfly-style sleeves—even as women in the Philippines were largely abandoning the wearing of ternos—a choice that spoke to the ways in which Filipinas' bodies represented the embryonic Phil-ippine nation and traditional culture in the United States (see figure 28).[136] Even non-Filipinas who were married to Filipinos wore Filipina ternos to better embody Filipina-ness. Many of the mostly white taxi dancers at the Rizal Social Club wore Filipina dresses, for example, at the Fourth of July Costume Contest hosted by the club in 1938.

When Anastacio ordered Angelina to change into her traditional Philip-pine dress in order to compete in the CDA queen contest, it was a moment rife with tensions that she remembered well. At a war bond rally a year after the

28. Helen Nava is crowned queen of the Filipino Community of Stockton in 1942. Angelina Bantillo, second woman from the left, who was forced to run as a candidate by her father, looks on glumly. Courtesy of the Angelina Bantillo Magdael family collection.

queen contest fiasco, Angelina donned another plain black dress. In a photograph published in the 1943 *Philippines Song Review*, a periodical that published Philippine popular and patriotic songs and photos of comely young second-generation Filipinas, the editor, Francisco G. Lomongo, included a photograph from the 1942 queen contest and made note of Angelina's "black tunic."[137] As Angelina understood all too well, Filipina bodies were used frequently as a way to raise funds for the Filipina/o American community. Few Filipinas protested, in part because queen contests were serious business, with the potential to raise thousands of dollars. For communitywide contests, such as the one for the title of Miss Philippines, "large amounts of money were spent for the candidates," remembered Terri Jamero, who was born in Little Manila. "Basically, one group would get together to back one girl and at the social box dance they would sometimes open their candidates' box at $1,000, and of course, during the dance all their *kababayans* [townmates] would take a turn at $20 to $100 a turn."[138] Campaigns were managed by men considered influential, rich, and/or powerful in the ethnic community. The investing of such large amounts of money in the contestants created some awkward situations and raised unrealistic expectations. Leatrice Bantillo Perez recalled that some queen contest campaign managers interpreted the acceptance of their thousands of dollars of investment as an engagement promise. Because contests often involved thousands of dollars, parents felt obligated to give their consent to an engagement.[139]

The contests promoted intense competition among Pinays and within the Filipina/o American community in general. Regional groups, ethnic organizations, fraternal lodges, labor camps, and regions in California would endorse candidates. A family's integrity and popularity would be measured through the number of tickets bought for its candidate. "Money was an important factor in getting one elected as queen," recalled Mary Arca Inosanto. "One had to have friends or sponsors who were willing to gamble or risk large sums of money. Sometimes lodges or associations can make the difference in sponsoring a candidate."[140] Regional conflicts would arise, recalled Flora Arca Mata. Queen contests became "contests between Ilocanos against Visayan candidates. Some contests became bitter rivalries among Ilocanos, Visayans, and Tagalogs."[141]

Filipina/o American newspapers discussed Pinays running against one another in various queen campaigns by comparing the candidates' femininity and beauty and promoted standards of beauty and behavior that were difficult for many young women to live up to. Queen contests in the Philippines during the same time period also relied on similar kinds of nostalgia for the shy, demure Filipina unchanged by Americanization, Roces argues.[142] In a *Filipino Pioneer* profile of "Vallejo's Sweetheart," the 1939 Miss Philippines queen candidate Flora Enero claimed that she yearned to be traditional. "When asked what her ambition is," the reporter wrote, "she blushed, and with an innocent twinkle of her pretty eyes she said she would rather be a good housewife. To a woman, she added, there is no career more lofty." Her "natural beauty" and her "evident Oriental demureness" made her a good choice for queen, the reporter wrote.[143] The glamorous future Hollywood extra Pacita Todtod of Oakdale took the crown. The losing candidates were Roseville Pinay; the CDA candidate, Eleanor Galvez; Stockton's Florence Ninonuevo; and Vivian Edwards, a mestiza from San Francisco.

Though most women remember the social box dances and queen contests as fun and profitable, some women, such as Angelina Bantillo Magdael, refused to be exploited. "Some parents objected to having their daughters in the contest because it was like selling merchandise," recalled Flora Mata. "The contestant had to dance with everyone who bought a ticket from her."[144] Terri Jamero refused to run in any queen contests. "The girls who ran would do it for family or the organization, but most often if they had a choice, they wouldn't have run," she said. "Money was [the] primary reason girls ran. There were a few who were running for queen and were constantly running for this contest or another, but as a whole, if the girl had anything to say, she would not run."[145]

Some Pinays, like Stockton's Trinedad Godinez, eschewed the whirl of social box dances and popularity and queen contests in favor of activities and issues that mattered to second-generation Filipinas, like cultural identity. In 1938 Godinez spearheaded a groundbreaking exhibit on Philippine art and culture at the Haggin Museum in Stockton, the region's main art and history museum. Previous exhibits on Filipinos in the United States had included the racist and exploitative 1904 St. Louis World's Fair exhibition of "native" Filipinos. "Here is an opportunity to show to the American people that our nation is possessed of a distinct culture," wrote the *Filipino Pioneer* in 1938. "The low regard other people have of us [is] partly due to the ignorance of the true measure of our culture. . . . If only to correct the mistaken notion the Americans have about us, the project deserves the wholehearted support of every Filipino."[146] The same year, Godinez organized her second-generation peers into the Daughters of the Philippines. As a reflection of the new ways these girls were thinking of their shifting gender roles, they changed the name to the Modern Girls Club, then settled on the Filipina Society of America.[147]

The activities of the members of this organization demonstrate the various ways young women in Little Manila were negotiating parental boundaries, American mass culture, and ethnic identity. Photographs of the young girls illustrate how they walked a fine line between cultural expectations and mainstream culture. During social events and in their free time and at school, young women wore fashions popular among most girls in the late 1930s and early 1940s. At a Filipina Society Easter Egg hunt, Godinez's brother noted cheekily in his column in the *Filipino Pioneer*, they had the audacity to wear shorts. But at community events, they wore Filipina ternos and sang traditional Tagalog, Visayan, and Ilocana/o songs to homesick audiences. At one social event, members sang jazz songs. They also yearned to learn about cultural identity; members participated in Lucia Cordova's Tagalog play and took her Tagalog classes.[148]

If traditional Filipinas were expected to be demure housewives, the members of the Filipina Society of America bucked these expectations. Trinedad Godinez and Teofila Sarmiento, another member, wowed Stockton audiences with their flying skills in the Filipino aviators' show in July 1938. The two young women, the only female members of a statewide Filipino network of aviator clubs, were the featured "bomb droppers" in the air bomb dropping contest.[149] That same month, Godinez organized the Filipino art exhibit at the Haggin Museum and was featured in a front-page photo wearing a traditional Filipina dress. The story about her participation in the air show was next to the photo. Apparently, Filipinas/os in Stockton were becoming accustomed to Filipinas challenging the boundaries of gender-role expectations and crafting a uniquely Filipina American identity.

WOMEN AND THE WAR

During World War II, the Filipina/o American community sprang into action to defend their twin allegiances: the United States and the Philippines. The men and women left behind in Californian Filipina/o communities contributed to the war effort with war bond rallies, where the main entertainment was provided by young Pinays. During the war, young women's bodies again symbolized the Philippine nation for Filipina/o Americans. At community and social events, war bond rallies, and dances across California, young Pinays were the draw, and they sang traditional Tagalog, Ilocano, and Visayan love songs; Filipino patriotic songs; and American standards. Young Pinay singers and the songs they performed at war bond events became so popular that an enterprising Filipino American radio programmer, Francisco Lomongo, periodically published a collection of song lyrics along with photos of California's most popular young Pinay singers.[150] Stockton Pinays aided the war effort in other ways. For example, Nancy Bayhon and Adeline Dalipe joined the Women's Ambulance Corps of America.[151]

In 1943 several Filipina/o American groups in Stockton organized the Great War Bond Drive, with a goal of selling enough war bonds to buy a fighter plane. Over several weekends on a portable stage in the heart of Little Manila, at El Dorado and Lafayette streets, young Pinays in traditional dresses sang Filipino songs for a musical program broadcast over the local radio station KGDM. The effort was led by one of Angelina Bantillo's younger sisters, Norma, and the CDA. The women were such a draw that the community ended up buying two planes. "We would sing Filipino songs and give a spiel on buying war bonds, and that would be a half-hour program. A whole event would last about an hour, and we would start like 6:30 or 7 o'clock [and go] until 8, at least one hour," Leatrice Perez remembered. "And we sold so many bonds, and by the time that that period of raising funds for the plane was finished, the Dimas Alang [CDA] had raised enough money to buy two war planes. And they called it "Spirit of Dimas Alang 1' and 'Spirit of Dimas Alang 2.' And we felt good about the fact that we had a big part in it."[152] Busloads of Pinays were brought to the Camp Cook and Fort Ord to keep morale high among soldiers. Many second-generation women married their soldier beaus before the men were sent to the Philippines.[153]

Their important roles in war bond rallies and military service inspired a new confidence among young postwar Pinays and Pinoys. Increasingly, Filipina/o youths began to demarcate the line between the old and new communities, going so far as to question the relevance of older ethnic institutions for younger Filipinas/os and demand more youth-centered activities. When a young delegate to a statewide Filipina/o conference in San José was ignored by elders in 1946, Filipina/o youths in Stockton wrote an angry open letter to the *Philippines Star-Press.* "They apparently think the youth hasn't the facilities to express his own opinion so consequently we were ignored," the youths wrote. "Yet the main topic of discussion of the 'Filipino Adults' is the 'Scandalous Youth.' It's a shame that we youth are always talked down by our own nationality." The Filipina/o youth of Stockton needed recreational facilities, the youths wrote. "Frankly, [we] would like to know what those organizations are actually doing for the betterment of the community," they continued. "We assure you we the youths will fully cooperate with you in any reform other than five dollar banquets if you would only provide something worthwhile."[154] Speaking before the Conference of Filipino Communities of the West Coast in 1944, Carmen Padilla, a Stockton Pinay, appealed to her elders: "Help us find ourselves.... Remove that veil of darkness which covers our eyes so that we may see the road ahead.... For we are part of the Filipino nation, and we are indeed proud of it."[155]

When adults failed to provide guidance, Filipina/o youth turned to other members of their own generation. Queen contests and social box dances still brought out crowds of families and single immigrant men, but young people wanted to socialize exclusively with their own peers, reflecting a larger trend in American youth culture of the 1940s and 1950s. The Depression-era Filipina Society of America paved the way for postwar coed youth organizations that sponsored their own dances and created their own rituals, fashions, and gatherings. Interest in athletics spurred by high school activities and mainstream culture inspired the rise of Filipina/o American athletic youth clubs in the 1940s, 1950s, and 1960s and areawide sports tournaments organized with other Pinays and Pinoys in California cities. A new Filipino American Youth Association was organized in Stockton in 1944, and the entire leadership, save one officer, were second-generation Pinays.[156] After the war, one of the leaders of the new organization was Sabas "Bob" A. Asis, a returning World War II veteran who had won a Purple Heart and Silver and Bronze stars for his heroic role in the liberation of the Cabanatuan prisoner of war camp as an Alamo Scout in the Philippines.[157]

Adults were invited to their events, but elders did not set the agenda for these Pinays and Pinoys, who traveled between Stockton and Watsonville, Los Angeles, and Salinas to play baseball, basketball, and volleyball with other second-generation Pinays and Pinoys. The clubs created an extensive peer network that helped young Filipina/o Americans gain a sense of place and identity. "Our parents belonged to clubs, regional or fraternal, that brought their generation together," wrote Terri Jamero. "They supported each other in whatever family crisis, need, or discrimination they encountered. We, in turn, did that for each other."[158] By the end of the war, almost every California community with a handful of Filipina/o families boasted a youth athletic club. The San José Agenda played the Salinas Filipino Youth Council, and the San Francisco Mangoes battled the Livingston Dragons and the Sacramento Static Six. The United Filipino Youth of Stockton held an annual dance that drew hundreds of people from all over California to Stockton each year. Unlike their parents, whose brittle relationships with Chinese and Japanese immigrants were at worst antagonistic and at best polite, Filipinas/os enthusiastically attended "All Oriental" invitational basketball tournaments with such teams as the San Francisco Chinese Saints, San José Nisei Zebras, and the Vallejo Val-Phi.[159]

Within this network, Pinays found a source of support and sisterhood. The younger sisters of the original Filipina Society of America formed the Filipina Athletic Club. Their studio portrait shows more than a dozen Pinays wearing pigtails and shorts, surrounded by tennis rackets, baseball bats, and basketballs. Second-generation Pinays played softball, volleyball, and tennis, participating wholeheartedly in organizing areawide tournaments with other Pinays in California communities such as San Francisco and Los Angeles. All-Pinay sports clubs organized in the 1940s and 1950s included the Filipina Athletic Club and the Fils boys' basketball team in Stockton, the Mangoettes of San Francisco, and the LVM Girls Club (LVM is an acronym for Luzon, Visayas, and Mindanao, the three largest islands in the Philippines) from the tiny Delta community of Isleton, and the Livingston Dragonettes volleyball team. "It was difficult for young girls to go anywhere without a brother or older woman . . . to chaperone us," recalled one member of the LVM Girls Club. "Parents in those days were very strict with their daughters. Sons, on the other hand, were able to go as they pleased. . . . We girls decided to form our own club so that we could become part of the Filipino American tournament circuit."[160]

Leatrice Perez recalled youth gatherings fondly. "A very popular group at that time was the Filipino Youth Association," she remembered. "On July 4th, we would hold these big [sports] tournaments and people from all over, Cali-

29. Second-generation Pinoys and Pinays formed their own sports organizations beginning in the 1930s, creating a large network of Filipino American sports clubs throughout the state that operated until the 1970s. The Filipina Athletic Club of Stockton was formed in the late 1930s. Courtesy of the Angelina Bantillo Magdael family collection.

fornia mostly, would come here and congregate in Stockton for the big tournament on July 4th and there was baseball, there was bowling, there was tennis." But it was the dancing — the socializing, music, and fun — that would bring out the entire community, she recalled: "Those were the times that the kids would really show off their talent and jitterbug. Even then, you brought the family with you to these dances, you weren't there alone. You know most of the people came with parents and it was a family affair."[161]

CRUISING EL DODO

But the burgeoning Filipina/o youth culture, and the new identities emerging from these peer networks, began to irk some immigrant parents in the same ways that other American teenagers irritated their parents in the 1940s and 1950s. The late 1930s and early 1940s found parents and teachers obsessed with fears of juvenile delinquency, as shown by films like *Reefer Madness* and such radio programs as *Young America in Crisis*.[162] Disrespect and insolence was creating a crisis, according to adults. In 1941 the editor of the *Philippines Mail*, Alex L. Fabros, wrote that "these tempestuous youths of ours are causing great concern in the ranks of our elders." Filipina/o youth were conducting themselves inappropriately, and he complained: "Terrible! Singularly terrible! Very embarrassing and disgusting! To dances and banquets, invited or not invited, they flick in reckless fashion in their rolled up dirty pants and body odor saturated sweaters!" These youths drank too much, wore too much makeup, and debased the community events organized by their elders. "It's my unbiased opinion that it's high time to curb this," Fabros wrote.[163] It was already too late. Some of the second-generation Pinoys were war veterans whose war service emboldened them.

One of these veterans was "The Buzzing Bee," a second-generation Pinoy who wrote a gossip column about Stockton's young social scene for the *Philippines Star-Press*. In one column, he railed against an elder who, at a community dance, had insulted and embarrassed his group of friends with a lengthy, public tirade in which he criticized their upbringing and lack of respect for elders. In the column, he accused the elder, who claimed to be an upstanding family man, of frequenting Little Manila's taxi-dance halls. "You and your group is supposed to set a good example for us, and have you?" he wrote. "You don't realize that the majority of boys you were insulting were veterans. We don't want another war with the older generation but if you start one, we'll be there to finish it."[164]

The Buzzing Bee's column followed the new youth-oriented postwar social scene. To the Buzzing Bee, Pinays and Pinoys were "hep" if they frequented dances; big parties became "jam sessions." The Little Manila area around Lafayette and El Dorado streets in Stockton became "El Dodo." In his *Philippines Star-Press* column, Buzzing Bee wrote about such peers as Constance Cano, a seventeen-year-old, who was "really a swell girl to meet and nice and friendly," he wrote. "A pure Pinay and proud of it, too! Not really hep, cause she's hardly ever seen at dances." Even marriage traditions were undergoing revision among the new generation. In the same column, Buzzing Bee reported on a wedding between two Stockton Filipinas/os in their early twenties. "After the ceremony the bride and groom and all the attendants got into a very sharp convertible, top down, and rode thru town," he wrote. "El Dodo [El Dorado Street] with horns ablast. . . . The reception was held at Eagles Hall with kids from Frisco and Vallejo joining in the fun. Some jam session really took place that night!"[165]

LOVE, ROMANCE . . . AND CHAPERONES

Unlike other teenagers of the same time period, Pinays and Pinoys did not "date" in the same ways their white peers did.[166] Like their Nisei and Mexican American counterparts, second-generation Filipinas yearned for the romance and love popularized in movies, magazines, and music of mainstream culture, but they were often constrained by the expectations of their parents and their traditional ethnic culture and Catholicism.[167] Elders strictly controlled courtship and marriage and maintained vigilance over their daughters and their chastity through the chaperonage system. Perhaps a product of Spanish colonial Catholic morality, the practice of chaperonage among Filipina/o American and Mexican American families was common. Ruiz describes chaperonage as "a manifestation of familial oligarchy whereby elders attempted to dictate the activities of youth for the sake of family honor."[168] Chaperonage, she argues, was a way in which families could exhibit social control over their daughters.

It was rare to see second-generation girls at community events, movies, and dances without their Filipina immigrant mothers or another relative such as a brother, sister, or cousin as chaperones. As Roman Catholics (a few Filipina/o families in Stockton were Protestants), and influenced by a restrictive Spanish-Filipina/o culture, the experiences of second-generation women were also similar to Mexican American women of the same time period. The Bantillo sisters, Leatrice and Angelina, remembered that when boys wanted to ask them to the movies, their beaus instead asked their mother if she was free. When she agreed, they would all — mother, daughter, and boy — proceed to the Fox Theater in downtown Stockton. At community social events and dances, the entire family was usually in attendance, and sons and daughters socialized and danced under the watchful eyes of their parents. "If a girl went to a dance without a chaperone of some sort, she was considered on the wild side, even if she was not," said Angelina Bantillo Magdael.[169]

Courtship was a family affair, and most Filipinas/os were accustomed to the rituals. Filipinos in their thirties and forties, often contemporaries of the girls' parents, would often come courting as soon as Pinays reached the age of thirteen or fourteen, bringing gifts of fruits and vegetables from the farms or salmon from the canneries, clothing, and jewelry, as discussed earlier this chapter. The sex ratio imbalance, which had radically changed how their mothers had married and created families, also shifted the balance of power toward young Pinays. Angelina Magdael's mother told her to be thankful to have been born at such an opportune time for young Filipinas "because no other time would you have all of your admirers."[170] Anita Bautista remembered that a labor contractor and family friend, "Uncle Terio," would buy her and her three sisters new holiday outfits every year and treat the family to dinner at the chop suey houses and to movies. One afternoon, Terio took the girls to the Fox Theater for a movie. "I was sitting next to him," Anita remembered. "I felt him grope for my hand in the darkness. I was shocked! I promptly got up and went to the ladies room and when I returned I sat in a different seat."[171] Bautista would later hide at a neighbor's house whenever her "uncle" would visit.

Bautista suggested that taxi dancers and prostitutes were, in fact, the "sexual saviors" of Filipina girls, who were often pressured to give in to the sexual and marriage demands of older Pinoy bachelors. "They were the ones who took the edge off the sexual needs of the Manongs, whether these women provided out and out sex or if they provided the Pinoy's need for a woman's warm companionship," said Bautista. "Otherwise, in the 1930s and 1940s in Stockton, we Filipina and mestiza teenagers, no matter how young, would have been aggressively pursued sexually by the Manongs." She remembered that her father insisted on chaperones — often one of her father's many cousins or other relatives — whenever she and her sisters went to town. "Daddee let it be known that he was a tough no-nonsense Pinoy and would not hesitate to literally kill anyone who disrespected him or his family," said Bautista. "He always had a shotgun displayed on the wall of our home." She fell in love with a successful Ilocano labor contractor and married him at the age of fifteen and a half. He was a dashing Pinoy who played sax in the Ernie Hernandez Jazz band at the Rizal Social Club.[172]

Immigrant parents resolutely protected their daughters from men of whom they did not approve. Older immigrant men, especially contractors, remembered Phyllis Cano Ente, were seen as more secure than younger, American-born Pinoys, and parents went to great lengths to keep young Pinoy suitors away from their daughters.[173] Most Filipinas acquiesced to the wishes of their families and married men who were agreeable to their parents. But like Mexican American young women chafing under the control of their families, a few Filipinas evaded the strict control of parents and eloped or married against their parents' wishes.[174] The number of elopements among second-generation Pinays illustrates how the contours of the Filipina/o American family were being transformed in this period. One Stockton Pinay, Susanna Caballero Mangrobang, recalls that her father was adamantly against her marriage to another Visayan, a second-generation Filipino, simply because his family was from a different province. To prevent the union, her father locked her in a room for several days, until her older brother entreated him to let her out so that she could get married.[175] Jerry Paular remembers that elders thought American-born Pinoys like him were unsuitable for marriage to their precious daughters. Jerry and his childhood sweetheart, Eleanor Engkabo, met in childhood and eloped when they were teenagers.[176]

When her father insisted she marry an older Visayan labor contractor, the second-generation Pinay Angeles Monrayo eloped with a Tagalog immigrant, Ray Raymundo, a suit salesman. On January 24, 1928, Monrayo and Raymundo met secretly in Little Manila and drove with good friends to Oakdale, where they found a justice of the peace who married them; the friends stood with them as Ninong and Ninang (godparents). In her diaries, Monrayo related the tension and fear surrounding her decision to defy her father by marrying Ray, who she nicknamed "Hon": "As soon as we got home the neighbor told us that Tatay [her father] has been here and he was furious, so very angry, that he wanted to kill Hon and me. Did you know he was fifteen minutes late after we were married? It's a good thing we left right after the ceremony." It took several years for her father to forgive her.[177]

Eleanor Galvez, the daughter of one of the oldest Filipina/o families in California, scandalized the entire community by eloping to Reno with the handsome Eddie Olamit, a Filipino immigrant, in 1942.[178] Her elopement was front-page news in the *Philippines Mail*, the same newspaper which three years earlier had lauded her as "the most typical and the most beautiful Pinay on the Pacific coast."[179] Olamit was a member of the Legionarios del Trabajo, and the Galvezes were leaders of the rival CDA. Eleanor's mother did not speak to her for a number of years after the marriage.[180] Lillian Bantillo, the youngest sister of Angelina Bantillo Magdael and Leatrice Bantillo Perez, eloped with another second-generation Filipina/o despite her father's insistence that his daughters marry only established, older, and stable immigrant men.[181]

As more second-generation youth matured, courtship became easier for Pinays. By the late 1940s and 1950s, the advent of Filipina/o sports tournaments had created a tight-knit network of Filipina/o American teenagers, and many young Pinays found spouses in this network.[182] But the preference that elders had for more stable and established husbands for their daughters had a ripple effect on the community. The sex ratio imbalance, antimiscegenation laws, family preferences for older husbands, and immigration patterns in which most women came to the United States after World War II created a family structure in the Stockton Filipina/o American community that Dorothy Cordova called the "late family phenomena," in which much older men married younger Pinays.[183] By World War II, it was common to see Filipinos married to Pinays ten to fifteen years younger than them, and by the 1960s and 1970s, many Filipina/o American families in Stockton consisted of three generations: the much older father; the younger, American-born or war bride wife; and their children.[184]

Gossip and society columns in the ethnic press also kept tabs on second-generation men and women in California, reporting romances, elopements, breakups, fashion faux pas, and other juicy items. Eno Godinez, Trinedad Godinez's brother, wrote a satirical column in the *Filipino Pioneer* in the late 1930s titled "For Men Only: But the Ladies May Read It Too." Full of wit and anecdotes about the trials and tribulations of courtship in Stockton, the column reflected young men's frustrations with the sex ratio imbalance. "This column is to better arm us men-folks against the whiles [*sic*] and whims and fastidiousness so common in women," wrote Godinez. His tip for hapless Filipino bachelors: "No matter how nuts you are about her, don't let on that your cranium has been the squirrel's favorite storehouse." In other words, play hard to get.[185] The gossip columns "Round the Town" in the *Filipino Pioneer* and "Miss Spotter" and "Merry-Go-Round" in the *Philippines Mail* gushed about different Pinays in California and commented freely on their clothing choices, beaus, and physical appearance.

The new Pinay of the late 1940s and 1950s—confident, independent, and athletic—alarmed older Filipinas/os, and elders quickly reminded young Filipinas of the standards of Filipina womanhood they were expected to uphold. In 1952 the *Philippines Mail* reminded young Pinays that "the ideal Filipino girl is not necessarily pretty of face and figure, but pretty within." The "Ideal Filipina" is refined, well-dressed, articulate, smiling and friendly, intelligent, educated, family-oriented, child-loving, and most important, industrious, the editor of the newspaper insisted. "If not sewing or cooking, she is writing or playing the piano," he wrote. "She loves music and children. When her hands are not busy, her mind is—with grand noble thoughts. The ideal Filipino girl is virtuous, not prudish: religious, not fanatical. . . . She is for sports, society, parties, but knows the limit. . . . She is alive and living, so much so that her face beams and a glow shines in her face, revealing a woman's soul."[186] The paper did not print any responses from young women, but as shown by their participation in sports tournaments and their jitterbugging and swing dancing, many resisted these edicts.

Filipina Americans had so profoundly transformed gender roles that some Pinoys stationed in the Philippines during World War II compared unfavorably the confident Filipina Americans they knew from home to the submissive, "real" Filipinas they encountered in the Philippines. "It is a well known fact that most of the Filipino younger generation in the states have nothing on the average real Filipino girl they have here in the Philippines," wrote Thomas Cabe, a personnel officer in the second Filipino Infantry Battalion, in the Stockton paper *Philippines Star-Press* in 1945. "Most solders say that Pinays in the states [*sic*] are more or less afflicted with a thing called superiority complex. . . . The girls in the islands are more reserved than the girls in the States . . . whereas the girls in the States seem to outgrow that old tradition of reservedness of the Filipinos."[187]

Second-generation Pinays, Cabe complained, had become too Westernized. "The average Filipino soldier will say, 'I will marry a Filipino girl from the Philippines first before that of a Pinay in the states [*sic*],'" wrote Cabe.

"They claim they will make better and more successful wives." Pinays in the United States, he concluded, "must add a certain ounce of that personality to catch up with the Pinay in the Philippines."[188] Hundreds of soldiers from the first and second Filipino Infantry Regiments, frustrated with the lack of marriageable Filipinas in the United States, brought home Filipina war brides.[189] The postwar arrival of thousands of new female immigrants would forever alter the sex ratio in the community, but the central role and power of Filipinas in their families and communities would endure.

CONCLUSION

In his memoir, *I Have Lived with the American People*, Manuel Buaken quotes an American white man. "'How many of you fellows have ever seen a Filipino woman?'" says Ted Leberthon, a lawyer in a trial that involved a Filipino-white couple. "'Not one of us apparently had ever seen a Filipino woman. It was as if we had all somehow thought of the Filipinos as an entirely male race, sprung directly from the earth.'"[190] On the eve of World War II, the sex ratio imbalance was still extreme. A Filipino woman "is as rare a specimen before the American public as a baby panda," reported the Stockton *Philippine Yearbook* in 1941.[191] The extreme imbalance of fourteen Filipino men to one woman in California radically shaped gender roles and how the wives of Filipino men—Filipina, white, Mexican, African American, and Native American women—and their daughters could wield power.

The small number of Filipinas and the material conditions in which Filipina/o men and women lived in Stockton in the early to the mid-twentieth century shifted the balance of power toward Filipinas, forcing both men and women to creatively adapt and transform gender roles and expectations brought from the Philippines. But Pinays faced challenges in addition to the ones faced by Filipino men, and their lives were circumscribed by gender, race, and class: they were women in a community dominated by men, brown people in a white society hostile to Filipinas/os, and migrant female workers during the Depression. In addition to the wage labor they performed in order to survive, they shouldered the primary responsibility for raising children and fostering family life, not only for their own relatives but also for many other Filipinas/os. Filipinas played many roles in the ethnic community: wage laborer, homemaker, mother, consumer, bearer and producer of culture, community organizer, and family gatekeeper.

Nationalist ideas about Filipina womanhood and authentic homeland culture were projected onto the bodies of young Pinays. The Filipina/o nationalist project, which in the 1930s advocated Philippine independence and during World War II victory over the Japanese, often used Pinay bodies as symbols of the Philippine homeland and, as such, expected them to uphold idealized gender roles. The tight control the community exerted over its young women and the resistance young Filipinas exhibited illustrates a tension between women's ideas about their own lives and identities and their elders' values. With the balance of power shifting toward them as a result of the sex ratio, Filipinas in Stockton were in a position of relative power within the Filipino American community. New attitudes about women's roles and abilities coupled with the new environment of the United States gave Filipinas an opportunity to make changes in their lives, marking paths radically different from what their mothers' had been. As queens of the domestic sphere and the larger community, and as highly valued wives and mothers, they were in a unique position in the community and forged powerful roles as cultural producers and community organizers. The influence of popular culture and ethnic culture brought multiple models of Filipina American identity for Pinays to draw on, negotiate, resist, and transform. Second-generation Pinays took in multiple influences—both mass culture, in the form of music, food, and clothing, and homeland Filipino and regional culture brought by their parents—to create a distinctly Filipina/o American ethnic identity in Stockton. The community these women forged helped Stockton's Filipinas/os weather the Depression and World War II.

CHAPTER 5

SEARCHING FOR SPIRITUAL SUSTENANCE

From the 1920s to World War II, the Arca family spent their Sunday mornings worshipping at two different churches in Stockton: the Roman Catholic St. Mary's Church on Washington Street, and the interdenominational Protestant church, the Lighthouse Mission, two blocks away on Lafayette Street, in Little Manila. The Arcas, a large Visayan/Tagalog family, had immigrated from Hawai'i in 1923 and settled in Little Manila, where José Arca worked as a labor contractor. Flora Arca Mata remembers that her mother, Victoria, would take her and her brothers and sisters to an early mass at St. Mary's Church downtown. After mass, the family, led by their father, José, trooped two blocks away to Little Manila, where Presbyterian, Methodist, Baptist, and Pentecostal Protestant missionaries offered religious services to Filipinas/os at the Lighthouse Mission.[1]

Flora, then a small girl, did not find it unusual that her family had both Catholic and Protestant members. Many other Filipinas/os around the country who had been baptized Catholic, either in the Philippines or the United States, also attended and joined Protestant churches. "My mother and father were not prejudiced about either religion," Flora said. Her older sister, Mary Arca, married the labor contractor and union leader Sebastian Inosanto, and they helped found Trinity Presbyterian Church, a mostly Filipina/o church. Eventually, even Victoria Arca, the family matriarch and staunch Catholic who raised the family alone after José's sudden death in 1930, left the Catholic Church and became a Presbyterian.

Flora and many others in her generation in Little Manila felt that the demands of immigrant life and the panoply of religious choices in America provided more fluid conceptions of religious identity for Filipinas/os. Although work, family, and community played important roles in the lives of immigrants and Filipina/o Americans, religion and faith were also important aspects of their lives in the United States, and both Protestant and Catholic churches were key institutions in the creation and maintenance of Filipina/o American ethnic and political traditions. Protestant churches and St. Mary's Church in Stockton provided sources of religious faith as well as gathering places for Filipinas/os.[2] As the historian Fred Cordova has observed, Christianity, and not necessarily denominational membership or the Catholic Church, was the glue that held many communities together. Novenas (nine days of rosaries), christenings, and funerals were rituals shared by early immigrants and their families, regardless of whether they were members of Protestant or Catholic churches.[3]

With the noted exception of Cordova's work and the groundbreaking research of Steffi San Buenaventura, few historians have written about the religious lives of Filipina/o immigrants, though religion and spirituality played central roles in the lives of most who lived in Little Manila, and ethnic traditions were often tied to religious practices and festivals. Only Steffi San Buenaventura has focused on early Filipina/o immigrants and their religious practices.[4] She writes that their spiritual life was shaped by "centuries of exposure to many forms of belief systems from contacts with other cultures in the home site."[5]

This chapter focuses on early Filipina/o American spirituality and religious practices in Little Manila and examines the conflicts and controversies surrounding race, gender, religion, spirituality, and church membership in the Stockton Filipina/o American community from the 1920s to the 1950s. It also explores the complex relationship of religion and spiritual practices to colonialism, assimilation, Americanization, gender roles, social movements, and class mobility among Filipinas/os in Little Manila. Immediately before and during World War II, Protestant missions and the Roman Catholic Archdiocese of San Francisco engaged in a protracted struggle for influence over the Filipina/o population. However, I argue that Filipinas/os were not victims of Protestant Americanization campaigns, nor were they pawns in the ever-changing power struggles between Protestant missionaries and Catholic bishops. Filipina/o Catholic organizations and Filipina/o American Protestant churches were spaces of spiritual sustenance from which Filipinas/os drew a wealth of emotional support, and sites within which they and religious leaders could organize other Filipinas/os to become politicized around issues of labor, unionization, and racial and social justice.

At the time of the American occupation, more than 90 percent of the population of the Philippines was Roman Catholic, and the overwhelming majority of immigrants arriving in Stockton from the 1920s to the 1960s had been baptized as Catholics. Under the Spanish, barrio life was centered around the activities of the Catholic Church and the ringing of the church bell. Spanish Catholicism had been adopted throughout most of the islands by the twentieth century (with the exceptions of the mostly Muslim south and in the highland areas), but the population infused the religion with indigenous animistic traditions and beliefs, creating a distinctly syncretic Filipino folk Catholicism.[6] Historians have found evidence that many Filipinas/os in provinces under Spanish control still had not converted to Catholicism in the late 1800s.[7] But after the American conquest and the defeat of Spain, hundreds of Spanish friars and priests abandoned the Philippines, leaving many villages without a priest. For Filipinas/os whose religiosity did not depend on institutional Catholicism and the delivery of the sacraments, the absence of clergy made little difference.[8] San Buenaventura argues that many Filipinas/os have historically chosen to embrace popular worship over "doctrinal directives" such as attending Sunday mass and obtaining the sacraments from priests.

Prior to the American occupation, it was illegal to proselytize about any other faith other than Roman Catholicism.[9] The advent of American colonialism in the Philippines in 1898 brought new secular and religious leaders, and their faiths and ideologies, to the islands. Religion—especially the belief that prevailed among most American Protestants that, as Catholics, Filipinas/os were only nominally Christian—played a key role in the debate in the United States over imperialism and the annexation of the Philippines. Indeed, the American colonial project in the Philippines had as one of its major aims the Christianizing of the Filipina/o people, and, according to Laura Prieto, missionaries found the prospect of going to an American territory "irresistible."[10] Early in the Spanish-American War, President William McKinley told Methodist church leaders that he felt it his duty to "educate the Filipinos, and uplift and civilize and Christianize them."[11] Some of the earliest proponents of the conquest of the Philippines were Protestant leaders and missionaries. Reverend Wallace Radcliffe embraced imperialism, going so far as to tell reporters: "I believe in imperialism because I believe in foreign missions. . . . The peal of the trumpet rings out over the Pacific. The Church must go where America goes."[12] The goals of Christianizing, Americanizing, and modernizing the Philippines were inseparable, as Prieto writes.[13]

A vocal proponent of imperial policy in the Philippines was F. F. Ellinwood, the director of all Presbyterian missions, who wrote that the American occupation of the Philippines was "a Providential event of the widest reach and of the most momentous consequences and on [the] whole a great step towards the civilization and evangelization of the world."[14] Missionaries even defended the atrocities committed by soldiers in the Philippines, calling Filipinas/os "treacherous and barbarous" and "defective in reasoning."[15] Some of the first Americans to arrive in the Philippines after the United States took possession of the islands were Protestant evangelicals. Only a week after the occupation of Manila, officers of the Young Men's Christian Association and army chaplains offered the first Protestant service in the Philippines.[16] Beginning in 1902, hundreds of women Protestant evangelicals streamed into the Philippines to work among women and children.[17] These missionaries set immediately to work, establishing missions, churches, social services, Bible study and English classes, hospital work, single-sex dormitories, and Sunday schools.

Catholic leaders in the United States bristled at the hubris of Protestant missionaries in the Philippines, with one archbishop suggesting that the Christianizing of the Philippines might be better accomplished by "good American priests."[18] Though the Philippines remained—and remains—staunchly Catholic, Protestants were able to win over a small population to whom the direct service work of the evangelicals was appealing, as well as those who embraced American colonial culture and associated modernity and Americanism with Protestant Christianity. Moreover, a strong anticlericalism was at the foundation of the Philippine Revolution, and many of the revolution's leaders—such as José Rizal, Andres Bonifacio, and Emilio Aguinaldo—were Masons and, therefore, not devout Catholics. The abuse and oppression of the local population by friars and priests and the rampant corruption in the Catholic Church in the Philippines might have also contributed to the conversion of thousands of Catholic Filipinas/os to Protestant faiths in the first decades of the twentieth century. Protestant penetration of the Philippines had been moderately successful by the time Filipinas/os began immigrating to California in the 1920s.

Some early immigrants had converted to Protestant denominations in the Philippines and completed their seminary training soon after they arrived in the United States in the 1920s and 1930s. These ministers included the Reverends Constantino Arpon, Vicente Zambra, Pablo Estrera, Apolonio Villa, Alejandro Ancheta, and Maurice B. S. Legare, all of whom traveled to Filipina/o communities in California after receiving missionary educations and seminary training in the Philippines and at various institutions in the United States.[19] These Filipino ministers and white Protestant missionaries in Stockton (some of whom had worked in the Philippines under the American occupation), turned their attention to the increasing numbers of Filipina/o immigrants arriving in Hawai'i and the United States after the occupation.

These missionaries had twin goals: they strove to save Filipina/o souls and to make Filipina/o immigrants into good Americans. Missionaries in Stockton established a wide-ranging campaign that included outreach to Filipina/o pensionados in the universities, farmworkers in the Delta, and families and single men in Little Manila. One of the first Filipino missionaries in the United States was Constantino Arpon, who graduated from Pasadena Nazarene College in 1916 and became an early community leader in Los Angeles. Arpon, with other white and Filipino missionaries, organized the Filipino Bible Class in 1918 in Los Angeles, which drew more than thirty members.[20] In many instances, missionaries stationed themselves near areas of large Filipina/o settlement and were quick to offer services to newly arrived immigrants.[21] Some Protestant missionary reformers believed that Filipinas/os, and other nonwhites, had the potential to be transformed into good, middle-class Americans if provided with proper Americanization and Christian religious education. Just as missionaries in the Philippines helped to transform Filipinas/os into good colonial subjects, Protestant missionaries and church leaders in the United States worked to transform Mexican, Asian, and European immigrants into Christian Americans.[22] Similar Americanization campaigns were conducted by missionaries among Chinese and Japanese immigrants and their families in Stockton.[23]

In Stockton, white and Filipina/o missionaries worked under the auspices of four Protestant institutions: the Lighthouse Mission, supported by Methodists and Presbyterians; the House of Friendship, supported by Methodists; the Filipino Christian Fellowship, supported by Presbyterians; and the Filipino Assemblies of the First Born, a Pentecostal, evangelical congregation sponsored by the Assemblies of God. These churches gained important footholds in the Filipina/o community through active outreach among Filipina/o immigrants, social welfare work among destitute Filipinas/os, and special programs geared toward children, families, and Filipina immigrants. Some of Stockton's most prominent citizens and church leaders played important roles in these storefront missions.

The oldest of the missions was the Lighthouse Mission, established in 1920 at 111 East Lafayette Street, between El Dorado and Hunter streets, by Dr. Henry C. Petersen and his wife, Cora (called "Mother") Petersen.[24] Henry Petersen was a prominent local obstetrician and pediatrician and former president of the Board of Education in Stockton who was the attend-

30. Filipina/o families gather in front of the Lighthouse Mission, a Protestant church, at 111 East Lafayette Street in 1933. The mission offered spiritual and moral support for Filipina/o immigrants and families. Courtesy of the Angelina Bantillo Magdael family collection.

ing doctor at several births of second-generation Filipinas/os in Stockton.[25] The Lighthouse Mission offered interdenominational religious services in its main hall and provided food and shelter in its basement. According to Sebastian Inosanto, who was active in the mission, Mother Petersen "loved the Filipino people and served them with love and devotion, [and] gave her time and money."[26] This work drew hundreds of Filipinas/os to the mission (see figure 30). Missionaries at the Lighthouse Mission included "Mother" Mary Hutchinson, who had lived in the Philippines when her husband was a colonel in the U.S. Army. Hutchinson was on call to Filipinas/os in need "twenty-four hours a day for social services," according to Inosanto.[27]

Several prominent white Stocktonians from the First Presbyterian Church of Stockton taught Sunday school and Bible classes at the Lighthouse Mission and visited the sick. The Filipino Christian Fellowship, founded in 1931 by the Visayan immigrant Vicente Zambra, met in the church in downtown Stockton on Sunday afternoons. Zambra had arrived in California in 1925 and attended Stockton High School. He earned a BA in theology from the San Francisco Seminary in San Anselmo and, after graduation, began conducting missionary work among Stockton and Sacramento Filipinos.[28] Zambra organized large Christian fellowship meetings, drawing dozens of Filipinas/os from across the Central Valley.[29] Other mainline Protestant organizations headed by Filipinas/os proliferated in the 1930s. From 1933 to 1936, Methodist missionaries organized the House of Friendship, led by the Filipina/o minister José Deseo, on San Joaquin Street in Little Manila. Missionaries offered children's activities, piano lessons, and even Tagalog classes.[30]

Although most other missionary efforts were led by mainline Protestants, Pentecostals made significant inroads into the immigrant community in the 1920s and 1930s. Julian Bernabe, who founded the Filipino Assemblies of the First Born, left his home in Ilocos Norte to go to Hawai'i in 1917 as a sakada.[31] In Hawai'i, Bernabe left Catholicism for evangelical Christianity. In 1924 he brought his wife and two children to California, where he began preaching to other Filipinas/os in the vineyards while they were harvesting grapes and on street corners and in tent services. Bernabe created a network of charismatic Filipina/o Christians throughout California and convened them at the Lighthouse Mission in Stockton on June 29, 1933. From that initial convention, tiny Filipino Pentecostal churches spread up and down the West Coast.[32] Stockton's Filipino Assembly of the First Born church, Bethany Temple, was formed when Pentecostal converts in the Lighthouse Mission, led by the Kentucky-trained Reverend Alejandro Ancheta, broke off to start their own church in the late 1930s.[33]

The mostly Catholic Filipina/o community turned to Protestant missionaries and services for varying reasons. Certainly, some Filipinas/os viewed their conversion to a Protestant denomination as part of their process of Americanization. The willingness of some of Stockton's most prominent white citizens to associate themselves with Filipinas/os on a weekly basis was impressive to many immigrants, particularly when most middle-class white citizens of Stockton never ventured into Little Manila. During the harrowing years of the late 1920s and the Depression, Protestant missionaries were some of the Filipina/o community's staunchest — and sometimes only — allies, which earned them the immigrants' trust and respect. White Protestant missionaries in Stockton might have been the first whites to treat Filipinas/os with a modicum of respect, however condescending and unequal the relations between white missionaries and Filipina/o churchgoers might have been. Allan Hunter, a missionary himself, noted that many Filipinas/os saw missionaries as the first "good" Americans they encountered; a missionary to some Filipinas/os was "an American who could treat you like a human being."[34]

But by exhorting Filipinas/os to call them "Mother," white women missionaries — who often represented American colonial power in the Philippines and the United States — certainly reinforced white maternalism and unequal power relations. Such strategies and relationships between women in minority racial and ethnic groups and white missionaries recall the power relationships between white women missionaries and women of color in

Peggy Pascoe's research.[35] Many of the white citizens of Stockton who were engaged in work with Filipinas/os, like the Petersen family, had been engaged in Progressive reform movements among the poor and other immigrants in the city. Missionaries like the Petersens, who had begun turning to Asian and Mexican immigrants in the late nineteenth and early twentieth centuries, saw their work as important in what Hunter termed "race reconciliation." "When men stand in line at employment bureaus . . . where they struggle in the fields for the right to a living wage—it is here that the spirit of Jesus must step in," he wrote in 1934, exhorting his fellow missionaries to work with Asian immigrants. "Consider some of the things our churches are doing for race reconciliation," Hunter wrote. "It is the voluntary church worker who steers the bewildered Oriental mother to the clinic where she can get free medical treatment for her children. It is in the Christian boys' camp that you find Orientals as leaders. . . . It is in the Americanization work of our churches that the Oriental comes to know what good citizenship really is."[36] The work of American missionaries, Hunter insisted, was key to helping people from new racial and ethnic groups assimilate.

MAKING GOOD AMERICANS

Protestant services, which were conducted in English, were a surprising contrast to the pre–Vatican II Latin masses to which immigrants were accustomed. Pete Valoria began attending services at the Lighthouse Mission soon after his arrival in Stockton in the late 1920s. He liked the English services and Bible studies offered by Protestants at the mission, which were very different from the Catholic masses offered in Latin. "I was a Catholic in the Philippines, but when I got here I started going to Protestant churches," he said. "And I like the way they express themselves. Because in the Catholic [Church], you cannot understand what they are talking about. In Protestant [churches], they really explain. In Catholic [mass], they say Latin words I cannot understand. I went to Catholic church I think one time here in Stockton, I don't understand [it]."[37]

Missionaries capitalized on the rapt attention and devotion of local Filipinas/os. Protestant workers dedicated a Filipino Reading Room and Recreation Hall at the Lighthouse Mission on October 23, 1926. The dedication program featured speeches in Tagalog and Visayan, musical performances, and prayers by "Mother" Petersen.[38] The earliest programs at the Lighthouse Mission also included ones aimed at children and women. By targeting young Filipina/o children with special Sunday school activities, missionaries appealed to mothers and families. Decades after the closing of the Lighthouse Mission, second-generation Filipinas/os, both Catholic and Protestant, recalled with fondness the Sunday afternoons they spent in their childhoods with the missionaries. During the Depression, when most Filipina/o American families were barely subsisting, missionaries delighted Filipina/o children with luxurious and expensive American treats like soda pop and cookies. "As a child, you know, it was fun to go to the Protestant church because you always got your cookies and your sodas," recalled Flora Arca Mata. "As a child, you looked [forward] to those goodies. So we were always ending up in the Protestant church."[39]

Music, games, and acting out Bible stories enraptured Filipina/o children. Mata and Angelina Bantillo Magdael and her sister Letty Bantillo Perez remember that white women missionaries used a sandbox and miniature figurines to dramatize Bible stories for the Filipina/o children, such as Moses' parting of the Red Sea. "They had a sandbox, and they used to tell the story of the Bible," recalled Mata. "All the Bible stories. They had those little figures all dressed up, they looked like little Arabs to me. I can remember that. [They acted out] the river, the ocean closing up after [Abraham]. That to me was very impressive. And of course, I loved the music, which we didn't have in the Catholic Church."[40] The missionaries also made sure that Filipina/o children and their families who lived outside Little Manila and far from the Lighthouse Mission could still attend services. Moreno Balantac, born in 1932, lived with his parents and siblings in a one-room house in rural French Camp, several miles from downtown Stockton. Each Sunday, church leaders from the Lighthouse Mission drove a bus that brought rural Filipina/o children like Moreno to Stockton for Sunday school.[41]

Missionaries were particularly successful in their efforts to reach out to Filipina immigrants. Filipinas traditionally held the role of spiritual leader in the family in the Philippines, and the religious choices made by grandmothers and mothers often reverberated throughout the family. The influence of their children and the outreach from missionaries had an effect on many Filipina immigrants, particularly a circle of pioneering Filipinas who had settled in Stockton with their families in the early 1920s, such as Virgilia Bantillo, Victoria Arca, and Rita Villaruz. Laura Lacy, a Stockton Baptist missionary, led women's Bible classes at 341 South Hunter Street, headquarters of the United Filipino Church, and many of these Filipina mothers were invited to attend.[42] Special Bible study classes for women appealed to some Filipinas, like Virgilia Bantillo, who attended them eagerly.[43] Though she had been raised a staunch Catholic, Bantillo left the Catholic Church and with her husband, Anastasio, joined her children on Sundays at the Lighthouse Mission. Virgilia's good friend Victoria Arca—Flora Arca's mother, who had been raised Catholic in Negros Occidental in the Visayas—became Protestant as well. "Eventually my mother, even my mother, would go to the Protestant church," remembered Flora Arca Mata. "Because all of her friends were Protestants."[44]

Protestant Americanization efforts continued throughout the 1930s, with the different missions offering Bible classes, piano lessons, and literary societies. But Filipina/o Protestant churches also became fertile ground for Filipina/o labor organizing. Sebastian Inosanto, a leader in the United Filipino Church, was also a well-respected labor contractor who advocated for better working conditions for Filipina/o laborers. In the spring of 1939, the United Filipino Church became involved in the largest agricultural strike in the history of San Joaquin Valley agriculture. That spring, asparagus growers refused to raise the wages of asparagus cutters from the year before. The strikers organized the Filipino Agricultural Laborer's Association and called a general strike on Good Friday, April 7, 1939. The United Filipino Church served as headquarters for the strike, and church members housed and fed the six thousand strikers. The strike is discussed at length in chapter 6, but it warrants a mention here because it illustrates how Filipina/o Protestants were supportive of the Filipina/o American labor movement.

THE BATTLE OVER THE SOULS OF LITTLE MANILA

The Catholic Church on the West Coast that Filipino immigrants encountered in the 1920s and 1930s must have seemed an alien institution in comparison to the small village churches, Iberian and Filipino priests, and the forms of popular piety and folk Catholicism the immigrants had been familiar with in the Philippines. Roman Catholicism was the state religion in the Philippines, and Philippinized Catholicism permeated every aspect of daily life in the Christian lowland regions. Immigrants found that American Roman Catholicism did not offer the same rituals, devotions, and celebrations as Philippine Catholicism. The forms of popular worship the immigrants had known in the Philippines included devotions to the Virgin of Antipolo (Mary) and the Santo Niño (the Christ child) figure; penitential rituals and devotions during January for the Feast of the Santo Niño, Lent, and Holy Week; and town fiestas, elaborate processions, pageants, and special celebrations on feast days and saint's days. These expressions of folk Catholicism brought entire villages and towns together for celebrations. Rites of passage such as births, baptisms, marriages, and funerals varied according to region and class in the Philippines.

Mexican immigrants, whose Catholic experiences and religious ethnic traditions were similar to those of Filipina/o immigrants, also experienced alienation from the American Catholic Church. The historian Jeff Burns writes that early Mexican immigrants felt that the church was a "cold, bewildering institution" and not the "village church they remembered from Mexico."[45] Filipina/o immigrants must have had much the same reaction. Without the stalwart spiritual guidance of local priests and staunchly Catholic female family members—mothers, grandmothers, wives, sisters, and daughters—the mostly male, young Filipino immigrant population probably felt little inclination to attend mass.

Roman Catholic Church leaders in California welcomed Filipina/o immigrants when they began arriving at the port of San Francisco in large numbers in the early 1920s. In 1922 Dr. H. F. Van Trump, a church lay leader, organized the Catholic Filipino Club at 1421 Sutter Street in San Francisco, a group that performed Catholic outreach to Filipinas/os in Northern California.[46] There were high hopes for the organization. In 1922 Van Trump told the Reverend Edward J. Hanna, then archbishop of San Francisco, he believed that "with the proper encouragement the Catholic Philippino [sic] Club can be made the strongest Catholic organization for any single body in the city of San Francisco." Van Trump maintained that the club was necessary, particularly in "the saving of our good Filipino boys from the propaganda of Protestants."[47] Little evidence survives about the impact of the club on new immigrants streaming into San Francisco. The social nature of the club may have attracted some immigrants. "They have some oldtimers that came before me staying there," recalled Sylvester Pili Mateo, who visited the club in 1928. "They have rooms and they have games . . . tennis, volleyball. They have billiards. They have ping-pong."[48] But the club may not have been the success that Van Trump had predicted, as the archdiocese sold its building for $60,000 in May 1928.[49]

In the nineteenth and early twentieth century, most Catholic congregations in American cities included large numbers of immigrants from Europe. Before Vatican II, the American Catholic Church was dominated by Irish American priests and parishioners. By the early twentieth century, Catholic churches in sizable cities like Stockton attracted mostly second- and third-generation European Americans: Irish, Southern Europeans, Italians, and Germans.[50] Stockton's St. Mary's Church had been founded in 1851 by Father Dominic Blaive, a French priest. Charles Weber, a Catholic German immigrant who founded the city of Stockton, donated two lots for the building of St. Mary's on Washington Street in the downtown area.[51] As the first Catholic parish in the San Joaquin Valley, St. Mary's was known as the Mother of All Catholic Churches in the northern end of the valley.[52] German, Irish, Italian, and some Mexican Catholics attended the church. From 1912 to the 1970s, all the pastors of St. Mary's Church were Irish American. In 1912 an

Irish American priest, William E. McGough, became pastor; his tenure lasted until World War II. In 1926 McGough was joined by Father William Walsh, a priest assigned to Catholics living on the remote Delta islands.[53]

Walsh was assigned to the Filipina/o population in Stockton (his biographer refers to this as his work among his "dusky" brethren), and he started a social club aimed at Filipinas/os.[54] The club was disbanded when Walsh was reassigned to a mission in Alaska and died in a freak plane accident in 1930.[55] No other club rose to replace Walsh's small group. Catholic leaders in Stockton and their superiors in the archdiocese in San Francisco puzzled over the Filipinas/os lack of interest in the church and tried numerous strategies to appeal to them, including the offering of special masses, to little success.[56] Northern California Catholic leaders bemoaned Filipinas/os' failure to attend church regularly.[57]

Certainly, the mostly Irish priests of the diocese and the Irish, German, and Italian American parishioners at old St. Mary's Church in downtown Stockton were less than enthusiastic about Filipinas/os worshipping next to them. St. Mary's was typical of other Catholic churches in American cities, which were highly segregated. The historian Chester Gillis notes that before Vatican II, priests and parishioners "perpetuated the sin of racism" by segregating their churches and/or shunning blacks and Latina/o and Asian immigrants. American bishops did not speak out against racism until 1958, when "Discrimination and the Christian Conscience," a critique of segregation, was published.[58] For example, "Mexican Only" signs attached to the back pews were prevalent in Southern California churches.[59] San Francisco's Archbishop Edward J. Hanna, who was also the president of the California State Commission on Immigration and Housing, supported restricting immigration from Mexico. The relationship between the archbishop and white organized labor, longtime foes of Mexican and Asian immigration, was particularly close.[60]

Racism against Filipinas/os within the church's leadership and among its parishioners was rarely addressed when Northern California Catholic leaders debated the "Filipino Problem" in the church. In letters to the archdiocese, priests argued that the migratory nature of Filipina/o labor and the youth of the immigrant population, the remoteness of the agricultural labor camps, and the way the immigrants spent Saturday nights — gambling, drinking, and carousing at the taxi-dance halls — prevented their enthusiastic participation at Sunday morning mass at St. Mary's. Surely, many Filipino bachelors did avoid mass on Sunday for these reasons. But the same men who were deemed to be too far from St. Mary's to attend church on Sunday mornings were carousing only blocks away on El Dorado Street on Saturday evenings.

And more important, hundreds of young, single, male Filipinos were enthusiastically attending Protestant missionary meetings on Sunday mornings.

A common complaint among Filipinas/os in California regarding the Catholic Church was the indifference of the clergy toward their problems, including anti-Filipina/o sentiment. The position the church took on Filipina/o repatriation and discrimination illustrates how its leaders sorely misinterpreted the best interests of their Filipina/o parishioners. Catholic leaders of the Archdiocese of San Francisco actively supported exclusion and the 1935 Filipino Repatriation Act. In the spring of 1935, the newly installed Archbishop of San Francisco, John J. Mitty, wrote Congressman Richard Welch to express his wholehearted support of the repatriation bill and to offer the assistance of the archdiocese. The archbishop assured Mitty that repatriation was in the best interest of Filipina/o immigrants: "I wish to emphasize my conviction, based upon Filipino sentiment, that repatriation will go far in solving the difficult Filipino problem," Mitty wrote to Welch.[61] Welch replied that he appreciated Mitty's help to "remove certain existing opposition" to the repatriation bill and that assured him that the Repatriation Act's purpose was humanitarian.[62] When Welch asked Mitty for help in researching steamship costs for the repatriates, Mitty's assistant forwarded Welch's correspondence to Rev. Edward B. Lenane, director of the Catholic Filipino club, writing, "This is to inform you of the progress of the movement on foot to transport your Filipino friends to their native habitat." Lenane complied with Welch's request.[63] Congress passed the act in July 1935.

These thinly veiled anti-Filipina/o attitudes on the part of the church's highest officials were also reflected in the ways the church regarded the important and powerful Filipina/o fraternal and Masonic lodges, and the thousands who were members of these organizations. Historically, the church has maintained that the principles of Freemasonry, which include the belief in the equality of all religions, are irreconcilable with church doctrine. Cardinal Joseph Ratzinger (Pope Benedict XVI), whom Pope John Paul II appointed the Prefect for the Congregation of the Doctrine of the Faith, affirmed the historic enmity between Freemasonry and the Catholic Church when he issued "A Declaration on Masonic Associations" in November 1983. In it, he repeated the church's historical position on Freemasonry and warned that "the faithful who enroll in Masonic associations are in a state of grave sin and may not receive Holy Communion."[64]

Strained relations between Catholic priests and Filipinas/os active in Masonic-style fraternal organizations like the Caballeros de Dimas Alang

(CDA) and Legionarios del Trabajo (LDT) contributed to the negative views many Filipinas/os had of the American Catholic Church. Catholic leaders often accused Filipina/o members of these organizations of being Freemasons and thereby anti-Catholic. In the 1950s, letters streamed back and forth between the CDA and the Archdiocese of San Francisco, with the church questioning the fraternity's relationship to freemasonry. The CDA's powerful and articulate grand master, San Francisco-based lawyer Celestino Alfafara, maintained that the CDA was not Masonic; rather, they were a patriotic organization dedicated to Philippine political independence and the preservation of Philippine language and culture, and they only copied Masonic insignia and regalia.[65] But the priests were unconvinced. In 1956 Reverend Donnell A. Walsh, Assistant Secretary to Archbishop Mitty, wrote Alfafara and asked for affidavits from Catholic clergy in the Philippines.[66] Alfafara charged that Catholic priests often refused to perform burial services for members of the CDA, and other members believed that they, as suspected Masons, were unwelcome at mass. In the affidavit, Alfafara swore the CDA was not Masonic and insisted that he was a good Catholic, "born and raised in a religious family."[67]

Rizaline Raymundo remembered that her father, Alejandro, a dedicated member of the Gran Oriente, a Filipina/o Masonic lodge based in San Francisco, was excommunicated from the Catholic Church during the Depression as a result of his membership.[68] Although the LDT and CDA were similar to Masonic organizations, the Gran Oriente was, and is, proudly Masonic.[69] Alejandro Raymundo was a member of the Mount Mayon chapter of the Gran Oriente lodge of Stockton. Born and raised in Tondo, near Manila, he had been baptized in the Catholic Church. He attended church in the United States until he joined the Gran Oriente and began wearing the organization's ring, which bore a distinctive Masonic symbol. "He said that one time he went to church, he had his ring and the priest saw it and . . . kicked him out," recalled Rizaline Raymundo. "Excommunicated him." She said that after the incident with the priest, her father never again attended mass and stepped inside a Catholic church only to attend a wedding or funeral.[70]

During the Depression, the Catholic hierarchy in Stockton was largely concerned with its white, middle-class worshippers, and Filipinas/os were not a priority. When Stockton's white middle class began to drift away from the city's core and toward the wealthy, white subdivisions in northwest Stockton in the late 1930s, Monsignor McGough proposed the construction of a new St. Mary's, a lavish new cathedral in northwest Stockton, and the demolition of the old St. Mary's Church. The bell from the old St. Mary's was moved to the shining new cathedral, but—for various reasons, among them the need for a downtown church during World War II — McGough was prevented from tearing down old St. Mary's and the new church was renamed the Cathedral of the Annunciation.[71] Certainly, serving the diverse, working-class Catholic population in downtown Stockton and the city's West End was not a priority for McGough.

"NOTHING TO OFFER IN THE WAY OF A SOLUTION"

By the late 1930s, Filipina/o Protestants were pushing for their own churches led by and for Filipinas/os. During World War II, no less than four Filipina/o-led Protestant churches served Little Manila. In 1938 many members of the Lighthouse Mission and the Filipino Christian Fellowship began to leave for ethnic Filipina/o, denominational churches. At that time, Filipinas/os who leaned toward the Presbyterian church formed the United Filipino Church, led by the Filipino ministers Pablo Estrera and Maurice B. S. Legare. They headquartered themselves on Hunter Street in Little Manila, officially organizing themselves as Trinity Presbyterian Church in October 1942 — striking Filipino from the church's name to become more inclusive.[72] Filipina/o Methodists formed the Filipino Methodist Church, led by a Filipino minister, Reverend D. F. Gonzalo. The church offered services only blocks away from the Lighthouse Mission, at 503 South Sutter Street. In 1946 the Filipino Full Gospel Church, two blocks away from the Methodist Church at 311 Center Street, offered two Sunday services, at 10 AM and 7:45 PM.[73] The Filipino Methodist Church changed its name to St. Peter's Methodist Church in the 1950s, and, under the leadership of Reverend Pat Stegall, became an important advocate for the poor and minority populations of South Stockton in the 1960s and 1970s.

While these Filipina/o Protestant churches were expanding in Stockton, there is little evidence to suggest that the Archdiocese of San Francisco was particularly concerned with Filipina/o immigrants until 1941. At that point, Monroe Sweetland — a leftist activist based in Portland, Oregon — sent a passionate, three-page letter to the National Catholic Welfare Conference in Washington, D.C. Sweetland had been a student radical and member of the socialist League of Industrial Democrats while in college in the 1930s. In the letter, he called the church's attention to the social conditions adversely affecting Filipinas/os on the West Coast and outlined in detail the severe racism and discrimination Filipina/o immigrants faced in all aspects of life in the United States. "I am sure that I am correct when I say that no national group in the United States finds its constitutional and human rights so frequently and flagrantly violated as our Filipinos," wrote Sweetland.[74] In his letter, he listed the injustices wreaked on Filipinas/os on the West Coast, including police abuse and false arrests, the existence of antimiscegenation laws, the lack of voting rights, incidents of mob violence, and their general ostracism by American society.

Sweetland argued that the social agencies of the Catholic Church had to address these problems, because the Communist Party had so far been the only group to come to the defense of Filipinas/os, and the majority of Filipinas/os were at least "nominal Catholics." "I think the American Filipinos are in desperate need of an effective defense agency and of an organization which will take an active interest in their training, education, and general economic and social advancement," he wrote. That agency, he stressed, should be the Catholic Church.[75] Stirred, Amleto G. Cicognani, the Archbishop of Laodicea and the Washington, D.C.–based Apostolic Delegate in the United States, forwarded the letter to Archbishop Mitty in January 1942, early in World War II. Cicognani asked Mitty to respond to Sweetland's letter and requested suggestions on how to respond to the issue of Filipinas/os in the Catholic Church.[76] As apostolic delegate, Cicognani was the pope's representative in the United States, and he was thus charged with the responsibility of overseeing the U.S. Catholic Church and its relationship with the state.

Archbishop Mitty pressured local priests to report back on the situation of Filipinas/os in the parish.[77] The response of Father McGough gives credence to the accusations that West Coast Catholic priests were at best naive about, and at worst willfully ignorant of, the problems facing Filipina/o immigrants and families. McGough relied solely on information provided from one Stockton-based Filipino immigrant, Salvatore Anuncion, to write a letter to Archbishop Mitty in late January 1942 that offered a view starkly opposed to that of Sweetland. McGough wrote that Filipinas/os themselves were to blame for their dwindling numbers at mass, and that they experienced no injustices at the hands of police or the courts.[78] Other organizations such as labor unions, could better serve the social needs of Filipinas/os than the church, McGough contended. Moreover, McGough notes, very few Filipinas/os married in the church. But McGough failed to realize that most Filipinos who married white and Mexican women could not obtain marriage licenses in California because of anti-miscegenation laws, and therefore, they could not get married at St. Mary's even if they were devout Catholics. McGough doubted that most went further than baptism in the Catholic faith. He reported that the parish clergy had gone so far as to form a club and offer a special mass and social events for Filipinas/os, but such efforts had been discontinued due to a lack of interest. McGough noted that Protestant missionary activity had been fervent among Filipinas/os; the Presbyterians, he wrote, visited Filipinas/os in their homes and offered social events, other entertainment, and Bible studies. Overall, McGough seemed resigned to the fact that Filipinas/os were only nominal Catholics, and he believed that there was little the church could do for them. "I regret I have nothing to offer in the way of a solution for these people," he concluded. As a final thought, McGough suggested that perhaps the church instead should go after Filipinas/os through "their own social customs."

Mitty took his cue from McGough and in rather defensive response, told the apostolic delegate that "the problem of Filipinos in California is not as black" as had been alleged.[79] Ignoring the tremendous discrimination aimed at Filipinas/os in California, Mitty parroted McGough's report, and told Cicognani that while there was some social discrimination, it was untrue that "human rights of the Filipinos are violated by false arrests, mob violence, individual violence, unjust treatment at the hands of the courts, juries and police."[80] In an early draft of this letter not sent to Cicognani, Mitty wrote that work among Filipinas/os was made difficult by "the instability of character of the Filipinos," "who left jobs and performed unsatisfactory work."[81] These same Filipinos, Mitty wrote, "want white collar jobs and flashy clothes." The final letter did not include those comments. Mitty closed by saying that he felt the heroism of Filipino troops in World War II was changing anti-Filipino attitudes.[82]

Mitty was correct. During World War II, as word of the heroism of Filipino soldiers in Bataan spread across the nation, it became increasingly unpopular to express anti-Filipina/o sentiment, at least publicly. The week of the Bataan Death March, as the incredible bravery of the Filipino soldiers made national headlines, the apostolic delegate wrote Mitty and made it clear that work among the Filipinas/os had to become a higher priority within the Archdiocese of San Francisco. Cicognani sent Mitty a blunt nine-point directive that pressed priests to take "a special interest in the Filipinos and their problems."[83] Cicognani advised priests to observe Philippine national holidays important to Filipinas/os, such as December 30, Rizal Day; August 19, the birthday of then-president Manuel Quezon; and November 30, National Heroes Day. Cicognani suggested that priests organize chapters of religious societies like the St. Vincent de Paul Society and the Legion of Mary among Filipinas/os, and to oversee their meetings.[84]

Cicognani wanted priests to work closely with diocesan charities to provide Filipinas/os with financial assistance and legal aid in emergencies, and he directed them to push harder wherever Protestant churches had made inroads with Filipinas/os and wherever Filipinas/os had established their own churches. "Every effort should be made to protect them from pernicious social and religious propaganda," he wrote. Filipinos, he continued, should be encouraged to marry in the church and to attain higher education, and all priests should work for citizenship for Filipina/o nationals.[85] This kind of work, the apostolic delegate implied, was already being done by Protestant missionaries working among Filipinas/os.

Mitty sent Cicognani's directive, titled "Priests for Work among the Filipinos," to the priests in the Archdiocese.[86] The directive pushed the clergy at St. Mary's to take a more active role in serving Stockton's Filipinas/os. In the fall of 1942, Monsignor McGough notified Mitty that he had organized a Filipino Catholic club through his chaplain, the Reverend John B. Mulligan. He reported that about 800 Filipinas/os had attended mass during the summer months, and they elected temporary officers, including R. T. Feria as president and, as treasurer, Mrs. M. D. Bautista, the European American wife of the community's prominent Filipino American doctor. McGough designated the 11 AM Sunday mass as the "Filipino Mass," and two officers were charged with forming a committee to visit Filipinas/os in their homes, "get the children for the sacraments," and encourage adults to attend Sunday mass.[87] The Filipino Catholic organization had renamed itself the Filipino Catholic Association by the mid-1940s. By then, the organization had recruited about forty members. In a pattern echoed by the Filipina/o Protestant groups, women and families dominated the membership.[88] Beginning in the 1950s, the Filipino Catholic Association hosted community events that appealed to Filipino Catholics, such as dances, processions, feasts and fiestas in honor of patron saints popular in the Philippines, and special devotions to the Virgin Mary (the annual Our Lady of Antipolo fiesta remains a popular feast and devotion). The organization continues to be active, and it now has members in several parishes throughout Stockton.

Despite this pressure, and the relative success of the Filipino Catholic Association of Stockton, the problems with Filipinas/os in the parish continued after World War II. In 1947 the Archdiocese of San Francisco sent a new priest to St. Mary's: Father Thomas McCullough, an Irish American priest fresh from St. Patrick's Seminary in Menlo Park, south of San Francisco. At St. Patrick's, McCullough—along with his boyhood friend Donald McDonnell—had been deeply influenced by a course on social justice that required them to read papal encyclicals focused on workers' rights and economic justice. According to biographers, McCullough remained deeply "loyal to the traditional Church and its teachings," but "that loyalty required, among other things, a devotion to social justice."[89] McCullough was assigned to work with children and youth. Though Local 7 of the United Cannery, Agricultural, Packing and Allied Workers of America led a huge asparagus strike in Stockton from 1948 to 1949—a strike headquartered a block from St. Mary's, at

Little Manila's Mariposa Hotel—McCullough did not get involved in it. However, he began ministering to Filipina/o and Mexican parishioners, most of whom were farmworkers.

What McCullough initially found among Filipina/o Catholics in Stockton must have disappointed him. In 1949 he reported to a priests' conference on Spanish-speaking Catholics that Filipinas/os in that city were not active in the church, and he implied that efforts to minister to them would be fruitless. McCullough reported that Filipinas/os should not be included in the grouping of "Spanish-speaking" because they preferred English, and "they are already lost to the church." He added that Filipinos had powerful lodges for unity, they were not poor, they practiced birth control, and their marriages—often to Mexican and white women—were illegal as a result of the state's stringent anti-miscegenation laws.[90] According to McCullough, the church needed to focus on Mexicans, who attended church in sizable numbers and were more dedicated Catholics than the Filipinas/os. By the end of World War II, it was evident to McCullough and St. Mary's other priests that Filipina/o Catholics were largely uninterested in attending mass. The several dozen members of the Filipino Catholic Association were a fraction of the Filipina/o population in Stockton, estimated at more than 15,000 by the end of World War II. As Catholic leaders plotted their next strategies in the race for the Filipina/o and Mexican souls of the Central Valley, Protestants continued to attract hundreds of Filipinas/os to their churches.

But as more Filipina/o Americans settled in Stockton and began having children after the war, they began to miss their traditional feast days and the celebrations and social gatherings associated with religious festivals. In the late 1940s, a group of Filipina/o Catholics in Stockton, many with roots in Cebu, began to informally celebrate the Feast of the Santo Niño, or the Christ child, traditionally celebrated in the Philippines beginning on the third Sunday of January. Members of the Daclan, Rabor, Manubag, Engkabo, Arcella, and Canete families attended mass and then invited friends and neighbors over for dinner. Devotees of the Santo Niño de Cebu—a statue of the Christ child brought to the island in 1521 by the Spanish and housed in a massive church in the middle of downtown Cebu—celebrate the feast with a week of masses, family celebrations, and joyous street dancing called *Sinulog*. In Aklan province, on the neighboring island of Panay, the Feast of the Santo Niño is married to the centuries-old annual indigenous festival called Ati-Atihan. The two festivals now draw thousands of visitors from across the Philippines and around the globe. In 1952 Rosauro Daclan traveled to Los Angeles with two of his daughters to learn how to organize a church fiesta. When he returned, he and the core group of families listed above founded the Santo Niño Association of Stockton and Vicinity, Inc. In that the group established a set of traditional rituals that are still celebrated the third week of January at St. Mary's Church: a mass, novenas, a living rosary, a community potluck dinner, and entertainment.[91]

FARM LABOR ACTIVISM AND THE CATHOLIC CHURCH, 1950S–1960S

Negative attitudes among St. Mary's clergy regarding Filipinas/os began to change in the mid-1950s. Several factors were key to this change: more staunchly Catholic Filipina/o families poured into Stockton and the surrounding areas, a group of Filipina Benedictine nuns arrived in Stockton and ministered to the Filipina/o population, and the parish experienced a change in leadership and in its memberships' ethnic composition that profoundly transformed the Filipina/o experience in Stockton and the history of the farm labor movement. Moreover, in the postwar period there was a profound shift in the church's attitudes toward the social and political needs of its poorest members. For the first time, priests in the Archdiocese of San Francisco were directed to work for social justice. One of the most significant organizations that grew out of this paradigm shift was the Spanish Mission Band, a group of priests who ministered directly to farmworkers in the camps of the Central Valley.

In June 1950 Fathers McCullough and McDonnell brought a radical proposition to Archbishop Mitty. The priests requested that they be allowed to leave their parish assignments and work as "priests to the poor" in the diocese.[92] Mitty agreed, and the Archdiocese of San Francisco created the Spanish Mission Band in that year. Several conferences of the Ministry to the Spanish Speaking in the late 1940s had already brought to light the misery experienced by *bracero* (Spanish for "strong arm") and migrant workers in the Central Valley (the bracero program, founded during World War II, authorized the importation of Mexican labor during shortages).[93] The band consisted of McCullough, McDonnell, and two of their old seminary friends, John Garcia and Ralph Duggan; it was based in St. Patrick's Seminary in Menlo Park. Initially, the band's duties remained strictly spiritual. The four priests were directed to offer mass, hear confessions, pray the rosary, teach catechism, and support the creation of devotions and Catholic organizations. McCullough was assigned to San Joaquin County, and he established a center in Stockton. His attitudes toward Filipinas/os changed as he spent more time in the San Joaquin Valley.[94] In fact, second- and third-generation Filipinas who attended St. Mary's have warm memories of him.[95]

McCullough's work among Mexican and Filipino farmworkers made a deep impression on him. Initially, the band worked primarily to prevent mostly Mexican Catholic farmworkers from leaving the church. In an interview, McCullough said, "During the first few years, our main concern was that [the migrants] were becoming lost to the Church: our concern with poverty was . . . that through poverty they were becoming morally disorganized . . . hurting themselves and losing the Faith." But as the priests in the band became aware of the larger context of farmworker poverty, they turned to "larger, structural problems."[96] As representatives of the church, McCullough and McDonnell began to testify at congressional and legislative hearings on behalf of farmworkers, and in opposition to the bracero program. By the early 1950s, the band had taken a radical stance on the situation of farmworkers. According to Burns, McCullough and McDonnell believed that it was only through unionization that farmworkers could achieve justice. Initially, the band tried to encourage the American Federation of Labor and Congress of Industrial Organizations (AFL-CIO) to organize farmworkers. When these efforts failed, the band's members concluded that they would be more effective if they organized workers themselves.[97] In their visits to the rural agricultural camps in the Central Valley, they became familiar with community leaders already trying to better the conditions of Mexican and Filipina/o farmworkers. In his work among Mexicans in San José, McDonnell met a charismatic young community leader, Cesar Chávez. In his work in Stockton, McCullough met a fiery young teacher and community organizer, Dolores Huerta, a parishioner at St. Mary's. According to Burns, the Spanish Mission Band formed a significant relationship with the Community Service Organization (CSO), a secular civil rights organization created in 1947 by community organizer Fred Ross to organize and politicize working-class communities of color. By 1952 the CSO was organizing Mexican Americans in rural areas. The priests introduced Huerta and Chávez to Ross, and the young activists soon became key leaders in the CSO.

A shift in St. Mary's leadership bolstered the work of the Spanish Mission Band among Mexican and Filipina/o farmworkers. McGough left St. Mary's to head the new Cathedral of the Annunciation, built to serve whites who had fled to the suburbs of Stockton. In 1955 the Franciscans—an order devoted to the service of the poor—were assigned to St. Mary's Church. The majority of parishioners at St. Mary's were now working-class people of color—Mexicans and Filipinas/os—and the congregation also included some working-class whites. The entrance of the Franciscans transformed the parish's attitudes toward its parishioners and neighborhoods. The new pastor at St. Mary's was Father Alan McCoy, a liberal Franciscan priest devoted to social activism. Soon after taking the helm at St. Mary's, he created a dining room that fed the poor of downtown.[98] The church focused its resources on Filipina/o workers and Mexican immigrants and their families, particularly braceros, who poured into the San Joaquin Valley from the 1940s to the 1960s.

In a letter to Archbishop Mitty in the late summer of 1956, McCoy was optimistic and upbeat about the progress the church was making among its Filipina/o parishioners. McCoy estimated that about 11,000 Filipinas/os lived in Stockton during the harvest season and that about 200 Filipino families were members of St. Mary's. He told Mitty that he believed McCullough's initial reaction to Filipina/o religiosity in Stockton had been an exaggeration. "When we first came to Stockton we heard that the vast majority of these people had been lost to the faith. However, we found that this was exaggerated," McCoy wrote. Even those Filipinos who had long abandoned St. Mary's for Protestant churches were coming back, he noted happily. Key to this return was the arrival of Filipino nuns, the Benedictine Sisters of Ilocos Sur. The sisters, McCoy noted, were a "tremendous blessing to the entire area."[99] The sisters offered preschool classes, visited Filipina/o families in their homes, ministered to Filipinas/os in agricultural camps, and created the Our Lady of Antipolo Society. Most of the babies born in the Filipina/o American postwar baby boom were being baptized at St. Mary's Church.

McCoy told Mitty that several key leaders in the Filipina/o community who had become Protestants had asked to be welcomed back to the Catholic Church and that several Filipina/o children had applied to enter the parish school. Overall, McCoy was enjoying his work in Stockton among Filipinas/os. Perhaps it was because McCoy approached the Filipina/o community without the prejudices and condescending attitudes of earlier priests that Filipinas/os in Stockton responded to him. He ended his letter to Mitty by saying that he found Filipinas/os to be a "most generous" and a "very likable people." He wrote: "Although I know it will take a long time to really understand them, the work with them has been most pleasant and gratifying." McCoy added that now that the Filipinos in the parish were better served, he concerned with better outreach to Chinese and black parishioners.[100]

As McCoy was making inroads with Filipina/o Catholics at St. Mary's, McCullough and Huerta were organizing Catholic farmworkers. After several years of pushing farmworker unionization, McCullough and Huerta formed the Agricultural Workers Association (AWA) in 1958. Not unlike a mutual-aid society, the new organization worked for the betterment of social and working conditions of farmworkers.[101] McCullough and Huerta organized by going house to house and by holding intimate meetings in people's homes; McCullough insisted that the organization would be ruled from the bottom up.[102] The AWA became so popular that even Filipinas/os who were not active Catholics — such as Cipriano "Rudy" Delvo, a founding member of Trinity Presbyterian Church and a veteran of the 1948 and 1949 asparagus strikes — became volunteers in the organization.[103]

As McCullough, Huerta, and Mexican and Filipino organizers were making headway with the AWA, the AFL-CIO leadership began to warm to the idea of allocating resources to organize farmworkers. Ernesto Galarza (a longtime labor organizer and academic), Jack Livingston (the AFL-CIO's director of organization), and McCullough met in San Francisco in March 1959 to plan for the new AFL-CIO farmworkers' union.[104] The meeting led to the creation of the Agricultural Workers Organizing Committee (AWOC). Because McCullough and Huerta had laid such a strong foundation in the area, it was decided that AWOC's headquarters would be in Stockton. That June, members of the AWA sensed it had become redundant and voted to dissolve, and they joined the newly formed AWOC, slated to be the farmworkers' union of the AFL-CIO. Among the first organizers of the AWOC were Huerta and two veterans of the Local 7 asparagus strikes, Rudy Delvo and Larry Itliong. Itliong was organizing AWOC grape workers in Delano when they voted to go on strike on September 8, 1965, which led to the creation of the United Farm Workers. Their story is told in the following chapter.

CONCLUSION

Though the vast majority of early Filipina/o immigrants were Catholic, many of them found spiritual sustenance with Protestants in Stockton for a number of reasons including the desire of some to embrace a more modern, American identity; racist indifference on the part of Catholic leaders; the lack of interest exhibited by the Catholic clergy in the social problems of Filipinas/os; and the scarcity of staunchly Catholic women in the Filipina/o community. The racism of local Catholic priests at St. Mary's — along with the strong pull of Protestant missionaries who were happy to provide Filipina/o immigrants with such social services as food, clothing, and shelter — helped to push a largely Roman Catholic immigrant group toward mainline and evangelical Protestant churches. As Catholic priests shut their doors to Filipinas/os, ignored the poverty the immigrants suffered through the Depression, and even supported anti-Filipina/o legislation, these Protestant missionaries reacted to the "Filipino Problem" by focusing their efforts on these immigrants, offering them food, shelter, salvation, and leisure-time activities that were alternatives to gambling, frequenting taxi-dance halls, relations with prostitutes, and engaging in other forms of vice.

These early Protestant missions, and the Filipina/o American Protestant churches that grew from these missionary efforts, offered Filipinas/os reared in Iberian Catholicism a new experience in Christian worship and spirituality. White, middle-class Protestant missionaries welcomed Filipinas/os into their homes and came into Little Manila to offer religious and social services, actions that impressed many Filipinas/os who had become accustomed to the rigid segregation of Stockton. To immigrant Filipina/o Catholics, many of whom had never entered a Protestant church before their arrival in the United States, the differences in worship traditions must have seemed revelatory. The social services provided by Protestant missionary programs, the targeting of women and children, and the missionaries' underlying message of Americanization appealed to early immigrants, particularly pensionados and immigrant families. Missionaries focused particularly on Filipina women and children through Bible study, Sunday school, after-school activities, Tagalog and English classes, and piano lessons. Women members of racial and ethnic minority groups, as many historians have noted, were often used as portals through which Americanization programs were brought to these groups.[105]

However, Protestant missionaries and their conversion tactics and Americanization programs were also sometimes condescending and paternalistic. Although it is unclear how wholeheartedly Filipina/o immigrants embraced the Americanization programs of white missionaries, it is evident that Filipinas/os gained social status and self-esteem through their relationships with Protestant missionaries, many of whom were leading white citizens in Stockton. By World War II, three separate Filipina/o American mainline and evangelical Protestant churches headed by Filipina/o ministers had been established in the city. This contrasted with the Catholic Church culture of San Joaquin County. Most priests at St. Mary's lacked an understanding of Filipina/o religious culture, popular piety, and folk Catholicism, and they displayed a shocking ignorance of the social conditions Filipinas/os endured. As attitudes about Filipinas/os changed during World War II, so did the Catholic Church's role in Filipina/o life in Stockton. The priests who practiced what Fred Cordova characterized as "indifference, if not benign condescension" were replaced after the war by spiritual leaders whose commitment to social justice and activism would provide a vision for and support of one of the most important social movements of the twentieth century: the farm labor movement.[106]

The Catholic Church and Protestant missions and Filipina/o Protestant churches played a variety of roles in the lives of Little Manila's Filipinas/os. They were organizing bases for militant farmworker organizing campaigns and havens from the rigors of daily life in Little Manila. Filipina/o Catholics used services offered by Protestant churches to take more control over their spiritual lives through Bible study and Christian fellowship meetings. These churches, which provided food, shelter, solace, and inspiration for their Filipina/o members, were important institutions.

Life in America — with its secularism, religious pluralism, and wide variety of religious choices — allowed Filipinas/os who were raised as Roman Catholics to step outside of conventional boundaries and transform their ideas of spirituality, religiosity, and the role of organized religion and churches in their lives. Filipinas/os in Little Manila attended Protestant services and Catholic masses to fulfill spiritual needs, but they also used these spaces to transform their political and social realities and possibilities. The advent of World War II, and the transformations that war brought in every aspect of Filipina/o life, would expand these possibilities for the community in more ways than anyone could have imagined at the time.

CHAPTER 6

THE WATERSHED OF WORLD WAR II

On December 10, 1943, the writer Carlos Bulosan sent a telegram to one of his great idols, the author and diplomat Carlos P. Romulo, who had been an aide-de-camp to General Douglas MacArthur and, with him, had watched the Philippines fall to the Japanese. Previously, Romulo served as the Philippine Commonwealth's secretary of information and public relations. "Enthusiasm of your coming to California is growing rapidly among our countrymen, especially in Stockton-Sacramento areas where American organizations and business groups are waiting for your presence," wrote Bulosan in the telegram. Bulosan promised Romulo an audience of 5,000 people and offered him contacts and assistance for his West Coast tour.[1] On April 9, 1944, to mark the second anniversary of the brutal Bataan Death March, Romulo paid the highly anticipated official visit to the Stockton Filipina/o community to drum up support for the war bond effort. Thousands of Filipinas/os in Stockton attended the event at Stockton's Civic Auditorium, because they ached to hear firsthand accounts of the war in the Philippines.

Romulo described in graphic terms the horror of the Bataan Death March and the brutalities suffered by whites and Filipinas/os together.[2] "In the foxholes of Bataan one would see a handsome, blonde American boy and a handsome, black-haired Filipino boy, their bodies lying in grotesque positions, their blood freely intermingling in the dust in the sacred cause of freedom, brothers and comrades in arms," he said.[3] Romulo then admonished whites to embrace Filipinas/os as their own brothers. "Take them into your hearts as the 17 million Filipinos took into their hearts the 7,000 American soldiers who fought for you, for us, for freedom in Bataan," he said. "Don't discriminate against them, please. Smile at them when you meet them in your street."[4]

Romulo's frank talk inspired thousands of Filipinas/os in Stockton who were chafing under white supremacy. Camila Carido felt that Romulo had sent a stinging message to local whites. "If Romulo didn't come over here and bawl out the people over here, they [would have been] still prejudiced to us," she said. "He tells them . . . American people died in their arms and that's the way you treat them!"[5] Asuncion Nicolas, who spent her adolescence and adulthood in Stockton and San Francisco, remembered the marked difference in the ways that Filipinas/os in Stockton were treated, particularly after Romulo's speech. "The government saw the bravery and the devotion of our Filipino people during the war," she remembered.[6] Indeed, World War II was a watershed moment for Filipinas/os in Stockton.

This chapter examines the changing fortunes of the Stockton Filipina/o American community during World War II and in the years immediately after it. The chapter first considers the community in the late 1930s, the nature of anti-Filipina/o racism in that period, and the burgeoning labor movement. Then it examines how Filipina/o American life in Stockton changed with the bombing of Pearl Harbor; advent of war in the Pacific, particularly the Philippines; and the internment of Japanese Americans. I argue that the war presented an opportunity for Filipinas/os to move beyond factionalism, reposition themselves in regard to the racial hierarchy in the San Joaquin Delta area, and stake their claim on Stockton as their home. The development of a more cohesive Filipina/o community, the burgeoning strength of the Filipina/o labor movement, the opportunities in labor and business provided by the forced removal of Japanese and Japanese Americans during World War II, and the changing attitudes of whites toward Filipinas/os in Stockton gave them more power and resources than ever before in San Joaquin County throughout the 1940s and 1950s. Goals that had seemed elusive prior to the war were almost immediately realized in the aftermath of Pearl Harbor—most specifically, landownership, citizenship rights, and labor justice.

LABOR MILITANCY AND UNITY

As the 1930s came to a close, those Filipinas/os in Stockton who had refused repatriation to the Philippines worked diligently to improve their lives and community. Their primary obstacles included struggles with the Japanese and white growers over wages and working conditions; continuing racist oppression; and internal factionalism, regionalism, and petty personal differences. All of these problems were slowing down community growth and strides toward Filipina/o self-determination. Throughout the 1930s, Filipinas/os across the United States had beseeched the resident commissioner—the representative of the Philippines in Congress—for help with labor problems and discrimination. In 1938 the resident commissioner was Joaquin M. Elizalde, a member of the Philippine elite for whom the job was a political plum; he was largely ineffectual.

In the summer of 1938, Filipinas/os gathered in Sacramento for the First Filipino National Convention. It was the first time Filipinas/os in the United States attempted to establish official solidarity with one another across regional origin, language group, and class. At the meeting, delegates demanded that Elizalde appoint someone to advocate for Filipinas/os in the increasingly hostile and bitter labor disputes.[7] In December of 1938, Francisco Varona—a former staff member for Commonwealth President Manuel Roxas—was appointed as a labor assistant to Elizalde.[8] Varona's reputation was so positive that in *America Is in the Heart,* Bulosan writes he was a "spectacular figure in Filipino life."[9]

Before his arrival in Washington, D.C., Varona, a native of Iloilo and graduate of the prestigious University of Santo Tomas, had a career as a highly respected journalist in the Philippines. In 1920, when he was sent to Hawai'i as a labor commissioner, he pushed for reforms for sakadas and held the first labor conference on labor migration to Hawai'i, but he was only moderately successful. In 1933 Manuel Quezon sent him along with a group of Philippine legislators to Washington, D.C., to negotiate the terms of Philippine independence.[10] Varona, as a member of the Philippine elite, was not always sympathetic to the problems of Filipinas/os in the United States. In 1938 he complained to a newspaper that the prejudice shown to Filipinas/os was of their own doing.[11] Regardless, his assignment as labor assistant was greeted with elation by Filipinas/os. Varona believed in independent racial unionism and opposed affiliation with the American Federation of Labor (AFL) or the Congress of Industrial Organizations (CIO).[12]

Soon after the appointment of Varona, Dr. Macario Bautista was elected the new president of the Filipino Community of Stockton. Bautista was the only licensed Filipina/o doctor in the Delta and San Joaquin County area, and probably one of just a few in California. Born in Imus, Cavite, in 1895, Bautista had earned a medical degree at the College of Physicians and Surgeons in San Francisco and was licensed to practice medicine in the United States, probably one of the first Filipina/o American doctors to achieve this distinction. He settled permanently in Stockton in 1929 and became sensitive to the needs and struggles of working-class Filipinas/os in Stockton because so many of them were his patients.[13]

The appointment of Varona and the election of the highly respected Bautista were sources of hope for a Stockton community wracked by internal and external pressures and conflicts.[14] The appointment of someone in Washington, D.C., whose sole job was to help Filipina/o labor could not have come at a better time. The union drives of the early 1930s had been crushed by grower and police repression. By the late 1930s, there was no labor union to represent Filipina/o workers in the San Joaquin Delta. The asparagus harvest of 1939 was a cause for great concern among Filipina/o laborers and community leaders: asparagus growers were setting wages at 10 cents less per hundred pounds of asparagus than the year before, and workers were still being given substandard housing. When his patients appealed to him, Bautista immediately wrote to Varona and asked for his help.[15]

Varona came quickly to Stockton and called a mass meeting of asparagus cutters on April 6, 1939. With Varona and Bautista facilitating the gathering, workers and contractors met for four hours at Japanese Hall on Washington Street and decided to organize an independent, all-Filipino union, the Filipino Agricultural Laborer's Association (FALA). The FALA demanded a 20 cent wage increase per hundred pounds of asparagus and called for a general strike of all asparagus workers for the next day, Good Friday, April 7.[16] Almost none of the 6,000 Filipino asparagus workers in Stockton reported for work on April 7, affecting thousands of acres of asparagus on Victoria Island, Union Island, Roberts Island, Stewart Tract, and Terminous Tract, and some areas of Sacramento and Yolo counties. The strike, called at the height of the season, caused a crisis in the industry, and most Japanese and white growers were taken completely by surprise by the unity of the Filipina/o workers. Anticipating the ruin of that season's multimillion-dollar asparagus crop, most growers capitulated within a day.[17]

The strike, which was unique in Filipina/o labor history in that it was completely nonviolent and did not use picketing, was a rousing success. Even the local press conceded that it had achieved a historic victory, and a front-page article in the *Stockton Daily Evening Record* commented at length, and in great surprise, at the organization and complete solidarity that Filipino workers had displayed: "It was the first time in the history of Filipino labor that a solid organization had been formed that would hold together against employers." Filipino strikers "displayed a solidarity and completeness unprecedented in the history of Filipino labor here."[18] Appreciative FALA members gave Varona a gold watch inscribed with "In Grateful Remembrance of April 7, 1939."

The organizers of the FALA stressed that all Filipinas/os shared the same labor conditions—poor wages, substandard living and working conditions, and dishonest white and Japanese farmers—and that unity with each other was imperative to defeat discrimination. The FALA leadership consisted of Ilocanos, Visayans, and Tagalogs and included respected leaders like Bautista, labor contractors, old-timers. It also included staunch trade unionists, such as Lamberto Malinab, general vice president; Sebastian Inosanto, general secretary; and Tomas Costales, general treasurer. Central Council members included such leaders as Primo Villaruz, the former president of the Filipino Community of Stockton.[19] In a statement issued after the strike, Bautista praised the "genius and leadership" of Varona and commented on the "miracle" of 6,000 united Filipina/o workers in Stockton:

> Never has such solidarity been shown before. . . . The growers were shocked when they realized the inspired unity of the Filipinos and the suddenness with which they achieved that unity. . . . We have achieved a beginning here towards the realization of our long-cherished dream of the Filipinos in this country to be united. The events that transpired convince me that the realization of that dream is not impossible. The Filipinos have been ready for that unity; all they needed was a leader upon whom they can repose the confidence and trust.[20]

In the FALA's official newspaper, the *Philippine Journal*, Juan "Johnny" C. Dionisio, the editor and an officer of the FALA, praised the organization's unity: "Filipinos in America are becoming convinced that individually they cannot hope to win their fight for recognition of their rights. More and more, they are becoming convinced that only through collective action can they win their fight."[21] A united Filipino front seemed to be spreading all over the San Joaquin Delta area and in surrounding communities.

UNION BUSTING

Japanese growers were shocked at the FALA's success. The Issei and Nisei left farm work to become growers in the 1930s, and Japanese and Filipina/o labor, social, and economic relations were already tenuous even before the Good Friday strike. As Eiichiro Azuma's research illustrates, white landowning elites were at the top of a rigidly enforced racial hierarchy. These elites owned most of the rich peat-soil land in the Delta, along with most of the shipping and marketing companies. In return for leasing thousands of acres to Japanese tenant farmers, the whites received intense loyalty and submission from the Japanese. By the late 1930s, Issei and Nisei farmers owned or leased much of the farmland on which Filipinas/os worked.[22] Ideas about Japanese racial superiority led Japanese leaders in the Delta to view themselves as racially, politically, and economically dominant in relation to the Chinese and Filipinas/os in the Delta. Many Issei perceived Filipinas/os as the racial enemy and were obsessed with maintaining the racial hierarchy in the Delta to serve Issei farming and merchant interests. Claro Candelario remembered bitterly that the Japanese treated Filipinas/os as if "we were below their feet!"[23] Camila Carido bitterly recalled the ways in which Japanese contractors treated Filipina/o laborers: "We were nothing to them!"[24]

Throughout the Depression, Azuma contends, Filipina/o immigrant laborers and Issei elites in San Joaquin County engaged in a "racial struggle" over power and resources.[25] Filipinas/os accused Japanese contractors of paying them less than other groups and of swindling them.[26] The Depression had been punctuated by militant Filipina/o strikes against Japanese and white farmers, coupled with boycotts of Japanese businesses in the Oriental Quarter in Stockton in order to pressure all segments of the Japanese community. For example, in 1936, Filipino laborers attempted an unsuccessful strike against Japanese celery farmers and launched an anti-Japanese boycott in Stockton when their demands were not immediately met. The strikes hurt Issei farmers, and numerous boycotts (in 1930, 1936, and 1939) organized by Filipinas/os against Japanese businesses bruised Japanese merchants in the Oriental Quarter. Therefore, it was against a backdrop of increasing hostility between the two groups that the Issei viewed the FALA's victory in the asparagus strike and the growing Filipina/o labor movement across the Delta.

From 1939 to 1941, Issei farmers worked diligently to break the union. Their overall plan, according to Azuma, was to remove troublesome, organized Filipino labor completely from the Delta labor equation and replace it entirely with the Nisei, who would bring back the "golden age" of Japanese agriculture in California that had existed in the 1910s, before Filipinas/os arrived.[27] In early October 1939, 250 Filipina/o pea and tomato pickers in nearby Concord who were affiliated with FALA walked out on their Japanese employers, who had refused a 35-cent-per-hour wage. The Japanese Association refused the workers' demands, calling Filipina/o workers "bums." The Concord Filipina/o community launched a boycott of Japanese businesses in the area, and Issei farmers retaliated by recruiting Mexican replacement workers.[28] Later that same month, the FALA attempted to organize Filipina/o and Mexican brussels sprouts workers in Pescadero, between San Francisco and Santa Cruz. The growers refused the workers' demand of 35 cents per hour. The strikers returned to work, only to strike again in December. To break the strike, the growers used 150 scabs, mostly Mexicans, recruited from Stockton. In that strike, two Filipino strikers were shot as they threw rocks at Mexican scabs.[29]

Undaunted, in the fall and winter of 1939, the FALA turned to organizing several thousand celery workers, mostly Filipinas/os. Working with the

31. Members of the Filipino Agricultural Laborer's Association union meet with local leaders in the fall of 1940. Courtesy of Holt-Atherton Special Collections, University of the Pacific Library.

Union of Cannery, Agricultural, Packing, and Allied Workers of America (UCAPAWA), a member of the CIO, the FALA won a significant victory.[30] The early success of the FALA earned the union a national reputation. In 1941, the labor scholar Harry Schwartz lauded the FALA, saying it "illustrates the success that a homogeneous group of farm workers can achieve if it has capable leadership and a unified membership."[31] By 1940 the FALA had organized branches in Concord, Sacramento, Pescadero, San Jose, San Juan Bautista, and Delano (see figure 31).[32]

When the Issei farmers were young, they had gained a reputation for their militant labor organizing.[33] But these were different times, and now the Issei moved both directly and covertly to crush any attempt to challenge their economic and racial position in the Delta. Hiring Mexican and Nisei strikebreakers was only one tactic used by Issei farmers to regain control over their labor supply. They found an ally in a Stockton Nisei woman, Kay Morimoto, the wife of a local leader of the Japanese American Citizen's League. Azuma and the Filipina/o American press describe Morimoto as an agent of Issei and white farmers whose main goal was the destruction of the FALA and the replacement of unionized Filipino workers with Japanese, Mexicans, and members of the conservative, anti-union Filipino Federation of America

(FFA). Morimoto's influence derived from her relationship with the federation and the alliance of Issei farmers and white landowners.

By 1939 the FFA had chapters throughout the West Coast and Hawai'i and owned a large building south of downtown, at 2049 South San Joaquin Street, which had been bombed by a white mob in 1930. Its leader, the charismatic Hilario Moncado, was anti-union, and the willingness of the group's members to serve as scab labor during strikes earned them the favor of growers and the enmity of other Filipina/o workers.[34] The editors of *Three Stars*, the pro-labor Stockton Filipina/o newspaper, considered the FFA a cult and wrote in 1928 that Moncado was a "human parasite" who "should be tarred and feathered" for training his largely uneducated followers to be docile and submissive. In the Tagalog section of *Three Stars*, the editors ridiculed the group's members as deluded, and laughed at Moncado's claim of holding three doctoral degrees.[35]

The alliance forged among white growers, Issei farmers, the FFA, and Morimoto served to deepen the antagonism between Japanese farmers and Filipina/o organized labor, weaken the FALA, and bolster the FFA's power and its reputation among Stockton's white elites. Morimoto recruited FFA strikebreakers during the 1939 celery strike, which had triggered a mass boycott of Japanese businesses by Filipinas/os in Stockton that winter. On November 30, 1939, Filipino strikers showed up in the Nihonmachi and Little Manila area holding anti-Japanese placards and dragged Filipinos out of Japanese stores.[36] In 1940 Morimoto told white growers that FALA members were "bad Filipinos," while FFA members were "good Filipinos." The bad ones, she said, resorted to strikes while the good ones believed in negotiating.[37] The strike is portrayed in Bulosan's *America Is in the Heart*: Carlos sees Claro holding up a sign reading: "PAISANOS! DON'T PATRONIZE JAP STORES! IT MEANS HUNGER!" Carlos asks Claro why the Japanese are being singled out in the asparagus strike. Claro angrily replies that a "Japanese woman is breaking it [the strike]. She is supplying laborers." Whenever Claro saw a Japanese face in Little Manila, "he became furious."[38]

In January and February 1940, the *Philippine Journal*'s editor, Johnny Dionisio, blasted Morimoto and the FFA on the paper's front page, accusing Morimoto of thinking Filipinas/os "dumb" calling the relationship between the FFA and Morimoto an "unholy alliance."[39] That spring, several Japanese growers refused to hire FALA members who had struck the year before and instead hired Japanese workers and FFA members.[40] Morimoto also worked to divide Filipinas/os across California. In August of 1940, the Associated Farmers, Union Island Growers, Delta Farms, and other big growers in the San Joaquin Delta gave Morimoto a large sum to help her efforts in breaking the FALA. She then donated a portion to a Filipina/o American sports bene-fit organized by Delfin Cruz, publisher of the Salinas *Philippines Mail*. Cruz's acceptance of the money enraged the FALA and its pro-labor allies, and the San Francisco and Sacramento delegations boycotted the benefit.[41]

In another union-busting tactic, Japanese landlords evicted pro-labor Fili-pinas/os in Little Manila. Bautista was evicted from his medical office at 241 South El Dorado Street; in the same office, Morimoto then created a farm labor employment agency for FFA members.[42] Outraged by Morimoto's strikebreaking work, Antonio Bustamante—a thirty-five-year-old member of FALA—fired ten shots at Morimoto's office, which she shared with her husband, a dentist. No one was hurt, and police immediately arrested the gunman. He told police that if they returned his gun, he'd "go back and fin-ish the job, and if he had a bomb he'd blow the office up."[43]

The FALA began suffering from factionalism and infighting during the celery strike in October 1940. Morimoto supplied strikebreakers to the growers during the strike. Feeling under siege, Bautista made a desperate and pragmatic, yet fatal, decision to ally with the AFL and changed the name of his group to the Federated Agricultural Laborer's Association.[44] In late October 1940, Bautista expressed his sadness to Varona. "I could see how that with the help of the AFL our chances of losing is [*sic*] very small, but the affiliation afterwards is the thing that will confront the situation," he wrote. "To me it looks like the end of an independent FALA."[45] Several FALA locals broke from the organization rather than affiliate with the notoriously anti-Filipina/o AFL. The Sacramento local of the FALA chose to organize itself in-stead as the Filipino Labor Supply Association of Sacramento and Superior California.[46] The AFL did negotiate important contracts for the FALA.[47] But the end of the celery season also brought another challenge for the FALA: Japanese farmers organized the California Farm Labor Union, an organi-zation of Nisei workers and Issei growers allied with white landowners, growers, and shippers.[48]

The FALA's rejection of the more radical CIO in favor of the AFL puzzled the savvy Filipino organizers with the Local 7 of the UCAPAWA, a CIO af-filiate in Seattle. In November 1940 they launched an attack on the FALA leadership, branding Bautista, Dionisio, and Varona as amateurs and sug-gesting that Bautista stick to medicine and Dionisio to writing.[49] The attacks from the militant salmon cannery workers' union were particularly painful. On March 12, Local 7's former president, Trinidad Rojo, and the current president, Vincent Navea, stopped in Stockton for a mass meeting of mem-bers of their union, which caused suspicion among the FALA leaders. "We are accused of causing disunity," Rojo and Navea stated. "On the contrary, we are here to help establish order out of chaos, unity of a mess created by the Stockton FALA amateur labor leaders."[50] With attacks coming from the left in the Filipina/o American labor community and from the FFA and the Issei and white elites on the right, the FALA was fighting for its life.

With the labor-organizing situation looking increasingly grim, the FALA's leaders turned to other endeavors. They took seriously their group's role as an organization that could bring Filipinas/os together, forging a common identity and collective vision among Ilocanas/os, Visayans, and Tagalogs. The FALA moved to help Filipinas/os save and invest their earnings by organizing the Philippine Mercantile Corporation, a cooperative general store in which FALA members bought stock at $5 a share. The store, located at 227 South Madison Street in downtown Stockton, sold groceries and imported Philippine products that members had been missing, such as rubber-soled slippers and canned mangoes and other fruit.[51]

Increasingly, the unity of the FALA reminded the community that factionalism impeded real progress. In January 1940, Eddie Wasan, a FALA member, addressed one of its meetings by demanding that the FALA leadership include an Ilocano representative who would look out specifically for Ilocano interests. His demand was greeted with silence. "You can no longer appeal to the Pinoys from the sectional standpoint," wrote Dionisio. "The FALA is not an organization for Visayans, Ilocanos, or Tagalogs. It is an organization for Filipinos only!"[52] By the fall of 1940, the FALA's leadership believed that worker solidarity as forged through the FALA could bring the entire population of farmworkers together. When Bautista wrote a desperate letter to Varona as the celery strike continued in the fall of 1940, Varona bolstered his spirits by reminding him how important the FALA victories had been not just for Filipinas/os but for all farm laborers. "You might not realize it because you are close to the movement, in fact you are the leader of it, but the FALA with its present gallant fight for the rights and for the protection of the interest [sic] of its members, is actually fighting for the cause of the entire farm labor [force] in California, if not the whole Pacific Coast," wrote Varona. "Your victory will be a vindication of the Filipino workingmen in this country and of the farm laborers of all races, including the Americans. In your moments of despair, Doctor, if you have any, think of this."[53]

STRUGGLES FOR CIVIL RIGHTS

It was the unity and strength among Filipinos forged in the FALA and the vibrant community of Filipinas/os in Stockton that led the Filipino Community of Stockton to optimistically boast in January 1941 that Little Manila was the "Model Filipino Community in America."[54] This "model community" maintained an active Filipino Community, Inc., all three Filipino fraternal orders (the Caballeros de Dimas Alang, Gran Oriente, and Legionarios del Trabajo), the Filipino Women's Club, dozens of hometown and regional groups such as the Numancia Aid Association and the Iloilo Circle, and a formidable union (the FALA). Despite meager resources in the years just before the war, these Filipina/o organizations held dances, fund-raisers, carnivals, sports tournaments, dinners, queen contests, and cultural events.

But Little Manila was still continually wracked with factionalism, and even the strength of the FALA in forging Filipina/o American unity in the Delta was waning by 1941. Even Filipina/o residents could not agree whether or not Stockton was a "model" for the rest of Filipina/o America. Writing in the Stockton/Sacramento Filipina/o newspaper, the *Philippine Record*, Simeon Doria Arroyo dismissed the assertion that Stockton was any kind of model for other Filipina/o communities. Filipino businessmen, he wrote, don't know their civic obligations, and Filipina/o families don't attend Filipino community meetings. Among Filipinas/os in Stockton, "there is too much sectionalism, fraternalism, and less of nationalism." His litany of complaints included the preponderance of pool halls, gambling dens, and "germ-infested parlors of clandestine hotels" which lined El Dorado and Lafayette streets, ill-educated Filipino youth, and immodest young Filipinas neglected by their parents.[55]

Attempting to shout over the infighting and factionalism were leftist Filipinas/os persisting in their efforts to achieve Philippine independence and Filipina/o naturalization rights. Leftist Filipinas/os in Los Angeles— including Bulosan, the writer and labor leader; Claro Candelario, a teacher turned labor activist; and Crispulo Mensalvas, the labor organizer—formed the Committee for the Protection of Filipino Rights (CPFR) in 1939 and launched a campaign to get 20,000 signatures in support of a bill for Filipino naturalization, sponsored by the radical New York Congressman Vito Marcantonio, who represented the American Labor Party.[56] The CPFR was an offshoot of the leftist American Committee for the Protection of the Foreign-Born, a significant Popular Front organization. The Popular Front was a radical social democratic movement founded in the Depression that brought together opponents of fascism and racism, proponents of the industrial unionism of the CIO, and artists and intellectuals, with the goal of shaping a new and radical culture and politics.

By the late 1930s, Bulosan had become a part of a circle of left-wing writers in Los Angeles that also included John Fante, William Saroyan, Carey McWilliams, and Louis Adamic.[57] Writing of the CPFR in *America Is in the Heart*, Bulosan stressed the need for a broad Filipina/o organization that

32. In 1940 the leftists Carlos Bulosan (left, in dark suit) and Claro Candelario (right, standing in hat) moved to Stockton to campaign for Filipino citizenship with the Committee for the Protection of Filipino Rights. Bulosan lived intermittently at 110 South El Dorado Street in Little Manila until his death in 1956. Candelario ran the Luzon Café and was president of the Filipino Community of Stockton, Inc. in the late 1940s. Here, they share a lighthearted moment with friends. Courtesy of NPA FANHS.

would allow local communities to work collectively for citizenship rights. Other Filipinas/os joined the CPFR's efforts. In the *Philippines Mail*, one Filipino directly challenged the notion of racial purity and naturalization laws that barred all but whites and blacks from citizenship: "When we back up the Marcantonio bill, we are fighting against this anomaly, this racial insult upon our people."[58] In backing the Marcantonio bill, Filipinas/os were facing a formidable alliance of racist groups such as the Associated Farmers and the Daughters of the American Revolution.

Sensing correctly that the critical mass of Filipinas/os was in Stockton, members of the CPFR—including Bulosan, Candelario, and Mensalvas—moved to Lafayette Street in the heart of Little Manila in 1940 (see figure 32) and brought with them their radical leftist newspaper, the *Commonwealth Times* (its publication had been based in Santa Maria, California, where Mensalvas was most likely organizing workers).[59] As Congress was debating the bill, another activist wrote a passionate plea to the *Philippines Mail*: "As long as we accepted low wages and intolerable working conditions, the exploiters professed to love us even more than their fellow countrymen white workers. But when we began to learn real Americanism, when we organized ourselves into unions . . . the exploiters became sick of indigestion due to sour grapes."[60] California congressmen aimed a worn anti-Filipina/o tirade at the bill, calling Filipinas/os "the most undesirable of our resident immigrants." The congressmen noted the poor character of Filipinas/os and their propensity for taking white workers' jobs, driving down wages, miscegenation, and crime, especially in districts like Little Manila, then banded together to block the bill.[61] Varona told advocates that Congress was "indifferent" to the demands of Filipina/o immigrants and that the California lawmakers in particular were "savagely against" consideration of the Marcantonio legislation.[62] Marcantonio promised to reintroduce it.[63] Resident Commissioner Elizalde responded by encouraging Filipinas/os to focus on their own communities.[64]

That summer Congress delivered a new blow to the Filipina/o community. With war imminent, Congress passed the Smith Act, also known as the Alien Registration Act. By requiring every alien aged fourteen and older to register and be fingerprinted, the act enabled the federal government to amass information on suspected alien Communists and spies, and enemy aliens such as Japanese, Italians, and Germans. Elizalde wrote to officials and asked for exemption for Filipinas/os, arguing that they should be considered nationals rather than aliens because the Philippines was still a colony of the United States. Secretary of the Interior Harold Ickes and Attorney General Robert Jackson responded that Filipinas/os were aliens and must register.[65] The Smith Act eventually led to the collection of information on almost five million noncitizens.

Undaunted by the death of the Marcantonio bill and the chilling effect of the Smith Act, the CPFR struggled on. Anticipating a Filipino labor shortage in the fall of 1941, an optimistic editorial in the *Commonwealth Times* again called for Filipina/o unionism and unity. "Filipinos are the most organized race group on the coast," wrote the editors. "The day is not far off when a united front of all Filipino organizations will be formed on a political basis. The farmers and growers must be prepared for this eventuality because the Filipino workers have nothing to lose but a shameful exploitation."[66] But by this time, the FALA had been weakened beyond repair by attacks from growers and by strikebreakers. The California Farm Labor Union, the Issei growers' organization, hired Japanese workers and members of the FFA for the asparagus season of 1941.[67]

Then members of the FALA were stunned when forty-four-year-old Francisco Varona died suddenly of a brain hemorrhage in a New York hospital, on June 28, 1941.[68] Filipinas/os across the nation gathered for memorial services for Varona, recalling his brave leadership and advocacy. The Third Filipino Inter-Community Council of the Western States Conference was under way in Oakland when the delegates—including Macario Bautista and Felipe Esteban of Stockton—received word of his death, and they ceased business to hold a short memorial service. Speeches and songs were delivered amid audible sobs.[69] In deep shock and mourning, the Filipina/o community and FALA attempted to reorganize and regroup. Earlier that summer, Bautista had taken a position as a West Coast representative of the resident commissioner's office.[70] On July 1, only days after Varona's death, the shaken members of the FALA gathered at the Stockton Civic Auditorium and elected Johnny Dionisio president.[71] But by this time, the FALA's influence was largely diminished. The union's last gasp occurred in the spring of 1942, when the San Joaquin Cannery Workers Union took over trusteeship of it and demanded from growers $1.50 per hundred pounds of asparagus.[72] World War II brought an end to the FALA, whose members left farm work to enlist or work in the defense industry, and wartime wages were relatively high.[73] In 1944 Dionisio was appointed as a western representative of the resident commissioner's office, and after the war he became a staff member of the first Philippine Consulate in San Francisco.[74]

Despite the early victories of the FALA, by the eve of World War II, Filipinas/os and their pleas for political recognition and fair wages and working conditions were still largely ignored or, as in the case of the Marcantonio bill, completely rebuffed. But activists like Bulosan and Candelario in Stockton had no idea that within a few years, their work would bear fruit. The movement for Filipina/o political empowerment and social mobility and acceptance in Stockton and on a national level would be hastened by the coming of the war. In late July 1941, Roosevelt called General Douglas MacArthur back into service and placed him in charge of organizing Filipino units into the U.S. forces in the Far East. Commonwealth President Roxas embraced MacArthur's promotion and what appeared to be a firm commitment from the United States to defend its colony.[75]

WAR COMES TO LITTLE MANILA

The bombing of Pearl Harbor on December 7, 1941, and the bombing of American military bases in the Philippines almost immediately afterward stunned the general U.S. public and threw the Oriental Quarter of Stockton into an uproar. Competing nationalisms, changing attitudes about race, and long-simmering tensions among the Filipina/o, Japanese, and Chinese communities erupted in the first few weeks of the war. Once seen as half-human, inferior savages, Chinese and Filipinas/os were suddenly America's allies, while the Stockton Japanese community immediately found itself the target of racist attacks from their Asian neighbors as well as whites. Once the favored racial minorities of white elites in the Delta, ethnic Japanese found themselves under racial attack and intense scrutiny in Stockton through the winter and spring of 1941–42. Filipinas/os and Chinese clamored to join the war effort through enlistment, relief work, work in the defense industries, and the purchase of war bonds.

Up and down the West Coast, Filipinas/os reacted with shock, anger, and fits of hysterical violence to the news of Pearl Harbor and the Japanese invasion and occupation of the Philippines. On the day of the Pearl Harbor attack, extra police cars patrolled the Oriental Quarter, and the San Joaquin County Sheriff was called to Terminous Tract north of Stockton, where tension had been reported between several hundred Japanese and smaller numbers of Filipinos.[76] Days after the bombing of Pearl Harbor and the invasion of the Philippines, the Filipino Community of Stockton, led by Teofilo Suarez, met at Rizal Hall (the Filipino-owned taxi-dance hall also known as the Rizal Social Club) at 138 East Lafayette Street. The members of the group pledged their loyalty to America, declared a boycott of all Japanese-owned businesses, ordered all Filipinas/os to move out of Japanese rooming houses, and suggested that all Filipinas/os wear identification buttons to prevent their being mistaken for Japanese. Dozens of Filipinas/os moved out of hotels owned or leased by Japanese immediately after the meeting.[77] The Caballeros de Dimas Alang made identification buttons that read "I AM FILIPINO" and were "swarmed" by Filipinas/os who desired to purchase them.[78]

Soon after the bombings, an editorial in the *Stockton Daily Evening Record* called on Filipinas/os and Chinese to "not take out their resentment on Nippon's racials."[79] But the *Record* was too late. Stockton Filipinas/os were prepared to arm themselves against the Japanese community, Camila Carido remembered. She supported Japanese internment because she believed removal of the Japanese would protect them from vengeful Filipinas/os who might hurt or kill them. "Oh, lotsa Filipinos were armed, ready to kill the Japanese," she remembered. "Lucky thing the Japanese were sent out to the camps, otherwise there would have been lotsa Japanese just fall out and died, and nobody knows! They had bad feeling against them, especially with all the killing in the Philippines. Lotsa Japanese here [in Stockton)] they just disappear! Good thing that President Roosevelt had that idea to bring the Japanese, even if you are an American citizen, to the camp. Otherwise, there were lotsa people killed!" Carido recalled arguing with friends and family members who were angry over the deaths of relatives in the Philippines and wanted to take their anger out on Japanese Americans: "I tell my husband, don't kill nobody!"[80] On February 20, 1941, the *Stockton Daily Evening Record* reported that at least two Japanese had been murdered mysteriously in the Oriental Quarter since the beginning of the war.[81]

An editor of the *Philippines Mail* berated Filipinas/o for their anti-Japanese racism: "Race hatred is . . . sheer stupidity. . . . There is still plenty we can do without inciting hysterical mob action."[82] His voice was drowned out by calls for nationwide boycotts and spontaneous walkouts of Filipina/o laborers working for Japanese farmers. Other Filipinos writing opinion pieces in the *Philippines Mail* justified the mass boycotts. One reasoned that Filipinas/os shouldn't work for or buy anything from the Japanese, as "any help the Japs get here will become an instrument to buy more bombs" and that Japanese settlement on the West Coast was part of Japan's world program.[83] Another insisted that a boycott prevented Japanese immigrants from rendering comfort and aid to Japan.[84] On December 27, a riot involving Filipinos and Japanese erupted in Little Manila, but there were no arrests or fatalities reported.[85] On New Year's Eve, 1941, Stockton police were alerted of a "huge racial riot" between Filipinas/os and Japanese in the downtown area.[86] It turned out to be only a rumor. However, according to Nelson Nagai, and as implied by Camila Carido, several Japanese residents of the Japantown or Little Manila neighborhoods were killed by Filipinos in the weeks after Pearl Harbor, but no one was ever arrested.[87]

In the first months of the Pacific war, the Japanese Imperial Army swiftly crushed the American forces in battle after battle. Stories of torture, starvation, beatings, and the brutality of the Japanese troops filtered back to Little Manila's residents through newspaper and radio accounts. All of Little Manila's residents had children or other relatives who were directly affected by the war or serving in the U.S. Armed Forces in the Far East (USAFFE). As soon as the war began, my father, Ernesto T. Mabalon, then only fifteen, enlisted in the USAFFE, claiming to be eighteen. He eventually rose to the rank of staff sergeant of E Company, 2nd Battalion, 66th Infantry, in the Sixth Military District.[88] When the Philippines fell and my father and his battalion went underground as guerrilla soldiers, he could no longer communicate with his mother, Isabel Mabalon, or his father, Pablo Mabalon, who was in Stockton.

FILIPINAS/OS, STOCKTON, AND WAR

During the war, Stockton, with its numerous military bases, became one of the most important cities on the West Coast, particularly in terms of shipbuilding and munitions work. The city's landscape and economy were transformed by the war and the influx of millions of dollars of military infrastructure and defense contracts. The War Department mandated that manufacture of military materiel be at least sixty miles from the coast to avoid enemy attacks. As the largest inland port on the West Coast, and close to three military installations, Stockton was strategically located for the defense industry, particularly shipbuilding. In 1944 Rough and Ready Island, in South Stockton, was transformed into a $20 million Naval Supply Depot, which supplied the Pacific Fleet. The army depot in sleepy French Camp, just south of Stockton, became the supply base of the Pacific. The historian Olive Davis argues that because of the concentration in shipbuilding and materiel, as well as its strategic position as a port and supply center, Stockton was considered the number one military target in California.[89]

After the Japanese bombing of Pearl Harbor and invasion of the Philippines, thousands of Filipinos rushed to their local recruiting offices, only to be turned away because they were aliens ineligible for citizenship. Writing that it was "disgusting that laws have been passed to bar them from more active participation in the war program," journalists at the *Commonwealth Times* demanded that a nationwide program for Filipino war relief be instituted and that Filipinos be allowed to enter the armed forces.[90] A turning point for the Filipina/o and Japanese communities in Stockton came in February 1942. On February 19 Filipinas/os in Stockton were finally given a chance to play a formal role in the war, and the "problem" of the Japanese on the coast was brought to a tragic resolution. Sensing a public relations opportunity that would lift morale in both the Philippines and the United States, President Franklin Roosevelt announced he was changing the draft law to allow Filipinos to join the military and work in the defense industry. An amendment to the Nationality Act of 1940 allowed Filipinos who enlisted in the military to become naturalized citizens.[91] In California approximately 16,000 Filipinos attempted to enlist in the U.S. Army, about two-fifths of the state's Filipino population. In keeping with the army's segregation policy, most of the 7,000 Filipinos who eventually enlisted were organized into two all-Filipino regiments in the spring of 1942: the First and Second Filipino Infantry Regiments.[92] Filipinos in Stockton also formed their own local Filipino unit of the National Guard.[93] Representatives of these groups marched proudly in the Fourth of July parade with other Filipina/o contingents during the war (see figure 33).

In language much different from the rhetoric used by lawmakers to rebuff moves toward Filipina/o naturalization only a few months earlier, Secretary of War Henry Stimson stated that the Filipino regiments were formed because of the "intense loyalty and patriotism" of Filipinos in the United

33. Members of the Teodoro Alonzo Lodge of the Legionarios del Trabajo remind Stockton of Bataan and Corregidor as they march proudly in Filipina dresses and in military uniforms at a Fourth of July parade during World War II. Courtesy of FANHS Stockton.

States.[94] The act of formally joining the U.S. military and, after decades of struggle, being granted the right to become an American citizen imbued enlisted Filipinos with a sense of pride and dignity, as well as intense feelings of patriotism and nationalism.[95]

The same day that he announced changes in the draft law, Roosevelt issued Executive Order 9066, which directed the incarceration of ethnic Japanese in concentration camps. By May 1942 the Japanese of Stockton had been imprisoned at the hastily built Assembly Center at the San Joaquin County fairgrounds and were awaiting transfer to the Rohwer camp, in Arkansas.[96] The handful of Stockton's mixed-heritage Filipino-Japanese families, such as the Espineda family, were also incarcerated.[97] Camila Carido remembered that several Filipinas/os broke into the hall in which the Japanese had stored their belongings and stole "all!" "The American people didn't care," she said.[98] Though newspaper reports do not corroborate Carido's memory of the incident, several community members, including Claro Candelario, repeated similar stories. Whether or not they are true is beside the point: these stories demonstrate that some Filipinas/os felt great pleasure and triumph in hurting the Japanese at their most vulnerable to avenge the treatment Filipinas/os had endured at the hands of Japanese farmers and merchants throughout the 1920s and the Depression, and to retaliate for the Japanese invasion and occupation of the Philippines.

Arguing that food production was essential for the war effort, in January 1942 Bautista called for changes in the state's Alien Land Law to allow Filipinas/os to lease farmland. Initially, there was no response to the proposal, but after the local Japanese were removed, the Alien Land Law was amended to allow noncitizen Filipinas/os, Mexicans, and Chinese to lease land. In addition, the Wartime Civilian Control Administration offered special Farm Security loans to Filipino farmworkers eager to lease land formerly farmed by the Issei.[99] With these changes, several Filipinos were able to take over the leases of formerly Japanese farms and become farmers and growers. In September 1944 Filipinas/os organized the San Joaquin Cooperative Growers Association. The organization's president was Anastasio B. Pagala, who had been the business agent of the FALA in its first year.

Filipina/o businesspeople also saw opportunity in the tragedy of Japanese removal. Alex Fabros, the editor of the Salinas-based *Philippines Mail*, encouraged Filipinas/os to jump at the opportunity provided by internment. "This is the best time for enterprising people to open new businesses now that the Japs who once controlled 90 to 95 percent of Pinoys' patronage have closed their [joints]," he wrote in January 1942.[100] Heeding Fabros's advice, and also on their own accord, Filipina/o merchants and entrepreneurs flourished as the city's wartime economy boomed and the city's Japanese American entrepreneurs were forced out. Japanese hotels, restaurants, employment agencies, and other businesses were transformed almost overnight into Filipina/o ones (see map 5).[101] In many cases, these Filipina/o entrepreneurs changed the Japanese names of businesses to patriotic Filipina/o ones or ones that reflected World War II heroism. For example, in an ironic twist, the office on the ground floor of the Japanese hotel at 241 South El Dorado Street — which had been the office of Dr. Bautista until Morimoto evicted him in 1940 — became in 1941 Fernando Buslon's Filipino employment agency. Filipinas/os took over the hotel's management and renamed it the Bataan Hotel sometime during the war. In 1946 the former Fukuokaya Hotel at 228 South El Dorado Street was taken over by Cirilo Juanitas, who renamed it the Quezon Hotel, after Manuel Quezon, the president of the Philippine Commonwealth. Immediately after the end of the war, dozens of Filipinas/os in Stockton pooled their resources and invested in a Filipina/o American development company called Bataan-Manila Enterprises, Inc. Soon after the war, the company owned two buildings. One was at 245 South El Dorado and

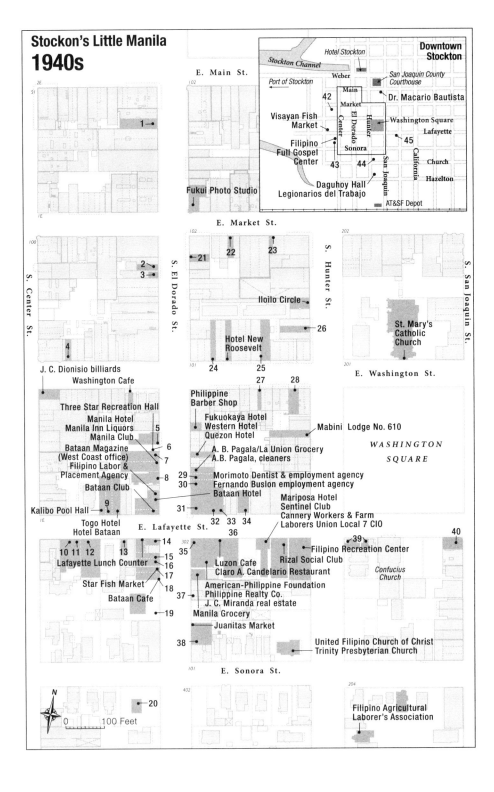

Stockon's Little Manila
1940s

E. Main St.

Downtown Stockton

Stockton Channel

Hotel Stockton

Port of Stockton

Weber

San Joaquin County Courthouse

Main

42

Market

Visayan Fish Market

El Dorado

Hunter

Dr. Macario Bautista

Washington Square

Lafayette

Filipino Full Gospel Center

Sonora

45

43

44

Church

Hazelton

San Joaquin

California

Fukui Photo Studio

Daguhoy Hall
Legionarios del Trabajo

AT&SF Depot

E. Market St.

S. Center St.

S. El Dorado St.

2E

SI

2E

100

IE

1

2
3

4

21

22

23

Iloilo Circle

26

Hotel New Roosevelt

24   25
      27   28

S. Hunter St.

St. Mary's Catholic Church

E. Washington St.

S. San Joaquin St.

202

201

J. C. Dionisio billiards
Washington Cafe

Three Star Recreation Hall
Manila Hotel
Manila Inn Liquors
Manila Club
Bataan Magazine
(West Coast office)
Filipino Labor & Placement Agency
Bataan Club

Kalibo Pool Hall

Togo Hotel
Hotel Bataan

IE

Philippine Barber Shop

Fukuokaya Hotel
Western Hotel
Quezon Hotel

A. B. Pagala/La Union Grocery
A.B. Pagala, cleaners

Morimoto Dentist & employment agency
Fernando Buslon employment agency
Bataan Hotel

Mabini Lodge No. 610

WASHINGTON

SQUARE

Mariposa Hotel
Sentinel Club
Cannery Workers & Farm
Laborers Union Local 7 CIO

5

6

7

8

29
30

9

31

32 33 34
36

E. Lafayette St.

10 11 12   13
Lafayette Lunch Counter

Star Fish Market

Bataan Cafe

35

14
15
16
17
18
19

302

Luzon Cafe
Claro A. Candelario Restaurant

American-Philippine Foundation
Philippine Realty Co.
J. C. Miranda real estate

Manila Grocery

Juanitas Market

39

Filipino Recreation Center

Rizal Social Club

Confucius Church

40

United Filipino Church of Christ
Trinity Presbyterian Church

37

38

101

E. Sonora St.

204

N

20

0   100 Feet

402

Filipino Agricultural Laborer's Association

5. Little Manila in the 1940s. The booming wartime economy and the internment of Japanese Americans, who had owned most of the businesses in the area, allowed Filipinas/os to open more businesses in Little Manila. SOURCE: POLK CITY DIRECTORIES, 1940–50. MAP BY BEN PEASE.

Numbers within parentheses indicate the businesses' chronological order at the sites.

1. Square Deal Store
2. Caruso (shoe shiner)
3. Sam Caruso (shoe shiner)
4. L. D. Cordova
5. Melecio Suguitan (barber)
6. (1) B.C. Magracia (barber); (2) Three Star Recreation Hall (pool hall); (3) Peter Patayan (pool hall); (4) Jos. Aurelio (pool hall); (5) Monaco Orellio (pool hall)
7. (1) P. D. Lazaro (dry goods); (2) Manila Inn Liquors
8. New Continent Fountain
9. Martin Carillo (pool hall)
10. Saurez Cleaners
11. Lapu Lapu Lodge
12. Lu Vi Min Social Club Inc.
13. Panay Apartments
14. (1) Fuertis (pool hall); (2) Filipino Club (pool hall)
15. Aklan Cleaners
16. J. P. Cabalteja (barber)
17. (1) C. S. Lonero (fish); (2) Star Fish Market
18. (1) Tamarao Club; (2) John Latosa Restaurant; (3) Bataan Café
19. (1) T. C. Supnet (auto repair); (2) Lincoln Super Service (auto repair)
20. Evans Service Station No.4
21. Hollywood Bath House and Barber Shop; (2) I. V. Labre (barber)
22. M. M. Balot (barber)
23. Agraciano Enriquez Restaurant
24. Victor's Barber Shop, Victor Catapang
25. (1) Pastor Engkabo (pool hall); (2) Pete Algas (CIO agent)
26. J. P. Cabalteja (barber) and C. B. Lacosta (pool hall)
27. Filipino Rooms
28. F. B. Marcelo and Eugenio Castillo (furnished rooms for rent) (1947–48) [to left, below 28]: N. L. Fuertis Grocery moved in after the Quezon Hotel [to left, below 28]: John Berzamina Restaurant and Michael Biniegla Restaurant both were onsite before the A. B. Pagala businesses
29. (1) Paul Porganan Cleaners; (2) Process Baylon (dry goods)
30. (1) La Union Supply Co. (grocery); (2) Roman Ordono Restaurant
31. El Dorado Market
32. Kaboyan Laundry and Cleaners
33. Andres Alvarico (restaurant)
34. E. R. Liwanag (auto repair)
35. (1) Alberca Bernabe (garage); (2) E. O. Viviano (garage)
36. (1) California Laundry; (2) Colonial Cleaners
37. Dioscoro Bonjoc (meats)
38. Dionicio Unsod (cleaners)
39. (1) Primitivo Reyes and family; (2) Mrs. Segunda C. Reyes Beauty Shop
40. L.V.M. Café
41. Reliable Farm Labor Supply
42. L. P. Canlis Restaurant
43. Daquiado & Co.
44. Raffanti's Inn
45. Kiliat Marceli (auto repair)

housed the Bataan Hotel, Bataan Cigar Stand, Bataan Pool Hall, and Bataan Club. The other building, at 227 South El Dorado, housed the Manila Hotel, Manila Inn, Manila Bar, Manila Cigar Stand, and Manila Club.[102]

During the war, public attitudes shifted racial discourse decisively in favor of Filipinas/os because China and the Philippines were important allies, and the Japanese became the new racial scapegoats. The three-month long battle of Bataan and the bravery of soldiers on the Bataan Death March and at Corregidor was reported in Stockton as front-page news, which noted American-Filipino bravery and heroism, moving and impressing whites. The *Stockton Daily Evening Record*'s pages were filled with stories of heroism in the Philippines and images of the exploits of Filipino and American soldiers during the valiant struggle for the Philippines.[103] The newspaper described Filipino soldiers as "heroic," "stoic," and "valiant," and published photos of the First Filipino Infantry in training at Camp San Luis Obispo.[104] When Jose Calugas, a 116-pound mess sergeant, was awarded the Congressional Medal of Honor for bravery during the fighting in Bataan, the *Stockton Daily Evening Record* gushed with praise: "The Filipinos won respect as hard fighters in Funston's time at the hinge of the century. Another generation of Filipinos—this time as comrades in arms—are proving their mettle."[105] Only a few years before, the same editors denigrated Filipinas/os as unassimilable sexual deviants and miscreants.

During the war, Stockton's elite began to welcome Filipinas/os into their homes as guests and not only as domestics. The Filipino-American Literary Club, a social organization formed in 1941 by Protestant missionaries connected with the Lighthouse Mission and second-generation Protestant Filipinas, met monthly to discuss the Bible and to pray together at Filipina/o and white homes. At the 1942 annual dinner, hosted in the home of an elite white family in North Stockton, the white women were pleasantly surprised to learn that Filipinas were civilized. "These women are just like we are!" exclaimed one attendee.[106] Stockton's elite white women of the north Stockton Philomathean Club, a philanthropic and social club, warmly welcomed Pilar Hildago-Lim, a mathematics professor at the University of the Philippines and the wife of Vicente Lim, Brigadier General of the Philippine Scouts and the first Filipino graduate of West Point, for a talk about the heroics of Filipino soldiers at Corregidor and postwar Philippine independence in January 1944.[107] Even First Lady Eleanor Roosevelt spoke about the brotherhood forged in the Philippines and the racial understanding that had been borne from the war. The courageous fighting in the Philippines, she said, "has been an excellent example of what happens when two different races respect each other. Men of different races and backgrounds have fought side by side and praised each other's heroism and courage."[108]

Filipinas/os reveled in their new status as "good" Asians, now that the Asians previously favored by white elites were imprisoned in concentration camps. The Filipino writer Manuel Buaken wrote in his memoirs: "No longer . . . do I feel myself in the presence of my enemies. We Filipinos are the same—it is Americans that have changed in their recognition of us."[109] Much like the black soldiers inspired by the black community's Double Victory campaign (the *Pittsburgh Courier's* wartime slogan of victory over fascism abroad and racism at home), many Filipinas/os saw their service in the war as a struggle for freedom from the Japanese occupation in the Philippines and anti-Filipina/o racism at home. "Oh Emancipating War!" wrote Fernando Taggoa, a Stanford student, in 1942. "Gone will be the thousands of Filipinos, particularly in California, relieved of the brunt of prejudice and injustice. No more shall the illiterate workers be oppressed, exploited and made to live in shacks and hovels, for they will have gone to fight and die for their freedom!"[110]

With public opinion now on their side, Filipinas/os took every opportunity to join whites in demonizing Japanese Americans. In the heady nationalism of the war, some Filipinas/os easily forgot that through the Depression, they had little reason to celebrate American ideals of liberty and civil equality. Smug Filipinas/os were now insisting that while the Japanese community had selfishly taken advantage of American opportunities and remained foreign, Filipinas/os had loyally assimilated and upheld American values. Many Filipinas/os supported internment for various reasons: some sympathetic to the Japanese felt that it protected them from racial violence; while others, bitter over Depression-era relations between the Japanese and Filipinas/os, derived personal satisfaction from seeing the Japanese lose their land and experience extreme racial repression.

Even Filipinas/os who blasted American imperialism and racism before Pearl Harbor now behaved as though they were still loyal colonial subjects who worshipped at the knee of Mother America, and they accused the Japanese of being sinister, anti-American fifth columnists. Buaken implied that Filipinas/os were better Americans than Japanese: "We have always wanted nothing more than to learn from America, to become good Americans." He went on to criticize Japanese American entrepreneurs who formed their own banks, ethnic stores, and Japanese schools: "We have striven to learn English, not to perpetuate foreign language schools and to teach foreign ideas to our children."[111] Nationalist Filipino leaders arrogantly compared themselves favorably to what they called the "disloyal," "alien," and "unpatriotic" Japanese. Vicente Villamin, an attorney, exhorted Japanese Americans interned in the camps to "intensify" their feelings of "gratitude for the United States for the opportunity in pre-war times to have lived, worked and prospered under its flag." Additionally, he wrote that internees should "overlook the legal and/or legalistic considerations surrounding American citizenship and its treatment while the emergency of the war lasted."[112]

In this atmosphere of positive Filipina/o sentiment, Bulosan, the Stockton Filipina/o American community's most famous writer, published an essay to accompany Norman Rockwell's painting *Freedom from Want*, referring to President Roosevelt's stirring wartime speech on "The Four Freedoms" (the other three were freedom from fear, freedom of speech, and freedom of worship) in the *Saturday Evening Post* and was thus discovered by the rest of the country, as August Espiritu writes.[113] Bulosan's essay was an eloquent and impassioned Popular Front plea for the American working class. "So long as the fruit of our labor is denied us, so long will want manifest itself in a world of slaves," he wrote. "It is only when we have plenty to eat—plenty of everything—that we begin to understand what freedom means." The essay also reflected some of the deep yearnings of Filipinas/os to live in the America they had idealized, and Bulosan's changing ideas about how that nation lived in the dreams of its denizens. "The America we hope to see is not merely a physical but also a spiritual and intellectual world," he wrote. "We are the mirror of what America *is*. If America wants us to be living and free, then we must be living and free. . . . We want to share the promises and fruits of American life. We want to be free from fear and hunger."[114] In retrospect, it was a daring essay that could not have been penned before the war, when attitudes toward Filipinas/os were more negative.

In April 1945 Johnny Dionisio addressed the California State Assembly, reminding its members of the heroism of Filipino soldiers in Bataan and appealing for legislation sympathetic to the more than 30,000 Filipina/o residents of the state. By then, Dionisio was an official in the San Francisco office of the resident commissioner. "They are the brothers, the cousins, the kinsfolk of the 21,000 Filipino soldiers who died for you—the American flag, in the foxholes of Bataan," he said. "They are law-abiding, industrious, respectful of the rights of others. I appeal to you: please remember them when you make your laws. . . . Filipino-American friendship has been sealed in blood and flowed together in the dust. . . . Filipino [and] American bodies were mangled by the same Japanese bombs, riddled by the same Japanese bullets. Please remember that we share the same hopes, dream the same dreams, fight the same fight for a better world to live in."[115]

Dionisio could deliver this speech in 1945 because attitudes toward Filipinas/os across the nation were the most positive they had ever been. With the war in the Philippines as their rallying point, the increasingly factionalized Filipina/o community in Stockton strove vainly to continue to live up to its self-proclaimed status as a model Filipina/o community. The annual dances, fund-raisers, dinners, potlucks, conferences, and conventions went on, albeit on a less grand scale with thousands of Filipino men missing, and with a nationalist consciousness and a heady awareness of the rising status of Filipinas/os in Stockton. Pinays in Stockton worked tirelessly for the war effort, organizing women's groups for war relief work, visiting Filipino soldiers undergoing training in Salinas, and organizing war bond drives that raised thousands of dollars for the war effort. In November 1944, Bautista, president of the Stockton Filipino Community, presented the Treasury Department with $97,075 in war bonds (approximately $1.24 million in 2012 dollars). This was an enormous amount, considering most Filipina/o wage earners were in farmwork.[116]

WAR WORK

The war also offered opportunities for Filipinos who did not enlist. Filipinas/os left agriculture by the thousands to work in defense-related industries. Filipina/o workers benefited greatly when, in 1942, Roosevelt created the Fair Employment Practices Commission and barred discrimination in all defense work hiring, bowing to pressure from A. Philip Randolph and other civil rights activists who had threatened a march on Washington if such practices were not banned.[117] Many Filipinas/os found work in shipbuilding and other war work. The exodus of Filipino laborers to the armed forces and to the defense industries threw area farmers, already reeling from the loss of Japanese tenant farmers, into a crisis. Employers who desired Filipina/o labor raised their wages so that their employees would not leave their jobs to enlist in the U.S. Army, but the shortage continued. For example, Filipinas/os working in the asparagus fields in the spring of 1942 left for the Alaska salmon canneries soon after the season ended, enticed by an overtime wage of $1 per hour and monthly wages ranging from $135 to $190.[118] Despite slavish pro-American rhetoric in the Filipina/o press, hardened Filipino laborers, tempered from the FALA struggles of the 1930s, persisted in their demands for better wages throughout the war. In the asparagus seasons of 1942 and 1943, faced with a labor shortage caused by thousands of Filipinos joining the army and hundreds more refusing to work unless wages were raised, asparagus farmers clamored for Filipina/o workers, eventually settling for several hundred Mexican laborers brought in to save the harvest.[119]

The growers in the Delta area, sensing an impending crisis in the shortage of Filipino labor, called on government officials to issue military deferments to Filipinos and promoted the importation of thousands of Mexican workers. By 1943 farmers were pushing the State Department to hasten the arrival of Mexican contracted bracero laborers to help harvest the year's crops, beginning a phenomenon that would bring thousands of Mexican farm laborers into the United States through the 1960s.[120] In 1943, 33,000 Mexican bracero laborers were promised to San Joaquin County growers, and grateful growers organized a welcome fiesta for the Mexican laborers who streamed into the valley that spring.[121] Filipino newspapers such as the *Philippines Mail* warned Filipinas/os engaged in farm labor to refrain from causing racial strife with Mexican laborers in the fields.[122]

The continued labor militance of Filipinas/os in Stockton worried leaders who were anxious to show white elites that Filipinas/os were fully cooperating with the war effort. Ever anti-union, the Filipino Federation of America in the spring of 1943 called on Filipinas/os to "stick to their jobs" and berated them for insisting on higher pay. E. C. Pecson, then the acting president of the FFA, told the *Stockton Daily Evening Record* that the Filipinos' refusal to work "is a deliberate aid to the enemy of democracies and an obstacle on the path of the victory which will win back for us our beloved Philippine Islands."[123] Evidently few Filipinas/os listened to Pecson because the same problems emerged in the asparagus harvest of 1944, prompting Reverend D. F. Gonzalo, a local Filipino Methodist pastor, to write to the *Record* in support of Filipinas/os' insistence on higher wages.[124] Filipina/o workers, confident in their value to area farmers, continued to stage walkouts and strikes. In June of 1946, a rice shortage brought on by wartime rationing pushed hundreds of Filipina/o workers to demand rice in their daily diets, or else they would walk off the asparagus fields. Hundreds of the 5,000 Filipinos working the asparagus that spring left their jobs.[125]

Pinays, already performing labor in the fields and in service-sector jobs in Little Manila as well as performing reproductive labor in the home, found themselves working even harder during wartime. Like all women in the United States during the war, they had to feed their families in spite of the rationing of such foods as meat and sugar, and doing without all luxury foods. Because Pinays traditionally controlled all aspects of the household budget, their ability to make ends meet during the war meant the survival of their households. Pinays found employment in jobs previously denied to women because of increased wartime opportunities. Segunda Reyes, the Cebuana teacher who had previously worked in agricultural labor, found work as a pipe welder in the Naval Supply Annex on Rough and Ready Island in Stockton, where 5,000 other Stocktonians, 18 percent of them women, also worked. "I was the only woman that can weld pipes!" she recalled.[126] Additionally, Filipinas sang patriotic songs and performed Filipino cultural dances at fund-raising dinners and war bond drives, as I discussed in chapter 4. The community, which had lost several leaders since the death of Francisco Varona and the demise of the FALA, overwhelmingly reelected Bautista the president of the Filipino Community of Stockton, Inc., in the spring of 1944. With the popular Bautista back at the helm, the community members seemed poised once again to commit themselves to community development. In the same month, Filipinas in Stockton organized the Filipino Community Women's Club, with the twin goals of building a better Stockton community and unifying all Filipinas/os in the city.[127]

But despite the more positive wartime attitudes about Filipinas/os in Stockton and on the West Coast, and though thousands of Americans nationwide were reading Bulosan's popular poetry collection, *Voice of Bataan*, Stockton's segregation was still rigidly enforced through the war, which was why Romulo's speech was such a stinging rebuke to Stockton's whites. The journalist Wallace Stegner and a camera crew from *Look* magazine visited the Filipina/o American community in Stockton in 1945 for a book, *One Nation*, which detailed the wartime racism and intolerance directed against minority groups in the United States. Stegner noted that Filipinas/os in Stockton owned their own small businesses in Little Manila, worked hard in the fields, were patriotic and loyal, had wholesome family lives, and had the same values as other Americans. A *Look* photographer snapped a photo of the front of a downtown hotel with the sign "Positively No Filipinos Allowed." The editor's caption was filled with irony: "How about our feeling towards the Filipinos?"[128]

Even through the war, movie theaters in Stockton still segregated Filipinas/os from other moviegoers. When Emily Rosal, born in Hawai'i, first arrived in Stockton in 1945, she was directed to the balcony when she went to see *Gone with the Wind* at the Fox Theater. "I learned that the segregation here in Stockton was pretty bad," she remembered. The white usher was adamant, telling Rosal that she and her girlfriends did not belong in a certain part of the theater. "I says, 'I beg your pardon? What do you mean we don't belong here?'" she recalled. "Finally, he won, so we sat in the corner where we were told." Rosal also discovered that buses were segregated in Stockton, even after the war. "When you ride a bus, you were told to sit in the back, and then I would say, 'Why?! I'm just as human as you guys!'" she recalled.[129]

As the war came to a close in 1945, the intense nationalism and loyalty (to both the United States and the Philippines) of the troops, as well as the bravery of Filipino soldiers in the Philippines, allayed some racial tensions between whites and Filipinas/os and bolstered Filipina/o nationalism and ethnic pride. Lingering bitterness over the racism of the 1930s and arrogance over their new position in the racial hierarchy fueled condescending sentiments about the returning Japanese. The Stockton City Council, reflecting attitudes popular around the country, passed a resolution in 1943 that expressed strong opposition to the return of Japanese to the State of California and the Pacific Coast. Such a return, wrote city councilmen, "would be detrimental to the best interest and general welfare of the State of California and the United States in general."[130] Japanese and Japanese Americans found themselves at the bottom of Stockton's racial hierarchy at the end of the war. Though Japanese Americans did return to Stockton in smaller numbers after the war, the resolution was not rescinded until 2000.

The pro-U.S. and pro-Philippines nationalism that arose out of the war effort transcended the petty factionalism and regionalism that had characterized the Stockton Filipina/o community prior to the war. As the "loyal" Asians, Filipinas/os were seen in a new light by Stockton's ruling elites. They used this new position in the country's racial hierarchy, and the Delta racial hierarchy, to demand civic equality for themselves and independence for the Philippines, and their efforts were rewarded. Filipina/o Americans were overjoyed when the U.S. Senate voted in December 1943 to give the Philippines independence following liberation of the islands. After a long battle against California's 1913 Alien Land Law, waged by the Filipino Inter-Community Council and San Francisco Filipino community leader Celestino T. Alfafara, the California Supreme Court in May 1945 ruled in *Alfafara v. Fross* that Filipinas/os were not aliens and could now officially own land. Alfafara had purchased land in San Mateo and the landowner had refused to transfer title to him, citing the Alien Land Law, Alfafara took the case all the way to the state Supreme Court.[131] The ruling was a boon for Filipinas/os. By the end of 1945, approximately 10,000 Filipino veterans had become citizens.[132] The swiftness of the political process was a stark contrast to Filipina/o life in Stockton before the war, when Filipinas/os had lived in constant repression under the hegemonic system of white supremacist rule and Japanese control over their labor.

AFTER THE WAR: EMBRACING THE AMERICAN DREAM
The end of the war brought immense relief and joy to Stockton's Filipina/o American community. Civil rights gains, sweeping changes in immigration and naturalization laws, more employment opportunities, the ability to live outside of Little Manila, and the benefits of the GI Bill would bring Fili-

pinas/os in the United States the opportunities and benefits of life in America for which they had been struggling for decades, such as citizenship, land-ownership, and family building. The most important change in the lives of Filipinas/os in the United States at the end of the war was the removal of the racial ban on citizenship for Filipinas/os. On July 2, 1946, President Harry Truman signed the Luce-Celler Act, which granted Filipinas/os and Indians racial eligibility for naturalization and increased the annual quota of Filipina/o entry visas to one hundred annually. Two days later, on July 4, 1946, the United States officially granted independence to the Philippines.

Filipinas/os in Stockton immediately scrambled to file for citizenship, prepare for their examinations, and have their citizenship application pictures taken at Bob's Studio and Carla Studio, two Filipina/o-owned photo studios on Main Street.[133] A special swearing-in program on May 19, 1949, honored more than two hundred new citizens, almost all of them Filipina/o Americans, at the Jackson School Auditorium, sponsored by the Board of Education, Stockton Evening High School, and Stockton College. Among those sworn in on that day were the community leaders Leo and Camila Carido, Claro Candelario, Pastor Engkabo Sr., and Pedro Adlao.[134] After the war, the sex ratio would finally be balanced, as postwar immigration brought over thousands of men and women annually: students, professionals, nurses, children of old-timers, and war brides married to current or former servicemen, as well as Filipina/o migrants from Hawai'i. Many Filipinas/os who had served in the U.S. military also settled in Stockton with their families because of the town's proximity to the Sharpe Army Depot in French Camp and the Rough and Ready Island Naval Station.

All of the Filipinas/os who had joined the U.S. military during the war were eligible for GI Bill benefits. The GI Bill of Rights, the brainchild of Warren Atherton—a Stockton attorney and the national commander of the American Legion—was the most wide-ranging set of social benefits ever offered by the federal government.[135] The GI Bill propelled millions, mostly whites, into the middle class through its educational benefits (college tuition and a stipend paid by the government, even up to a doctoral degree), job training programs, no-down-payment and low- or no-interest loan programs for single family homes and businesses, and unemployment benefits of $20 per week for up to one year.[136] But like African Americans and other veterans of color, Filipinas/os did not benefit from the GI Bill in the same ways as whites. For example, most Filipinas/os were barred by restrictive covenants and devious real estate agents from purchasing homes in white neighborhoods. Also, for the many older Filipina/o veterans, the college benefits that the GI Bill offered came two decades too late. For example, like their African American and Mexican American counterparts, most Filipinas/os lacked high school degrees and/or the proper preparation to attend college, and instead they had to return to work immediately after the war in order to support their families.

But Filipina/o American veterans who served in the First and Second Filipino Infantry and in other branches of the military were somewhat better off than their counterparts in the Philippines. Receiving the worst postwar benefit package were the more than 250,000 Filipino veterans who had joined the USAFFE in the Philippines, among them my father, Ernesto Mabalon. In 1946 Congress passed the Rescission Act, which declared that their service "shall not be deemed to be or to have been service in the military or national forces of the United States or any component thereof or any law of the United States conferring rights, privileges or benefits," even though President Roosevelt had promised them full equity with other veterans. My father, a veteran of the campaigns on the island of Panay, considered the Rescission Act a deep insult. He passed away in 2005, four years before Congress voted to issue a $15,000 one-time payment to each eligible Filipino veteran—a payment some felt was insulting in its implication that the veterans were mercenaries instead of loyal soldiers who were serving their Commonwealth and country.

WAR BRIDES AND FAMILY REUNIFICATION

The new naturalization laws and resulting population explosion after the war made the community grow in leaps and bounds. Though the Luce-Celler Act only allowed one hundred immigrants to enter per year, the dramatic increase came from immigrants arriving as a result of family reunification, the immigration of war brides, and Filipino enlistees in the U.S. Navy and Army. With citizenship, those who had enlisted could now bring over their immediate family members. A provision of the 1924 Immigration Act allowed citizens to welcome their immediate relatives (spouses, parents, and children) as nonquota immigrants. Citizens began the process by filing a petition to the Immigration and Naturalization Service (INS) for an alien relative to obtain an immigrant visa. Now that Filipinas/os could become citizens, they could petition their parents, spouses, and children and reunify their families. Moreover, citizenship and new legislation such as the War Brides Act, passed in 1945, allowed many Filipinos to finally marry and start families. After 1947 the Military Bases Agreement between the Philippines and the United States allowed the military to recruit up to 2,000 Filipinas/os a year; the majority were U.S. Navy seamen. Also among these postwar arrivals were college stu-

34. My grandmother Isabel Tirona Mabalon and grandfather Pablo Magdaluyo Mabalon pose on Lafayette Street to commemorate their reunion in 1947. My father, Ernesto Mabalon, carried this photo in his wallet for much of his life. On the back, he had written: "Mother and Father reunited after 17 years apart." Author's personal collection.

dents, who were allowed to study for graduate degrees in the United States as a result of the U.S. Information and Educational Exchange Act of 1948.[137]

Between 1946 and 1960, approximately 21,912 Filipinas/os immigrated to the United States, and Stockton was one of the main West Coast cities where they chose to settle—along with Seattle, Salinas, Vallejo, San Diego, San Francisco, and Los Angeles.[138] Census numbers tell the story of Filipina immigration and Filipina/o American family formation in the postwar years. In 1940 only 1,502 Filipinas were known to be living in the United States. In 1950 the Census counted 5,141 Filipinas. In 1940 the Census counted only 5,327 married Filipinas/os; in 1950 the number was 17,616.[139]

One of the first to apply for citizenship was my grandfather, Pablo "Ambo" Mabalon, who quickly moved to reunify his transnational family. As soon as he became a citizen in 1946, he petitioned his wife (my grandmother Isabel Tirona Mabalon) and his youngest son, Eutiquio ("Tex"). They arrived in San Francisco on September 24, 1947, and went immediately to Stockton for an emotional reunion (see figure 34). It was the first time that Pablo had seen his wife and youngest son in seventeen years. Still in the Philippines was his oldest daughter, Florencia; her husband, Genaro; and his oldest son, my father Ernesto, who had been honorably discharged from the military and was beginning medical school at the University of Santo Tomas. As his family began to gather around him, Pablo's long decades of solitude came to an end. The war years were profitable ones for his restaurant in Little Manila, the Lafayette Lunch Counter, and the postwar years were prosperous and happy as well. The Lafayette Lunch Counter continued to be a bustling center of life in Little Manila. The postwar boom had been so good for business that in 1947 he managed to buy a three-bedroom home on West Jefferson Street in South Stockton.

Another new citizen who moved quickly to bring his family together was Claro Candelario, who in 1949 was the newly elected president of the Filipino Community of Stockton, Inc. Claro, who ran the Luzon Café at 148 East Lafayette Street, had left his wife and two children behind in La Union when he left his position as a vice principal in a high school and had traveled to California in 1930. After the war, he invited his teenage daughter, Angelina, to visit him in Stockton. Soon after she arrived in Stockton, she decided she wanted to stay and attend the University of the Pacific. "I didn't really know if I was going to stay, but at that point in my life, I also knew my life back home was not going to be the same as when my mom and her sisters were [young adults], the same social status," she recalled.[140]

War brides also constituted a significant number of postwar immigrants to Stockton. The War Brides Act allowed servicemen to bring their wives to the United States with no quota restriction. Approximately 118,000 spouses, among them several thousand Filipinas, came over as a result of the act.[141] Many women also came over in later decades when Filipino Americans took advantage of their new status as citizens, which allowed them to travel back to their hometowns to find a spouse. These families reflected the "late family phenomenon" that was common in many Filipina/o American communities, according to Dorothy Cordova.[142] Even up to the late 1970s, single Pinoys in their sixties and seventies traveled to the Philippines on vacations to find wives and establish families.

As Vince Reyes argues, many Pinoys saw their service in the Philippines as a perfect opportunity to find brides and start families.[143] Most units were chosen for counterintelligence units, the Alamo Scouts of the 6th Army Division, or the Philippine Civil Affairs Units, or PCAU. The PCAU were sent to villages and towns to help in the mop-up efforts, rebuild, and assist civilians with procuring basic needs such as water and food. As the war wound down, thousands of Filipinos serving in the U.S. military used their free time to visit the families they had not seen in almost two decades and to court Filipinas they met in the towns and barrios. Stockton resident Leo Giron was among the thousands of Filipino soldiers who met his wife while serving in the Philippines. When the First and Second Filipino Infantry Regiments were established in 1942, a very select few, such as the Stockton resident Leo Giron, were assigned to top-secret counterintelligence units who were dropped into the Philippines before the return of General MacArthur in the spring of 1945.

Before World War II, only prostitutes would dare be seen with American military men in the Philippines. In the jubilation at the war's end, Caridad Vallangca writes, such taboos about romance with servicemen were abandoned, especially when the suitor was also Filipino, from the United States, and came bearing gifts to the families.[144] Even so, as Vallangca and Emily Porcincula Lawsin argue, many of these women were ridiculed that they would be "*hanggang* pier" only, or wives "up to the pier" only—an insinuation that they would be left behind once their serviceman sweetheart shipped back to the United States.[145] However, because Filipino veterans were desperate for a Filipina wife, most women who were courted by Filipino servicemen did end up marrying their suitors and emigrating to the United States. Filipinos were careful to also court the parents and other relatives of the women they wanted to marry, but, as Reyes writes, these suitors had to engage in abbreviated romances because their tours of duty were so limited. Women, many of whom were ten to twenty years younger than their suitors, had little time to ponder their responses.[146]

Many of the PCAU units were stationed on Leyte, in the Visayas, and Filipino soldiers took every advantage to meet and court Filipinas there on their days off. Modesto Lagura, a veteran of the First Filipino Infantry, said that Visayans used to joke about the many marriages between the mostly Ilocano soldiers and women from the towns of Leyte. The PCAU were sent to Leyte toward the end of the war to mop up the Japanese, Lagura said, but instead they focused on mopping up the countryside clean of marriageable women. They "cleaned up the women from Leyte!" he laughed. "Not the Japanese!"[147] One of the PCAU servicemen sent to mop up Leyte was my maternal grandfather, Delfin Bohulano, a native of Kalibo, in Capiz province, who had lived in California since 1929. Delfin met my grandmother at a dance in her mother's hometown of Palompon, Leyte, where her family stayed during the war. "We were so excited, we just entertain anybody who comes to help us and protect us from the Japanese," my grandmother Concepcion Moreno Bohulano remembered. Delfin brought gifts of food and groceries to the family and won them over with his generosity and industriousness, and Concepcion remembered that he would talk about his life in the United States. When he proposed, Concepcion hesitated, but her relatives insisted that Delfin was a good man. The love came later, she said. Wartime deprivation meant that my grandmother, an expert seamstress, had to fashion a wedding dress from an old parachute. "He had some pigs, chickens somebody raised for him, and we had a big feast on our wedding day," she remembered.[148]

In contrast to other couples who left for the United States soon after the war, my grandparents stayed in the Philippines and used the GI Bill to finish their college educations, relying on their extended family and household help to help them take care of their growing family. In retrospect, this was a smart choice, because the cost of living in the Philippines was low, and they might never have been able to finish their degrees if they had gone immediately to the United States and were forced to work alongside their college studies. Delfin finished a degree in business administration at Far Eastern University in Manila, and Concepcion finished a degree in education at San Carlos University in Cebu. A son, Delfin Jr., was born in 1946; my mother, Cristina, was born in 1947 (her name was later changed to the more American Christine). The family settled in Concepcion's hometown of Cebu City, where she worked as a high school teacher, and Delfin started a grocery store cooperative. In 1950 Delfin heard word from Stockton: wages were rising, and he itched to go back. Emily Lawsin writes that many families did not encourage their daughters to emigrate; this was the case for my grandmother. Concepcion's older brother cried and begged her not to leave, saying that the sacrifice of their parents in working hard to leave them a significant amount of land would be wasted once she left. But Concepcion, who was raised and educated under the American regime, had always dreamed of seeing America. Delfin reached the United States first, in June 1952, and the rest of the family followed him, arriving on the U.S.S. *President Wilson* in San Francisco in August.

Atanasio Alcala met his wife when he was a teletype operator for General MacArthur, on the island of Leyte. They set up camp right next to Maria Cabugayan's home village. "Their romance was set to the backdrop of World War II," said their daughter, Alma Alcala. "He was Ilocano and she was Visayan, and that's why so many of the two tribes came together—because of the war." Atanasio courted Maria in English, the only language they had in common, since he could speak only English, Tagalog, and Ilocano, and she could speak only Waray and English. "My mother said she was glad to marry an Ilocano because all the Visayan boys, they just want to party and spend money," Alma Alcala said. "'Ilocanos are very thrifty and hardworking,' she said."[149] The couple married on Leyte and had a daughter. After the

35. Members of the newly created Manuel A. Roxas Post of the American Legion gather with their families at Washington Square Park in the late 1950s. The post was named after the first president of the Philippine Republic. First row, left to right: Ernest Cabañero, Laura Cabañero, Aurora Cabañero, Laureña Cabañero, Leo Cabañero, and Connie Sajulan. Second row, left to right: Teri Cabañero, Nora Alcala, Alma Alcala, Conching Sajulan. Standing, left to right: unknown man, Martin Atad, Sid Samporna, Mr. Yurong, Rory Alcala, three unknown people, Atanasio Alcala and his son, Lucresio Cabañero, Irene Cabañero. Courtesy of Laurena Cabañero/FANHS.

war, Atanasio left for Stockton. Maria and their oldest daughter followed. In 1948 Atanasio helped to found an American Legion post in Stockton just for Filipino veterans, named initially after Anastacio "Bo" Bantillo Jr., a second-generation Pinoy from Stockton who was killed while serving in the Navy during the war. It was later renamed Manuel A. Roxas Post No. 798, after the first president of the Philippine Republic. Soon after, the war brides and wives of veterans organized themselves into the Manuel Roxas ladies auxiliary (see figure 35).[150]

Other migrant and immigrant Filipinas/os who swelled the population after World War II were from other regions of the U.S. mainland and Hawai'i. In October 1945—having been summoned by her sister, Mrs. Antonio Cruz, a Little Manila businesswoman with a new baby—Emily Behic left her home in Ewa, on Oahu in Hawai'i, and arrived in San Francisco on a steamship teeming with returning veterans. While on El Dorado Street, she met a handsome second-generation Pinoy, a veteran of the First Filipino Infantry, Toribio "Terry" Rosal.[151] They met again at a dance at the new Filipino Recreation Center at Lafayette and Hunter streets. Terry followed her back to Hawai'i and formally asked her family for her hand. Emily and Terry were married in a large Legionarios del Trabajo wedding ceremony in Stockton and settled in South Stockton.

After the war, due to the influx of new immigrants and migrants like Emily Rosal, war brides, students and servicemen, Little Manila residential and street life boomed. The Japanese American community did not return to the West End or Oriental Quarter, and the foothold that the Filipinas/os had established in the district became stronger. During the 1940s and 1950s, the Little Manila district boasted the most businesses in the history of the neighborhood. New immigrants from the Philippines arrived in Stockton each day, lured to El Dorado Street by the stories of the close-knit community there. The Little Manila district was bustling with activity as new Filipina/o immigrants poured into Stockton and families experienced a postwar baby boom. Filipinas/os who lived in the suburban neighborhoods on the South Side still frequented Little Manila on the weekends and after work, shopping at its grocery stores, filling up their cars with gas there, and eating at its numerous restaurants.

When Angelina Candelario arrived in Stockton just after World War II to join her father, Claro, she was stunned when she saw Little Manila. She expected she would encounter a country that was a melting pot of different races living in harmony. She expected the waitresses in her father's Luzon Café to be blondes and redheads. What she saw—the segregated Little Manila community—surprised her. "I thought that Filipinos were living with the Americans, an integrated community," she said. "It's not the America I expected it to be. That was my expectation, the America of my dreams."[152] Emily Rosal's first visit to Stockton was both startling and exhilarating. "I was in another world!" she remembered. "It was so different! El Dorado Street at that time—it was booming, [I'd] never seen anything like it. Lots of Filipinos gathering at 4 or 5 o'clock in the afternoon, with their suits and zoot suits. It was something to see, and I'll never forget it."[153]

Veterans and their war brides and the new immigrants who settled in nearby neighborhoods and cities continued to visit to Little Manila to socialize, eat in the Filipina/o and Chinese restaurants, shop for Filipino groceries, play pool or gamble, and get a haircut at one of the many Filipino barbershops. Little Manila street life, especially on El Dorado Street, was a welcome relief from the monotony and loneliness of a hotel room or the campo, especially in the broiling summers and freezing winters of the Central Valley, and from the bland South Side suburban developments where many Filipinas/os made their homes after the war.

The opportunities and civil rights enjoyed by Filipinas/os in the postwar period transformed their lives, but only to a point. Thousands of them returned to the San Joaquin Delta and found that despite their experience in defense industry work, wartime service, and/or college educations, the only jobs available to them were still in the fields. In 1952 my grandfather Delfin Bohulano was again a labor contractor, in Tracy, a small town just south of Stockton. Living in the country with him was my grandmother Concepcion Bohulano and her two children—Delfin Jr. and Christine, my mother. Soon, two more children followed: Virginia, born in 1955, and Adeline, born in 1957. Because she had been a pampered, middle-class girl, Concepcion found the struggle to survive in America to be overwhelming.

Other highly educated Filipinas who immigrated after World War II suffered similar experiences of occupational downgrading and underemployment. Lawsin's study of Seattle war brides shows that they, too, were doing manual labor like domestic work and manufacturing work in the city's factories, even though many had college degrees.[154] My grandmother Concepcion's first job in America was in the celery fields near Stockton. She was clumsy and slow, and the old-timers ridiculed her. "They called out to me, 'Pinay, you better look at what you are doing!'" she recalled. They said "'Maybe you are not used to working, huh?'"[155] Her next job, which she held for many years, was as a cook for my grandfather's farm labor crew in Tracy. Concepcion, who had never cooked before, struggled to learn how to make Philippine dishes and dozens of tortillas for the Mexican workers.

In Little Manila, she ran into a friend from her mother's hometown of Palompon, Leyte, who remembered her as a daughter of one of the town's richest families. "He said to me: 'You have been a señorita, but now you are a *kusinera* [cook]!'" The family was so poor in their first years that Concepcion suggested that they take on an extra job picking green tomatoes, for extra money. "It was 27 cents a box, but we tried it, but I cannot get up anymore, even to put some soda in the refrigerator," she recalled. "I cannot do it. It is hard, heavy; you know my back hurts and everything." She then found a job at a cannery near Stockton, with many other postwar Filipina immigrants. She worked long hours on her feet for almost ten years in the canneries in Stockton and Modesto and joined the cannery workers' union. Early on, she struggled. "I'm not used to it, you know," she said. "I would try to work in the cannery and every four hours, [even] before four hours, I'm tapped by a floor lady and [she] tells me to go home after lunch hour."[156] To try to supplement the family income, she also knit socks to sell. In 1962, on the encouragement of my mother's teacher, who was surprised to learn that my grandmother had a college degree, she applied and was hired at the Delta Island School in Tracy, becoming one of the first Filipina American public school teachers in the area.[157]

THE 1948–49 ASPARAGUS STRIKE

As war brides like my grandmother, students, servicemen, veterans, and other migrants were settling into their new community and experiencing the many novelties of the postwar world, such as the ability to purchase farmland and single-family houses in suburban neighborhoods, citizenship, voting, and landowning rights, farmworkers still continued to suffer from the same low wages and poor conditions that they had experienced since the 1910s. In the days before the war ended, members of Local 7 of the United Cannery, Agricultural, Packing and Allied Workers of America gathered to discuss plans for organizing an asparagus drive in Stockton.[158] The Seattle-based union, an affiliate of the Congress of Industrial Organizations (CIO), had organized Filipino salmon workers beginning in 1934 and had allied itself briefly with the FALA in 1940. Local 7 was originally chartered as the Cannery Workers and Farm Laborers Union, Local 18257 of the American Federation of Labor (AFL). In 1937 the union allied itself with the CIO and became the UCAPAWA. That union transformed itself in 1944 into the Food, Tobacco, Agricultural and Allied Workers of America (FTA), in the CIO.[159] Leaders of Local 7 included veterans of the 1930s organizing campaigns and of the FALA: Seattle-based Chris Mensalvas, Ernesto Mangaoang, and Larry Itliong and Stockton-based Cipriano "Rudy" Delvo. Almost as soon as organizers descended on Stockton to unionize workers, a rival group met at the Rizal Social Club in Little Manila and the alliances and factions within the Filipina/o American community threatened to destroy worker unity.[160]

Local 7 called a mass meeting at the Japanese Temple at 148 West Washington Street, in Japantown, at the height of the asparagus season in April 1948, where they agreed on demands, according to the historian Arleen de Vera: a guaranteed minimum wage for the season negotiated by a union committee and the growers; an end to the holdback system, in which the bulk of the workers' pay was held back until the end of the season; housing that met a guaranteed minimum standard; and a 25 percent wage increase, retroactive to the beginning of the season. The growers refused all the demands, and the workers called for a strike to begin on Tuesday, May 4. "If you complained you didn't come back to work there the next year," Delvo, a crew boss turned strike leader (see figure 36), told a reporter from *Workers World* newspaper

36. Rudy Delvo, a native of Carcar, Cebu, was a FALA veteran, an organizer for the Local 7 asparagus strike in 1948, a founder of the Agricultural Workers Association in 1956, and the first Filipino American organizer hired by the Agricultural Workers Organizing Committee, AFL-CIO, in 1960. Courtesy of Dillon Delvo.

on May 17. "We were helpless. That's why we have organized into a union."[161] Delvo was a veteran of the FALA.

The strike was the largest that had hit the area since the FALA struck in 1939. More than 4,000 workers walked off their jobs and formed picket lines. Philip Vera Cruz, who hailed from Delano, went on strike for the first time in his life. "I was so naïve I didn't even know the name of the union organizing the strike, but I knew it was part of the CIO and the leaders were Filipino," he wrote in his autobiography. "The most important memory I have of that strike was the leadership of Chris Mensalvas." Mensalvas, Vera Cruz wrote, was one of the most outstanding labor leaders of his time. Vera Cruz participated in the strike until he ran out of money and had to go back to Delano.[162]

Citing a law against picketing, Sheriff Carlos Sousa threatened strikers that they would be arrested if they tried to talk to workers, and the police escorted workers past the picket lines.[163] On May 5 the union used an airplane to rain leaflets on the remaining workers. Angry growers evicted hundreds of striking workers the next day. One of them was Rudy Delvo, who had been living on Union Island and working for the asparagus growers Mussi, Del Arringa, and Gianini. Delvo lost all of his belongings: his trailer, clothing, cooking utensils, bedding, radio, and groceries totaling more than $1,000.[164]

37. Members of Local 7 march in downtown Stockton in 1948 in one of the biggest agricultural strikes in California history. Courtesy of the Stockton Chapter of FANHS.

Representatives of asparagus growers appeared before the Board of Supervisors meeting on May 6 to commend Sousa's crackdown on the strikers.[165] The sheriff began mass arrests of strikers on Sunday, May 9. By the next week, approximately forty-four strikers had been arrested. The brutality of the police and growers began to bring the Filipina/o community together, and even the anti-union Filipino Federation of America voted to support the strike. On Saturday, May 14, 1,500 strikers and supporters marched through downtown Stockton, led by Filipino veterans of World War II (see figure 37).[166] But the strike failed when, at the end of May, the growers announced the end of the season. They had lost $4 million.[167]

In late 1948 Carlos Bulosan and Chris Mensalvas went to Stockton to organize again for the next season. That year, they headquartered the union in the heart of Little Manila, at what would eventually be named the Mariposa Hotel at 130 East Lafayette Street. A mass meeting of the heads of all the fraternal and community organizations in Stockton was called next door, at the Filipino Recreation Center at Hunter and Lafayette streets. At the meeting, Filipino Community President Claro Candelario urged the community to side with the union (see figure 38). However, some community members were suspicious of the radical union. The *Bataan News*, an anti-communist newspaper edited by the conservative Manuel Insigne, accused

38. Filipino Community of Stockton President Claro Candelario exhorts community members to back the Local 7 union in 1949. Courtesy of Angelina Candelario Novelozo/FANHS.

Local 7 of being a communist union and denounced its organizers as "communist stooges" in a special issue dedicated to denigration of the union and a proposed 1949 asparagus strike.[168] However, the 1949 negotiations with the growers were successful. They agreed to recognize the union, accepted a minimum wage agreement, and promised to improve housing. Growers also agreed to pay the workers the $50,000 in wages they had lost when on strike, and the holdback system was made less draconic.[169] It was the most significant victory in the fields since the FALA strike in 1939.

However, according to Arleen de Vera, anticommunism crushed efforts to organize Filipino workers after World War II. After the 1948 strike and the 1949 organizing campaign, the INS targeted the leaders of the Local 7 for deportation. After a protracted struggle, the deportation attempts failed, but the passage of the anti-union Taft-Hartley Act and red-baiting and union-busting activities of the INS, the growers, the Federal Bureau of Investigation (FBI), and the sheriffs in Stockton killed radical Filipina/o union activity through the 1950s. Angelina Candelario Novelozo remembered coming from school to the Luzon Café one afternoon in 1949 to find two FBI agents in suits escorting her father, Claro Candelario, to San Francisco for several days of questioning. When her father returned, he told Angelina that he had been

39. Larry Itliong was an organizer with Local 7 and president of the Filipino Community of Stockton in the 1950s. Rudy Delvo recruited him to the Agricultural Workers Organizing Committee in Stockton in 1960. Itliong went on to organize the Delano Grape Strike in 1965. Courtesy of NPA FANHS.

a member of the Communist Party with Carlos Bulosan, Chris Mensalvas, and other friends from Los Angeles, and that they had met regularly at the Los Angeles Public Library. Candelario was never deported, but in the late 1940s, the FBI also began surveillance on Bulosan.[170]

CONTINUING THE FIGHT IN THE FIELDS

In the midst of the repression of leftist Filipinos, a handful of organizers pressed on. Local 7 was reconstituted as Local 37 of the International Long-shoreman's and Warehouse Workers Union (ILWU), and the radical labor leader Chris Mensalvas, who had been targeted for deportation in 1952 by the FBI and the INS, was elected president. The union's vice president in 1953 was a Stockton organizer, Larry Itliong (see figure 39).[171] Modesto "Larry" Itliong had been born into a poor Ilocana/o farming family in 1913 in San Nicolas, in the province of Pangasinan, and had arrived on the West Coast at the age of fifteen on April 6, 1929. He immediately went to work in the fields and then the Alaskan salmon canneries.[172] He had only a sixth-grade education, but he had dreamed of being a lawyer and politician. He spoke nine Philippine dialects, a skill that made him a formidable organizer among Filipinas/os.[173]

Known in Little Manila as "Seven Fingers," a nickname based on an accident in an Alaskan salmon cannery that claimed three of his fingers, the cigar-chomping Itliong had spent decades working in the Filipino farm labor movement. He had helped found the Alaska Cannery Workers Union, which became Local 7 of UCAPAWA, then Local 37 of ILWU, and helped found the Cannery Workers in the sardine industry in San Pedro. In 1933 he was organizing lettuce workers during strikes in Salinas.[174] During World War II, Itliong served as a messman on a U.S. Army transport ship out of San Francisco; he settled in Stockton after the war.[175] As an organizer with the UCAPAWA, Itliong had helped organize the 1948–49 Local 7 asparagus strikes in Stockton, with Delvo, Mensalvas, and Candelario.[176]

As soon as he settled in Stockton after the war, Itliong was elected secretary of the Filipino Community of Stockton, a post he held from 1946 to 1950. He was president from 1954 to 1956. He joined the Legionarios del Trabajo and was elected president of the Filipino Voters League in Stockton in 1957.[177] Itliong married and raised a family in Stockton, where he lived amongst many Filipina/o families on the South Side on Kohler Street, and joined Trinity Presbyterian Church. He continued to serve Local 37 throughout the 1950s as its vice president and in 1957, its dispatcher, and in 1956, he organized a relatively ineffectual union, the Filipino Farm Labor Union in Stockton.[178]

In the late 1950s, the academic and labor organizer Ernesto Galarza; Father Thomas McCullough, of St. Mary's Church in Stockton; and the local teacher and organizer Dolores Huerta began to pressure the leadership of the national AFL-CIO (the two organizations united in 1955) to organize farmworkers.[179] McCullough, Huerta, and Rudy Delvo had organized the Agricultural Workers Association (AWA) in Stockton in the late 1950s, as I discussed in chapter 5. At the time that the AWA was putting pressure on the AFL-CIO, the AFL's only attempt to help unionize Filipina/o farmworkers had been its short-lived alliance with the FALA in 1940. Most Filipinas/os still had bitter memories of the AFL's racist and anti-Filipina/o stance on immigration and labor, and the exclusion of Filipina/o members from AFL unions (the only exceptions being Local 20221 in Stockton in 1937, and the FALA, during the brief affiliation in 1940).

Angelina Novelozo remembers her father, Claro Candelario, directing an invective-laced tirade at an AFL representative in 1949, at a dinner in the middle of the Local 7 asparagus strike. Candelario argued that not only had the AFL never supported Filipina/o labor, but it had played a central role in their exclusion and deportation, and it had advocated denying citizenship rights to Filipinas/os for decades. He said "that the AFL had said that the Filipinos are a group of people who lowers the American standard of living, because they are paid such a low wage and therefore they can eat nothing but rice and fish," Novelozo recalled. "My dad said: 'If the AFL will only allow us to become members of his union and be paid higher wages then we don't have to be lowering the standard of the American way of life, all we need is to be given a chance.'"[180]

The AFL-CIO succumbed to the pressure and chartered the Agricultural Worker's Organizing Committee (AWOC) in Stockton in 1959 and brought in the veteran organizer Norman Smith as its head. Working closely with McCullough and Huerta, Smith assembled a team of organizers, including the former AWA organizers Dolores Huerta and Rudy Delvo.[181] By then, the Spanish Mission Band, the Northern California priests who had first organized farmworkers in California, had been broken up by the San Francisco Archdiocese, and its members were scattered. McDonnell went to Mexico, and McCullough, under strict orders to cease his involvement in farm labor organizing, was sent to an inner-city parish in Oakland.[182]

To recruit union members, Delvo began walking through the Little Manila and West End districts daily, and he showed films on the labor movement every Thursday night at the El Verano Club in Little Manila at East Lafayette Street and El Dorado.[183] At the end of 1959, an invigorated Delvo wrote his old friend Chris Mensalvas, who was then president of the ILWU's Local 37, the Alaskan salmon cannery union, and told him that "things are different now," since AWOC would accomplish for laborers what past organizations never could. "It is not like in 1948 when we put up a fight here," he wrote. "At that time we were alone. No other nationality was with us. Our finances were so limited. . . . Our mistakes taught us a lesson and this time . . . it is going to be us to designate the time, place and the kind of weapon."[184] Excited by the prospect of a new union, Delvo approached his old friend and Legionarios del Trabajo brother, Larry Itliong, and asked him to become an AWOC organizer. Itliong agreed, and Smith quickly hired him.[185] Itliong's long history in the labor movement and in local community affairs had made him a trusted and respected figure in Little Manila. Delvo and Itliong were the only Filipino organizers in the first years of the AWOC, but as the union progressed, other Filipinos were added, including Ben Gines of Salinas and Philip Vera Cruz and Pete Velasco of Delano.[186] The membership and leadership of the AWOC was heavily Filipino, but the union also included whites, Arabs, blacks, and Mexicans. Many of the organizers, like Itliong and Delvo, were veterans of the strikes of the past forty years. By the mid-1960s, Sam Kushner writes, the AWOC was the "center of activity" for Filipino trade unionists.[187] With his long history of labor activism in the Central Valley and his strong relationship with Filipina/o farmworkers, Itliong became an effective and trusted organizer.

From its founding, the AWOC aimed its ire at the bracero program.[188] Growers preferred braceros because they were easily exploited, cost less than American farmworkers, and were not unionized. Furthermore, the growers claimed there was a shortage of American farmworkers. Organizers of the AWOC argued that there was plenty of labor, but the growers refused to negotiate with the union and hire union labor. In 1965 the AWOC attempted a strike in the asparagus fields, but the union did not win recognition among the growers. By then, Itliong had been appointed the AWOC's southern regional director and moved his family to the southern San Joaquin Valley to live in Delano, where he began organizing the mostly Filipino grape workers. In Delano was his former AWOC colleague, Dolores Huerta, who was organizing the National Farm Workers Association (NFWA). In the late summer of 1965, Itliong and Pete Velasco were organizing Filipino grape workers in Delano and had won a wage increase to $1.40 per hour in the Coachella Valley.[189] The workers then moved to the Delano grape harvest, where Delano growers offered $1 per hour and refused to budge.

On the night of September 7, 1965, Filipino grape workers, all rank and file members of the AWOC, voted to go on strike the following day. Itliong warned the strikers that there were many Mexican workers who would provide scab labor and that the likelihood of success was slim. "We told them, you're going to suffer a lot of hardship, maybe you're going to get hungry, maybe you're going to lose your car, maybe you're going to lose your house," he said. "They said, 'We don't care.' They feel that they're not being treated fairly by their employers so they took a strike vote."[190] As Itliong predicted, the strike was brutal and violent. Several days after the strike began, Itliong approached Cesar Chávez and Dolores Huerta to convince the NFWA to join it.[191] Itliong argued that if the Mexicans did not stand with the Filipinas/os, if they were scabs while the Filipinas/os struck, then when the Mexicans went on strike, the Filipinas/os would be scabs. Huerta said that the NFWA organizers were worried that the violence would force the Filipinas/os to abandon the strike. "Some of them were beaten up by the growers [who] would shut off the gas and the lights and the water in the labor camps," she said.[192]

Chávez and Huerta consulted the NFWA members, and on September 16 they joined the grape strike. The Delano grape strike and national boycott of grapes, which was directed by Itliong, gave the plight of farmworkers a global audience. Letters and donations poured in, and Itliong answered many personally from the beginning of the strike to the early 1970s.[193] In 1967 the AWOC and the National United Farm Workers Union merged to form the United Farm Workers Organizing Committee (UFW), with Chávez as director and Itliong as assistant director.[194] Although the strike action was located mainly in Delano, the AWOC established a Stockton office at El Dorado and Lafayette streets. After the AWOC and the National Farm Workers Union merged, the UFW maintained an office in Little Manila through the 1970s. Throughout the late 1960s and early 1970s, Itliong, as the national coordinator of the grape boycott, traveled throughout the country, organizing cities and communities to support the boycott. In 1970 he went back to Stockton and organized the second-generation youth and old-timers to back the boycott and put pressure on the local Safeway stores.[195] Passionate and articulate, Itliong brought in allies and thousands of dollars in donations.

But Filipinas/os felt squeezed out of the union almost immediately after the merger. The years of seniority that they had achieved in the AWOC were wiped out when the unions merged.[196] Almost all of the Filipina/o veteran organizers of the Delano Grape Strike left, including Gines, and only four Filipinos remained on the UFW board by 1967: assistant director Itliong and vice presidents Andy Imutan, Philip Vera Cruz, and Pete Velasco. Differences between the leadership and the rank and file in regard to organizing styles and priorities, philosophies of organizing, and strategy began to pull the coalition apart. Kushner argues that many of the civil rights activists who rushed to Delano were turned off by the approach of the AWOC Filipino organizers, who saw the grape strike as a traditional trade-union strike. The deeply religious approach of the Chicanas/os in the NFWA, with its social movement style and civil rights focus, attracted more media and activist attention.[197]

For example, Filipina/o strikers, accustomed to the militancy that was the result of decades of shoot-outs, fascist police action, and violent confrontations with growers and scabs, felt that it made no sense to adhere to nonviolence. In his account of the Delano grape strike, Eugene Nelson recalled that in one violent confrontation with growers, there had been one hundred Filipino strikers with knives drawn, waiting to defend themselves. They had to be begged to stay nonviolent, avoid self-defense, and put their knives away.[198] Many of the veteran Filipina/o and some Chicana/o and white organizers of the AWOC felt that the strike—with its emphasis on Catholic religiosity and nonviolence, and its social-movement style—did not adhere to traditional trade-union strategies and refused to join the new union.[199] Moreover, as Marissa Aroy has shown in her documentary *The Delano Ma-*

nongs and as Matt Garcia points out in his book on the grape strike, Filipino workers became increasingly disgruntled with the new union, particularly with the hiring hall system the UFW enforced, which disempowered Filipino contractors, who had been central to Filipina/o American farm work culture and militancy for decades. Many Filipinos, including Gines, abandoned the UFW in favor of the Teamsters Union.[200]

Because of these factors, the UFW was largely unsuccessful with Filipina/o workers in Stockton. When I asked my father why he did not join the UFW, especially when Gines and Itliong were his Legionarios lodge brothers, he retorted: "Marching 350 miles behind a statue of the Virgin Mary is not a strike! That's not a labor union!"[201] When interviewed by the *Stockton Record* in March 1971, Johnny Latosa, a labor contractor and then the president of the Filipino Community of Stockton, said he doubted that workers could be organized in Stockton. Latosa said that he was godfather to one of Itliong's sons. "Larry Itliong is my compadre," Latosa told the newspaper. "We've known each other 35 years. I keep telling him don't go too far. It'll take maybe five years to organize this union."[202] But by the time Latosa expressed his views to the *Stockton Record*, his compadre Larry Itliong was already in private disagreement with Chávez and the direction of the UFW. On October 15, 1971, Itliong resigned from the union. Itliong had been struggling with several issues within the union and with Chávez himself, including the situation with Filipino contractors, the UFW's refusal to reimburse his expenses, the lack of power of Filipinas/os in the union, and the UFW leadership's ambivalence toward the aging Filipino rank and file. "[But] my biggest disappointment is that the Organization I participated in to fight for Justice and Dignity is not turning [out] as planned," he told Bill Kircher, a fellow organizer. "So I had to go in order to save my reputation (insignificant as it may [be]) and my conscience. . . . Many of the workers around here, Filipinos and Chicanos, are very unhappy on how the union is being operated."[203] Itliong's departure, which followed the resignations of other organizers, such as Gines, meant that the UFW had lost its most seasoned labor organizer.

Filipina/o dissatisfaction with the new union notwithstanding, the AWOC and its merger with the UFW, grape strike, and boycott brought the struggle of the farmworkers to people around the globe. The farmworkers' movement of the 1960s and 1970s—founded by Filipinas/os and Mexicans from Stockton such as Itliong, Delvo, Gines, and Huerta—was the culmination of more than four decades of struggle in the Filipina/o American labor movement of Stockton, and it could not have taken place without the civil rights gains of World War II and the organizing lessons learned from the FALA.

CONCLUSION

The Filipina/o exclusion movement of the early to mid-1930s and the passage of the Tydings-McDuffie Act and the Repatriation Act had been turning points for the Filipina/o community. Those who refused to be deported abandoned the idea of returning to the Philippines and turned seriously to building a strong and viable community in Stockton. Prior to the bombing of Pearl Harbor and the invasion of the Philippines in December 1941, Stockton's thriving Filipina/o community boasted of its strong community, growing families, and numerous organizations in several Filipina/o American publications. Hailing itself as the "Model Filipino Community in America," the Stockton Filipina/o community in the late 1930s looked forward to Philippine independence and relished Little Manila's prominence among other Filipina/o communities on the Pacific Coast. The rise of the FALA in the late 1930s and early 1940s demonstrates the savvy and unity that the community had built in the long, hard 1920s and 1930s. The growing unity of the larger West Coast Filipina/o American community was also evidenced by the large coalition organizations such as the Committee for the Protection of Filipino Rights, which fought for naturalization, and the Filipino Inter-Community Council of the Western States, which lobbied for landownership rights for Filipinas/os in America.

In World War II, the Little Manila community experienced a watershed moment, one that would forever alter its members' racial position in Stockton in myriad ways. Examining the impact of the war on the Filipina/o community in Stockton reveals a complex portrait of wartime existence. Friction and violence between Filipinas/os and Japanese erupted immediately after the bombing of Pearl Harbor and subsided only after Japanese American incarceration in concentration camps. The scapegoating of Japanese Americans and the widely publicized heroism of Filipino soldiers in the Pacific theater shifted discourses on race; Filipinas/os previously viewed as savages unfit for independence or citizenship were quickly welcomed into the American body politic, while Japanese Americans were imprisoned in camps. Filipinas/os in Stockton jumped at the opportunity to act on their long-standing grudges against Japanese contractors and merchants, directing violence, boycotts, and accusations of disloyalty at the general Japanese American community. The tension revealed the ongoing antagonism and competing nationalisms between Asian immigrant groups in Stockton that had been continuing throughout the Depression. A look beneath the surface of positive change reveals that Filipina/o economic growth, at least in agriculture, came at expense of Japanese Americans, who had to abandon their homes, businesses, and agricultural lands because of wartime incarceration.

The rising tide of Filipina/o nationalism and the war effort unified what had been an increasingly factionalized Filipina/o community; forged a stronger, more militant Filipina/o American identity and community; and bolstered Filipina/o American claims on the American dream. With the war in the Philippines and the war effort in the United States as the rallying points for Filipinas/os, and with their antagonists — the Issei farmers and merchants — in internment camps, Filipina/o Americans found an increasingly unified and stronger voice with which to advocate for Philippine independence, Filipina/o American civil and political equality, and justice in the fields. Changes in immigration law and a baby boom after the war swelled the Filipina/o American population in the United States, especially in Stockton. Veterans and their war brides, other veterans and servicemen, second-generation couples, and newly reunified families produced second and third generations. The Filipina/o American community exploded between 1945 and 1960. About half of the postwar immigrants were women.[204]

Building on the Filipinas/os' postwar political and economic gains, unions such as Local 7, the Agricultural Workers Organizing Committee, and the United Farm Workers attempted to end, once and for all, the system of virtual slavery in the fields that had kept Filipinas/os in miserable conditions. This new postwar attitude was demonstrated in the militant, highly organized asparagus strikes in 1948 and 1949 and in the work of the Agricultural Worker's Organizing Committee and its 1965 grape strike in Delano. With the hardship and struggle of the Depression and the sacrifices and tensions of the war behind them; and armed with the benefits of union representation, citizenship, voting rights, and landownership, Filipinas/os in Stockton and their growing families and community organizations hoped for a promising future.

PART III DESTRUCTION AND DISPLACEMENT

1950s–2010

Everybody was sorry to lose El Dorado. It's beautiful before. They should not have destroyed that. The state highway should have went farther from the town.... [Politicians] are not [for our] community.... That's how they separated the Filipinos.

— *Carmen Saldevar*

It touched my heart when I see our people ... they're living in a hotel, they're dying without people knowing that they're dead. They stink before they [are] found. That's why we have the Filipino Plaza, because of what I saw.

— *Eulogio "Ted" Lapuz*

CHAPTER 7

LOSING EL DORADO STREET

The Ilocana immigrant Carmen Saldevar's happiest memories came from her years as a pool hall operator in the Little Manila district (see figure 40). A former schoolteacher, she arrived in Stockton in 1952 after meeting and marrying Fernando Saldevar, a World War II veteran. "I was so happy!" she recalled. "The people walking around were all Filipinos! When I look at the street, from the shop, my goodness, it looks like the Philippines!" All of the businesses on El Dorado Street were owned by Filipinas/os, she remembered. "All the buildings there, Filipinos!" she said. "Downstairs, Filipinos! Upstairs, the Filipinos, living there, who were working the farms, all the way down to Lafayette. All you could see is Filipinos. Walking there. Standing there. Talking there."[1] The Saldevars ran a barbershop and a pool hall in Little Manila, both of which drew their fellow Ilocanos in large numbers.

For my Lolo Pablo "Ambo" Mabalon, the owner of and cook at the Lafayette Lunch Counter since 1931, the postwar years were prosperous and happy as well. The Lafayette Lunch Counter continued to be a bustling center of life in Little Manila life. Though my grandmother Isabel Mabalon died of cancer in 1952, only four years after her reunion with my grandfather, the arrival of my father, Ernesto, in 1963 and the birth of his youngest son Tex's two children, Tex Jr. and Cynthia, helped ease my grandfather's loneliness. The change in immigration laws in 1965 allowed Pablo to petition his daughter, Florencia, and her husband, Genaro. They then petitioned all nine of their children. The Mabalon family was finally coming together after decades apart.

The general mood and prosperity of the Saldevar and Mabalon families echoed those of other Filipinas/os in Stockton. The Sal-

40. Carmen Saldevar in front of her pool hall in the 1960s. Courtesy of the Saldevar family.

devars' New Deal Barbershop was only one of four Filipino-owned barbershops that lined El Dorado Street from Washington to Lafayette streets in the 1960s, and their Stockton Pool Hall was one of several Filipina/o-owned pool halls remaining in the neighborhood in the late 1960s. Saldevar remembered that her husband's barbershop often hummed with activity until past midnight several nights a week.[2] The barbershops, along with Filipino-owned or -managed pool halls, restaurants, hotels, card rooms, and grocery stores, met the retail and social needs of Little Manila's elderly old-timers as well as the larger Filipina/o community (see figure 41).

But the happy atmosphere and bustling street life of Little Manila would soon be replaced by the cacophony of falling bricks and the growl of the federal bulldozer. With the help of millions of dollars in federal subsidies for slum clearance, the city's white elite of politicians, planners, developers, and business owners set out to transform downtown's turn-of-the-century landscape and clear its ethnic and working-class neighborhoods, which members of the elite regarded as blighted slums. The massive postwar redevelopment projects in the city's West End—in the form of slum clearances and demolitions in Little Manila and Chinatown and highway construction projects— almost destroyed the city's Filipina/o American community in the 1960s and 1970s.

In this chapter, I discuss and examine the urban redevelopment policies that led to the destruction of most of Little Manila by the late 1960s. I ar-

41. Lafayette and El Dorado streets in the 1950s, before redevelopment and freeway construction decimated the Little Manila neighborhood. Courtesy of the Bank of Stockton Historical Photograph Collection.

gue that local officials targeted Filipinas/os, as well as other racial and ethnic groups and poor whites, for removal from the downtown. Urban redevelopment in Stockton was a strategy used by the city's power elite to rid the West End of its poorest citizens and its people of color. The city's Redevelopment Agency, with its ambitious and ultimately damaging West End Redevelopment Project, which targeted Little Manila and Chinatown, evicted the area's businesses and residents and cleared nine city blocks. More than 1,000 single men were displaced, and dozens of businesses shut their doors. The project decimated Chinatown and Little Manila, and when the Crosstown Freeway was built in 1974, it further damaged the area. By the late 1970s, fewer than two blocks of Little Manila were left.

Since Filipinas/os leased their stores and hotels, they lost their businesses when building owners sold their structures to the Redevelopment Agency. Ultimately, Filipinas/os in the West End and Little Manila were powerless to stop the bulldozers, since the agency, using the power of eminent domain and federal subsidies for slum clearance, wrested the land and property from even those powerful white landowners who opposed urban redevelopment. This chapter documents how Filipinas/os in Stockton weathered the city's assault on their neighborhood and community.

A number of factors, including racist and elitist attitudes about the conditions of the urban poor and racial or ethnic minorities, ideas about the eradication and prevention of slums and blight, the movement of the white middle class from urban areas to all-white suburbs, and the pressure to squeeze more property-tax dollars out of poor neighborhoods, contributed to the postwar rush to clear and then redevelop inner cities. Like cities across the United States after World War II, Stockton was transformed by white flight to the suburban subdivisions, the emergence of suburban shopping malls, and massive freeway construction. New postwar federal programs, such as the Federal Housing Authority (FHA) loans and veterans' loans provided by the GI Bill, were aimed at helping returning veterans purchase homes in these new suburban neighborhoods. Suburban developments began to proliferate across the Stockton area and, indeed, the country.[3] The privately owned, single-family detached home became both the American ideal and national policy, to the detriment of residential hotels and dense, mixed-use districts like Little Manila.[4] Generous tax subsidies on mortgage interest made it even easier to own a home.[5] By 1972, 63 percent of Americans owned their own homes.[6]

In a frenzy of postwar suburban development, Stockton developers invested massively in subdivisions such as Lincoln Village and Weberstown on the city's northern periphery, north of the Calaveras River—which had historically separated urban Stockton from the agricultural fields.[7] A typical deed for these new suburban homes, such as the ones in the exclusive Lincoln Village, contained covenant provisions prohibiting its sale to African Americans and members of other minority groups. Residents and real estate agents believed that all-white neighborhoods enforced via racially restrictive covenants were key to maintaining property values. In fact, the FHA recommended and endorsed such covenants in order to protect property values.[8] Natalie Molina argues that restrictive covenants, racially exclusive FHA policies and the racialized housing and loan policies of the Home Owners Loan Corporation, had lasting effects on segregation and housing in Los Angeles; Thomas Sugrue makes a similar argument in his work about the ways in which Detroit kept African Americans out of white neighborhoods.[9]

Because FHA lending practices favored loans in white neighborhoods, and restrictive covenant laws barred most Filipina/o, Chinese, Japanese, Mexican, and African American Stocktonians from owning homes in the exclusive suburban housing developments on the city's north side, instead they bought modest homes or rented apartments in older, working-class neighborhoods in downtown or in South or East Stockton. Most Stocktonians living in those areas were people of color, many of whom lived at or below the federal poverty level and were untouched by the prosperity north of the Calaveras River.[10] If, as historians argue, the inclusivity of the white suburban neighborhoods played a central role in racializing Jews, Catholics, and ethnic Europeans as whites, then the South Side of Stockton played a similar role in the racialization of its mostly African American, Filipina/o, Chinese, Japanese, and Mexican residents as brown others who shared experiences of segregation, exclusion, poverty, and oppression.[11]

After World War II, the families of veterans and war brides and of the second generation were outgrowing the cramped Little Manila district. With citizenship came the right to buy and own land—a right long denied Filipinas/os in the United States—but most were barred from the North Side subdivisions by restrictive covenants and prohibitive costs. Soon, Stockton developers saw profits in building suburban developments in the fields around South Stockton for the Mexican, African American, Filipina/o, Japanese American, and Chinese American residents of the South Side. Most of the homes that Filipinas/os moved into were located in the residential South Side neighborhoods around Charter Way and north of the French Camp slough, such as Homestead Tract, around Hazelton School near Charter Way—the main artery that bisected the city's South Side core—and Corona Park, just south of Charter Way.

In 1955, the city of Stockton annexed farmland south of the city for a new subdivision, Lever Village, at Stockton's southern border, off Eighth Street and Turnpike Road.[12] The Nomellini-Ferroggiaro Company developed the homes. In "A Home for Everyone," their Lever Village promotional brochure, the developers subtly announced that all Stocktonians, regardless of race, would be welcome there. Nomellini-Ferroggiaro built ranch-style, three-bedroom, one-bathroom houses with clean lines and modern architecture that imitated the more expensive Eichler homes built in more affluent neighborhoods in California, for only $8,500 ($73,365 in 2012 dollars) with no down payment required for veterans and FHA loans available for nonveterans.[13] Filipinas/os also bought homes in other new South Side developments, including the Corona Park subdivision, north of McKinley Park.[14] Living in these new suburban homes, with their several bedrooms, fireplaces, ceramic tile, modern kitchens, and expansive yards in front and back, allowed local lower-middle class and middle-class Filipinas/os to take part in the nation's postwar suburbanization and its booming consumer economy.[15]

The neighborhoods of Corona Park, Homestead Tract, McKinley Park, and Lever Village became a suburban counterpart to Little Manila, in which Filipinas/os built a world of their own. By the 1960s, the majority of the

42. After World War II, Filipinas/os bought homes in South Stockton, and these homes became gathering places for the relatives who immigrated to the United States in the 1950s and 1960s. Here, the Bohulano family entertained the Villegas, Jhao, and Rembulat families and other relatives in the early 1960s at their home at 633 Chicago Avenue in Lever Village. Concepcion Bohulano is in the center in a white blouse. Delfin Bohulano is behind her. Author's personal collection.

homeowners in these neighborhoods were Filipina/o. In these homes, families grew, and extended families came together for celebrations and backyard barbecues in the expansive backyards. In 1956 my maternal grandparents, the Bohulanos, bought a home in Lever Village on a corner lot on Chicago Avenue (see figure 42). The purchase of such an expansive and beautiful home meant so much to my grandmother that she saved the promotional flier for the Lever Village development among her most important belongings. In the floor plan on the flier, she penciled in her paint color choices: "powder blue," white, and coral for the three bedrooms.[16] My grandparents then encouraged their relatives and friends to move to Lever Village. Other Filipina/o American families reached out to their extended networks and did the same. By the 1960s, there were so many Filipinas/os in the subdivision that they organized themselves by the streets they lived on. For example, my grandparents and their neighbors around the corner named themselves the Boston Avenue Association. Lever Village's children went to nearby Taylor Elementary School and Marshall Middle School. In 1955 St. George's Church, in a Catholic parish on Sixth Street, was built to serve the growing Catholic population of the South Side—mainly the Corona Park, McKinley Park, and Lever Village neighborhoods. By the 1960s the church was more than half Filipina/o.[17]

THE DEATH OF DOWNTOWN

The racialization of space in Stockton resulted in deep divisions—cultural, economic, political, and geographic—between white, suburban North Stockton and the brown and black West End and South Side. After World War II, city elites lavished investment and attention on the North Side, thereby contributing to the decline and neglect of downtown and the South Side. For example, on Christmas Eve in 1955, when the nearby Mormon Slough overflowed its banks during a rainstorm, the city rushed to sandbag the downtown area but left all of the South Side underwater. More than 3,000 residents were evacuated.[18] Similarly, across the country, as the suburbs grew, the inner cities, starved of resources, slowly deteriorated.

Federal policies played a central role in the racialization of downtown and integrated neighborhoods as slums where dark-skinned people lived, surrounded by decay. The Home Owners Loan Corporation—the New Deal agency created in 1933 that was the forerunner of the FHA—created the practice of redlining, or denying federal insurance to banks and federal loan programs that issued loans and mortgages to people and businesses in racially mixed neighborhoods.[19] As Molina writes in her study of Mexicans in Los Angeles, appraisers for the Home Owners Loan Corporation, assessed the value of a home in relationship to its occupant. Racially mixed neighborhoods containing Mexicans and African Americans were considered undesirable and were appraised accordingly.[20]

The FHA and GI Bill loan programs in the postwar period picked up where Home Owners Loan Corporation left off and ensured that thirty-year, fixed-rate mortgages would be available to middle-class whites aspiring to live in the suburbs, to the detriment of inner-city neighborhoods. The FHA made loans only in all-white subdivisions and officially refused to guarantee loans in neighborhoods that were racially mixed or in downtown districts in which mixed use was common. According to Kenneth Jackson, the FHA "exhorted segregation and enshrined it as public policy."[21] Thomas Sugrue's research on Detroit and Scott Kurashige's book on African Americans in Los Angeles illustrate these patterns of residential segregation via federal and local policies and programs.

White Stocktonians' attitudes toward the West End and South and East Sides were somewhere between neglect and outright hostility. The dozen city blocks west of the central business district (including Little Manila) were dubbed Skid Row by middle-class whites; area residents preferred the name West End. The urban historian Paul Groth notes that Americans began using Skid Row as a pejorative term in the 1950s for what should be more accurately called "single laborers' zones." In Stockton's West End, as in single laborers' zones in other West Coast cities (Seattle, San Francisco, and Los Angeles all had sizable zones), single residential occupancy hotels, cheap rooming houses, and businesses catering to working-class people and families were abundant.[22] City planners and business leaders in Stockton argued that if the gritty West End could be cleared and rebuilt, the city could remake its downtown into a more attractive and economically viable district.

The post–World War II rush to remake cities by clearing them of slums and blight in the wake of frenzied suburban development had its origins in the public housing movements of the nineteenth and early twentieth centuries and in the movement of the affluent to exclusive suburbs beginning in the 1920s. The federal government responded to a strange alliance of public housing proponents concerned with improving the housing of the poor, and business interests intent on downtown slum clearance, and passed the 1949 Housing and Slum Clearance Act. This legislation authorized more than $1 billion in loans and grants to cities for the acquisition of blighted land and redevelopment, with "blight" defined as any area that was in economic decline or racially mixed.[23] Though the act was purported to be the federal government's remedy for slums, the legislation was backed by influential realtors, bankers, builders, and business groups, all of which had lobbied relentlessly for the act's passage, a "shotgun wedding between enemy lobbying groups", as Alexander von Hoffman writes.[24] Cities across the nation participated wholeheartedly in the program: approximately 912 cities launched 1,912 redevelopment projects from 1949 to 1968.[25]

The State of California had already passed a redevelopment law in 1945; the 1949 federal act brought federal approval and money to an idea already in the works in the state. The promise of federal money to clear the city's core galvanized Stockton's power elite of white city planners, politicians, businesspeople, and developers, all of whom pushed for a redevelopment plan for the city's downtown. In 1952 the Stockton City Planning Commission prepared a report for the city council, advocating the use of federal funds for redevelopment. Using the example of aboriginal Australians and Africans who burned their villages to the ground periodically in order to start clean, the 1952 report advocated for a redevelopment plan in downtown Stockton that would clear out the city's "infested" areas.[26]

But getting the federal money for urban redevelopment projects took several steps. A city had to create a local redevelopment agency in order to be eligible for federal redevelopment funds. The agency then designated an area as a urban renewal zone, and renewal plans were sent to Washington, D.C., for approval. City officials, using the power of eminent domain, could obtain land in the redevelopment zone. The Supreme Court ruled that eminent domain could be used if the projects were deemed beneficial to the public. Once the city owned the land, demolition could commence. The federal government paid for two-thirds of the cost of the redevelopment—usually funds for acquisition of the land and demolition. Each municipality met the remainder of the cost with funds allocated for public works improvements, such as roads, sewers, parks, parking lots, and other public facilities. To attract investment, cities then sold the land at less than acquisition cost to private developers. Proponents believed that taxes from the rebuilt areas would compensate for this outlay.[27]

Nationwide, urban power elites remade their downtowns into sanitized landscapes by destroying historic buildings and neighborhoods in massive efforts to bring investment into the central cities and shore up city tax revenue. Within the first decade of federal urban redevelopment programs, critics began assailing the net effect of the programs on American cities. "Blight" in Stockton, as in the rest of the nation, was defined broadly, and the neighborhoods that were targeted in cities like San Francisco, New York, Boston, Detroit, and Philadelphia were most often stable neighborhoods of working-class African Americans, Latinas/os, and Asians—far from the blighted, decrepit slums that urban renewal boosters claimed they were. Many stable communities of color were destroyed because only one-fifth—a small portion—of an entire neighborhood had to be considered blighted to make the entire community eligible for destruction.[28] Because it focused so harshly and disproportionately on urban African American communities, urban renewal's harshest critics dubbed the program "Negro removal."[29]

Critics on the left and right charged that the program displaced the poor (especially poor African American and Latina/o families), forced small businesses to close their doors, contributed to unemployment, tore down ethnic and working-class neighborhoods, and left downtown cores empty of street life, community cohesion, and vitality.[30] Writing in the early 1960s, the scholar Martin Anderson, a conservative critic of urban renewal, estimated that it destroyed more housing than it created (particularly low-income housing) and made overall housing conditions worse. More than 126,000 units of housing were destroyed by these programs from 1950 to 1960.[31] In the early 1960s, William Slayton, commissioner of the Urban Renewal Administration, estimated that his agency's programs would displace more than a million families during that decade. On the East Coast, more than two-thirds of those displaced were African American or Puerto Rican.[32] More than 100,000 small businesses were displaced, and most were forced to close.[33] Between 1949, when urban renewal began, and 1968, 425,000 units of low-income housing had been destroyed across the country. The 125,00 new units that had been built were not replacement housing; the majority of them were luxury apartments.[34] For example, an area in the Chavez Ravine that had been razed for public housing instead was used for the baseball stadium for the Los Angeles Dodgers.[35]

DESTROYING THE WEST END

In 1954 Stockton Mayor Dean de Carli authorized the formation of an Urban Blight Committee to study problems involving law enforcement, alcoholism, and public health in the city's West End and named Angelo Sanguinetti, a downtown business owner and former mayor, as its chair.[36] The report of the committee concluded that clearances were necessary in order to eliminate blight and bring economic revival to downtown Stockton. The committee regarded the working-class and ethnic neighborhoods in the West End as eyesores; the blocks of hotels, bars, and small businesses were areas of blight, "a cancer-like growth," that needed to be swept clean. "Blight has far-reaching effects on Stockton—both economic and social," the committee reported. "Blighted neighborhoods mean blighted lives—like the bad boy in school who requires so much of the teacher's attention—throw a heavy burden on public agencies at the expense of the rest of the community." The committee found that law enforcement and the justice system had not succeeded in reducing vagrancy, crime, and drunkenness in the West End. The only answer was clearance.[37]

Stockton elites believed that wholesale clearance of the West End would alleviate poverty and alcoholism, a belief shared by the staff members of other redevelopment agencies who cleared their cities' ghettoes on the premise that redevelopment would alleviate social ills by ridding the landscape of the physical manifestations of poverty. In 1961, the Planning Commission pressured the city to close the area's flophouses, bars, Christian mission soup kitchens and to move farm laborers who daily assembled in the area, looking for work to an area outside of the downtown.[38] Instead of offering better public education and college opportunities, employment programs, social services, and other social welfare programs, redevelopment proponents believed that pushing out the poor, demolition, and rebuilding would best serve both the urban residents and Stockton's elite and middle class.

But where elites saw a slum, residents saw a bustling, diverse, working-class community in Stockton's West End (see map 6). The area was home to mostly poor and working-class people, who were the engines of the area's agricultural economy. Contractors seeking laborers for farm work traditionally recruited workers in the West End's pool halls, bars, restaurants, park, and recreation halls. In the Chinatown and Little Manila neighborhoods, workers and families ate in the cheap Chinese, Filipina/o, and American restaurants. After a day at work, men relaxed in the bars, card rooms, diners, and pool halls. Workers and their families lived in the hotels; men and women played pool in the Filipina/o- and Chinese-owned pool and gambling halls; and families and members of community organizations danced and relaxed in the area's numerous recreation centers. Working-class families from all backgrounds held picnics, religious festivals, and parades in Washington Square Park, which was also home to the area's thriving farmer's market. The West End was full of residential hotels and beautiful, historic buildings, many of them built with of locally made red brick, earning the city its nickname, The Brick City.[39] But redevelopment proponents in Stockton portrayed the working-class and minority men and families of the West End as bums, transients, and winos, who were poor, shiftless, alcoholic, and lethargic by choice, not circumstance. Police were aggressive and abusive toward the residents of the West End. For example, the Northern California Chapter of the American Civil Liberties Union filed a complaint with the city in 1955 when Stockton police began arresting unemployed men living in the West End who refused to work as field laborers.[40]

It came as no surprise, then, that the West End Redevelopment Project, created in 1956, targeted the city's West End and central business district.[41] The city's Redevelopment Agency and the City Council worked quickly to apply for more than $5 million in federal funds in 1960. The original plans proposed to clear almost the entire downtown; eventually, the City Planning Commission identified for total clearance a nine-block area in the West End considered the worst of Skid Row. In the spring of 1960, the Stockton's application for $5.3 million in federal redevelopment funds was approved. But as the money flowed into the city, some city leaders began to have misgivings. Edna Gleason—liberal, outspoken, and the only woman on the City Council—was adamantly opposed. "I think the whole thing is radically wrong—you'll never get my vote," she said.[42] After the city notified West End business owners that they would receive only $3,000 each for relocation, opposition to redevelopment began to crystallize. The San Joaquin County Taxpayers Association began advocating for owners to rehabilitate the West End buildings. Sanguinetti, alarmed by the idea of total clearance, organized West End business owners into a new Committee on Rehabilitation. In the spring of 1961, Sanguinetti and John H. Jacobs, director of the Stockton Re-

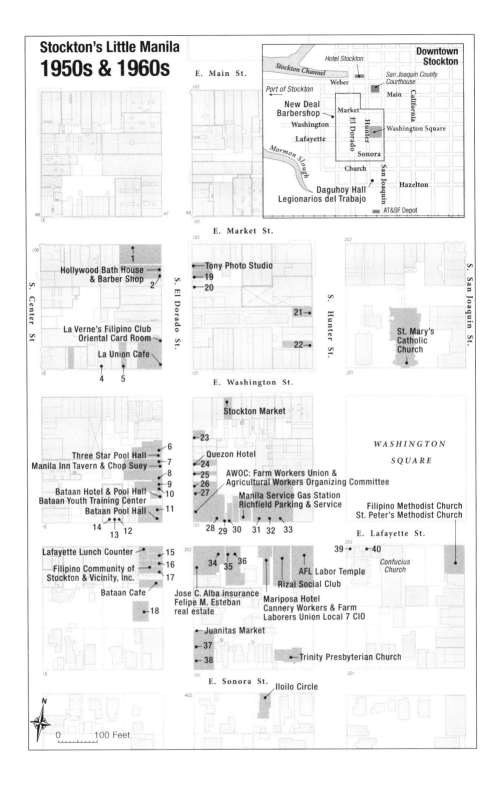

Stockton's Little Manila
1950s & 1960s

Downtown Stockton

Hotel Stockton
Stockton Channel
Port of Stockton
Weber
San Joaquin County Courthouse
Main
California
New Deal Barbershop
Market
Washington
El Dorado
Hunter
Washington Square
Lafayette
Mormon Slough
Sonora
Church
San Joaquin
Hazelton
Daguhoy Hall
Legionarios del Trabajo
AT&SF Depot

E. Main St.

E. Market St.

1
Hollywood Bath House & Barber Shop
2

Tony Photo Studio
19
20

21
22

St. Mary's Catholic Church

La Verne's Filipino Club Oriental Card Room
La Union Cafe

4   5

E. Washington St.

S. Center St.

S. El Dorado St.

S. Hunter St.

S. San Joaquin St.

Stockton Market

Three Star Pool Hall
Manila Inn Tavern & Chop Suey
6
7
8
9
Bataan Hotel & Pool Hall
Bataan Youth Training Center
10
Bataan Pool Hall
11

14   12
13

23
Quezon Hotel
24
25
26
27
AWOC: Farm Workers Union & Agricultural Workers Organizing Committee
Manila Service Gas Station
Richfield Parking & Service

28 29 30   31 32 33

WASHINGTON

SQUARE

Filipino Methodist Church
St. Peter's Methodist Church

E. Lafayette St.

Lafayette Lunch Counter
15
16
Filipino Community of Stockton & Vicinity, Inc.
17
Bataan Cafe

18

39   40

Confucius Church

34 35 36

Jose C. Alba insurance
Felipe M. Esteban real estate

AFL Labor Temple
Rizal Social Club

Mariposa Hotel
Cannery Workers & Farm Laborers Union Local 7 CIO

Juanitas Market
37
38

Trinity Presbyterian Church

E. Sonora St.   Iloilo Circle

N

0   100 Feet

6. Little Manila in the 1950s and 1960s. The dispersal of Filipinas/os into the South Side neighborhoods and pressure from redevelopment and freeway construction began to affect the Little Manila neighborhood. The West End Redevelopment Project's impact is shown on map 7, p. 338. SOURCE: POLK CITY DIRECTORIES, 1950–70. MAP BY BEN PEASE.

Numbers within parentheses indicate the businesses' chronological order at the sites.

1. Savoy Lunch and Club
2. Golden Gate Dept. Store
3. Philippine Rooms
4. Atonilco Pool Hall
5. (1) Corregidor Barber Shop; (2) Ceso's Cigars
6. Melecio Suguitan (barber)
7. J. R. Bagtos (shoe shiner)
8. (1) Manila Club (cigars); (2) Stockton Pool Hall and Cigar Stand
9. Cuizon's Restaurant
10. Madera (barbershop)
11. Republic Jewelry
12. Aklan Hotel
13. Elk Cleaners
14. Kalibo Pool Hall
15. (1) Horseshoe Fountain; (2) Leta's Place
16. Public Relations Bureau
17. Tommy's Barber Shop
18. Lincoln Super Service Garage
19. Sim's Barber Shop
20. (1) Hollywood Bath House, Shoe Shine Stand, and Barber Shop; (2) Sim's Barber Shop
21. Aloha Hotel
22. Mrs. L. I. Osencio Restaurant
23. The Philippines
24. The Quezon Hotel
25. Pacific Cleaners
26. Modern Barber Shop
27. (1) Roman Ordono Restaurant; (2) Frank Sarmiento Restaurant
28. (1) Snack Shop; (2) Luz Vi Minda Café
29. (1) Andres Alvarico Restaurant; (2) La Perla del Oriente Restaurant
30. Johnnie's Family Market
31. Luneta Pool Room
32. (1) Felipe M. Esteban (real estate); (2) Leyte Café
33. Juliana Apartments
34. Alberca Bernabe (gas station) and E. O. Viviano (auto repair)
35. (1) Luzon Café; (2) N & L Fish Market
36. Colonial Cleaners
37. (1) Dionicio Unsod (cleaners); (2) Manila Cleaners
38. Binatilan Hotel
39. Luz Paragas
40. St. Benedict Convent

development Agency, engaged in a debate on redevelopment at a meeting of the city's real estate agents, the local Realty Board. Sanguinetti, the early architect of the city's redevelopment, became the West End Redevelopment Project's most ardent opponent.[43]

Opposition to the project gained momentum after the more than $5 million for redevelopment funds had been approved. Even James Gardner, the City Planning Director, had second thoughts about the demolitions, which he believed would have a detrimental effect on the central business district. Redevelopment proponents organized themselves into the Citizen's Committee for the Elimination of Skid Row, and Sanguinetti's opposition group was joined by Donald Boscoe, a local attorney and downtown business owner. By late 1961, the battle over the West End was heating up. Several business owners who wanted to stay in the West End and who opposed displacement and demolition simply refused to give in to the Redevelopment Agency.

On December 1, 1961, Sanguinetti, Boscoe, and other business owners went to Superior Court to halt redevelopment proceedings. The trial was moved to Tuolumne County when local judges recused themselves from the case. Among the criticisms leveled at the city during the trial was the relocation plan for the 1,200 single men in the West End. Two camps in desolate areas of the city several miles from downtown had been planned as relocation camps: one was at the San Joaquin County Fairgrounds, and the other was on Turnpike Road, in South Stockton. Boscoe complained that the substitute housing offered to these men was even worse than the housing in the West End. He told the court that the camps were too remote for these men, who would be far from work and commercial areas: "Conditions there are so deplorable that one cannot find, even in the West End, conditions that compare with the blight there." Living quarters on Turnpike Road allowed for twenty square feet per man, while the state required at least forty-five square feet per jail inmate in its prisons.[44]

Critics of redevelopment pointed to the new shopping centers planned for the suburban North Side and questioned whether or not the West End clearance could really kick-start downtown renewal. The Redevelopment Agency rebuffed such criticisms; Edwin Manuel, an agency member, assured critics that the project would be successful despite the mushrooming of shopping malls in the north and major retailers' defections from downtown. City politicians were quick to reiterate their support of redevelopment. "We thank our lucky stars we voted for redevelopment when we did," City Councilman Jacob Fetzer told the *Stockton Daily Evening Record* in February 1962. "Otherwise, we'd be getting the blame for those stores going out there [to shopping malls on the North Side]."[45]

In January 1963, Judge Ross Carkeet ruled in favor of the Redevelopment Agency and blamed West End residents for the deterioration of the neighborhood. "The single farmworker who prefers to try and find some other quarters in an area of 'Skid Row' atmosphere is at liberty to do so," Carkeet said. "But he has no constitutional right to jeopardize the well-being, health and welfare of the remaining population by insisting on his right to live in squalor, filth and degradation."[46] At word that the redevelopment project was given a green light, Mayor Elmer Boss was "jubilant," reported the *Record*.[47]

Two weeks later, the City Council voted 5 to 3 in favor of redevelopment. Former mayor Dean de Carli, now head of the Redevelopment Agency, was elated. "I felt confident all along we'd win," he told the *Record*. "I feel that we were both morally and legally right. This is one of the biggest things in the city's history. If we're going to invite industry to Stockton, we'd better clean up our house first."[48] Angry West End business owners appealed the decision to the Third District Court of Appeals in Sacramento and moved to block the land purchases with a stay of execution, but they were unsuccessful. Resigned, Boscoe told the *Record* on March 5, 1965, that "further resistance seemed futile." A defeated Sanguinetti told the newspaper he did not want to "see the project held back. I hope it will be successful."[49]

The Redevelopment Agency and the city had been so confident that the court would rule in their favor that they had begun acquiring and demolishing property in the West End long before Judge Carkeet's decision. After the decision, when business and property owners demanded to stay in the West End and refused to sell their buildings to the Redevelopment Agency, the city began filing condemnation suits against property owners who were unwilling to sell.[50] If a building was condemned, the agency could force the owners to sell their land and the building could be demolished. The strategy worked, and demolitions in the West End began in early February 1964.[51] For more than two years, buildings fell like dominoes and block after block was cleared. In 1966 the *Stockton Daily Evening Record* reported that the area looked like "a bombed out World War II section of London."[52] At the end of the demolition, only three buildings remained because they were considered historic and/or architecturally unique: the Nippon Hospital, built in the 1920s to serve Japanese Americans, and two historic warehouses: the Sperry Flour Mill and the Eureka Grain and Farmer's Union Warehouse.[53]

THE VICTIMS OF URBAN RENEWAL

Although bankers and real estate developers could measure the success of the West End renewal through their financial statements, assessing the emotional and psychological toll of displacement on the residents of the West End is more difficult. Those who were displaced from their neighborhood experienced deep grief, sorrow, and loss. In a study of the working-class Italian Americans who were displaced from Boston's West End, researchers noted that the residents felt extreme hopelessness, anger, and psychological distress.[54]

In Stockton, almost no money went to ensure that businesses and residents were relocated. A similar pattern emerged in redevelopment districts nationwide. Relocation assistance constituted only half of a percent of the

$2.2 billion federal budget for redevelopment.[55] In April 1964 the Redevelopment Agency's relocation administrator reported that forty-four businesses, fifty-nine single residents, and nine families had relocated from the West End. Some residents moved into hotels in other parts of downtown such as the last remaining blocks of Chinatown and Little Manila south of Washington Street, which only exacerbated blight and overcrowding among the poor of downtown. Officials who had believed that the majority of West End residents were vagrants, transients, and seasonal workers now learned that many of the hotel residents had been living at the same address for six to nine years, and most had nowhere else to go.[56] City officials believed they were acting sensitively, and in the best interests of both powerful local farmers and the city's laborers, by planning the demolitions during the winter, when most of the migratory farm laborers would be away.[57] But when the laborers returned in the spring and summer to work the crops, they found they had nowhere to live.

The demolitions displaced and dispersed much of the Filipina/o community in and near the West End and Little Manila. Filipina/o business owners especially hard hit by the demolitions were the Saldevars, who owned the New Deal Barber Shop on Center Street. Though they knew the West End demolitions were imminent, Fernando was confident that they could find a place to move. Carmen recalls that African American, Mexican, Filipino, Chinese, and white customers lined up all night for haircuts from Fernando Saldevar or Melecio Suguitan, one of the two other barbers in his shop. When they received notice of the impending demolition in the mid-1960s, Fernando was forced to relocate the barbershop. "They said they have to build up the skid row place," remembered Carmen. "That's what they say, because the nine-block area is composed of different businesses of the colored, Japanese, Chinese, Filipinos, and Mexicans. . . . The sidewalks are filled up with people."[58] She speculated that the city cleared the area because too many members of minority groups lived and conducted business there, and because it was too noisy.

Preferring to stay downtown, where he had a steady clientele, Fernando and Carmen walked south of the West End to Little Manila to find a suitable shop. When they found a barbershop they could purchase on El Dorado Street, they were elated: they would be in the heart of the city's Filipina/o community. When the Stockton Pool Hall, a Visayan-owned pool hall located across the street from the barbershop went up for sale, the Saldevars bought it. Carmen managed the pool hall, and Fernando ran the barbershop. The Ilocanos who lived in Little Manila began to flock to the Stockton Pool Hall. After the Saldevar family took over, Carmen remembered that "everybody I see is Ilocano!" She said, "And they're happy because we're with our own people. You could hardly walk in front of the pool hall. You could hardly get in. Inside, you could hardly walk."[59] Filipinas/os greeted each other with, "Are you Ilocano?" she recalled. Their shared heritage and language bound the Saldevars to their clients, and the elderly Ilocano old-timers began asking Carmen to act as their translator and representative at trials, the Social Security and Veterans Administration offices, and their visits to Nicanor Bernardino, a Filipino doctor in downtown. Carmen was happy to oblige.

When the pool hall and barbershop were flourishing in the late 1960s and early 1970s, Filipinas/os were clinging tenaciously to the intersection of Lafayette and El Dorado streets and the four remaining blocks of Little Manila, which had miraculously been spared the West End's wrecking ball. Many of the old-timers were beginning to retire from farm work, preferring to spend their last years in the comfort of their hotel rooms, surrounded by familiar faces and businesses, living on their meager Social Security checks. Alma Alcala cherished the memories of the afternoons of her girlhood when she accompanied her father, Atanasio, to visit the old-timers on El Dorado Street in the 1960s. "When I was very little, every time my dad would get a paycheck, we would go to downtown Stockton, go to Gan Chy on El Dorado, and we'd eat Chinese food, and we'd pass the old-timers and my dad would talk to them in Ilocano," she remembered. As she recalled the street scene, she was overcome with emotion and began to cry: "It was so much fun to hear them talk, and they would be so animated, and then afterwards their eyes would get so sad, and I would see them standing on the street, always so sad and lonely. I could feel their pain."[60] Many of these elderly residents of Little Manila did not know that within a few years, the community they knew and loved would be gone.

THE FIGHT OVER THE CROSSTOWN FREEWAY, 1961–75

Some members of the Filipina/o community had heard rumblings about the impending construction of a freeway nearby, but few knew the plans. From the 1910s through the 1980s, freeway construction went hand in hand with the transformation of America's cities and the mushrooming of the country's suburbs. The passage of the 1956 Interstate Highway Act—a result of relentless pressure from powerful auto, oil, rubber, and asphalt lobbies, as well as Cold War defense needs—funded the construction of more than 40,000 miles of highways and freeways, further spurring the growth of suburbs.[61] By the 1960s, massive freeway construction throughout California had spurred increased decentralization and the attendant deterioration of the state's downtowns and inner cities. Ironically, elites and planners saw freeways as the panacea for decaying central cores. Suburbanites would use the thoroughfares to speed into downtowns, leave their cars in the new parking garages, and pour their money into downtown entertainment and shopping. In fact, the opposite occurred. Freeways, most scholars and city planners now concur, accelerated suburbanization and sprawl and destroyed neighborhoods by uprooting and displacing communities, particularly the neighborhoods of poor people of color.[62]

Soon after the passage of the Interstate Highway Act, the California Highway Commission presented its plans for Interstate 5, a freeway that would run from Canada south to Mexico, and through Washington, Oregon, and California. This freeway would bisect Stockton's West Side.[63] Included in the plans was a $20 million dollar Crosstown Freeway that would connect the new I-5 and the state's old north-south mainstay, Highway 99, through downtown Stockton. Highway officials, politicians, businessmen, and urban planners who supported the construction of the Crosstown Freeway envisioned it transforming Stockton into the center of a transportation hub linking Northern, Central, and Southern California. The Crosstown would cut through Stockton's downtown and directly through two of the four remaining blocks of Little Manila (see figure 43). City leaders were won over when they were convinced that the freeway would bring more people into downtown and add to the revitalization of the already cleared West End, directly to the north of the planned freeway.

In the 1950s and 1960s, freeway proponents were optimistic. Planners believed freeways were positive for urban communities.[64] Highway planners and engineers claimed that the Crosstown Freeway would not divide the city of Stockton, and that the artery would, instead, revitalize the downtown. The State Division of Highways offered several options but favored the Washington-Lafayette corridor. This route cut through the remains of Little Manila and Chinatown and through five other neighborhoods whose residents were mostly people of color, where many families subsisted on less than $3,000 per year. In 1970, $4,000 was the poverty line in California.[65] The route would eliminate 461 homes, 126 businesses, six churches, the seventy-year-old Washington Square Park in front of the venerable St. Mary's Church, a school, and 80 acres of farmland.[66]

The State Division of Highways sponsored a public hearing on proposed freeway routes on Thursday, June 1, 1961 at the Civic Auditorium, which drew howls of protest from downtown residents. More than 175 residents of Little Manila, Chinatown, and the other five affected neighborhoods came to the public hearings to protest the freeway route. None of the proposed routes garnered any major support, but the route that aroused the most ire was the

43. Redevelopment and demolition for the Crosstown Freeway couldn't completely displace the Filipino old-timers who, for decades, had called Little Manila home. Here, Manong Johnny (right) and a friend pose on Washington Street in the 1970s. Photograph by and from Laurena Cabañero.

Washington-Lafayette corridor that bisected downtown into two separate neighborhoods: a white one north of the freeway, and a brown one to its south. For more than four hours, state highway officials and residents battled over the proposed freeway route. Only two supporters of the Washington-Lafayette corridor attended the public hearing: George Hench of the Greater Stockton Chamber of Commerce, and John Jacobs of the Stockton Redevelopment Agency. Opposition to the freeway came from all sectors of the downtown community: ministers, landowners, businesspeople, community leaders, attorneys, and residents voiced loud protests to the state officials. Those opposing the freeway included Charles M. Weber, grandson of the city's founder, Charles Weber, who owned Washington Square Park, opposite St. Mary's Church; members of the Japanese American Buddhist church; and several attorneys representing the Japanese American and Chinese American communities, whose neighborhoods would be destroyed by the freeway. Filipinas/os had no attorney present.

Those opposing the freeway cited numerous issues with its proposed route. Residents bemoaned the destruction of their community institutions and homes, while business owners felt that the freeway would kill an already deteriorating downtown. Residents were suspicious of the planned location, which would rip through the mostly poor, black, Asian and Mexican American sections of Stockton and displace mostly poor and minority residents. "'Why there?' we asked. Why not through the Mormon Slough, just a few blocks away?" recalled Angelina Bantillo Magdael, one of the few Filipinas/os who attended the public hearing and spoke against the Washington-Lafayette corridor.[67] Opponents were troubled by the possibility of the freeway becoming a "Chinese Wall" that would divide the city into two camps. Growth would be hindered, too many people would be displaced or otherwise affected, and the freeway would be an "eyesore," according to dissenters.[68] The opposition noted that one of the city's busiest parks, Washington Square Park, would vanish.

Despite the vocal opposition to the Washington-Lafayette route, a majority of the pro-redevelopment City Council favored the freeway route.[69] When the State Division of Highways chose the Washington-Lafayette Street corridor and the City Council approved the route in a 6–2 vote on December 27, 1961, the area's residents were incensed but resigned.[70] Throughout much of the 1960s, city and state highway officials battled over the design of the Crosstown Freeway. Stockton city leaders continued their demands that the freeway be elevated and open underneath, so as to avoid the freeway becoming a "Chinese Wall" and therefore lessening the freeway's impact. State highway division officials balked at the extra $5 million in costs incurred by an elevated freeway. In December 1966, Mayor Jimmie Rishwain appointed a ten-man Crosstown Freeway Task Force to offer suggestions regarding the conflict between the city and state.[71] An open design was finally agreed upon.

In July 1965 the State Division of Highways created a new program that provided between $50 and $200 as compensation for families affected by highway construction.[72] Though construction of the Crosstown Freeway would not take place until the early 1970s, residents of the South and East Stockton neighborhoods most affected by the freeway pushed the city leadership to begin considering the impact of the freeway demolitions. In the summer of 1967, five churches in South and East Stockton, organized into the South Stockton Parish, demanded the formation of a relocation task force. Mayor Rishwain formed a Mayor's Crosstown Freeway Relocations Committee in September 1967; eleven men on the new committee had also served on the original Crosstown Freeway Task Force in 1966. One Filipino, Jose Alba, represented the community's interests on the task force. Rishwain asked the task force to help the city and its residents prepare for the relocation problems expected by the freeway.[73]

The committee convened in the fall of 1967. At their first meeting, the

Division of Highways notified the Relocation Committee that the area west of El Dorado Street would be vacated as soon as January 1968. The committee members set out to survey the relocation and housing needs of the residents of the area and surmised that approximately 416 families lived in the area.[74] Two interns from the South Stockton Parish surveyed an eight-block area that included four blocks of Little Manila. Their findings revealed that the area was home to almost 1,000 residents living in rooming houses and residential hotels. Most of the residents were Filipina/o, with smaller numbers of Mexican, Chinese, and black residents. They averaged $1,500 to $3,000 in annual income, and paid from $28 to $35 per month for their hotel rooms. More than 70 percent were more than sixty-five years old.[75]

The task force did not feel that it was the city's responsibility to find replacement housing for the migrant laborers who lived in the area for only part of the year, so they concluded that only 81 residents would have to be relocated prior to 1968. The Task Force recommended that the city establish a relocation assistance office staffed with bilingual personnel, and that demolition be delayed so as to not interfere with the influx of farm laborers during the spring and summer harvest time.[76] The city had also taken the harvest time influx into account when planning the West End Redevelopment Project demolitions.

Obviously, though the area's economy still relied heavily on agriculture, the city cared little about the housing needs of Filipina/o and Mexican migrant laborers. Instead of creating a solution for the labor housing problem and making plans for immediate replacement housing for the soon-to-be-displaced agricultural workforce, the committee members suggested that the demolition take place when most workers would be out of town. Committee members reported that "if vacation and demolition of structures can be timed to coincide with the off-agricultural season, the impact of displacement will be lessened."[77] In the end, the committee did almost nothing to help the Filipina/o American community.

FILIPINAS/OS AND THE FREEWAY

Though Little Manila lay directly in the path of the freeway, Filipinas/os made no substantive or organized opposition to it. A number of factors contributed to their silence. As former colonials with a long tradition of deference to white Americans, and as the victims of years of racial discrimination at the hands of Stockton elite, police, and government officials, many Filipinas/os felt powerless to stop the demolitions. In many ways, even in the 1960s and 1970s, some of the older generation of Filipinas/os in Stockton still felt like colonial subjects and guests in Stockton despite their status as citizens, their long presence in the community, and the central role they played in the area's agriculture. Community leaders hesitated to make any real demands on elected officials, provoke any real confrontations, or lodge any formal complaints to try to influence redevelopment or the freeway. And organized opposition to the freeway was unlikely, given the factionalism, poverty, racism, and political powerlessness experienced by the community in the postwar years.

By the 1960s, the large Filipina/o organizations, such as the fraternal orders, seemed reluctant to involve themselves in local politics. Moreover, although mutual-aid and hometown organizations proliferated after World War II, their immediate goals included financial support for those left behind in the Philippines and the creation of purely social networks among new immigrants and established residents. As a result, they wielded little political power in Stockton. A conservative, "don't rock the boat" attitude had developed among the early generation as a survival mechanism in the 1920s and 1930s. The left-wing, militant, politically powerful labor leaders that had changed the face of farm labor unionism across the state had been silenced and crushed by McCarthyism and red baiting. The last militant farmworkers strike in Stockton had occurred in 1949, and many of the formerly radical workers now had wives and children. Former radical leaders such as Larry Itliong, Macario Bautista, and Claro Candelario had families and were now keeping lower profiles.

In the ways they revered white elected officials, the leaders of the Filipino Community of Stockton, Inc., the powerful umbrella organization, replicated the kind of patron-client relations that proliferated in Philippine politics and reflected internalized colonialism and internalized racism.[78] American imperial culture, deeply embedded in these men and women in their youth, influenced the ways that Filipinas/os regarded white elected officials. The leaders of the community had reverent relationships with local politicians — such as John McFall, a member of the U.S. House of Representatives, and Carmen Perino, a member of the City Council — and feared angering them. McFall and Perino were simply patrons who would court Filipina/o voters by showing up at their banquets, dinners, and ribbon-cutting events, for which Filipinas/os acted extremely grateful.

Filipinas/os in Stockton in the late 1960s were still at the bottom of the class and racial hierarchy in Stockton, and as such, they saw their positions in Stockton as precarious. In the late 1960s, racial covenants and Stockton's continuing segregation still barred Filipinas/os from buying homes in exclusive North Side developments. Their children and grandchildren attended the highly segregated South Side schools with other Filipina/o, Asian, Mexican, and African American children. Most Filipinas/os were still unable to find jobs outside of farm work or domestic work, or to be employed in professional work commensurate to their degrees and experience. In his study of Filipinas/os in Salinas in the 1970s and 1980s, Edwin Almirol found that older Filipinas/os were reluctant to become politically involved because they felt that the political process was beyond their influence. As a result, their powerlessness lead to even more intense malaise about the possibility of political power and change.[79] A similar situation happened among Filipinas/os in Stockton. The special social world that they created for themselves in the 1920s that insulated them from the vicious racism in Stockton helped them to survive, but it also created a situation in which many of them acquired little political savvy or experience in attempting to influence local politics and local policy.

Economics also played a substantial role in the lack of organized opposition. Because citizenship came so late for members of the Filipina/o community, and because of their low wages in farm and domestic work, few actually owned any land downtown. Filipina/o American business owners leased their spaces, and their fates were tied to the decisions of their white landlords, who were profiting from the sale of their buildings to the Redevelopment Agency and the State Highway Commission. A Filipino American Chamber of Commerce had yet to be established, and Filipina/o business owners were not organized as a group. Most Filipinas/os saw fighting the freeway as a losing battle, for even the most powerful members of Stockton's white elite who opposed the freeway, such as the Weber family, could not stop the freeway. Moreover, the idea that freeways and urban redevelopment marked the progress of the postwar American modern age — an ideology that most Americans embraced — convinced many Filipinas/os that demolition and displacement were inevitable. Many seemed to think that they — working-class, brown-skinned immigrants in Stockton with no political power — should not try to stand in the way of progress.

"EVERYBODY WAS SORRY TO LOSE EL DORADO"

Demolitions in preparation for the freeway construction began in the winter of 1967–68. In February 1968, bulldozers demolished the White Hotel, a four-story, brick residential hotel located at Lafayette and Center streets in Little Manila.[80] Newspaper accounts provide no information on where the residents were relocated. In 1970 Lawrence M. Bjornstad, an assistant district engineer with the State Division of Highways, told the *Stockton Daily Evening Record* that the state was attempting to ensure that all those displaced by the freeway would be relocated "with a minimum of inconvenience and discomfort."[81] Those business owners who would be displaced could apply for relocation grants of up to $5,000, and tenants could get up to $1,500 to find replacement housing. This extra money had been set aside by the state's legislature in response to complaints that the state cared little for the people it displaced in favor of freeways. There is little evidence that the Mayor's Crosstown Freeway Relocations Committee or the local Relocation Office, the state's bureaucrats assigned to help relocation, assisted a significant number of Filipinas/os in finding replacement housing.

Freeway engineers were optimistic about the impact the freeway would have on downtown Stockton and its residents. As demolitions were winding down, state highway engineers told the *Stockton Daily Evening Record* that the freeway would enhance redevelopment efforts and reduce blighted buildings, and that those hundreds of people displaced by the freeway would suffer "little or no hardship."[82] They were wrong. Low-cost replacement housing was difficult to find in Stockton, since most residential hotels in the West End had already been razed, and few replacement houses under $50,000 could be found in the city. In the spring of 1972, the State Division of Highways reported that 430 residents and 81 businesses had been removed from seven blocks, and that it had paid out $605, 619 in relocation money.[83] The state could promise replacement housing and business relocation, but it could not offer a replacement for the loss of community that the Filipina/o and Chinese populations suffered as a result of the Crosstown Freeway.

The personal stories of loss and grief that accompanied the demolitions give a sense of the incredible blow that urban redevelopment and freeway construction dealt to the Little Manila community. In the early 1970s, Carmen and Fernando Saldevar received notification from the State Division of Highways that their pool hall and barbershop would be obliterated by the freeway. Less than five years before, the previous location of their barbershop had been demolished by West End redevelopment. The Saldevar family businesses, the New Deal Barbershop and the Stockton Pool Hall, both at El Dorado and Lafayette streets, would have to relocate yet again. While searching for a new location, Carmen kept her always busy pool hall open. One day in 1971, she returned from an errand to find a puzzled crowd standing in front of the pool hall. An employee told her that a man from the state highway had come and taken two of her pool tables. She first went to the City Council and asked for permission for an extension of her use permit for the pool hall, saying she was having trouble finding a new location; the council members assured her that they would grant her a new use permit for a new location if there was no opposition from her new neighbors. Immediately after that, she went to an attorney who was working with the soon-to-be-displaced business owners; he told her to go to the State Division of Highways and demand that her tables be returned.

Carmen, a diminutive woman barely five feet tall, walked into the division office and demanded to speak to the man who had taken her pool tables. "I said, 'I am the owner of the Stockton Pool Hall. I am surprised why you took my pool tables,'" she recalled. "He said, 'You have to close the business.' I said, 'Close the business, why? How could I take out the pool tables without a place to put them?' And then he didn't speak up. I said, 'Sir, I need the pool table. Bring it back. I am looking for a place to move my pool tables. Please, bring it back.'"[84] The state highway official was unmoved, and Carmen finally returned home. When she attempted to relocate downtown, near Little Manila on Market Street, she applied for a use permit, only to be faced with opposition from an Italian American business owner who objected to a Filipina/o pool hall near his business. The city council rejected her permit application and suggested that she move her business outside of town. Saldevar balked at this: "I said to the council, 'Outside town? My customer lives inside town! And it's hard for them, and they live in those hotels around the area where I like to be.'"

She continued to run her pool hall at the old location, and dozens of Ilocano old-timers and more recent immigrants still flocked there. Eventually she found a new location at the Lee Center, at El Dorado and Washington streets, a Chinese-themed, low-income residential and commercial building erected by a local attorney on one of the Chinatown blocks cleared for the West End redevelopment. After she found the new location, the State Division of Highways returned her pool tables. Saldevar's was one of the last Filipina/o pool halls in Little Manila, an area that was once filled with pool halls, and when it closed in the 1970s after a short stint in the Lee Center, it signaled the end of an era in Stockton's Filipina/o American history.

Because Stockton's elites were concentrated in neighborhoods north of Main Street, the impact of the Crosstown Freeway on the poor and minority communities of downtown and the South and East Sides went largely unnoticed by them until the construction of the thoroughfare was imminent. In May 1971, the *Stockton Daily Evening Record* ran a series of stories on the impact of the freeway on those whom it displaced. Marjorie Flaherty, one of the paper's reporters, found that business owners in Chinatown and Little Manila viewed the freeway construction as bittersweet. Some business owners jumped at the chance to find new locations, while others bemoaned the loss of the Asian American communities that had been rooted in the Washington-Lafayette corridor since the nineteenth century.[85] Several business owners opted for relocation in the area, and the state offered them relocation assistance. If businesses could show that relocation would necessitate a loss, state relocation assistance payments could total $5,000. The state also offered a going-out-of-business payment. Several businesses took that money, since they could find no other suitable place to operate.

The *Stockton Daily Evening Record* found that many of the Filipina/o farmworkers forced to leave their hotel rooms had lived in them for ten to thirty years. Many were forced to find housing in a downtown without much affordable housing left. Flaherty interviewed two old-timers, both of whom were lucky enough to find replacement housing in the downtown area. Santiago Manzig told Flaherty that he was happy with the studio apartment he had found in the Lee Center. Magdaleno S. Ybono found an apartment in the downtown that he shared with other old-timers. Ybono told Flaherty that he was happy to be near his favorite restaurants, card rooms, and the bus station.[86] Some Filipina/o residents moved into the handful of residential hotels in the downtown that had survived the West End redevelopment. Most businesses closed altogether. Most people moved in with friends or relatives, or into the homes and boardinghouses of their mutual-aid associations and fraternal orders, such as the Daguhoy Lodge, the Iloilo Circle building that had been relocated to Hunter and El Dorado streets, the Caballeros de Dimas Alang building on Hunter, or the Numancia Aid house on the South Side. Eventually, many would live in the Filipino Center, built in 1972, which I will discuss in chapter 8.

Without an outlet to express their fear, indignation, and outrage at being displaced, and feeling helpless in the face of the city's power and as a result of their place in the city's class and racial hierarchy, Filipinas/os kept relatively quiet during the demolitions. In the opening scenes of the classic 1972 boxing film *Fat City*, filmed in Little Manila and downtown Stockton during the Crosstown Freeway demolitions in 1971, the camera pans over the freeway construction to show glimpses of elderly Filipinas/os watching the destruction with a mixture of sadness, resignation, and bewilderment. In fact, some scenes were filmed inside the Juanitas family's Quezon Hotel on El Dorado Street not long before the hotel was demolished.[87]

Emily Rosal, who arrived in Stockton from Hawai'i in 1945, still feels hurt and angry because she and others in the community felt so helpless. "The people—we were all scared, we were all frustrated," she remembered. "It hurts to know that there's nothing [we can do], we can't even fight throughout that thing. It shouldn't have happened. Today, I still think about it, and I still think that we've been mistreated."[88] My father remembered that his father, Pablo Mabalon, did not openly express any emotions about the destruction, but he was probably relieved that the freeway spared his Lafayette

Lunch Counter. His other business did not fare as well. Pablo leased and managed the Aklan Hotel on Lafayette Street from an Italian American who owned the building, and when that building lay in the path of the freeway, he could do nothing to oppose its demolition and the eviction of all of his tenants. In fact, he allowed the State Highway Commission to demolish the hotel with all of the furniture inside, and didn't bother to claim one piece of property from inside the building—all the beautiful wood furniture was destroyed, remembered my cousin, Lourdes Tumbokon Sobredo.[89] Perhaps he had nowhere to store the items.

Luna Jamero was in her early twenties when she moved to Stockton in 1967 to take a job as a social worker. Jamero, a graduate of California State University, Stanislaus, was a single mother from Livingston, a farm town an hour south of Stockton, whose family ran a campo and had deep kinship ties to the Stockton Filipina/o community. Since she had been a small girl, she had loved to go up and down El Dorado Street visiting with friends and family. But when she returned to Stockton in 1967, almost everything had been destroyed. "When I moved to Stockton that was in the [midst of the] redevelopment was going on, all of downtown Stockton looked like a war zone because all of the parts that I remember were being torn down," she said. "Everything was just totally gone. I couldn't believe it. What happened to all the businesses, where'd they all go? Where are all the people living?"[90]

Also among those moved by the plight of the Filipinas/os in Little Manila was Ted Lapuz, a Navy veteran and native of Batangas province who moved with his wife, Africa, to Stockton in the late 1960s to join his brother, Dr. Narciso Lapuz, who worked at the Alpine Meat Company in Stockton. Lapuz saw that the old-timers in Little Manila were neglected and had the least access of any group to resources and political power. "Well, most of them, you know, they . . . most of them are not educated, they cannot stand up for themselves," he remembered. City officials just offered pittances to the residents of Little Manila, he recalled. "You know, they just said, 'You're a good boy, we'll give you a little money, you go ahead and move out,'" he said. "That's all. That's why [when] I asked them, 'Where are you going?' they would say, 'I don't know, they're just giving me this much money.'" Ted Lapuz was moved by their plight. "So, that's why I felt so bad for them because, here they are, they don't know how to look for an apartment. They always live together in a community. And here they are, they're trying to tell them to get out, they're trying to tell them to find their own place. When I saw that, I said, 'This is not fair,' you know. These people, they have always lived together, they're sending them out."[91]

It was too painful to watch the demolitions, said Carmen Saldevar. Decades later, the injustice of them continued to haunt her. "We were so sad," she said wistfully. "I did not even go and see it. I remember how bad it is, to lose a business. And it's not only the money I'm after—I was helping the Filipinos there with their problems." The close-knit Filipina/o community on El Dorado Street disappeared. "They were scattered," she says of the old-timers of Little Manila. "No more. They even cried." The loss of the bustling community was heartbreaking for Saldevar. No longer would she see her elderly Ilocano customers, who loved to speak the dialect with her and stuff dollar bills into her young son's hands. When she saw some of the last of the old-timers who remained in the area after redevelopment, they would greet each other with deep sadness, and the anger would build up in Saldevar. "When I saw them, the more I am mad," she said. "I can't sleep. I would say [to them], 'I'm sorry. We used to be together here, now we are separated.'"[92]

The demolitions, for Saldevar, were insulting to the Filipinas/os who had long toiled in Stockton, and the wasteful destruction of perfectly good, beautiful buildings was detrimental to downtown's beauty. "I don't know why they moved the freeway close to town . . . Imagine those hotels that were demolished!" she said. "Everybody was sorry to lose El Dorado. It's beautiful before. They should not have destroyed that. The state highway should have went farther from the town, but they don't like to destroy houses. How about the hotels, that makes the town more beautiful, and more decent? [Politicians] are not [for our] community. We should have not elected them. That's how they separated the Filipinos. Some are mad [at] the Filipinos maybe, how come they do that? They don't remember what the Filipinos have done for California? What made California prosperous? The Filipinos, working in the farm!"[93]

A year after the state promised to build housing for each family affected by the freeway construction, funds began to dry up. By 1971 inflation and the economic downturn had begun to affect state and federal budgets. A once-flush Division of Highways found its budget slashed when $100 million in freeway funds were diverted to other state and federal programs by Jerry Brown, the new governor who supported mass transit.[94] The freeway stretch through Little Manila and Chinatown scheduled for completion in July 1972 was pushed back to 1974, though the state continued to acquire property, evict residents, raze buildings, and clear the area through the early 1970s (see figure 44). By April 1972, all buildings save one had been cleared for the freeway.[95] That fall, Congress delayed funding for the construction of the freeway to 1974.[96] The first stretch of the Crosstown Freeway was finally dedicated in 1976. Budget woes delayed its construction further, and the freeway did not link Interstate 5 and Highway 99 until 1993.

44. The Crosstown Freeway cut a wide swath through Stockton, leaving only two blocks of Little Manila. Courtesy of FANHS Stockton.

CONCLUSION

The hulking, intimidating Crosstown Freeway became, and continues to be, a physical barrier between two vastly different Stocktons. The Crosstown divides the city between the affluent, white North Side, and the poorer, working-class South Side, whose residents were predominantly African American, Latina/o, and Asian.[97] The elevated design of the freeway, considered so crucial for some residents and officials early in the design process, still became the "Chinese Wall" that its critics feared it would be. In a private conversation with me in 2002, a city official who asked to be unnamed referred to the freeway as the "Great Wall of Downtown."[98] It became a physical manifestation of the segregation that already existed in Stockton. The two remaining blocks of Little Manila were cut off from the rest of downtown, psychologically as well as physically. In 1972, as the dust cleared from continuous demolitions, the bustling, vibrant Little Manila neighborhood was torn asunder. Save for two lonely blocks, its businesses were devastated and its residents scattered. On one of those blocks, Pablo struggled to keep the Lafayette Lunch Counter open for business through the 1970s. Only a few key businesses and buildings, such as the Lafayette Lunch Counter, Iloilo Circle, Daguhoy Lodge, Caballeros de Dimas Alang lodge, several barbershops and grocery stores, and only a handful of residential hotels remained, such as the Mariposa, Liberty, and MacArthur.

Stockton's Filipinas/os did not protest eviction and redevelopment in the same ways that their counterparts did in San Francisco. The activists in San Francisco who protested redevelopment in the Western Addition and in the South of Market area in the late 1960s saw redevelopment projects through the lenses of class, race, and power, and linked their movement against redevelopment with revolutionary anticolonial, civil rights, and social justice movements. Beginning in 1968, a coalition of Filipina/o and other residents responded to redevelopment and the 1977 eviction of Filipina/o and Chinese senior citizens from San Francisco's International Hotel with a militant movement for affordable housing and social justice.[99] But by the time the San Francisco activists began their work, it was already too late in Stockton—most of the buildings were already gone, and the freeway was as good as built. Filipinas/os in Stockton had felt helpless to stop the demolitions. Decades of political powerlessness, their position as renters and not owners, their place at the bottom of the racial hierarchy in Stockton, and the conservatism and colonial mentality of their community leaders prevented them from launching any meaningful response to or attack on the policies that decimated their neighborhood. It would take a new generation and the arrival of new immigrants in Stockton in the 1960s for Filipinas/os in the city to take on the city's politicians and elites, as I will discuss in the next chapter.

The remaining two blocks of Little Manila gradually decayed as the old-timers died and businesses closed. My grandfather sold the Lafayette Lunch Counter in 1983 to another Filipina/o American family. A new generation of Filipina/o Americans—I count myself part of this group—was born and raised in Stockton with little or no knowledge of the vibrant urban landscape that had been home to the most populous Filipina/o community in the nation. Urban redevelopment and highway construction had destroyed the beloved community of thousands of Filipinas/os in Stockton and obscured the history of Filipinas/os in Stockton for new residents and new immigrants.

CHAPTER 8

BUILDING A FILIPINA/O AMERICAN MOVEMENT IN STOCKTON

In late 1967 two Filipino members of St. Mary's Church in the West End—Eulogio "Ted" Lapuz, a businessman, and Jose Bernardo, an engineer—surveyed the area surrounding Little Manila and St. Mary's Church in the West End as part of the annual parish survey of the Roman Catholic Diocese. What they saw shocked them to tears: elderly men living out their last years in cramped, dilapidated housing about to be displaced by the Crosstown Freeway. They both saw a pressing need for low-income housing for the soon-to-be-displaced Filipinas/os. Their survey found that 72 families and 462 single, elderly men—most of them Filipino—needed to be relocated as a result of the demolitions for the redevelopment of the West End and the pending demolitions for the freeway.[1] Lapuz and Bernardo began eliciting community support for a new idea: a low-income housing and retail project by and for Filipinas/os, a "Filipino Center," paid for with low-income housing funds from Great Society urban housing programs and collectively owned by the entire Filipina/o American community in Stockton. No other Filipina/o community in the United States had attempted such an ambitious project. But Lapuz and Bernardo soon faced opposition from local, state, and federal officials determined to delay or crush the movement for the Center, and the suspicion and hostility of the community's conservative old-timers.

This chapter examines the struggle to build a unified movement behind the Filipino Center in the wake of the demolitions of the West End and the destruction of Little Manila to build the Crosstown Freeway. The story of how the Stockton Filipina/o American community responded to the demolitions and displacements of urban redevelopment through fighting for the construction of the

Filipino Center illustrates how racial or ethnic communities in urban places struggled over space, power, and resources in the wake of postwar urban redevelopment projects that decimated their communities. It was a challenge to build the movement to support the Filipino Center. Filipinas/os in Stockton had mustered no formal opposition to the redevelopment project that destroyed the West End or to the Crosstown Freeway. Hindered, as I argued in chapter 7, by conservatism and colonial mentality, many of them did not think they had enough power or resources to be politically influential. Furthermore, they were divided by the panoply of ethnic organizations that had only multiplied since World War II, mutual mistrust, language differences, class, generation, and status as either newcomer or old-timer. But with new leadership from the second and third generation and from a mix of pioneers and newcomers, this fractious community began to make its demands with a united voice.

From 1967 to 1972, the struggle for a Filipino Center brought together a strategic alliance of progressive old-timers, educated postwar immigrants, and second- and third-generation Filipina/o American college students radicalized by the burgeoning Filipina/o American movement. Galvanized by anger over the displacements of urban renewal and freeway construction, these seemingly disparate groups drew on their community networks, organizing experience, and passion for Filipina/o American community development to forge a formidable alliance that challenged the white and Filipina/o power structure in Stockton, as well as the notion that Filipinas/os should remain second-class citizens. The struggle for the Filipino Center in Stockton became a flashpoint of the larger Filipina/o American movement throughout the West Coast in the late 1960s and early 1970s.

THE STRUGGLE FOR CONSENSUS

The coming of age of the second and third generations and the arrival of new immigrants after 1965 brought increasing diversity to the Filipina/o American community in Stockton in the late 1960s, but this diversity further hindered efforts to come together as a unified, politically powerful community. The 1965 Immigration Act brought two streams of Filipina/o immigrants to the United States: highly educated workers and family members of Filipinas/os who were American citizens or permanent residents. The law's preference for skilled workers in occupations considered in short supply encouraged the arrival of Filipina/o doctors, nurses, accountants, teachers, engineers, and other educated professionals. Some of the new arrivals had been able to go to college because they had relatives in the United States who had sent money back to the Philippines for that purpose. Professionals constituted about half of all Filipina/o immigrants arriving in the United States between 1966 and 1975.[2] Nurses dominated the earliest groups of immigrants. As the historian Catherine Ceniza Choy writes, the American colonial regime established nursing training in the Philippines in the first decade of the twentieth century, and these nursing schools answered the demand for nurses in the United States. Between 1966 and 1985, more than 25,000 Filipina nurses immigrated.[3] There were fewer job opportunities for highly educated professionals and their family members in agricultural areas such as San Joaquin County. Immigrants began to flock to other areas, such as Los Angeles and the Bay Area, where they found work in medicine, engineering, and accounting.[4]

Provisions in the 1965 act continued to allow all Filipina/o American citizens and Filipina/o permanent residents to petition their spouses, parents, siblings, and children above the quotas set for each nation. Many of those arriving in the 1960s and 1970s were the family members of pre-1965 immigrants, including the children, grandchildren, parents, and siblings of the immigrant community's earliest residents and spouses. By 1980, 80 percent of the new immigrants arriving in the United States came over as family-preference immigrants.[5] By the 1970s Stockton was no longer home to the largest Filipina/o American community in the nation; that designation had gone to the San Francisco Bay Area, where educated professionals were in demand. However, Stockton's reputation in the Philippines as a mecca for immigrants persisted, and thousands of new arrivals still came to Stockton to join family members. In 1968 so many professionals had arrived in Stockton, many of them teachers, that a new organization was founded: the Association of Filipino American Professionals, whose membership consisted of newcomers, second-generation Pinoys and Pinays who had become professionals, and a handful of old-timers who had finally been given opportunities to use their college degrees thanks to the civil rights movement and the rapidly expanding economy of the postwar era (see figure 45).

Deep divisions of class, both real and imagined, separated the old-timers from the newcomers, even within families. As the sociologist Antonio Pido notes, new postwar immigrants came in time to take full advantage of citizenship, civil rights legislation such as affirmative action, the outlawing of segregation and discrimination in hiring, widening job opportunities, and an expanding postwar economy. The newcomers, whose upbringings in the Philippines still carried the effects of American colonialism, imagined life in America much the way the old-timers had in the 1920s: the United States was a land of limitless possibilities for success. Lacking a complex understanding of the larger political and economic context of the relatively privileged

45. The membership of the Association of Filipino American Professionals reflected the immigration of Filipina/o professionals to Stockton after World War II, as well as a new environment in which earlier immigrants and their children could, at last, use their educations and skills. Courtesy of FANHS Stockton.

position they occupied in the immigrant community, and not realizing that the benefits of life in the United States that they took for granted had been denied to the pioneering generations, the newcomers tended to blame the old-timers for their poverty and lack of education. Many newcomers were ignorant of the struggles that the Filipina/o community had weathered from the 1920s through the postwar era.[6] Some immigrants brought with them the deep class and urban elitism and prejudices of the Philippines, and they arrogantly looked down on the mostly uneducated, provincial farm laborers from the Ilocos and Visayas who made up the bulk of the Stockton Filipina/o community. To them, the old-timers' grand adventure in coming to America had been a monumental failure: after decades in the land of opportunity, they were largely uneducated and poor. Class-conscious newcomers were reluctant to associate themselves with farmworkers and former sakadas.

These intense class divisions wracked the community, remembered Lillian Galedo, a second-generation Pinay born in Stockton. She recalled that most of the newcomers were Tagalog speakers, and the mostly Ilocana/o and Visayan community conversed largely in their dialects and English, so the language barrier compounded the conflict. Since most community members' last contact with the Philippines had been in the 1920s or 1930s, or just after World War II, they were relatively unfamiliar with the modern Philippine culture and society in which the newcomers had been raised. "The newer immigrants felt that the previous immigrants hadn't hung on to their culture," Galedo said. "And in a way treated them like they were sort of sorry for them—that their children didn't speak whatever dialect they came here with, that they didn't seem to know a lot of the cultural nuances of the Philippines—and made some assumption about their educational level and by extension their intelligence." Galedo said that the newcomers were standoffish, arrogant, and disrespectful of the community they encountered. "The generation who had immigrated here in the thirties and forties, they wanted [their] institutions to be respected and their role in establishing and sustaining those institutions to be respected," she said.[7]

New immigrants were haughty, remembered Luna Jamero, who was born and raised in Livingston on her parents' campo and began a job as a social worker in Stockton in 1967, after attending California State University, Stanislaus. "And of course there were the assholes, too, that came over from the Philippines who were full of it, full of themselves because they were the elites in the Philippines, and they grew up with a lot more than a lot of Pinoys we knew who grew up in the provinces," she said. In the early 1970s, Jamero was one of the young board members of the newly organized Filipino Multi-Service Center in downtown Stockton. On the board with her were her revered elders, or manongs (older male relatives in Ilocana/o and Visayan). At one meeting, a lawyer was being interviewed as a potential board member. When asked why he wanted to join the board, Jamero recalled: "He very arrogantly says, with all the arrogance he could muster, 'Well, because you know I am a lawyer, which is better than being a farmworker.' And I just looked him in the eye and said, 'You know what Leonard, I'll tell you something, if it wasn't for the backs of the manongs and Filipino farmworkers, you wouldn't be standing there right now, so you just get the fuck out of here.' I just told him to leave." Luna remembered that Isidro Samporna, a long-time community leader, became enraged. "He said, 'She is right, you don't know our history, you don't know what we have done in this country,'" she remembered. "'You know nothing about us, just because we're not lawyers. We didn't have a chance to get your education, and if not for us you wouldn't be in that city hall.'"[8]

My grandmother Concepcion Moreno Bohulano, herself a middle-class teacher who hailed from Cebu City, felt angry and insulted at the way she and my grandfather and their pre-1965 generation of pioneers were disdained by the new immigrants. In the 1950s and early 1960s, my college-educated grandparents worked in manual labor: Concepcion, a graduate of San Carlos

University in Cebu who worked as a schoolteacher, toiled in the canneries and as a campo cook and farmworker; my grandfather, who had gone to Far Eastern University in Manila on the GI Bill, worked as a contractor on a farm in Tracy. In 1962, Concepcion was hired as an elementary school teacher in nearby Tracy. But my grandmother still felt the condescension of the newcomers, and their disdain for the local community. "When the newcomers came, they think they are so big! [But they were really] big mouths, and they think they are so very good, that they are better off . . . than we were," she recalled bitterly. "Because they said we could have been [better] organized. But we were just happy before they came. I call them 'intruders.' They think they are so great. They belittled us."[9]

ENVISIONING A FILIPINO CENTER

Because of the attitudes of the newcomers, the old-timers treated them with suspicion and were on guard against interlopers, frauds, and arrogant new immigrants who might threaten their leadership and the cohesion of the community. St. Mary's Church members Jose Bernardo and Ted Lapuz carried none of the condescension and elitism of some of the newcomers. Nonetheless, the general conceit of the newcomers stigmatized Bernardo and Lapuz. Lapuz had retired from the U.S. Navy and become a local businessman. Bernardo's father was a farm labor contractor in the Delta, and father and son had worked together in the potato, celery, and tomato crops. After serving in Korea with the Navy, Bernardo had attended Stockton College and the University of California, Berkeley; he now owned his own engineering firm.[10] Both men were homeowners, with families and successful careers. Neither had been the leaders of any Filipina/o American organizations in Stockton. "I just had a world of my own," Bernardo said. "Come Sunday, we'd go to church. After that we'd take off. . . . We never really went to the community. And so I really didn't know that many people, and my contact with the Filipino people was up to the church."[11]

Bernardo and Lapuz had not spent much time in the hotels, bars, pool halls, and restaurants in what remained of Little Manila after the demolitions for the West End's redevelopment and the Crosstown Freeway. So when they saw the deplorable living conditions in the area's remaining residential hotels, they were appalled. "We knocked on those doors in a full block of the four block area known as 'Little Manila,'" Lapuz said in 1969. "If we didn't see with our own eyes, we wouldn't believe the living conditions there. It opened our eyes to our own people. That was quite a traumatic experience seeing our own people in unspeakable housing conditions."[12] Lapuz saw tiny, suffocating rooms in filthy, dilapidated, fleabag hotels that were stifling in the summer and freezing in the winters, and the staggering loneliness of life as a senior citizen without family. "Since they don't have any families, they live in small rooms in those hotels," he said, overcome with emotion. Many died, alone, in their hotel rooms, he remembered: "Several times, they don't see them and until they smell [up] the room that they're dead [in] that's when they found out. They don't miss them, they're old people and there's no accommodation for them."[13]

Bernardo, too, was shocked at the conditions Filipinas/os endured in the residential hotels. "If you had told me [prior to the survey] that this condition exists on El Dorado Street where people were living, I'd tell you, 'You're fibbing,'" he said. "Because I wouldn't have believed the condition that those people were in. That was the first time I was exposed to it. . . . How could people possibly live that way?"[14] Lapuz and Bernardo believed that they should try to effect some kind of change. "So, when I saw . . . their living condition, I said, when we went back to the church, I said, 'Compadre, something has to be done,'" Lapuz said. "That is how we got started on the idea of the Filipino Plaza."[15]

Galvanized, Lapuz and Bernardo then met Ted Lee, who had just completed work with displaced African Americans and Japanese Americans in San Francisco, where several hundred acres of buildings had been demolished in a slash-and-burn redevelopment project in the Western Addition and the Fillmore neighborhood. Lee agreed to help in Stockton.[16] The three men began developing plans for a federally funded, low-income housing and retail project to be located in a newly cleared block in the West End Renewal Area, at Main and Center streets. The landmark Housing and Urban Development Act of 1968 earmarked new federal funds for low-income housing to increase homeownership and units for low-income renters.[17] Lee found that the act provided a federal subsidy to defray interest payments on mortgages for nonprofit developers who would provide low-income rental housing. The act eventually was responsible for more housing than federal public housing programs.[18] The Filipino Center, Lee suggested, could be built with these new funds. In March 1968, when Lee asked the Redevelopment Agency to reserve land for a Filipino development, the agency asked him for a proposal and a deposit of $10,150, approximately 5 percent of the land's value.[19]

Lee, Lapuz, and Bernardo then embarked on a mission to convince the Filipina/o community to invest in the project. Decades of oppression and a deeply ingrained colonial mentality had made the old guard Filipina/o American leadership hesitant to challenge the status quo and white elite in Stockton, as shown by their unwillingness to formally oppose downtown redevelopment and the Crosstown Freeway. Lapuz knew he was a newcomer challenging the leadership of a formidable faction of the community in proposing a Filipino Center.[20] He and Bernardo were attempting a community organizing and education campaign in Stockton during a time of massive social transformations nationwide, and in Filipina/o American communities throughout the West Coast.

A FILIPINA/O AMERICAN MOVEMENT IN STOCKTON

Lapuz and Bernardo's first allies came from the generation that came of age after World War II, the Filipina/o American baby boomers, who were wholeheartedly in favor of the Filipino Center. The members of the second and third generations were the daughters and sons of the small number of families that had arrived before and immediately after World War II, and the children of veterans and their war brides. Many of these families in Stockton were the result of marriages between Ilocanas/os, Tagalogs, and Visayans or the marriages of Filipinas/os with whites, African Americans, ethnic Mexicans, ethnic Asians, and Native Americans. Regionalism was largely obsolete for the children of these families, who saw little utility in retreating solely into their Ilocana/o or Visayan clans and communities as their parents did. Most did not speak Ilocana/o, Visayan, or Tagalog, and they lacked the strong hometown and provincial ties of their parents. In school, they socialized with and dated other Filipinas/os and were racialized as Filipinas/os. They thought of themselves not as Ilocanas/os or Visayans, but as Filipina/o Americans. During the first stages of the Filipino Center project, the support and enthusiasm of the second and third generations were central to its success.

Some members of this generation were deeply influenced by the civil rights, feminist, and antiwar movements of the 1960s and became heavily involved in the burgeoning Filipina/o American movement that followed, in the late 1960s and early 1970s. The left-leaning and radical politics of some members of the second and third generations was a reaction to the deeply conservative atmosphere in which most of them had been raised in Stockton in the 1950s. As the historian Estella Habal argues, postwar Filipina/o American parents deemphasized language skills and traditional ethnic culture and emphasized instead assimilation and Americanization to help shield their children from the humiliation of racism.[21] "It was a generation within our community's history that emphasized being American," Lillian Galedo recalled. "You were now American so you will act like an American."[22] In the early 1960s, Rene Latosa and his parents—Juan (also known as "Johnny"), a labor contractor, and Purita, a homemaker—left Stockton to live in a mostly white suburban neighborhood in Lodi, immediately north of Stockton. "I could see it now, my parents tried to mirror what an American family lives like," remembered Rene. "You have a living room, you have a kitchen, and you go to school, and you drink milk, and you do all these things that an American family would do. It's like they took the culture away from us, so that we could live the American way. So we wouldn't stick out the way they did, [we] wouldn't suffer the type of discrimination that they did."[23]

Most postwar immigrants insisted that their children speak only English and did not teach Philippine dialects to their children. Because Tagalog did not become the national language of the Philippines until after World War II, most of those who immigrated to Stockton before 1965 had only a rudimentary grasp of Tagalog and were more comfortable in their dialects of Ilocano, Illonggo, Cebuano, or other dialects of the Visayas and Ilocos regions, and in the English they had learned in public schools in the Philippines during the colonial period. In marriages between Ilocanos and Visayan women, or between Visayans who spoke different dialects, English might be the language of choice anyway, as it was for the Bohulanos, my mother's family. Even those who spoke the same dialect, such as the Boholano parents of Lillian Galedo, did not pass the dialect of Cebuano on to their children. "Our generation really didn't retain our parents' language; it was not something that they forced us to do," said Galedo. "I don't think I ever remember my mother ever saying, you know, she wanted us to learn Visayan or Boholano. Even though they [my parents] spoke that to each other." Lillian Galedo's oldest sister had been born in the Philippines and immigrated to Stockton after the war, but she soon forgot her Cebuano dialect. My mother, Christine Bohulano, arrived in Stockton in 1952 as a four-year-old who spoke only Cebuano; within two years, she spoke only English.

This postwar emphasis on conformity and Americanization shaped the Filipina/o American postwar generation in myriad ways. Some members of the generation embraced American middle-class culture, married non-Filipinas/os, and/or left Stockton. Others—especially those who were swept up in civil rights, social justice, and antiwar movements, like Luna Jamero, Laurena Cabañero, Mel LaGasca, Morris Artiaga, Alma Alcala, Vince Reyes, Remy Galedo Reyes, and Lillian Galedo—rebelled against their parents' conservatism and emphasis on assimilation by becoming radicalized and politically conscious. They were part of a burgeoning Filipina/o American movement that consisted of second-generation and immigrant Filipinas/os who were highly influenced by the cultural, political, and social movements and identity politics of the 1960s and 1970s in the United States and the Philippines. Many were increasingly drawn into antiwar movements, and in the 1970s, the feminist movement; gay and lesbian movements; struggles for ethnic studies and open admissions policies at the University of California, Berkeley, and San Francisco State University; the farmworkers' movement, which boasted Filipina/o leadership in the form of three leaders of the United Farm Workers, UFW Assistant Director Larry Itliong, Philip Vera Cruz, and Pete Velasco; and Filipina/o cultural and arts projects, as well as opposition to the U.S.-supported Ferdinand Marcos regime and martial law in the Philippines.

The Filipina/o American movement (also called the Pilipino American movement, with the substitution of *P* for *F* being an anticolonial statement that acknowledged the lack of an *F* in the Tagalog language) grew by the early 1970s into a cultural and political movement that affirmed Filipina/o American ethnic identity and history, embraced Filipina/o American and Philippine cultures, promoted the production of Filipina/o American literature and art, opposed the Marcos dictatorship, and proclaimed solidarity with left and Third World movements.[24] Several Filipina/o American movement leaders hailed from Stockton: Larry Itliong, assistant director of the United Farm Workers and president of the Filipino American Political Association; some of the founders of the Pilipino American Collegiate Endeavor at San Francisco State University; Vince Reyes, who taught Filipino American studies at Sacramento State University in the early 1970s; and the University of California, Davis, students Lillian Galedo and Laurena Cabañero all hailed from Stockton.[25]

Many of Stockton's second-generation Filipinas/os were exposed to the campus politics of the late 1960s when they attended the campuses of the University of California (UC) and the California State University with the support of the Educational Opportunity Program (EOP), an affirmative action program that recruited promising Latina/o, African American, and Asian American low-income, first-generation college students to the two universities with full scholarships, tutoring, and counseling. Lillian Galedo—a graduate of Edison High School, like most of her Filipina/o American generation on the South Side—had planned to follow her older sister to San Jose State College (now San Jose State University). She was surprised when an EOP recruiter offered her a full scholarship to UC Davis. Lillian was in the first large group of EOP recruits to UC Davis, with a number of other bright Stockton Filipinas/os—including Laurena Cabañero and my mother, Christine Bohulano, an aspiring artist.

At UC Davis, Galedo and my mother took their first Asian American studies classes. My mother remembers the exhilaration of reading about Filipina/o American history.[26] The rise of ethnic studies and Asian American and Filipina/o American studies classes at colleges and universities up and down the West Coast in the late 1960s transformed and radicalized Asian

American youth. "I walked in the room, and it was a room full of Asians and it was so empowering just to see I could've just broken down and cried," Galedo remembered. "All you have to do is go home and talk to your parents and find out what's going on in your community, write it down, and this is it, the Asian American history." The emphasis in Asian American studies on community-based history and studies was revelatory for Galedo and other Filipinas, such as my mother, who remembered writing papers for her Asian American studies classes at UC Davis by drawing on our family's histories and experiences in the fields. "Then right around the same time the antiwar movement is really picking up and it hits Davis and we're doing exchanges in between Davis and Berkeley and Berkeley seemed like it, you know the center of the universe," Lillian remembered. "I wanted to live in Berkeley and San Francisco."[27]

A central part of the growing Filipina/o American movement, as Habal argues, was the discovery of and deep respect for the struggles of the old-timer generation—the Manongs and Manangs—as Filipina/o American activists came to call the pioneering generation of Filipina/o immigrants. Rejecting their parents' middle-class aspirations and emphasis on Americanization, many young people in the burgeoning Filipina/o American movement found profound meaning in the buried past of the Filipino proletariat. Their rediscovery of Carlos Bulosan's classic *America Is in the Heart*—with its vivid descriptions of American colonial rule, economic dislocation in the Philippines, and the racist brutality of life in the 1920s and 1930s for Filipinas/os—was key to this reawakening, as Habal argues.[28] When Bulosan died in Seattle in 1956, he was better known by some Filipina/o Stocktonians for his drinking binges, Communist politics, and poverty than his brilliant writing. The annual Filipino People's Far West Conventions, which kicked off in Seattle in 1971, established a network of Filipina/o American community organizers in California who were working on political issues, the farmworker's movement, social justice issues, and arts and culture in Filipina/o American communities along the West Coast.

For progressive Filipinas/os in Northern California, the struggle over the International Hotel—on Kearny Street in San Francisco's Manilatown—which began in 1968, was a flashpoint in the burgeoning Filipina/o American movement. A developer's plan to evict the mostly elderly Filipina/o and Chinese residents of the hotel and the Filipina/o American community's radical resistance drew Filipina/o American activists to Kearny Street from 1968 to 1977 the way aspiring hippies were drawing flower children to Haight Street in the same period. Students and activists in San Francisco picketed, marched, and rallied to prevent the eviction of the International Hotel's tenants and called attention to the plight of seniors who were being targeted by urban redevelopment. Luna Jamero, Alma Alcala, James Villadores, Lillian Galedo, and other activists often went back and forth between Little Manila and Manilatown in San Francisco, organizing residents to oppose displacement, Laurena Cabañero remembered.[29]

But the political environment in Stockton was much more conservative than the one in San Francisco. In contrast to the raucous and militant International Hotel struggle, the Stockton Filipina/o community's response to local demolitions in the 1960s and early 1970s was one of bewilderment and repressed anger; instead of taking to the streets, they instead embarked on a federally funded community center project. Despite its conservatism, Stockton's Little Manila was an important front in the Filipina/o American movement in Northern California. If the Filipina/o American movement was about reclaiming the proletarian politics of the pioneering generation of Filipinas/os, championing the struggles of the farmworkers, and veneration of the Manong generation, Stockton was ground zero for Filipina/o American history, Rene Latosa argues: "We were where the pavement hits the road." The distant, academic approach in his Filipino American history course at Delta College left him disappointed. "We were *in* Stockton, we related to the migrant workers, the festivals after the harvest, the reality of working in the fields," he said. "They didn't talk about the actual people doing the job, you know doing the work. Getting on the bus at 4 o'clock in the morning, getting out to the pear field, asparagus field, to the peaches, and working that all day long in the hot sun. Getting their card stamped for how many boxes they picked."[30]

What Latosa didn't find in the Filipino American studies courses he sought in the practice of arnis escrima—the ancient martial arts of stick, hand, and blade fighting in the Philippine archipelago—which was experiencing a renaissance in Stockton in the late 1960s. The revival of escrima as a formally taught martial arts practice in Stockton emerged as part of the Filipina/o American movement of the late 1960s and 1970s, when Filipinas/os, as Habal writes, were developing a new consciousness about traditional Philippine arts, culture, icons, symbols, and values.[31] The most obvious expression of this in Stockton and elsewhere on the West Coast was the dance troupes that proliferated across the country in Filipina/o American communities, especially after the world-famous Bayanihan Dance Company made its first acclaimed world tour in 1959. Stockton had its share of Philippine dance groups, including the Sampaguita Dance Troupe, led by postwar Ilocana immigrant Carmen Tomek, just after World War II; and the Luzviminda Dance Troupe, led by Voltaire Gungab, who had been a member of the Filipininana Folk Dance Troupe at the University of the Philippines. Gungab brought dances from the northern and southern non-Christian tribes to Stockton for the first time.[32]

But what made Stockton unique in the flowering of Philippine and Filipina/o American arts and culture in the United States in the late 1960s was the community's central role in the revival of escrima through the nation's first formal schools and exhibitions of the art. Many of the earliest immigrants to Stockton had brought with them the knowledge of different regional systems of escrima. One of the most knowledgeable and skilled escrimadors in Stockton was Angel Cabales, a native of Antique province, Panay, who settled in Stockton after World War II. Cabales drew on his training in boxing and escrima from elders to develop his own style, called Cabales *serrada escrima*, which he taught informally above a restaurant in Little Manila. In March 1967—encouraged by Max Sarmiento and Dentoy Revillar, two second-generation Pinoys, and assisted by Lynn Sarmiento— Cabales opened the first public Filipino Martial Arts academy in the United States on Harding Way in Stockton.[33] Around the same time, Leo Giron, a highly skilled escrimador and World War II hero with the First Filipino Infantry Regiment, was prompted to revive escrima as a form of self-defense when eight student nurses, two of them Filipina, were brutally raped, beaten, tortured, and murdered in Chicago in 1966. In September 1968 Giron opened up his own escrima school in Tracy, south of Stockton, to teach his *largo mano* system. He moved the school to South Stockton in 1973, and the club was formally named the Bahala Na Filipino Martial Arts Club in 1979.[34]

One of the most prominent escrimadors to emerge from Stockton was Dan Inosanto, the son of the labor contractors and union activists Sebastian and Mary Inosanto. After college, Dan joined the military. When he was stationed in Kentucky, a knowledgeable instructor encouraged him to explore Philippine escrima. Inosanto returned to Stockton and began to study with the old masters, including Giron and Cabales (see figure 46). As he writes in his groundbreaking 1980 book *The Filipino Martial Arts*, the escrimadors in Stockton who began to teach him and others the art of escrima in the 1960s and 1970s included Cabales, Giron, John LaCoste, and Regino Ellustrisimo. In 1964 Inosanto met Bruce Lee and acted as his training partner until Lee's untimely death in 1973.[35] Inosanto is widely known as one of the most skilled martial arts teachers in the world, and his Southern California martial arts school, the Inosanto Academy of Martial Arts, is widely credited with bringing escrima to Hollywood films.

Rene Latosa, who became an escrima grand master, began his training with Angel Cabales, a close family friend, in the late 1960s. But soon he found

46. In this photo taken in the 1960s, a legendary escrima master, Leo Giron (left), plays with one of his protégés, Stockton-born Dan Inosanto. Courtesy of Antonio E. Somera.

other old-timers willing to share their secret arts. "There were lots of old-timers," Rene Latosa remembers, "in the Filipino Community Center and the Iloilo Circle, and everywhere else where there were card rooms and old Filipinos all out on the street, but they were reluctant to say that they knew anything because that would be a fatal blow to their strategy of surprise and being a warrior and drawing attention to yourself. But as they found out that I was learning [escrima], they would come by, and as I was working out in the buildings in the Filipino community, they would come by and show me things." Unbeknownst to Rene, his father, Johnny Latosa, had been a highly skilled and renowned escrimador in his home province of Antique and was famous among the old-timers in Stockton.[36] When Rene asked his father to be a stand-in during a routine backyard escrima practice, Johnny Latosa responded with swift, crushing blows on his son's skull, much to Rene's surprise. Rene Latosa now teaches escrima worldwide.

Along with the escrimadors, those especially revered by those in the Filipina/o American movement were the Filipina/o American leaders of the farmworkers movement of the mid- to late 1960s. If Martin Luther King Jr. and Cesar Chávez became heroes to the African American and Mexican American communities, so did Larry Itliong, Philip Vera Cruz, Pete Velasco, and the other Filipina/o founders of the United Farm Workers to the young Filipina/o American activists. The activists embraced the farmworker's movement, making it a part of their own, just as Chicanas/os had made it an integral part of the Chicana/o movement. In his time as assistant director of the United Farm Workers and national grape boycott coordinator, Itliong spoke at innumerable Filipino community conferences, especially those involving students and other young people, imparting his wit and wisdom and helping the next generation learn how to organize around political issues. "Itliong constantly challenged young Filipino American activists to understand they needed specific objectives to successfully organize themselves in the difficult struggle for equality," writes Dorothy Cordova.[37]

Itliong bridged a significant generation gap in Stockton. As an old-timer, farmworker, and contractor who was a former secretary and president of the Filipino Community of Stockton, Inc., and as a longtime organizer with the Local 7 cannery workers' union, he had close ties to and the trust of the earlier, more conservative generation. For example, he was the compadre of Johnny Latosa, the longtime president of the Filipino Community, and was an active member of the Legionarios del Trabajo lodge in Stockton. But as the radical leader of the farmworker movement and a member of the brave, passionate vanguard of the Filipinas/os in that movement, he became a hero to young Filipinas/os who were rediscovering the proletarian roots of Filipina/o American history and Filipina/o radical movements in the United States. Mel LaGasca, a second-generation Filipino-black mestizo, remembers that Itliong empowered them to realize the difference that individual consumers could make when they chose to not buy grapes.[38] When Itliong, citing bad health, quit the United Farm Workers in 1971 over deep philosophical and political differences with Chávez and the other union leaders, Pete Velasco took over for Itliong as the Stockton field office representative.[39] But Itliong continued to organize in the Filipina/o American community, founding the Filipino American Political Association (which encouraged Filipinas/os to get involved in politics) and coming back to Stockton in 1972 to speak at the Far West Convention.[40]

In Stockton, activists in their late teens and twenties like Luna Jamero, Laurena Cabañero, Lillian Galedo, Morris Artiaga, Hedy Yurong, Sonny Olaso, Mel LaGasca, Alma Alcala, and James Villadores began gathering behind the Filipino Center project. Bernardo and Lapuz received some of their most stalwart support from these young people and other immigrant and second-generation Filipina/o American college students who were attending nearby UC Davis and the local colleges—the private University of the Pacific and the local community college, San Joaquin Delta College. Their identities as native-born American citizens, their racialization as Filipinas/os in Stockton, their experiences in the Filipina/o American movement and the social transformations wrought by the civil rights movement and the Great Society social programs shaped the worldview of the second- and third-generation youth. They were convinced that community power and unity was an achievable goal, and that the Filipino Center was not only necessary, but possible. By joining with older progressive Filipinas/os—including immigrants, labor organizers, veterans, war brides, and old-timers, they created a powerful coalition that spoke louder to elite power in Stockton than any previous generation had done.

BUILDING A COALITION

Though these college students and radicalized Filipinas/os were quick to support Lapuz and Bernardo, the old guard in Stockton was more hesitant. Because of their newcomer status, Lapuz and Bernardo were viewed as outsiders by some in the close-knit community. In contrast to the two men, several families and leaders like Filipino Community President Johnny Latosa and former president Claro Candelario had established a foundation of leadership and spheres of influence in the community that long predated World War II. But though Lapuz and Bernardo's idea for a Filipino Center seemed like a radical departure from Stockton Filipina/o American community politics of the 1960s, in fact such a center was not a new goal. Since the 1920s, Filipinas/os in Stockton had been trying to raise funds for a community hall, although their attempts had been scattered and fruitless. The Filipino Community of Stockton organization had spearheaded a fund-raising drive in the 1930s, when Macario Bautista, the respected doctor, was its president. Through social box dances and queen contests, several thousand dollars had been raised and set aside in a building fund.[41]

The massive Filipino Center project—slated to be eight stories tall and fill an entire city block with affordable housing and retail—aroused jealousies and suspicions. Lapuz recognized early on that the conflict with the old guard was not about the need for a center, but about who would be able to take the credit for the project, if it was successful. Other organizations, including the Manuel Roxas post, the local Filipino post of the American Legion, had been saving money for their own buildings since the 1950s, for example. "So, the conflict is, who is this man who came to Stockton and [is] trying to do this, and here we are—for the longest time, we have the dances, and things like that, trying to raise money for a building," Lapuz remembered. "Actually, they're not against the idea. The only thing is that [the] wrong persons are trying to get it built. Who am I? I just came to Stockton in 1965."[42]

The displacements of the West End Redevelopment Project and the Crosstown Freeway made the need for a building for the entire community even more pressing. Only a handful of Filipina/o American organizations in Stockton owned their own buildings in Little Manila. The Filipino Community of Stockton, Inc., opened the Filipino Community Hall in the mid-1960s, next to Gleason Park at 443 South Sonora Street. The powerful and wealthy Filipino fraternal order, the Legionarios del Trabajo, constructed its Grand Lodge several blocks from Little Manila on South San Joaquin Street in 1964; the Filipino Federation of America had occupied a huge compound across the street at 2049 South San Joaquin Street since the late 1920s; and the Caballeros de Dimas Alang Regidor Lodge and the Iloilo Circle maintained small buildings on East Sonora Street, near Hunter, in Little Manila.

Lillian Galedo remembered that it was difficult to convince separate organizations to throw their support behind one large project, especially those that already had a building or were saving for one. "There were certain organizations that had, actually, more advanced community development achievements that had a building, you know—had property and things like that—and I think when the Center was proposed, some of those groups felt threatened. For one thing they felt excluded, and they also felt threatened in a kind of narrow view of our own community," she said. "[As if] you couldn't have more than one center. And so if it wasn't going to be yours, if you couldn't, like, get the money to build yours up more, then you weren't necessarily going to be very supportive about someone else doing it." Some of the differences were regional and factional, but the divisions, Galedo recalled, were largely due to personal issues, jealousies, egos, and ambitions. "Some of it was totally personal, in terms of individuals' personal ambitions and personal connections and things like that," she remembered. "Some of the resistance had to do with kind of sharing the stage with another organization, and then this project was just so much more ambitious than the others. That it would really overshadow all the other accomplishments that other groups had made."[43]

Despite these difficulties, there had been some success: some Filipinas/os were warming to the idea of a Filipino-owned center, and others became wholeheartedly supportive. Lapuz and Bernardo embarked on a door-to-door campaign to woo the members and leaders of the thirty-plus Filipina/o American organizations in Stockton and to raise the $10,150 they needed. It was a daunting task. Lapuz and Bernardo attended meeting after meeting, armed with mimeographed information sheets describing the project. Some community members were receptive to the idea, but many others were lukewarm or adamantly opposed to it. The sum was "a lot of money back then, and all these organizations didn't have money in their treasuries or were saving for their own buildings," recalled Laurena Cabañero, a second-generation Stockton Pinay who was one of the UC Davis undergraduates documenting the progress of the project. "To give up money for one big effort took a lot."[44]

Many community members distrusted Lapuz and Bernardo's motives because similar proposals for Filipino community halls in the past had failed, though Lapuz and Bernardo continually assured people that the Center could be realized. Several community members began to openly oppose the project, and at least one organization was torn apart by the debate over whether or not to invest in it. Old-guard community leaders questioned Lapuz and Bernardo's motives. The leaders wanted to know who would control the Center after its construction, if each organization would have equal say in its operations, and whether the project was worth the money they had saved for their own buildings.

My grandmother Concepcion Bohulano remembers when Bernardo and Lapuz approached her and my grandfather Delfin Bohulano in early 1968, asking them to support the Filipino Center. My grandparents were active members in no fewer than seven Filipina/o American community organizations in Stockton: the American Legion's Manuel Roxas Post and Auxiliary, the Filipino Catholic Association of Stockton, the Santo Nino Association of San Joaquin County and Vicinity (a Filipino religious association devoted to the Santo Nino, or Christ Child), the Numancia Aid Association, the Iloilo Circle, the Filipino Community of Stockton, and the Legionarios del Trabajo. They embraced the project and accompanied Bernardo and Lapuz to community meetings to convince the organizations of which they were members to join in the effort. The Bohulanos helped to convince the members of the Manuel Roxas Post and Auxiliary of the American Legion to put their building savings fund toward the Filipino Center seed money. "They approached the Auxiliary while I was the president," my grandmother remembered. "There was a woman I fought with because she would not support the idea [of getting money] from the government, $2 million, to build that plaza. They are opposed to that, but I'm campaigning for that to help everybody." She then went to the Iloilo Circle, a hometown organization where she served as secretary. The Iloilo Circle members were unwilling to believe that the federal government would invest that much in the Filipina/o community. "And I went to Iloilo Circle; they don't want nothing [to do with it])," she recalled. "They said, 'They won't give you that amount of money.'" She told them that if they invested their building money in a larger project, it would benefit the entire community: "'This one will not be ours, but it will be for the whole community of Filipinos.' I made enemies," she admitted.[45]

My grandfather Delfin became the first Filipina/o businessperson to commit to renting retail space at the Center. Delfin's dream was to have a Philippine grocery store at the Filipino Center, if it could ever be built.[46]

But after several months, only the Filipino Catholic Association, the American Legion Manuel Roxas Post and Auxiliary, the Filipino Women's Club, and the Santo Nino Association of San Joaquin County and Vicinity had signed onto the project and offered portions of the seed money. Those groups were only five of the more than thirty Filipina/o organizations in Stockton. Representatives from these organizations formed an organizing committee for the Center. The committee was a cross-section of the community. Some members came from old Stockton families, such as the Caridos and Daclans. Other members of the organizing committee came from more recent, postwar immigrant families, or families that consisted of old-timer fathers who were World War II veterans and war bride mothers, like the Jusas, Yurongs, and Bohulanos.

On April 4, 1968—the day that Martin Luther King Jr. was assassinated—Lapuz, Bernardo, and their supporters unveiled their plans for the Filipino Center to the Redevelopment Agency. They proposed a 150-unit, low-income housing project featuring a child-care center, retail space, and a community meeting hall. They promised to return in thirty days with the required $10,150 deposit as their seed money. At the meeting, a Filipino community member spoke passionately in favor of the project. "I have lived here 25 years and I have found that my people have had a hard time to locate a place where they could live decently," he told the representatives of the agency. "When Mr. Lee extended the project to us, I was so happy to have a place we could enjoy and where we could live decently."[47]

The project's supporters told city officials that their plans for a multimillion-dollar commercial and apartment center would be a cooperative venture of up to forty local Filipino organizations. This was an idealistic projection and an exaggeration, for only four organizations had made a formal and monetary commitment to the Center. The site they wanted, a block bounded by Commerce, Center, Main, and Market streets, was on the edge of the West End renewal zone and only a few blocks from the heart of Little Manila at El Dorado and Lafayette streets (see map 7 in the epilogue). Agency members expressed a keen interest in the project and asked the staff of the agency to assist the Filipina/o community.[48] The following month, Lee, Lapuz, Bernardo, and representatives of the five organizations proudly returned to the Redevelopment Agency with a check for $10,150. It was a triumphant moment for the Filipina/o American community in Stockton. According to the uc Davis student researchers, the Filipina/o community believed that the Center could be constructed in two years. However, it eventually took more than four.[49]

ORGANIZING STRATEGIES FOR THE FILIPINO CENTER

The Filipinas/os supporting the Filipino Center project believed that their biggest obstacle had been overcome: they had convinced at least a significant portion of the community to support the project and raised a considerable sum of money for the deposit. But if the struggle to achieve consensus on the Filipino Center proposal had been maddening for the project's advocates, the four-year battle for federal funding pitched Filipinas/os in Stockton against federal bureaucrats, elected officials, and Stockton's business and political elite. The fight almost destroyed the fragile coalition of Filipina/o American community groups in the city, and it forced community members to come to terms with, and challenge, their status as second-class citizens in Stockton.[50] Soon after receiving the $10,150 check, the Redevelopment Agency made a formal request to the Sacramento office of the Federal Housing Administration (FHA) to study the feasibility of the project. However, FHA officials were unsupportive. Community members then began an exhausting and confusing attempt to navigate a bureaucratic labyrinth.

The headaches for the Filipino Center advocates began when FHA staff dragged their feet on the issue of a feasibility study. The staff's constant requests for additional information established a frustrating pattern of relations between the FHA and the Center advocates. For the next three years, the FHA sent repeated requests for information, indicating that a feasibility study would commence as soon as the required information had been submitted. When the Filipina/o community provided the information that had been requested, the FHA would respond unfavorably, each time discounting the information as incomplete or irrelevant. The FHA rejected applications for a feasibility study of the Filipino Center project three times in three years; each rejection forced the coalition of Center advocates to regroup, reassess, and recommit to the dream of the Center.[51]

The uc Davis researchers who had followed the Center proposal from 1968 to 1970 noted that the four years it took for the Center to be constructed embittered several community members but proved a revelation to those who had been complacent about the conditions in which Filipinas/os had been forced to live in Stockton. In the years it took to build the Center, Stockton's Filipinas/os learned how to confront bureaucrats and elected officials, and how to speak to power with a unified voice. In her speech for the dedication ceremony, Deanna Daclan Balantac talked about the struggle that the board endured to learn how to make the project happen. "It was a whole new way of thinking, a whole new language of procedures, meetings, surveys, estimates, contracts, feasibility studies, and more meetings and procedures," she said. "This was a perplexing undertaking, since few people on the committee attained a high school education and even fewer had any experience with federal programs."[52]

After the proposal's initial rejection in October 1968, the organizing committee for the Filipino Center embarked on a massive campaign to win the entire Filipina/o community's support and prove the necessity of the Center to Stockton city officials and the FHA. For the next nine months, committee members worked tirelessly to provide evidence of this necessity to the FHA. In March 1969, with the help of James Smyth, a sociology professor at Delta College, committee members conducted their own census of Filipinas/os in San Joaquin county. College students, Filipina nuns, and committee members conducted door-to-door surveys in the evenings, after work, in every town in the county. The committee found that 80 percent of Filipinas/os in Stockton supported the idea of a Filipino Center, and 90 percent supported having low-income housing for the elderly and poor. Most Filipinas/os in Stockton had been born in the Philippines, the census takers discovered, were over the age of forty, married, and homeowners. Most worked as farm laborers, and most of the remainder were federal employees. Soon after the organizing committee submitted the new information, Roland Sherman and Charles Barnaby, officials in the Sacramento office of the FHA, wrote to the committee, saying the information was too brief and not pertinent to the proposal.[53]

Committee members felt that the FHA had turned a deaf ear to the proposal because of its lack of faith in the Filipina/o American community. The committee also suspected that the delays were related to the struggles of the Lee Center, the low-income housing and retail building constructed as a consolation for the destruction of Chinatown, only two blocks from the planned Filipino Center. Since only a little more than half of the Lee Center's apartments had been rented, the FHA failed to see the need for more low-income housing in the area. In the fall of 1969, the committee decided to put pressure on Congressman John McFall, a moderate Democrat whose district included Stockton. McFall, who was gearing up for his campaign for his eighth term in the U.S. House of Representatives, promised a congressional inquiry. McFall's pressure may have paid off; in any case, the FHA finally granted an application for a feasibility study.

The community mood was sour, however. Almost two years of work toward the feasibility study had only brought them to the application process, which would take several months more. Several disenchanted community members gave up at this point; to them, the idea that the Center could become a reality was "just another silly idea someone thought up and abandoned," wrote the UC Davis researchers.[54] Lapuz, Bernardo, and a core of dedicated committee members decided to continue to fight and put pressure on McFall.

Politicians like McFall were held in high regard by immigrant and old-timer Filipinas/os in Stockton, and little up to that point — beyond minor personal favors or appearances at dinners — had been asked of political leaders in Stockton. Following the traditions they had brought from the Philippines, immigrants afforded elected officials deep respect, regardless of their politics or their relationship with the Filipina/o community. This attitude frustrated the younger activist Filipinas/os, like Luna Jamero. If younger or more progressive Filipinas/os dared to criticize local politicians, she remembered, the old guard would defend them. "The old guard, they would always come back and say, 'Well, you know, after all he has done a lot of things for the Filipino community!'" she recalled. "[And I would say] 'What, named a park after you?'" Luna remembered that the old guard craved the personal attention and small favors that they received from politicians. This relationship between elected officials and their constituents reflects Filipina/o relations of political power in the Philippines, where politicians were patrons, not representatives, of their constituents. "It was that same mentality that they had brought from the Philippines," Jamero said. "If they went to a politician and asked for a personal favor, then that politician was okay." But the younger generation felt that this attitude could not persist, according to Jamero. She and her generation of activists demanded that their elected officials act for the good of their constituents. "In our opinion, as people that were of a different mind-set, we felt politicians were not there to do personal favors," she said. "They're supposed to be doing something for the greater good, not for you personally."[55]

Asking McFall to get involved, then, was a significant step for the community. Though McFall had represented Stockton since 1957, he knew little about the Filipinas/os in his district. After the new application was submitted to the FHA, he called a communitywide meeting for January 25, 1970, to be held at the home of Jose Bernardo. Committee members remembered that McFall arrived late, and that what he told the community "had little substance."[56] County Supervisor Carmen Perino was also at the meeting. Community members in attendance offered evidence of the need for the Center. Lillian Galedo and Laurena Cabañero, the Stockton-based UC Davis researchers and activists, made a dramatic presentation, in which they showed how the planned Crosstown Freeway would obliterate what had been left of Little Manila after West End redevelopment demolitions. According to Galedo and Cabañero, half of all Filipina/o businesses in Stockton would be destroyed, and hundreds of Filipino single men would be displaced. Those attending the meeting were stunned. Although many of them had known that freeway construction was pending, few had realized the devastation the freeway would bring to the last blocks of Little Manila.

However, even McFall's influence proved useless, because the FHA denied the Center's feasibility application in mid-February 1970. The agency pointed to the failure of the nearby Lee Center to attract enough tenants to fill its units and quibbled about the amount of parking planned for the Center and the amount of commercial space, which it deemed unnecessary.[57] Soon after receiving word from the FHA, the director of the Redevelopment Agency, Ed Griffith, told Ted Lee that his agency wished to put the block reserved for the Filipino Center back on the market, since the FHA's rejection seemed so final.[58] Lee was undaunted and insisted on the need for housing for families displaced by the Crosstown Freeway, the Stockton school district's interest in a child-care facility, the need for retail space, the availability of parking in the area, and the Filipina/o American community's unequivocal support for the Center. The FHA responded to Lee with an unequivocal no.[59] Lee next contacted Arthur Timmel, director of the regional office of the FHA in San Francisco. A community meeting with Timmel, Ed Griffith of the Redevelopment Agency, and the Center committee was planned for April 2, 1970. The *Stockton Record* ran a story on the project and the meeting, but the paper published an incorrect meeting date.

Despite this mistake, more than fifty Filipina/o community members—including senior citizens and college students and other young people—attended the meeting, where they went head-to-head with Timmel, other officials from the FHA, and Griffith. Though the meeting was supposed to be a pivotal one, Congressman McFall was absent. Timmel told the crowd that his main concern was the planned location of the Center in the old Skid Row, and the possibility that the Center would attract the old undesirables back to downtown. An elderly Filipino rose to challenge Timmel:

> [Ted] Lee did not choose this site; the people picked this site. This site was chosen because it is in the vicinity where many of the elder Filipinos already live. This site has been the focal point of Filipino activities ever since their migration into this country. It is less expensive living in this area, especially for elder Filipinos since it is in close proximity to the services they want and need. The Greyhound bus station is right there. . . . If

he wants to buy bagoong [salted, fermented shrimp paste, a popular condiment], he can go down the street, because the shops where he buys his special foods are right there.[60]

The same man added that Filipino immigrants were coming to Stockton in large numbers, and they also needed housing. A Filipino American Delta College student was insulted by Timmel's questions and asserted that Filipinas/os "just wanted to be with their own people."[61] Lee reiterated the need for the Center, particularly in light of the Crosstown Freeway demolitions.

Community members in support of the project remained steadfast in their belief that the Center could be built. The rejections from FHA were a result of racism and economic discrimination, some Center supporters concluded. "There's no reason why our project should have taken this long," one community member said in July 1970. "We have all of the qualifications. But look at what happens. We've been at it for two and one half years. A project like this could be turned up in six months. FHA, if they wanted to, could have cleared it up in six months. But you see what they've done to us?"[62] Despite the idealistic view that there had been progress in race relations in Stockton, the obstacles placed in the path of the Center project smacked of racism. "The only thing that we could really think of right now is that FHA in Sacramento just really has something against this project," said one community member. "Maybe it's because we're Filipino people. The Filipino people have never done a project like this. Maybe they're afraid of that?"[63]

After years of complex negotiations and political wrangling, the FHA approved the concept of the Center in June 1970 but withheld a decision on whether or not they would fund it. Unfazed, the Center advocates pressed on through the winter of 1970–71, convinced that the agency would fund the $2.8 million dollar project because it was the only proposal from San Joaquin County. When the FHA offered to provide a sum well below the estimate for construction, advocates challenged the agency with evidence that other projects had been given ample funding. Six months later, in December, the Filipino Center committee hired the services of a contractor, and Center advocates and the original organizing committee formed a nonprofit organization on February 4, 1971, called the Associated Filipino Organizations of San Joaquin County, Inc. (AFO). The Filipino Medical and Allied Professionals also joined the original five organizations.[64]

Official incorporation was a significant step for the committee. Its officers reflected the diversity of the Filipina/o American population in Stockton in the 1970s, and this consensus was key to holding together the tenuous coalition of Ilocanas/os, Visayans, and Tagalogs; men and women; farmworkers and professionals; and postwar immigrants, old-timers, and American-born Filipinas/os. Ted Lapuz was elected president, and Rosauro Daclan, who had immigrated to Stockton in the 1920s, was elected vice president. Carmen A. Griggs, a second-generation Filipina and daughter of the longtime community leaders Camila and Leon Carido, was elected secretary; and Concepcion Bohulano, my grandmother, was elected assistant secretary. The Pinay business owner Iluminada Unsod was elected treasurer, and the old-timer and World War II veteran Tomas Jusa was her assistant. Jose Bernardo served as the technical adviser for the Center.[65] However, as the AFO board moved closer to its goal, conflicts in the community over the organization's legitimacy and Bernardo's motives threatened to delay the project further.

A COMMUNITY IN CONFLICT

The members of the AFO board who had been elected in 1970 soon found themselves in direct conflict with the officers and members of the Filipino Community of Stockton and Vicinity, Inc. As described previously, this organization was a powerful umbrella group that had been formed in 1927 with the goal of consolidating the community's different factions and regional groups into one organization. The Filipino Community, then, served as the Filipina/o American community's representative to the larger public. Every other major Filipina/o community in the United States had, and continues to have, similar organizations. The leadership of Stockton's Filipino Community consisted of old-timers who had been the founders of the Filipina/o organizations of the 1920s and 1930s. Soon, the Stockton Filipina/o American community was split in two over the fate of the Filipino Center: on one side was the old guard, the mostly conservative old-timers who were the members and leaders of the Filipino Community and other organizations, such as the fraternal orders; on the other side was a loose coalition that I call the "progressives," including more liberal and politicized Filipinas/os, the AFO, college students and other young people, second- and third-generation Filipinas/os in their twenties and thirties, postwar immigrants, professionals, and some old-timers who believed in the Center and cared little for the politics, petty divisions, and loyalties of the past.

The old-guard leaders of the Filipino Community viewed the rise of the AFO, which represented a new energy and leadership in Stockton, as a challenge to the status quo. The president of the Filipino Community, the business owner and labor contractor Johnny Latosa, led the opposition to the Center. Latosa and other members of the old guard—including my father, Ernesto T. Mabalon, who revered Latosa—did not trust newcomers like Jose Bernardo and questioned his motives. According to the leadership of the Filipino Community, Bernardo failed to respect that organization and did not get the proper support of its officers for the Center. "They were so opposed, and there was so much at stake," recalled Alma Alcala, whose family supported the Center. "There were a lot of stories put out there, that Jose just wanted to do it for his own glory."[66]

Alcala felt that the opposition of the Filipino Community to the Center was born out of fear: members of the organization saw that their social hall, and their organization itself, might become irrelevant if the Center proved successful. "The Filipino Community didn't understand what their role would be in the Filipino Center," Alcala said. "It was a pride thing. They said, 'What does [the Center] do to us? We don't have a role?' That kind of wanting to maintain some semblance of authority and reputation, saving face."[67] Conservative ideas about the use of taxpayer funds and an aversion to government social programs also influenced the opposition of the Filipino Community to the Center. My father, who was one of the officers of the Filipino Community at the time, argued that the organization's leaders were opposed because they felt that federal funds were being used to benefit only Filipinas/os, and the Filipino Community's leaders did not want to be accused of discriminatory behavior. Any federally funded housing project, they argued, should benefit all members of the Stockton community, regardless of racial and ethnic background.[68] In a statement to the City Council, one Filipina said that she detested the idea of a federally funded Filipino Center because it was tantamount to a "handout" that would be detrimental to the community and would set Stockton back thirty years in terms of race relations. "We must not rock the boat," the community member told the City Council.[69]

But the Filipino Community lacked the political savvy and determination of the progressive Filipinas/os who demanded the Center as a payback for the demolitions and displacements of the 1960s and early 1970s. New programs and funds from the War on Poverty's Community Action Council grants supported the creation of the Central Stockton Community Center, a resource center for those affected by downtown displacement. Progressive Filipinas/os jumped at the opportunity to influence the politics and policies of downtown Stockton and gain skills in community organizing and policymaking. Jamero, Artiaga, and Bernardo sat on the Community Action Council, and they tapped Alma Alcala—a University of the Pacific graduate and second-generation Filipina—to lead the Central Stockton Community Center. Alma Alcala's parents, Atanasio and Maria Alcala, were founders of the Filipina/o American Legion post that had given the Filipino Center its earliest support and seed money.[70] It was at this time that Laurena Cabañero and Lillian Galedo, then undergraduates at UC Davis who had been advocates for the

Center, began researching the history of Stockton and the movement for the Center for a paper for an Asian American studies class. "We're going to fight; we're going to get this center," Bernardo told Galedo and Cabañero in 1970.[71]

These political upheavals had a deep impact on Filipina/o organizations, and the divisions affected every aspect of Filipina/o American life in the community, from organizational leadership to family relations in Stockton. Many families were torn between support of the new leadership provided by the AFO and the promise of the Filipino Center, on the one hand, and the status quo represented by the Filipino Community, on the other hand. Alma Alcala's godmother, the influential and powerful Filipino Community officer Segunda Reyes, was vehemently opposed to the Center. My family was divided over the Center, too. With the Giva family, my grandparents Concepcion and Delfin Bohulano had planned to open a Filipino grocery store in the Center called the B&G Market. The entire Bohulano family—including Concepcion and Delfin's oldest daughter Christine, who became my mother—supported the Center unequivocally, and Concepcion was a founding AFO board member. In 1971 Christine married Ernesto T. Mabalon, the man who became my father and a protégé of Johnny Latosa and up-and-coming leader in the Filipino Community. Family relations were strained under the pressures of divergent community alliances. Family gatherings could explode in screaming matches between my grandmother and father.[72]

Luna Jamero clearly remembered the opposition of the Filipino Community to the Center, and Bernardo's firm resolve to see the project through. "They already made up their minds," she said. "I would just shake my head and think, they're not going to listen to me—you know, we just got to do what needs to be done. Just go for it." Jamero remembered that Bernardo refused to allow the acrimony that had developed between the AFO, including him, and the Filipino Community derail the project. "That's what Jose's mind-set was all about," Jamero recalled. "He said: 'You know there's more people against me and what this center is all about. But you know what when it's built, they'll understand there will be a living monument to them as well. Even though they're not for it and that's the reality of it.'"[73] The struggle for the Center continued through the spring and summer of 1971.

APPROVAL FOR THE CENTER

By the midsummer 1971, the AFO's negotiations with the FHA had been successful, and the two organizations signed a contract on July 23. Bernardo and Lapuz's determination to build a center that featured low-cost housing and a social gathering place proved too much for even the most stubborn members of the old guard. The coalition that Lapuz and Bernardo had pieced together,

47. The board of the Associated Filipino Organizations celebrate the August 1971 groundbreaking for the Filipino Center at 6 West Main Street. Leaders of the project were Ted Lapuz and Jose Bernardo. From left to right: unknown, Fred Yurong, Maxie Yurong, unknown, Lapuz, two officials from the Department of Housing and Urban Development, Rosauro Daclan, Naty Jusa, Concepcion Bohulano, Bernardo, unknown, and Tom Jusa. From the author's personal collection.

beginning in 1968, had achieved an enormous victory. The groundbreaking ceremonies were held on July 24, 1971 (see figure 47). On that day, more than 500 community members gathered at the Center site to hear speeches and observe the ceremonial turning of earth. The vice president of the Philippines, Fernando Lopez, was visiting the area at the time and was a guest of honor at the groundbreaking. Old-timers present clamored to shake Lopez's hand, some of them brushing away tears. The vice president broke the earth, offered heartfelt congratulations to the community, and referred to the community's historical factionalism and its efforts to unify to build the Center. "Here you can forget the factionalism of the islands and be just Filipinos," he told the crowd.[74]

In a powerful show of community solidarity, even those Filipina/o organizations that had refused to join the AFO and those naysayers who had abandoned the project early on joined the celebration. Even Johnny Latosa was present at the groundbreaking. The leaders of the Filipina/o fraternal orders—Antonio Santos of the Legionarios del Trabajo, and Marion Rayray of the Filipino Federation of America—were also part of the welcoming delegation of community leaders at the groundbreaking. After the ceremony, the AFO board sponsored a community reception that featured lechon (roast pig); Filipina/o American folk dancing; The Third Wave, a local Pinay singing group; and community speakers.[75] "Until they actually broke ground, I don't think people really believed it, because it took so long," recalled Laurena Cabañero.[76] Along with the AFO board members, federal, state, and local officials were present, including Congressman McFall, Stockton Mayor Arnold Rue, FHA officials, and Secretary of Housing and Urban Development George Romney. Representatives from the state chapters of the Filipino-American Council and the Filipino-American Political Association were also present.[77]

For community members, especially the leaders of the AFO, the groundbreaking must have been an emotional moment, for the construction of the Center represented decades of struggle, and four years of pitched battle, for an elusive unity among Filipinas/os in Stockton and recognition from the federal and local governments that Filipinas/os were a force to be recognized. The groundbreaking had a ripple effect nationwide, and Filipina/o American community organizers and left-wing activists across the country pointed to the significance of the Center to the budding Filipina/o American movement. Among all other Filipina/o communities nationwide, Stockton became the "chief barangay," Alma Alcala recalled, using the Tagalog word that means community, village, and boat.[78]

Kalayaan International, a new, left-wing Filipina/o American newspaper based in San Francisco, published a major piece on the Center's groundbreaking by Lillian Galedo. *Kalayaan*'s editors, most of them radical Filipina/o American activists in their twenties and thirties, lauded the Stockton community's struggle to create consensus and their challenge of the status quo in order to build the Center. In an editorial, *Kalayaan* was careful to note that the Center came not as a benevolent handout from the federal government, but as the result of a sustained Filipina/o American political movement: "This center is not the result of any extraordinary benevolence on behalf of the Redevelopment Agency of Stockton or the Federal Housing Administration, but rather is due to the persistent efforts of the Filipino community in Stockton." The editors hoped the Center would be a tool for community unity.[79] Though most members of the AFO would not have aligned themselves with *Kalayaan*'s leftist politics, the organization's members understood that they had accomplished an incredible feat and that the building of the Center represented a powerful community movement.

Although the young Filipina/o activists in Stockton learned from and respected the ultraleft radical activists in the Bay Area, especially those involved in the struggle over the International Hotel and Manilatown displacements, the Stockton activists preferred to keep their politics more moderate. "One of the marked differences that I see in the way the Bay Area Filipino communities and our area took care of business is that we weren't quite as radical," Alma Alcala said. "We honored how they wanted to do things, but we always worked more with the [larger] community." Alcala remembered that her generation resisted, at least in public, the ultraleft politics embraced by Bay Area and Los Angeles Filipina/o activists because they didn't want to completely alienate the deeply conservative, older generations of Filipinas/os in Stockton, whose support for the Center was critical. "We had a Filipino community," she said. "What they did was they came together, they put their money, their hearts, their lives on the line to build this center. Working in the system."[80] Although Stockton activists took advantage of the existing system, they also noted the more radical organizing against displacements taking place in San Francisco. There, activists staged rallies, protests, and sit-ins and committed acts of civil disobedience to protest the massive displacement of Filipinos in San Francisco's Manilatown in 1977. But Stockton's Filipinas/os answered the bulldozers with a call for unity behind the Center. "Really, the Filipino Center crystallized as our solution to the whole redevelopment thing, the displacement of the Manongs," Alcala said. "We [could] have our own Filipino Center, and we could really take care of our people. The Filipino Center really was the protest. It was our resolution to all that was going on."[81]

Almost four decades after the community struggles, Lapuz harbored no ill feelings toward those bitter opponents of the Center who had had a change of heart. "I think, even though they're opposing us, there is no animosity, no hard feelings," Lapuz said. "I mean, we're just focused on what we have in mind of what we're doing, because if we sway one way or another, the government will not give us the funding for the Center. So, we just said, 'Hey, we are serious about what we're doing here and we're not going to give up.' And we did not give up. Can you imagine, three years? And we just kept pursuing it!"[82] Indeed, most of the old guard and leaders of the Filipino Community came around and eventually embraced the Center. Some of my earliest memories include my father, then a vice president of the Filipino Community, taking me in the early 1970s to visit my grandparents at their B&G Market on the ground floor of the Filipino Center, and next door to the Foo Lung deli for fried rice and Chinese barbecued pork.

FILIPINA/O POLITICAL POWER
Emboldened by the groundbreaking of the Center, members of the progressive wing of the Filipina/o American community decided to launch the most

provocative challenge ever to white political power in Stockton: they de-cided to run Jose Bernardo against the longtime county supervisor, the Ital-ian American Carmen Perino, in the fall of 1971. No Filipina/o had ever run for public office in Stockton, much less dared to run against someone who was considered a patron of the old guard. This was the ultimate challenge to the white and Filipina/o status quo in Stockton. The fact that Bernardo dared to run against Perino, the longtime political patron of local Filipinas/os and guest of honor at many events sponsored by the Filipino Community, signaled the eroding power of the Filipina/o American old guard and was a powerful rejection of the deference that politicians had always expected from Filipinas/os. Perino, an opponent of the Center, was closely allied with the Filipino Community leadership. The struggle between the old guard and the new guard, the Filipino Community and the AFO, and the Filipino Com-munity building and the Filipino Center came to a head that fall. If the two groups — the old guard and the progressives — were already divided by ideol-ogy, strategy, and perspective — then the race for who would best represent Filipinas/os on the Board of Supervisors raised the stakes even higher.

Luna Jamero remembered the deep respect the old guard felt for Perino. "The Filipinos in Stockton revered him, they *revered* him," she recalled. "The old guard revered Perino. The ones that knew better did not, and they were the ones behind Jose."[83] Jamero remembered how the old guard would de-fend Perino, crediting his numerous appearances at Filipina/o social func-tions, but these appearances meant nothing to the progressive wing of the community. "They would say, 'After all you know, Perino, he is there for us, he is always a dignitary at our functions.' So what! What does that mean? Who cares?" Jamero said.[84] Alma Alcala remembered the acrimony that had developed between the two groups by that point. The Filipino Community saw Bernardo's challenge to Perino as another threat to their control. "They were so in love with Carmen Perino," said Alcala. Through his attendance at Filipina/o events and the personal favors he doled out, Perino had earned the blind loyalty of the Filipino Community leadership, according to Alcala. "I think it was this feeling that somehow he was this hero who could answer all the questions, and so they put their faith and trust in him," she said. Alcala re-called that Perino doled out only personal favors and appearances that were "enough to keep them faithful."[85]

Bernardo symbolized a new political direction, according to Alcala: "But see, what Jose did was dare to come out and say, 'We don't need you. We can do it ourselves.'" "And then of course Filipinos are very loyal," Alcala said. "They didn't want to incur the wrath of someone who had supported them, but the only way he supported them was coming and speaking at the parties and at the events. And that was supposed to be good enough. Well, I'm sorry. That wasn't good enough."[86] Progressive Filipinas/os, including my grand-parents Delfin and Concepcion Bohulano, came out wholeheartedly for Bernardo. College students and other young people, as well as Filipinas/os in their twenties and thirties, walked through precincts, campaigning for him. Bernardo lost, but only by approximately two hundred votes. "It was really disheartening, but you know it was really part of the journey," remembered Jamero.[87] Bernardo's run for the Board of Supervisors represented the coming of age of Filipina/o American political awareness, central to which was an unwillingness to rely on the patronage of local politicians, who had believed for decades that Filipina/o loyalty to them was unquestioned.

POWER THROUGH UNITY

The Filipino Center was under construction for an entire year, from the summer of 1971 to August 1972. Watching the building rise was an emotional experience for Bernardo, the project coordinator. When the construction workers went home for the day, Bernardo would go to the site, sit, and "just look at it."[88] Filipinas/os across the nation were watching as well. The organizers of the Far West Convention, the Filipina/o American activist-oriented convention first held the year before in Seattle, chose Stockton as the site for its 1972 meeting.

Luna Jamero remembered how she and a group of young Filipinas/os scrambled to pull the convention together with little time and few resources. The theme for that year was "Power through Unity/*Lakas ng Pagkakaisa*," which reflected the struggle that had only recently ended in Stockton with the building of the Filipino Center, a powerful physical manifestation of the theme.[89] In conjunction with the AFO board, Alma Alcala, Luna Jamero, and Morris Artiaga planned the Filipino Center dedication ceremonies on August 12, the convention's last day. The University of the Pacific in Stockton was chosen as the site, and Alcala, Jamero, and Artiaga sat on the convention's steering committee. Publicity materials for the convention described unity, political empowerment, and liberation as the main goals of the Filipina/o American movement.

The committee welcomed several hundred young people, activists, and organizers to Stockton for the convention. It included a cultural night called *Kaisahan* (Unity), which was headlined by the Sampaguita Dance Troupe. Al Robles of San Francisco, one of the activists involved in the International Hotel struggle, performed a poem, "Magellan's Ship."[90] The convention themes and workshops reflected the growing political savvy of the Filipina/o American movement: there were workshops on grant proposal writing;

community research skills; political campaigning; federal programs beneficial to Filipinas/os; youth programming; and issues surrounding youth, the elderly, and a proposed national Filipina/o American organization. An entire track of the convention was dedicated to the issues and challenges facing women. Pete Velasco and Philip Vera Cruz also led a workshop on the problems and needs of the United Farm Workers Organizing Committee.[91] Other presenters included Fred Cordova, a Stockton native who founded the Filipino Youth Activities and the FYA Drill Team in Seattle, and local educators Andrea Nicolas, John Fabionar, and Frank LaGasca. One of the highlights of the convention was a rousing speech by the former president of the Filipino Community of Stockton, Larry Itliong, the assistant director and cofounder of the United Farm Workers.

By taking out a full-page ad in the *Stockton Record* on August 11, 1972, the AFO invited attendees and the entire Stockton community to the dedication of the Filipino Center the following day, which symbolized for all the optimism of the next generation of Filipina/o Americans nationwide. Present at the momentous event were hundreds of nattily dressed old-timers, whose downtown apartments had only recently been razed for the Crosstown Freeway and urban redevelopment. Most had lived in the downtown area for decades and had been waiting a long time for a community building like the Filipino Center. On this sweltering August day, they watched the ceremonies from the shade of the second-floor balcony of the Center.[92] The Sampaguita Dance Troupe performed Filipina/o American dances, and Samuel Jackson, assistant director of the U.S. Department of Housing and Urban Development, was the keynote speaker. The celebration, which lasted all afternoon, was called a "barrio fiesta," and it also included escrima demonstrations and a mass. Community members held a dinner and dance in the evening.

The community certainly had much to celebrate. The Center was its pride and joy, featuring 128 units of low-income housing and 26,000 feet of commercial space. Its brown stucco structure, designed by Jose Bernardo to mimic the shape of a Philippine bamboo *nipa* hut, rose ten stories and dominated the downtown skyline (see figure 48). By the dedication, almost all of the retail spaces had been occupied. Businesses included a Filipina/o American travel agency; Trade East Imports, Ted Lapuz's Philippine import shop; a Chinese bakery called Yet Bun Heong and a Chinese delicatessen (the West End Redevelopment Project had forced both businesses, which had many Filipino clients, to relocate); a dental lab; a child-care center; and Delfin Bohulano and Narciso Giva's B&G Market, a Filipina/o American grocery store. Full occupancy of the housing units was expected by the following month.[93]

Filipino Center, Stockton, California

48. Postcard of the Filipino Center in 1972. From the author's personal collection.

The AFO members knew that the Center had national and international significance. "It showed that we are united, that we can work together for the prosperity of all Filipinos," said my grandmother Concepcion Bohulano, who was an AFO board member at the time of the dedication.[94] It was the largest project of its kind undertaken by Filipinos outside of the Philippines, and it addressed key needs in the Filipina/o American community: it was a social gathering point and a retail center, and it offered low-cost housing. The victory of the Center's construction represented the elusive dream of community unity, and the Center became a model for Filipina/o American communities nationwide. In her dedication speech, AFO member Deanna Daclan Balantac, a second-generation Filipina whose parents, Paula and Rosauro Daclan, had been two of the original supporters and coalition members, spoke of the Center's significance nationally, as well as locally. "The struggle for the Filipino Center has indirectly involved, included and affected every Filipino in the city of Stockton, and as the more aware community people see it, it affects every Filipino community in the United States," Balantac told a crowd of several hundred at the ceremony. "It is the first undertaking of its kind by a community of Filipinos in the United States, and may it be only the beginning."[95]

CONCLUSION

When the Filipino Center held its opening celebration in August 1972, it was a joyous end to almost four years of heartbreak, sacrifice, and community conflict. After more than seven decades of struggles toward unity in Stockton, the movement behind the Filipino Center was the most significant demonstration of solidarity that the Filipina/o American community in Stockton had ever made. The West End demolitions, Crosstown Freeway displacements, and struggle to build the Center forced Filipinas/os in Stockton to endeavor to change their longtime status as second-class citizens in Stockton.

But at the beginning, most local Filipinas/os were hesitant, skeptical, suspicious, and scared by the idea of the Center. Only a fraction of the community's leaders jumped on Lapuz and Bernardo's bandwagon. Many leaders, including the heads of the powerful Filipina/o umbrella group, the conservative Filipino Community of Stockton and Vicinity, Inc., refused to support the Center because they opposed the use of federal funds for a Filipina/o American housing project. The Federal Housing Administration; the city's Redevelopment Agency; and local, state, and federal officials and legislators stalled the project for three years. It took a steep learning curve, courage, and impassioned refusal to give up on the part of the Filipina/o community for the Filipino Center to be realized. In the end, the momentum behind the project became so powerful that even the opposition from the leadership of the Filipino Community could not prevent the Center from being built.

But the building and dedication of the Filipino Center was only part of the community's victory. The journey from idea to dedication became the political coming of age of the Filipina/o American community in Stockton. Ironically, it was Lapuz and Bernardo's newcomer status to community politics and their relative inexperience that made the project ultimately successful, because they were not hindered by political loyalties and past failures of community struggles toward unity and political power. The gains of civil rights, Great Society legislation, the Filipina/o American movement, and Lapuz and Bernardo's willingness to create a coalition of progressive Filipinas/os to challenge the second-class citizen status of Filipinas/os in Stockton made the project successful.

Indeed, as Balantac asserted in her dedication speech, the Filipino Center has become a model for other community centers of its kind all over the nation. In the last two decades, other Filipina/o American communities opened their own community centers: the Filipino Community Center in Waipahu, Hawaii; San Francisco's Bayanihan Community Center; and Manilatown Center in San Francisco all had concepts similar to that of the Filipino Center, with affordable housing mixed with community and retail space. The Barrio Fiesta celebration held at the Center's grand opening in August 1972 has been held annually on the second weekend in August since then, to mark the Center's anniversary. Thousands of San Joaquin County residents attend the

fiesta each year, which features a mass, religious procession, cultural performances, escrima demonstrations, and food booths. In the 1980s and 1990s,
other communities, including San Francisco, Los Angeles, and Seattle, instituted their own annual summer community gatherings in Barrio Fiesta style.
"I think that the experience in the Filipino community of Stockton actually
has a lot of lessons for the Filipino community everywhere," reflected Lillian
Galedo, who has served as the executive director of Filipinos for Affirmative
Action in Oakland for more than three decades. "It isn't this backwater experience. The same dynamics sort of play themselves out in communities all
over the country. There's a lot of lessons to be learned about what happened
in Stockton for those that want to build some lasting institution and symbol
of the Filipino community in places like San Francisco."[96]

From its earliest years, members of the community had worked toward a
sense of unity and common purpose and identity. In the struggle for the Filipino Center, they learned how to navigate bureaucracy; overcome factionalism, petty jealousies, and grudges; and challenge the entrenched power of the
white elite. Though much of the Little Manila neighborhood they loved had
been destroyed, the community rallied around the Filipino Center, placing
in its completion all of their hopes and dreams for a new beginning in their
hometown. However, the unity forged among Filipinas/os in the struggle for
the Center was short-lived. A few weeks after the Center's grand opening,
on September 23, 1972, President Ferdinand Marcos declared martial law
in the Philippines. The politics of martial law and the Marcos dictatorship
ripped the Filipina/o American community apart, cleaving the community
in two once again. The impact of the politics of martial law in Stockton and
on Filipina/o American communities throughout the United States is a story
yet to be fully explored.

COMING HOME TO LITTLE MANILA

That restaurant, that building, that place, was the beginning of all of us.
That was where we all came from.

— ERNESTO TIRONA MABALON

In my most painful memory of Stockton's Little Manila, it is
May 18, 1999, and I am standing in front of the brick building
that once housed the Lafayette Lunch Counter, watching the
press conference and demolition kickoff festivities for the Gateway Project. In a struggle that a local journalist compared with
some irony to the almost decade-long effort to demolish the block,
City Council members took almost a dozen swings with a ceremonial, gold-painted sledgehammer to break a piece of glass hung
on one of the walls of the buildings to signal the beginning of the
demolition. The council member who finally succeeded in breaking the glass was Vice Mayor Gloria Nomura, whose family had
lived in the Little Manila area and owned a pool hall there before World War II. The Redevelopment Agency had dubbed this
project the Gateway Project, as the block was in front of the downtown exit from Interstate 5 and was thus the gateway to Stockton. The project displaced dozens of elderly and poor residents
and replaced the block's residential hotels, restaurants, and grocery stores with a McDonald's and a Union 76 gas station. The city
poured $4 million into the project to try to resurrect the moribund
downtown.[1]

It seemed that no one in Stockton had remembered the tragedies of the 1960s West End Redevelopment Project and the Crosstown Freeway demolitions. When this block was targeted for clearance and redevelopment in the mid-1990s, it was one of the last

two remaining of Little Manila. It had taken seven years to clear the block, which was surrounded by Center, El Dorado, Lafayette, and Sonora streets. Eventually, the city prevailed in lawsuits filed by owners and took the buildings by eminent domain, forcing decades-old businesses to move or shut down altogether, including residential hotels and the legendary Mexican American dive, Arroyo's Café (which, ironically, had moved to that site when the original building was demolished by the Crosstown Freeway). The residents of the Fox, Delta, and MacArthur Hotels—some of them Filipinas/os in their eighties and nineties—were evicted in sweeps that recalled the evictions of the 1960s and 1970s. Clearing the block that had once housed my grandfather's restaurant and countless other businesses took a little more than two months. The prewar brick buildings that were home to generations of Filipinas/os and other Stocktonians vanished in a cloud of dust as bulldozers pushed in walls with efficient ruthlessness. After the dust settled, almost three-quarters of the block lay in rubble. Now, the downtown exit of the Crosstown Freeway deposits motorists onto a landscape that few who lived in Little Manila in the 1930s would recognize.

Though my grandfather had retired and had sold his restaurant in the early 1980s after almost fifty years of continuous ownership, the building in which it stood was a constant reminder of my family and community's history. My father, Ernesto Mabalon, choked back tears as we watched the doors of our family's old restaurant collapse under the bulldozer on a hot spring morning. "That restaurant, that building, that place, was the beginning of all of us," he said, his voice breaking. "That was where we all came from." And then he turned away, so I could not see his tears. What he meant was that the restaurant was the symbol of my grandparents' dreams. The restaurant funded college educations for my father and his siblings; paid for two homes in South Stockton that housed many generations of the family; and made possible the immigration of my grandmother, my father, his brother, his sister and brother-in-law, their children, and those children's spouses and children's children, over the course of five decades.

But even beyond the block's significance for our family, my father knew that it was an important historic place, a place worth remembering and preserving. In this book I have been able only to scratch the surface of my community's history, telling a tale that has been long overdue. With this book, I have offered a portrait of one Filipina/o American community's struggles toward cohesion, in the hope that this project is a contribution toward the collective labor of uncovering what the late historian Yuji Ichioka called a "buried past."[2] This book has attempted to understand the processes of identity and community formation among early Filipina/o immigrants in a California city. The immigrants and their descendants in Stockton struggled from the 1920s to the 1970s toward building a cohesive community and identity in a physical as well as an emotional, cultural, political, and spiritual sense. To do this, they had to surmount myriad divisions of class, gender, ethnicity, religion, and generation, all within the larger context of racism and colonialism.

What is left of Little Manila after the 1999 demolitions are several blocks of older buildings, some original to the Little Manila neighborhood and others built in the past fifty years (see map 7). They include the Iloilo Circle card room and apartments; the Caballeros de Dimas Alang building; the Filipino Community Building; the Mariposa Hotel, a single room occupancy hotel that had been a significant meeting place for Filipino labor unions and organizations; the Legionarios del Trabajo's Daguhoy Temple, landmarked by the city in 2002; the now-shuttered Emerald Restaurant, formerly the Filipino Recreation Center; and a long-vacant building that once housed the Rizal Social Club, a popular Filipino nightclub. The neighborhood around the buildings is approximately 46 percent Asian, and the median annual income of its residents falls far below the average: $14,000 compared to $25,000 in 1997.[3] In the 1970s and 1980s, drug dealers moved in to the adjacent Gleason Park area, and homeowners and residents have engaged in a protracted battle to take back their neighborhood. In 2010 only two blocks of the historic Little Manila neighborhood remains, dwarfed by the Crosstown Freeway.

In the spring of 1999, I contemplated the issues that Dolores Hayden discusses at length in *The Power of Place*. Hayden writes that when sensitively and carefully researched and written, urban landscape history "can help to reclaim the identities of deteriorating neighborhoods where generations of working people have spent their lives." She argues for the centrality of space and place in uncovering the histories of working-class people and those of color in urban landscapes, because "places make memories cohere in complex ways."[4] How could I describe the evictions and demolitions of the 1960s, indicting the Redevelopment Agency in my research and criticizing urban redevelopment policies, yet ignore the continued injustice the agency was wreaking on historic Little Manila and its current residents? I realized that a community worth writing about was a community worth preserving. That spring of 1999, I joined the Stockton chapter of the Filipino American National Historical Society, and the chapter began a movement to designate the four-block area around the intersection of El Dorado and Lafayette streets as the Little Manila Historic Site and to place markers around the area. We rather naively believed that such a designation would protect the neighborhood from further displacements and demolitions.

My dissertation research did double duty by forming the basis on which

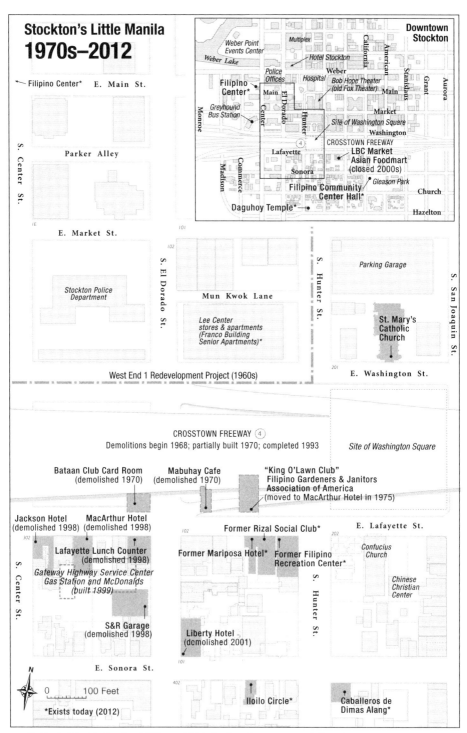

Stockton's Little Manila
1970s–2012

Filipino Center*   E. Main St.

S. Center St.

Parker Alley

E. Market St.

Stockton Police Department

West End 1 Redevelopment Project (1960s)

S. El Dorado St.

Mun Kwok Lane

Lee Center stores & apartments (Franco Building Senior Apartments)*

S. Hunter St.

Parking Garage

St. Mary's Catholic Church

E. Washington St.

S. San Joaquin St.

Downtown Stockton

Weber Point Events Center
Weber Lake
Police Offices
Hotel Stockton
Filipino Center*   Main
Greyhound Bus Station
Multiplex
Weber
Hospital
Bob Hope Theater (old Fox Theater)   Main
Market
Site of Washington Square
Washington
CROSSTOWN FREEWAY
LBC Market
Asian Foodmart (closed 2000s)
Gleason Park
Filipino Community Center Hall*
Daguhoy Temple*–
Church
Hazelton

Monroe
El Dorado Center
Hunter
Lafayette
Madison
Commerce
Sonora
California
American
Stanislaus
Grant
Aurora

CROSSTOWN FREEWAY (4)
Demolitions begin 1968; partially built 1970; completed 1993

Site of Washington Square

Bataan Club Card Room (demolished 1970)

Mabuhay Cafe (demolished 1970)

"King O'Lawn Club" Filipino Gardeners & Janitors Association of America (moved to MacArthur Hotel in 1975)

Jackson Hotel (demolished 1998)

MacArthur Hotel (demolished 1998)

Former Rizal Social Club*

E. Lafayette St.

Lafayette Lunch Counter (demolished 1998)

Gateway Highway Service Center Gas Station and McDonalds (built 1999)

Former Mariposa Hotel*   Former Filipino Recreation Center*

Confucius Church

S. Center St.

S&R Garage (demolished 1998)

Liberty Hotel (demolished 2001)

S. Hunter St.

Chinese Christian Center

E. Sonora St.

N

0   100 Feet

*Exists today (2012)

Iloilo Circle*

Caballeros de Dimas Alang*

7. Little Manila in the 1970s to 2010. Redevelopment and the Crosstown Freeway decimated the neighborhood, but some businesses and organizations hung on. MAP BY BEN PEASE.

I crafted a historic site designation proposal. The Filipina/o American National Historical Society and many other community groups, including the Legionarios del Trabajo, helped to bring together a broad coalition of Filipinas/os in Stockton—old-timers; descendants of the early settlers; newer immigrants; local historians, including Marilyn Guida, then a curator at the Haggin Museum, the local history museum; students; and activists—to support the proposal for the designation as a historic site. Several hundred letters and e-mail messages of support poured in from people all over the nation, and we packed City Council meetings with dozens of community members, some driving from as far as the San Francisco Bay Area and Sacramento, in favor of the designation.

We expected opposition to come from white Stocktonians. What was shocking was the negative reaction we received from some leaders of the Asian American and Filipina/o American community. Although most Asian American leaders in Stockton were supportive, some Japanese and Chinese American leaders disputed the boundaries of Little Manila as outlined by our historic site proposals and our preservation campaigns.[5] Some even went so far as to contend that Filipinas/os had been just a transient population in the area, and Chinese Americans and Japanese Americans had owned most of the businesses, gambling halls, restaurants, and hotels. We countered that while Filipinas/os may not have owned all of the businesses, it was Filipinas/os who made Lafayette and El Dorado their own from the 1930s to the 1970s.

We accomplished a significant victory on October 17, 2000, when the City Council voted unanimously to designate the area around El Dorado and Lafayette streets the Little Manila Historic Site, the nation's first city-designated Filipina/o American historic site. One elderly council member, a descendant of a farming family, gave us what he thought was a compliment: he said he remembered what good and happy workers Filipinos had been. We smiled gamely, then gathered outside of the chambers to cheer and exchange hugs. We believed that we had gained a measure of political power, that the historic site designation would save the residents from displacement and the neighborhood from further demolition. We were wrong.

The 2001 eviction of the residents of the Liberty Hotel and its immediate demolition broadsided us. The Liberty Hotel was across the street from the Gateway Project and was the site of some of the earliest Filipina/o American businesses. Many poor people still lived in the hotel. That year, ten residential hotels, some of them historic and meaningful to our community, such as the Mariposa Hotel, were closed and condemned as a result of a building-code crackdown that was the brainchild of Mayor Gary Podesto and his city manager, Mark Lewis, who were intent on clearing the downtown area of

49. In 2002 a banner featuring my grandfather Pablo Mabalon standing in front of his Lafayette Lunch Counter was placed where the restaurant used to stand. The block is now taken up by a McDonalds and a gas station. Photograph by the author.

poor people and older buildings. Because the city did not provide replacement housing and gave the hotel residents bus tickets out of Stockton, the California Rural Legal Assistance brought a successful lawsuit against the city that stopped the widespread evictions and hotel crackdowns. However, the damage and displacement had already been done.[6]

Chilled and angered by the Liberty Hotel demolition, Dillon Delvo and I formed the Little Manila Foundation to advocate for the preservation and revitalization of the Little Manila Historic Site. Our board members represented the diversity of Filipina/o Stocktonians: students and other young people; recent immigrants; and Filipina/o Americans of the first, second, and third generations. In order to raise public awareness about the history of Little Manila, we sold Little Manila T-shirts at the annual Barrio Fiesta. With the profits, we created light pole banners featuring historic photographs around the neighborhood (see figure 49). The city's Cultural Heritage Board helped us to place signs around the neighborhood, designating the area as the Little Manila Historic Site (see figure 50). On October 26,

50. The Crosstown Freeway obliterated much of Little Manila. Here, in a photograph taken in 2010, the entrance to the freeway and the Little Manila Historic Site marker frame the last remaining block of Little Manila. The remaining original buildings of Little Manila are on the right. Photograph by the author.

2002, we dedicated the historic markers and banners in a community celebration that drew almost a thousand people.

In the spring of 2003, a Filipino American landscape architect and developer notified us that he, along with a group of wealthy Asian investors, wanted to build a six-block strip mall called the Asia Pacific Center in the middle of the Little Manila and Chinatown areas. The strip mall would feature an enormous Asian grocery store and retail outlets like Goldilocks Bakery, a popular Philippines-based bakery that was proliferating in the Filipina/o American suburbs. This, he said proudly, would be the New Little Manila. "The Chinese are hot and heavy" in favor of this project the developer, a post-1965 Filipino immigrant, told me. "Don't be left out—it's better to be on the inside."[7] But the plan outlined the demolition of eight blocks of downtown—including the Iloilo Circle and the Caballeros de Dimas Alang building. The project would displace dozens of homeowners in the area, mostly working-class people of color. The last original buildings of Little Manila—the Filipino Recreation Center, the Rizal Social Club, and the Mariposa Hotel—would be demolished for a parking lot.[8] Other historic and culturally significant community buildings, including the ornate and historic Confucius Church, would also have to be razed. Angry and alarmed at the prospect of demolitions initiated by our own community, we rejected the development group's offer of partnership and turned to the National Trust for Historic Preservation for help.

That spring, the National Trust put the Little Manila Historic Site on its annual list of the "11 Most Endangered Historic Places in America," because of the threat of the strip mall project. On June 3, 2003, the Stockton City Council offered the developers and the Little Manila Foundation four months to develop redevelopment proposals for the neighborhood. That summer was a crash course in urban historic preservation for all of us. I found myself learning how to become a cultural preservationist, community developer, and community organizer, engaged in scholarly and community organizing practices in which I was toeing a fine line between analysis and advocacy, inquiry, and intervention. We threw ourselves into grassroots organizing and community education among both Filipinas/os and other groups in Stockton. We led town-hall meetings with residents, and—working with urban planning consultants—we developed our own proposal for historic preservation, revitalization, and affordable housing in the area. We packed City Council and Redevelopment Agency meetings and held fundraisers.

Stockton, now a city of more than 400,000, is typical of the Central Valley in its conservatism. The city hadn't witnessed such a militant and protracted battle over historic preservation since the 1980s, when preservationists won a battle to save the Fox Theater, a 1930s art deco gem, in downtown. But the battle over Little Manila was more than a campaign to preserve a building or a neighborhood; it became a class and generational battle over whose experiences and whose memories and stories best represented Filipina/o American history in Stockton. We found that the barriers to unity that prevented Filipinas/os, and other Asian Americans, from protesting redevelopment in the 1950s and 1960s remained in place to prevent the community from coming together to support preservation. It was immediately apparent that we had to mount a massive campaign to educate the community on the history of Little Manila, and to spread awareness that demolition was not the only option.

We assembled a coalition to support preservation that included the old-timers of the Legionarios del Trabajo and the Bahala Na Escrima club, high school and college students, young people in their twenties and thirties, Bridge Generation Filipina/o Americans, and progressive post-1965 immigrants. However, the Little Manila neighborhood had little meaning for the vast majority of Filipinas/os in Stockton—those of the second, third, and fourth generations as well as post-1965 immigrants—because they had no knowledge that anything of any importance took place there or that the history of Filipina/o Americans was worthy of study or recognition. There are no monuments to Filipina/o American history in Stockton. Filipinas/os in the public and private schools in Stockton do not learn about local or national Filipina/o American history. Young people across the country in Asian American studies and Filipina/o American studies courses know more about Filipinas/os in Stockton than Stocktonians do. We were living in the heart of Filipina/o American history, in what was once the West Coast's most Filipina/o American city, surrounded by the memories of our community's leaders, yet most Stocktonians knew next to nothing about any of that history. Worse, many did not care to either preserve or demolish the neighborhood. The answer to this paradox lies in this community's historical amnesia; its history of factionalism; the decades-old scorched-earth policy of redevelopment in Stockton; and the racist, imperialist, and colonial context from which the city's Filipina/o community emerged.

In many ways, Little Manila and Stockton's Asian American community are haunted by the divisions of the past as well as the present. Ignorance of Filipina/o American local history and divisions of class and generation, which have split the community in past decades, remain entrenched. Resistance to the preservation of Little Manila has come from all corners of the Asian American community, including professionals, new immigrants, elected officials, and Filipinas/os of all generations who think that total clearance of the area and complete assimilation is the answer. Some of the most ardent opposition to saving Little Manila came from Filipinas/os and other Asian Americans in Stockton. Ironically, some of these opponents had deep roots in downtown Stockton. One second-generation Filipina whose family fought militantly for the construction of the Filipino Center once asked a Little Manila board member: "Why do you want to save a whorehouse?"

Given these divisions and community issues, the campaign to save Little Manila took on a new turn. We weren't merely arguing about money and economics with the city's Redevelopment Agency and the white elite. Instead, we were battling over issues of space, resources, community identity and history, and memory with other Asian Americans and Filipina/o Americans in California as well as in Stockton, and bringing up decades-long antagonisms: Who called the Oriental Quarter home? Where did the boundaries lie between Chinatown, Japantown, and Little Manila? Who decides the contours of Filipina/o American history and identity in Stockton, and what elements make up that history and identity? Whose history, and what kind of history, is worth saving? What is the relationship between memory and history? The historical amnesia the community had suffered since the first demolitions in Chinatown, Japantown, and Little Manila in the 1960s shook our movement to its core.

The battles over the significance of place and power, naming, and historical memory in Little Manila mirror other recent conflicts in the Asian American community in the San Francisco Bay Area. The battle over the Northgate neighborhood near 24th and Telegraph streets in Oakland is only one example. In the late 1980s and early 1990s, Korean-owned businesses organized into a merchants' district organization, which paid for security, graffiti abatement, and other services. In 2009 the board named the area Koreatown and put up banners that read "Oakland's Got Seoul," triggering howls of protest. The area, whose population was mostly African American according to the 2000 Census, includes a diversity of businesses, including an Ethiopian market, a Middle Eastern grocery, soul food restaurants, a mosque, and art galleries. The merchants removed the banners in February 2010. It took more than two years for a new name, and new look, for the neighborhood. In May 2012, the neighborhood threw Oakland a 160th birthday party and unveiled its new name: Koreatown Northgate, or KONO. The ribbon-cutting ceremony formally unveiled more than a dozen new art murals and street banners and celebrated more than eighty newly planted trees around the neighborhood.[9]

Memory, place, power, identity, and history were also central themes in the 2008 controversy over the naming of a strip of businesses in San Jose. Various groups — including Vietnamese immigrants, Vietnamese Americans, and non-Vietnamese residents and business owners — have clashed over "Little Saigon," "Vietnam Business District," and "Saigon Business District." In March 2008 almost a thousand concerned citizens crowded into San Jose City Hall to back "Little Saigon" for sentimental and historical reasons, among them a deep attachment to the city that is now named Ho Chi Minh City. The San Jose City Council eventually brokered a peace agreement between warring factions that allowed community members to erect their own privately funded "Little Saigon" sign.[10]

THE STRUGGLE OVER LITTLE MANILA INTENSIFIES

The naming of the Little Manila Historic Site to the National Trust's list of America's Most Endangered Places brought a media spotlight to our small city in the summer of 2003. Huell Howser, of the popular California public television program *California's Gold*, produced a half-hour program on the community's history that aired across the state that fall. The History Channel produced a segment on Little Manila for its *Save Our History* program. The *San Jose Mercury News*, *Filipinas* magazine, the *Los Angeles Times*, the *San Francisco Chronicle*, and *The Record* ran prominent stories on the history of Little Manila and the controversy over its future. In the glare of media attention, neither the pro-development nor the pro-preservation side conceded any ground. That summer, Asian Americans in Stockton quickly chose sides. Some wrote letters to the editor of the *Record* and were interviewed by local and national media. The strip mall development was embraced by conservatives in the Asian American community, especially elected officials and wealthy landowners in Chinatown and Little Manila. To bolster their position, some conservative community leaders in the community challenged the idea that the neighborhood had really been Filipina/o arguing that we had no claim to preserve the area.[11]

But the Little Manila Foundation had allies among some of the oldest Chinese American families in the area. When the Asian strip mall plan, which proposed demolishing Confucius Church was revealed that summer, presidents of the venerable Chinese family associations, most of them with Gold Rush–era roots in the area, spoke out to defend the preservation of Little Manila and Chinatown. The Wong Family Association and the Suey Sing Family Association were particularly incensed at the threat to their historic Confucius Church, one of the few original buildings of Chinatown still standing, and the building where the acclaimed writer Maxine Hong Kingston went to Chinese school. "If you tear down the whole thing, you wipe out six family associations," Henry Yip, then seventy-six and president of the Suey Sing Family Association, told the local newspaper. "We want to preserve history."[12] Members of the Soares family, owners of Chapel of the Palms, a funeral home that had generously served the local community for many decades, were also angered and shocked to learn that their business was included in the redevelopment zone, especially considering they had already been moved by the city's postwar West End Redevelopment Project to their current location.

That summer, the fledgling Little Manila Foundation and the Stockton chapter of the Filipino American National Historical Society (FANHS) allied with the neighborhood's residents and progressive Filipina/o and Asian American local leaders who supported the concept of cultural and historic preservation. We had preservation and urban planning help from our contacts in Los Angeles and the Bay Area. In slide shows, we demonstrated to Stocktonians how historic and cultural preservation and innovative methods of adaptive reuse had revitalized Seattle's International District, Los Angeles's Little Tokyo, San Francisco's Chinatown, and New York's Lower East Side. We held these neighborhoods up as examples of how other communities had opposed redevelopment and mounted successful preservation and revitalization projects in their historic neighborhoods.

But some conservative community old-timers viewed our relative youth, passion, and radical politics with a critical eye and a good deal of mistrust. Our tactics, our radicalism, and the new ways we used marketing—including our Little Manila T-shirts, website, and use of e-mail, social media, photographs, and use of digital filmmaking—made us suspect. Such tactics and politics came from Dillon's and my many years of learning community organizing in Los Angeles and the Bay Area and from our mentors, who had led the campaign for the International Hotel in San Francisco. Moreover, Dillon had trained in digital filmmaking, graphic design, and web design. Some Stocktonians believed that what we were attempting to do was naive and idealistic, as well as too radical. Similar criticisms from conservative factions in the community had been aimed at activists in the 1960s who attempted to build the Filipino Center, the first Filipina/o American affordable housing and retail project to be funded by the U.S. Department of Housing and Urban Development.[13] Now the Center is the oldest Filipina/o American center and one of the oldest and most successful Asian American publicly funded affordable-housing projects in the nation. In August 2012, the Associated Filipino Organizations board paid off the forty-year mortgage and now owns the building.

Some of the more recent Filipina/o American immigrants in Stockton exhibited opposition, apathy, or condescension to preservation. As I discussed in chapter 8, immigrants arriving in Stockton after 1965 were more educated, urban, professional, middle class, and politically conservative than earlier generations.[14] When immigrants arrived in California in the late 1960s and early 1970s, some expressed surprise that thousands of Filipinas/os were working at the most menial jobs, in agriculture and the service sector, and that they lacked education. Many of the newer arrivals set themselves apart from working-class Filipinas/os in the late 1960s by organizing professional associations such as the Filipino American Professionals Association, Filipino American Educators Association, and Filipino Medical and Allied Professionals Association. Beginning in the late 1970s, as a result of the civil rights movement, Filipinas/os were able to buy homes in the white suburbs of north Stockton. As a result, many had never set foot in Little Manila or South Stockton, where most working-class Filipinas/os in Stockton had lived prior to the 1970s.

Some of these newer arrivals saw Little Manila as a ghetto filled with homeless criminals and drug addicts as well as elderly, poor, uneducated, working-class Filipinas/os who had limited options. Lacking connections to downtown and the city's working-class South Side, many of these new immigrants and their descendants argued that Little Manila should all just be demolished for a shining new strip mall that would be like other middle-class

Bay Area Filipina/o American enclaves such as Fremont, Milpitas, and Daly City — the new Little Manilas, which were the only Little Manilas that resonated with some of the newer immigrants at all.

Their position was best represented by the developer behind the strip mall, who told us that we were calling attention to a past that was bad because it was marked with racism, discrimination, and segregation. Community members of all generations and immigrant experiences said, in letters to the editor and e-mail messages to us, that they wanted no part of a history of Little Manila because they, as professionals, didn't want a connection with farmworkers or laborers, or people who frequented such unsavory institutions as gambling and taxi-dance halls — or the buildings that had housed such activities. They could see nothing of significance, either personal or historical, in the preservation of Little Manila. Some believed that they, as educated professionals, occupied a more respectable place in the social hierarchy than the Filipina/o laborers of an earlier time. When a Little Manila Foundation board member invited a Filipina community member to a symposium on the contributions of the labor leader Larry Itliong at the local community college, she responded with great condescension: "Why do I care? I'm not descended from those sakadas."

Typical of this elitist position was Oscar Domagas, a Filipino resident of Stockton who was moved to write to the editor of *The Record* to oppose the preservation of Little Manila in 2003. Domagas believed that highlighting the history of racism against Filipinos reminded young Filipinas/os that they came from "inferior stock":

> What's the big deal about preserving an old hotel and two other structures . . . ? To honor the first Filipino immigrants in Stockton, proponents have the wrong symbol. I understand the hotel is a former bordello. This isn't exactly edifying. . . . I'll concede if the buildings were icons of the workers' struggle to free themselves from virtual bondage, but there was no such struggle. At best, the buildings only underscore the Filipino workers' miserable plight — the abuses and insults they suffered. Remembering them out of pity . . . sends a wrong message to Filipino youth that they come from inferior stock.[15]

Domagas went on to exhort the community to leave its past behind and disconnect itself from its working-class history. He insisted that the focus should instead be on "a new generation of Filipino professionals contributing to the progress of the nation in all aspects. Instead of dwelling on the dark past, let's accentuate the positive by showing our capacity and willingness to blend in rather than insulate ourselves to preserve our Filipino identity."[16]

Domagas's misinformed assumption that no labor struggle took place flies in the face of the true history of the area. The Mariposa Hotel was the headquarters of the 1948–49 asparagus strike, whose leaders included Ernesto Mangaoang, Chris Mensalvas, Larry Itliong (the future founder of the United Farm Workers), the local labor leader Cipriano "Rudy" Delvo, and Carlos Bulosan. Philip Vera Cruz participated in the strike. The most offensive of Domagas's assumptions was his racist, elitist belief that the "miserable plight" of the early immigrants was because they came from "inferior stock."

Echoing Domagas's position was Vice Mayor Gloria Nomura, who told *Preservation* magazine in 2003 that the Little Manila area represented a negative era of Filipina/o American history and that nothing in the area was worth saving. "Little Manila was just an area we went to," she said. "We were restricted to it. Today I have the opportunity to go wherever I want to go — that's the important thing. Do those three buildings signify what I struggled through as a Filipino? I'd have to say no."[17] She told the *Los Angeles Times* that her decision to back the Asian strip mall developers was based on cold, hard economics: "Faced with well-funded developers on one side and a grass-roots group with big dreams to preserve the integrity of the area, but with no money, which way do you think most cities would go?"[18]

Undaunted, we assembled a proposal that outlined an ambitious plan to revitalize the neighborhood through the development of small businesses, historic and cultural preservation, the construction of affordable housing, and the establishment of the Filipino American National Museum in the historic Emerald Restaurant and former Rizal Social Club. We began to realize that our campaign was about more than the three original buildings: it was about building political power, and a progressive voice, through a broad coalition of Filipinas/os in Stockton. In many ways, our campaign has been successful. A regime change in Stockton's elected leadership, media pressure, and community support ultimately saved Little Manila. The Asian American investors dropped their development proposal in 2004, and the city has never formally responded to our proposal.

The recession of 2008–11 has been both a boon and curse. I write this conclusion as we emerge from the nation's worst economic collapse since the Depression, and Stockton felt the brunt of it acutely. In the 1990s and early 2000s, developers had turned thousands of acres of farmland around Stockton into subdivisions, and when the housing bubble burst in 2008, Stockton was one of the hardest-hit cities in the state. Stockton had one of the nation's highest foreclosure and unemployment rates through the entire recession. Budget cuts have decimated the city's police force, fire stations, and city workforce. In 2010, *Forbes* magazine ranked Stockton at number 1 on its annual list of the most miserable cities in America.[19] In 2012, Stockton became the largest American city to declare bankruptcy. The recession brought redevelopment in the area to a halt and the buildings are no longer as threatened, especially since the state cut all funding for redevelopment agencies to balance its budget. Money for historic preservation has all but dried up, and we have been forced to put on hold our dreams of purchasing the buildings and an expensive rehabilitation for them, and for a museum in one of them. Yet we persevere. We come from resilient stock.

We have helped to paint and clean two buildings in the Little Manila Historic Site, the Iloilo Circle, and the Daguhoy Temple. Hundreds come to Stockton annually and tour Little Manila and the exhibit in the basement of the Daguhoy Temple that was created by Tony Somera. We continue to raise funds and write grants to help us purchase the buildings, and we are working to designate the area as a state and national historic landmark site. The Little Manila Foundation, with the local chapter of FANHS, continues to work to educate the community about local Filipina/o American history, to remind old-timers to struggle against forgetting, and to bring our history to young people. The director Patricio Ginelsa and the pop group Black Eyed Peas set their music video for "Bebot" in a recreated, 1930s-era Rizal Social Club in Little Manila and filmed their exterior shots in front of it and throughout the neighborhood in 2007. In 2008 the Little Manila Foundation brought the Obie Award-winning, New York–based Ma-Yi Theatre Company's production of Carlos Bulosan's "The Romance of Magno Rubio" to the Bob Hope Fox Theatre. The play, which is set in Stockton's agricultural fields, tells the story of a naive, lonely Pinoy bamboozled by a blonde, buxom scam artist (a powerful allegory of the early Filipina/o American experience) and brought the audience of almost 700 to their feet, giving long-overdue recognition to Bulosan, who lived in Stockton for many years. The play reminded the audience that our experiences in Stockton loom large in the cultural and historical memories of Filipinas/os elsewhere in the country.

The Little Manila Foundation, with the Stockton FANHS, publishes a calendar each year that lists important dates in Philippine and Filipina/o American history in Stockton, in an attempt to make our history a daily part of our community's lives. In 2010, we launched our Little Manila Afterschool Program, in which several dozen South Side high school students learn our local Filipina/o American history from our former Little Manila interns, Alma Riego, Brian Batugo, and Aldrich Sabac, now local school teachers. The next generation of Filipina/o Americans in Stockton will know their history.

I am still deeply involved in our fight against forgetting and our struggle to save the neighborhood from the wrecking ball. One of the great gifts of straddling the border between scholarship and activism is that I have been able to discover that the current community divisions and the attempts to create community unity and identity have deep roots in debates over historical memory, class struggles, factionalism, rivalries, and ideological and political divisions of the past. We saved Little Manila—for now—but not without serious challenges. The writing of this book and the struggle to save the neighborhood have taught me that Filipinas/os in Stockton are still struggling to find solidarity with one another and political power, and they face the same dynamics that threatened to tear earlier generations apart: divisions of class and regional differences, political ideologies, generation, and immigrant and American-born experiences, within the context of American imperialism and enduring racism against Filipinas/os in Stockton. I never realized this more fully than in the past ten years, as we mounted the massive campaign of community education for the preservation and revitalization of the Little Manila neighborhood, and now, as I complete this book.

I know now that the struggle to create and maintain community is an ongoing one. Ethnic culture and identity are only a few of the threads that bind a community together. In addition, memories, shared victories, experiences, and losses; stories of survival; and disagreements and divisions have shaped our Filipina/o American and Asian American community in Stockton. As I finish this book, millions of Filipinas/os all over the globe are writing new chapters in the story of the Filipina/o diaspora and community settlement as they make new Little Manilas in places like Daly City, Virginia Beach, Queens, Chicago, Tokyo, London, Dubai, Rome, and Hong Kong. And as they build these new places, we Filipinas/os of the second, third, fourth, and fifth generations continue to struggle to preserve our community history in places where Filipina/o footprints are deep, like New Orleans, Los Angeles, Salinas, Seattle, San Francisco, and my hometown of Stockton.

As we dig in our heels and continue fighting to save Little Manila's last residents and buildings, I realize more clearly that our campaign is not just a struggle to preserve what is left of our community. Our campaign to remember, reclaim, and revitalize Little Manila is part of the historic and ongoing struggle to create and sustain a Filipina/o American community, a struggle I have attempted to document in this book.[20] The struggle over these buildings and space, and the memory of this place, is really a metaphor for the historical struggles of our larger Filipina/o American community and Asian American community to achieve social and economic justice, political power, and real, meaningful visibility in the United States. It is my hope that the love, respect, and commitment we feel for our historic community runs deeper than anything that can divide us. Little Manila will always be in our hearts.

NOTES

ABBREVIATIONS

AASF   Archives of the Archdiocese of San Francisco, St. Patrick's Seminary, Menlo Park, Calif.

BIA   Records of the Bureau of Insular Affairs, National Archives and Records Administration, College Park, Md.

JEWP   James Earl Wood Papers, Manuscripts, Special Collections, Bancroft Library, University of California, Berkeley

FANHS   Manuscript, Ephemera and Photograph Archives, Stockton Chapter, Filipino American National Historical Society

FOHP   Interviews, Filipino Oral History Project, Inc., Stockton, Calif.

LHC   Local History Collection, Cesar Chavez Central Library, Stockton, Calif.

NARA   National Archives and Records Administration, Washington, D.C.

NPA FANHS   Photograph Collection, Manuscripts, Personal, City, Organizational and Subject Files, and documents, Demonstration Project for Asian Americans, National Pinoy Archives, Filipino American National Historical Society, Seattle, Wash.

RG   Record Group

INTRODUCTION

1. Vicente S. Roldan, "Filipinos Contributed to Stockton's Economic Well-Being," Filipino carnival program, Stockton, Calif., 1937. See also Fred Cordova, "Stockton: From Whence the San Joaquin Flows in the Wellspring of Filipino American History," Hellman Goldman Foundation Lecture, Haggin Museum, April 19, 1997, NPA FANHS.

2. Interview with Frank Perez by author. See also Perez's weekly columns in the *Philippine Examiner* (1940s–1950s, Stockton, Calif.) and the *Philippines Mail* (1940s–1980s, Salinas, Calif.).

3. Frank Perez, "Mr. Little Manila," *Philippines Press USA* 5, no. 5 (San Jose), August 1987.

4. Lillian Galedo, Laurena Cabanero, and Brian Tom, "Roadblocks to Community Building: A Case Study of the Stockton Filipino Center Project" (Working Publication No. 4, Asian American Research Project, University of California, Davis, 1970), 8.

5. Donald Walker, "Race Relations and Specialty Crops: San Joaquin County Horticulture, 1900–1925," master's thesis, California State University, Sacramento, 1992), 270.

6. Carey McWilliams, *Brothers under the Skin* (Boston: Little, Brown, 1964), 238.

7. David Blight, "DuBois and the Struggle for American Historical Memory," in *History and Memory in African American Culture*, ed. Genevieve Fabre and Robert O'Meally (New York: Oxford University Press, 1994), 46.

8. Dolores Hayden, *The Power of Place: Urban Landscapes as Public History* (Cambridge: MIT Press, 1997), 8.

9. Michael Frisch, *A Shared Authority: Essays on the Craft and Meaning of Oral and Public History* (Albany: State University of New York, 1990), 16.

10. Ibid.

11. Michael Omi and Howard Winant, *Racial Formation in the United States: From the 1960s to the 1980s*, 2nd ed. (New York: Routledge, 1994), 55.

12. Paul A. Kramer, *The Blood of Government: Race, Empire, the United States and the Philippines* (Chapel Hill: University of North Carolina Press, 2006), 124.

13. Ibid., 5–6.

14. George Sanchez, *Becoming Mexican American: Ethnicity, Culture and Identity in Chicano Los Angeles, 1900–1945* (New York: Oxford University Press, 1993), 11.

15. Steffi San Buenaventura, "Filipino Folk Spirituality and Immigration: From Mutual Aid to Religion," *Amerasia* 1, no. 22 (1996): 2. See also Steffi San Buenaventura, "Filipino Folk Spirituality and Immigration: From Mutual Aid to Religion," in *New Spiritual Homes: Religion and Asian Americans*, ed. David K. Yoo (Honolulu: University of Hawai'i Press, with the UCLA Asian American Studies Center, 1999), 53.

16. Sanchez, *Becoming Mexican American*, 11–12.

17. See Ronald Takaki, *Strangers from a Different Shore* (Boston: Little, Brown, 1989); and Carlos Bulosan, *America Is in the Heart* (Seattle: University of Washington Press, 1973). For an argument regarding the durability of local and regional analysis, see Sau-Ling Wong, "Denationalization Reconsidered: Asian American Cultural Criticism at a Theoretical Crossroads," *Amerasia* 21, nos. 1–2 (1995): 1–27.

18. Takaki, *Strangers from a Different Shore*, 336. In her critique of Takaki, the historian Linda España-Maram writes that Takaki, and Carey McWilliams, who makes a similar argument, miss the point. España-Maram posits that Filipinas/os created "networks of portable communities," as the nature of their migratory work depended on mobility (see "Negotiating Identity: Youth, Gender and Popular Culture in Los Angeles' Little Manila, 1920s–1940s" [PhD diss., University of California, Los Angeles, 1996], 45).

19. On Seattle, see Dorothy Fujita-Rony, *Colonial Workers, American Power* (Berkeley: University of California Press, 2003); Linda España-Maram, *Creating Masculinity in Los Angeles's Little Manila: Working Class Filipinos and Popular Culture, 1920s–1950s* (New York: New York University Press, 2007); and Catherine Ceniza Choy, *Empire of Care: Nursing and Migration in Filipino American History* (Durham: Duke University Press, 2003). Arleen de Vera explores Japanese-Filipina/o relations in Stockton and reactions to anti-Filipina/o sentiment in "The Tapia Saiki Incident: Interethnic Conflict and Filipino Responses to the Filipina/o Exclusion Movement," in *Over the Edge: Remapping the American West*, ed. Valerie J. Matsumoto and Blake Allmendinger (Berkeley: University of California Press, 1999), 172–200. Valerie Matsumoto discusses young Nisei girls and urban culture in "Japanese American Women and the Creation of Urban Nisei Culture in the 1930s," in Matsumoto and Allmendinger, *Over the Edge*, 291–306. Eiichiro Azuma has written a groundbreaking study of Filipina/o and Japanese competing nationalisms:

"Racial Struggle, Immigrant Nationalism, and Ethnic Identity: Japanese and Filipinas/os in the California Delta," *Pacific Historical Review* (May 1998): 163–99. For other published sociological and anthropological approaches to Filipina/o American communities, see Rick Bonus, *Locating Filipino Americans: Ethnicity and the Cultural Politics of Space* (Philadelphia: Temple University Press, 2000); Benito M. Vergara, *Pinoy Capital: The Filipino Nation in Daly City* (Philadelphia: Temple University Press, 2009); Yen Le Espiritu, *Home Bound: Filipino American Lives across Cultures, Communities and Countries* (Berkeley: University of California Press, 2003); and Joseph Galura and Emily P. Lawsin, eds., *Filipino Women in Detroit: Oral Histories from the Filipino American Oral History Project of Michigan* (Ann Arbor: OCSL Press of the University of Michigan, 2002).

20. See Maria P. P. Root, ed., *Filipino Americans: Transformation and Identity* (Thousand Oaks, Calif.: Sage, 1997).

21. Matt Garcia, *A World of Its Own: Race, Labor and Citrus in the Making of Greater Los Angeles, 1900–1970* (Chapel Hill: University of North Carolina Press, 2001); Mark Wild, *Street Meeting: Multiethnic Neighborhoods in Early Twentieth-Century Los Angeles* (Berkeley: University of California Press, 2005); Allison Varzally, *Making a Non-White America: Californians Coloring outside Ethnic Lines* (Berkeley: University of California Press, 2008); and Scott Kurashige, *The Shifting Grounds of Race: Black and Japanese Americans in the Making of Multiethnic Los Angeles* (Princeton: Princeton University Press, 2008).

22. Bulosan, *America Is in the Heart*, 289.

23. Alessandro Portelli, "What Makes Oral History Different," in *The Oral History Reader*, ed. Robert Perks and Alistair Thompson (New York: Routledge, 1998), 69.

24. See Antoinette Burton, *Dwelling in the Archive: Women Writing House, Home and History in Late Colonial India* (Oxford: Oxford University Press, 2003), 5; and Hayden, *The Power of Place*, 8.

25. See Jesse G. Quinsaat, ed., *Letters in Exile: An Introductory Reader on the History of the Pilipinos in America* (Los Angeles: UCLA Asian American Studies Center, 1976); or Royal F. Morales, *Makibaka: The Pilipino American Struggle* (Los Angeles: Mountainview, 1974).

26. See Fujita-Rony, *American Workers, Colonial Power*, xviii; and Teresa Amott and Julie Mattaei, *Race, Gender and Work: A Multicultural Economic History of Women in the United States* (Boston: South End, 1991), 239–49.

27. Stanley Garibay, "On the Word 'Pinoy,'" NPA FANHS.

28. "Special Filipino Women Students' Number," *Filipino Student Bulletin*, April–May 1926.

29. Bulosan, *America Is in the Heart*, 327.

CHAPTER 1. FROM THE PROVINCES TO THE DELTA

1. Reynaldo Ileto writes that conservative estimates place the deaths at 109,461. See Reynaldo C. Ileto, "Cholera and the Origins of the American Sanitary Order," in *Discrepant Histories: Translocal Essays on Filipino Cultures*, ed. Vicente L. Rafael (Philadelphia: Temple University Press, 1995), 54. David Silbey estimates that anywhere from 150,000 to 200,000 people died from cholera throughout the Philippines. See Silbey, *A War of Frontier and Empire: The Philippine American War, 1899–1902* (New York: Hill and Wang, 2007), 200. Capiz province was one of those places affected in the first phase of the epidemic. See Matthew Smallman-Raynor and Andrew D. Cliff, "The Philippines Insurrection and the 1902–4 Cholera Epidemic: Part II — Diffusion Patterns in War and Peace," *Journal of Historical Geography* 24, no. 2 (1998): 188–210.

2. Pablo Magdaluyo Mabalon interview by Nina T. Cordova, 1981, FOHP.

3. Florencia Mabalon Pastrana interview by author. "Puring" remembers that her Uncle Sacarias "acted like the Spanish way of living, very strict."

4. Ernesto Tirona Mabalon interview by author, May 10, 1997.

5. Pablo Mabalon sold the land to the Villanueva family. David Villanueva, heir to his family's land, now operates an exclusive cemetery called Golden Sunset on the land that caters to *balikbayan* (those Filipinas/os living abroad who are returning to the Philippines) families. My aunt Florencia Mabalon Pastrana was interred there in 2010.

6. Pablo Magdaluyo Mabalon interview by Nina T. Cordova, 1981, FOHP; and Ernesto Mabalon interview by author.

7. Florencia Pastrana interview by author.

8. Ernesto Mabalon interview by author.

9. Dorothy B. Fujita-Rony, *American Workers, Colonial Power: Philippine Seattle and the Transpacific West, 1919–1941* (Berkeley: University of California Press, 2003), 27.

10. Floro L. Mercene, *Manila Men in the New World: Filipino Migration to Mexico and the Americas from the Sixteenth Century* (Quezon City: University of the Philippines Press, 2007).

11. Eloisa Gomez Borah, "Filipinos in Unamuno's California Expedition of 1587," *Amerasia Journal* 21, no. 3 (1995), 175–183. See also Lorraine Jacobs Crouchett, *Filipinos in California: From the Days of the Galleons to the Present* (El Cerrito, Calif.: Downey Place, 1982).

12. Marina E. Espina, *Filipinos in Louisiana* (New Orleans: A. F. LaBorde, 1988). See also Fred Cordova, *Filipinos: Forgotten Asian Americans, A Pictorial Essay; 1763–Circa 1963* (Dubuque, Iowa: Kendall/Hunt, 1983), 1–2.

13. Paul A. Kramer, *The Blood of Government: Race, Empire, the United States, and the Philippines* (Chapel Hill: University of North Carolina Press, 2006), 36–37.

14. Stuart Creighton Miller, *Benevolent Assimilation: The American Conquest of the Philippines, 1899–1903* (New Haven: Yale University Press, 1992), 33. See also Felix B. Regalado and Quintin B. Franco, *History of Panay* (Central Philippine University, 1973).

15. John N. Schumacher, S.J., *The Propaganda Movement, 1880–1895* (Quezon City: Ateneo de Manila University Press, 1997). See especially 172–81 in regard to freemasonry.

16. Renato Constantino, *The Philippines: A Past Revisited, Vol. 1* (Manila: Tala Pub. Services, 1975), 1:206.

17. Luzviminda Francisco, "The Philippine-American War," in *The Philippines Reader: A History of Colonialism, Neocolonialism, Dictatorship, and Resistance*, ed. Daniel B. Schirmer and Stephen Rosskam Shalom (Boston: South End, 1987), 9; Silbey, *A War of Frontier and Empire*, 15.

18. Constantino, *The Philippines*, 223.

19. Miller, *Benevolent Assimilation*, 13–24.

20. Luzviminda Francisco, "The Philippine-American War," in Schirmer and Shalom, *The Philippines Reader*, 22. The speech was not published until 1903. See General James Rusling, "Interview with President William McKinley," *Christian Advocate*, January 22, 1903, 22–23.

21. Rudyard Kipling, "White Man's Burden," *McClure's Magazine* 12, no. 4 (1899), 290–91.

22. Constantino, *The Philippines*, 293; Stanley Karnow, *In Our Image: American Empire in the Philippines* (New York: Ballantine, 1990), 82; Paul Kramer, *The Blood of Government: Race, Empire, the United States and the Philippines* (Chapel Hill: University of North Carolina Press, 2006), 13–14; Willard B. Gatewood, Jr., *"Smoked Yankees" and the*

Struggle for Empire: Letters from Negro Soldiers, 1898–1902 (Urbana: University of Illinois Press, 1971), 13.

23. Miller, *Benevolent Assimilation*, 61.

24. Emilio Aguinaldo, "To the Philippine People," in Schirmer and Shalom, *The Philippines Reader*, 20.

25. Karnow, *In Our Image*, 140. The Library of Congress used "Philippine Insurrection" as a subject heading in its catalog until 1997, when the term was finally changed to "Philippine-American War."

26. Kramer, *The Blood of Government*, 146–51. See also Miller, *Benevolent Assimilation*; Silbey, *A War of Frontier and Empire*.

27. Francisco, "The Philippine-American War," in Schirmer and Shalom, *The Philippines Reader*, 13.

28. Silbey, *A War of Frontier and Empire*, 197–201; Warwick Anderson, *Colonial Pathologies: American Tropical Medicine, Race and Hygiene in the Philippines* (Manila: Ateneo de Manila University Press, 2007), 68; Pablo Mabalon interview by Nina T. Cordova.

29. Frank Hindman Golay, *Face of Empire: United States-Philippine Relations, 1898–1946* (Manila: Ateneo de Manila University Press, 1997), 93.

30. A growing body of work is appearing on the effects of U.S. colonization on the Philippines. Memoirs produced by former colonial officials include Dean C. Worcester, *Philippines: Past and Present*, first published in 1914 (New York: Macmillan, 1930); and W. Cameron Forbes, *The Philippine Islands*, first published in 1928 (Cambridge: Harvard University Press, 1945). The most recent monograph-length studies on U.S. colonialism in the Philippines include Golay, *Face of Empire*; Vicente L. Rafael, *White Love and Other Events in Filipino History* (Durham: Duke University Press, 2000); and Kramer, *The Blood of Government*.

31. Constantino, *The Philippines: A Past Revisited*, 316–17.

32. Worcester, *Philippines*, 399.

33. The Government of the Philippine Islands, Department of Public Instruction, Bureau of Education, *Thirty-Second Annual Report of the Director of Education for the Calendar Year 1931* (Manila: Bureau of Printing, 1932), 2, BIA, RG 350.

34. Quoted in Anne Paulet, "To Change the World: The Use of American Indian Education in the Philippines," *History of Education Quarterly* 27, no. 2 (2007): 177–78.

35. Worcester, *Philippines*, 398–99. See also Constantino, *The Philippines*, 315.

36. Constantino, *The Philippines*, 315.

37. James F. Smith, "Address of James F. Smith to the Second Convention of Division of Superintendent of Schools," *Philippine Teacher* 1, no. 2, January 15, 1905, BIA, RG 350.

38. Mary Racelis, "Bearing Benevolence in the Classroom and Community," in *Bearers of Benevolence: The Thomasites and Public Education in the Philippines*, ed. Mary P. Racelis and Judy Celine Ick (Pasig City, Philippines: Anvil, 2001), 4.

39. Government of the Philippine Islands, *Thirty-Second Annual Report of the Director of Education*, 2.

40. Quoted in Paulet, "To Change the World," 177–78. See also David Wallace Adams, *Education for Extinction: American Indians and the Boarding School Experience, 1875–1928* (Lawrence: University Press of Kansas, 1997).

41. Paulet, "To Change the World," 174.

42. Quoted in Steffi San Buenaventura, "The Colors of Manifest Destiny," in "Essays into American Empire in the Philippines," special issue, *Amerasia* 24, no. 3 (1998): 7.

43. Government of the Philippine Islands, *Thirty-Second Annual Report of the Director of Education*, 2.

44. Kramer, *The Blood of Government*, 204–5.

45. Constantino, *The Philippines*, 317.

46. Renato Constantino, "The Miseducation of the Filipino," excerpted in Schirmer and Shalom, *The Philippines Reader*, 46.

47. Nick Joaquin, *The Aquinos of Tarlac: An Essay on History as Three Generations* (Manila: Solar, 1988), 91.

48. Concepcion Moreno Bohulano interview by author, November 27, 1992, and Camila Labor Carido interview by author, July 12, 2002.

49. Catherine Ceniza Choy, *Empire of Care: Nursing and Migration in Filipino American History* (Durham: Duke University Press, 2003), 33–34.

50. See Laura Shapiro, *Perfection Salad* (Berkeley: University of California Press, 2008).

51. Camila Carido interview by author, February 19, 1996.

52. Emily Porcincula Lawsin, "Pensionados, Paisanos and Pinoys: An Analysis of the *Filipino Student Bulletin*, 1922–1939," *Filipino American National Historical Society Journal* 4 (1996), 33. See also Barbara M. Posadas and Roland L. Guyotte, "Unintentional Immigrants: Chicago's Filipino Foreign Students Become Settlers, 1900–1941," *Journal of American Ethnic History* 9, no. 2 (1990): 26–48; and Catherine Ceniza Pet, "Pioneers/Puppets: The Legacy of the Pensionado Program," (bachelor's thesis, Pomona College, 1991).

53. H. Brett Melendy, *Asians in America: Filipinos, Koreans, and East Indians* (Boston: Twayne, 1977), 31–33; Constantino, *The Philippines*, 316. See also Pet, "Pioneers/Puppets"; and Lawsin, "Pensionados, Paisanos and Pinoys."

54. Posadas and Guyotte, "Unintentional Immigrants," 27.

55. See letter from F. L. Parker, chief, Bureau of Insular Affairs, to James Earl Wood, May 26, 1932, Box 2, JEWP; and Lawsin, "Pensionados, Paisanos and Pinoys."

56. Frank Perez and Leatrice Bantillo Perez, "Pioneer Filipino Families and Leaders," in special issue, ed. Frank Perez and Leatrice Bantillo Perez, *San Joaquin Historian* 8, no. 4 (1994): 9–13.

57. Choy, *Empire of Care*, 36–37.

58. D. B. Ambrosio, "Filipino Women in U.S. Excel in Their Courses: Invade Business, Politics," *Filipino Student Bulletin, Special Filipino Women Students' Number* 5.8 (April-May 1926): 1, NPA FANHS.

59. Joan May Cordova and Alexis Canillo, eds., *Voices: A Filipino American Oral History* (Stockton, Calif.: Filipino Oral History, 1984); interviews and questionnaire, Box 2, JEWP.

60. Quoted in Honorante Mariano, "The Filipino Immigrants in the United States" (master's thesis, University of Oregon, 1933), 9.

61. Anastasio B. Pagala interview by David Magdael, 1981, FOHP.

62. Segunda Reyes interview by Mary Inosanto, 1981, FOHP.

63. Camila Carido interview by author, July 12, 2002.

64. Unnamed interviewee as quoted in Cordova and Canillo, *Voices*, unpaginated.

65. Pablo Mabalon interview by Cordova.

66. Felipe Napala interview by Joan May T. Cordova, 1981, FOHP.

67. Claro Candelario interview by author (unless otherwise noted, all subsequent quotes from Candelario have been taken from this interview); *Manifest of Passengers Arriving in the St. Albans, Vermont, District through Canadian Pacific Ports, 1929–1949*, NARA, microfilm publication M1465, 25 rolls, Records of the Immigration and Naturalization Service, RG 85, National Archives, Washington, D.C., www.ancestry.com, accessed November 13, 2012.

68. Cited in Melendy, *Asians in America*, 32.

69. Manuel Adeva, "Filipino Students in the United States," *Filipino Student Bulletin*, May–June 1931, BIA, RG 350.

70. George Montero interview by Joan May T. Cordova, 1981, FOHP.

71. Nemesio D. Paguyo interview by Joan May T. Cordova, 1981, FOHP.

72. Mary Dorita Clifford, "The Hawaiian Sugar Planters Association and Filipino Exclusion," in *Letters in Exile: An Introductory Reader on the History of the Pilipinos in America*, ed. Jesse G. Quinsaat (Los Angeles: UCLA Asian American Studies Center, 1976), 75; and Patria P. Ramos, "Filipino Women in Hawaii: Where We Were, Where We Are Now," in *Filipina: Hawaii's Filipino Women*, ed. Pepi Nieva (Honolulu: Filipino Association of University Women, 1994), 21–25. See also Dean T. Alegado, "The Filipino Community in Hawai'i: Development and Change," *Social Process in Hawaii* 33 (1991): 12; and Lawrence H. Fuchs, *Hawaii Pono: A Social History* (New York: Harcourt, Brace and World, 1961).

73. Henry T. Lewis, *Ilocano Rice Farmers: A Comparative Study of Two Philippine Barrios* (Honolulu: University of Hawaii Press, 1971), 26.

74. Constantino, *The Philippines*, 307.

75. Antonio J. A. Pido, *The Pilipinos in America: Macro/Micro Dimensions of Immigration and Integration* (New York: Center for Migration Studies, 1986), 61.

76. Elizabeth Uy Eviota, *The Political Economy of Gender: Women and the Sexual Division of Labour in the Philippines* (London: Zed, 1992), 70–71.

77. Lewis, *Ilocano Rice Farmers*, 24–25.

78. Mariano, "The Filipino Immigrants in the United States," 13–15.

79. Miriam Sharma, "The Philippines: A Case of Migration to Hawai'i, 1906 to 1946," in *Labor Immigration under Capitalism: Asian Workers in the United States before World War II*, ed. Lucie Cheng and Edna Bonacich (Berkeley: University of California Press, 1984), 340; Luis V. Teodoro, *Out of This Struggle: The Filipinos in Hawaii* (Honolulu: University Press of Hawaii, 1981), 13–18.

80. Hermenegildo Cruz, *The Activities of the Bureau of Labor* (Manila: Bureau of Printing, 1930), 105, BIA, RG 350.

81. Mariano, "The Filipino Immigrants in the United States," 14.

82. Lewis, *Ilocano Rice Farmers*, 24–25; William Henry Scott, *Ilocano Responses to American Aggression, 1900–1901* (Quezon City: New Day, 1986), 201–3.

83. Lewis, *Ilocano Rice Farmers*, 24–25.

84. Ibid., 6.

85. Sharma, "The Philippines," 341–42.

86. Ibid., 344.

87. Ibid., 350.

88. Ibid., 351; Lewis, *Ilocano Rice Farmers*, 25–26.

89. While my paternal grandfather Pablo Mabalon was in the United States, his wife — my grandmother Isabel Tirona Mabalon — worked as a weaver and tobacco trader in Numancia, Aklan (Ernesto Mabalon interview by author).

90. Carlos Bulosan, *America Is in the Heart: A Personal History* (Seattle: University of Washington Press, 1973), 14–15.

91. Ibid., 32–33.

92. Juan "Johnny" Dionisio interview by Ben Menor, June 27, 1981, Mililani, Hawai'i, NPA FANHS.

93. Felipe Napala interview by Cordova.

94. Nemesio Paguyo interview by Cordova.

95. Pablo Mabalon interview by Cordova.

96. Concepcion Bohulano interview by author, November 27, 1992.

97. Frank Perez and Letty Perez, "The Long Struggle for Acceptance: Filipinos in San Joaquin County," in special issue, *San Joaquin Historian* 8, no. 4 (1994): 5.

98. Frank Perez interview by David Magdael, 1981, FOHP.

99. Louis Bloch, *Facts about Filipino Immigration into California* (San Francisco: State of California, Department of Industrial Relations, April 1930), 12.

100. Steffi San Buenaventura, "Filipino Immigration to the United States," in *Asian American Encyclopedia*, ed. Franklin Ng (New York: Marshall Cavendish, 1995): 445–46.

101. Bloch, *Facts about Filipino Immigration into California*, 32.

102. Eudosia Bravo Juanitas interview by author.

103. For a thorough discussion of push factors in Filipina immigration before World War II, see Dorothy Cordova, "Voices from the Past: Why They Came," in *Making Waves: An Anthology of Writings by and about Asian American Women*, ed. Asian Women United of California (Boston: Beacon, 1989), 42–49.

104. Camila Carido interview by author, February 19, 1996.

105. Paula Dizon Daclan interview by author.

106. Eudosia Juanitas interview by author.

107. Quoted in "Girls Won't Come Abroad," *Commonwealth Times*, November 14, 1941.

108. Eviota, *The Political Economy of Gender*, 72.

109. Bloch, *Facts about Filipino Immigration into California*, 26.

110. Maria "Terri" Torres, "Juanitas Family Partial History Booklet," compiled for the Juanitas Reunion, 2002, personal collection of the author; passenger list for the SS *Lurline*, February 22, 1916, National Archives, Washington, D.C., www.ancestry.com, accessed August 2, 2010.

111. Melendy, *Asians in America*, 33; Ruben Alcantara, "The First Sakada," in *Filipinos in Hawaii: The First 75 Years: A Commemorative Book*, ed. Juan C. Dionisio, (Honolulu: Hawai'i: Filipino News Specialty Publications, 1981), 37.

112. Alcantara, "The First Sakada," 36–37.

113. Ibid., 44.

114. Ibid. Thanks to Jonathan Okamura for his conversations with me on the topic of the preponderance of early emigration of Visayan families and early Visayan emigration to Hawai'i.

115. John A. Larkin, *Sugar and the Origins of Modern Philippine Society* (Manila: New Day, 2001), 78.

116. Miriam Sharma, "Labor Migration and Class Formation among the Filipinos in Hawai'i, 1906–1946," in Cheng and Bonacich, *Labor Immigration under Capitalism*, 582.

117. Alcantara, "The First Sakada," 44.

118. Felix Tapia interview with James Earl Wood, Field Notes, Box 2, JEWP.

119. Fuchs, *Hawai'i Pono*, 142.

120. Luna Jamero interview by author.

121. Alegado, "The Filipino Community in Hawai'i," 12.

122. Manuel Buaken, *I Have Lived with the American People* (Caldwell, Idaho: Caxton Printers, 1948), 36–39.

123. Virgilio Menor Felipe, *Hawai'i: A Pilipino Dream* (Honolulu: Mutual, 2002), 105.

124. Ibid. See also Lewis, *Ilocano Rice Farmers*, 26.

125. Angeles Monrayo, *Tomorrow's Memories: A Diary*, edited by Rizaline R. Raymundo (Honolulu: University of Hawai'i Press, 2003).

126. Alberta Alcoy Asis interview, NPA FANHS.

127. Fuchs, *Hawai'i Pono*, 141.

128. Bienvenido D. Junasa, "The Great Filipino Migration," in *Filipinos in Hawai'i: The First 75 Years*, ed. Juan C. Dionisio (Honolulu: Hawai'i Filipino News Specialty Publication, 1981), 54.

129. Fuchs, *Hawaii Pono*, 143–44.

130. Melinda Tria Kerkvliet, "Pablo Manlapit's Fight for Justice," in "The Filipino American Experience in Hawai'i, in Commemoration of the 85th Anniversary of Filipino Immigration to Hawai'i," special issue, *Social Process in Hawai'i* 33 (1991): 154–55. See also Melinda Tria Kerkvliet, *Unbending Cane: Pablo Manlapit, A Filipino Labor Leader in Hawai'i* (Honolulu: Office of Multicultural Student Services, University of Hawaii Press, 2002); John E. Reinecke, *The Filipino Piecemeal Sugar Strike of 1924–1925* (Honolulu: Social Science Research Institute, University of Hawaii Press, 1996); and Ronald Takaki, *Pau Hana: Plantation Life and Labor in Hawaii* (Honolulu: University of Hawaii Press, 1983).

131. Jonathan Okamura, "Filipino American History in Hawai'i: A Young Visayan Woman's Perspective," in Angeles Monrayo, *Tomorrow's Memories: A Diary, 1924–1928*, ed. Rizaline Raymundo (Honolulu: University of Hawaii Press, 2003), 230–31.

132. Helen Lagrimas Liwanag, Flora Arca Mata, and Rizaline Monrayo Raymundo interviews by author. See also Okamura, "Filipino American History in Hawai'i," in Monrayo, *Tomorrow's Memories*, 240.

133. Monrayo, *Tomorrow's Memories*, 110.

134. Alberta Asis interview.

135. Helen Liwanag interview by author.

136. Polk city directories for Stockton, California, 1930–31, Cesar Chavez Central Branch, Stockton-San Joaquin County Public Library, Stockton, Calif.; Flora Mata interview by author.

137. Flora Mata interview by author; 1930 Census of the United States, National Archives and Records Administration, San Bruno, Calif.

138. Author's notes, Ming Hsu, speech at the dedication of the Grand Re-Opening of the Angel Island Immigration Station, February 15, 2009; Dollar Steamship Line history, http://www.apl.com/history/html/timeline_02.html#4, accessed November 13, 2012.

139. Quoted in Bruno Lasker, *Filipino Immigration to the Continental United States and to Hawaii* (Chicago: University of Chicago Press, 1931), 212–17.

140. Ibid., 217.

141. Quoted in Lasker, *Filipino Immigration*, 246.

142. Mariano, "The Filipino Immigrants in the United States," 13–15.

143. Unnamed interviewee, in Cordova and Canillo, *Voices*, unpaginated.

144. Perez and Perez, "The Long Struggle for Acceptance," 4.

145. D. L. Marcuelo, "Filipinos Must Stop Coming to America," *Three Stars*, May 1931.

146. Sixto Nicolas interview by David Magdael, 1981, FOHP.

147. *Seattle, Washington, Passenger and Crew Lists, 1882–1957*, database online on www.ancestry.com. Original source: *Seattle, Washington, Passenger and Crew Lists of Vessels Arriving at Seattle, Washington, 1890–1957*, NARA, microfilm publication M1383, 357 rolls, Records of the Immigration and Naturalization Service, RG 85, National Archives, Washington, D.C., accessed November 13, 2012.

148. Ernesto Mabalon interview by author.

149. The English translation for the Aklanon word "kabanua" is "countrymen," but since Filipina/o languages are not gender-specific, it means both men and women. The Tagalog word is "kababayan."

150. The Freedom Hotel was renamed the Eastern Hotel after 1944. It is listed on the National Register of Historic Places and now houses the Carlos Bulosan Memorial Exhibit (see http://www.bulosan.org/html/eastern_hotel.html).

151. Pablo Mabalon interview by Cordova, FOHP.

152. Ernesto Mabalon interview by author, May 1997.

153. Carol Hemminger, "Little Manila: The Filipino In Stockton Prior to World War II," *Pacific Historian* 24, no. 1 (1980): 24. The activist and writer Carey McWilliams calls Stockton the *"Manila of California"* in *Brothers under the Skin* (Boston: Little, Brown, 1964), 238.

154. Roger Daniels, *Guarding the Golden Door: American Immigration Policy and Immigrants since 1882* (New York: Hill and Wang, 2004), 51, 67.

CHAPTER 2. THE "VALLEY OF OPPORTUNITY"

1. D. L. Marcuelo, "Who's Who in Business," *Three Stars*, October 1928. See also U.S. Selective Service System, World War I Selective Service System Draft Registration Cards, 1917–1918, M1509, Records of the Immigration and Naturalization Service, NARA. Marcuelo's last sentence is a paraphrase of a well-known proverb.

2. Ninonuevo had moved to Porterville by 1930. James Earl Wood, Field Notes, Box 2, JEWP.

3. Donald Walker, "Race Relations and Specialty Crops: San Joaquin County Horticulture, 1900–1925" (master's thesis, State University, Sacramento, 1992), 270.

4. Bruno Lasker, *Filipino Immigration to the Continental United States and to Hawaii* (Chicago: University of Chicago Press, 1931), 217; Carey McWilliams, *Brothers under the Skin* (New York: Little, Brown, 1964), 235.

5. Carol Hemminger, "Little Manila: The Filipino in Stockton Prior to World War II," *Pacific Historian* 24, no. 1 (1980): 17.

6. Walker, "Race Relations and Specialty Crops," 273.

7. McWilliams, *Brothers under the Skin*, 241.

8. George P. Hammond, *The Weber Era in Stockton History* (Berkeley: Issued for the Friends of the Bancroft Library, University of California, 1982), 9; Olive Davis, *Stockton: Sunrise Port on the San Joaquin* (Sun Valley, Calif.: American Historical Press, 1998), 21.

9. Works Progress Administration and the City of Stockton, "History of Stockton and San Joaquin County, 1938," LHC. See also Susan Lee Johnson, *Roaring Camp: The Social World of the California Gold Rush* (New York: W. W. Norton, 2000).

10. Davis, *Stockton*, 25.

11. W. C. Ramsey, "Stockton: The Chicago of the Far West," *Overland Monthly*, September 1895, 297–314.

12. Sucheng Chan, *This Bittersweet Soil: The Chinese in California Agriculture, 1860–1910* (Berkeley: University of California Press, 1986), 158–67; Sylvia Sun Minnick, *Samfow: The San Joaquin Chinese Legacy* (Fresno, Calif.: Panorama West Publishing, 1987), 65–69.

13. Chan, *This Bittersweet Soil*, 163.

14. Davis, *Stockton*, 44.

15. See Stuart Marshall Jamieson, *Labor Unionism in American Agriculture*, U.S. Department of Labor Bulletin no. 836 (Washington: U.S. Government Printing Office, 1945); Kevin Starr, *Endangered Dreams: The Great Depression in California* (New York: Oxford University Press, 1996); Carey McWilliams, *Factories in the Fields: The Story of Migratory Farm Labor in California* (Santa Barbara, Calif.: Peregrine, 1971); Walker, "Race Relations and Specialty Crops"; and Cletus E. Daniel, *Bitter Harvest: A History of California Farmworkers, 1870–1941* (Berkeley: University of California Press, 1982).

16. Walker, "Race Relations and Specialty Crops"; Daniel, *Bitter Harvest*; and McWilliams, *Factories in the Fields*.

17. Stockton Gurdwara Sahib official website (http://www.stocktongurdwarasahib.com/2/).

18. Chan, *This Bittersweet Soil*, 162.

19. McWilliams, *Factories in the Fields*, 183.

20. Alfred Marks, "Stockton," *Mercantile Guide: Business Directory of the Principal Cities of California*, 1924, vol. 24 (San Francisco: Alfred Marks), 588.

21. Davis, *Stockton*, 75–76; Architectural Resources Group, "Stockton Downtown Historic Resources Survey," September 1, 2000, LHC.

22. Louis Bloch, *Facts about Filipino Immigration into California* (San Francisco: State of California, Department of Industrial Relations, April 1930), 12.

23. Quoted in McWilliams, *Factories in the Fields*, 118. "Hindu" was the name erroneously used by many farmers and even the U.S. Census to categorize and racialize all South Asian immigrants, regardless of their religious affiliation.

24. Ibid., 103; Walker, "Race Relations and Specialty Crops," 273.

25. Japanese farming settlements, or "colonies," included Livingston and the Yamato and Cortez communities. See Valerie J. Matsumoto, *Farming the Home Place: A Japanese American Community in California, 1919–1982* (Ithaca: Cornell University Press, 1993), 22–31.

26. Davis, *Stockton*, 60.

27. Matsumoto, *Farming the Home Place*, 31.

28. Starr, *Endangered Dreams*, 62.

29. Quoted in Wood, Field Notes, Box 2, JEWP.

30. Walker, "Race Relations and Specialty Crops," 270. See also McWilliams, *Factories in the Fields*; and Daniel, *Bitter Harvest*.

31. Wood, Field Notes, Box 2, JEWP.

32. Quoted in ibid.

33. Alma Alcala interview by author.

34. Stockton Township, 1930 U.S. Census, National Archives and Records Administration, San Bruno, Calif.; Alma Alcala interview by author.

35. Alma Alcala interview by author.

36. Quoted in Wood, Field Notes, Box 2, JEWP.

37. Quoted in ibid.

38. George Montero interview by Joan May T. Cordova, 1981, FOHP.

39. Fausto Rabaca interview by David Magdael, 1981, FOHP.

40. Nemesio D. Paguyo interview by Joan May T. Cordova, 1981, FOHP.

41. Harry Hammond interview, Wood, Field Notes, Box 2, JEWP.

42. Honorante Mariano, "The Filipino Immigrants in the United States" (master's thesis, University of Oregon, 1933), 30; State Relief Administration of California, "Migratory Labor in California," California State Labor Federation Papers, Folder 10, Box 15, Labor Archives and Research Center, San Francisco State University.

43. Wood, Field Notes, Box 2, JEWP.

44. Starr, *Endangered Dreams*, 63.

45. George Montero interview by Cordova.

46. Carey McWilliams, "Exit the Filipino," *Nation*, September 4, 1935, 265.

47. Quoted in Wood, Field Notes, Box 2, JEWP.

48. Dorothy Fujita-Rony, *American Workers, Colonial Power: Philippine Seattle and the Transpacific West, 1919–1941* (Berkeley: University of California, 2003), 92–93.

49. Benicio T. Catapusan, "Filipino Social Adjustment in the United States" (PhD diss., University of Southern California, 1940), 69; *One Nation*, ed. Wallace Stegner and the editors of *Look* (Boston: Houghton Mifflin, 1945).

50. Ignacio Sabedra interview by Mary Arca Inosanto, 1981, FOHP. For the Alaskan salmon canning industry and Filipino workers, see Donald L. Guimary, *Marumina Trabajo: A History of Labor in Alaska's Salmon Canning Industry "Dirty Work"* (New York: iUniverse, 2006); and Thelma Buchholdt, *Filipinos in Alaska, 1788–1958* (Anchorage: Aboriginal, 1996).

51. Pablo Mabalon interview in *Voices: A Filipino American Oral History*, ed. Joan May Cordova and Alexis Canillo (Stockton, Calif.: Filipino Oral History, 1984).

52. My cousins and uncles returned from Alaska each fall with shiny golden cans of salmon. We would devour the contents — chunks of luscious, pink salmon — with hot rice.

53. For unionization efforts in the Alaskan canned salmon industry, see Jack Masson and Donald Guimary, "Asian Labor Contractors in the Alaskan Canned Salmon Industry: 1880–1937," *Labor History* 22, no. 3 (1981): 377–97; Chris Friday, *Organizing Asian-American Labor: The Pacific Coast Canned-Salmon Industry, 1870–1942* (Philadelphia: Temple University Press, 1994); Crystal Fresco, "Cannery Workers' and Farm Laborers' Union 1933–39: Their Strength in Unity" (Seattle Civil Rights Project, 1999, http://depts.washington.edu/civilr/cwflu.htm).

54. Gessie Gesulga Bowden, "Growing Up Brown," journal writing project, NPA FANHS.

55. Walker, "Race Relations and Specialty Crops," 238, 241.

56. Wood, Field Notes, Box 2, JEWP.

57. Bloch, *Facts about Filipino Immigration into California*, 13.

58. Ibid., 69.

59. All wage figures are taken from Vicente Roldan, "Filipinos Contributed to Stockton's Economic Well Being," in the program of the Filipino Carnival, Stockton, Calif., 1937, 26–29, Angelina Bantillo Magdael Family Collection. See also Starr, *Endangered Dreams*, 67.

60. Starr, *Endangered Dreams*, 67.

61. Ted Gabales, "The Impact of Filipino Farm Labor and Organization on San Joaquin County Agriculture," Independent Study Project Working Paper, July 30, 1985, unpaginated, NPA FANHS.

62. Jamieson, *Labor Unionism in American Agriculture*, 72; Bloch, *Facts about Filipino Immigration into California*, 12.

63. Hemminger, "Little Manila," 24.

64. Quoted in Wood, Field Notes, Box 2, JEWP.

65. Quoted in ibid.

66. Bloch, *Facts about Filipino Immigration to California*, 71.

67. Wood, Field Notes, Box 2, JEWP.

68. Iloilo Circle incorporation papers, housed at the Iloilo Circle, 128 E. Sonora Street, Stockton, Calif.

69. Wood, Field Notes, Box 2, JEWP.

70. Interview with Mr. Cinco, Wood, Field Notes, Box 2, JEWP.

71. Interview with Mrs. D. L. Marcuelo, ibid.

72. Gabales, "The Impact of Filipino Farm Labor and Organization on San Joaquin County Agriculture"; Bloch, *Facts about Filipino Immigration into California*, 61.

73. Hemminger, "Little Manila," 26.

74. *Stockton Record*, March 28, 1971.

75. Manuel Buaken, *I Have Lived with the American People* (Caldwell, Idaho: Caxton, 1948), 196.

76. Jerry Paular interview by author.

77. George Montero interview by Cordova.

78. Bloch, *Facts about Filipino Immigration into California*, 62.

79. Buaken, *I Have Lived with the American People*, 87.

80. D. L. Marcuelo, "A Tip to the Filipino Workers," *Three Stars*, September 1, 1928.

81. Wood, Field Notes, Folder 3, Box 2, JEWP.

82. Lorenzo Romano Sr. interview by author.

83. George Montero interview by Cordova.

84. Jerry Paular, interview by author. See also Gabales, "The Impact of Filipino Farm Labor and Organization on San Joaquin County Agriculture."

85. Cipriano Parlone Insular interview by Terri Jamero, NPA FANHS.

86. Nemesio Paguyo interview by Cordova.

87. Wood, Field Notes, Box 2, JEWP.

88. Camila Labor Carido interview by author, January 15, 1996.

89. Jimmy Ente interview by author.

90. Bob Cabigas, "The Tomato Field," *Stockton Chapter Newsletter*, Stockton Chapter, FANHS, newsletter. 11 no. 4 (October 2005), 4–5.

91. Quoted in Wood, Field Notes, Box 2, JEWP.

92. Hemminger, "Little Manila," 10.

93. George Montero interview by Cordova.

94. Sebastian Inosanto, listed as "Sebastian Imosanto," arrived on June 10, 1925, in Seattle on the President Grant. *Seattle, Washington, Passenger and Crew Lists, 1882–1957*, database online on www.ancestry.com, accessed November 10, 2012. Original source: *Seattle, Washington, Passenger and Crew Lists of Vessels Arriving at Seattle, Washington, 1890-1957*, NARA, microfilm publication M1383, 357 rolls, Records of the Immigration and Naturalization Service, RG 85, National Archives, Washington, D.C.

95. Quoted in Gabales, "The Impact of Filipino Farm Labor and Organization on San Joaquin County Agriculture," unpaginated.

96. Ulpiano Morania interview by Mary Arca Inosanto, 1981, FOHP.

97. George Montero interview by Cordova.

98. Nemesio Paguyo interview by Cordova.

99. Ibid.

100. Author's notes taken during speech by Anita Navalta Bautista, at panel presentation for a visit of college students from San Francisco State University to Stockton, March 22, 2009, Stockton, Calif.

101. Mr. and Mrs. Felipe Napala interview by Joan May T. Cordova, 1981, FOHP.

102. Segunda Reyes interview by Mary Arca Inosanto, 1981, FOHP.

103. "Our Housings," Rizaline Raymundo letter to author, August 2006.

104. Anita Bautista interview by author.

105. Leo Giron, *Giron Escrima: Memories of a Bladed Warrior* (Los Angeles: Empire, 2006). See also Dan Inosanto, *The Filipino Martial Arts as Taught by Dan Inosanto* (Los Angeles: Know How, 1980); Antonio Somera, *Giron Arnis Escrima* (Boston: Tuttle, 1998); and Mark V. Wiley, *The Secrets of Cabales Serrada Escrima* (Boston: Tuttle, 2001), and *Filipino Martial Culture* (Boston: Tuttle, 1997).

106. Giron, *Giron Escrima*, 6–7.

107. Ibid., 7; Antonio Somera, "Tools of the Trade," unpublished paper.

108. Somera, "Tools of the Trade."

109. Giron, *Giron Escrima*, 88.

110. Somera, "Tools of the Trade."

111. Giron, *Giron Escrima*, 9; see also 10–13.

112. Perry William Kelly, *Dan Inosanto: The Man, The Teacher, The Artist* (Boulder, Colo.: Paladin, 2000), 5.

113. Rene Latosa interview by author.

114. Daniel Inosanto, "Foreword," in Antonio Somera, *The Secrets of Giron Arnis Escrima* (Boston: Tuttle, 1998), ix–x.

115. Trinidad Rojo, Report of the First Filipino Convention, Sacramento, California, 1938. Trinidad Rojo papers, NPA FANHS.

116. Linda España-Maram, *Creating Masculinity in Los Angeles' Little Manila: Working Class Filipinos and Popular Culture, 1920s–1950s* (New York: New York University Press, 2006).

117. Greg Bankoff, "Redefining Criminality: Gambling and Financial Expediency in the Colonial Philippines, 1764–1898," *Journal of Southeast Asian Studies* 22, no. 2 (1991): 267–81.

118. Pete Valoria interview by author.

119. Angelina Bantillo Magdael interview by Cheryl Magdael, July 1, 1981, FOHP.

120. Quoted in Fred Cordova, *Filipinos: Forgotten Asian Americans, A Pictorial Essay; 1763–Circa 1963* (Dubuque, Iowa: Kendall/Hunt, 1983), 212.

121. Peter Jamero, *Growing Up Brown: Memoirs of a Filipino American* (Seattle: University of Washington Press, 2006), 47–49.

122. "Cockfight Nets 170 Filipinos," *Stockton Daily Evening Record*, May 10, 1943.

123. Pete Valoria interview by author.

124. Luna Jamero interview by author.

125. Carlos Bulosan, *America Is in the Heart: A Personal History* (Seattle: University of Washington Press, 1973), 159.

126. Quoted in Wood, Field Notes, Box 2, JEWP.

127. Buaken, *I Have Lived with the American People*, 116.

128. Both quoted in Wood, Field Notes, Box 2, JEWP.

129. Rhacel Salazar Parreñas, "'White Trash' Meets 'Little Brown Monkey': The Taxi Dance Hall as a Site of Interracial and Gender Relations between White Working Class Women and Filipino Immigrant Men in the 1920s and 1930s," *Amerasia* 24, no. 2 (1998): 128.

130. Wood, Field Notes, Box 2, JEWP.

131. Howard A. DeWitt, *Violence in the Fields: California Filipino Farm Labor Unionization during the Great Depression* (Saratoga, N.Y.: Century Twenty One, 1980), 17.

132. Lasker, *Filipino Immigration to the Continental United States and to Hawaii*, 56.

133. All quoted in Wood, Field Notes, Box 2, JEWP.

134. Daniel, *Bitter Harvest*, 109.

135. DeWitt, *Violence in the Fields*, 7.

136. Jamieson, *Labor Unionism in American Agriculture*, 71–79.

137. Quoted in John Gregory Dunne, *Delano: The Story of the California Grape Strike* (New York: Farrar, Straus and Giroux, 1967), 40.

138. David J. Pivar, "The American Federation of Labor and Filipino Exclusion: 1927–1934," in *The Filipino Exclusion Movement*, ed. Josefa M. Saniel (University of the Philippines, 1967), 32.

139. Legionarios del Trabajo Blue Book, 1940 National Convention, author's personal collection.

140. *California Passenger and Crew Lists, 1893–1957*, NARA, Records of the Immigration and Naturalization Service, RG 85, National Archives, Washington, D.C.

141. Gabales, "The Impact of Filipino Farm Labor and Organization on San Joaquin County Agriculture"; Melinda Tria Kerkvliet, *Unbending Cane: Pablo Manlapit, A Filipino Labor Leader in Hawaii* (Honolulu: Office of Multicultural Student Services, University of Hawai'i Press, 2002), 66–69; DeWitt, *Violence in the Fields*, 80.

142. Manuel M. Insigne and D. L. Marcuelo, "Filipino Labor between Hell and Fire," *Philippine Advertiser*, February 29, 1928, 8, RG 350, File No. 26671-61, Box 1103, BIA.

143. Pivar, "The American Federation of Labor and Filipino Exclusion," 36.

144. "Asparagus Question Still Unsolved — Strained Relations between Growers and Laborers," *Philippine Advertiser*, February 29, 1928, 10, RG 350, File No. 26671-61, Box 1103, BIA.

145. Bloch, *Facts about Filipino Immigration into California*, 58–59.

146. Juan Malumay Macahilas interview by author.

147. "Mga Anak Ng Bukid to Hold Their Convention Here," *Three Stars*, December 1, 1928.

148. Wood, Field Notes, Folder 2, JEWP.

149. "Mga Samahang Pangbayan Inanyayahang Magunawaan," *Three Stars*, September 1, 1928.

150. Juan Macahilas interview by author.

151. D. L. Marcuelo, *Three Stars*, January 1929.

152. "J. Y. Billones, Filipino Leader, Makes a Tour of Asparagus Fields," *Three Stars*, May 1, 1930.

153. Pivar, "The American Federation of Labor and Filipino Exclusion," 30.

154. Paul Scharrenberg, "The Philippine Problem," *Pacific Affairs* 2 no. 2 (February 1929): 49–54.

155. Ibid., 53; DeWitt, *Violence in the Fields*, 13.

156. See H. Brett Melendy, "California's Discrimination against Filipinos," in *Letters in Exile: An Introductory Reader on the History of the Pilipinos in America*, ed. Jesse G. Quinsaat (Los Angeles: UCLA Asian American Studies Center, 1976), 35–44. See also Howard A. DeWitt, *Anti-Filipino Movements in California: A History, Bibliography and Study Guide* (San Francisco: R and E Research Associates, 1976).

157. Commonwealth Club of California, "Filipino Immigration," *Transactions of the Commonwealth Club of California* 24, no. 7 (November 5, 1929): 307–78.

158. Mae M. Ngai, *Impossible Subjects: Illegal Aliens and the Making of Modern America* (Princeton: Princeton University Press, 2004), 109.

159. Davis, *Stockton*, 78; Starr, *Endangered Dreams*, 223. See also James N. Gregory, *American Exodus: Dust Bowl Migration and Okie Culture in California* (New York: Oxford University Press, 1991).

160. Juan Macahilas interview by author.

161. Camila Carido interview by author, January 15, 1996.

162. "Eight Wounded in Race War as Old Year Ends," *Stockton Daily Evening Record*, January 1, 1926. See also Gabales, "The Impact of Filipino Farm Labor and Organization on San Joaquin County Agriculture," 2.

163. Bulosan, *America Is in the Heart*, 143.

164. Lasker, *Filipino Immigration to the Continental United States and to Hawaii*, 13–15.

165. Quoted in Wood, Field Notes, Box 4, JEWP.

166. As quoted by Emory S. Bogardus in "Anti-Filipino Race Riots," in *Letters in Exile:*

An Introductory Reader on the History of Pilipinos in America, ed. Jesse Quinsaat (UCLA Asian American Studies Center, 1976), 52–53.

167. Ibid., 55; DeWitt, *Anti-Filipino Movements in California*, 50.

168. "White Youth Stabbed by Islanders," *Stockton Daily Evening Record*, January 24, 1930.

169. "Filipino Center Here Dynamited," *Stockton Daily Evening Record*, January 29, 1930.

170. "Luneta Service — Huge Mass Meeting," *Manila Times*, January 31, 1930.

171. "Mammoth Crowd Predicted," in *Manila Bulletin*, February 2, 1930, quoted in "'Humiliation Day' Observed on Luneta," *Manila Bulletin*, February 3, 1930.

172. "Filipinos Mass in Protest," *New York Times*, February 3, 1930.

173. Quoted in "10,000 in Manila Protest Rioting in California," *New York Herald Tribune*, February 3, 1930.

174. D. L. Marcuelo, "Watsonville's Problem, Its Causes and Solution," *Three Stars*, February 5, 1930.

175. Lawrence Litwack, *Trouble in Mind: Black Southerners in the Age of Jim Crow* (New York: Knopf, 1988).

176. Hyung-chan Kim and Cynthia C. Mejia, *The Filipinos in America, 1898–1974* (Dobbs Ferry, N.Y.: Oceana), 14.

177. Quoted in Wood, Field Notes, Box 2, JEWP.

178. *The Three Stars*, August 15, 1930.

179. D. L. Marcuelo, "Two Filipinos Hanged and One Was Burnt," *The Three Stars*, August 15, 1930.

180. Walker, "Race Relations and Specialty Crops," 267; Glenn Alvin Kennedy, *It Happened in Stockton* (Stockton, Calif.: Kenco Reproduction, 1967), 2:216.

181. Jerry Paular interview by author.

182. Juan Macahilas interview by author.

183. Camila Carido interview by author, January 15, 1996.

184. Rene Latosa interview by author.

185. "Filipino Influx Called Menace," *Los Angeles Times*, March 26, 1930.

186. "Urges Filipino Exclusion: Representative Welch of California Sees 'Invasion' of Coast," *New York Times*, March 26, 1930, 20.

187. Starr, *Endangered Dreams*, 82.

188. DeWitt, *Violence in the Fields*, 7. See also Hemminger, "Little Manila," 12.

189. Polk city directories for Stockton, California, 1927 and 1928, Cesar Chavez Central Branch, Stockton–San Joaquin County Library, Stockton, Calif.

190. Starr, *Endangered Dreams*, 72.

191. DeWitt, *Violence in the Fields*, 18.

192. Crystal Fresca, "Cannery Workers' and Farm Laborers' Union, 1933–39: Their Strength in Unity," Seattle Civil Rights Project Website, http://depts.washington.edu/civilr/cwflu.htm, accessed November 13, 2012.

193. McWilliams, *Factories in the Field*, 214–15.

194. Daniel, *Bitter Harvest*, 109, 117.

195. DeWitt, *Violence in the Fields*, 17.

196. "Filipino Labor Groups in Fight," *Sacramento Bee*, June 6, 1932.

197. McWilliams, "Exit the Filipino," 265.

198. Howard DeWitt, "The Filipino Labor Union: The Salinas Lettuce Strike of 1934," *Amerasia* 5, no. 2 (1978): 1–21.

199. Jamieson, *Labor Unionism in California Agriculture*, 129.

200. Ibid. See also California Labor Federation Collection, Box 11, Folder 9, Labor Ar-

chives and Research Center, San Francisco State University. On Mensalvas's radicalism, see Stephen Schwartz, *From West to East: California and the Making of the American Mind* (New York: Free Press, 1998), 273, 396.

201. Jamieson, *Labor Unionism in California Agriculture*, 143.

202. "Asparagus Workers on Union Island Strike," *Filipino Pioneer*, March 15, 1937, Records of the Immigration and Naturalization Service, RG 85, File 464, National Archives and Records Administration, Washington, D.C.

CHAPTER 3. MAKING A FILIPINA/O AMERICAN WORLD

1. Carey McWilliams, *Brothers under the Skin* (Boston: Little, Brown, 1964), 238; "Whites and Filipinos Urge Peace," *Stockton Daily Evening Record*, January 30, 1930; John F. Wilson, "The Filipino as I Know Him," in "Filipino Immigration," The Commonwealth Club, *Transactions of the Commonwealth Club of California* 24, no. 7 (November 5, 1929): 327.

2. Linda España-Maram, *Creating Masculinity in Los Angeles' Little Manila: Working-Class Filipinos and Popular Culture, 1920s–1950s* (New York: Columbia University Press, 2006).

3. H. Brett Melendy, *Asians in America: Filipinos, Koreans, and East Indians.* (Boston: Twayne, 1977), 29.

4. Mary Arca Inosanto Journals, NPA FANHS.

5. See Angeles Monrayo, *Tomorrow's Memories: A Diary, 1924–1928*, ed. Rizaline R. Raymundo (Honolulu: University of Hawai'i Press, 2003).

6. Perry William Kelly, *Dan Inosanto: The Man, The Teacher, The Artist* (Boulder, Colo.: Paladin, 2000), 4. On Itliong, see Patricia Leigh Brown, "Forgotten Hero of Labor Fight: His Son's Lonely Quest," *New York Times*, October 18, 2012.

7. Mae Ngai, *Impossible Subjects: Illegal Aliens and the Making of Modern America* (Princeton University Press, 2004), 108.

8. Quoted in "Stockton Free of Filipino Riot Theats," *Stockton Daily Evening Record*, January 27, 1930.

9. Ibid.

10. "Whites and Filipinos Urge Peace," *Stockton Daily Evening Record*, January 30, 1930.

11. Quoted in James Earl Wood, Field Notes, Box 2, JEWP.

12. "Filipino Center Here Dynamited," *Stockton Daily Evening Record*, January 29, 1930; "Whites and Filipinos Urge Peace," *Stockton Daily Evening Record*, January 30, 1930. See also Frank Perez and Leatrice Bantillo Perez, "Filipinos in San Joaquin County," in "The Long Struggle for Acceptance: Filipinos in San Joaquin County," ed. Frank Perez and Leatrice Bantillo Perez, special issue, *San Joaquin Historian* 8, no. 4 (1994): 10.

13. Quoted in Wood, Field Notes, Box 2, JEWP.

14. "Filipinos Stay Parade Plans," *Stockton Daily Evening Record*, February 7, 1930.

15. "Attorney on Tour to Centers of Filipino Labor; Stopped in Stockton," *Stockton Daily Evening Record*, September 29, 1930.

16. See Lillian Galedo, Laurena Cabanero, and Brian Tom, "Roadblocks to Community Building: A Case Study of the Stockton Filipino Community Center Project," Working Publication No. 4, Asian American Research Project, University of California, Davis, 1970.

17. Emory Bogardus, "American Attitudes towards Filipinos," *Sociology and Social Research* 14 no. 1 (September-October 1929): 66.

18. Fred Cordova, *Filipinos: Forgotten Asian Americans* (Dubuque, Iowa: Kendall/Hunt, 1983), 175.

19. Jon D. Cruz, "Filipino American Community Organizations in Washington, 1900–1930s," in *Peoples of Color in the American West*, ed. Sucheng Chan (Lexington, Mass.: D.C. Heath and Company, 1994), 235–45.

20. See Edwin B. Almirol, "Filipino Voluntary Associations: Balancing Social Pressures and Ethnic Images," *Ethnic Groups* 2, 1978, 65–92, and his study of Salinas, *Ethnic Identity and Social Negotiation: A Study of a Filipino Community in California* (New York: AMS, 1985); Jonathan Okamura, "Filipino Organizations: A History," in *The Filipinos in Hawaii: The First 75 Years*, ed. Juan C. Dionisio (Honolulu: Hawaii Filipino News Specialty Publications, 1981), 72–75); Scott Morgan, "Nostalgia and the Present: Filipino Hometown and Provincial Associations in California," in *Patterns of Migration in Southeast Asia*, ed. Robert R. Reed (Berkeley: University of California, Centers for South and Southeast Asian Studies, 1990), 258–81; and Steffi San Buenaventura, "Filipino Folk Spirituality and Immigration," in *New Spiritual Homes*, ed. David Yoo (Honolulu: University of Hawai'i Press with the UCLA Asian American Studies Center, 1999).

21. Legionarios del Trabajo Blue Book, 1940, author's personal collection; San Buenaventura, "Filipino Folk Spirituality and Immigration," 81; Leo Giron, *Giron Escrima: Memories of a Bladed Warrior* (Los Angeles: Empire, 2006), 61; Ernesto Tirona Mabalon interview by author, January 1996. Mabalon, a former LDT vice grand master and supreme minister, discussed the deep influences of freemasonry on the LDT.

22. Legionarios del Trabajo Blue Book, 1940; see also San Buenaventura, "Filipino Folk Spirituality and Immigration," 55.

23. Christine N. Halili and Maria Christine Halili, *Philippine History* (Manila: Rex Bookstore, 2004); Antonio Santos interview by David Magdael, 1981, FOHP.

24. Legionarios del Trabajo Blue Book, 1940.

25. Nina van Zandt, a Chicago socialite turned labor radical, married the labor activist August Spies in 1887 as he served a prison term for conspiracy to murder a police officer. Spies had been accused of throwing a bomb into a group of police during a meeting of labor union members on May 4, 1886, at Haymarket Square in Chicago. See Henry David, *The History of the Haymarket Affair* (New York: Farrar and Rhinehart, 1936), 453.

26. "History of the Daguhoy Lodge," application for City of Stockton Landmark Designation, Stockton City Archives, Office of the City Clerk, Stockton, Calif.

27. Legionarios del Trabajo Blue Book, 1940.

28. Letter from J. K. Butler to James Earl Wood, July 10, 1931, Wood, Field Notes, Box 1, JEWP.

29. San Buenaventura, "Filipino Folk Spirituality and Immigration," 55.

30. Ibid., 55–56. See also souvenir program, Filipino Federation of America National and State Convention Banquet, Saturday, July 5, 2003, personal collection of the author.

31. Quoted in Wood, Field Notes, Box 2, JEWP.

32. San Buenaventura, "Filipino Folk Spirituality and Immigration," 55.

33. Legionarios Del Trabajo Blue Book, 1940; Regidor Lodge #5 Photo Album, The Haggin Museum, Stockton, Calif.

34. Vicente L. Rafael, *White Love and Other Events in Filipino History* (Durham: Duke University Press, 2000), 76–102.

35. Joan May T. Cordova with Dawn B. Mabalon, "History of the Numancia Aid Association, Inc.," seventy-fifth anniversary souvenir program of the Numancia Aid Association, September 2007, Stockton, Calif., personal collection of the author; Fausto Rabaca interview by David Magdael, 1981, FOHP; Iloilo Circle incorporation papers, FANHS.

36. See Galedo, Cabanero, and Tom, "Roadblocks to Community Building," "Appendix B: Filipino Organizations of Stockton, California."

37. Fausto Rabaca interview by Magdael.

38. Nemesio D. Paguyo interview by Joan May T. Cordova, 1981, FOHP.

39. Jimmy Ente interview by author.

40. Fred Cordova interview by author.

41. "Filipinos Plan Hospital Project," *Philippine Advertiser*, February 28, 1928, 20, RG 350, National Archives and Records Administration, College Park, Md.; Wood, Field Notes, Box 2, JEWP.

42. "Macario Darvin Bautista, M.D.," *Ten Outstanding Filipino Americans In San Joaquin County*, Maharlika Management Corporation souvenir program, 1983 (The Haggin Museum, Stockton, Calif.).

43. "Walang Kamatayang Pag-Ibig," 1937 Filipino Carnival souvenir program, Angelina Bantillo Magdael family collection, 10.

44. See Jean Vengua Gier, "Bibliography and Locator: Selected Periodicals, 1903 to 1946," in "The Commonwealth Cafe: U.S. Filipino Writing in the Early 20th Century's Blog," http://www.commonwealthcafe.info/bibliography/, accessed June 1, 2011.

45. Art Irish, "Unwholesome Commercial Recreation Survey in the City of Stockton," paper for urban sociology class, 1939, UOP Archives Record Group 7.2.J17, Students and Student Projects, Box 1 (A–J), Jacoby Papers, Special Collections, University of the Pacific Holt-Atherton Library.

46. Anita Bautista, "El Dorado Street: An Experience in Filipino American History," 1, FANHS.

47. Sylvia Sun Minnick, *Samfow: The San Joaquin Chinese Legacy* (Fresno, Calif.: Panorama West, 1988), 39.

48. "Japanese Quarters: Market Street the Future Home of the Japanese," *Stockton Independent*, March 15, 1907. See also Nelson Nagai, "The Death of Nihonmachi," *Nikkei Heritage* 12–13 (Fall 2000–Winter 2001): 10–11.

49. Rudy Guevarra Jr., "'Skid Row': Filipinos, Race and the Social Construction of Space in San Diego," *Journal of San Diego History* 54, no. 1 (2008): 27.

50. Fred Cordova interview by author.

51. Carlos Bulosan, *America Is in the Heart: A Personal History*, 2nd ed. (Seattle: University of Washington Press, 1973), 116.

52. Monrayo, *Tomorrow's Memories*, 153.

53. Bautista, "El Dorado Street," 1.

54. Fred Cordova interview by author.

55. Frank Perez, "This Is Stockton," *Philippine Examiner*, March 31, 1944.

56. Japanese American local history materials, The Haggin Museum, Stockton, Calif.

57. Stockton Japanese American Directory and Japanese American local history materials, The Haggin Museum, Stockton, Calif. See also Minnick, *Samfow*, 187–211.

58. D. L. Marcuelo, "Filipinos in San Joaquin Valley," *Three Stars*, September 1, 1928.

59. Tomas Espanola, World War I draft registration card, accessed at www.ancestry.com.

60. Polk city directory, 1927; 1930 U.S. Census, Stockton Township, Microfilm at NARA, San Bruno, Calif.

61. Pastor Engkabo, World War I draft registration card, 1917–1918; World War II draft registration card, accessed at www.ancestry.com.

62. Polk city directories, 1922–26.

63. 1930 U.S. Census.

64. Nelson Nagai interview by author.

65. Policarpo Porras interview by David Magdael, 1981, FOHP.

66. Polk city directories, 1920–35.

67. Polk city directories, 1926–42. See also Wood, Box 1, JEWP.

68. Quoted in Wood, Field Notes, Box 1, JEWP.

69. Advertisement for Japanese Restaurant, "Caters to Filipinos," *Philippine Advertiser,* February 28, 1928, 9. For the centrality of sinigang to Philippine cuisine, see Doreen G. Fernandez, *Tikim: Essays on Philippine Food and Culture* (Pasig City, Philippines: Anvil, 1994), 37.

70. Claro Candelario interview by author.

71. Gussie Gesulga Bowden, journals, journal writing project, circa 1985, NPA FANHS.

72. Flora Arca Mata interview by author; 1930 U.S. Census.

73. Peter Jamero, *Growing Up Brown: Memoirs of a Filipino American* (Seattle: University of Washington Press, 2006), 51.

74. Rizaline Monrayo Raymundo interview by author.

75. Jerry Paular interview by author.

76. Fred Cordova interview by author.

77. Jerry Paular interview by author.

78. Fred Cordova interview by Dominic Cordova, NPA FANHS.

79. Galedo, Cabanero, and Tom, "Roadblocks to Community Building," 7.

80. Pete Valoria interview by author.

81. Trinidad Rojo, "Rojo Offers Suggestions to Mr. Varona," *Philippines Mail,* January 23, 1939.

82. Jamero, *Growing Up Brown,* 51.

83. Fred Cordova interview by Dominic Cordova.

84. Jerry Paular interview by author.

85. Corky Pasquil, director, *The Great Pinoy Boxing Era* (San Francisco: Center for Asian American Media, 1994).

86. España-Maram, *Creating Masculinity in Los Angeles' Little Manila,* 83.

87. Cordova, *Filipinos,* 93; Pasquil, *The Great Pinoy Boxing Era*; España-Maram, *Creating Masculinity in Los Angeles' Little Manila,* 76.

88. España-Maram, *Creating Masculinity in Los Angeles' Little Manila,* 98.

89. My grandfather and I clashed over what to watch on television when I was a toddler: I wanted cartoons and *Sesame Street,* and he wanted boxing and football. My father was also a passionate boxing fan.

90. Peter Bacho, *Dark Blue Suit and Other Stories* (Seattle: University of Washington Press, 1997), 110.

91. Quoted in España-Maram, *Creating Masculinity in Los Angeles' Little Manila,* 101.

92. Bacho, *Dark Blue Suit and Other Stories,* 110.

93. See "Speedy Dado," on the boxing statistics website BoxRec, http://boxrec.com /list_bouts.php?human_id=9907&cat=boxer&pageID=2.

94. "Stockton Program to Feature Stars," *Three Stars,* December 25, 1932. See also "Chato Laredo," BoxRec, http://boxrec.com/list_bouts.php?human_id=41924&cat=boxer.

95. Pasquil, *The Great Pinoy Boxing Era.* See also "Ceferino Garcia," BoxRec, http:// boxrec.com/list_bouts.php?human_id=9601&cat=boxer.

96. Jerry Paular interview by author.

97. Program of the Filipino American historical reunion, "Pilgrimage of the American Born Filipino," October 1989, Filipino American Historical Institute, Stockton, Calif., author's personal collection.

98. Pasquil, *The Great Pinoy Boxing Era.*

99. "California Bars Filipino Boxers," *New York Times,* January 30, 1930.

100. "Editorial," *Stockton Daily Evening Record,* January 30, 1930.

101. España-Maram, *Creating Masculinity in Los Angeles' Little Manila*, 100.

102. "Dempsey Batters and Drops His Adversary to Canvas in 4th," *Three Stars*, April 1931.

103. Jamero, *Growing Up Brown*, 51.

104. Anita Navalta Bautista interview by author.

105. Anita Bautista, "The Chop Suey with the Mostest 1950's Style," *Stockton Chapter Newsletter*, Stockton Chapter, Filipino American National Historical Society 12 no. 2 (April 2006): 6. After its original building was torn down for the Crosstown Freeway, the restaurant moved to 146 South Sutter Street, where it remains today. For the history of chop suey and Chinese restaurants in urban enclaves in the West, see Andrew Coe, *Chop Suey: A Cultural History of Chinese Food in the United States* (Oxford: Oxford University Press, 2009); and Jennifer 8 Lee, *The Fortune Cookie Chronicles* (New York: Hachette, 2008).

106. Pasquil, *The Great Pinoy Boxing Era*.

107. Quoted in Wood, Field Notes, Box 2, JEWP.

108. Pete Valoria interview by author.

109. Policarpo Porras interview by Magdael.

110. Quoted in Wood, Field Notes, Box 2, JEWP.

111. P.C. Morantte, "A Writer Visits the Gambling Joints," *Filipino Pioneer*, May 16, 1938.

112. "Wild Race Riot Threatens Havoc in Chinatown," *Stockton Daily Evening Record*, January 4, 1924.

113. Bulosan, *America Is in the Heart*, 116–17.

114. Letter from Luis Agudo to James Earl Wood, September 1930, Box 1, JEWP.

115. McWilliams, *Brothers under the Skin*, 239.

116. Trinidad Rojo, "Report of the First Filipino Convention, Sacramento, California, 1938," Trinidad Rojo papers, NPA FANHS.

117. "Arresting Filipinos an Empty Gesture," *Three Stars*, June 15, 1930.

118. Policarpo Porras interview by Magdael.

119. Vicente Roldan, "Filipinos Contributed to Stockton's Well Being," 1937 Filipino Carnival souvenir program, 29.

120. Paul G. Cressey, *The Taxi-Dance Hall: A Sociological Study in Commercialized Recreation and City Life* (Chicago: University of Chicago Press, 1932).

121. Ibid.; Rhacel Salazar Parreñas, "'White Trash' Meets the 'Little Brown Monkeys': The Taxi Dance Hall as a Site of Interracial and Gender Relations between White Working Class Women and Filipino Immigrant Men in the 1920s and 1930s," *Amerasia* 24, no. 2 (1998): 115–34. See also España-Maram, *Creating Masculinity in Los Angeles' Little Manila*, 105–33.

122. Anita Bautista, "Sex and the Single Pinay," FANHS.

123. Modesto Lagura interview by author.

124. Parreñas, "'White Trash' Meets the 'Little Brown Monkeys.'"

125. España-Maram, *Creating Masculinity in Los Angeles' Little Manila*, 109.

126. Barbara M. Posadas and Roland L. Guyotte, "Unintentional Immigrants: Chicago's Filipino Foreign Students Become Settlers, 1900–1941," *Journal of American Ethnic History* 9, no. 2 (1990): 26–48. Paul Cressey noted that Filipinos used "going to class" as a euphemism for going to the dance halls; most Filipinas/os in Chicago were college students (*The Taxi-Dance Hall*, 34–35).

127. Quoted in Wood, Field Notes, Box 2, JEWP.

128. Quoted in ibid.

129. "Judge Smith's Los Angeles Ruling," *Stockton Daily Evening Record*, March 6, 1930.

130. Policarpo Porras interview by Magdael.

131. Cressey, *The Taxi-Dance Hall*, 43.

132. Quoted in Wood, Field Notes, Box 2, JEWP.

133. Carlos Bulosan, "The Romance of Magno Rubio," *Amerasia* 6, no. 1 (1979): 33–50. See also Carlos Bulosan Papers, Special Collections, University of Washington. Seattle, Wash.

134. "Dance Hall is Scene of Near-Riot; Filipino Boycott, Picketing Leads to Arrest of Pair," *Stockton Daily Evening Record*, July 8, 1937.

135. "Two Filipinos Knifed in Battle," *Stockton Daily Evening Record*, March 9, 1938.

136. Jimmy Ente interview by author.

137. *Stockton Daily Evening Record*, July 8, 1937; advertisement for the Rizal Social Club, 1937 Filipino Carnival souvenir program.

138. "Community Moves vs. Newly Opened 'Clubs,'" *Filipino Pioneer*, March 15, 1937.

139. Quoted in "Community Moves vs. Newly Opened 'Clubs,'" *Filipino Pioneer*, March 15, 1937.

140. Advertisement for the Rizal Social Club, 1937 Filipino Carnival souvenir program, 10.

141. Leslie Crow, Historic Site Survey Report for the Rizal Social Club, October 1, 2003, author's personal collection.

142. Ibid., *Stockton Daily Evening Record*, August 28, 1937.

143. Quoted in "Change of Judges for Dance Hall Hostesses Sought," *Stockton Daily Evening Record*, November 18, 1937.

144. "Demetrio M. Ente," Bohol Circle Souvenir Program, 1949, private collection of Caroline Bulawit Gray; Jimmy Ente interview by author. See also Polk city directories, 1937–40.

145. Photograph of the Rizal Social Club, 1938, Stockton Chapter, FANHS Photograph Archives.

146. Nelson Nagai interview by author.

147. Nelson Nagai interview by author.

148. Jimmy Ente interview by author.

149. Leatrice Bantillo Perez interview by author, June 2003.

150. Much more research needs to be done on same-sex relationships in Filipina/o American communities. This story about gay Pinoys in Little Manila was related to me by my father, who, in the 1960s, would drive one of his uncles to the Fox Theater, where he could meet other men.

151. Carol Hemminger, "Little Manila: The Filipino in Stockton Prior to World War II," master's thesis, San Joaquin Delta College, 1978, 26.

152. Fred Cordova interview by author.

153. Ibid.

154. Quoted in Wood, Field Notes, Box 2, JEWP.

155. Quoted in ibid.

156. Angelina Bantillo Magdael interview by author.

157. Duncan Aikman, "Filipino Sheiks Arouse Hatred in California," *Baltimore Sun*, January 30, 1930. See also "Filipino Laborers for U.S.," newspaper clipping, Box 1103, 26668, 1 to 7 to 26671-38 to 9, Part 1, RG 350, BIA, National Archives and Records Administration, College Park, Md.

158. Hemminger, "Little Manila," 26–30. Mae Ngai makes a similar argument (*Impossible Subjects*, 109).

159. Quoted in Wood, Field Notes, Box 2, JEWP.

160. Quoted in ibid.

161. "Race Riot at Exeter Ends," *Stockton Daily Evening Record*, October 26, 1929.

162. Donald E. Anthony, "Filipino Labor in Central California," *Sociology and Social Research* 16, no. 2 (1931): 156.

163. Leatrice Perez interview by author, December 2000.

164. Billy Carson and John Montgomery, "Philippino [*sic*] Problems," n.d., UOP Archives Record Group 7.2.J17, Students and Student Projects, Box 1 (A–J), Jacoby Papers, Special Collections, University of the Pacific Holt-Atherton Library.

165. Wallace Stegner and the editors of *Look*, *One Nation* (Boston: Houghton Mifflin, 1945), 43.

166. Policarpo Porras interview by Magdael.

167. Eudosia Juanitas interview by author.

168. Quoted in Galedo, Cabanero, and Tom, "Roadblocks to Community Building," 10.

169. Alma Alcala interview by author.

170. Buster Villa interview by author.

171. Nemesio Paguyo interview by Joan May T. Cordova, undated, FOHP.

172. Personal notes, Tony Somera, presentation for visiting college students at the Daguhoy Temple, Stockton, Calif., March 22, 2009.

173. Jorge Bacobo, "Freedom Drive Futile If Disgrace Continues," *Philippine Herald*, July 17, 1930. See also "Filipino Laborers for U.S."

174. Quoted in "Filipinos Held to Blame for Plight Abroad," *Wheeling News-Register*, September 2, 1938. See also Francisco Varona file, Box 665 Entry 21, Personal Name Information File, 1914–1945, RG 350, BIA, National Archives and Records Administration, College Park, Md.

175. See Howard DeWitt, *Anti-Filipino Movements in California: A History, Bibliography, and Study Guide* (San Francisco: R and E Research Associates, 1976).

176. Matthew Fry Jacobsen, *Whiteness of a Different Color: European Immigrants and the Alchemy of Race* (Cambridge: Harvard University Press, 1998). See also James A. Tyner, "The Geopolitics of Eugenics and the Exclusion of Philippine Immigrants from the United States," *Geographical Review* 89, no. 1 (1999), 54–73.

177. Quoted in Tyner, "The Geopolitics of Eugenics and the Exclusion of Philippine Immigrants from the United States," 66.

178. David Barrow, "The Desirability of the Filipino," in The Commonwealth Club, *Transactions of the Commonwealth Club of California* 24, no. 7 (November 5, 1929): 321–23.

179. C. M. Goethe, "Filipino Immigration Viewed As a Peril," *Current History*, June 1931, 129–30. See also Alexandra Minna Stern, *Eugenic Nation: Faults and Frontiers of Better Breeding in Modern America* (Berkeley: University of California Press, 2005), 134–35.

180. Paul A. Kramer, *The Blood of Government: Race, Empire, the United States, and the Philippines* (Chapel Hill: University of North Carolina Press, 2006), 424.

181. Record of Primitivo Gonzales, RG 85, Series ACF, Box 3271, Folder 34028/16-5, Records of the Immigration and Naturalization Service, National Archives and Records Administration, San Bruno, Calif.

182. See the files of the Filipinas/os who landed on Angel Island in May 1934, RG 85, Series ACF, Box 3271.

183. Letter to Mr. Modesto Pascua from W. W. Brown, May 2, 1935. RG 85, accession number 58A734, File 55874, Box 697, Folder 464A, Records of the Immigration and Naturalization Service, National Archives and Records Administration, Washington, D.C.

184. At the same time, the INS, in collusion with local officials, was deporting ethnic

Mexicans. See George Sanchez, *Becoming Mexican American: Ethnicity, Culture and Identity in Chicano Los Angeles, 1900–1945* (New York: Oxford University Press, 1993), 209–26; and Ngai, *Impossible Subjects*, 120.

185. See press releases and telegrams to local field offices and newspapers from the INS, RG 85, accession number 58A734, File 55874, Box 697, Folders 464A-D, Records of the Immigration and Naturalization Service, National Archives and Records Administration, Washington, D.C. See also Casiano Pagdilao Coloma, "A Study of the Filipino Repatriation Movement," master's thesis, University of Southern California, 1939.

186. Radio address of Edward H. Cahill, August 19, 1935, KQW, San Jose, Calif., RG 85, accession number 58A734, File 55874, Box 697, Folder 464A, Records of the Immigration and Naturalization Service, National Archives and Records Administration, Washington, D.C.

187. Letter from Edward Cahill to William MacCormack, August 25, 1935, RG 85, accession number 58A734, File 55874, Box 697, Folder 464A, Records of the Immigration and Naturalization Service, National Archives and Records Administration, Washington, D.C.

188. Emory Bogardus, "Filipino Repatriation," *Sociology and Social Research* 21, no. 1 (1936): 70.

189. "We're Like Prisoners, Repatriate [*sic*] Protest," *Filipino Pioneer*, March 15 and March 27, 1937.

190. See the correspondence between Resident Commissioner Quintin Paredes and Deputy Commissioner of the Field Service of the INS, and between the San Francisco and Washington offices of the INS, RG 85, File 88674, Files 464 and 464A-C, Records of the Immigration and Naturalization Service, National Archives and Records Administration, Washington, D.C.

191. Carey McWilliams, "Exit the Filipino," *Nation*, September 4, 1935, 265.

192. Steffi San Buenaventura, "Filipino Immigration to the United States," in *Asian American Encyclopedia*, ed. Franklin Ng (New York: Marshall Cavendish, 1995), 445–46. McWilliams writes that 2,190 Filipinas/os took the offer (*Brothers under the Skin*, 244).

193. George Montero interview by Joan May T. Cordova, 1981, FOHP.

CHAPTER 4. WOMEN AND THE SECOND GENERATION

1. Camila Carido's father's given name was Manuel. She joked that he did not want to be called "Manuel Labor" and changed his name to "Epifiano." Camila Carido interview with author, January 15, 1996.

2. Ibid.

3. Ibid.

4. Dorothy Cordova, "Voices from the Past: Why They Came," in *Making Waves: An Anthology of Writings by and about Asian American Women*, ed. Asian Women United of California (Boston: Beacon, 1989), 42.

5. Visayan family preponderance in Hawai'i is discussed by Jonathan Okamura in "Filipino American History in Hawai'i: A Young Visayan Woman's Perspective," in Angeles Monrayo, *Tomorrow's Memories: A Diary, 1924–1928*, ed. Rizaline Raymundo (Honolulu: University of Hawai'i Press, 2003), 230. Jerry Paular also maintains that most, if not all, of the early families in Stockton came from Hawai'i and were Visayan. Jerry Paular interview with author.

6. 1930 U.S. Census, National Archives and Records Administration, San Bruno, Calif.

7. Louis Bloch, *Facts about Filipino Immigration into California* (San Francisco: State of California, Department of Industrial Relations, April 1930), 32.

8. Numerous scholars in Asian American studies comment on the effects of the sex ratio imbalance in the early experiences of Asian American communities. See Yen Le Espiritu, *Asian American Women and Men: Labor, Laws and Love* (Thousand Oaks, Calif.: Sage, 1997); Judy Yung, *Unbound Feet: A Social History of Chinese Women in San Francisco* (Berkeley: University of California Press, 1995); Asian Women United of California, eds., *Making Waves: An Anthology of Writings by and about Asian American Women* (Boston: Beacon, 1989); Evelyn Nakano Glenn, *Issei, Nisei, War Bride: Three Generations of Japanese American Women in Domestic Service* (Philadelphia: Temple University Press, 1986); and George Anthony Pfeffer, *If They Don't Bring Their Women Here: Chinese Female Immigration before Exclusion* (Urbana: University of Illinois Press, 1999).

9. Fred Cordova, *Filipinos: Forgotten Asian Americans, A Pictorial Essay; 1763–Circa 1963* (Dubuque, Iowa: Kendall/Hunt, 1983), 153.

10. Toribio B. Castillo, "The Changing Social Status of Filipino Women during the American Administration" (master's thesis, University of Southern California, 1942), 49.

11. Ofelia Regala Angangco, Laura L. Samson, and Teresita Albino, *Status of Women in the Philippines: A Bibliography with Selected Annotations* (Quezon City: Alemar-Phoenix, 1980), xviii.

12. Cited in Catherine Ceniza Choy, *Empire of Care: Nursing and Migration in Filipino American History* (Durham: Duke University Press), 36–38.

13. Fe Mangahas, "From Babaylans to Suffragettes: The Status of Filipino Women from Pre-Colonial Times to the American Period," in *Kamalayan: Feminist Writings in the Philippines*, ed. Pennie S. Azarcon (Quezon City, Philippines, 1987), 11. See also Elizabeth Uy Eviota, *The Political Economy of Gender: Women and the Sexual Division of Labour in the Philippines* (London: Zed, 1992).

14. Mangahas, "From Babaylans to Suffragettes," 14.

15. Sara M. Evans, *Born for Liberty: A History of Women in America* (New York: Free Press, 1989), 147–52.

16. Mangahas, "From Babaylans to Suffragettes," 18. See also Catherine Ceniza Choy's pathbreaking study of nursing in Filipina/o American history *Empire of Care*.

17. Castillo, "The Changing Social Status of Filipino Women during the American Administration," 45.

18. Quoted in Eviota, *The Political Economy of Gender*, 73.

19. Belen T. G. Medina, *The Filipino Family: A Text with Selected Readings* (Manila: University of the Philippines Press, 1991), 65–67.

20. Angelina Bantillo Magdael interview by Cheryl Magdael, 1981.

21. Benicio T. Catapusan, "Filipino Social Adjustment in the United States," PhD dissertation, University of Southern California (June 1940), 78. See also Benicio T. Catapusan, "Filipino Intermarriage Problems in the United States," *Sociology and Social Research* 22, no. 3 (January 1938): 265–72.

22. Anita Bautista interview by author.

23. Nellie Foster, "Legal Status of Filipino Intermarriages in California," *Sociology and Social Research* 16, no. 5 (1932): 441–54; Henry Empeno, "Anti-Miscegenation Laws and the Pilipino," in *Letters in Exile: An Introductory Reader on the History of the Pilipinos in America*, ed. Jesse G. Quinsaat (Los Angeles: UCLA Asian American Studies Center, 1976), 63–71; Leti Volpp, "American Mestizo: Filipinos and Anti-Miscegenation Laws in California," in *Mixed Race America and the Law: A Reader*, ed. Kevin R. Johnson (New York: New York University Press, 2003). See also Allison Varzally, *Making a Non-White America: Californians Coloring outside Ethnic Lines, 1925–1955* (Berkeley: University of California Press, 2008).

24. George Montero interview by Joan May T. Cordova, 1981, FOHP.

25. Claro Candelario interview by author.

26. James Earl Wood, Field Notes, Folder 2, JEWP. See also Arleen de Vera, "The Tapia-Saiki Incident: Interethnic Conflict and Filipino Responses to the Anti-Filipino Exclusion Movement," in *Over the Edge: Remapping the American West*, ed. Valerie J. Matsumoto and Blake Allmendinger (Berkeley: University of California Press, 1999), 201–14.

27. Varzally, *Making a Non-White America*, 95.

28. Camila Carido interview by author, January 15, 1996.

29. George Montero interview by Cordova.

30. Quoted in Wood, Box 2, Folder 5, JEWP.

31. Asuncion Guevarra Nicolas interview by author.

32. Hellen Rillera, "The Filipina in Filipino Society," *Philippines Mail*, 1934, reprinted at www.commonwealthcafe.info/editorials-and-essays/.

33. Paula Dizon Daclan interview by author.

34. Okamura, "Filipino American History in Hawai'i," 234.

35. See ibid., 234–35. See also "In the Grand Old Days They Stole Wives Not Money: The Story of Kauai's Grand Old Lady Mrs. Joséfina Cortezan," in *Filipinos in Hawai'i: The First 75 Years 1906–1981*, ed. Juan C. Dionisio (Honolulu: Filipino News Specialty Publications, 1981), 100; Patria P. Ramos, "Filipino Women in Hawai'i: What We Were, Where We Are Now," in Nieva, *Filipina Hawai'i*, 24–25.

36. Alberta Alcoy Asis interview, NPA FANHS.

37. Angeles Monrayo, *Tomorrow's Memories: A Diary* (Honolulu: University of Hawai'i Press, 2003), 72–73.

38. Asuncion Nicolas interview by author.

39. Eudosia Bravo Juanitas interview by author; Maria "Terri" Torres, "Juanitas Family Partial History Booklet," compiled for the Juanitas Reunion, 2002, personal collection of the author.

40. Eudosia Juanitas interview by author.

41. Concepcion Bulawit Lagura interview by author.

42. Rillera, "The Filipina in Filipino Society."

43. Trinidad Rojo, "Social Maladjustment among Filipinos in the United States," *Sociology and Social Research* 21, no. 5 (1937): 447.

44. Camila Carido interview by author, January 15, 1996.

45. See Valerie J. Matsumoto, "Redefining Expectations: Nisei Women in the 1930s," *California History*, Spring 1994, 45–53.

46. Aunt Dearie, "In the Valley of the Moonstruck," *Philippines Mail*, September 11, 1933.

47. Rillera, "The Filipina in Filipino Society."

48. "The Most Gruesome Murder Staged in Rodeo City," *Three Stars* (Stockton, Calif.), June 1929.

49. "Filipino Schoolgirl Slain by Enraged Lover," *Three Stars*, November 15, 1929.

50. Anita Bautista, "Sex and the Single Pinay," unpublished essay, FANHS. See also Anita Bautista, "Love in the Time of Taxi Dancers," *Filipinas*, October 2007, 43–44.

51. Alex S. Fabros Jr. and Katherine S. Fabros, "Jersey Island Murder Case," *Filipinas*, October 1997, 66–69.

52. "Pair Planned to Flee to Escape Cult's Wrath," *Stockton Daily Evening Record*, April 3, 1933; Fabros and Fabros, "Jersey Island Murder Case," 67.

53. "Dead Filipino Woman Feared Lodge Members," *Stockton Daily Evening Record*, April 8, 1933; Fabros and Fabros, "Jersey Island Murder Case," 67.

54. Fabros and Fabros, "Jersey Island Murder Case," 68.

55. "Witnesses Relate Inside Facts about Burial," *Philippines Mail*, April 10, 1933.

56. "Not Guilty Pleas Entered by Seven in Navarro Case," *Philippines Mail*, May 15, 1933.

57. "Trial of Mrs. Novarro's Slayers Put Over," *Philippines Mail*, June 26, 1933.

58. "Dead Filipino Woman Feared Lodge Members."

59. Newspaper reports from April to July 1933 in the *Stockton Daily Evening Record* and the *Philippines Mail* provide detailed discussions.

60. "Unfaithful Wife Buried Alive," *Stockton Daily Evening Record*, April 3, 1933.

61. "Seven Filipinos Are Indicted on Murder Charge," *Stockton Daily Evening Record*, April 4, 1933.

62. "Causes and Circumstances of Crimes," *Philippines Mail*, April 10, 1933.

63. "No Fanatical 'Cults' among Filipinos, Reports Branded Untrue," *Philippines Mail*, April 10, 1933.

64. Quoted in "Stockton in Protest over 'Color' News," *Philippines Mail*, April 10, 1933. See also "Filipino Colony Voices Protest," *Stockton Daily Evening Record*, April 7, 1933.

65. Fabros and Fabros, "Jersey Island Murder Case," 68.

66. Quoted in "Attorneys for Defense Said Planning Numerous Surprises at Resumption of Martinez Living Burial Case Tuesday," *Philippines Mail*, July 24, 1933.

67. "Filipinos Are Acquitted of Living Burial," *Philippines Mail*, August 14, 1933.

68. *Philippines Mail*, November 27, 1933.

69. F. Cordova, *Filipinos*, 147.

70. Camila Carido interview by author, February 19, 1996.

71. Elizabeth Uy Eviota, *The Political Economy of Gender: Women and the Sexual Division of Labour in the Philippines* (London: Zed, 1992), 152.

72. Glenn, *Issei, Nisei, War Bride*, 192. See also Mina Davis Caulfield, "Imperialism, the Family and the Cultures of Resistance," *Socialist Revolution* 20 (October 1974): 67–85.

73. Eudosia Juanitas interview by author.

74. Micaela di Leonardo, *The Varieties of Ethnic Experience: Kinship, Class and Gender Among California's Italian Americans* (Ithaca: Cornell University Press, 1984), 191–229.

75. Camila Carido interview by author, January 15, 1996.

76. Angelina Bantillo Magdael, journals, NPA FANHS.

77. On *compadrazgo*, see Rosalinda Gonzáles, "Chicanas and Mexican Immigrant Families, 1920–1940: Women's Subordination and Exploitation," in *Decades of Discontent, 1920–1940*, ed. Lois Scharf and Joan M. Jenson (Westport, Conn.: Greenwood Press, 1983), 75–76. See also Bonnie Thornton Dill, "Fictive Kin, Paper Sons and Compadrazgo: Women of Color and the Struggle for Family Survival," in *Women of Color in U.S. Society*, ed. Maxine Baca Zinn and Bonnie Thornton Dill (Philadelphia: Temple University Press, 1994), 149–70.

78. F. Cordova, *Filipinos*, 133.

79. 1930 U.S. Census, Table 14, "Filipino Gainful Workers 10 Years Old and Over, by Occupation, by Age and Sex." See also Wood, Field Notes, Box 2, JEWP.

80. Louise A. Tilly and Joan Wallach Scott, *Women, Work, and Family* (New York: Routledge, 1987), 104. See also Glenn, *Issei, Nisei, War Bride*, 207–8; and Valerie J. Matsumoto, *Farming the Home Place: A Japanese American Community, 1919–1982* (Ithaca: Cornell University Press, 1993).

81. F. Cordova, *Filipinos*, 152.

82. Eudosia Juanitas interview by author.

83. Asuncion Nicolas interview by author.

84. Flora Arca Mata interview by author and Joan May T. Cordova, May 24, 2002, Stockton, Calif.

85. Angelina Bantillo Magdael interview by author, November 1999.

86. Paula Daclan interview by author.

87. Camila Carido interview by author, January 15, 1996.

88. Glenn, *Issei, Nisei, War Bride*, 207–8; Matsumoto, *Farming the Home Place*.

89. Angel Bantillo Magdael interview by Cheryl Magdael, FANHS.

90. Leatrice Bantillo Perez interview by author, November 1999.

91. Angelina Magdael interview by author, November 1999.

92. Mary Arca Inosanto, journals, 1985, NPA FANHS.

93. Eleanor Galvez Olamit interview by author.

94. Camila Carido interview by author, February 19, 1996.

95. Segunda Reyes, Stockton, Calif., 1980, FOHP.

96. Segunda Reyes interview by author.

97. Angel Magdael interview, 1980, FOHP.

98. F. Cordova, *Filipinos*, 148.

99. Asuncion Nicolas interview by author.

100. Virgilia Marello Bantillo, diaries, Bantillo family personal papers, Stockton, Calif.

101. Leatrice Bantillo Perez interview by author, November 1999.

102. Bantillo diaries.

103. F. Cordova, *Filipinos*, 109.

104. Quoted in ibid. See also Catherine Bilar Autentico oral history, NPA FANHS.

105. Camila Carido interview by author.

106. Paula Daclan interview by author.

107. Di Leonardo, *The Varieties of Ethnic Experience*, 191–229.

108. Mary Inosanto, journals, 1985, NPA FANHS.

109. Camila Carido interview by author, January 15, 1996.

110. Eleanor Olamit interview by author.

111. Legionarios del Trabajo Blue Book, 1940, author's personal collection.

112. Camila Carido interview by author, January 15, 1996.

113. Ibid.

114. Bantillo diaries.

115. *The Philippine Yearbook, 1941*, ed. Simeon Doria Arroyo (*Philippine Record*, 1941), 10, author's personal collection.

116. George Sanchez, *Becoming Mexican American: Ethnicity, Culture and Identity in Chicano Los Angeles, 1900–1945* (New York: Oxford University Press, 1993, 149.

117. Camila Carido interview by author, February 19, 1996.

118. 1937 Filipino Carnival souvenir program, Angelina Bantillo Magdael family collection, 10.

119. Susan Kalcik, "Ethnic Foodways in America: Symbol and Performance," in *Ethnic and Regional Foodways in the United States: The Performance of Group Identity*, ed. Linda Brown and Kay Mussel (Knoxville: University of Tennessee Press, 1984), 38.

120. Bantillo diaries.

121. Eleanor Olamit interview by author.

122. Asuncion Nicolas interview by author.

123. Camila Carido interview by author.

124. Deanna Daclan Balantac interview by author.

125. Angelina Bantillo Magdael interview by Cheryl Magdael, 1981, FOHP.

126. F. Cordova, *Filipinos*, 157. Only Mexico has sent more immigrants than the Philippines to the United States since immigration laws were changed in the 1965 Immigration Act.

127. Ibid., 165.

128. Joseph F. Kett, *Rites of Passage: Adolescence in America, 1790 to the Present* (New York: Basic, 1977); and Grace Palladino, *Teenagers* (New York: Basic, 1996).

129. See Shirley Jennifer Lim, *A Feeling of Belonging: Asian American Women's Public Culture: 1930–1960* (New York: New York University Press, 2005); Matsumoto, *Farming the Home Place*, and her "Desperately Seeking Deirdre: Gender Roles, Multicultural Relations, and Nisei Women Writers of the 1930s," *Frontiers: A Journal of Women Studies* 12, no. 1 (1991), 19–32; Matsumoto, "Redefining Expectations" and "Japanese American Women and the Creation of Urban Nisei Culture in the 1930s," in *Over the Edge: Remapping the American West*, ed. Valerie Matsumoto and Blake Allmendinger (Berkeley: University of California Press, 1999), 291–306; Vicki L. Ruiz, *From Out of the Shadows: Mexican American Women in Twentieth Century America* (New York: Oxford University Press, 1998); Sanchez, *Becoming Mexican American*; and Yung, *Unbound Feet*.

130. Ruiz, *From Out of the Shadows*, 50.

131. Matsumoto, "Japanese American Women and the Creation of Urban Nisei Culture in the 1930s."

132. Toribio "Terry" Rosal interview with author, February 18, 1996, Stockton, Calif.

133. Celestino Alfafara, "The Ideal Pinay," *Three Stars*, November 15, 1929.

134. "Ma! The Ladies Are Here Again!" *Philippine Yearbook*, 1941, 1.

135. Mina Roces, "Gender, Nation, and the Politics of Dress in Twentieth Century Philippines," in *The Politics of Dress in Asia and the Americas*, ed. Louise Edwards and Mina Roces (Portland, Ore.: Sussex Academic Press, 2010), 19–41.

136. Flora Mata, journals, 1985, NPA FANHS. See also Roces's descriptions of the terno ("Gender, Nation, and the Politics of Dress in Twentieth Century Philippines," 24).

137. F. G. Lomongo, *Philippines Song Review*, 1943 (Salinas, Calif.), Angelina Bantillo Magdael family collection.

138. Terri Jamero, journals, 1985, NPA FANHS.

139. Leatrice Perez interview by author, November 1999.

140. Mary Inosanto, journals.

141. Flora Mata, journals.

142. Roces, "Gender, Nation, and the Politics of Dress in Twentieth Century Philippines," 28.

143. "Flora Enero of Vallejo Gains Popularity in Contest," *Filipino Pioneer*, August 5, 1938.

144. Flora Mata, journals.

145. Terri Jamero, journals.

146. "A Worthy Project," *Filipino Pioneer*, March 14, 1938.

147. Angelina Magdael and Leatrice Perez interviews by author, November 1999.

148. Eno Godinez, "For Men Only: But the Ladies May Read It Too," *Filipino Pioneer*, July 1, 1938.

149. "Flyers to Hold Big Air Show" and "First Filipino Art Exhibit a Success," *Filipino Pioneer*, July 1, 1938.

150. Lomongo, *Philippines Song Review*, 1943.

151. "Two Stockton Girls Volunteer in Defense," *Philippines Mail*, March 10, 1942.

152. Leatrice Perez interview by author, November 1999. See also Frank Perez and

Leatrice Bantillo Perez, "Filipinos in San Joaquin County," in "The Long Struggle for Acceptance: Filipinos in San Joaquin County," edited by Frank Perez and Leatrice Bantillo Perez, special issue, *San Joaquin Historian* 8, no. 4 (1994): 16.

153. See the "Miss Spotter" and "Society Notes" columns in the *Philippines Mail*, from 1943 to 1944.

154. "Open Letter to Stockton," *Philippines Star-Press*, May 18, 1946.

155. Quoted in *Philippine Examiner*, September 30, 1944.

156. "Stockton News Briefs," *Philippines Mail*, July 31, 1944.

157. In a conversation with me about the Filipino Youth Association, Leatrice Bantillo Perez told me that Bob Asis was one of its first presidents. Leatrice Bantillo Perez, conversation with the author, Stockton, Calif., October 30, 2010. See also the obituary of Sabas "Bob" Alcoy Asis at http://bonneywatson.com/obituaries/detail.html?id=1781, accessed November 5, 2012.

158. Terri Jamero, "Welcome," souvenir program, Grand Reunion of Filipino American Athletic Youth Clubs, 1940s–1970s, November 1, 1991, San Ramon Marriott, San Ramon, Calif., 1. Author's personal collection.

159. Ibid.

160. "The LVM Girls Club, Isleton, Calif.," ibid., 29.

161. Leatrice Bantillo Perez interview by author, November 1999.

162. See Palladino, *Teenagers*, 82.

163. Alex L. Fabros, "Thorns and Roses," *Philippines Mail*, September 30, 1941.

164. "The Buzzing Bee: Stockton Sagas," *Philippine Star-Press*, January 11, 1947.

165. Ibid.

166. Palladino, *Teenagers*, 7–8.

167. See Matsumoto, "Japanese American Women and Nisei Culture," 296.

168. Ruiz, *From Out of the Shadows*, 52.

169. Angelina Magdael interview by Cheryl Magdael.

170. Angelina Magdael interview by author, November 1999.

171. Bautista, "Sex and the Single Pinay."

172. Ibid.

173. Phyllis Cano Ente interview by author.

174. Ruiz, *From Out of the Shadows*, 60–61.

175. Susanna Caballero Mangrobang interview by author.

176. Jerry Paular interview by author.

177. Monrayo, *Tomorrow's Memories*, 179.

178. "Roseville Beauty Marries in Reno," *Philippines Mail*, May 31, 1942.

179. "Inspiration," *Philippines Mail*, August 30, 1939.

180. Eleanor Olamit interview by author.

181. Angelina Magdael and Leatrice Perez interviews by author, November 1999.

182. Jamero, "Welcome."

183. Quoted in Emily Porcincula Lawsin, "Beyond 'Hanggang Pier Only': Filipina War Brides of Seattle," *FANHS Journal* 4 (1996): 50D.

184. My own father, Ernesto T. Mabalon, was twenty-five years older than my mother, Christine Bohulano.

185. Godinez, "For Men Only."

186. "The Ideal Filipino Girl," *Philippines Mail*, June 1952.

187. Thomas C. Cabe, "Filipino Girls in US vs. Filipino Girls in the Philippine Islands, *Philippines Star-Press*, March 31, 1945.

188. Ibid.

189. Vince Reyes, "The War Brides," *Filipinas*, October 1995, 22–24.

190. Quoted in Manuel Buaken, *I Have Lived with the American People* (Caldwell, Idaho: Caxton, 1948), 132.

191. *Philippine Yearbook, 1941.*

CHAPTER 5. SEARCHING FOR SPIRITUAL SUSTENANCE

1. Flora Arca Mata interview by author, May 24, 2002, Stockton, Calif.

2. In her article on Italian American Catholics in Providence, Rhode Island, the historian Evelyn Savidge Sterne reminds historians to recognize that the church played dual roles in the lives of working-class people. Scholars often separate religion and the church in their analyses, with religion as a set of beliefs and the church as an institution. However, Sterne argues that the two must be considered together: Catholics relied on the church as a source of spiritual sustenance and moral activism; and the church provided a gathering space in which these ideas could inspire moral activism within the ethnic community. See Sterne, "Religion in Working-Class History," *Social Science History*, 24, no. 1 (2000): 149–82.

3. Fred Cordova, *Filipinos: Forgotten Asian Americans: A Pictorial Essay, 1763–Circa 1963* (Dubuque, Iowa: Kendall Hunt, 1983).

4. Steffi San Buenaventura, "Filipino Religion at Home and Abroad: Historical Roots and Immigrant Transformations," in *Religions in Asian America: Building Faith Communities*, ed. Pyong Gap Min and Jung Ha Kim (Walnut Creek, Calif.: Altamira, 2002), 143–84. Several studies by pensionados focus on the religious practices of early immigrants. See Severino Corpus, "An Analysis of Racial Adjustment Activities and Problems of the Filipino-American Christian Fellowship in Los Angeles," master's thesis, University of Southern California, 1938; and Mario Paguia Ave, "Characteristics of Filipino Social Organizations in Los Angeles," master's thesis, University of Southern California, 1956. Ave discusses important organizations in Los Angeles, including regional and hometown associations and the ritualistic lodges. For a discussion of Filipina/o Protestants and the role of religion in early Filipina/o American communities on the West Coast, see F. Cordova, *Filipinos*. A useful essay on early Filipina/o American religious practices in Stockton is Steffi San Buenaventura, "Filipino Folk Spirituality and Immigration: From Mutual Aid to Religion," *Amerasia* 22, no. 1 (1996): 1–30. San Buenaventura examines the powerful Filipino Federation of America, a fraternal lodge with chapters nationwide that functioned simultaneously as a mutual aid organization and religious group.

5. San Buenaventura, "Filipino Religion at Home and Abroad," 143.

6. Ibid. See also Kenton J. Clymer, *Protestant Missionaries in the Philippines: An Inquiry into the American Colonial Mentality* (Urbana: University of Illinois Press, 1986), 4; Peter G. Gowing, *Islands under the Cross: The Story of the Church in the Philippines* (Manila: National Council of Churches in the Philippines, 1967), 53; and John Leddy Phelan, *The Hispanization of the Philippines: Spanish Aims and Filipino Responses, 1565–1700* (Madison: University of Wisconsin Press, 1967), 72–89.

7. San Buenaventura, "Filipino Religion at Home and Abroad," 146. San Buenaventura cites the Philippine historian William Henry Scott, who writes that large areas of the Philippines had yet to be Christianized in the late nineteenth century, though official documents of the Spanish regime argued otherwise. See William Henry Scott, *Cracks in the Parchment Curtain and Other Essays in Philippine History* (Quezon City: New Day, 1982), 1, 18.

8. San Buenaventura, "Filipino Religion at Home and Abroad," 154–55.

9. Clymer. *Protestant Missionaries in the Philippines*, 4.

10. Laura Prieto, "Stepmother America: The Woman's Board of Missions in the Philippines, 1902–1930," in *Competing Kingdoms: Women, Mission, Nation and the American Protestant Empire, 1812–1960*, ed. Barbara Reeves-Ellington, Kathryn Kish Sklar, and Connie A. Shemo (Durham, N.C.: Duke University Press), 343.

11. General James Rusling, "Interview with President William McKinley," *Christian Advocate*, January 22, 1903.

12. Quoted in Stuart Creighton Miller, *Benevolent Assimilation: The American Conquest of the Philippines, 1899–1903* (New Haven: Yale University Press, 1982), 18–19 and 248–49.

13. Prieto, "Stepmother America," 349.

14. Quoted in Miller, *Benevolent Assimilation*, 248.

15. Quoted in ibid., 249.

16. Ibid., 5.

17. Prieto, "Stepmother America," 342.

18. Quoted in Miller, *Benevolent Assimilation*, 19.

19. Sebastian N. Inosanto, *The Story of Trinity Presbyterian Church*, rev. ed. (Stockton, Calif: Trinity Presbyterian Church, 1992), 3.

20. Rodney Reno Jr., "Old Timers of Little Manila: An Interview with Rev. Constantino Arpon," in souvenir program, Celebration of the Fourth Anniversary of the Philippine Commonwealth, Los Angeles, personal collection of Stanley B. Garibay.

21. The missionary Allan Hunter writes that missionaries would identify newly arrived Filipinas/os arriving in San Francisco and would direct them to a Filipino Christian mission at the University of California, Berkeley. See Hunter, *Out of the Far East* (1934, reprinted San Francisco: R and E Research Associates, 1972), 10.

22. See Vicki L. Ruiz, *From Out of the Shadows: Mexican Women in Twentieth-Century America* (New York: Oxford University Press), 1998, chap. 2. See also George Sanchez, "Go after the Women: Americanization and the Mexican Immigrant Woman, 1915–1929," in *Unequal Sisters: A Multi-Cultural Reader in U.S. Woman's History*, ed. Vicki Ruiz and Ellen Carol DuBois, 2nd ed. (New York: Routledge, 1994), 250–63.

23. See Hunter, *Out of the Far East*. Peggy Pascoe's *Relations of Rescue: The Search for Female Moral Authority in the American West, 1874–1939* (New York: Oxford University Press, 1990) describes Donaldina Cameron's missionary work. Judy Yung discusses the impact of the YMCA and Protestant Christianity on Chinese women throughout *Unbound Feet: A Social History of Chinese Women in San Francisco* (Berkeley: University of California Press, 1995). Pascoe's and Yung's discussions of Donaldina Cameron's Presbyterian Mission Home point to the ways that Americanization and missionary efforts coincided.

24. S. Inosanto, *The Story of Trinity Presbyterian Church*, 19.

25. George Tinkham, "Henry Christian Petersen, M.D.," in *History of San Joaquin County, California* (Los Angeles: Historic Record Company, 1923), 1247; and birth certificate of Albert Liwanag, personal papers of Helen Liwanag, Stockton, Calif.

26. S. Inosanto, *The Story of Trinity Presbyterian Church*, 8.

27. Ibid., 6.

28. Clifford Merril Drury, *Ninety Years of History: First Presbyterian Church*, March 17, 1940, LHC; S. Inosanto, *The Story of Trinity Presbyterian Church*, 8.

29. Photographs of Zambra's fellowship meetings are featured in F. Cordova, *Filipinos*, 166–70.

30. S. Inosanto, *The Story of Trinity Presbyterian Church*, 9.

31. Myrtle O. Agatep, *A Glimpse of Our Heritage* (N.p.: Filipino Assemblies of the First Born, 1992).

32. Ibid.

33. "Reflections on the Ordinary That Became Unusual," in Agatep, *A Glimpse of Our Heritage*, 50.

34. Hunter, *Out of the Far East*, 15.

35. Pascoe's *Relations of Rescue* is a fascinating history of unequal power relations between women in minority groups and white women missionaries in the West.

36. Hunter, *Out of the Far East*, 93.

37. Pete Valoria interview by author.

38. "Reading Room of Filipinos Is Dedicated," *Stockton Independent*, October 27, 1926.

39. Flora Mata interview by author, 14 May 2002, Stockton, Calif.

40. Ibid.

41. Moreno Balantac and Deanna Daclan Balantac interview by author.

42. S. Inosanto, *The Story of Trinity Presbyterian Church*, 7.

43. Virgilia Marello Bantillo, diaries, Bantillo family collection, Stockton, Calif.

44. Flora Mata interview by author.

45. Jeff Burns, "The Mexican Catholic Community in California," in *Mexican Americans and the Catholic Church*, ed. Jay P. Dolan and Gilberto M. Hinojosa (Notre Dame, Ind.: University of Notre Dame Press, 1994), 130.

46. Catholic Filipino Club file, AASF.

47. Letter from Dr. H. F. Van Trump to Archbishop Edward J. Hanna, August 16, 1922, Catholic Filipino Club file, AASF.

48. Quoted in F. Cordova, *Filipinos*, 171.

49. Letter from Monsignor James P. Cantwell to Jas W. Doherty, Realtor, May 21, 1928, Catholic Filipino Club file, AASF. However, the club continued to operate at the building until at least until 1935 (letter from Father Edward B. Lenane to Most Reverend John J. Mitty, April 12, 1935, Catholic Filipino Club file, AASF).

50. Chester Gillis, *Roman Catholicism in America* (New York: Columbia University Press, 1999), 60–61.

51. St. Mary's Church, Landmark Designation file, Cultural Heritage Board, LHC.

52. St. Mary's of the Assumption Church, "St. Mary's Church" souvenir program, 150th anniversary, Stockton, Calif., author's personal collection.

53. Robert Glody, *A Shepherd of the Far North: The Story of William Francis Walsh (1900–1930)* (San Francisco: Harr Wagner, n.d.), 71.

54. Letter from the Right Reverend Monsignor W. E. McGough to Reverend William J. Flanagan, January 28, 1942, "Filipinos," AASF.

55. Glody, *A Shepherd of the Far North*, 71.

56. Correspondence between priests at St. Mary's Church and the archdiocese of San Francisco concerning Filipinas/os dates from the early 1930s to the 1950s. See the Filipinos file, AASF.

57. Correspondence between Archbishop John J. Mitty and local Catholic clergy regarding the problems of Filipinos and church attendance date from 1922 to the 1950s. See the Catholic Filipino Club file and Filipinos file, AASF.

58. Gillis, *Roman Catholicism in America*, 81.

59. Burns, "The Mexican Catholic Community in California," 133.

60. Ibid., 207–8.

61. Letter from John J. Mitty, Archbishop of San Francisco, to the Honorable Richard Welch, United States Congressman, March 23, 1935; Catholic Filipino Club file, AASF.

62. Letter from Richard Welch to the Right Reverend John J. Mitty, D.D., April 1, 1935, Catholic Filipino Club file, AASF.

63. Telegram from Richard J. Welch, M.C., to Right Reverend John J. Mitty, D.D., Archbishop of San Francisco, April 5, 1935; letter from Chancellor of the Archdiocese of San Francisco to Rev. Edward N. Lenane, April 9, 1935; letter from Edward B. Levane to the Most Reverend John J. Mitty, April 12, 1935, Catholic Filipino Club file, AASF.

64. Cardinal Joseph Ratzinger, "Declaration on Masonic Associations," November 26, 1983, issued by the Office of the Sacred Congregation for the Doctrine of the Faith, Rome. Accessed at http://www.vatican.va/roman_curia/congregations/cfaith/documents/rc_con_cfaith_doc_19831126_declaration-masonic_en.html.

65. Letter from C. T. Alfafara to Father Gabriel J. Zavatarro, August 14, 1956, Filipinos file, AASF.

66. Letter from Reverend Donnell A. Walsh to Celestino T. Alfafara, August 22, 1956, Filipinos file, AASF.

67. Affidavit from the Grand Lodge of the Caballeros de Dimas-Alang, Inc., dated April 14, 1944, Filipinos file, AASF.

68. Rizaline Monrayo Raymundo interview by author, November 16, 2000.

69. Ernesto Tirona Mabalon interview by author, December 1996.

70. Rizaline Monrayo Raymundo interview by author.

71. St. Mary's of the Assumption Church, "History of St. Mary's Church" souvenir program, 150th anniversary.

72. S. Inosanto, *The Story of Trinity Presbyterian Church*, 19.

73. Ibid.; listings of local churches, *Stockton Daily Evening Record*, March 30, 1946, Folder Four: Local Filipinos, Pearl Shaffer Sweet Papers, Photographs and Manuscripts, Special Collections, University of the Pacific Holt-Atherton Library.

74. Letter from Monroe Sweetland to Mr. Bruce M. Mohler, National Catholic Welfare Conference, October 14, 1941, 1, Filipinos file, AASF.

75. Ibid., 2.

76. Letter from A. G. Cicognani, Archbishop of Ladodicea, Apostolic Delegate, to Most Reverend John J. Mitty, D.D., Archbishop of San Francisco, January 2, 1942, AASF.

77. Letter from John J. Mitty, Archdiocese of San Francisco, to Reverend William J. Flanagan, Catholic Charities, San Francisco, Filipinos file, AASF.

78. Letter from Right Reverend W. E. McGough to Rev. William J. Flanagan, January 28, 1942, Filipinos file, January 1942, AASF.

79. Letter from John J. Mitty, Archbishop of San Francisco, to His Excellency, Most Reverend Amlete G. Cicognani, D.D., Washington, D.C., January 31, 1942, Filipinos file, AASF.

80. Ibid., 1.

81. Draft "Points Concerning Filipinos," Archbishop Mitty to Archbishop Cicognani, January 1942, Filipinos file, AASF.

82. Ibid.

83. Letter from Archbishop A. G. Cicognani, Archbishop of Laodicea, Apostolic Delegate, to The Most Reverend John J. Mitty, D.D., Archbishop of San Francisco, Filipinos file, April 8, 1942, AASF.

84. Ibid.

85. Ibid.

86. "Priests for Work among the Filipinos," letter from Archbishop Mitty to all priests in the Archdiocese of San Francisco, 1942, Filipinos file, AASF.

87. "Report on Filipino Organization," letter from Right Reverend W. E. McGough to Most Reverend John J. Mitty, Archbishop of San Francisco, October 16, 1942, Filipinos file, AASF.

88. Based on a group photograph of the Filipino Catholic Association, circa 1940s, FANHS.

89. Joan London and Henry Anderson, *So Shall Ye Reap: The Story of Cesar Chavez and the Farm Workers' Movement* (New York: Thomas Y. Crowell, 1970), 82–83.

90. Thomas McCullough, "Priest's Conference on Spanish Speaking, St. Charles Church," February 10, 1949, Spanish Mission Band, Box A67, Folder 2, AASF, 1.

91. Deanna Daclan Balantac, "History of the Santo Niño Association of Stockton and Vicinity, Incorporated," *Stockton Chapter Filipino American National Historical Society Newsletter,* January 2007, 5.

92. London and Anderson, *So Shall Ye Reap*, 83.

93. Burns, "The Mexican Catholic Community in California," 213–15.

94. Ibid., 215.

95. Violet Juanitas Dutra told me this in a conversation about St. Mary's Church, October 2001, Stockton, Calif.

96. Quoted in Leo Grebler, Joan W. Moore, Ralph C. Guzmán, and Jeffrey Lionel Berlant, *The Mexican American People: The Nation's Second Largest Minority* (New York: Free Press, 1970), 483.

97. Burns, "The Mexican Catholic Community in California," 219.

98. St. Mary's of the Assumption Church, "St. Mary's Church."

99. Letter from Father Alan McCoy, O.F.M., to the Most Reverend John J. Mitty, D.D., Archbishop of San Francisco, August 30, 1956, Filipinos file, AASF, 1.

100. Ibid., 3.

101. For the relationship between the AWA, AWOC, and the UFW, see the History page of the United Farm Workers website, "Rise of the UFW," http://www.ufw.org/_page.php ?menu=research&inc=history/03.html, accessed November 5, 2012.

102. London and Anderson, *So Shall Ye Reap*, 91.

103. Ibid., 93.

104. Ibid., 95.

105. Sanchez, "Go after the Women."

106. F. Cordova, *Filipinos*, 171.

CHAPTER 6. THE WATERSHED OF WORLD WAR II

1. Telegram from Carlos Bulosan to Carlos P. Romulo, December 10, 1943, Carlos P. Romulo Papers, Box 1, Carlos P. Romulo Papers, Special Collections, University of the Philippines, Diliman.

2. Photograph of Bataan Day Memorial program, Visual Communications archives, Los Angeles, Calif.

3. Quoted in J. C. Dionisio, "Colonel Romulo Pleads for Tolerance for Filipinos on Pacific Coast," *Philippine Examiner*, April 30, 1944.

4. Ibid.

5. Camila Labor Carido interview by author, January 15, 1996.

6. Asuncion Guevarra Nicolas interview by author.

7. FALA Yearbook, Second Annual Convention, July 7–8, 1940, Macario Bautista Papers, Trinidad Rojo Papers, NPA FANHS.

8. "F. Varona Arrives in Washington, D.C.," *Philippines Mail*, February 6, 1939.

9. Carlos Bulosan, *America Is in the Heart: A Personal History* (Seattle: University of Washington Press, 1973), 277.

10. On the Philippine independence mission, see Frank Hindman Golay, *Face of Empire: United States-Philippine Relations, 1898–1946* (Manila: Ateneo de Manila University

Press, 1998), 318–27; "Francisco Varona," Entry 21, Personal Name Information File, 1914–1945, Box 665, RG 350, BIA; Lawrence H. Fuchs, *Hawaii Pono: A Social History* (New York: Harcourt, Brace and World, 1961), 148, 441.

11. "Filipinos Held to Blame for Plight Abroad," *Wheeling News Register*, September 2, 1938, in "Francisco Varona."

12. Stuart Marshall Jamieson, *Labor Unionism in American Agriculture*, Bulletin 836 (Washington, D.C.: Government Printing Office, 1945), 180.

13. "Macario Darvin Bautista, M.D.," in program for the "1983 Ten Outstanding Filipinos in San Joaquin County," Maharlika Management Company, Stockton, Calif., Special Collections, The Haggin Museum, Stockton, Calif. See also the Macario Bautista Papers. Dr. Bautista was the doctor for my grandfather Pablo Mabalon, who listed the doctor on his World War II draft registration card as his contact in case of emergency.

14. "Francisco Varona."

15. FALA Yearbook, 1940.

16. "Strike Ties up Half of Grass Harvest," *Stockton Daily Evening Record*, April 8, 1939.

17. Ibid.; FALA Yearbook, 1940; Alexis Canillo and Joan May Cordova, *Voices: A Filipino American Oral History* (Stockton, Calif: Filipino Oral History, Inc., 1984), unpaginated.

18. "Strike Ties up Half of Grass Harvest."

19. FALA Yearbook, 1940.

20. Macario Bautista, *Philippines Mail*, April 22, 1939.

21. Juan C. Dionisio, "Need for United Filipino Front," *Philippine Journal*, August 26, 1939.

22. "Japanese Own Little Land in County," *Stockton Daily Evening Record*, April 8, 1942.

23. Claro Candelario interview by author, February 15, 1993.

24. Camila Carido interview by author, January 15, 1996.

25. Eiichiro Azuma, *Between Two Empires: Race, History and Transnationalism in Japanese America* (New York: Oxford University Press, 2005).

26. Donald Walker, "Race Relations and Specialty Crops: San Joaquin County Horticulture, 1900–1925," master's thesis, California State University, Sacramento, 1992, 269.

27. Azuma, *Between Two Empires*, 203.

28. Juan C. Dionisio, "Concord Filipinos on Strike! Workers Walk Out as Japanese Refuse $.35 Hr. Wage Boost; Japanese Association Refuses Demand; Filipinos Solidly United Together in Fight for 'Rights,'" *Philippine Journal*, October 7, 1939.

29. Jamieson, *Labor Unionism in American Agriculture*, 183.

30. Ibid., 184; Azuma, *Between Two Empires*, 196.

31. Harry Schwartz, "Recent Developments among Farm Labor Unions," *Journal of Farm Economics* 23, no. 4 (1941): 833–42.

32. FALA Yearbook, 1940.

33. The 1903 sugar beet strike of the Japanese Mexican Labor Association is a prime example of Japanese immigrant labor militancy. See Tomas Almaguer, *Racial Faultlines: The Historical Origins of White Supremacy in California* (Berkeley: University of California Press, 2009), 185 and 199.

34. See Steffi San Buenaventura, "Filipino Folk Spirituality and Immigration: From Mutual Aid to Religion," *Amerasia* 1, no. 22 (1996).

35. D. L. Marcuelo, "Moncado Should Be Tarred and Feathered," and "Tungkol Kay Moncado at Kaniyang 'Federation,'" *Three Stars*, October 15, 1928.

36. "Celery Men in Protest over Filipino Leader," *Stockton Daily Evening Record*, November 30, 1940; Azuma, *Between Two Empires*, 198.

37. "Filipino Labor to Be Replaced by Other Types," *Philippines Mail*, August 12, 1940. See also Azuma, *Between Two Empires*, 198.

38. Bulosan, *America Is in the Heart*, 275–76.

39. Juan C. Dionisio, "Poor Mrs. Morimoto; She Must Think Filipinos Dumb," *Philippine Journal*, January 23, 1940; Juan C. Dionisio, "More about Asparagus," *Philippine Journal*, February 15, 1940.

40. Juan C. Dionisio, "Displacement of Workers Most Serious Threat to Asparagus Labor Peace," *Philippines Journal*, February 15, 1940.

41. "Mrs. Morimoto Is Invited to Fete," *Philippines Mail*, August 12, 1940.

42. Azuma, *Between Two Empires*, 202; Polk city directories, 1941–42.

43. Quoted in "Striking Member of FALA Creates Sensation in Protest against Mrs. Morimoto's Activities in Delta Asparagus Strike; Office of International Employment Agency, Filipino Federation of America Damaged," *Philippines Mail*, December 9, 1940.

44. Jamieson, *Labor Unionism in American Agriculture*, 185.

45. Letter from Macario Bautista to Francisco Varona, October 26, 1940, Macario Bautista Papers, NPA FANHS.

46. "Dissolution Considered as Mere Formality after AFL Affiliation with Central Body," *Philippines Mail*, January 30, 1941.

47. "News and Views," *Philippine Journal*, June 30, 1941.

48. Azuma, *Between Two Empires*, 203–4.

49. "CIO, Maritime Urge Varona Ouster," *Philippines Mail*, January 30, 1941.

50. Quoted in "Misrepresentation of Desperation Quotations and Misquotations from Rojo And Navea," *Philippines Mail*, March 14, 1941.

51. FALA Yearbook, 1940.

52. Juan C. Dionisio, "No Sectionalism Please!," *Philippine Journal*, February 15, 1940.

53. Letter from Francisco Varona to Dr. Macario Bautista, October 24, 1940. Macario Bautista Papers, NPA FANHS.

54. *The Philippine Yearbook of 1941*, Stockton, Calif.

55. Simeon Doria Arroyo, *Philippine Record*, November 13, 1941.

56. Claro Candelario interview by author; "Move to Support Marcantonio Citizenship Bill Is Strengthened," *Philippine Journal*, August 26, 1939; "Society Notes," *Philippine Journal*, November 11, 1939.

57. See Michael Denning, *The Cultural Front: The Laboring of American Culture in the Twentieth Century* (London: Verso, 1996), xviii, 17, 60, 222–26, 237–39, and 280–81. For more about Bulosan, see Susan Evangelista, *Carlos Bulosan and His Poetry: A Biography and Anthology* (Quezon City, Philippines: Ateneo de Manila University Press, 1985); and E. San Juan, ed., *On Becoming Filipino: Selected Writings of Carlos Bulosan* (Philadelphia: Temple University Press, 1995).

58. "I Favor the Marcantonio Bill," *Philippines Mail*, November 27, 1939.

59. Claro Candelario interview by author; "Society Notes," *Philippine Journal*, November 11, 1939.

60. "An Appeal for U.S. Citizenship," *Philippines Mail*, February 26, 1940.

61. "Short Cuts," *Philippines Mail*, May 11, 1940.

62. "Marcantonio Bill Killed; Author Seeks to Introduce New Measure; Committee Hearings Ditch Citizenship Issues to Filipinos; Pinoys Plan to Carry on Fight and Do More Campaigning," *Commonwealth Times*, (Salinas, Calif.), April 15, 1940.

63. Ibid.

64. "Short Cuts."

65. Letter from Harold Ickes, Secretary of the Interior to J. M. Elizalde, August 17, 1940; letter from J. M. Elizalde to the Secretary of the Interior, Harold Ickes, August 20, 1940; letter from Robert H. Jackson to J. M. Elizalde, September 9, 1940, reprinted in *Philippines Mail*, October 14, 1940.

66. "Filipino Labor Shortage," *Commonwealth Times*, November 14, 1941.

67. Azuma, *Between Two Empires*, 204.

68. "Francisco Varona"; *Philippines Mail*, July 9, 1941.

69. "Varona Dies in New York Hospital," *Philippines Mail*, July 11, 1941.

70. Letter from J. M. Elizalde to Dr. Macario Bautista, September 17, 1941, Macario Bautista Papers, NPA FANHS.

71. "Dionisio Wins in Recent Election," *Philippines Mail*, July 11, 1941.

72. "Cannery Workers Back FALA," *Stockton Daily Evening Record*, March 13, 1942.

73. Letter to Fred Cordova from Juan C. Dionisio, March 9, 1983, Juan C. Dionisio Papers, NPA FANHS.

74. Maxine Gonong Papers, San Francisco History Center, San Francisco Public Library, Calif.

75. Stanley Karnow, *In Our Image: America's Empire in the Philippines* (New York: Ballantine, 1989), 282–83; and David A. Kennedy, *Freedom from Fear: The American People in Depression and War, 1929–1945* (New York: Oxford University Press, 1999), 510–11.

76. "Stockton Mobilizes Emergency Defense; Japanese Association Pledges Support," *Stockton Daily Evening Record*, December 8, 1942.

77. "Filipinos Pledge Aid to America; Mass Meeting Also Boycotts Japanese," *Stockton Daily Evening Record*, December 13, 1941; "Japanese Here Feel Pinch," *Stockton Daily Evening Record*, December 10, 1941; and "Stockton Pinoys Pledge Aid to the United States," *Philippines Mail*, December 22, 1941.

78. "CDA Mobilizes for P.I. Defense," *Commonwealth Times*, December 18, 1941.

79. Editorial, *Stockton Daily Evening Record*, December 8, 1941.

80. Camila Carido interview by author, January 15, 1996.

81. "Second Japanese Is Murdered; Rooming House Proprietor Shot in Dark Hall," *Stockton Daily Evening Record*, February 20, 1942.

82. Victorio Valasco, "For National Sanity," *Philippines Mail*, December 22, 1941.

83. "Why Boycott the Japanese?" *Philippines Mail*, December 22, 1941.

84. "Total Boycott Declared against Japs," *Philippines Mail*, January 31, 1942.

85. Carey McWilliams, "California and the Japanese," *New Republic*, March 2, 1942, 295.

86. "1941 Passes Quietly; Police Find Little to Do; Race Riot Rumor," *Stockton Daily Evening Record*, January 1, 1942.

87. Nelson Nagai interview by author.

88. "E" Company, Box 759, Record Group 407, Records of the Adjutant General's Office, Philippine Archives Collection, USAFFE, Sixth Military District, National Archives and Records Administration, College Park, Md.

89. Olive Davis, *Stockton: Sunrise Port on the San Joaquin* (Sun Valley, Calif.: American Historical Press, 1998), 81–82. See also Raymond Hillman, *Stockton through the Decades* (Stockton, Calif.: Vanguard, 1981), 29.

90. "War and the Filipinos in America," *Commonwealth Times*, December 18, 1941.

91. Steffi San Buenaventura, "Filipino Immigration to the United States," in *Asian American Encyclopedia*, ed. Franklin Ng (New York: Marshall Cavendish, 1995), 448.

San Buenaventura notes that the act specifically excluded those Filipinos serving in U.S. forces in the Philippines.

92. See Fred Cordova, "Filipinos: Forgotten Asian Americans," Demonstration Project for Asian Americans (Dubuque, Iowa: Kendall Hunt, 1982), 217–26.

93. "Filipinos Form Militia Here," *Stockton Daily Evening Record*, April 23, 1942.

94. Quoted in Bienvenido Santos, "Filipinos in War," *Far Eastern Survey* 2 (November 30, 1942): 249.

95. Ronald Takaki, *Double Victory: A Multicultural History of America in World War II* (Boston: Little, Brown, 2001), 123.

96. "Japanese Advised to Keep Calm in Disposing of Farms, Equipment," *Stockton Daily Evening Record*, March 30, 1942; "Every Japanese Must Leave City," *Stockton Daily Evening Record*, May 8, 1942.

97. Simeon Espineda and Tsuru Saito Panoncialman Espineda and their children, among them Josephine S. Paular, were forced to live in the Rohwer internment camp. Obituary of Josephine S. Paular from the *Sacramento Bee*, August 23–26, 2009. Accessed at http://www.legacy.com/obituaries/sacbee/obituary.aspx?pid=131730223#fbLoggedOut, on October 4, 2012.

98. Camila Carido interview with author, January 15, 1996.

99. "Filipinos Request Privilege of Leasing Farm Land," *Stockton Daily Evening Record*, January 26, 1942; "Japanese Land Awaits New Operators," *Stockton Daily Evening Record*, April 16, 1942; "Two New Rules on Japanese Land; All Filipinos May Obtain Loans," *Stockton Daily Evening Record*, April 17, 1942.

100. Alex S. Fabros, "Thorns and Roses," *Philippines Mail*, January 31, 1942.

101. Polk city directories, 1944–45.

102. Polk city directories, 1940–50; *Bohol Circle Yearbook*, Stockton, Calif., 1949, Bulawit family collection.

103. The Associated Press noted that the "gallant" American-Filipino defenders of the Bataan Peninsula were closing a "heroic" three-month battle. See "Weary Troops Overwhelmed; Corregidor Continues Battle; 36,530 Americans, Filipinos Face Death or Capture on the Isle, Stimson Reveals," *Stockton Daily Evening Record*, April 9, 1942.

104. Significant *Stockton Daily Evening Record* articles include "Bravery in Jungle Fighting Upholds Traditions of Philippine Scouts," February 16, 1942; "Igorote Tribesmen Having Field Day with No Strings on Killing Japs," February 20, 1942; "Filipino Pilots Are Defenders of Bataan," April 3, 1942; "The End at Bataan," April 9, 1942; "Filipino Infantry Unit Eager to Retake Isles," April 10, 1042; "Would Avenge Defenders of Bataan," April 17, 1942.

105. "To a Filipino Sergeant," *Stockton Daily Evening Record*, February 19, 1942.

106. Irving Martin Jr., "Mrs. Lacy and the Filipino Club," *Stockton Daily Evening Record*, May 30, 1942.

107. Idamae Johnson, "Philippine Independence Is Example for Postwar World," *Stockton Daily Evening Record*, January 22, 1942.

108. Quoted in Ronald Takaki, *In the Heart of Filipino America: Immigrants from the Pacific Isles* (New York: Chelsea House, 1995), 96.

109. Quoted in ibid., 97.

110. Quoted in San Buenaventura, "Filipino Immigration to the United States," 448.

111. Manuel Buaken, *I Have Lived with the American People* (Caldell, Idaho: Caxton, 1948).

112. Vicente Villamin, "If I Were a Japanese American," *Philippines Mail*, July 31, 1944.

113. August Fauni Espiritu, *Five Faces of Exile: The Nation and Filipino American Intellectuals* (Stanford: Stanford University Press, 2005), 50.

114. Carlos Bulosan, "Freedom from Want," *Saturday Evening Post*, March 6, 1943, 12–13.

115. Quoted in "Dionisio Addresses State Assembly on Filipino-American Friendship," *Philippines Star-Press*, April 28, 1945.

116. Letter from Dr. Macario D. Bautista to A. B. Warfield, Brigadier General, U.S.A., Rtd., Chairman of the War Finance Committee of Northern California, November 20, 1944, Macario Bautista Papers, NPA FANHS.

117. Cornelius Bynum, *A. Philip Randolph and the Struggle for Civil Rights* (Urbana-Champaign: University of Illinois Press, 2010), 172–73.

118. "Top Wages Given Cannery Workers," *Philippines Mail*, June 23, 1942.

119. "Labor Shortage Menaces County Asparagus Crop," *Stockton Daily Evening Record*, February 26, 1942; "Asparagus Crop Faces Labor Shortage Threat; Decrease in Filipino Workers, Probable Removal of Japanese, Main Factors," *Stockton Daily Evening Record*, March 5, 1942; "Delta Farms Operator Urges Mexican Labor; Deferment of Filipinos Also Proposed in Senate Committee Hearing Here," *Stockton Daily Evening Record*, April 24, 1942.

120. "Shortage of Field Laborers Seen," *Philippines Mail*, August 31, 1942.

121. "33,000 Mexicans to Be Imported into California to Harvest Crops," *Stockton Daily Evening Record*, May 7, 1943; "Welcome to Our Mexican Friends," *Stockton Daily Evening Record*, May 29, 1943.

122. "Mexican Workers," *Philippines Mail*, August 25, 1943.

123. Quoted in "Filipinos' Head Urges Work," *Stockton Daily Evening Record*, May 14, 1943.

124. D. F. Gonzalo, "Asparagus Picture," *Stockton Daily Evening Record*, February 22, 1944.

125. *Stockton Daily Evening Record*, June 9, 1946.

126. Segunda Reyes interview by Mary Arca Inosanto, FOHP. See also Hillman, *Stockton through the Decades*, 29; and Davis, *Stockton*, 81–82.

127. "Stockton Merry-Go Round," *Philippines Mail*, February 25, 1944.

128. Wallace Stegner and the editors of *Look*, *One Nation* (Boston: Houghton Mifflin, 1945).

129. Emily Behic Rosal interview by author.

130. Resolution no. 13746, June 21, 1943, Stockton City Archives, Office of the City Clerk, Stockton, Calif.

131. See *Alfafara v. Fross*, 26 Cal2d. 358. Accessed at the Stanford University Law School website, http://scocal.stanford.edu/opinion/alfafara-v-fross-29287, on November 11, 2012. Discussed at length by Lisa Suguitan Melnick, "The Sky Is the Limit: The Legacy of Celestino T. Alfafara," a paper presented at the Filipino American National Historical Society Fourteenth Biennial Conference, Albuquerque, New Mexico, June 29, 2012. Melnick is Alfafara's granddaughter. Author's notes.

132. Steffi San Buenaventura and Linda S. Revilla, "Filipino Veterans and Naturalization," in *Asian American Encyclopedia*, ed. Franklin Ng (New York: Marshall Cavendish, 1995), 469.

133. *Philippine Examiner*, June 30, 1946.

134. "I Am an American," program honoring new citizens, May 18, 1949, Stockton file, NPA FANHS.

135. Ira Katznelson, *When Affirmative Action Was White: The Untold History of Racial*

Inequality in Twentieth Century America (New York: Norton, 2005). See also Edward Humes, *Over Here: How the G.I. Bill Transformed the American Dream* (Orlando, Fla.: Harcourt, 2006).

136. James Patterson, *Grand Expectations: The United States, 1945–1974* (New York: Oxford University Press, 1996), 68; on race and the GI Bill, see Ira Katznelson, *When Affirmative Action Was White: The Untold History of Racial Inequality in Twentieth Century America* (New York: W. W. Norton, 2005).

137. James P. Allan, "Recent Immigration from the Philippines and Filipino Communities in the United States," *Geographical Review* 67, no. 2 (1977): 196 and 199.

138. Caridad Vallangca, *The Second Wave: Pinay and Pinoy, 1945–1960* (San Francisco: Strawberry Hill, 1987), 73. A number of community studies have been published that discuss postwar Filipino settlement in California cities. See Rudy P. Guevarra Jr., "'Skid Row': Race and the Social Construction of Space in San Diego," *Journal of San Diego History* 54, no. 1 (2008), 26–38. For Salinas, see Edwin B. Almirol, *Ethnic Identity and Social Negotiation: A Study of a Filipino Community in California* (New York: AMS, 1985). For San Francisco, see James Sobredo, "From Manila Bay to Daly City: Filipinos in San Francisco," in *Reclaiming San Francisco: History, Politics, Culture*, ed. James Brook, Chris Carlsson and Nany J. Peters (San Francisco: City Lights, 1998), 273–86); Estella Habal, *San Francisco's International Hotel: Mobilizing the Filipino Community in the Anti-Eviction Movement* (Philadelphia: Temple University Press, 2008); and Filipino American National Historical Society, Manilatown Heritage Foundation, and Pin@y Educational Partnerships, *Filipinos in San Francisco* (Charleston, S.C.: Arcadia, 2011). For Vallejo, see Mel Orpilla, *Filipinos in Vallejo* (Charleston, S.C.: Arcadia, 2005). For the East Bay, see Evangeline Canonizado Buell, Evelyn Luluquisen, Lillian Galedo, and Eleanor Hipol Luis, *Filipinos in the East Bay* (Charleston, S.C.: Arcadia, 2008). For Los Angeles, see Mae Respicio Koerner, *Filipinos in Los Angeles* (Charleston, S.C.: Arcadia, 2007).

139. Vince Reyes, "The War Brides," *Filipinas*, October 1995, 24.

140. Angelina Candelario Novelozo interview by author.

141. Vallangca, *The Second Wave*, 57.

142. Quoted in Emily Porcincula Lawsin, "'Beyond Hanggang Pier Only': Filipina War Brides of Seattle," *FANHS Journal* 4 (1996): 50D.

143. Reyes, "The War Brides," 22.

144. For more about Filipina war brides, see ibid.; Vallangca, *The Second Wave*; and Emily Porcincula Lawsin, "Hanggang Pier Na Lamang: Filipina War Brides of Seattle," *Filipino American National Historical Society Journal* 4 (1996): 50A–50G.

145. Vallangca, *The Second Wave*, 33; Lawsin, "Hanggang Pier Na Lamang," 50C.

146. Reyes, "The War Brides," 22.

147. Modesto Lagura interview by author.

148. Concepcion Moreno Bohulano interview by author, 1992.

149. Alma Alcala interview by author.

150. Ibid.

151. Emily Rosal interview by author.

152. Angelina Novelozo interview by author.

153. Emily Rosal interview by author.

154. Lawsin, "Hanggang Pier Na Lamang," 50F.

155. Concepcion Bohulano interview by author, 2000.

156. Ibid.

157. Ibid.

158. Arleen de Vera, "An Unfinished Agenda: Filipino Immigrant Workers in the Era of McCarthyism; A Case Study of the Cannery Workers and Farm Laborers Union, 1948–1955," master's thesis, University of California, Los Angeles, 1990, 8.

159. Ibid., 5.

160. Ibid., 20.

161. "Why Asparagus Workers Strike: Grievances Told at Citizens Meeting," *Daily People's World*, May 21, 1948. Delvo had run unsuccessfully for several FALA officer positions in the elections of July 1941. "Dionisio Wins in Recent Election," *Philippines Mail*, July 11, 1941.

162. Philip Vera Cruz, *A Personal History of the Farmworkers Movement* (Seattle: University of Washington Press, 2000), 17.

163. "4,000 Strike in Farm Area; Sheriff Threatens Pickets," *Daily People's World*, May 5, 1948.

164. C. Delvo, Field Boss, Personal Losses—on Evictions, Papers of the FTA, Box 272, Folder 12, Labor Archives and Research Center, San Francisco State University, San Francisco, Calif.

165. "Farmers Praise Sheriff in Strike," *Stockton Daily Evening Record*, May 7, 1948.

166. "They're Making Labor History in the San Joaquin Valley," *Daily People's World*, May 21, 1948.

167. de Vera, "An Unfinished Agenda," 30.

168. "Public Decency Condemns Commie Strike in Asparagus Fields; FBI Investigation Is Suggested as FTA-CIO Threatens Strike of Asparagus Cutters in the Delta," *Bataan News*, February 1949, Labor Archives and Research Center.

169. de Vera, "An Unfinished Agenda," 38.

170. Marilyn C. Alquizola and Lane Ryo Hirabayashi, "Bulosan's Laughter: The Making of Carlos Bulosan," *Our Own Voice*, March 2006, http://www.oovrag.com/essays/essay2006a-5.shtml. See also Emil Guillermo, "Hounded to Death: The FBI File of Carlos Bulosan," *Asian Week*, November 8, 2002. Special thanks to my colleague Trevor Griffey for speaking with me about Bulosan's FBI file.

171. "1953–1954 Local 37-ILWU Annual Election," Larry Itliong Papers, NPA FANHS.

172. Résumé of Larry Itliong, Larry Itliong Papers; *Seattle, Washington, Passenger and Crew Lists, 1890–1957*, database online on www.ancestry.com. Original source: *Seattle, Washington, Passenger and Crew Lists of Vessels Arriving at Seattle, Washington, 1890–1957*, NARA, microfilm publication M1383, 357 rolls, Records of the Immigration and Naturalization Service, RG 85, National Archives, Washington, D.C., accessed November 13, 2012.

173. Stephen Magagnini, "New Recognition for Labor Leader," *Sacramento Bee*, December 28, 1996.

174. Ibid.; Ernesto Tirona Mabalon, interview by author, October 23, 2003; résumé of Larry Itliong.

175. *California Passenger and Crew Lists, 1893–1957*, NARA, Records of the Immigration and Naturalization Service, RG 85, National Archives, Washington, D.C., record for Modesto Itliong, accessed at www.ancestry.com on August 2, 2010.

176. Sam Kushner, *Long Road to Delano* (New York: International, 1975), 82–83; résumé of Larry Itliong.

177. Résumé of Larry Itliong; Reels 8 and 9, Collections of the United Farm Workers of America. Series 2, Papers of the United Farm Workers of America, 1969–1975 [microform], Doe Library, University of California, Berkeley.

178. Résumé of Larry Itliong; Magagnini, "New Recognition for Labor Leader"; Kushner, *Long Road to Delano*, 82–83.

179. Susan Ferriss and Ricardo Sandoval, *The Fight in the Fields: Cesar Chavez and the Farmworkers Movement* (New York: Harcourt, Brace, 1997), 70.

180. Angelina Novelozo interview by author.

181. Reels 1–3, Papers of the Agricultural Worker's Organizing Committee [microform], Doe Library, University of California, Berkeley.

182. Joan London and Henry Anderson, *So Shall Ye Reap: The Story of Cesar Chavez and the Farm Workers' Movement* (New York: Thomas Y. Crowell, 1970), 96–97.

183. Daily logs of Norman Smith and Rudy Delvo, Reels 1–3, Papers of the Agricultural Worker's Organizing Committee; AWOC *Organizer*, September 1959–October 26, 1960, Main Library (Gardner Stacks), University of California, Berkeley.

184. Letter from Cipriano Delvo to Mr. Chris Mensalvas, December 29, 1959, Reel 1, Papers of the Agricultural Worker's Organizing Committee.

185. Conversation with Dillon Delvo about his father, Larry Itliong, and the AWOC, March 2003.

186. Reels 1–3, Papers of the Agricultural Worker's Organizing Committee.

187. Kushner, *Long Road to Delano*, 108.

188. "AWOC Organizes Farm Labor," Reel 1, Papers of the Agricultural Worker's Organizing Committee.

189. Kushner, *Long Road to Delano*, 123.

190. Quoted in Ferriss and Sandoval, *Fight in the Fields*, 87.

191. See Kushner, *Long Road to Delano*; London and Anderson, *So Shall Ye Reap*; and Ferriss and Sandoval, *Fight in the Fields*.

192. Quoted in Magagnini, "New Recognition for Labor Leader."

193. Correspondence, Box 1, Folders 1–14; Larry Itliong Collection, UFW Collection, Walter P. Reuther Library of Labor and Urban Affairs, Wayne State University, Detroit, Michigan.

194. I eagerly anticipate Marissa Aroy's film *The Delano Manongs*. I thank her sincerely for generously sharing with me her research in the Larry Itliong Papers at Wayne State University.

195. Conversation with Mel LaGasca, Stockton FANHS chapter meeting, October 2, 2010.

196. Dan Gonzales, labor symposium at San Joaquin Delta College, Stockton, Calif., April 7, 2005.

197. Kushner, *Long Road to Delano*, 137.

198. Eugene Nelson, *Huelga! The First Hundred Days of the Great Delano Grape Strike* (Delano, Calif.: Farmworkers, 1966).

199. Kushner, *Long Road to Delano*, 159.

200. Marissa Aroy, rough clip of *The Delano Manongs* (New York: Media Factory, 2012). See also Matt Garcia, *From the Jaws of Victory: The Triumph and Tragedy of Cesar Chavez and the Farmworker's Movement* (Berkeley: University of California Press, 2012), 119–20.

201. From a conversation with my father, Ernesto Tirona Mabalon, in 1998 when I began research for this book. When Philip Vera Cruz published his autobiography, *Philip Vera Cruz: A Personal History of Filipino Immigrants and the Farmworkers Movement* with Craig Scharlin and Lillia Villanueva in 1994, I attended his book launch at UCLA, purchased his book, and had him sign it for me. On a visit home to Stockton, I showed my father my treasured copy: a signed first edition. My father eagerly borrowed it from me, read it, then asked to bring it to his annual Legionarios del Trabajo convention to be held in Salinas that year because his lodge brother Ben Gines, and other former UFW orga-

nizers, were eagerly anticipating it. Gines had disagreed with Vera Cruz on many issues. I assume that Gines and fellow former organizers found the book an engrossing read, because I never saw my treasured book again.

202. Quoted in "The Filipino: A Real Pro Where Men Toil in the Fields," *Stockton Record*, March 28, 1971.

203. Quoted in Garcia, *From the Jaws of Victory*, 120.

204. San Buenaventura, "Filipino Immigration to the United States," 448–49.

CHAPTER 7. LOSING EL DORADO STREET

1. Carmen Saldevar interview by author.

2. Ibid.

3. The classic, and still the best, history of suburbanization is Kenneth T. Jackson, *Crabgrass Frontier: The Suburbanization of the United States* (New York: Oxford University Press, 1985).

4. Paul Groth, *Living Downtown: The History of Residential Hotels in the United States* (Berkeley: University of California Press, 1994), 253.

5. Jackson, *Crabgrass Frontier*, 173.

6. Ibid., 215.

7. Olive Davis, *Stockton: Sunrise Port on the San Joaquin* (Sun Valley, Calif.: American Historical Press, 1998), 87–88.

8. Professor Richard Bastear, San Joaquin Delta College, lecture on racial covenants and segregation in local neighborhoods in Stockton, in Political Science 10, Fall 1991, author's notes. On the FHA and racially restrictive covenants, see Jackson, *Crabgrass Frontier*, 208–9. Thomas Sugrue discusses how restrictive covenants were used by whites to keep African Americans out of certain neighborhoods in *The Origins of the Urban Crisis: Race and Inequality in Postwar Detroit* (Princeton: Princeton University Press, 1996).

9. Natalie Molina, *Fit to Be Citizens? Public Health and Race in Los Angeles, 1879–1939* (Berkeley: University of California Press, 2006); and Sugrue, *The Origins of the Urban Crisis*.

10. Lillian Galedo, Laurena Cabanero, and Brian Tom, "Roadblocks to Community Building: A Case Study of the Stockton Filipino Community Center Project" (Working Publication No. 4, Asian American Research Project, University of California, Davis, 1970), 4–5. See also Harold F. Wise Associates, *Urban Blight in Stockton, California: A Report to the City of Stockton*, Urban Blight file, CAT 3, Stockton Municipal Records 43, Stockton City Archives.

11. See David Roediger's discussions about whiteness and the suburbs in *Working towards Whiteness: How America's Immigrants Become White* (New York: Basic, 2005).

12. City of Stockton Resolution 19,745, *Lodi News-Sentinel*, December 2, 1955.

13. Nomellini-Ferroggiaro Development Company, "A Home for Everyone," Lever Village promotional brochure, Concepcion Moreno Bohulano personal papers, Bohulano family collection.

14. Galedo, Cabanero, and Tom, "Roadblocks to Community Building," 115–16.

15. "A Home for Everyone."

16. Ibid.

17. Lillian Galedo interview by author.

18. Davis, *Stockton*, 88.

19. Jackson, *Crabgrass Frontier*, 198–201.

20. Molina, *Fit to Be Citizens?*, 180–81.

21. Jackson, *Crabgrass Frontier*, 206–13.

22. Groth, *Living Downtown*, 151.

23. Alexander Von Hoffman, "A Study in Contradictions: The Origins and Legacy of the Housing Act of 1949," *Housing Policy Debate* 11 no. 2 (2000): 318.

24. Ibid., 299.

25. Von Hoffman, "A Study in Contradictions," 317; John A. Jakle and David Wilson, *Derelict Landscapes: The Wasting of America's Built Environment* (Savage, Md.: Rowman and Littlefield, 1992), 131.

26. City Planning Commission, "Redevelopment," a report prepared for the City of Stockton, Calif., February, 1952, Harold S. Jacoby Papers, Photographs and Manuscripts, Special Collections, University of the Pacific Holt-Atherton Library, 1.

27. Ibid.

28. Jakle and Wilson, *Derelict Landscapes*, 131.

29. Martin Anderson, *The Federal Bulldozer* (Cambridge: MIT Press, 1964), 4.

30. Jane Jacobs and Herbert Gans were two of the earliest and most influential critics of urban redevelopment policies. See Jane Jacobs, *The Life and Death of Great American Cities* (New York: Random House, 1961); and Herbert Gans, *The Urban Villagers: Group and Class in the Life of Italian Americans*, rev. and expanded ed. (New York: Free Press, 1982). See also James Q. Wilson, ed., *Urban Renewal: The Record and the Controversy* (Cambridge: MIT Press, 1966).

31. Martin Anderson, "The Federal Bulldozer," in Wilson, *Urban Renewal*, 494.

32. Ibid., 495.

33. Jakle and Wilson, *Derelict Landscapes*, 131.

34. Scott Kurashige argues that these policies disproportionately and negatively affected African Americans in Los Angeles in *The Shifting Grounds of Race: Black and Japanese Americans in the Making of Multiethnic Los Angeles* (Princeton: Princeton University Press, 2008), 224–29.

35. Von Hoffman, "A Study in Contradictions," 318.

36. The other members included Dr. Harlan Rayburn, educator; David B. Epstein and Charles Wagner, businessmen; Charles A. James, attorney; Jalwant Singh, labor contractor; Dr. J. Ford Lewis and Rev. Juan M. Oronoz, ministers; and Mrs. R. Kenneth Wells, a local housewife. Minutes, Mayor's Committee on Urban Blight, January 20, 1954, Urban Blight files, Box 1162, Folder 2, CAT 3, SMA 43, Stockton City Archives, Office of the City Clerk, Stockton, Calif.

37. Report on Urban Renewal, August 1, 1955, Urban Blight files, Box 1162, Folder 2, CAT 3, SMA 43, Stockton City Archives, Office of the City Clerk, Stockton, Calif.

38. "The West End Story: A 'Wide Open' Town," unsigned thesis, San Joaquin Delta College, n.d., 29–34, Photograph and Manuscript Archives, Bank of Stockton, Stockton, Calif., 33.

39. R. Coke Wood and Leonard Covello, *Stockton Memories: A Pictorial History of Stockton, California* (Fresno, Calif.: Valley, 1977).

40. Minutes of the City Council Meeting, September 26, 1955, Stockton City Archives.

41. Minutes of the City Council Meeting, November 21, 1955, and July 23, 1956, Stockton City Archives.

42. Quoted in "The West End Story: A 'Wide Open' Town," 29.

43. Ibid., 29–34.

44. Quoted in "Relocation of Single Men Is Under Fire," *Stockton Daily Evening Record*, April 5, 1962.

45. Quoted in "West End Redevelopment Essential Despite Moves North, Agency

Told," *Stockton Daily Evening Record*, February 21, 1962. See also West End Redevelopment Project press clippings, Stockton City Archives.

46. Quoted in "Renewal Plan Ruled Legal: Judge Removes Barrier to Erasing of 'Skid Row' Blight," *Stockton Daily Evening Record*, January 4, 1963.

47. "Mayor Happy Way Cleared for Renewal," *Stockton Daily Evening Record*, January 4, 1963.

48. Quoted in "Renewal Plan Ruled Legal."

49. "Litigation Appears Over in West End Renewal Legality," *Stockton Daily Evening Record*, March 3, 1965.

50. "Condemnation Suit Filed on West End Property In Renewal," *Stockton Daily Evening Record*, August 13, 1963; West End Redevelopment Project press clippings.

51. "Long Awaited Demolition of W. End Buildings Starts," *Stockton Daily Evening Record*, February 11, 1964.

52. "Just Kindling Now," *Stockton Daily Evening Record*, February 14, 1966.

53. Davis, *Stockton*, 105.

54. Chester Hartman, "The Housing of Relocated Families," in Wilson, *Urban Renewal*, 359. See also Gans, *The Urban Villagers*.

55. Hartman, "The Housing of Relocated Families," 321.

56. "West End's People Are Relocating," *Stockton Daily Evening Record*, April 3, 1964.

57. "Renewal Area Demolition Halt Ordered; Migrant Housing Units Affected," *Stockton Daily Evening Record*, June 17, 1964.

58. Carmen Saldevar interview by author.

59. Ibid.

60. Alma Alcala interview by author.

61. Jackson, *Crabgrass Frontier*, 248–49.

62. Raymond A. Mohl, "Shifting Patterns of American Urban Policy since 1900," in *Urban Policy in Twentieth Century America*, ed. Arnold R. Hirsch and Raymond A. Mohl (New Brunswick, N.J.: Rutgers University Press, 1993), 16; and Andres Duany, Elizabeth Plater-Zyberk, and Jeff Speck, *Suburban Nation: The Rise of Sprawl and the Decline of the American Dream* (New York: North Point, 2000), 130.

63. "West Side Freeway Path Set," *Stockton Daily Evening Record*, January 30, 1960.

64. Loran C. Vanderlip, "Freeways: Role? Necessity? Cost? Location? Impact?" *Commonwealth* 38, no.5 (1961): 36.

65. Galedo, Cabanero, and Tom, "Roadblocks to Community Building," 4.

66. "Washington-Lafayette Route for Freeway Is Opposed," *Stockton Daily Evening Record*, June 2, 1961.

67. Angelina Bantillo Magdael interview with author, August 17, 2001.

68. Quoted in *Stockton Daily Evening Record*, June 2, 1961.

69. "Crosstown Freeway Site Decision Near: Washington St., Lafayette Route Proposal Made," *Stockton Daily Evening Record*, November 15, 1961.

70. "Washington-Lafayette Route Is Approved by City Council," *Stockton Daily Evening Record*, December 27, 1961.

71. "City Council Position on Crosstown Freeway Hit," *Stockton Daily Evening Record*, December 7, 1961.

72. "10 Get Paid for Moving Costs," *Stockton Daily Evening Record*, October 1, 1965.

73. Mayor's Crosstown Freeway Relocations Committee Interim Report, November 1967, Crosstown Freeway files, Papers of Harold S. Jacoby, Special Collections, Holt-Atherton Library, University of the Pacific, Stockton, Calif.

74. Mayor's Crosstown Freeway Relocations Committee, Minutes of Subcommittee Chairmen, October 4, 1967, Crosstown Freeway files, Papers of Harold S. Jacoby.

75. Ibid., 4.

76. Minutes, Mayor's Crosstown Freeway Relocations Committee Meeting, November 8, 1967, and the Mayor's Crosstown Freeway Relocations Committee Interim Report, November 1967, Crosstown Freeway files, Papers of Harold S. Jacoby.

77. Ibid., 7.

78. The phrase "and Vicinity" was added to the organization's name in the 1960s.

79. Edwin B. Almirol, *Ethnic Identity and Social Negotiation: A Study of a Filipino Community in California* (New York: AMS, 1985), 156.

80. "Rooms with a View," *Stockton Daily Evening Record*, February 9, 1968.

81. "Freeway Plans Take Shape," *Stockton Daily Evening Record*, February 4, 1970.

82. Quoted in "Crosstown Freeway's Ecological Impact," *Stockton Daily Evening Record*, June 6, 1971.

83. "Pathway for the Freeway," *Stockton Daily Evening Record*, April 4, 1972.

84. Carmen Saldevar interview by author.

85. Marjorie Flaherty, "'Sweet and Sour' of Business Relocation," *Stockton Daily Evening Record*, May 2, 1971.

86. Marjorie Flaherty, "People in Freeway's Path: The Human Side of Relocation," *Stockton Daily Evening Record*, May 3, 1971.

87. *Fat City* (DVD, Culver City, Calif.: Columbia Pictures, 2002); conversation with Maria "Terri" Torres, August 2003, Stockton, Calif.

88. Emily Rosal interview by author.

89. Conversation with Lourdes Tombokon Sobredo, October 2002, Stockton, Calif.

90. Luna Jamero interview by author.

91. Ted Lapuz interview by author, August 2008, Stockton, Calif.

92. Carmen Saldevar interview by author.

93. Ibid.

94. "Fund Delays Stall Crosstown Freeway until 1974," *Stockton Daily Evening Record*, May 2, 1971.

95. "Pathway for the Freeway."

96. "No Federal Aid: Crosstown Freeway Stalled," *Stockton Daily Evening Record*, October 20, 1972.

97. See Mayor's Crosstown Freeway Relocations Committee Interim Report.

98. City official (name withheld), interview by author, August 26, 2002, Stockton, Calif.

99. Estella Habal, *San Francisco's International Hotel: Mobilizing the Filipino Community in the Anti-Eviction Movement* (Philadelphia: Temple University Press, 2008).

CHAPTER 8. BUILDING A FILIPINA/O AMERICAN MOVEMENT

1. Deanna Daclan Balantac, "A Brief History of the Filipino Center of Stockton, California," August 12, 1972, family archives of Alma Alcala, Stockton, Calif.

2. James P. Allan, "Recent Immigration from the Philippines and Filipino Communities in the United States," *Geographical Review* 67, no. 2 (1977): 198.

3. Catherine Ceniza Choy, *Empire of Care: Nursing and Migration in Filipino American History* (Durham: Duke University Press, 2003).

4. Allan, "Recent Immigration from the Philippines and Filipino Communities in the United States," 196.

5. Yen Le Espiritu, *Home Bound: Filipino American Lives across Cultures, Communities and Countries* (Berkeley: University of California Press, 2003), 33–34.

6. Antonio J. A. Pido, *The Pilipinos in America: Macro/Micro Dimensions of Immigration and Integration* (New York: Center for Migration Studies, 1986), 92.

7. Lillian Galedo interview by author.

8. Luna Jamero interview by author.

9. Concepcion Moreno Bohulano interview by author, December 2, 2000.

10. Keith Reid, "Building a Home for Their History," *Stockton Record*, May 28, 2011.

11. Quoted in Lillian Galedo, Laurena Cabañero, and Brian Tom, "Roadblocks to Community Building: A Case Study of the Stockton Filipino Community Center Project," Working Publication No. 4. Asian American Research Project, University of California, Davis, 1970, 22.

12. Quoted in "History of the Filipino Center," Barrio Fiesta 25th Anniversary Celebration program, Filipino Plaza, 1997, Stockton, Calif., author's personal collection.

13. Eulogio "Ted" Lapuz interview by author, August 29, 2008.

14. Quoted in Galedo, Cabañero, and Tom, "Roadblocks to Community Building," 23.

15. Ted Lapuz interview by author.

16. Galedo, Cabañero, and Tom, "Roadblocks to Community Building," 23.

17. For a description of the Housing and Urban Development Act of 1968 and an explanation of Section 236, the Rental Housing Insurance Program, see the Department of Housing and Urban Development website, at http://archives.hud.gov/budget/fy04/cjs /renthouse.pdf. For a history of federal housing policy since 1949, see Alexander von Hoffman, "A Study in Contradictions: The Origins and Legacy of the Housing Act of 1949," *Housing Policy Debate* 11, no. 2 (2000): 299–326.

18. Von Hoffman, "A Study in Contradictions," 319.

19. Galedo, Cabañero, and Tom, "Roadblocks to Community Building," 25.

20. Ted Lapuz interview by author.

21. Estella Habal, *San Francisco's International Hotel: Mobilizing the Filipino Community in the Anti-Eviction Movement* (Philadelphia: Temple University Press, 2008), 68.

22. Lillian Galedo interview by author.

23. Rene Latosa interview.

24. Filipinas/os from Stockton have played a significant role in the Filipina/o American movement and the larger Asian American and third world movements of the 1960s and 1970s. For example, Filipina/o American students from Stockton were leaders in the 1968 San Francisco State College Third World Strike. See Karen Umemoto, "On Strike! San Francisco State College Strike, 1968–69: The Role of Asian American Students," *Amerasia* 15, no. 1 (1989): 3–41. For general overviews of the Filipina/o American and Asian American movements of the 1960s to the 1980s, see Habal, *San Francisco's International Hotel*; see also Steve Louie and Glenn Omatsu, eds., *Asian Americans: The Movement and the Moment* (Los Angeles: UCLA Asian American Studies Center, 2001); and Fred Ho, Carolyn Antonio, Diane Fujino, and Steve Yip, eds., *Legacy to Liberation: Politics and Culture of Revolutionary Asian Pacific America* (San Francisco: Big Red Media and AK Press, 2000). Filipina/o involvement in the movement against martial law through the radical organization Kilusan Demokratikong Pilipino is discussed in Helen Toribio, "We Are Revolution: A Reflective History of the Union of Democratic Filipinos," in "Essays into American Empire in the Philippines: Part 1—Legacies, Heroes, and Identity," ed. Enrique dela Cruz, centennial commemorative issue, *Amerasia* 24, no. 2 (1998): 155–78.

25. Laurena Cabañero interview by author; Lillian Galedo interview by author. See

also Karen Umemoto, "'On Strike!': San Francisco State College Strike, 1968–69: The Role of Asian American Students," *Amerasia* 15, no. 1 (1989): 3–41.

26. Conversation with Christine Bohulano Bloch, July 2001.

27. Lillian Galedo interview by author.

28. Habal, *San Francisco's International Hotel*, 27–28. See Carlos Bulosan, *America Is in the Heart: A Personal History* (Seattle: University of Washington Press, 1973).

29. Laurena Cabañero interview by author.

30. Rene Latosa interview by author.

31. Habal, *San Francisco's International Hotel*, 28.

32. Program for "Pamana," Luzviminda Dance Troupe performance at Stockton Junior High School Auditorium, May 4 and 5, 1973, Concepcion Bohulano papers, author's personal collection.

33. Mark V. Wiley, *The Secrets of Cabales Serrada Escrima* (Boston: Tuttle, 2000), 14–15. See also Leo Giron, *Giron Escrima: Memories of a Bladed Warrior* (Los Angeles: Empire, 2006), 86–87; and Dan Inosanto, *The Filipino Martial Arts* (Los Angeles: Know Now, 1980), 17–22.

34. Giron, *Giron Escrima*, 87; and Antonio Somera, *The Secrets of Giron Aris Escrima* (Boston: Tuttle, 1998), 13.

35. D. Inosanto, *The Filipino Martial Arts*, 9 and 21–29.

36. Rene Latosa interview by author.

37. Dorothy Cordova, "Biography of Larry Itliong," NPA FANHS.

38. Conversation with Mel LaGasca, Stockton FANHS chapter meeting, October 1, 2010.

39. "Official Notice to All Members of the United Farm Workers AFL-CIO," memo from Cesar Chavez to the UFW rank and file, 1971, Larry Itliong Collection, Box 1, Folder 9, UFW Collection, Walter P. Ruether Library, Wayne State University, Detroit, Michigan.

40. In 1977 Larry Itliong passed away suddenly at the age of sixty-four, a relatively young age given that many of his peers would live into their nineties. The Stockton community mourned the loss of one of its most impassioned and brilliant leaders. See Larry Itliong file, NPA FANHS.

41. Galedo, Cabañero, and Tom, "Roadblocks to Community Building," 20.

42. Ted Lapuz interview by author.

43. Lillian Galedo interview by author.

44. Laurena Cabañero interview by author.

45. Concepcion Bohulano interview by author, December 2002.

46. Ibid.

47. Quoted in Galedo, Cabañero, and Tom, "Roadblocks to Community Building," 26.

48. "New Proposal for Complex in West End; Filipino Groups Sponsor Plans," *Stockton Record*, April 5, 1968.

49. Galedo, Cabañero, and Tom, "Roadblocks to Community Building," 42–46.

50. Alma Alcala interview by author.

51. Galedo, Cabañero, and Tom, "Roadblocks to Community Building," 42–46.

52. Balantac, "A Brief History of the Filipino Center of Stockton, California," 3.

53. Galedo, Cabañero, and Tom, "Roadblocks to Community Building," 32.

54. Ibid., 33.

55. Luna Jamero interview by author.

56. Galedo, Cabañero, and Tom, "Roadblocks to Community Building," 34.

57. Ibid., 36.

58. Galedo, Cabañero, and Tom, "Roadblocks to Community Building," 36.

59. Ibid., 37.

60. Quoted in ibid., 39.

61. Quoted in ibid., 40.

62. Quoted in ibid., 46.

63. Quoted in ibid.

64. Balantac, "A Brief History of the Filipino Center of Stockton, California," 5.

65. Minutes, Board of Directors meeting, Associated Filipino Organizations of San Joaquin County, February 4, 1971, Concepcion Bohulano personal papers, Bohulano family collection.

66. Alma Alcala interview by author.

67. Ibid.

68. Conversation with Ernesto Tirona Mabalon by author, February 2003, Stockton, Calif.

69. Quoted in Galedo, Cabañero, and Tom, "Roadblocks to Community Building," 19.

70. Alma Alcala interview by author.

71. Quoted in Galedo, Cabañero, and Tom, "Roadblocks to Community Building," 22.

72. Concepcion Bohulano interview with author, September 2000.

73. Luna Jamero interview by author.

74. Quoted in "Filipino Fete at Mall Site," *Stockton Record*, July 25, 1971.

75. Ibid.

76. Laurena Cabañero interview by author.

77. "Filipino Center Groundbreaking Sat.," *Stockton News*, July 21, 1971.

78. Alma Alcala interview by author.

79. Quoted in Lillian Galedo, "Pinoy Power in Stockton," in *Filipino American Architecture, Design and Planning Issues*, ed. Anatalio C. Ubalde (Vallejo, Calif.: Flipside, 1996), 59.

80. Alma Alcala interview by author.

81. Ibid.

82. Ted Lapuz interview by author.

83. Luna Jamero interview by author.

84. Ibid.

85. Alma Alcala interview by author.

86. Ibid.

87. Luna Jamero interview by author.

88. Quoted in Galedo, "Pinoy Power in Stockton," 65.

89. Program for the 1972 Filipino People's Far West Convention, Far West Conventions files, NPA, FANHS.

90. *Kaisahan* program, Concepcion Bohulano personal papers, Bohulano family collection.

91. 1972 Filipino People's Far West Convention poster and program, Stockton, Calif., Stockton file, NPA, FANHS.

92. "Big Day for Stockton's Filipinos," *Stockton Record*, August 13, 1972.

93. "Dedication Held for Filipino Center," *Stockton Record*, August 12, 1972.

94. Concepcion Bohulano interview by author, December 2, 2002.

95. Balantac, "A Brief History of the Filipino Center of Stockton, California," 7.

96. Lillian Galedo interview by author.

1. Amy Starnes, "Corner of History Falls to Progress: Little Manila Gone but Not Forgotten," *Stockton Record*, May 19, 1999.

2. Yuji Ichioka, "A Buried Past: Early Issei Socialists and the Japanese Community," *Amerasia Journal* 1 no. 2 (1971): 1–25.

3. "Gleason Park Redevelopment Plan," City of Stockton, 1998, author's personal collection.

4. Dolores Hayden, *The Power of Place: Urban Landscapes as Public History* (Cambridge: MIT Press, 1997), 43.

5. Notes from phone meeting with Marilyn Guida of the Haggin Museum on August 8, 2000, author's personal collection.

6. Rick Delvecchio, "Big Push to Save Little Manila," *San Francisco Chronicle*, July 16, 2003.

7. Notes from meeting with Manuel Fernandez, 2003.

8. Emil Guillermo, "Left Out in Little Manila: Filipino Group to Lobby for Preservation, Fair process," *The Record*, June 3, 2003.

9. Carolyn Jones, "Seoul Searching for New Name in Oakland," *San Francisco Chronicle*, February 1, 2010; Maria Carle, "Oakland Koreatown Northgate Gives Birthday Present to Oakland for 160th Birthday," Oakland Local.com, accessed at http://oaklandlocal.com/posts/2012/04/oaklands-koreatown-northgate-gives-birthday-present-city-160th-birthday, on November 18, 2012.

10. Steve Rubenstein, "1,000 Jam Hearing, Most Like 'Little Saigon,'" *San Francisco Chronicle*, March 5, 2008; John Cote, "'Little Saigon' Battle May Be Over," *San Francisco Chronicle*, March 14, 2008.

11. Notes from Guida meeting.

12. Quoted in Emil Guillermo, "Little Manila Foundation Finds Competing Group," *The Record*, July 27, 2003.

13. Lillian Galedo, Laurena Cabañero, and Brian Tom, "Roadblocks to Community Building: A Case Study of the Stockton Filipino Community Center Project," Working Publication No. 4, Asian American Research Project, University of California, Davis, 1970.

14. Antonio J. A. Pido, *The Pilipinos in America: Macro/Micro Dimensions of Immigration and Integration* (New York: Center for Migration Studies, 1986), 81.

15. Oscar Domagas, "History Is Now for Filipinos," *The Record*, July 6, 2003.

16. Ibid.

17. Quoted in Stephen Howie, "It Has Come to This: But Little Manila, Stockton Ca.'s Once Vibrant Filipino Enclave, Does Not Lack for Champions," *Preservation*, November–December 2003, 37.

18. Quoted in John Glionna, "Saving a Harsh Picture of the Filipinos' Past," *Los Angeles Times*, May 31, 2003.

19. Evelyn Nieves, "Stockton, California Is Foreclosureville, U.S.A; Has One of the Worst Foreclosure Rates in the United States," *Huffington Post*, January 10, 2010, http://www.huffingtonpost.com/2010/01/10/stockton-california-is-fo_n_417704.html.

20. I deeply appreciate the support and example of Estella Habal, whose life as an activist and historian in the International Hotel struggle in San Francisco has been an inspiration for this project and for how I position myself as both scholar and activist. See her important book, *San Francisco's International Hotel: Mobilizing the Filipino Community in the Anti-Eviction Movement* (Philadelphia: Temple University Press, 2008).

BIBLIOGRAPHY

SPECIAL COLLECTIONS AND ARCHIVES

Agricultural Worker's Organizing Committee: Records, 1959–1966, Walter P. Reuther Library, Wayne State University, Detroit, Michigan; Microfilm, Doe Library, University of California, Berkeley.

Archdiocese of San Francisco: Archives, St. Patrick's Seminary, Menlo Park, Calif. Bank of Stockton: Photograph and Manuscript Archives, Stockton, Calif.

Carlos Bulosan: Papers, Special Collections, University of Washington, Seattle, Wash.

Bureau of Insular Affairs: Records, National Archives and Records Administration, College Park, Md.

Demonstration Project for Asian Americans: Photograph collection and documents, National Pinoy Archives, Filipino American National Historical Society, Seattle, Wash.

Filipino American Experience Research Project: CD-ROM, San Francisco State University, San Francisco, Calif.

Filipino American National Historical Society: Manuscript, Ephemera, and Photograph Archives, Stockton Chapter, Stockton, Calif.

Maxine Gonong: Papers, San Francisco History Center, San Francisco Public Library, Calif.

Hoover Institution: Manuscripts, Hoover Institution, Stanford University, Stanford, Calif.

The Haggin Museum: General files, Filipinos file, Caballeros de Dimas Alang file, Japanese Internment files, Chinese American files, Manuscript and Photograph Archives, Stockton, Calif.

Immigration and Naturalization Service: Records, National Archives and Records Administration, San Bruno, Calif.; records, National Archives and Records Administration, Washington, D.C.

Larry Itliong: Papers, United Farm Workers of America Collection, Walter P. Reuther Library, Wayne State University, Detroit, Mich.

Harold S. Jacoby and Pearl Shaffer Sweet: Papers, photographs, and manuscripts, Holt-Atherton Special Collections, University of the Pacific Library, Stockton, Calif.

Labor Archives and Research Center: Local 7 files, California Federation of Labor files, Filipino Labor File, *El Macriado* newspaper, *Daily People's World*, and additional manuscript collections and photographs, San Francisco State University, San Francisco, Calif.

Local History Collection: Cesar Chavez Central Branch, Stockton–San Joaquin County Public Library, Stockton, Calif.

National Pinoy Archives: Photographs, individual files, Stockton file, Labor files, Trinidad Rojo Papers, Juan C. Dionisio Papers, community organizations files, *Filipino Student Bulletin* Collection, Filipino American National Historical Society, Seattle, Wash.

Numancia Aid Association: Photographs and documents, Stockton, Calif.

Philippine Archives Collection: National Archives and Records Administration, College Park, Md.

Carlos P. Romulo: Papers, Special Collections, University of the Philippines, Diliman

Stockton City Archives: Office of the City Clerk, Stockton, Calif.

U.S. Census (1930): National Archives and Records Administration, San Bruno, Calif.

Visual Communications Archives: Photograph and Document Collection, Los Angeles, Calif.

U.S. Selective Service System, World War I Draft Registration Cards, 1917–1918, M1509, National Archives and Records Administration, Washington, D.C.

James Earl Wood: Papers, Manuscripts, Special Collections, Bancroft Library, University of California, Berkeley.

AUDIOTAPED AND VIDEOTAPED INTERVIEWS BY DAWN BOHULANO MABALON

Alma Alcala, October 6, 2002, Manteca, Calif.

Manuel Antaran, February 18, 1996, Stockton, Calif.

Moreno Balantac and Deanna Daclan Balantac, July 2001, Stockton, Calif.

Anita Navalta Bautista, March 11, 2003, Stockton, Calif.

Christine Bohulano Bloch, May 9, 1997, Stockton, Calif.

Concepcion Moreno Bohulano, November 27, 1992, Corona, Calif., and December 2, 2000, Stockton, Calif.

Laurena Cabañero, August 15, 2001, Sacramento, Calif.

Claro Candelario, February 15, 1993, Stockton, Calif.

Camila Labor Carido, January 15, 1996, February 19, 1996, and July 12, 2002, Stockton, Calif.

Dorothy Cordova, June 17, 2002, Seattle, Wash.

Fred Cordova, June 17, 2001, Seattle, Wash.

Paula Dizon Daclan, January 17, 1997, Stockton, Calif.

Jimmy Ente, January 30, 2007, Stockton, Calif.

Phyllis Cano Ente, January 30, 2007, Stockton, Calif.

Lillian Galedo, August 2001, Oakland, Calif.

Luna Jamero, August 21, 2010, Livingston, Calif.

Eudosia Bravo Juanitas, April 6, 1997, Stockton, Calif.

Concepcion Bulawit Lagura, July 8, 2001, Stockton, Calif.

Modesto Lagura, July 8, 2001, Stockton, Calif.

Eulogio "Ted" Lapuz, August 29, 2008, Stockton, Calif.

Rene Latosa, April 2008, San Francisco, Calif.

Helen Lagrimas Liwanag, July 9, 2001, Stockton, Calif.

Ernesto Tirona Mabalon, January 1996; May 1996; February 2003; October 23, 2003; Stockton, Calif.

Juan Malumay Macahilas, January 1, 1996, Stockton, Calif.

Angelina Bantillo Magdael and Leatrice Bantillo Perez, November 1999, Stockton, Calif.

Angelina Bantillo Magdael, August 17, 2001, Stockton, Calif.

Susanna Caballero Mangrobang, August 1999, Stockton, Calif.

Flora Arca Mata, May 24, 2002, Stockton, Calif., with Joan May T. Cordova

Nelson Nagai, November 26, 2001, Stockton, Calif.

Asuncion Guevarra Nicolas, January 1996, Stockton, Calif.

Angelina Candelario Novelozo, August 29, 2008, Stockton, Calif.

Eleanor Galvez Olamit, February 19, 1996, Stockton, Calif.

Florencia Mabalon Pastrana, May 1996, Stockton, Calif.

Jerry Paular, August 6, 2001, Sacramento, Calif.

Frank Perez, May 1999, Stockton, Calif.

Leatrice Bantillo Perez, December 2000; June 2003, Stockton, Calif.

Rizaline Monrayo Raymundo, November 16, 2000, San Jose, Calif.

Segunda Reyes, January 18, 1997, Stockton, Calif.

Lorenzo Romano Sr., August 14, 2001, Stockton, Calif.

Emily Behic Rosal, April 2007, Stockton, Calif.

Toribio "Terry" Rosal, February 18, 1996, Stockton, Calif.

Carmen Saldevar, September 2002, Stockton, Calif.

Pete Valoria, July 10, 2001, Stockton, Calif.

Buster Villa, July 2003, Stockton, Calif.

ADDITIONAL ORAL HISTORY INTERVIEWS

Filipino Oral History Project Interviews, Stockton, California, 1976–1982

Mary Arca Inosanto	Anastasio B. Pagala
Pablo Magdaluyo Mabalon	Nemesio D. Paguyo
Angelina Bantillo Magdael	Frank Perez
Flora Arca Mata	Policarpo Porras
George Montero	Fausto Rabaca
Ulpiano Morania	Segunda Reyes
Mr. and Mrs. Felipe Napala	Ignacio Sabedra
Sixto Nicolas	Antonio Santos

Filipino American National Historical Society Interviews, Seattle, Washington

Alberta Alcoy Asis	Cipriano Parlone Insular
Donnie Bilar	Maxima M. Marzan
Fred Castillano	Natividad Pacificar Moquite
Fred Cordova	Angelina Bantillo Magdael
Juan "Johnny" Dionisio	Remedios Tenedor

NEWSPAPERS

Commonwealth Times (Santa Maria, Calif.)
Filipino Journal (Stockton, Calif.)
Filipino Pioneer (Stockton, Calif.)
Filipino Student Bulletin (Seattle, Wash.)
Philippine Advertiser (Stockton, Calif.)
Philippine Examiner (Stockton, Calif.)
Philippine Journal (Stockton, Calif.)

Philippines Mail (Salinas, Calif.)

Philippines Press USA (San Jose, Calif.)

Philippines Star-Press (Stockton, Calif.)

The Record (1994–present, Stockton, Calif.)

Sacramento Bee (Sacramento, Calif.)

Stockton Daily Evening Record (1904–69, Stockton, Calif.)

Stockton Independent (Stockton, Calif.)

Stockton Record (1969–93, Stockton, Calif.)

Three Stars (Stockton, Calif.)

PUBLISHED SOURCES

Adams, David Wallace. *Education for Extinction: American Indians and the Boarding School Experience, 1875–1928*. Lawrence: University Press of Kansas, 1997.

Agatep, Myrtle O. *A Glimpse of Our Heritage*. Privately printed. Filipino Assemblies of the First Born, 1992.

Agoncillo, Teodoro. *A Short History of the Philippines*. New York: New American Library, 1969.

Aguilar, Filemino V., Jr. *A Clash of Spirits: The History of Power and Sugar Planter Hegemony on a Visayan Island*. Honolulu: University of Hawai'i Press, 1998.

Alamar, Estrella Ravelo and Willi Red Buhay. *Filipinos in Chicago*. Chicago: Arcadia Press, 2001.

Alcantara, Ruben. "The First Sakada." In *Filipinos in Hawaii: The First 75 Years*, edited by Juan C. Dionisio. Honolulu: Hawai'i Filipino News Specialty Publication, 1981.

Alegado, Dean T. "The Filipino Community in Hawaii: Development and Change." *Social Process in Hawaii* 33 (1991): 12–38.

Allan, James P. "Recent Immigration from the Philippines and Filipino Communities in the United States." *Geographical Review* 67, no. 2 (1977): 195–208.

Almaguer, Tomas. *Racial Faultlines: The Historical Origins of White Supremacy in California*. Berkeley: University of California Press, 2009.

Almario, Virgilio S., et al., eds. *100 Events That Shaped the Philippines*. Quezon City: National Centennial Commission, 2000.

Almirol, Edwin B. *Ethnic Identity and Social Negotiation: A Study of a Filipino Community in California*. New York: AMS, 1985.

———. "Filipino Voluntary Associations: Balancing Social Pressures and Ethnic Images." *Ethnic Groups* 2, no. 1 (1978): 65–92.

Amott, Teresa, and Julie Mattaei. *Race, Gender and Work: A Multicultural Economic History of Women in the United States*. Boston: South End, 1991.

Anderson, Benedict. "Hard to Imagine: A Puzzle in the History of Philippine Nationalism." In *Cultures and Texts: Representations of Philippine Society*, edited by Raul Pertierra and Eduardo F. Ugarte. Manila: University of the Philippines Press, 1994.

———. *Imagined Communities: Reflections on the Origin and Spread of Nationalism*. London: Verso, 1985.

Anderson, Karen. *Changing Woman: A History of Racial Ethnic Women in Modern America*. New York: Oxford University Press, 1996.

Anderson, Martin. *The Federal Bulldozer*. Cambridge: MIT Press, 1964.

———. "The Federal Bulldozer." In *Urban Renewal: The Record and the Controversy*, edited by James Q. Wilson. Cambridge: MIT Press, 1966.

Anderson, Warwick. *Colonial Pathologies: American Tropical Medicine, Race, and Hygiene in the Philippines*. Manila: Ateneo de Manila University Press, 2007.

Angangco, Ofelia Regalia, Laura L. Samson, and Teresita Albino. *Status of Women in the Philippines: A Bibliography with Selected Annotations*. Quezon City: Alemar-Phoenix, 1980.

Anthony, Donald E. "Filipino Labor in Central California." *Sociology and Social Research* 16, no. 2 (1931): 149–56.

Aptheker, Bettina. *Tapestries of Life: Women's Work, Women's Consciousness, and the Meaning of Daily Experience*. Amherst: University of Massachusetts Press, 1989.

Asian Women United of California, eds. *Making Waves: An Anthology of Writings by and about Asian American Women*. Boston: Beacon, 1989.

Azuma, Eiichiro. *Between Two Empires: Race, History and Transnationalism in Japanese America*. New York: Oxford University Press, 2005.

———. "Racial Struggle, Immigrant Nationalism, and Ethnic Identity: Japanese and Filipinos in the California Delta." *Pacific Historical Review* (May 1998): 163–99.

Baca Zinn, Maxine, and Dill, Bonnie Thornton, eds. *Women of Color in U.S. Society*. Philadelphia: Temple University Press, 1994.

Bacho, Peter. *Dark Blue Suit and Other Stories*. Seattle: University of Washington Press, 1997.

Balantac, Deanna Daclan. "History of the Santo Niño Association of Stockton and Vicinity, Incorporated." *Stockton Chapter Filipino American National Historical Society Newsletter*, January 2007, 5.

Bankoff, Greg. "Redefining Criminality: Gambling and Financial Expediency in the Colonial Philippines, 1764–1898." *Journal of Southeast Asian Studies* 22, no. 2 (1991): 267–81.

Bautista, Anita. "Love in the Time of Taxi Dancers." *Filipinas* (October 2007): 43–44.

Blight, David. "DuBois and the Struggle for American Historical Memory." In *History and Memory in African American Culture*, edited by Genevieve Fabre and Robert O'Meally, 45–75. New York: Oxford University Press, 1994.

Bloch, Louis. *Facts about Filipino Immigration into California*. State Department of Industrial Relations, April 1930.

Bodnar, John. *The Transplanted: A History of Immigrants in Urban America*. Bloomington: Indiana University Press, 1985.

Bogardus, Emory S. "American Attitudes towards Filipinos." *Sociology and Social Research* 14, no. 1 (September–October 1929): 59–69.

———. "Anti-Filipino Race Riots: A Report Made to the Ingram Institute of Social Science, of San Diego, by E. S. Bogardus, University of Southern California, May 15, 1930." In *Letters in Exile: An Introductory Reader on the History of Pilipinos in America*, edited by Jesse Quinsaat, 51–62. Los Angeles: UCLA Asian American Studies Center, 1976.

———. "Citizenship for Filipinos." *Sociology and Social Research* 29, no. 1: 51–54.

———. "Filipino Immigrant Attitudes." *Sociology and Social Research* 14, no. 5: 469–79.

———. "Filipino Repatriation." *Sociology and Social Research* 21, no. 1 (1936): 67–71.

Bonacich, Edna, and Lucie Cheng. *Labor Immigration under Capitalism: Asian Workers in the United States before World War II*. Berkeley: University of California Press, 1984.

Bonus, Rick. *Locating Filipino Americans: Ethnicity and the Cultural Politics of Space*. Philadelphia: Temple University Press, 2000.

Borah, Eloisa Gomez. "Filipinos in Unamuno's California Expedition of 1587." *Amerasia* 21, no. 3 (1996), 175–83.

Buaken, Manuel. *I Have Lived with the American People*. Caldwell, Idaho: Caxton, 1948.

Buchholdt, Thelma. *Filipinos in Alaska: 1788–1958*. Anchorage: Aboriginal, 1996.

Bulosan, Carlos. *America Is in the Heart: A Personal History*. 2nd ed. Seattle: University of Washington Press, 1973.

———. "Freedom from Want." *Saturday Evening Post*, March 6, 1943, 12–13.

———. *On Becoming Filipino: Selected Writings of Carlos Bulosan*. Edited by E. San Juan. Philadelphia: Temple University Press, 1995.

———. "The Romance of Magno Rubio." *Amerasia Journal* 6, no. 1 (1979): 33–50.

Burns, Jeff. "The Mexican Catholic Community in California." In *Mexican Americans and the Catholic Church*, edited by Jay P. Dolan and Gilberto M. Hinojosa, 128–233. University of Notre Dame Press, 1994.

Burton, Antoinette. *Archive Stories: Facts, Fictions, and the Writing of History*. Durham: Duke University Press, 2005.

———. *Dwelling in the Archive: Women Writing House, Home and History in Late Colonial India*. Oxford: Oxford University Press, 2003.

Bynum, Cornelius. *A. Philip Randolph and the Struggle for Civil Rights*. Urbana: University of Illinois Press, 2010.

Catapusan, Benicio T. "Filipino Immigrants and Public Relief in the United States." *Sociology and Social Research* 23, no. 6 (1939): 546–54.

———. "Filipino Intermarriage Problems in the United States." *Sociology and Social Research* 22, no. 3 (January 1938): 265–72.

Chan, Sucheng. *Asian Americans: An Interpretive History*. London: Prentice Hall, 1991.

———. *This Bittersweet Soil: The Chinese in California Agriculture, 1860–1910*. Berkeley: University of California Press, 1986.

Choy, Catherine Ceniza. *Empire of Care: Nursing and Migration in Filipino American History*. Durham: Duke University Press, 2003.

Clifford, Mary Dorita. "The Hawaiian Sugar Planters Association and Filipino Exclusion." In *Letters in Exile: An Introductory Reader on the History of the Pilipinos in America*, edited by Jesse Quinsaat, 74–89. Los Angeles: UCLA Asian American Studies Center, 1976.

Clymer, Kenton J. *Protestant Missionaries in the Philippines, 1898–1916: An Inquiry into the American Colonial Mentality*. Urbana: University of Illinois Press, 1986.

Coe, Andrew. *Chop Suey: A Cultural History of Chinese Food in the United States*. Oxford: Oxford University Press, 2009.

Cohen, Lizabeth. *Making a New Deal: Industrial Workers in Chicago, 1919–1939*. New York: Cambridge University Press, 1990.

Collins, Patricia Hill. *Black Feminist Thought: Knowledge, Consciousness, and the Politics of Empowerment*. Boston: Unwin Hyman, 1990.

Commonwealth Club of California. "Filipino Immigration." *Transactions of the Commonwealth Club of California* 24, no. 7 (November 5, 1929): 307–78.

Constantino, Renato. "The Miseducation of the Filipino." Excerpted in *The Philippines Reader: A History of Colonialism, Neocolonialism, Dictatorship, and Resistance*, edited by Daniel B. Schirmer and Stephen Rosskam Shalom, 45–49. Boston: South End, 1987.

Constantino, Renato, and Letizia R. Constantino. *The Philippines: A Past Revisited*. Vol. 1. Manila: Tala Pub. Services, 1975.

Cordova, Dorothy. "Voices from the Past: Why They Came." In *Making Waves: An Anthology of Writings by and about Asian American Women*, edited by Asian Women United of California, 42–49. Boston: Beacon, 1989.

Cordova, Fred. *Filipinos: Forgotten Asian Americans, A Pictorial Essay; 1763–Circa 1963*. Dubuque, Iowa: Kendall/Hunt, 1983.

Cordova, Joan May, and Alexis Canillo, eds. *Voices: A Filipino American Oral History*. Stockton, Calif.: Filipino Oral History, 1984.

Cortes, Rosario Mendoza. *Pangasinan: 1901–1986: A Political, Socioeconomic and Cultural History*. Quezon City, Philippines: New Day Publishers, 1975.

Cressey, Paul G. *The Taxi-Dance Hall: A Sociological Study in Commercialized Recreation and City Life*. Chicago: University of Chicago Press, 1932.

Crouchett, Lorraine Jacobs. *Filipinos in California: From the Days of the Galleons to the Present*. El Cerrito, Calif.: Downey Place, 1982.

Cruz, Jon D. "Filipino American Community Organizations in Washington, 1900–1930s." In *Peoples of Color in the American West*, edited by Sucheng Chan, 235–45. Lexington, Mass.: D. C. Heath and Company, 1994.

Daniel, Cletus E. *Bitter Harvest: A History of California Farmworkers, 1870–1941*. Berkeley: University of California Press, 1982.

Daniels, Roger. *Guarding the Golden Door: American Immigration Policy and Immigrants since 1882*. New York: Hill and Wang, 2004.

Davis, Olive. *Stockton: Sunrise Port on the San Joaquin*. Sun Valley, Calif.: American Historical Press, 1998.

de Jesus, Melinda, ed. *Pinay Power: Peminist Critical Theory*. New York: Routledge, 2006.

de la Cruz, Enrique. Centennial Commemorative Issue, Essays into American Empire in the Philippines: Part 1—Legacies, Heroes, and Identity. *Amerasia Journal* 24, no. 2, Summer 1998.

de la Cruz, Enrique, with Pearlie Rose S. Baluyot and Rico J. Reyes. *Confrontations, Crossings and Convergence: Photographs of the Philippines and the United States*. University of California Asian American Studies Center and the UCLA Southeast Asia Program, 1998.

Denning, Michael. *The Cultural Front: The Laboring of American Culture in the Twentieth Century*. London: Verso, 1996.

de Vera, Arleen. "The Tapia-Saiki Incident: Interethnic Conflict and Filipino Responses to the Anti-Filipino Exclusion Movement." In *Over the Edge: Mapping the American West*, edited by Valerie J. Matsumoto and Blake Allmendinger, 201–14. Berkeley: University of California Press, 1999.

————. "Without Parallel: The Local 7 Deportation Case, 1949–1955." *Amerasia Journal* 20, no. 2 (1994): 1–25.

DeWitt, Howard A. *Anti-Filipino Movements in California: A History, Bibliography, and Study Guide*. San Francisco: R and E Research Associates, 1976.

————. "The Filipino Labor Union: The Salinas Lettuce Strike of 1934." *Amerasia* 5, no. 2 (1978): 1–21.

————. *Violence in the Fields: California Filipino Farm Labor Unionization during the Great Depression*. Saratoga, N.Y.: Century Twenty One, 1980.

Di Leonardo, Micaela. *The Varieties of Ethnic Experience: Kinship, Class and Gender among California's Italian Americans*. Ithaca: Cornell University Press, 1984.

Dill, Bonnie Thornton. "Fictive Kin, Paper Sons and Compadrazgo: Women of Color and the Struggle for Family Survival." In *Women of Color in U.S. Society*, edited by Maxine Baca Zinn and Bonnie Thornton Dill, 149–70. Philadelphia: Temple University Press, 1994.

Duany, Andrés, Elizabeth Plater-Zyberk, and Jeff Speck. *Suburban Nation: The Rise of Sprawl and the Decline of the American Dream*. New York: North Point, 2000.

Dunne, John Gregory. *Delano: The Story of the California Grape Strike*. New York: Farrar, Straus and Giroux, 1967.

Empeno, Henry. "Anti-Miscegenation Laws and the Pilipino." In *Letters in Exile: An Introductory Reader on the History of the Pilipinos in America*, edited by Jesse G. Quinsaat, 63–71. Los Angeles: UCLA Asian American Studies Center, 1976.

España-Maram, Linda. *Creating Masculinity in Los Angeles' Little Manila: Working-Class Filipinos and Popular Culture, 1920s–1950s*. New York: Columbia University Press, 2006.

Espina, Marina E. *Filipinos in Louisiana*. New Orleans: A. F. Laborde, 1988.

Espiritu, August Fauni. *Five Faces of Exile: The Nation and Filipino American Intellectuals*. Stanford: Stanford University Press, 2005.

Espiritu, Yen Le. *Asian American Women and Men: Labor, Laws and Love*. Thousand Oaks, Calif.: Sage, 1997.

———. *Filipino American Lives*. Philadelphia: Temple University Press, 1995.

———. *Home Bound: Filipino American Lives across Cultures, Communities and Countries*. Berkeley: University of California Press, 2003.

Evangelista, Susan. *Carlos Bulosan and His Poetry: A Biography and Anthology*. Quezon City, Philippines: Ateneo de Manila University Press, 1985.

Evans, Sara M. *Born for Liberty: A History of Women in America*. New York: Free Press, 1989.

Eviota, Elizabeth Uy. *The Political Economy of Gender: Women and the Sexual Division of Labour in the Philippines*. London: Zed, 1992.

Fabre, Genevieve, and Robert O'Meally, eds. *History and Memory in African American Culture*. New York: Oxford University Press, 1994.

Fabros, Alex S., Jr., and Katherine S. Fabros. "Jersey Island Murder Case." *Filipinas*, October 1997, 66–69.

Felipe, Virgilio Menor. *Hawai'i: A Pilipino Dream*. Honolulu: Mutual, 2002.

Feria, R. T. "War and the Status of Filipino Immigrants." *Sociology and Social Research* 31, no. 1 (September–October 1946): 48–53.

Fernandez, Doreen G. *Tikim: Essays on Philippine Food and Culture*. Pasig City, Philippines: Anvil, 1994.

———. *Palayok: Philippine Food Through Time, On Site, In the Pot*. Manila: Bookmark, 2000.

Ferriss, Susan, and Ricardo Sandoval. *The Fight in the Fields: Cesar Chavez and the Farmworkers Movement*. New York: Harcourt, Brace, 1997.

Filipino American National Historical Society, Central Valley Chapter. *Talk Story: Anthology of the Stories by Filipino Americans of the Central Valley of California*. Merced, Calif.: Carpenter Printing, 2008.

"Filipino Immigration." *The Commonwealth—Part II*. Vol. 5, no. 45, November 5, 1929, San Francisco, Calif.

Findley, Sally E. *Rural Development and Migration: A Study of Family Choices in the Philippines*. Brown University Studies in Population and Development. Boulder, Colo.: Westview Press, 1987.

Fischer, Michael M. J. "Ethnicity and the Post-Modern Arts of Memory." In *Writing Culture: The Poetics and Politics of Ethnography*, edited by James Clifford and George Marcus. Berkeley: University of California Press, 1986.

Forbes, W. Cameron. *The Philippine Islands*. Cambridge: Harvard University Press, 1945 (originally published in 1928).

Foronda, Marcelino A., Jr. "America Is in the Heart: Ilokano Immigration to the United States (1906–1930)." De La Salle University Occasional Paper No. 3, August 1976.

Foster, Nellie. "Legal Status of Filipino Intermarriages in California." *Sociology and Social Research* 16, no. 5 (1932): 441–54.

Francisco, Luzviminda. "The Philippine-American War." In *The Philippines Reader: A History of Colonialism, Neocolonialism, Dictatorship, and Resistance*, edited by Daniel B. Schirmer and Stephen Rosskam Shalom, 8–19. Boston: South End, 1987.

Friday, Chris. *Organizing Asian-American Labor: The Pacific Coast Canned-Salmon Industry, 1870–1942*. Philadelphia: Temple University Press, 1994.

Frisch, Michael. *A Shared Authority: Essays on the Craft and Meaning of Oral and Public History*. Albany: State University of New York, 1990.

Fuchs, Lawrence H. *Hawaii Pono: A Social History*. New York: Harcourt, Brace and World, 1961.

Fujita-Rony, Dorothy B. *American Workers, Colonial Power: Philippine Seattle and the Transpacific West, 1919–1941*. Berkeley: University of California Press, 2003.

Galedo, Lillian. "Pinoy Power in Stockton." In *Filipino American Architecture, Design and Planning Issues*, edited by Anatalio C. Ubalde, 59–65. Vallejo, Calif.: Flipside, 1996.

Galedo, Lillian, Laurena Cabañero, and Brian Tom. "Roadblocks to Community Building: A Case Study of the Stockton Filipino Community Center Project." Working Publication No. 4. Asian American Research Project, University of California, Davis, 1970.

Galura, Joseph, and Emily P. Lawsin, eds. *Filipino Women in Detroit: Oral Histories from the Filipino American Oral History Project of Michigan*. Ann Arbor, OCSL Press of the University of Michigan, 2002.

Gans, Herbert. *The Urban Villagers: Group and Class in the Life of Italian-Americans*, rev. and expanded ed. New York: Free Press, 1962.

Garcia, Matt. *A World of Its Own: Race, Labor and Citrus in the Making of Greater Los Angeles, 1900–1970*. Chapel Hill: University of North Carolina Press, 2001.

Gardner, Leonard. *Fat City*. New York: Lescher & Lescher, 1969.

Gatewood, Willard B., Jr. *"Smoked Yankees" and the Struggle for Empire: Letters from Negro Soldiers, 1898–1902*. Urbana: University of Illinois Press, 1971.

Gillis, Chester. *Roman Catholicism in America*. New York: Columbia University Press, 1999.

Giron, Leo. *Giron Escrima: Memories of a Bladed Warrior*. Los Angeles: Empire, 2006.

Glenn, Evelyn Nakano. "From Servitude to Service Work: Historical Continuities in the Racial Division of Paid Reproductive Labor." *Signs* 18, no. 1, 1992.

———. *Issei, Nisei, War Bride: Three Generations of Japanese American Women in Domestic Service*. Philadelphia: Temple University Press, 1986.

Glody, Robert. *A Shepherd of the Far North: The Story of William Francis Walsh (1900–1930)*. San Francisco: Harr Wagner, n.d.

Goethe, C. M. "Filipino Immigration Viewed as a Peril." *Current History*, June 1931, 129–30.

Golay, Frank Hindman. *Face of Empire: United States-Philippine Relations, 1898–1946*. Manila: Ateneo de Manila University Press, 1997.

Gonzáles, Rosalinda. "Chicanas and Mexican Immigrant Families, 1920–1940: Women's Subordination and Exploitation." In *Decades of Discontent, 1920–1940*, edited by Lois Scharf and Joan M. Jenson, 59–84. Westport, Conn.: Greenwood Press, 1983.

Gonzalo, D. F. "Social Adjustments of Filipinos in America." *Sociology and Social Research* 14 (2): 166–73.

Gowing, Peter G. *Islands under the Cross: The Story of the Church in the Philippines*. Manila: National Council of Churches in the Philippines, 1967.

Grebler, Leo, Joan W. Moore, Ralph C. Guzmán, and Jeffrey Lionel Berlant, *The Mexican American People: The Nation's Second Largest Minority*. New York: Free Press, 1970.

Gregory, James N. *American Exodus: Dust Bowl Migration and Okie Culture in California*. New York: Oxford University Press, 1991.

Groth, Paul. *Living Downtown: The History of Residential Hotels in the United States*. Berkeley: University of California Press, 1994.

Guevarra, Rudy, Jr. "'Skid Row': Filipinos, Race and the Social Construction of Space in San Diego." *Journal of San Diego History* 54, no. 1 (2008): 26–38.

Guillermo, Emil. "Hounded to Death: The FBI File of Carlos Bulosan." *Asian Week*, November 8, 2002.

Guimary, Donald L. *Marumina Trabajo: A History of Labor in Alaska's Salmon Canning Industry*. New York: iUniverse, 2006.

Guyotte, Ronald L., and Barbara Posadas. "Celebrating Rizal Day: The Emergence of a Filipino Tradition in Twentieth Century Chicago." In *Feasts and Celebrations in North American Ethnic Communities*, edited by Ramon A. Gutierrez and Genevieve Fabre, 111–27. Albuquerque: University of New Mexico Press, 1995.

Habal, Estella. *San Francisco's International Hotel: Mobilizing the Filipino Community in the Anti-Eviction Movement*. Philadelphia: Temple University Press, 2008.

Halili, Christine N., and Maria Christine Halili. *Philippine History*. Manila: Rex Bookstore, 2004.

Hammond, George P. *The Weber Era in Stockton History*. Berkeley: Issued for the Friends of the Bancroft Library, University of California, 1982.

Handlin, Oscar. *The Uprooted: The Epic Story of the Great Migrations That Made the American People*. Boston: Little, Brown, 1951.

Hayden, Dolores. *The Power of Place: Urban Landscapes as Public History*. Cambridge: MIT Press, 1997.

Hemminger, Carol. "Little Manila: The Filipino in Stockton Prior to World War II." *Pacific Historian* 24, no. 1 (1980): 12–26.

Hillman, Raymond. *Stockton through the Decades*. Stockton, Calif.: Vanguard, 1981.

Ho, Fred, Carolyn Antonio, Diane Fujino, and Steve Yip, eds. *Legacy to Liberation: Politics and Culture of Revolutionary Asian Pacific America*. San Francisco: Big Red Media and AK Press, 2000.

Hondagneu-Sotelo, Pierrette. *Gendered Transitions: Mexican Experiences of Immigration*. Berkeley: University of California Press, 1994.

hooks, bell. *Feminist Theory: From Margin to Center*. Boston: South End, 1984.

Howie, Stephen. "It Has Come to This: But Little Manila, Stockton Ca.'s Once Vibrant Filipino Enclave, Does Not Lack for Champions." *Preservation*, November–December 2003, 34–37.

Humes, Edward. *Over Here: How the G.I. Bill Transformed the American Dream*. Orlando, Fla.: Harcourt, 2006.

Hunter, Allan. *Out of the Far East*. 1934. Reprinted San Francisco: R and E Research Associates, 1972.

Ichioka, Yuji. "A Buried Past: Early Issei Socialists and the Japanese Community." *Amerasia Journal* 1 no. 2 (1971): 1–25.

Ileto, Reynaldo C. "Cholera and the Origins of the American Sanitary Order." In *Discrepant Histories: Translocal Essays on Filipino Cultures*, edited by Vicente L. Rafael, 54. Philadelphia: Temple University Press, 1995.

————. *Pasyon and Revolution: Popular Movements in the Philippines, 1840–1910*. Quezon City: Ateneo de Manila University Press, 1979.

Inosanto, Dan. *The Filipino Martial Arts as Taught by Dan Inosanto*. Los Angeles: Know Now, 1980.

Inosanto, Sebastian N. *The Story of Trinity Presbyterian Church*. Rev. ed. Stockton, Calif.: Trinity Presbyterian Church, 1992.

Jackson, Kenneth T. *Crabgrass Frontier: The Suburbanization of the United States*. New York: Oxford University Press, 1985.

Jacobs, Jane. *The Life and Death of Great American Cities*. New York: Random House, 1961.

Jacobsen, Matthew Fry. *Whiteness of a Different Color: European Immigrants and the Alchemy of Race*. Cambridge: Harvard University Press, 1998.

Jakle, John A., and David Wilson, *Derelict Landscapes: The Wasting of America's Built Environment*. Savage, Md.: Rowman and Littlefield, 1992.

Jamero, Peter. *Growing Up Brown: Memoirs of a Filipino American*. Seattle: University of Washington Press, 2006.

Jamieson, Stuart Marshall. *Labor Unionism in California Agriculture*. U.S. Department of Labor Bulletin 836. Washington, D.C.: Government Printing Office, 1945.

Jenkins, J. Craig. *The Politics of Insurgency: The Farm Worker Movement in the 1960s*. New York: Columbia University Press, 1985.

Joaquin, Nick. *The Aquinos of Tarlac: An Essay on History as Three Generations*. Manila: Solar, 1988.

Jocano, Landa F. *Growing up in a Philippine Barrio*. New York: Holt, Rhinehart and Winston, 1969.

Johnson, Susan Lee. *Roaring Camp: The Social World of the California Gold Rush*. New York: W. W. Norton, 2000.

Junasa, Bienvenido D. "The Great Filipino Migration." In *Filipinos in Hawaii: The First 75 Years*, ed. Juan C. Dionisio. Honolulu: Hawai'i Filipino News Specialty Publication, 1981. 53–54.

Kalcik, Susan. "Ethnic Foodways in America: Symbol and Performance." In *Ethnic and Regional Foodways in the United States: The Performance of Group Identity*, edited by Linda Brown and Kay Mussel, 37–65. Knoxville: Temple University Press, 1984.

Kaplan, Amy, and Donald E. Pease, eds. *Cultures of United States Imperialism*. Durham: Duke University Press, 1993.

Karnow, Stanley. *In Our Image: America's Empire in the Philippines*. New York: Ballantine, 1990.

Katznelson, Ira. *When Affirmative Action Was White: The Untold Story of Racial Inequality in Twentieth Century America*. New York: W. W. Norton, 2005.

Kelly, Perry William. *Dan Inosanto: The Man, The Teacher, The Artist*. Boulder, Colo.: Paladin, 2000.

Kennedy, David A. *Freedom from Fear: The American People in Depression and War, 1929–1945*. New York: Oxford University Press, 1999.

Kennedy, Glenn Alvin. *It Happened in Stockton*. 2 vols. Stockton, Calif.: Kenco Reproduction, 1967.

Kerkvliet, Benedict J. *The Huk Rebellion: A Study of Peasant Revolt in the Philippines*. Berkeley: University of California Press, 1977.

Kerkvliet, Melinda Tria. "Pablo Manlapit's Fight for Justice." In "The Filipino American Experience in Hawaii, in Commemoration of the 85th Anniversary of Filipino Immigration to Hawai'i" special issue. *Social Process in Hawaii* 33 (1991): 153–68.

⸺. *Unbending Cane: Pablo Manlapit, A Filipino Labor Leader in Hawaii*. Honolulu: Office of Multicultural Student Services, University of Hawai'i Press, 2002.

Kett, Joseph F. *Rites of Passage: Adolescence in America, 1790 to the Present*. New York: Basic, 1977.

Kibria, Nazli. *Family Tightrope: The Changing Lives of Vietnamese Americans*. Princeton: Princeton University Press, 1993.

⸺. "Migration and Vietnamese American Women: Remaking Ethnicity." In *Women of Color in U.S. Society*, edited by Maxine Baca Zinn and Bonnie Thornton Dill, 247–61. Philadelphia: Temple University Press, 1994.

Kim, Hyung-chan, and Cynthia C. Mejia. *The Filipinos in America, 1898–1974: A Chronology and Fact Book*. Dobbs Ferry, N.Y.: Oceana, 1976.

Koerner, Mae Respicio. *Filipinos in Los Angeles*. Charleston, S.C.: Arcadia, 2007.

Kramer, Paul A. *The Blood of Government: Race, Empire, the United States, and the Philippines*. Chapel Hill: University of North Carolina Press, 2006.

Kurashige, Scott. *The Shifting Grounds of Race: Black and Japanese Americans in the Making of Multiethnic Los Angeles*. Princeton: Princeton University Press, 2008.

Kushner, Sam. *Long Road to Delano*. New York: International, 1975.

Kwantes, Anne C. *Presbyterian Missionaries in the Philippines: Conduits of Social Change (1899–1910)*. Quezon City, Philippines: New Day Publishers, 1989.

Larkin, John A. *Sugar and the Origins of Modern Philippine Society*. Manila: New Day, 2001.

Lasker, Bruno. *Filipino Immigration to the Continental United States and to Hawaii*. Chicago: University of Chicago Press, 1931.

Lawsin, Emily Porcincula. "Hanggang Pier Na Lamang: Filipina War Brides of Seattle." *Filipino American National Historical Society Journal* 4 (1996): 50A–50G.

⸺. "Pensionados, Paisanos and Pinoys: An Analysis of the *Filipino Student Bulletin*, 1922–1939." *Filipino American National Historical Society Journal* 4 (1996): 33A–33P.

Lee, Jennifer 8. *The Fortune Cookie Chronicles*. New York: Hachette, 2008.

Leonard, Karen Isaksen. *Making Ethnic Choices: California's Punjabi Mexican Americans*. Philadelphia: Temple University Press, 1992.

Lewis, Henry T. *Ilocano Rice Farmers: A Comparative Study of Two Philippine Barrios*. Honolulu: University of Hawai'i Press, 1971.

Lim, Shirley Jennifer. *A Feeling of Belonging: Asian American Women's Public Culture, 1930–1960*. New York: New York University Press, 2005.

Limerick, Patricia Nelson. *The Legacy of Conquest: The Unbroken Past of the American West*. New York: W. W. Norton, 1987.

Litwack, Lawrence. *Trouble in Mind: Black Southerners in the Age of Jim Crow*. New York: Knopf, 1988.

Liwanag: Literary and Graphic Expressions by Filipinos in America. San Francisco: Liwanag Publishing, 1975.

London, Joan, and Henry Anderson. *So Shall Ye Reap: The Story of Cesar Chavez and the Farm Workers' Movement*. New York: Thomas Y. Crowell, 1970.

Lott, Juanita Tamayo. *Common Destiny: Filipino American Generations*. Lanham, Md.: Rowman and Littlefield, 2006.

Louie, Steve, and Glenn Omatsu, eds. *Asian Americans: The Movement and the Moment*. Los Angeles: UCLA Asian American Studies Center Press, 2001.

Mananzan, Sr., Mary John, ed. "Essays on Women." Women's Studies Series 1, Institute of Women's Studies, St. Scholastica's College, 1991.

Mangahas, Fe. "From Babaylan to Suffragettes: The Status of Filipino Women from Pre-Colonial Times to the Early American Period." *Kamalayan: Feminist Writings in the Philippines* (1987): 8-20.

Marks, Alfred. "Stockton." In *Mercantile Guide: Business Directory of the Principal Cities of California*. Vol. 26. San Francisco, 1928.

Masson, Jack, and Donald Guimary. "Asian Labor Contractors in the Alaskan Canned Salmon Industry: 1880–1937." *Labor History* 22, no. 3 (1981): 377–97.

Matsumoto, Valerie J. "Desperately Seeking Deirdre: Gender Roles, Multicultural Relations, and Nisei Women Writers of the 1930s." *Frontiers: A Journal of Women Studies* 12, no. 1 (1991): 19–32.

———. *Farming the Home Place: A Japanese American Community in California, 1919–1982*. Ithaca: Cornell University Press, 1993.

———. "Japanese American Women and the Creation of Urban Nisei Culture in the 1930s." In *Over the Edge: Remapping the American West*, ed. Valerie J. Matsumoto and Blake Allmendinger, 291–306. Berkeley: University of California Press, 1999.

———. "Japanese American Women during World War II." *Frontiers: A Journal of Women Studies* 8, no. 1 (1984): 6–14.

———. "Redefining Expectations: Nisei Women in the 1930s." *California History*, no. 1 (1994): 44–53.

Matsumoto, Valerie J., and Blake Allmendinger. *Over the Edge: Remapping the American West*. Berkeley: University of California Press, 1999.

Mazumdar, Sucheta, "General Introduction: A Woman Centered Perspective on Asian American History." In *Making Waves: An Anthology of Writings by and about Asian American Women*, edited by Asian Women United of California, 1–22. Boston: Beacon, 1989.

McWilliams, Carey. *Brothers under the Skin*. Boston: Little, Brown, 1964.

———. "California and the Japanese." *New Republic*, March 2, 1942, 295.

———. "Exit the Filipino." *Nation*, September 4, 1935, 265.

———. *Factories in the Field: The Story of Migratory Farm Labor in California*. Santa Barbara, Calif.: Peregrine, 1971.

Medina, Belen T. G. *The Filipino Family: A Text with Selected Readings*. Manila: University of the Philippines Press, 1991.

Meister, Dick, and Anne Loftis. *A Long Time Coming: The Struggle to Unionize America's Farm Workers*. New York: Macmillan, 1977.

Melendy, H. Brett. *Asians in America: Filipinos, Koreans, and East Indians*. Boston: Twayne, 1977.

———. "California's Discrimination against Filipinos." In *Letters in Exile: An Introductory Reader on the History of the Pilipinos in America*, edited by Jesse G. Quinsaat, 35–44. Los Angeles: UCLA Asian American Studies Center, 1976.

Meñez, Herminia. *Explorations in Philippine Folklore*. Manila: Ateneo de Manila University Press, 1996.

Mercene, Floro L. *Manila Men in the New World: Filipino Migration to Mexico and the Americas from the Sixteenth Century*. Quezon City: University of the Philippines Press, 2007.

Miller, Sally M., and Mary Wedergaertner. "Breadwinners and Builders Part II: Stockton's Immigrant Women." *The Californians*, September–October 1986.

Miller, Stuart Creighton. *Benevolent Assimilation: The American Conquest of the Philippines, 1899–1903*. New Haven: Yale University Press, 1982.

Milner, Clyde A., II, ed. *Major Problems in the History of the American West: Documents and Essays*. Lexington, Mass.: Heath, 1989.

Minnick, Sylvia Sun. *Samfow: The San Joaquin Chinese Legacy*. Fresno, Calif.: Panorama West, 1988.

Mohl, Raymond A. "Shifting Patterns of American Urban Policy since 1900." In *Urban Policy in Twentieth Century America*, edited by Arnold R. Hirsch and Raymond A. Mohl, 1–45. New Brunswick, N.J.: Rutgers University Press, 1993.

Molina, Natalia. *Fit to Be Citizens? Public Health and Race in Los Angeles, 1879–1939*. Berkeley: University of California Press, 2006.

Monrayo, Angeles. *Tomorrow's Memories: A Diary, 1924–1928*. Edited by Rizaline R. Raymundo. Honolulu: University of Hawai'i Press, 2003.

Morales, Royal F. *Makibaka: The Pilipino American Struggle*. Los Angeles: Mountainview, 1974.

Morgan, Scott. "Nostalgia and the Present: Filipino Hometown and Provincial Associations in California." In *Patterns of Migration in Southeast Asia*, edited by Robert R. Reed, 258–81. Berkeley: University of California, Centers for South and Southeast Asian Studies, 1990.

Nagai, Nelson. "The Death of Nihonmachi." *Nikkei Heritage* 12–13 (Fall 2000–Winter 2001): 10–11.

Nakpil, Carmen Guerrero. *Woman Enough and Other Essays*. Quezon City, Philippines: Vibal Publishing House, 1963.

Navarro, Jovina. "Immigration of Pilipino Women to America." In *Lahing Pilipino: Pilipino American Anthology*. Sacramento: University of California at Davis, 1977.

Nelson, Eugene. *Huelga! The First Hundred Days of the Great Delano Grape Strike*. Delano, Calif.: Farmworkers, 1966.

Ngai, Mae M. *Impossible Subjects: Illegal Aliens and the Making of Modern America*. Princeton: Princeton University Press, 2004.

Okamura, Jonathan. "Filipino American History in Hawai'i: A Young Visayan Woman's Perspective." In Angeles Monrayo, *Tomorrow's Memories: A Diary, 1924–1928*, edited by Rizaline Raymundo, 230–31. Honolulu: University of Hawai'i Press, 2003.

———. "Filipino Organizations: A History." In *The Filipinos in Hawaii: The First 75 Years*, edited by Juan C. Dionisio, 73–77. Honolulu: Hawaii Filipino News Specialty Publications, 1981.

———. *Imagining the Filipino American Diaspora: Transnational Relations, Identities, and Communities*. New York: Garland, 1998.

Okamura, Jonathan, Amefil R. Agbayani, and Melinda Tria Kerkvliet, guest eds. "The Filipino Experience in Hawai'i: In Commemoration of the 85th Anniversary of Filipino Immigration to Hawai'i." Special issue of *Social Process in Hawaii* 33 (1991).

Omi, Michael, and Howard Winant. *Racial Formation in the United States: From the 1960s to the 1980s*. 2nd ed. New York: Routledge, 1994.

Orpilla, Mel. *Filipinos in Vallejo*. Charleston, S.C.: Arcadia, 2005.

Palladino, Grace. *Teenagers*. New York: Basic, 1996.

Palmer, Albert W. *Orientals in American Life*. New York: Friendship Press, 1934.

Parreñas, Rhacel Salazar. "'White Trash' Meets the 'Little Brown Monkeys': The Taxi Dance Hall as a Site of Interracial and Gender Relations between White Working Class Women and Filipino Immigrant Men in the 1920s and 30s." *Amerasia* 24, no. 2 (1998): 115–34.

Pascoe, Peggy. *Relations of Rescue: The Search for Female Moral Authority in the American West, 1874–1939*. New York: Oxford University Press, 1990.

Pasquil, Corky, dir. *The Great Pinoy Boxing Era*. San Francisco: Center for Asian American Media, 1994.

Patterson, James. *Grand Expectations: The United States, 1945–1974*. New York: Oxford University Press, 1996.

Paulet, Anne. "To Change the World: The Use of American Indian Education in the Philippines." *History of Education Quarterly* 27, no. 2 (2007): 173–202.

Perez, Frank, and Leatrice Bantillo Perez, guest editors. "The Long Struggle for Acceptance: Filipinos in San Joaquin County." Special issue, *San Joaquin Historian* 8, no. 4 (1994).

Pfeffer, George Anthony. *If They Don't Bring Their Women Here: Chinese Female Immigration before Exclusion*. Urbana: University of Illinois Press, 1999.

Phelan, John Leddy. *The Hispanization of the Philippines: Spanish Aims and Filipino Responses, 1565–1700*. Madison: University of Wisconsin Press, 1967.

Pido, Antonio J. A. *The Pilipinos in America: Macro/Micro Dimensions of Immigration and Integration*. New York: Center for Migration Studies, 1986.

Pivar, David J. "The American Federation of Labor and Filipino Exclusion: 1927–1934." In *The Filipino Exclusion Movement*, edited by Josefa M. Saniel, 30–39. University of the Philippines, 1967.

Polk city directories for Stockton, Calif., 1920–75, Cesar Chavez Central Branch, Stockton-San Joaquin County Public Library, Stockton, Calif.

Portelli, Alessandro. "What Makes Oral History Different." In *The Oral History Reader*, edited by Robert Perks and Alistair Thompson, 63–74. New York: Routledge, 1998.

Posadas, Barbara M. "Crossed Boundaries in Interracial Chicago: Pilipino American Families Since 1925." *Amerasia Journal* 8, no. 2 (1981): 31–52.

———. *The Filipino Americans*. Westport, Conn.: Greenwood, 1999.

Posadas, Barbara M., and Roland L. Guyotte. "Unintentional Immigrants: Chicago's Filipino Foreign Students Become Settlers, 1900–1941." *Journal of American Ethnic History* 9, no. 2 (1990): 26–48.

Prieto, Laura. "Stepmother America: The Woman's Board of Missions in the Philippines, 1902–1930." In *Competing Kingdoms: Women, Mission, Nation and the American Protestant Empire*, edited by Barbara Reeves-Ellington, Kathryn Kish Sklar, and Connie A. Shemo, 342–66. Durham: Duke University Press, 2010.

Quinsaat, Jesse G., ed. *Letters in Exile: An Introductory Reader on the History of the Pilipinos in America*. Los Angeles: UCLA Asian American Studies Center, 1976.

Racelis, Mary, and Judy Celine Ick, eds. *Bearers of Benevolence: The Thomasites and Public Education in the Philippines*. Pasig City, Philippines: Anvil, 2001.

Rafael, Vicente L., ed. *Discrepant Histories: Translocal Essays on Filipino Cultures*. Manila: Anvil Publishing, 1995.

———. *White Love and Other Events in Filipino History*. Durham: Duke University Press, 2000.

Ramsey, W. C. "Stockton: The Chicago of the Far West." *Overland Monthly* (September 1895): 297–314.

Ratzinger, Joseph. "Declaration on Masonic Associations." November 26, 1983. Rome: Office of the Sacred Congregation for the Doctrine of the Faith.

Regalado, Felix B., and Quintin B. Franco. *History of Panay*. Central Philippine University, 1973.

Reinecke, John E. *The Filipino Piecemeal Sugar Strike of 1924–1925*. Social Science Research Institute, University of Hawai'i, 1996.

Revilla, Linda. "Filipino American Women." In *Asian American Encyclopedia*, edited by Franklin Ng. New York: Marshall Cavendish, 1995.

Reyes, Vince. "The War Brides." *Filipinas*, October 1995, 22–24.

Roces, Mina. "Gender, Nation, and the Politics of Dress in Twentieth Century Philippines." In *The Politics of Dress in Asia and the Americas*, edited by Mina Roces and Louise Edwards, 19–41. Eastbourne, Great Britain: Sussex Academic Press, 2010.

Roediger, David. *Working towards Whiteness: How America's Immigrants Become White*. New York: Basic, 2005.

Rojo, Trinidad. "Social Maladjustment among Filipinos in the United States." *Sociology and Social Research* 21, no. 5 (1937): 447–57.

Root, Maria P. P., ed. *Filipino Americans: Transformation and Identity*. Thousand Oaks, Calif.: Sage, 1997.

Ruiz, Vicki L. *From Out of the Shadows: Mexican Women in Twentieth-Century America*. New York: Oxford University Press, 1998.

Said, Edward. *Orientalism*. New York: Vintage, 1979.

Salomon, Larry. "Filipinos Build a Movement for Justice in the Asparagus Fields." *Third Force* 2, no. 4 (October 31, 1994): 30.

San Buenaventura, Steffi. "The Colors of Manifest Destiny." In "Essays into American Empire in the Philippines," special issue, *Amerasia* 24, no. 3 (1998): 1–26.

———. "Filipino Folk Spirituality and Immigration: From Mutual Aid to Religion." *Amerasia* 1, no. 22 (1996): 1–30.

———. "Filipino Folk Spirituality and Immigration: From Mutual Aid to Religion." In *New Spiritual Homes: Religion and Asian Americans*, edited by David K. Yoo, 52–86. Honolulu: University of Hawaii Press with the UCLA Asian American Studies Center, 1999.

———. "Filipino Immigration to the United States." In *Asian American Encyclopedia*, edited by Franklin Ng, 445–48. New York: Marshall Cavendish, 1995.

———. "Filipino Religion at Home and Abroad: Historical Roots and Immigrant Transformations." In *Religions in Asian America: Building Faith Communities*, edited by Pyong Gap Min and Jung Ha Kim, 143–84. Walnut Creek, Calif: Altamira, 2002.

San Buenaventura, Steffi, and Linda S. Revilla. "Filipino Veterans and Naturalization." In *Asian American Encyclopedia*, edited by Franklin Ng, 468–69. New York: Marshall Cavendish, 1995.

Sanchez, George. *Becoming Mexican American: Ethnicity, Culture and Identity in Chicano Los Angeles, 1900–1945*. New York: Oxford University Press, 1993.

———. "Go after the Women: Americanization and the Mexican Immigrant Woman, 1915–1929." In *Unequal Sisters: A Multi-Cultural Reader in U.S. Woman's History*, edited by Vicki Ruiz and Ellen Carol DuBois, 250–63. 2nd ed. New York: Routledge, 1994.

San Juan, E. *The Philippine Temptation: Dialectics of Philippines-U.S. Relations*. Philadelphia: Temple University Press, 1996.

Santos, Bienvenido. "Filipinos in War." *Far Eastern Survey* 2 (November 30, 1942): 249–50.

Saxton, Alexander. *The Indispensable Enemy: Labor and the Anti-Chinese Movement in California*. Berkeley: University of California Press, 1971.

Scharlin, Craig, and Lilia V. Villanueva. *Philip Vera Cruz: A Personal History of Filipino Immigrants and the Farmworkers Movement*. Los Angeles: UCLA Labor Center, Institute of Industrial Relations and UCLA Asian American Studies Center, 1992.

Scharrenberg, Paul. "The Philippine Problem." *Pacific Affairs* 2 no. 2 (February 1929): 49–54.

Schirmer, Daniel B., and Stephen Rosskam Shalom, eds. *The Philippines Reader: A History of Colonialism, Neocolonialism, Dictatorship and Resistance*. Boston: South End, 1987.

Schumacher, John N., s.j. *The Propaganda Movement, 1880–1895*. Quezon City: Ateneo de Manila University Press, 1997.

Schwartz, Harry. "Recent Developments among Farm Labor Unions." *Journal of Farm Economics* 23, no. 4 (1941): 833–42.

Schwartz, Stephen. *From West to East: California and the Making of the American Mind.* New York: Free Press, 1998.

Scott, William Henry. *Cracks in the Parchment Curtain and Other Essays in Philippine History*. Quezon City: New Day, 1982.

———. *Ilocano Responses to American Aggression, 1900–1901*. Quezon City: New Day, 1986.

Seller, Maxine Schwartz, ed. *Immigrant Women*. Philadelphia: Temple University Press, 1981.

Shapiro, Laura. *Perfection Salad*. Berkeley: University of California Press, 2008.

Sharma, Miriam. "Labor Migration and Class Formation among the Filipinos in Hawaii, 1906–1946." In *Labor Immigration under Capitalism: Asian Workers in the United States before World War II*, edited by Lucie Cheng and Edna Bonacich, 579–615. Berkeley: University of California Press, 1984.

———. "The Philippines: A Case of Migration to Hawaii, 1906 to 1946." In *Labor Immigration under Capitalism: Asian Workers in the United States before World War II*, edited by Lucie Cheng and Edna Bonacich, 337–58. Berkeley: University of California Press, 1984.

Silbey, David J. *A War of Frontier and Empire: The Philippine-American War, 1899–1902*. New York: Hill and Wang, 2007.

Smallman-Raynor, Matthew, and Andrew D. Cliff. "The Philippines Insurrection and the 1902–4 Cholera Epidemic: Part II — Diffusion Patterns in War and Peace." *Journal of Historical Geography* 24, no. 2 (1998): 188–210.

Sobredo, James. "From Manila Bay to Daly City: Filipinos in San Francisco." In *Reclaiming San Francisco: History, Politics, Culture*, edited by James Brook, Chris Carlsson, and Nancy J. Peters, 273–86. San Francisco: City Lights, 1998.

Somera, Antonio. *The Secrets of Giron Arnis Escrima*. Boston: Tuttle, 1998.

Starr, Kevin. *Endangered Dreams: The Great Depression in California*. New York: Oxford University Press, 1996.

Stegner, Wallace, and the editors of *Look*. *One Nation*. Boston: Houghton Mifflin, 1945.

Stern, Alexandra Minna. *Eugenic Nation: Faults and Frontiers of Better Breeding in Modern America*. Berkeley: University of California Press, 2005.

Sterne, Evelyn Savidge. "Religion in Working-Class History." *Social Science History*, 24, no. 1 (2000): 149–82.

Sugrue, Thomas. *The Origins of the Urban Crisis: Race and Inequality in Postwar Detroit*. Princeton: Princeton University Press, 1996.

Takaki, Ronald. *Double Victory: A Multicultural History of America in World War II*. Boston: Little, Brown, 2001.

———. *In the Heart of Filipino America: Immigrants from the Pacific Isles*. New York: Chelsea House, 1995.

———. *Pau Hana: Plantation Life and Labor in Hawaii*. Honolulu: University of Hawai'i Press, 1983.

———. *Strangers from a Different Shore*. Boston: Little, Brown, 1989.

Teodoro, Luis V., Jr. *Out of This Struggle: The Filipinos in Hawaii.* Honolulu: University of Hawai'i Press, 1981.

Tilly, Louise A. and Joan Wallach Scott, *Women, Work, and Family.* New York: Routledge, 1987.

Tinkham, George. "Henry Christian Petersen, M.D." In *History of San Joaquin County, California.* Los Angeles: Historic Record Company, 1923.

Tiongson, Tony, ed. *Positively No Filipinos Allowed: Building Communities and Discourses.* Philadelphia: Temple University Press, 2006.

Toribio, Helen. "We Are Revolution: A Reflective History of the Union of Democratic Filipinos." In "Essays into American Empire in the Philippines: Part 1 — Legacies, Heroes, and Identity," ed. Enrique dela Cruz, centennial commemorative issue, *Amerasia* 24, no. 2 (1998): 155–78.

Tyner, James A. "The Geopolitics of Eugenics and the Exclusion of Philippine Immigrants from the United States." *Geographical Review* 89, no. 1 (1999): 54–73.

Umemoto, Karen. "'On Strike!': San Francisco State College Strike, 1968–69: The Role of Asian American Students." *Amerasia* 15, no. 1 (1989): 3–41.

Vallangca, Caridad. *The Second Wave: Pinay & Pinoy, 1945–1960.* San Francisco: Strawberry Hill, 1987.

Vallangca, Roberto. *Pinoy: The First Wave.* San Francisco: Strawberry Hill Press, 1977.

Varzally, Allison. *Making a Non-White America: Californians Coloring outside Ethnic Lines, 1925–1955.* Berkeley: University of California Press, 2008.

Vera Cruz, Philip. *A Personal History of the Farmworkers Movement.* Seattle: University of Washington Press, 2000.

Vergara, Benito M. *Pinoy Capital: The Filipino Nation in Daly City.* Philadelphia: Temple University Press, 2009.

Volpp, Leti. "American Mestizo: Filipinos and Anti-Miscegenation Laws in California." In *Mixed Race America and the Law: A Reader,* edited by Kevin R. Johnson, 86–93. New York: New York University Press, 2003.

Von Hoffman, Alexander. "A Study in Contradictions: The Origins and Legacy of the Housing Act of 1949." *Housing Policy Debate* 11, no.2 (2000): 299–326.

Weatherford, Doris. *Foreign and Female: Immigrant Women in America: 1840–1930.* New York, Schocken, 1986.

Wild, Mark. *Street Meeting: Multiethnic Neighborhoods in Early Twentieth-Century Los Angeles.* Berkeley: University of California Press, 2005.

Wiley, Mark V. *Filipino Martial Culture.* Boston: Tuttle, 1997.

———. *The Secrets of Cabales Serrada Escrima.* Boston: Tuttle, 2001.

Wilson, James Q., ed. *Urban Renewal: The Record and the Controversy.* Cambridge: MIT Press, 1966.

Wolff, Leon. *Little Brown Brother: How the Americans Conquered the Philippines, 1898–1902.* New York: Doubleday, 1960.

Wong, Sau-Ling. "Denationalization Reconsidered: Asian American Cultural Criticism at a Theoretical Crossroads." *Amerasia* 21, nos. 1–2 (1995): 1–27.

Wood, R. Coke, and Leonard Covello. *Stockton Memories: A Pictorial History of Stockton, California.* Fresno, Calif.: Valley, 1977.

Worcester, Dean C. *The Philippines: Past and Present.* New York: McMillan, 1930 (originally published in 1914).

Yung, Judy. *Unbound Feet: A Social History of Chinese Women in San Francisco.* Berkeley: University of California Press, 1995.

UNPUBLISHED PAPERS, THESES, AND DISSERTATIONS

Ave, Mario Paguia. "Characteristics of Filipino Social Organizations in Los Angeles." Master's thesis, University of Southern California, 1956.

Bohulano, Virginia. "The Struggle of Filipino Farm Workers to Improve Working Conditions from 1939 to 1949." Unpublished paper, April 16, 1971. Bohulano family collection.

Castillo, Toribio B. "The Changing Social Status of Filipino Women during the American Administration." Master's thesis, University of Southern California, 1942.

Catapusan, Benicio T. "Filipino Social Adjustment in the United States." PhD diss., University of Southern California, 1940.

Coloma, Casiano Pagdilao. "A Study of the Filipino Repatriation Movement." Master's thesis, University of Southern California, 1939.

Cordova, Dorothy. "Filipino Women in America." Unpublished manuscript, NPA FANHS.

Corpus, Severino. "An Analysis of Racial Adjustment Activities and Problems of the Filipino-American Christian Fellowship in Los Angeles." Master's thesis, University of Southern California, 1938.

de Vera, Arleen. "An Unfinished Agenda: Filipino Immigrant Workers in the Era of McCarthyism; A Case Study of the Cannery Workers and Farm Laborers Union, 1948–1955." Master's thesis, University of California, Los Angeles, 1990.

España-Maram, Linda. "Negotiating Identity: Youth, Gender and Popular Culture in Los Angeles' Little Manila, 1920s–1940s." PhD diss., University of California, Los Angeles, 1996.

Gabales, Ted. "The Impact of Filipino Farm Labor and Organization on San Joaquin County Agriculture." Independent Study Project Working Paper, July 30, 1985. National Pinoy Archives, Seattle, Wash.

Hemminger, Carol. "Little Manila: The Filipino in Stockton Prior to World War II." Master's thesis, San Joaquin Delta College, 1978.

Juarez, Ophelia Lynn Paciente Juarez. "Filipino American Family Research Paper: Lucia Cordova." Undergraduate paper, University of Washington.

Lim, Shirley Jennifer: "Girls Just Wanna Have Fun: The Politics of Asian American Women's Public Culture, 1930–1960." PhD diss., University of California, Los Angeles, 1998.

Mariano, Honorante. "The Filipino Immigrants in the United States." Master's thesis, University of Oregon, 1933.

Somera, Antonio. "Tools of the Trade." Unpublished paper.

Unknown, "The West End Story: A 'Wide Open' Town." Unpublished essay for History 10, San Joaquin Delta College, no date. Bank of Stockton Archives, Stockton, Calif.

Walker, Donald. "Race Relations and Specialty Crops: San Joaquin County Horticulture, 1900–1925." Master's thesis, California State University, Sacramento, 1992.

Wallovits, Sonia Emily. "The Filipinos in California." PhD diss., University of Southern California, June, 1966.

GOVERNMENT SOURCES

State of California, Department of Industrial Relations. "Facts about Filipino Immigration into California." Special Bulletin, no. 3. San Francisco: State of California, Department of Industrial Relations, 1930.

U.S. Census (1930). National Archives and Records Administration, San Bruno, Calif.

U.S. Congressional Records, Seventy-fourth Congress, First Session, 1935, vol. 79, Part XIV, Public No. 202.

U.S. Department of Commerce, Bureau of the Census. *Fifteenth Census of the United States*: 1930, vol. 3, pt. 2. Washington, D.C.: Government Printing Office, 1932.

INDEX

Aception, E. V., 117

Adamic, Loyus, 227

Adeva, Manuel, 39

Adlao, Pedro, 245

Adobo, 82, 85

African Americans, 112, 132, 138; and civil rights movement, 312; and Crosstown Freeway, 297; and EOP program, 308; and GI Bill, 245; intermarriage with, 155–56, 306; in Koreatown Northgate, 344; in Little Manila, 284; and segregation and restrictive covenants, 272–73, 275, 290–91, 394n8; on the South Side, 273; teenagers, 190; and urban redevelopment, 277–78, 305

Agapeto Restaurant, 117

Agricultural Labor Bureau of San Joaquin Valley, 89

Agricultural Workers Association, 213, 259

Agricultural Workers Organizing Committee, AFL-CIO, 214, 255, 258; AWOC and UFW, 259–63; charter of, 260–62, 265; headquarters, 280

Agricultural Workers Union, Local 20221, 98–99

Agudo, Luis, 97–98, 131

Aguinaldo, Emilio, 29, 31, 195

Aklan Cleaners, 237

Aklan Hotel, 281, 295

Aklanon language, 1, 103–4

Aklan province: Ati-Atihan festival in, 210; as place of origin for immigrants, 3–4, 10; steamship ticket agents in, 49. *See also* Capiz, Philippines

Alamo Scouts, 182, 247

Alaska: cannery workers union, 97; as part of labor migration circuit, 5, 61, 70–71; wartime work, 241; work conditions in, 70–71

Alba, Jose C., 280, 288

Albano, Francisco T., 90

Alcala, Alma, 67, 141, 250, 251, 285; and Central Stockton Community Center, 324; conservatism in Stockton, 328; county supervisor race, 329–30; and Filipina/o American movement, 307, 313; groundbreaking of Filipino Center, 327; opposition to Filipino Center, 324

Alcala, Maria Cabugayan, 250, 324

Alcala, Nora, 251

Alcala, Rory, 251

Alcos, Melecia, 121

Alfafara, Celestino T., 176, 205, 244

Algas, Pete, 237

Alien Land Law, in California (1913), 62, 169; amended act, 235

Alien Registration Act (Smith Act), 229

Almirol, Edwin, 291

Aloha Hotel, 281

Alzona, Encarnacion, 153

America Is in the Heart, 1, 2, 20–21, 114, 123, 130; celery strike and Japanese boycott in, 224; Committee for the Protection of Filipino Rights in, 227; poverty of Ilocanas/os in, 44; rediscovery by Filipina/o American youth, 309

American Federation of Labor, 92, 98, 143, 212, 214, 219; and anti-Filipina/o senti-

American Federation of Labor (*continued*) ments, 92, 259–60; and organization of the AWOC, 259–60

American Indians, 33; boarding school education as a model for the Philippines, 33. *See also* Native Americans

American Legion, 96, 143. *See also* Manuel Roxas Auxiliary; Manuel Roxas Post

American-Philippine Foundation, 236

Amianan Pool Hall, 120

Amistad, Felipe, 111

Anak ng Bukid, 90–91, 97, 104, 116, 131

Ancheta, Alejandro, 195, 198

Andres Alvarico Restaurant, 237, 281

Ang Bantay (newspaper), 90

Angel Island, 60, 144–45

Angel, Concepcion, 117

Anthony, Donald, 140

Anti-miscegenation laws, 8, 86, 155–58, 207, 210

Antique province, 47, 48, 103, 117, 119, 159, 311, 312

Arca, Albert, 123

Arca, Cecil, 123

Arca, Conching, 123

Arca, Felicidad, 123

Arca, Flora. *See* Mata, Flora Arca

Arca, Jose, 54, 192

Arca, Mary. *See* Inosanto, Mary Arca

Arca, Victoria Salcedo, 54, 123, 192, 200

Archdiocese of San Francisco, 204, 209; and Filipina/o exclusion and repatriation, 204–5; and freemasonry, 205

Arnis. *See* Escrima

Aroy, Marissa, 262–63

Arpon, Constantino, 195

Arroyo, Simeon Doria, 227

Arroyo's Café, 336

Artiaga, Morris, 307, 313

Asian Americans, 6; Census figures, 6; movement, 308–9; students, 308; studies, 308–9

Asis, Alberta Alcoy, 51, 53, 159

Asis, Genario, 51, 53

Asis, Sabas "Bob" A., 182

Asparagus, 5; farms, 72; harvest of, 68–69, 77; strikes of 1948–1949, 254–58; wages and box rates, 74–75

Assemblies of God. *See* Filipino Assemblies of the First Born

Associated Farmers, 89, 96, 224, 228

Associated Filipino Organizations of San Joaquin County, Inc. (AFO): conflict with Filipino Community of Stockton and Vicinity, Inc., 323–25; founding, 322; groundbreaking 326; mortgage for Filipino Center, 346; officers, 323

Association of Filipino American Educators (AFAE), 16, 346

Association of Filipino American Professionals, 301, 346

Atad, Martin, 251

Ateneo de Manila University, 38

Atherton, Warren, 73

Athletic clubs, 182–84

Atonilco Pool Hall, 281

Azuma, Eiichiro, 11, 221–22

B&G Market, 325, 331

Baccus, Francisca, 121

Bacobo, Jorge, 94, 142

Bacon Island, 62

Bagtos, J. R., 281

Bahala Na Escrima, 14, 85, 311, 342. *See also* escrima

Balantac, Deanna Daclan, 173, 318, 332, 333

Balantac, Moreno, 200

Balot, M. M., 121, 237

Balucas, Margarita, 118

Bantillo, Anastacio, 121, 139, 173, 200

Bantillo, Anastacio "Bo" Jr., 251

Bantillo, Lillian, 188

Bantillo, Norma, 181

Bantillo, Virgilia, 85, 167, 168, 171, 199

Barrio Fiesta, 331, 333–34, 340

Barrows, David, 143

Bataan Café, 236, 237, 280

Bataan Cigar Stand, 238

Bataan Club, 236, 338

Bataan Death March, 217, 238, 240

Bataan Hotel, 236, 280

Bataan Magazine, 236

Bataan-Manila Enterprises, Inc., 235–36

Bataan News, 256

Bataan Pool Hall, 237, 280

Bataan Youth Training Center, 280

Basado, M. B., 120
Baseball, 123, 183
Basilio Boja Restaurant, 116
Basketball, 183
Bath House Barber Shop, 121
Bautista, Anita Navalta, 82, 113, 115, 129, 133, 156; courtship and dating, 161, 186
Bautista, E., 121
Bautista, Isabelo, 121
Bautista, Macario, 111, 119, 120, 290, 314; as Filipino Community President, 219; as head of the FALA, 219–30; office, 236
Bayanihan Community Center (San Francisco), 333
Bayanihan Dance Troupe, 310
Bayhon, Nancy, 181
Bellosillo, Simon, 131
Benevolent Assimilation Policy, 29, 31
Benigno, Delgado, 121
Bernabe, Alberca, 237, 281
Bernabe, Julian, 198
Bernardo, Jose: as adviser to Filipino Center project, 323; background, 304, 314; candidacy in county supervisor race, 329–30; construction of Filipino Center, 330; groundbreaking of Filipino Center, 326; parish survey, 299; relationship with community, 314, 324
Bethany Temple, 198
Bernardino, Nicanor, 285
Beveridge, Alfred, 29
Biko, 85, 172
Bilinario, Simplicio, 67
Billiards, 116, 117
Billones, John Y., 91, 104–6, 116, 119, 158
Billones Photography Studio, 119
Binalonan, Pangasinan, 17
Binangkal, 85
Binatilan Hotel, 281
Black Eyed Peas, 349
Blight. *See* Urban redevelopment
Blight, David, 6
Bloch, Christine Bohulano, 250, 308, 325
Bob's Studio, 245
Bogardus, Emory, 106
Bohol, 48, 49, 56, 57, 83, 103, 108, 110, 151; immigrants from, 128
Bohol Circle, 110

Bohulano, Concepcion Moreno, 3, 35; AFO board, 323; conflict with new immigrants, 303–4; emigration to U.S., 55, 253–55; on Filipino Center, 316–17; Filipino Center groundbreaking, 326; marriage, 249–50
Bohulano, Delfin, 3, 46, 127, 249–50; emigration to Tracy, Calif., and Stockton, 253–55, 304
Bohulano, Delfin, Jr., 250
Boja, Basillo, 117
Bombing: of bunkhouses, 93–94; Filipino Federation building in Stockton, 93–94; 104–5. *See also* violence
Bonus, Rick, 12
Bonifacio, Andres, 28, 108, 195
Bonjoc, Dioscoro, 237
Boscoe, Donald, 282
Boss, Elmer, 282
Bowden, Gussie, 123
Boxing, 15, 102, 127–29
Bracero program, 211, 241–42; AWOC opposition, 261
Bridge Generation, 174
Buaken, Manuel, 49–50, 75, 86, 239; novel, 190
Bulosan, Carlos, 1, 12, 13, 20, 129, 130, 217; and Committee for the Protection of Filipino Rights, 227–28; as Communist, 2, 97, 258; death and reputation in Stockton, 309; essay in the *Saturday Evening Post*, 240; as Stockton resident, 2
Buslon, Fernando, 235
Bustamante, Antonio, 225
Bustamente, Pablo, 161

Cabaccang, V. S., 121
Cabales, Angel, 84; founding of *serrada escrima*, 311
Caballero, Joey, 128
Caballero, "Sleepy," 128
Caballeros de Dimas Alang: building, 16, 120, 315, 337; and Catholic church, 204; Cecelia Navarro murder case and, 161–63; in Little Manila, 294; organization, 107; queen contests, 173; Regidor Lodge, 120, 121, 315; rivalry with LDT, 188; Spirit of Dimas Alang plane, 181; Travel Bureau, 120; and World War II, 231

Caballo, Pedro, 117

Cabalteja, J. P., 237

Cabañero, Aurora, 251

Cabañero, Ernest, 251

Cabañero, Irene, 251

Cabañero, Laura, 251

Cabañero, Laurena, 251, 307; in the
Filipina/o American movement, 308, 310,
312; fundraising for the Filipino Center,
315–16; UC Davis research project, 319–25

Cabañero, Leo, 251

Cabañero, Lucresio, 251

Cabañero, Teri, 251

Cabe, Thomas, 189–90

Cabebe, V. J., 121

Cabigas, Bob, 79

Caesar, Sar, 117, 118

Cahill, Edward, 145

Calape, Bohol, immigrants from, 8

California Delta Farms, 73

California Filipino Farmers Association,
location in the 1920s, 116

California Highway Commission, 286

California Laundry, 237

California Rural Legal Assistance, 340

California State Federation of Labor, 92

California State University, 308

Camarillo, Albert, xii

Camp Cook, 181

Campo, conditions on, 79–80, 82

Canete, Rufo, 97–98

Canillo, Alexis, xii

Canion, Josephine Tenio, 137

Candelario, Claro, 46, 122, 123, 130–31, 248,
290; AFL and anti-Filipino sentiment,
259–60; asparagus strike, 256; as character in America Is in the Heart, 12, 39; and
Committee for the Protection of Filipino
Rights, 227–29; communism and FBI surveillance, 257–58; leadership in the Filipino Community of Stockton, Inc., 314;
naturalization, 245; wartime antagonism
towards Japanese, 234

Cannery and Agricultural Workers Industrial Union (CAWIU), 96, 98

Cannery Workers' and Farm Laborers
Union, Local 7, 97, 236

Cano, Constance, 185

Capiz, Philippines, emigrants from, 25, 36,
45, 46, 47, 249. See also Aklan entries

Carcar, Cebu, 17, 161; emigrants from, 51

Cariaga, Ramon, 159

Carido & Luisen Billiards, 120

Carido, Camila Labor, 35–36, 78, 95, 151, 157,
160, 163; as AFO board member, 323; antagonism towards Japanese during World
War II, 231–34; food and cooking, 173;
housing discrimination, 169; importance
of women's organizations, 171; labor in
the fields, 168; labor in the home, 164–65;
naturalization, 245; World War II, 218

Carido, Leon, 151, 169, 245, 323

Carla Studio, 245

Castillo, Eugenio, 237

Castillo, J. M., 117

Catapang, Victor, 237

Catapusan, Benicio, 39, 155

Catholic Filipino Club, 202

Cebu, Philippines, 3, 8, 17, 28, 51, 53, 57, 110,
154, 250; Dollar Steamship Line ticket
agents in, 53; and HSPA recruitment, 49;
as island of origin for emigrants, 40–42,
210

Cebu-American Hotel, 120

Cebu City, 3, 17

Cebuano, 103–4, 307

Celebrations, 172

Census: 2010 and Filipinas/os, 6

Central Luzon, 8

Central Stockton Community Center, 324

Ceso's Cigars, 281

Chan, Sucheng, 65

Chang, Gordon, xii

Chapel of the Palms, 345

Chávez, Cesar, 212, 261–63, 312, 313

Chinatown, 6, 15, 112–15; competition for
Filipina/o business, 122–23; and Crosstown Freeway, 292–94; gambling dens in,
91, 129–32; in Los Angeles, 84; and redevelopment, 284–85; restaurants in, 122

Chinese Americans, 112, 115; and anti-
miscegenation law, 156; and Crosstown
Freeway, 287–89; in Hawai'i, 48; and
housing discrimination, 272–73; intermarriage with, 156; at the International
Hotel, 298, 309–10; as laborers in the San

Joaquin Delta, 65–66; and Lee Center, 293; in Little Manila, 284; and the Little Manila Historic Site, 339–45; and missionaries, 196; and parish survey, 289; and racial hierarchy in the Delta, 221; relations with Filipinas/os, 183; school segregation and, 175–76; and St. Mary's Church, 213; and World War II, 230–31, 235

Chinese Christian Center, 338

Cholera: as result of Philippine-American War, 5, 25, 31, 353n1

Chop suey, 122, 129

Choy, Catherine Ceniza, 11, 35

Cicognani, Amleto G., 207–9

Cipano, E. M., 121

Citizens Committee for the Elimination of Skid Row, 282

Citizenship, 245

Civil rights: and anti-imperialism, 30; and CSO, 212; and Fair Employment Practices Commission, 241; and housing, 346; movement, 298, 306–7, 313–14, 333; and post-1965 Filipina/o immigrants, 301; and UFW, 262; after World War II, 244, 253, 263

Clarin-Tubigon-Calape Association, 110

Class, conflict amongst old and new immigrants after 1965, 301–4

Coboy-coboy, 51, 159

Colonial Cleaners, 237, 281

Colonialism: American colonial period, 5, 7–8, 17, 31–40, 59; colonial mentality, 13, 300; education and, 26, 31–40; and emigration, 27–28; Philippine economy and, 41–45; and racialization, 7; Spanish-era, 27–28

Cockfights, 82, 84–86; wages lost through cockfights, 84

Committee for the Protection of Filipino Rights, 12, 227, 264

Committee on Rehabilitation, 279

Commonwealth Club, 92, 143

Commonwealth Times, 229

Communist Party, 89, 96, 98, 258

Community Action Council, 324

Community Service Organization, 212

Compadrazgo system, 165

Concord, Calif., 222

Conference of Filipino Communities of the West Coast, 182

Confucius Church, 338

Congress of Industrial Organizations (CIO), 99, 212, 219. See also labor; strikes

Constantino, Renato, 41

Contracting: encloso system, 74–75; Filipinas/os, 74–76; respect for, 76; and strikes, 88; unscrupulous practices in, 74–76

Cordova, Braulio, 57

Cordova, Dorothy Laigo, xii, 11, 152, 188

Cordova, Fred, xii, 11, 111, 115, 124, 126, 138, 163, 174; and compadrazgo system, 165; religion, 174;

speaker at the Far West Convention, 331

Cordova, Joan May T., xii

Cordova, Leoncio C., 237

Cordova, Lucia, 111, 138, 180

Cordova, Marcelina, 121

Corona Park, 273

Corregidor, 238

Corregidor Barber Shop, 281

Costales, Tomas, 221

Courtship: chaperonage and, 185–86; religion, 186; rituals, 156–57

Cristobal, Silbia, 121

Crosstown Freeway, 1, 269; completion, 296; Crosstown Freeway Relocation Committee, 288–89; demolitions for, 291–92; elevated design for, 288; as "Great Wall," 297; impact on Little Manila, 286–96, 321; impact on local residents, 292–96; opposition to, 286–88; plans for, 285–86; Washington-Lafayette route, 287–88

Cruz, Delfin, 225

Cruz, Hermenegildo, 37–38

Cruz, Ray, 121

Cuban Revolution, 29

Cuizon's Restaurant, 281

Daclan, Paula Dizon, 47, 158, 167, 173, 332

Daclan, Rosauro, 158, 173, 323, 326, 332

Daguhoy, Francisco, 108

Daguhoy Lodge, 108, 120; basement museum, 14, 349; building, 16, 108, 236, 280, 294, 337

Dagupan, Pangasinan, 17

Daily Worker, 96
Dalipe, Adeline, 181
Daly City, Calif., 11, 347, 350
Dancel, Daniel, 67
Dances, 170
Daniel, Cletus 88
Dato, Bruno E., 104, 117
Daughters of the Philippines, 126, 180
Daquiado & Co., 237
Davao (Mindanao), 17
De Carli, Dean, 278
De Jesus, Jose, 94
Delano, Calif., 84, 125; FALA chapter, 223; Grape Strike, 261–63
De Las Yslas, Roque, 145
Delta Farms, 224
Delta Hotel, 336
De Vera, Arleen, 11, 254
De Witt, Howard, 89
Delvo, Cipriano "Rudy," 214; asparagus strikes, 254–56, 348; organizer with AWOC, 260
Delvo, Dillon, 340, 346
Demonstration Project for Asian Americans, 15
Department of Housing and Urban Development, 305, 326, 331, 346
Desano, C., 117
Deseo, José, 198
Detroit, Filipino Community in, 12
Dewey, George, 29
Diniguan, 117–18
Dionisio, Juan "Johnny," 45, 112, 224; address to the California State Assembly by, 240; billiard hall of, 236; grocery store of, 120; and *Philippine Journal* and FALA, 221, 225–26; as president of FALA, 230
Dollar Steamship Company, 54–55, 57
Domagas, Oscar, 347–48
Domestic labor, 8, 36. *See also* Labor
Domestic science, 35–36
Double Victory Campaign, 239
Dubai, United Arab Emirates, 350
DuBois, W. E. B., 30
Dumangas Restaurant, 121
Dust Bowl migrants to Stockton, 92

Edison High School, 308
Education: and American colonialism, 17, 31–40; and emigration to the U.S., 37, 59; Thomasites, 31; use of English in, 33–34
Educational Opportunity Program, 308
El Dorado Market, 237
Elite Jewelry and Novelty, 121
Elizalde, Joaquin Miguel, 142, 219
Elk Cleaners, 281
Ellustrisimo, Regino, 311
Elorde, "Flash," 129
Emerald Restaurant. *See* Filipino Recreation Center
Encloso system, 74–75
Enero, Flora, 179
Engkabo, Pastor: billiards, 116, 118, 237; naturalization, 245
English, fluency amongst emigrants, 9, 27
Ente, Demetro, 134, 136–38
Ente, Jimmy, 78, 111, 134, 135
Ente, Phyllis Cano, 187
Enriquez, Agraciano, 237
Ernado, Cotleco, 117
Escrima, 14; in the campo, 82–84; first schools, 311; implements, 83; regional systems, 83; among second-generation Filipinas/os, 310–12
España-Maram, Linda, 11, 84, 128, 133
Espanola, Tomas 90, 116, 117,
Espiritu, Yen Le, 12
Esteban, Felipe, 280, 281
Estrera, Pablo, 195, 206
Ethnic identity, 3, 170–71, 191, 306–14
Ethnic studies, 307
Eugenics: and empire, 30; and exclusion, 143
Eugenio, Martisano, 117
European Americans, 112, 132, 196, 202; as boxers, 129; and Catholic Church, 205–6; changing attitudes after World War II, 218; intermarriage with, 143–44, 155–57, 190, 207, 210; labor competition with, 92; missionaries, 196–200; racial violence of, 92–95, 97, 104–5, 139, 141–42; and segregation, 170, 176, 272–73, 275–76; and sexual relations with Filipinos, 132–38, 140; as whites, 273
Evans Service Station No. 4, 237
Eviota, Elizabeth Uy, 153
Exclusion of Asian immigrants from United States, 28, 48, 54, 60

Exclusion of Filipinas/os from United States, 91–92, 143–47, 264
Exeter, Calif., 93

Fabionar, John, 331
Fabros, Alex, Sr., 184, 235
Fair Employment Practices Commission, 241
Families: in the campo, 81–82; *coboy-coboy* practice, 51; and emigration, 45–46; gender, power, and labor in, 164; kinship and emigration, 46; late family phenomenon, 188, 248; as a network for survival, 9; women's financial control within, 168; women's side businesses, 168–69. *See also* Anti-miscegenation law; Courtship; Gender; Marriage
Fante, John, 227
Farmers: Chinese American, 65–66; European American, 65; and exploitation of Filipinas/os, 70–82; and the FALA, 220–26; farmers' market in Little Manila, 279; and immigration exclusion, 60, 228; Japanese American, 65–66, 157, 221–26, 232, 235, 265; and labor militancy, 88–91, 96–99, 221–26; in the Philippines, 41–43; in the San Joaquin Delta, 5, 63–66; South Asian American, 65–66; and West End Redevelopment, 284; and World War II, 241–42
Fat City, 294
Federal Bureau of Investigation, 257
Federal Housing Authority, 272, 275; and Filipino Center project, 318–22
Felipe, Virgilio, 50
Feria, R. T., 209
Fernando Buslon Employment Agency, 236
Filipina Athletic Club, 183
Filipina/o, use of term, 19
Filipina/o American Movement, 300, 307; and Far West convention in Stockton, 330
Filipinas Café, 121
Filipinas magazine, 344
Filipina Society of America, 180
Filipino Agricultural Laborer's Association, 99, 111, 168, 201; charter with AFL, 225; end of union, 230; founding of, 220; headquarters of, 236; strike activity of, 221–30
Filipino American Experience Research Project, 16

Filipino American Political Association, 308
Filipino-American Literary Club, 238
Filipino American National Historical Society: Seattle headquarters, 15; Stockton chapter, 337, 349
Filipino American Youth Association, 182
Filipino Assemblies of the First Born, 196
Filipino Catholic Association, 209, 316
Filipino Center: Barrio Fiesta dedication ceremony, 331–32; community backers of, 316–17; concept for, 299, 317; construction of, 330; down payment for, 315–16; and Federal Housing Administration, 318–21, 325; groundbreaking, 326–27
Filipino Center Restaurant, 120, 121
Filipino Christian Fellowship, 196
Filipino Club, 237
Filipino Community of Stockton and Vicinity, Inc., 3, 135, 219, 226; building of, 315, 337; founding of, 106; headquarters of, 280; and opposition to Filipino Center project, 323–25; political activity of, 329–30; and presidency of Larry Itliong, 259; and presidency of Primo Villaruz, 37; and reaction to Crosstown Freeway displacements, 290; and relationships with local politicians, 290–91; and support of Filipino Center, 328
Filipino Employment Agency, 61, 116, 118
Filipino Farm Labor Union, 259
Filipino Federation of America, 16; as antiunion, 223–24; band, 126; bombing in 1930 of, 93, 104–5; criticism of, 109; Filipino Center groundbreaking, 326; founding, 107, 109–10; labor attitudes during World War II, 242; location, 116; strict guidelines of, 109
Filipino Full Gospel Church, 206, 236
Filipino Independent Labor Union, 98
Filipino Industrial Club, 116
Filipino Information Bureau, 116
Filipino Inter-Community Council of the Western States, 264
Filipino Hospital, 111
Filipino Labor Agency, 116
Filipino Labor Association, 98
Filipino Labor Supply Association of Sacramento and Superior California, 225

Filipino Labor Supply Association of Stockton, 98

Filipino Labor Union, 98

Filipino Medical and Allied Professionals, 322, 346

Filipino Methodist Church, 206, 280

Filipino Multi-Service Center, 303

Filipino National Convention, 219

Filipino Oral History Project, 15

Filipino People's Far West Convention, 309; in Seattle, 309; in Stockton, 330–31

Filipino Pioneer, 112, 119, 135, 145; gossip column, 189

Filipino Presbyterian Church, 120

Filipino Repatriation Act (1935), 10, 144–46, 264; and Archdiocese of San Francisco, 204; reaction to, 145–47

Filipino Recreation Center, 16, 138, 238, 251, 256; as AFL Labor Temple, 280; as Emerald Restaurant, 337; proposed demolition, 341

Filipino Rooms, 237

Filipino Sales Promotion and Service, 117

Filipino Voters League, 259

Filipino Workers and Businessmen's Protective Association, 116

Filipino Workers Delegation, 90

Filipino Youth Activities (Seattle) Drill Team, 331

Fils Basketball Club, 183

First Filipino Infantry Regiment, 3, 84, 233, 238

First Presbyterian Church, 197

Flaviano, Vergara 84

Florita, Jimmy, 128

Florita, M. M., 121

Food: in the campo, 82; at cockfights, 85; home cooking, 172–73; restaurants, 118–19; as symbol of ethnic culture, 172

Food, Tobacco, Agricultural, and Allied Workers of America (FTA, CIO), 254

Fort Ord, 181

Fourth of July parades in Stockton, 15, 125

Fox Hotel, 336

Fox Theater, 140, 243, 342

Francisco, Machila, 121

Frank Sarmiento Restaurant, 281

Freemasonry, 28; and Catholicism, 195, 204–5

Freeways, 1; negative impacts, 286. *See also* Crosstown Freeway

Fremont, Calif., 347

French Camp, Calif., 233

French Camp Slough, 273

Fresno, Calif., 125

Frisch, Michael 6

Fuertis Pool Hall, 237

Fujita-Rony, Dorothy, 11, 27

Fukui Photo Studio, 120

Fukuokaya Hotel, 120

Funerals, 111

Galarza, Ernesto, 214, 259

Galea, C., 121

Galedo, Lillian, 303; Americanization and ethnic identity, 306; on community divisions, 315; Filipina/o American movement, 308, 313; groundbreaking of Filipino Center, 327; UC Davis research project, 319–25

Galleon Trade, 28

Galura, Joseph, 12

gambling: in the campo, 82–84; in Little Manila, 102, 129–32; wages lost from, 84, 131–32

Gan Chy Restaurant, 124, 129, 285

Garcia, Ceferino, 128

Garcia, Matt, 12

Gateway Project, 2, 335–39

gender: and clothing, 177; and community leadership, 172; and education in the Philippines, 35–37; gender role transformations in U.S., 173; and migration, 46–48, 245; queen contests and, 176–80; and roles in Philippines, 154; sex ratio imbalance and, 151–52; sexual division of labor in the home, 163–65; and women's organizations, 170–72; and women's networks, 172; after World War II, 189

General Ricarte Lodge, 121

German immigrants, 65

GI Bill, 244–46, 304

Gier, Jean Vengua, 112

Gines, Ben, 260, 263

Giron, Leo, 84, 249; and founding of Bahala Na, 311

Giva, Bernie and Narciso, 325

Gleason, Edna, 279

Gleason Park, 337

Godinez, Eno, 188

Godinez, Trinedad, 180

Golden Gate Department Store, 280

Gonzales, Primitivo, 144

Gonzalez, Philip, 121

Gonzalo, D. F., 206, 242

Goo-goos, Filipinos as, 8

Gran Oriente Filipino, 107–9, 205

Grape boycott, 313. *See also* United Farm Workers Union

Great Depression, 5, 10, 100, 102, 115, 144; and Filipina/o workers, 68

Great Society, 333

Griggs, Carmen, 323, 326

Grocery stores, 120

Guadalupe, Calif., 91

Guam, 29

Guida, Marilyn, 339

Guilledo, Francisco "Pancho Villa," 129

Guindulman Syndicate of America, 116

Gungab, Voltaire, 310–11

Habal, Estella, 306

Haggin Museum of Stockton, 180, 339

Hanna, Edward J., 202; anti-Mexican attitudes of, 203

Hawai'i: anti-Filipina/o racism in, 51–52; emigrants' experiences in, 48–54; first Filipina/o immigrants to, 48; immigration to, 9, 41; labor organizing in, 52–53; labor recruitment for, 40; labor unrest in, 89; sugar plantations in, 15, 26

Hawai'ian Sugar Planters Association, 40; recruitment of Filipinas/os, 48–49

Hawai'ianas/os, 49–50, 55

Hayden, Dolores, 6, 337

Hernandez, Ernie, 137, 187

Hidalgo-Lim, Pilar, 238

Hiligaynon, 103

Hispolito, Sajonia, 121

Historical memory, 6

History Channel, 344

Holly Sugar Company, 89

Hollywood Bath House and Barber Shop, 237

Hollywood Tailoring Co., 120

Homestead Tract, 273

Hometown associations, 110

Hong Kong, Republic of China, 350

Horseshoe Fountain, 281

Hotel Dorin, 121

Hotel Franklin, 117

Hotel New Roosevelt, 236

House of Friendship, 197

Housing and Slum Clearance Act, 276

Housing and Urban Development Act, 305

Howser, Huell, 344

Hutchinson, Mary, 197

Ibajay, Aklan, 17

Ichioka, Yuji, 336

Ilocanas/os: in agricultural labor, 63; conflict with other Filipinas/os, 52, 134, 141, 179; emigration to Hawai'i, 40–41; and ethnic identity, 8–9, 63, 157, 307; experiences in Hawai'i, 50–52; in the FALA, 221, 226; immigrants, 129, 134, 141, 173, 179, 187, 221, 226; in Little Manila, 269, 284, 285, 295–96; marriage to other Filipinas/os, 158, 187, 250, 307; organizations in Stockton, 110; stereotypes about, 52; and World War II, 249

Ilocano language, 57, 67, 103–4, 112, 181, 307

Ilocos region, 42, 45, 46, 67, 68, 83, 85, 97, 198, 213, 302; and colonial economy, 40; Dollar Steamship ticket agents in, 54–55; and escrima, 83; HSPA recruiters in, 40, 48–50; as place of origin for emigrants, 3, 4, 8, 27; 41–50, 55, 57

Iloilo, Philippines: Dollar Steamship ticket agents in, 55; as farm laborers, 73; HSPA recruiters in, 49; immigrants from, 2, 73, 77, 103, 119, 122, 127, 158, 219;

Iloilo Circle: and Asia Pacific Center proposal, 341; building, 16, 294, 297, 312, 315, 337, 349; and Filipino Center project, 316; organization, 73, 110, 227, 316; relocation after Crosstown Freeway, 294, 315

Illonggo: language, 1

Illustrados, 28

Immigration Act of 1924. *See* National Origins Act

Immigration and Naturalization Act of 1965, 300–301; impact on Filipinas/os, 301–2

Immigration and Naturalization Service, 144–46, 246

Imperial Valley, Calif., 70

Imutan, Andy, 262

Indios, 7, 27, 28

Industrial Workers of the World, 96, 116

Inosanto, Daniel, 84, 311

Inosanto, Mary Arca, 67, 70, 84, 103, 166, 179; agricultural labor, 168; in the ethnic community, 170; and religion, 192; as a teacher, 166

Inosanto, Sebastian, 80, 84, 90, 192, 201; and FALA, 221; and Lighthouse Mission, 197

Insigne, Manuel, 90, 145, 256–57

Insular, Cipriano, 77

Inter-Filipino Community Conferences, 172; in Oakland, 230

International Café, 117

International Hotel, 298, 309–10; 327–28

International Longshoreman's and Warehouse Workers Union (ILWU), Local 37, 258

International Photo Studio, 117

Interstate 5, 286

Interstate Highway Act, 285

Irish Americans, 202

Isleton, Calif., 176

Italian immigrants, 65

Itliong, Larry Dulay, 13, 14, 71, 214, 290, 348; asparagus strikes, 254; Delano Grape Strike, 262; departure from UFW, 263; emigration, 258; at the Far West Convention, 331; in the Filipina/o American movement, 308; as founder of Filipino American Political Association, 308; and ILWU, Local 37, 258; labor organizing, 259; life in Stockton, 259–60; as member of Legionarios del Trabajo, 313; organizing with the AWOC, 260–62; relationship with Filipina/o American youth, 312; resignation from UFW, 313

Jackson Hotel, 338

Jacobs, John H., 279–80

Jamero, Ceferino, 49, 125

Jamero, Luna, 49, 86; class conflict, 303; in the Filipina/o American movement, 307, 313; and Filipino Center project, 325; frustration with local politicians, 320; 1971 county supervisor race, 329; reaction to redevelopment in Little Manila, 295

Jamero, Peter, 85, 123, 124, 129

Jamero, Terri, 178, 179, 183

Jamieson, Stuart 89

Japanese Americans: anti-Japanese racism after World War II, 244; celery strike and boycott against, 224; farmers in the San Joaquin Delta, 66, 218–26; Filipina/o boycotts against, 157, 222; as foremen and contractors, 73–74, 88; as immigrants to Stockton, 65; incarceration/internment of, 233–35; as laborers in Hawai'i, 48; as merchants in Little Manila, 122; opposition to the Crosstown Freeway, 287; and Pearl Harbor, 230–34; relations with Filipinas/os, 157, 218–26; as strikebreakers, 223

Japantown, 6, 15, 112–13. *See also* Nihonmachi

Jazz, 82, 119, 132, 137, 187

J. C. Miranda Real Estate, 236

Jeepneys, 16

Jim Crow, 92, 94, 112

John Benzarmina Restaurant, 237

Johnnie's Family Market, 281

Jos, Rado, 121

Jos. Aurelio Pool Hall, 237

Juanitas, Cirilo Yongque, 48, 159; candy store, 116; Quezon Hotel, 235

Juanitas, Eudosia Bravo, 35, 47, 159; as a nurse, 166, 167; work in the campo, 168

Juanitas Market, 236, 280

Juliana Apartments, 281

Jusa, Natividad, 326

Jusa, Tomas, 323, 326

Kaboyan Laundry and Cleaners, 237

Kalayaan International, 327

Kali. *See* Escrima

Kalibo, Aklan, 17

Kalibo Pool Hall, 236, 281

Katipunan, 28, 107

Kinaray-a, 103

King, Martin Luther, Jr., 312, 317

King O' Lawn Club (Filipino Gardeners & Janitors Association of America), 338

Korean Americans, laborers in Hawai'i, 48, 344

Koreatown-Northgate District (Oakland, Calif.), 344

Kramer, Paul, 8
Ku Klux Klan, 95, 126
Kurashige, Scott, 12

Labor: agricultural labor, 8, 68–82; contractors, 75; domestic 8, 68; fruit and vegetable harvest seasons, 71; and gender, 190–91, 242–43; migration of agricultural workers, 70–71; recruitment in Little Manila, 125; service work, 8; shortage during World War II, 241
Labor unions, 2, 63; communism and Filipina/o unions, 96–97; early labor organizing efforts, 96–98; founding of the FALA, 219–30; militancy of workers, 18, 88–91, 97; and red baiting, 257–58; white labor and Filipinas/os, 91–93
Labre, I. V., 237
Lacaste, Juanito, 84
Lacosta, 237
LaCoste, John, 311
Lafayette and El Dorado Streets. *See* Little Manila
Lafayette Lunch Counter 1, 2, 118, 120, 236; banner, 340; after Crosstown Freeway, 297–98; demolition, 335; after World War II, 269
LaGasca, Frank, 331
LaGasca, Mel, 307, 313
Lagrimas, E. G., 132, 136; 237
Lagrimas, Helen Liwanag, 52
Lagura, Concepcion Bulawit, 160
Lagura, Modesto, 133, 249
Lai, T. C., 121
Language: and class, 302–3; among Filipinas/os, 101–3; use of English amongst Visayans, Ilocanas/os and Tagalogs, 307
La Perla del Oriente Restaurant, 281
Lapu Lapu Lodge, 237
Lapuz, Eulogio "Ted," 267; background, 304; groundbreaking, 326; idea for Filipino Center, 314–15; and opposition to the Filipino Center, 328; parish survey, 299; reaction to Filipina/o displacement, 295
Lathrop, 3, 139
Latosa, Juan "Johnny," 74, 95, 306; compadre to Larry Itliong, 313; as an escrimador, 312; and labor organizing, 263; opposi-

tion to Filipino Center, 323; president of the Filipino Community of Stockton and Vicinity, Inc., 314; restaurant, 237
Latosa, Purita, 306
Latosa, Rene, 84, 95, Americanization, 306–7; escrima training, 311–12
La Union, Philippines, 55
La Union Grocery, 236
La Union Supply Company, 237
La Verne's Filipino Club/Oriental Card Room, 280
Lawsin, Emily Porcincula, 12, 249, 250, 253
Lazaro, Juliana, 47, 122, 169, 170
Lazaro, Placido D., 117, 120, 122, 169; dry goods store, 237
LBC Market/Asian Foodmart, 338
lechon, 172
Lee, Bruce, 311
Lee, Ted, 293, 321
Lee Center, 293, 338
Legare, Maurice B. S., 195, 206
Legionarios del Trabajo 3, 13, 16, 252; building, 315; and Catholic church, 205; and Filipino Center groundbreaking, 326; founding of, 107; labor organizing origins of, 89; in Little Manila, 120, 121; and rivalry with CDA, 188; and support of Little Manila preservation, 342; women's lodges of, 170
Leta's Place, 281
Lever Village, 273–75
Leyte, Philippines, 3, 151
Leyte Café, 281
Lezo, Aklan, 17
Liberty Hotel, 298, 338
Liga Filipina 28
Lighthouse Mission, 116, 196–201, 206, 238
Lim, Vicente, 238
Lincoln Super Service, 237
L. I. Osencio Restaurant, 281
Little Manila, 1, 2, 6, 8; businesses during World War II in, 232–36; and California's Gold episode, 344; campaign to save Little Manila, 342–48; and Crosstown Freeway, 289–98; and demolitions for Gateway Project, 335–36; and demolition of Liberty Hotel, 339–40; earliest businesses, 116–17; early settlement in, 101–2,

Little Manila (*continued*)
112–13; *History Channel* episode, 344;
housing conditions in, 304–5; loss of, 7;
naming of, 4, 113, 115; opposition to preservation of, 345–48; postwar growth of,
252–53; and proposal for Asia Pacific Center, 341–43; as Skid Row, 9, 112; violence
against Filipinas/os in, 139–43; and West
End Redevelopment Project, 283–85
Little Manila After School Program, 349
Little Manila Foundation: founding, 340–41;
preservation work, 348–49
Little Manila Historic Site, 337; banners,
340–41; beautification efforts, 349; cam-
paign for, 339–40; as one of 11 Most En-
dangered Historic Places in America, 342
Little Saigon (San Jose, Calif.), 344
Livingston, Calif., 49, 85, 124
Livingston, Jack, 214
Livingston Dragons and Dragonettes, 183
Liwanag, Helen Lagrimas, 52–53
Loboc (Bohol), 17
Local 7. *See* United Cannery and Packing
and Allied Workers Union
Local 37, 71
Lodi, 81; racism in, 176
Lonero, C. S., 237
London, 350
Look Magazine, 243
Lopez, Fernando, 326
Lordsburg, New Mexico, 155
Los Angeles, 5–6, 46, 107, 247
Los Angeles Times, 344, 348
Los Filipinos Tailoring Shop, 116, 119, 122, 169
Lower East Side (New York City), 345
L. P. Canlis Restaurant, 237
Luce-Celler Act, 245
Lumpia, 168–69
Luneta Pool Room, 281
Lu-Vi-Min Club, 132, 134, 136, 237
Luzon, 27, 28
Luzon Café, 122, 123, 236, 281
LVM Girls' Club, 183
LVM Restaurant (Café), 116, 117, 237, 281

Mabalon, Cynthia, 2, 269
Mabalon, Ernesto Tirona, 1, 14, 76, 115; atti-
tudes towards UFW, 263; demolition of
Lafayette Lunch Counter, 336; emigra-

tion of, 3; opposition to Filipino Cen-
ter project, 323, 325; reaction to Gateway
Project, 335–36
Mabalon, Francisco 26
Mabalon, Florencia. *See* Pastrana, Florencia
Mabalon
Mabalon, Guillermo, 25
Mabalon, Isabel Tirona, 25, 232; arrival in
Stockton, 247
Mabalon, Pablo Magdaluyo, 1, 2, 76, 247;
during World War II, 232; education, 38;
emigration to the United States, 45–46;
family reunification, 247; historic site
banner of, 340; impact of Philippine-
American War on, 25, 31; reaction to
Crosstown Freeway, 294–95; and restau-
rant ownership, 118–19; reunification of
the Mabalon family, 336; youth in Manila,
25
Mabalon, Rodrigo, 26
Mabalon, Teqio "Tex," 26, 76, 247, 269
Mabalon, Tex, Jr., 269
Mabini, Apolinario, 108
Mabini Lodge (Legionarios del Trabajo),
236
Mabuhay Café, 338
Macahilas, Juan Malumay, 90–91, 95
MacArthur, Douglas, 218, 249
MacArthur Garage, 124
MacArthur Hotel, 298, 336
Madera Barber Shop, 281
Mafea, V. J., 117
Magdael, Angelina Bantillo, 85, 139; and
courtship and dating rituals, 186; labor in
the home, 165; opposition to Crosstown
Freeway, 288; and Protestant missionar-
ies, 200; and queen contests, 173–80; and
work, 166, 167–68
Magellan, Ferdinand, 28
Magracia, B. C., 121, 237
Makato, Aklan, 17
Main Street, 141
Malinab, Lamberto, 221
Malolos, Bulacan, 29
Mancao, Frank, 102, 122
Mangahas, Fe, 153
Mangaoang, Ernesto, 96–97, 254
Mangrobang, Susanna Caballero, 187
Manila, 17, 25, 54

Manila Bar, 238

Manila Barber Shop, 120

Manila Bulletin, 50

Manila Cigar Stand, 238

Manila Cleaners, 281

Manila Club, 238

Manila Electric Company, 89, 108

Manila Grocery Co., 116, 236

Manila Hotel, 238

Manila Inn, 238

Manila Inn Liquors, 236, 237

Manila Inn Tavern & Chop Suey, 280

Manila Rooms, 120

Manila Service Gas Station/Richfield Parking & Service, 280

Manilatown Center (San Francisco), 333

Manlapit, Pablo, 52, 89

Manong/Manang: usage, 19

Manuel Roxas Auxiliary, American Legion, 316

Manuel Roxas Post, American Legion, 251, 314; support of the Filipino Center project, 316

Mapa, V. G., 117

Marcantonio, Vito, 227–29

Marceli, Kiliat, 237

Marcelo, F. B., 237

Marcos, Ferdinand: dictatorship, 308; martial law and anti-Marcos movement, 334

Marcuelo, D. L., 57, 61, 74, 75, 90–91, 94, 97, 105, 112, 117

Maria Clara Lodge (Caballeros de Dimas Alang), 161–63, 170

Mariano, Honorante, 56

Mariposa Hotel, 16, 108, 210, 236, 298, 338; proposed demolition, 341; as strike headquarters, 256, 280

Marmelino, Inez, 121

Marriage, 154; elopement, 187; among Filipinas/os and other groups, 155. *See also* Anti-miscegenation law; Courtship; Gender; Sexuality

Martin Carillo Pool Hall, 237

Martin, Robert B., 94

Martisano, Eugenio, 121

Maruico, Catalico, 121

Masinloc, Zambales, 17

Masonic organizations, 107, 204–5. *See also* Freemasonry

Mata, Flora Arca, 54, 67, 123, 166, 179; first Asian American public school teacher in Stockton, 166; Protestant missionaries, 200–201; religion, 192, 200; as a student, 166

Mateo, Sylvester Pili, 202

Matsumoto, Valerie J., 175

Ma-Yi Theatre Company, 349

Mayon Restaurant, 116, 118

McClatchy, V. S., 143

McCoy, Alan, 212–14

McCullough, Thomas, 209–14, 259

McDonalds, 2, 338, 340. *See also* Gateway Project

McFall, John, 290, 319, 321

McGough, William E., 203, 205–8

McIntosh suit, 56, 124, 157, 177

McKinley, William 29

McKinley Park, 273

McWilliams, Carey, 5–6, 69, 131, 145

Medallo, E. D., 117, 121

Menda's Soft Drink Parlor, 116

Mendiola, J. S., 121

Mensalvas, Chris (also Crispulo), 71, 96–98, 348; activism with the Committee for the Protection of Filipino Rights, 227–29; and asparagus strikes, 254–57; red-baiting of, 257–58

Merced County, 86

Merida, S. J., 121

Methodists, 196–97

Mexican Americans, 9–10, 15, 65, 140, 253; agricultural labor, 70, 73, 74, 80; and Agricultural Workers Association, 213–14; and Agricultural Workers Organizing Committee, 260; alliance with Filipinas/os in UFW, 261–63; and amendment to Alien Land Law, 235; and Border Patrol, 60; boxers, 127–28; Catholicism and, 201–3, 210; chaperonage and, 186; and *compadrazgo*, 165; courtship and marriage, 185–87, 190; and Crosstown Freeway, 288–89; as dancers in taxi-dance halls, 132; and ethnic identity, 172; and GI Bill, 246; immigrants in Stockton, 65, 112; intermarriage with, 155–57, 207, 306; labor competition with, 66; labor during World War II, 241–42; labor organizing among, 96–98; and missionaries, 196, 199; as prostitutes

Mexican Americans (*continued*) in Stockton, 138; repatriation of, 373n184; second generation, 185–86; and segregation, 272–73, 275; and Spanish Mission Band, 211–12; used as strikebreakers, 222–23

Mexican-American War, 65

Mexico, 28

Michael Biniegla Restaurant, 237

Military Bases Agreement, 246

Milpitas, Calif., 347

Mindanao, 17

Ministers, 195

Missionaries: among immigrants in Stockton, 195–201, 214–15; as Pentecostals, 198; in the Philippines, 194–95

Mitty, John Joseph, 205, 207–9, 213; and Spanish Mission Band, 211

Mocordo, Garcalea, 121

Modern Barber Shop, 281

Modesto, Calif., 253

Moncado, Hilario Camino, 107, 109; as anti-union, 224; criticism of, 224

Monico Orellio Pool Hall, 237

Monrayo, Angeles, 51–53, 101, 159; elopement of, 187–88

Monrayo, Valeriano, 159

Monrayo, Enarciso, 52, 115

Monrayo, Julian, 115

Montano, P. R., 117

Montermeso, Juan, 67

Montero, George, 40, 68, 69, 75, 76, 146, 157

Moquite, Natividad, 170

Morania, Ulpiano, 80

Morantte, P. C., 130

Morimoto, Kay, 223–25

Morimoto Dentist and Employment Company, 236

Morro Bay, Calif., 28

Mothers of the Philippines, 170–72

mutual aid associations, 107, 110

N & L Fish Market, 281

Nagai, Nelson, 232

Napala, Felipe, 39, 80–81

Napala, Ramona, 80

Naranda, Fortunata Montayre, 53

National Day of Humiliation, 94

National Farm Workers Union, 261

National Labor Relations Act (Wagner Act), 89

National Origins Act (Immigration Act of 1924), 60, 61, 143, 246

Nationalism, Philippine, 8

nationals: American Indians and Filipinas/os as, 33; Filipinas/os as, 5, 8

National Trust for Historic Preservation, 342

Native Americans, intermarriage with, 155–56, 190, 306

Native Sons of the Golden West, 143

Nava, Helen, 178

Navalta, Jose and Francisca, 155–56

Navarro, Cecelia, 161–63

Navea, Vincent, 225

Naranda, Fortunata Montayre, 53

Negros, Philippines, 29

Nemecio, Bueno, 117

New Continent Fountain, 237

New Deal Barbershop, 270, 280, 292

New Orleans, 350

newspapers, 112; gossip columns, 189

Ngai, Mae, 92

Nicolas, Andrea, 331

Nicolas, Asuncion Guevarra, 47, 122, 158, 159, 167, 168

Nicolas, Sixto, 57, 167

Nihonmachi (Japantown), 101, 113, 137, 369n48. *See also* Oriental Quarter

Ninonuevo, Eleno, 61, 118

Ninonuevo, Flora, 179

N. L. Fuertis Grocery, 237

Nomura, Gloria, 335, 348

Norman, Casil, 121

Novelozo, Angelina Candelario, 12, 248, 252, 257, 260

Numancia, Aklan (formerly Capiz): immigrants from, 8, 25, 58, 91, 144; as source of emigration, 3, 8, 17, 25, 45, 46, 47. *See also* Capiz

Numancia Aid Association, 110, 227, 316; building, 294

Nueva Ecija, 17

Nueva Vizcaya, 17

Nurses, 35, 154, 245, 300–301, 311

Oakdale, 188

Oakland, Calif., 344

Okamura, Jonathan, 159

O'Keefe, Jack, 137
Okies, 92. *See also* Dust Bowl migrants
Olamit, Eddie, 188
Olamit, Eleanor Galvez, 168, 179; elopement, 188
Omi, Michael, 7
Opialdo, Marcelino, 117
Oposa, Pedro, 117
Oriental Quarter, 113–15, 120–23, 131
Ortega, Connie Amado, 85
Osias, Camilo, 95

Pacific Cleaners, 281
Padilla, Carmen, 182
Pagala, Anastasio, 38, 235; cleaners and grocery, 236
Paguyo, Nemesio, 40, 68, 77–78, 80, 111, 142
Pajaro, Calif., 93
Palmos, Max, 121
Palompon, Leyte, 8
Paminsan, Damaso, 121
Panay, Philippines, 4
Panay Apartments, 237
Pangasinan, Philippines, 40
Paragas, Luz, 281
Parino, Policarpo, 121
Parreñas, Rhacel Salazar, 87
Pastrana, Florencia Mabalon, 26, 248, 269
Paul Porganan Cleaners, 237
Paular, Jerry, 75, 76, 95, 124, 128, 187
Pasquil, Corky, 127
Patayan, Peter, 237
Pearl Harbor, 218; Filipina/o reaction to, 230–32
Pecson, E. C., 242
Pelago Perlas Billiards, 116
Pensionadas/os, 4; impact on emigrants, 38; origins of program, 36
Perez, Frank, 4, 46, 56–57; on Little Manila, 115
Perez, Leatrice "Letty" Bantillo, 46, 167–68, 178–79, 181, 183, 186; Protestant missionaries, 200
Perez, Steph, 117
Perino, Carmen, 290, 320; county supervisor race, 329–30
Pescadero, Calif., 222
Petersen, Henry C., 196
Petersen, Cora, 196, 199

Philippine Advertiser, 90, 111
Philippine-American War, 5, 7, 8, 9, 30; casualties of, 31; and cholera epidemic, 5, 31; and race, 30–33; violence of, 25, 31
Philippine Barber Shop, 117, 121, 236
Philippine Bureau of Labor, 37
Philippine Civil Affairs Units, 248
Philippine Examiner, 112
Philippine folk dance, 310–11
Philippine Journal, 112, 221
Philippine Mercantile Corporation, 226
Philippine Normal School, 39
Philippine Realty Co., 236
Philippine Record, 227
Philippine Republic, 29
Philippine Revolution, 29
Philippine Rooms, 281
Philippine Scouts, 31
Philippine Yearbook, 160
Philippines, 8, 16
Philippines Mail, 158, 160, 188–89; anti-Japanese sentiments, 232; gossip column, 189; and naturalization rights, 228
Philippines-Star Press, 185, 189
Philip's Philippine Billiard Parlor, 116
Philomathean Club, 238
Phoenix, 155
Pilipina/o, 19
Pilots, 180
Pinoy/Pinay, earliest usage of, 20, 37
Podesto, Gary, 339
Ponce, Domingo, 107–8
Popular Front, 227
Porras, Policarpio, 119, 129–30, 131, 134
Portuguese immigrants, 65
Posadas, Diosdado, 127–28
Positively No Filipinos Allowed sign, 243
Presbyterians, 194–95. *See also* Lighthouse Mission; Trinity Presbyterian Church
Process Baylon Dry Goods, 237
Prostitution: in the campo, 86–87; race and prostitutes, 87; in West End, 132–38
Pruning, 5
Public Relations Bureau, 281
Puerto Rico, 29

Queen contests, 170, 314; gender roles and, 173–80; inter-regional rivalries and, 179
Queens, New York, 350

Quezon, Manuel, 145, 219, 235
Quezon City, 93
Quezon Hotel, 235, 236, 280; as location for *Fat City* film, 294

Rabaca, Fausto, 68, 110
Rabang, G. R., 121
Race and racialization: and boxing, 128–29; and exclusion, 143–44; and Filipinas/os, 3, 7, 6, 8, 10, 63, 97, 102, 313; and gender, 190; and marriage and relationships, 155; and Philippine-American War, 8, 30, 102; and South Stockton, 273; and suburbanization of Stockton, 273–75; and urban redevelopment, 277–78; and World War II, 23–32
Race riots: 104, 128, 141, 155; between Chinese and Filipinos, 130; in Watsonville, 95, 105–6, 142; during World War II, 232
Racism, against Filipinas/os, 94–96, 102. *See also* Race riots; Segregation; Violence; *Exclusion entries*
Rafael, Vicente, 116
Raffanti's Inn, 237
Railroads, 4
Randolph, A. Philip, 241
Ramos, Victor, 121
Rayray, Marion, 326
Religion: and American colonialism, 194–95; Catholicism among Filipina/o immigrants, 193; Islam, 194; in the Philippines, 194–95; Protestant denominations, 192; Protestant missions, 193
Remigio, Prudencio, 50
Repatriation Act (1935). *See* Filipino Repatriation Act
Rescission Act, 246
Reyes, Primitivo, 237
Reyes, Remy Galedo, 307
Reyes, Segunda, 47; beauty shop, 237; opposition to the Filipino Center, 325; work in the campo, 167, 168; during World War II, 242–43
Reyes, Vince, 248, 307
Ricarte, Artemio, 108
Rillera, Helen, 158
Rizal, José, 28, 109, 154, 176; as a Mason, 195
Rizal Barber Shop, 117
Rizal Social Club, 16, 120, 134, 135–37, 177, 231, 236, 280, 338; proposed demolition, 341

Raymundo, Alejandro, 205
Raymundo, Rizaline Monrayo, 82
Recomio, Pony, 121
Reliable Farm Labor Supply, 237
Republic Jewelry, 281
Resident commissioners, 92
Revillar, Dentoy, 311
Reyes, Segunda, 35, 81
Rilorcasa, Melecio, 121
Rishwain, Jimmie, 288
Roberts Island, 62
Robinal, Marcelo, 117, 121
Robles, Al, 330
Roces, Mina, 177
Rohrback, D. W. 93
Rohwer Concentration Camp, 234
Rojo, Trinidad, 125, 160, 225
Roldan, Salvador, 4
Roldan, Vicente 4, 112, 131
Romance of Magno Rubio: play, 349; short story, 134
Romano, Lorenzo, Sr., 76
Roman Catholicism, and courtship, 186. *See also* Religion
Roman Ordono Restaurant, 237, 281
Rome, 350
Romeo, Autentico, 117
Romulo, Carlos P., 217–18
Roosevelt, Eleanor, 238
Roosevelt, Franklin D., 241
Rosal, Emily Behic, 243, 251–52; reaction to Crosstown Freeway, 294
Rosal, Toribio "Terry," 175–76, 251–52
Roxas, Manuel, 219
Rough and Ready Island Naval Station, 233, 242, 245
Ruiz, Vicki, 175
Ryer Island, 62

S & R Garage, 338
Sabong. See cockfighting
Sacramento, Calif., 217, 220; FALA chapter, 223
Sacramento Bee, 97
Saiki, Alice, 157
Sajonia, Hoyolito, 67
Sajulan, Conching, 251
Sakadas, 49, 60, 66, 158. *See also* Hawai'i
S. G. Gavarra Billiards, 116

Saldevar, Carmen, 267, 269, 284; Crosstown Freeway displacement, 292–96

Saldevar, Fernando, 284; Crosstown Freeway displacement, 292–93

Salinas, Calif., 11, 247, 350; labor migration to, 70; lettuce strike, 97–98; politics, 291

Salinas Filipino Youth Council, 183

Salvador, Carrasco, 121

Sambahang Filipino Mission, 117

Sampaguita Dance Troupe, 310, 330

Samporna, Isidro "Sid," 251, 303

San Buenaventura, Steffi, xii, 193, 194

Sanchez, George, 9, 172

Sanguinetti, Angelo, 278–83

San Francisco, 4, 6, 54, 60, 125; Chinatown, 345; Filipina/o community in, 11, 350; International Hotel, 298, 327–28; Manilatown, 328; Western Addition redevelopment, 298

San Francisco Mangoes and Mangoettes, 183

San Diego, Calif., 11, 12, 247

San Joaquin Cannery Workers Union, 230

San Joaquin Cooperative Growers Association, 235

San Joaquin County, 5

San Joaquin Delta, 3, 5, 8; agriculture in, 17, 65–69; peat soil in, 73, 77

San Joaquin Delta College, 13, 310, 313

San Joaquin Valley, 5, 27

San Jose, 4, 125, 182; anti-Filipina/o violence in, 93; FALA chapter, 223; Little Saigon controversy, 344

San Jose Mercury News, 344

San Jose State University (also, College), 308

San Juan Bautista, Calif., 223

Santa Maria, Calif., 98

Santo Niño Association, 210–11, 316

Santos, Antonio, 326

Santos, Respicio, 117

Sar Caesar Billiards, 116

Sarmiento, Lynn, 311

Sarmiento, Max, 311

Saroyan, William, 227

Savoy Lunch and Club, 281

Scharrenberg, Paul, 92

Seattle, 2, 5, 54; Filipina/o community in, 11, 134, 247, 350; International District, 345

Second Filipino Infantry Regiment, 189, 233

Segregation: Federal Housing Authority policies, 275; North Stockton and South Stockton, 272–76; in Stockton, 112, 140–41, 147, 168, 170, 243

Sex ratio imbalance: courtship and, 185–88, 189; among Filipinas/os, 8, 132, 190; after World War II, 245

Sexuality: hypersexuality of Filipinos, 87; same-sex relationships, 138, 372n150; and white prostitutes, 86–87; 132–38, 187

Sharpe Army Depot, 245

Shima, George, 66

Shipping lines, voyages on, 57–58. *See also* Dollar Steamship Line

Short-handled hoe, 79

Shortridge, Samuel, 143

Sibunga Association, 110

Sikhs, 65. *See also* South Asians

Simeon, Sawat, 121

Sinigang, 173

Siquijor Association, 110

Smith, Norman, 260

Sobredo, Lourdes T., 295

social box dances, 176–77, 314

Sollis, Bonansio, 117

Sons of Batac, 110

Sons of Catalina, 110–11

Sons of Naga, 110

Somera, Antonio "Tony," Jr., 14, 83–84, 312, 349

Sosona, V., 121

South Asians, 28, 65–66

Southern California, 5

Southern Pacific Railroad, 89

South Stockton, 3, 252

Spain and colonization of the Philippines. *See* Colonialism: Spanish-era

Spanish-American War, 29

Spanish Mission Band, 211–12

Stanford University, 239

Star Fish Market, 236

St. Benedict Convent, 281

Stegner, Wallace, 243

St. George's Church, 274–75

Stimson, Henry, 233

St. Louis World's Fair, 180

St. Mary's Catholic Church, 116, 192, 202, 205–6, 215, 280; parish survey, 299

Stockton: bankruptcy, 249; emigration to, 59, 62; and Great Recession, 348; most

Stockton (*continued*)
  miserable city in the U.S., 348; Port of
  Stockton, 66
Stockton, Commodore Robert F., 65
Stockton Barber Shop, 121
Stockton Box Factory, 88
Stockton City Council: Little Manila His-
  toric Site, 339; West End Redevelopment
  Project, 279
Stockton Civic Auditorium, 95, 127, 128, 217
Stockton Cultural Heritage Board, 340
Stockton Filipino Community Center, 116,
  118
Stockton High School, 68; Filipino Club,
  67
Stockton Labor Council, 68
Stockton Labor Journal, 90
Stockton Market, 280
Stockton Police Department, 130–31; bru-
  tality against Filipinas/os, 141
Stockton Pool Hall and Cigar Stand, 281,
  284; relocation, 292
Stockton Redevelopment Agency: and Asia
  Pacific Center proposal, 342–42; and Fili-
  pino Center, 317–18; and Gateway Project,
  336–37; and West End redevelopment,
  279–83
St. Patrick's Seminary, 209
St. Peter's Methodist Church, 206, 280
Strikes, 88; asparagus strikes of 1948–1949,
  254–58; AWU celery strike, 1936, 98–99;
  during the Depression, 98; FALA aspara-
  gus, pea, and celery strikes, 220–25; Lodi
  grape workers, 88; Piecemeal Sugar Strike,
  52–53; Salinas lettuce, 97–98; Union
  Island asparagus strike, 1937, 99; wildcat
  and gang strikes, 88
Students, working in farm labor, 68. See also
  Pensionadas/os
Suarez Cleaners, 237
Suburbanization: FHA policies and, 272–73;
  in North Stockton, 272; and race in South
  Stockton, 273–75; shopping centers in
  North Stockton, 282
Suey Sing Association, 345
Suguitan, Melecio, 238, 281, 284
Supnet, T. C., 237
Sweetland, Monroe, 206–7

Tactacan, L. L., 121
Taft, William Howard, 31
Taft-Hartley Act, 25
Tagalog language, 1, 8, 19, 57, 103–4, 199, 250,
  302, 307, 308; classes in, 180, 181, 198, 215;
  newspapers, 112, 224; play in, 112; songs
  in, 180–81
Tagalogs: and boxing, 128; conflict with
  other Filipinas/os, 52, 57, 97, 103, 179; and
  escrima, 83; and ethnic identity, 3, 8–9, 63,
  97, 101, 103, 147; experiences in Hawai'i,
  50–51; and FALA, 221, 226; and food,
  118–19, 122, 173; HSPA recruitment of im-
  migrants, 49; immigrants, 19, 31, 52–54, 73,
  111, 124, 187, 192; intermarriage with other
  Filipinas/os, 306; stereotypes about, 139
Tagbilaran, Bohol, 17
Taggoa, Fernando, 239
Takahashi, Chuzo, 121
Takaki, Ronald, 11
Talisay (Cebu), 17
Talisay Association, 110
Tamarao Club, 237
Tapia, Felixberto, 49, 138, 157
Tarlac Province, 8
Taxi-dance halls, 102, 132–38
Taxi-dancers, 177
Teamsters Union, 263
Tenedor, Remedios, 53
Tenio, Rudy, 137
Tennis, 183
Teodora Alonzo Lodge (Legionarios del
  Trabajo), 109, 170–72
Terminous, Calif., 85
The Third Wave, 327
Three Star Pool Hall, 120, 236, 237, 280
Three Stars (newspaper), 57, 61, 74, 75, 90,
  91, 94, 105, 112, 115; location of publishing
  house, 116, 131, 160
Tigayol Pool Hall, 121
Thomasites, 31. *See also* Education
Tracy, Calif., 3, 124, 252
Trade East Imports, 331
Treaty of Paris, 29
Tobera, Fermin, 93–94, 106
Tokyo, 350
Tolio, D., 90
Ton, Victoriano, 83

Tonie, C., 99
Tony Photo Studio, 280
Tomatoes, 5
Tomek, Carmen, 310
The Torch, 112
Trinity Presbyterian Church, 192, 206, 236, 280
Trinidad, Estrella, 117
Tulare County, 93
Twain, Mark, 30
Tydings-McDuffie Act (1934), 5, 144–46, 264

Unsod, Dionicio, 237, 281
Unsod, Illuminada, 323, 326
United Cannery and Packing and Allied Workers Union, Local 7, 98, 209, 223, 265; asparagus strikes of 1948–1949, 254; headquarters in Little Manila, 280; relations with FALA, 225
United Farm Workers Union, 214, 262, 265, 312–13, 331. *See also* Agricultural Workers Organizing Committee; Labor; Strikes
United Filipino Church, 120, 200, 201, 206, 236
United Filipino Youth of Stockton, 183
United Sons of Catalina, 110
United States Army, 246
United States Armed Forces of the Far East (USAFFE), 232, 245
United States Border Patrol, 60
United States Information and Educational Exchange Act, 247
United States Navy, 246
University of California, Berkeley, 4, 62, 143
University of California, Davis, 3, 308, 313
University of California, Los Angeles, 1
University of the Pacific, 4, 13, 62, 313
University of the Philippines, 38, 93
University of Santo Tomas (Manila), 3, 38
Union Island Growers, 224
Urban redevelopment: criticism of, 277–78; in Stockton, 2, 6, 270–71, 276–77, 335; Urban Blight Committee, 278. *See also* West End Redevelopment Project

Vallangca, Caridad, 249
Vallejo, Calif., 185, 247

Vallejo Val-Phi Club, 183
Valley Fruit Growers of San Joaquin County, 89
Valoria, Pete, 85–86, 124, 129, 199
Varona, Francisco, 142–43; death of, 229–30; and FALA, 219–26; and Marcantonio bill, 229; Allyson Varzally, 12, 157
Velasco, Pete, 260, 262, 312, 313, 331
Ventura, Filipe, 120
Vera Cruz, Philip, 255, 260–62; asparagus strike of 1948, 312, 331, 348
Vergara, Benito, 12
Veteran's Administration, 3, 285
Victor's Barber Shop, 237
Vietnamese Americans, 344
Villa, Apolonio, 195
Villa, Buster, 141
Villadores, James, 310, 313
Villamin, Vicente, 106, 240
Villamor, Anastasia, 121
Villanueva, Esteban, 121
Villanueva, Louis, 121
Villanueva, N. C., 90
Villareal, 4
Villaruz, Arthur, 37
Villaruz, Primo, 36–37, 105, 107; and FALA, 221
Villaruz, Rita, 170, 200
Vineyards, 5
Violence: bombing of Filipino Federation Building, 104–5; in California, 93–96; and Delano Grape Strike, 262; among Filipinas/os, 97; intra-Asian, 130; and jealousy, 134; in Little Manila, 139–43; in Lodi, 94; police brutality, 141; in San Francisco, 94; in the San Joaquin Valley, 94; and racial terror, 95; white vigilantes, 94–96. *See also* Race riots
Virginia Beach, 350
Visayan Fish Market, 236
Visayan Grocery, 120
Visayan language, 19, 57, 103–4, 165, 199, 302, 306
Visayas: HSPA recruitment in, 49; as source of emigrants, 2, 3, 4, 26–27, 42–46, 47, 49
Visayans, 101, 103, 111, 119, 124, 151, 152, 187, 192, 197; and AFO, 322; and boxing, 128–29; conflict with other Filipinas/os, 52,

Visayans (*continued*)
134, 141, 179; and escrima, 83; ethnic identity, 8–9, 147, 307; experiences in Hawai'i,
50–52; and FALA, 221–26; food of, 85,
118, 119, 173; intermarriage with other
Filipinas/os, 158, 187, 250, 306; in Little
Manila, 114; songs of, 180–81; and violence, 97, 134;World War II, 249
Viviano, E. O., 237, 281
Volleyball, 82

Waipahu, Hawai'i, 333
Walang Kamatayang Pag-Ibig, 112, 180
Walnut Grove, Calif., 176
Waray-Waray, 103
War bond rallies, 181, 243
War brides, 249–50
War Brides Act, 246, 248
War on Poverty, 324
Wasan, Eddie, 135, 226
Washington State Aural/Oral History
     Project, 15
Washington Square Park, 147, 279
Watsonville, Filipino Community in, 11
Watsonville riots, 93, 104, 139
Weber, Charles, 65, 202
Welch, Richard, 92, 143–44; and Repatria-
     tion Act, 204. *See also* Tydings-McDuffie
     Act; *Exclusion entries*
West End, Stockton, 6, 112, 270, 275
West End Redevelopment Project, 275–85;
     creation of, 279; court challenge, 282–

83; demolitions for, 283; and Gateway
Project, 335; impact on Little Manila,
284–85; opposition to, 279–82; and Plan-
ning Commission, 278; reaction of Fili-
pinas/os to, 283–85; relocation plans for,
282–83; and Urban Blight Committee,
278–79
Wild, Mark, 12
Winant, Howard, 7
Women. *See* Gender
Women's organizations, 170–72
Wong Family Association, 345
Wood, James Earl, 16, 122
World War I, 62
World War II 4, 8–9, 20, 107; Filipinas/os
     and, 232–44; labor shortage during, 241–
     42; Pearl Harbor and aftermath, 230–32;
     war bonds sales and, 241

Ybono, Magdaleno S., 294
Yet Bun Heong bakery, 331
Yokohama, Japan, 54
Youth culture, 176
Yurong, Fred, Sr., 251, 326
Yurong, Maxie, 326
Yurong, Hedy, 313

Zambales, 17
Zambra, Vicente, 195, 197
Zandt, Nina Van, 108
Zoot suits, 177
Zuckerman Farms, 167